Hyman Hurwitz

A grammar of the Hebrew language

Hyman Hurwitz

A grammar of the Hebrew language

ISBN/EAN: 9783337729066

Printed in Europe, USA, Canada, Australia, Japan

Cover: Foto ©Paul-Georg Meister /pixelio.de

More available books at **www.hansebooks.com**

ELEMENTS

OF

THE HEBREW LANGUAGE.

BY HYMAN HURWITZ,
PROFESSOR OF HEBREW IN UNIVERSITY COLLEGE, LONDON,
AUTHOR OF
"VINDICIÆ HEBRAICÆ," "HEBREW TALES," ETC.

Fourth Edition.

LONDON:
PRINTED FOR TAYLOR AND WALTON,
BOOKSELLERS AND PUBLISHERS TO UNIVERSITY COLLEGE,
28, UPPER GOWER STREET.
M.DCCC.XLVIII.

CONTENTS.

	PAGE.
Preface	iii.
Mode of Writing and Reading	3
Nature of the Alphabet	4
Manner of Indicating the Vowels	ib.
Sh'va	5
Dagesh	5 - 6
Sounds and their Representatives	7
Table containing the Alphabet	9
Observations on ditto	10
Division of Letters	11
Formation of the Letters	12 — 14
Vowel-points	14 — 15
Observations on ditto	16
Combination of the Vowels with the Consonants	17 — 20
Syllables	21
On the Letters אהוי	22
Syllables beginning with two Consonants	23 — 24
Semi-vowels or Substitutes for Sh'va	25 — 26
Syllables terminating in a Consonant at the End of a Word	27 — 28
Syllables beginning with Two Consonants and terminating in one	29
Syllables terminating in Two Consonants at the End of Words	ib.
Syllables terminating with a Consonant in the Middle of a Word	30
Sh'va in the Middle of a Word	23 — 34
Dagesh Kal	35 — 36

A *

CONTENTS.

	PAGE.
Dagesh Hazak	37
Rules to distinguish Sh'va Initial from Sh'va Final	38—39
Rules to distinguish short (ָ o) and (· i) from long (ָ) ā and (· ī)	39—42
Remarks on the Vowel (וּ) when preceded by שׂ s, or followed by שׁ sh	42—45
Reading Lessons	47
Analysis of the first four Verses of Genesis	48—54
Reading Lessons with the Literal Translation	55—78
Accents.—Introductory Observations	79
Table containing the Forms, Position, and Names of the Accents	80
Nature and Importance of the Accents	81—85
Use of the Accents in shewing the Relations of Words considered as Members of a Sentence	85—90
Familiar Phrases, in which the Pronouns, and the Verb TO BE are exemplified	91—96

PREFACE.

I DEEM it unnecessary to offer an apology for this little work. If it prove useful, I shall have earned the reader's thanks; and if worthless, an apology will be but an additional waste of his time. I proceed at once, therefore, to specify its object, and the persons for whom it is designed.

It is intended for students desirous of acquiring the Hebrew Language, and as yet unacquainted with the rudiments; and its object is to facilitate the acquisition of that tongue by a methodical unfolding of its constituent parts, and a simplification of its rules; providing the learner, at the same time, with such preparatory information as may enable him to proceed with ease to the Etymology and Syntax, and to enter with advantage on the study of larger and more recondite works.

Many, indeed, are the works that have already been published on this subject; but whether their learned authors had forgotten the obstacles which they themselves must be supposed to have encountered, or whether they measured the average capacity of students by their own, or whatever else might be the cause, it is certain that their labours do not provide the learner with those aids of which he stands most in need at the commencement of his career. Nay, the very display of learning which distinguishes many of these works, renders them unfit for beginners, who are distracted by the multitude of facts crowded on their minds, whilst yet unprepared by previous discipline to receive them; and whose attention is thus frequently diverted from the main object of pursuit.

What would be thought of an anatomical professor who should attempt to explain all the intricacies of the vascular system before auditors to whom even the structure of the skeleton is as yet unknown? Such, however, is the method generally adopted in communicating a knowledge of the Hebrew Language. The attempt also to explain every thing on theoretical principles, even to the denial of any anomaly—just as if the Hebrew, granting even its immediate Divine origin, had not been for ages the common medium of intercourse between a multitude of frail human beings, whose imaginations neither will nor can be confined within the narrow limits of theoretical rules—has, in no small degree, contributed to entangle the subject, and to retard, if not entirely to check, the progress of the learner.

I have endeavoured to avoid these defects, by introducing nothing in the following sheets but what experience has taught me it is necessary for the beginner to know: while, on the other hand, I have been no less anxious to omit nothing that is really useful.

As the Orthography, owing to the strangeness of the Hebrew characters, and the peculiar system of the vowel-points, is by far the most perplexing and the least inviting part of the language, I have endeavoured to lessen the difficulties, by familiarising the learner with the system, in the introductory sections, by plain and progressive rules, accompanied with numerous examples, the pronunciation of which is given in English characters; and by the introduction of short vocabularies, which, while they further exemplify the rules, serve at the same time to make the student acquainted with the signification of numerous words. And here I cannot too strongly recommend to the young beginner, to learn to write the Hebrew characters (directions for which he will find in page 12—13) before he proceeds to combine them with the vowel-points; then to continue the practice with both, till they are as familiar to him as the English letters.

Those who learn the language without the aid of a living instructor, will find the *Analysis* of the first four verses of *Genesis* (page 48—54) particularly useful, as it will remove the hesitation which the self-instructed ever feel respecting correct pronunciation.

This little work further contains Progressive Reading Lessons, selected from Scripture, accompanied by a literal translation ; not, indeed, as if I wished it to be understood that a critical knowledge of any language, and especially of such a one as the Hebrew, can be obtained by mere literal translations, unaided by grammatical learning, but, because I am persuaded that they are, when analytically conducted, the surest means of giving the student a real insight into the use and application of words, and the peculiar idiom of a language.

With this view, the letters expressing the modification of the Hebrew words, together with their corresponding English equivalents, have been printed in a type differing from that of the principal words; so that the pupil may easily ascertain the real meaning of every compound, and become gradually acquainted with the mechanism of the language.

As the most correct editions of the Hebrew Bibles are printed with the accents, so that the student cannot open a page without their being presented to his view—the accents being likewise intimately connected with the vowel-points, without which, no critical knowledge of the Hebrew can be obtained—it has been thought most advisable to explain them, and to describe their use.

Lastly, a few pages have been added, containing familiar phrases in which the verb TO BE, and the PRONOUNS, are exemplified; not only on account of their frequent occurrence, but also because they are the elements from which the greater part of those fragments which express the modifications of words are taken; and consequently they cannot be too early acquired. Thus prepared, the student will be able to pursue the Etymology and Syntax with ease and satisfaction; and ultimately to reap those advantages from the Sacred Records which their interpretation, founded on philological and grammatical rules, is sure to yield.

ELEMENTS OF THE HEBREW LANGUAGE.

CHAPTER I.

§ 1.—Introductory Observations.

Mode of Reading and Writing.

1. In our mode of writing we proceed from the left hand to the right; but the Hebrews, in common with several other Oriental nations, proceed in a contrary direction.

The consequence of this arrangement is, that their words and lines begin where ours end, and their books commence where ours terminate, and *vice versâ*.

Thus, instead of writing a, b, c, d, etc., they write their own characters — { $\overset{4}{d}$, $\overset{3}{g}$, $\overset{2}{b}$, $\overset{1}{a}$, etc.
ד ג ב א }

Thus, also, instead of writing the word *Abraham* in this manner, they would write it in their own characters = $\overset{5}{m}\ \overset{4}{h}\ \overset{3}{r}\ \overset{2}{b}\ \overset{1}{a}$ (omitting the vowels); and read it $\overset{3}{mah}$-$\overset{2}{ar}$-$\overset{1}{ba}$, = Abraham.

Nature of the Alphabet.

2. Their Alphabet, which is given at large in page 10, consists of consonants only, because in ancient times they wrote their words without vowels, these being supplied by the reader.

Every Hebrew knew, from practice, the vocal sounds with which the consonants were pronounced in the different words, in the same manner as every Englishman knows the different sounds of *a* in *hat, hate, all, was*, etc., and that *knt* is pronounced *knight*. The words "*long live the king*" would, in their manner of writing, be *lng lv th kng*; or rather in the reverse order—

$$\underset{\text{gnk}}{\text{קנג}} \quad \underset{\text{ht}}{\text{ת}} \quad \underset{\text{vl}}{\text{לב}} \quad \underset{\text{gnl}}{\text{לנג}}.$$

Mode of Indicating the Vowels.

3. This mode of writing and reading continued as long as the language was vernacular; but when it ceased to be so, and could only be attained, like every other dead language, through a written medium, the necessity of having visible marks for the vowel sounds was strongly felt: but, as all their ancient records were written without vowels, and their alphabet was already fixed*, they could not extend it by the addition of new letters, without disarranging the whole system, and remodelling their written document; and these they held in too great veneration to attempt the slightest change in them.

---

* See the alphabetical Psalms xxv., xxxiv, cxix.

Instead, therefore, of inventing letters to represent the vowel-sounds, they contented themselves with indicating them by points and small strokes placed above, below, or in the middle of the consonants.

Thus they represent the sound of
o in *no*, by a dot above the consonant, ṅ, ṡ, ġ, l̇, = no, so, go, lo,
e in *me*, by a dot under the consonant, ḅ, ḥ, ṃ, ṣḥ, = be, he, me, she,
a in *may*, by 2 dots under the consonant, b̤, d̤, g̤, m̤, = bay, day, gay, may,
e in *bed*, by 3 dots under the consonant, bd̥, fd̥, mt̥, = bed, fed, met.
In a similar manner they represent the rest of the vowels. (See page 15.)

Sheva or Sh'va.

4. To indicate that a consonant was to be pronounced conjointly with the succeeding or preceding syllable, they placed two dots (:) denominated *Sh'va*, under the unvowelled consonant: as, blow, bread, asleep, admire, bold, abrupt.

Dagesh.

5. As the Hebrew letters corresponding with our *b, g, d, c, p,* and *th*, were in ancient times pronounced either aspirated or unaspirated, according to the place they occupied in a word, a small stroke (-), denominated *Raphe**, was placed over them when they were

---

* This is only found in ancient Hebrew Manuscripts; in printed books it is omitted.

to be aspirated; thus, בֿ b, = bh or v; פֿ p = ph or f. A dot (denominated *dagesh*) was placed in the middle of these letters when they were pronounced unaspirated: as, בּ b, פּ p.

This dot is by Hebrew grammarians called *dagesh kal*, the *light* or *simple dagesh*, as it only removes the aspiration.

6. By a dot in these or any other letters occurring in the middle of a word preceded by a vowel-point, they indicated that such consonants were pronounced like double letters: as, baner = banner, dager = dagger.

This dot is by way of distinction called *dagesh hasak*, *hard* or *strong dagesh*.

Accents.

7. Besides the marks before described, the Hebrews have several others, called accents, by which they indicate the relative connection between words, considered as members of a sentence, and point out at the same time the syllable on which the stress of the voice is to be laid. They perform, therefore, the same office as our accents, comma, semicolon, colon, period. To understand them thoroughly, requires a complete knowledge of the language. For the mere beginner it is sufficient to know, that, generally, wherever they occur, there the stress of the voice must be laid. Further explanation respecting them will be given in the progress of the work.

§ 2. — Consonants.

Sounds and their Representatives.

1. Most of the sounds employed in the Hebrew are similar to those used in our own language, but they are represented by different characters: thus—

b is represented by	בּ
v	ב
g, as in *go*	גּ ג
d	דּ ד
h, as in *he*	ה
w, as in *we*	ו
z	ז
t	ט
y, as in *yes*	י
c as in *can*, or *ch* in *chord**, or ך { at the end of words.	כּ
l	ל
m	מ ,, ם ,,
n	נ ,, ן ,,
s, as in *so*	ס
p	פּ
f	פ ,, ף ,,

---

* This letter without the point (כּ), is pronounced like ח. See page 8.

k is represented by ק

r .... ר

sh .... שׁ

s .... שׂ

th or t .... ת

The following Hebrew characters represent sounds which we have not in our language, or for which we have no character.

א represents the sound heard in emitting the breath, somewhat similar to the *e* in *echo*. The Hebrews appear to have considered it as the basis of all the vocal sounds. It occupies the first place in the alphabetical series, and is pronounced either *a*, *e*, *i*, *o*, or *u*, according to the vowel-point annexed (see p. 15). In writing the Hebrew in Roman characters, we shall represent it by a dot under the vowel, thus *ạ, ẹ, ị, ọ,* &c.

ח a guttural sound, similar to the rough sound of the German *ch* in *ach*, *nach*. We shall represent it by the letter *ḥ* with a dot under.

ע generally pronounced like *gn* at the beginning of words and syllables, and like *ng* at the end of them. Some pronounce it like א. We shall indicate it by a dot over the vowels ȧ ė, ï, ȯ, u̇.

צ, or at the end of words ץ, sounds like *ts*, by which we shall represent it.

HEBREW LANGUAGE.

2. The following table contains the Hebrew consonants in alphabetical order, their names, forms, and powers.

FORMS.		NAMES.	POWERS.	NUMERICAL VALUE.
א	*א	Aleph ..	....	1
ב	ב	Beth ...	b, v	2
ג	ג	Gimel ..	g in *go*	3
ד	ד	Daleth..	d	4
ה	ה	He	h in *he*	5
ו	ו	Wav ...	w or v	6
ז	ז	Zain ...	z	7
ח	ח	Heth ...	ch {in the German word *Nacht*.	8
ט	ט	Teth ...	t	9
י	Final Letters. י	Yod ...	y in *ye*	10
כ	ך כ	Caph ...	ch in *chord* .	20
ל	ל	Lamed..	l	30
מ	ם מ	Mem ...	m	40
נ	ן נ	Nun ...	n	50
ס	ס	Samech .	s in *so*	60
ע	ע	Ayin ...	....	70
פ	ף פ	Pe	f or p	80
צ	ץ צ	Tsadi ..	ts	90
ק	ק	Koof ...	k	100
ר	ר	Resh ...	r	200
ש	ש	Shin ..	sh	} 300
ש	ש	Sin	s	
ת	ת	Thav ...	th or t	400

* This column contains the *Rabbinical* characters.

Observations on the Alphabet.

3. The Hebrew words *Aleph* or rather *Aluph*, an ox; *Beth*, a house; *Gimel*, or rather *Gamal*, a camel; *Daleth*, a door; *Wav*, a hook or plug; were originally given to the respective letters, in consequence of a real or fancied resemblance between their shape and the natural form of the object so denominated. As, however, the beginner cannot be supposed to know the signification of these words, he had better pass them over for the present, and name the letters by their powers: thus, א č', ב b'.

מ ל כ י ט ח ז ו ה ד ג ב א
m' l' k' h' y' t' h' z' w' h' d' g' v' b' č'

ת ת ש ש ר ק צ פ פ ע ס נ
t' th' s' sh' r' k' ts' p' f' č' s' n'

4. All the above letters, excepting צ ע מ נ י ו ו ג ן, appear frequently in manuscripts and printed books under a lengthened form: thus—

ת ר ם ל ד א

5. The following letters require particular attention on the part of the learner, on account of their similarity.

ב....b   ג....g   ד....d   ט....t
כ....h   נ....n   ר....r   מ....m

HEBREW LANGUAGE. 11

ה....h	ו....w	ך *final h*	ס....s
ח....ḥ	ז....z	ע....ʻ	ם *final m*
פ....f	י....y	צ....ts	שׁ....sh
ת....th	ן *final n*	ץ *final ts*	שׂ....s

Division of Letters.

6. Letters are divided according to the organ by which they are chiefly formed: thus —

א ה ח ע are denominated *Gutturals.*
ב ו מ פ . . . . . . *Labials.*
ג י כ ק . . . . . . *Palatals.*
ד ט ל נ ת . . . . . *Linguals.*
ז ס שׁ ר צ . . . . . *Dentals.*

Obs.—Letters pronounced by the same organ, are sometimes substituted for one another. This is likewise the case with the letters א ה ו י, which are denominated *quiescents.* See chap. ii. § 2.

For the division of letters into *radicals* and *serviles,* see Etymology, chap. i. § 2.

7. The letters בגד כפת, without a dot, were anciently pronounced aspirated: thus, ב bh, or v; ג gh; ד dh; כ ḥ, like ח; פ ph; ת th; but with the dot they were pronounced unaspirated: thus, ב b, ג g, ד d, כ k, פ p, ת t. This distinction is, by the Spanish Jews, whose pronunciation is generally adopted by the learned, retained only in כ and פ. The German Jews retain it in ב and ת likewise.

8. The characters ץ ף, ן ם, ך, standing for נ, מ, כ, צ, פ, occur only at the end of words, and are, therefore, called *finals*.

Formation of Letters.

9. In learning to form the Hebrew letters, attend to the following Elements :—

    1ˢᵗ·—The broad point ` ` ` ` `
    2ⁿᵈ·—The perpendicular | |
    3ʳᵈ·—The horizontal ¯ ¯ ¯ ¯ ¯
    4ᵗʰ·—The diagonal ＼ ＼ ＼
    5ᵗʰ·—The curve כ ى ל ל ך

From the 1st ׳, and 2nd ן, are formed :—

    ׳ y, ו w, ג g, ז z, ן n, ן *n final*.

From the 1st ׳, and 4th ＼ ＼ ╱, are formed :—

    א e, ע è, צ ts, ץ *ts final*.

From the 3rd ¯ and 2nd (ן are formed :—

ד d, ה h, ב b, ח h, כ h, ך *h final*,
ר r, ף *f final*, ם *m final*, and ת.

From the 5th כ ى, 1st ׳, 2nd ן, & 3rd ¯ ى, are formed :—

    מ m, ט t, פ f, ל l, ק k, ס s, and ש sh.

Practice.

Write the following characters:—

n	m	l	ḥ	y	t	ḥ	z	w	h	d	g	b	e

א ב ג ד ה ו ז ח ט י ך כ ל מם נן

th	t	s	sh	r	k	ts		p	e	s

ס ע ף פ ץ צ ק ר ש ש ת ת

Write the English letters corresponding to the following Hebrew characters:—

אל בם בס גג גן דם הפ הך עו זץ וץ חץ
טר יש יש כת תך

Write the corresponding Hebrew characters to the following English:—

w, k, y, th, t, z, sh, s, r, ph, p, n, m, l, h,
g, f, d, c, b, ĕ.

Write the English characters corresponding to the following Hebrew letters:—

פפף תת בכ וף הה ח בכךך לל
מם ש ש תשרק צפעס נמלך יטחז
והדג בא ד ס ז ו ף ץ בכ דרך גון

בראשית ברא אלהים את השמים ואת
הארץ : והארץ היתה תהו ובהו וחשך
על פני תהום ורוח אלהים מרחפת על
פני המים :

ויאמר אלהים יהי אור ויהי אור :
וירא אלהים את האור כי טוב ויבדל
אלהים בין האור ובין החשך :

ויקרא אלהים לאור יום ולחשך קרא לילה
ויהי ערב ויהי בקר יום אחד :

§ 3.—Vowels.

1. The vowels are represented in Hebrew by small strokes and points variously arranged, and placed either above or below the consonants. They are ten in number; five long and five short. The following table contains their names (which the beginner

may disregard for the present), forms, position, and power.

LONG.

NAMES.	FORMS.	POSITION.	POWER.
KAMETS	ָ	under the consonant } as אָ בָּ	~~a in father~~
TSERE	ֵ	under as אֵ בֵּ	â in *ale*
HIRIK	ִ or ִי	under as אִי, אִ, בִּי	î in *machine*
HOLEM	וֹ or ֹ	above as אוֹ or אֹ, בֹּ	ô in *no, so*
SHUREK	וּ	in the middle of the letter } as אוּ, רוּ	û in *rule*

SHORT.

NAMES.	FORMS.	POSITION.	POWER.
PATHAH	ַ	under as אַ, דַ da	a in *what*
SEGOL	ֶ	under as אֶ, דֶ de	e in *met, set*
SHORT HIRIK	ִ	under as אִ, בִּ bi	i in *pin*
KAMETS HATAPH	ֳ or ָ	under as אֳ or אָ, בָּ bo	o in *son*
KIBUTS	ֻ	under as אֻ, בֻּ bu	u in *bull**

* The above scale is according to the pronunciation of the Portuguese and Spanish Jews; the German and Polish Jews pronounce (ָ) like *o* in *bone*, (ֵ) like *i* in *bind*, and (וּ) like *ow* in *vow*; the other vowels they pronounce like their Spanish brethren.

Observations on the Vowel Points.

2. The ו which supports the point representing long ō is frequently omitted, and the dot (placed above the left of the consonant) retained: as, בֹּ bō גֹּ gō, דֹּ dō.

3. The י following long (ִ) î, is frequently omitted. To distingish it in such cases from the short (.) i, rules will be given in the progress of the work. The same observation will apply to short (ֳ) o, the two dots being frequently omitted; and to וּ, for which (ֻ) is sometimes substituted. See chap. ii. § 7, No. 2—4.

4. The use of the vowel points being only to indicate how the consonants are pronounced; it follows that they cannot form a syllable without the consonants. To represent, therefore, the sounds of a, e, i, etc., the corresponding vowel points must be added to the letter א: thus, אָ ā, אֶ e, אִ î, אוּ ū, etc.

5. The consonants must be sounded before the vowel points: as בָּ bā (not ab), גָּ gā (not ag). See the next page.

Practice.

Write the vowels corresponding to the following vowel points — ָ ֵ ִ וּ יִ - ְ ֳ ִ ֻ ֹ וּ

Write the vowel points corresponding to the following vowels, ā, a, â, e, ū, i, u, î, o, ō, ū, ŭ, ā, a, i, î, u, ō, o.

§ 4.—CONSONANTS AND VOWELS.

Scale of the Alphabet with the Vowel Points and their corresponding sounds, according to the pronunciation of the Spanish and Portuguese Jews.

לָ	כָ	בָּ	יָ	טָ	חָ	זָ	וָ	הָ	דָּ	גָּ	בָּ	אָ	} *a* in
lā	hā	chā	yā	tā	ḥā	zā	wā	hā	dā	gā	bā	ā	*father.*
תָ	שָׂ	שָׁ	רָ	קָ	צָ	פָ	פָּ	עָ	סָ	נָ	מָ		
thā	sā	shā	rā	kā	tsā	fā	pā	á	sā	nā	mā		

לַ	כַ	בַּ	יַ	טַ	חַ	זַ	וַ	הַ	דַּ	גַּ	בַּ	אַ	} *a* in
la	ha	cha	ya	ta	ḥa	za	wa	ha	da	ga	ba	a	*what.*
תַ	שַׂ	שַׁ	רַ	קַ	צַ	פַ	פַּ	עַ	סַ	נַ	מַ		
tha	sa	sha	ra	ka	tsa	fa	pa	á	sa	na	ma		

לָ	כָ	בָּ	יָ	טָ	חָ	זָ	וָ	הָ	דָּ	גָּ	בָּ	אָ	} *a* in
lâ	hâ	châ	yâ	tâ	ḥâ	zâ	wâ	hâ	dâ	gâ	bâ	â	*ale.*
תָ	שָׂ	שָׁ	רָ	קָ	צָ	פָ	פָּ	עָ	סָ	נָ	מָ		
thâ	sâ	shâ	râ	kâ	tsâ	fâ	pâ	á	sâ	nâ	mâ		

לֶ	כֶ	בֶּ	יֶ	טֶ	חֶ	זֶ	וֶ	הֶ	דֶּ	גֶּ	בֶּ	אֶ	} *e* in
le	he	che	ye	te	ḥe	ze	we	he	de	ge	be	e	*set.*
תֶ	שֶׂ	שֶׁ	רֶ	קֶ	צֶ	פֶ	פֶּ	עֶ	סֶ	נֶ	מֶ		
the	se	she	re	ke	tse	fe	pe	á	se	ne	me		

לִי	כִּי	בִּי	יִי	טִי	חִי	זִי	וִי	הִי	דִּי	גִּי	בִּי	אִ	} *i* in
lī	hī	chī	yī	tī	ḥī	zī	wī	hī	dī	gī	bī	i	*field.*
תִּי	שִׂי	שִׁי	רִי	קִי	צִי	פִי	פִּי	עִי	סִי	נִי	מִי		
thī	sī	shī	rī	kī	tsī	fī	pī	í	sī	nī	mī		

18 ELEMENTS OF THE

לִ	כִּ	בִ	פִּ	יִ	טִ	חִ	זִ	וִ	הִ	דִ	גִ	בִ	אִ	} i in
li		chi	hi	yi	ti	hi	zi	wi	hi	di	gi	bi	i	pin.
תִ	שִׂ	שִׁ	רִ	קִ	צִ	פִ	פִּ	עִ	סִ	נִ	מִ			
thi	si	shi	ri	ki	tsi	fi	pi	i	si	ni	mi			

לֹ	כֹ	בֹ	יֹ	טֹ	חֹ	זֹ	הֹ	דֹ	גֹ	בֹ	אֹ	} o in
lō	hō	chō	yō	tō	hō	zō	hō	dō	gō	bō	ō	no.
תֹ	שֹׂ	שֹׁ	רֹ	קֹ	צֹ	פֹ	פֹּ	עֹ	סֹ	נֹ	מֹ	
thō	sō	shō	rō	kō	tsō	fō	pō	ō	sō	nō	mō	

לָ	כָ	בָ	יָ	טָ	חָ	זָ	וָ	הָ	דָ	גָ	בָ	אָ	} o in
lo	ho	cho	yo	to	ho	zo	wo	ho	do	go	bo	o	son.
תָ	שָׂ	שָׁ	רָ	קָ	צָ	פָ	פָּ	עָ	סָ	נָ	מָ		
tho	so	sho	ro	ko	tso	fo	po	o	so	no	mo		

לוּ	כוּ	בוּ	יוּ	טוּ	חוּ	זוּ	וּ	הוּ	דוּ	גוּ	בוּ	אוּ	} u in
lū	hū	chū	yū	tū	hū	zū	wū	hū	dū	gū	bū	ū	rule.
תוּ	שׂוּ	שׁוּ	רוּ	קוּ	צוּ	פוּ	פּוּ	עוּ	סוּ	נוּ	מוּ		
thū	sū	shū	rū	kū	tsū	fū	pū	ū	sū	nū	mū		

לֻ	כֻ	בֻ	יֻ	טֻ	חֻ	זֻ	וֻ	הֻ	דֻ	גֻ	בֻ	אֻ	} u in
lu	hu	chu	yu	tu	hu	zu	wu	hu	du	gu	bu	u	bull.
תֻ	שֻׂ	שֻׁ	רֻ	קֻ	צֻ	פֻ	פֻּ	עֻ	סֻ	נֻ	מֻ		
thu	su	shu	ru	ku	tsu	fu	pu	u	su	nu	mu		

Scale of the Alphabet with the Vowels and their corresponding English sounds, according to the pronunciation of the German and Polish Jews.

בָּךְ	כָּ	יָ	טָ	חָ	זָ	וָ	הָ	דָ	גָ	בָ	אָ	} o in
ko	cho	yo	to	ho	zo	vo	ho	do	go	vo	bo	o	bone.
תָ	תָ	שָׁ	רָ	קָ	צָ	פָ	פָּ	עָ	סָ	נָ	מָ	לָ
so	to	so	sho	ro	ko	tso	fo	po	o	so	no	mo	lo

HEBREW LANGUAGE.

אִ בִּ וִּ גִּ דִּ הִ חִ טִ יִ כִּ לִ } *i* in
i bi vi gi di hi ḥi ṭi yi ki li } bind.

מִ נִ סִ ע פִּ פִ צִ קִ רִ שִׁ שִׂ תִּ תִ
mi ni si i pi phi tsi ki ri shi si ti si

אוֹ בּוֹ בוֹ גוֹ דוֹ הוֹ וּ זוֹ חוֹ טוֹ יוֹ כּוֹ } *ow* in
ow bow vow gow dow how vow zow how tow yow kow } vow.

כוֹ לוֹ מוֹ נוֹ סוֹ עוֹ פּוֹ פוֹ צוֹ קוֹ רוֹ
how low mow now sow ow pow phow tzow kow row

שׁוֹ שׂוֹ תּוֹ תוֹ
show sow tow sow

אִי בִּי בִי גִּי דִי הִי וִי זִי חִי טִי יִי כִּי כִי לִי } *i* in
מִי נִי סִי עִי פִּי פִי צִי קִי רִי שִׁי שִׂי תִּי תִי } field.*

אוּ בּוּ בוּ גוּ דוּ הוּ וּ זוּ חוּ טוּ יוּ כּוּ כוּ לוּ } *u* in
מוּ נוּ סוּ עוּ פּוּ פוּ צוּ קוּ רוּ שׁוּ שׂוּ תּוּ תוּ } rule.

אַ בַּ בַ גַ דַ הַ וַ זַ חַ טַ יַ כַּ כַ לַ } *a* in
מַ נַ סַ עַ פַּ פַ צַ קַ רַ שַׁ שַׂ תַּ תַ } what.

אֶ בֶּ בֶ גֶ דֶ הֶ וֶ זֶ חֶ טֶ יֶ כֶּ כֶ לֶ } *e* in
מֶ נֶ סֶ עֶ פֶּ פֶ צֶ קֶ רֶ שֶׁ שֶׂ תֶּ תֶ } set.

אִ בִּ בִ גִ דִ הִ וִ זִ חִ טִ יִ כִּ כִ לִ } *i* in
מִ נִ סִ עִ פִּ פִ צִ קִ רִ שִׁ שִׂ תִּ תִ } pin.

אָ בָּ בָ גָ דָ הָ וָ זָ חָ טָ יָ כָּ כָ לָ } *o* in
מָ נָ סָ עָ פָּ פָ צָ קָ רָ שָׁ שָׂ תָּ תָ } son.

אֻ בֻּ בֻ גֻ דֻ הֻ וֻ זֻ חֻ טֻ יֻ כֻּ כֻ לֻ } *u* in
מֻ נֻ סֻ עֻ פֻּ פֻ צֻ קֻ רֻ שֻׁ שֻׂ תֻּ תֻ } bull.

---

* See pages 17 and 18.

Practice.

Write the English characters corresponding with the following syllables: —

אָ אֶ אִי אֵ א אֱ אוֹ אָ אֲ בְּ בָּ בֻּ גְ
גוֹ גְ גִי דְ דָ דֶ דֻ דוֹ דַ דָה הֲ הֶ הֹ הוֹ הִי וְ
נְ זוֹ זֻ חֹ חַ חְ טֶ טֲ יְ יַ יוֹ כֻּ כְ כָּ לוֹ
לִי לְ לוֹ לָ מָ מְ נְ נֶ סְ סוֹ סֶ סָ סַ עֲ עַ עֵי
עוֹ עֲ עַ פִּי פֵּ פְ צוֹ צִי קְ קָ קֻ רְ רָ רְ שׁוּ שַׁ שֶׁ
תְּ תָ תְ תֶ תּוֹ

Write the following syllables in Hebrew characters: —

bā ba bī bi gâ ge dō ho wō zū tu yā ya yâ ye kī ki lō nō sō mo so ru sā sa sâ se shī shi pī pi fū ā a â e i ī ō u o ū

Read the following words, and write the corresponding English characters: —

אָבִי בְּכִי גָּאוּ דּוֹדִי הָיוּ וָוֵי זָדוּ טוּבוֹ יָדוֹ כּוֹסִי לֶחִי
מֶשִׁי נֵרוֹ סוֹדִי עֵינִי צוּרִי רוּחִי אָנֹכִי בָּנִיתִי גָּבְרוּ
הוֹדְךָ חָלִינוּ טוּבְךָ יָחוֹגוּ כָּמוֹהוּ פָּנֵינוּ צָמְחוּ רָאִינוּ
שָׁרֶיהָ תּוֹרָתוֹ אוֹתוֹתָךְ גּוֹרָלֵנוּ הֵינִיקָהוּ יָגִילוּ זוּלָתָךְ
תּוֹרָתֵינוּ כָגִינֵנוּ הוֹדִיעוּ עֵדְוֹתָיךְ :

CHAPTER II.

§ 1.— SYLLABLES AND WORDS.

Introductory Observations.

Syllables are either simple or compounded, accented or unaccented.

1. Simple syllables are such as terminate in a vowel: as, בְּ ba, נָ nā, גְּלוּ* glu; or in a quiescent letter: as, לֹא lō, זֶה zeh, מָה mah. See the following section.

2. Compounded are such as terminate in a consonant: as, אֶל el, אַט at, בְּלֶד bled, רוּל rule, פָּל pull. See § 4, page 27.

3. Accented syllables are such as have any of the accents; a list of which the reader will find in chap. iii.

4. Every Hebrew word must have an accent, either on the last syllable, as בִּינָה bī-nā′h, *understanding;* or on the one before the last, as בִּינָה bī′nāh, *understand thou.*

Except when a word is joined to the following by a small stroke (-) denominated (*Mak-keph*), as בִּי־לִי kī-lī′, in which case the last word receives the accent.

---

* This denomination of the grammarians is retained for the sake of distinction, although, strictly speaking, *glu* is as much a compound syllable as אֶל *al.*

5. A small perpendicular stroke (ֽ) denominated *metheg* (*a bridle*), is frequently added to a vowel to give it its full sound, and to prevent its being slurred over in the rapidity of utterance: as, לִידִידִי li-dī-dī′.

This mark may be considered as a secondary accent, and is mostly used to distinguish simple from compound syllables; and hence, when a letter following it happens to have *sh'va*, the *sh'va* is *initial*. See § 5, chap. ii.

We shall indicate the Hebrew accent, whenever it is on the penultima, by the following mark (׳). and omit it entirely when it is on the last syllable. In all words, therefore, where the accent is omitted, it must be considered as being on the last syllable.

§ 2.—*On the Letters* א ה ו י.

These letters frequently lose their consonantal sounds, and are then said to be *quiescent* or *mute*.

1. א and ה are always *mute* unless they have a vowel point: as, בָּא bā, בֹּא bō, בִּיא bī, הוּא hū, הִיא hī, לֵא lé, לֹא lō, רֵא rā, הֵא hā, זֶה zé, שֶׂה sé, פֹּה pō, מַה ma, לָה lā, נֶה né, נָה nā.

2. ה occurs sometimes with a dot in it (הּ), when it is pronounced like *h* in *ah!* as, בָּהּ bāh, לָהּ lāh.

This dot is by grammarians called Mappik.

3. ו is *mute* when it represents the vowel *holem* or *shurek*: as, אוֹ ō, בוֹ bō; אוּ ū, בוּ bū.

ו at the beginning of words is pronounced like א ū: as, וּמִי *u-mi*, not *vu-mi*; וּפָרָה *u-fā-rā*, not *vu-fā-rā*.

4. י is *mute* after (ִ), (ֵ), (ֶ): as, בִּי bī, נִי nī, נֵי nâ, נֶי né; also after (ָ) when followed by ו: as, עָלָיו ālāv,

פָּנָיו pā-nāv. In all other cases it is pronounced, and its sound is similar to *y* in *yes* when it begins a syllable: as, יוֹמוֹ yō-mō; and to *y* in *boy* when it terminates it: as, אֵלַי â-lay, גּוֹי gōy.

Additional Examples.

bō ..	בֹּא	kā-rā'..	קְרָא	sū-sī'	סוּסִי	â-bī ..	אָבִי
kō-vâ'	קוֹי	bā-thī'	בָּאתִי	pé-le	פֶּלֶא	bī-nā'	בִּינָה
kō-nà'	קְנֵה	kā-rū'	קְרוּא	pō ..	פֹּה	lō-vē..	לוֹוֶה
yā-mâ'-nū	יָמֵינוּ	hō-ré-cha	הוֹרֶיךָ	â-lē'-hā ..	אֵלֶיהָ
a-hé-hā ..	אַחֶיהָ	rā-shâ-nū	רָאשֵׁינוּ	tū-bō'....	טוּבוֹ
		ko-dā-sha'nu ..	קָדְשֵׁנוּ	ōrō-thā'nū ..	אוֹרוֹתֵינוּ

Practice.

בּוֹא בָּא מָה מַה פֶּה פֹּה פָּא פֶּא הֶא הִיא הוּא לוֹ לֹא
לוּ זֶה שָׁא שָׂא פָּלֵא כְּלֵא מָלֵא מָלֹא פָּנֶה פָּנָה פָּנֶה פְּנֵי
פָּנֵי פָּנָיו יוֹכִי יָמֵי יָכְיו יָמֶיהָ יוֹצֶיהָ רֹאשֵׁי רָאשֵׁי רָאשֵׁי
אֵלַי אֵלָיו אֵלַי גָּלָה גֹּלֶה גָּלוּי תָּלוּי קוֹנֶה קֹנֶי קֹנִי
קוֹנֶךְ קֹנִי קְנוֹ הוֹי גּוֹי אוֹי קְרָא קָרוּא שָׁלוּ וּבָנָיו
וּמֵאָחִיו וּמֵאַחֶיהָ

§ 3.—Syllables beginning with Two Consonants.

drā ..	דְּרַ	glā ..	גְּלַ	blā ..	בְּלַ	*a* in *far*.
mrā ..	מְרַ	frā ..	פְּרַ	trā ..	תְּרַ	

dlâ .. דְּל	glâ .. גְּל	blâ .. בְּל	} *a* in *ale*.
clâ .. כְּל	prâ .. פְּר	slâ .. שְׁלִי	
tree .. טְרִי	grī .. גְּרִי	blī .. בְּלִי	} *ī* in
prī .. פְּרִי	mrī .. מְרִי	krī .. קְרִי	*machine*
rdō .. רְדוֹ	glō .. גְּלוֹ	blō .. בְּלוֹ	} *ō* in *no*.
drō .. דְּרוֹ	srō .. שְׂרוֹ	slō .. שְׁלוֹ	
threw . תְּרוּ	brew . בְּרוּ	blū .. בְּלִי	} *ū* in *rule*.
prū .. פְּרוּ	trū .. טְרוּ	klū .. קְלוּ	
shra .. שְׁרַ	gla .. גְּל	bla .. בְּל	} *a* in *what*.
bra .. בְּר	tra .. טְר	cla .. כְּל	
fre .. פְּר	pre .. פְּר	ble .. בְּל	} *e* in *set*.
dle .. דְּל	cle .. כְּל	swe .. שְׁו	
fri .. פְּר	pri .. פְּר	bli .. בְּל	} *i* in *pin*.
kri .. קְר	dri .. דְּר	gri .. גְּר	
dlo .. דְּל	glo .. גְּל	blo .. בְּל	} *o* in *son*.
bro .. בְּר	pro .. פְּר	fro .. פְּר	
cru .. כְּר	glu .. גְּל	blu .. בְּל	} *u* in *bull*.
m'ru . מְר	plu .. פְּל	swu .. סְו	

Observe.—The two dots (:) under the first of the two consonants are called *sh'va initial*, because the consonants under which they are placed begin the syllable. In giving the Hebrew words in English characters, we shall indicate the initial sh'va by ('), as בְּל b'lo, &c.

Practice.

גַּל בַּל בָּל בְּלִי בְּלוּ בְּל בְּל בְּל גְּל

גְּל גְּלִי גְּל גְּלוּ גְּל גְּלִי דְּךְ דְּרָא דְּר

דְּרִי דְּרוּ דְּרוֹי דְּלוּ דְּמִי דְּמֶ דְּשׁ וְל וְלֶ וְלִי וְרוּ
וְרִי זְרִי זְרַ זֶר טְלַ טְלִי טְרִי יְמֵי יְמוֹ כְּלוּ כְּךָ לְרוּ
לְרֹ מְרִי מְךָ מְר גְּוֶ נְבוּ כְרוּ סְלִי סְרִי פְּרִי פְּרוּ צְל צְרִי
קְרוּ שֶׁל שְׁמֶ שְׂרֶ רְדִי רְדוּ תְרוּ תְלוּ תְמִי תְפִי תְרֹא
קְרָא קְהָה קְהוּ בְּלֹא מְצֹא מְצָא רָאָה רְאִי רְאוּ נְסָה
נְשִׂיא נְשִׂי״אֵי קְדוּ״אֵי שְׁרוּ״פֵי גְּבוּ״רָה גְּבִי״רָה בְּרָ״כָה
שְׁפָ״תַי מְלָ״כֵי בְּרוּכָה גְּלִי״לֵי דְּרוּשֵׁי שְׁנָנָה רְפוּאָה
צְדָקָה תְּנוּפָה תְּרוּמָה

Substitutes for Sh'va Initial or Semi Vowels —

(⁻ְ), (ֱ), (ֳ)*.

2. When the first of the two consonants is one of the gutturals ע, ח, ה, א†, which do not easily combine with the following letter, (-), (ֱ), or (ֳ) is added to the (ְ) that they may be uttered more distinctly. These marks may be considered as *semi-vowels*. They never form a syllable, but must be pronounced with the following syllable, in the same manner as letters having *sh'va initial*.

---

* They are denominated (ֲ) *ḥataph pataḥ*; (ֱ) *ḥataph segol*; (ֳ) *ḥataph kamets*.

† In a few instances the semi-vowels occur also under non-gutturals: as, וְזָהָב Gen. ii. 12, &c.

Examples.

אֲנִי ... ‎ אֲרִי ... ‎ אֳנִי ... ‎ אֲנִי ... ‎ הֲלֹא
עֲלִי ... ‎ חֳרִי ... ‎ אֱלִי ... ‎ חֳלִי ... ‎ הֲלִי
חֳלִי ... ‎ עֳנִי ... ‎ אֱמוּנָה ... ‎ ĕmū-nā

3. When the semi-vowels occur in the middle of a word, as וַאֲנִי wa-ănī, then the preceding vowel receives *metheg*. See page 22.

Examples.

ō-hăbī .... אֹהֲבִי ‎ ba-hălō-mī .... בַּחֲלֹמִי
be-ĕmū-nāh .. בֶּאֱמוּנָה ‎ zā-ăkū ...... זָעֲקוּ
tzā-ăkū........ צָעֲקוּ ‎ thō-ămî ...... תֹּאֲמִי
ā-hŏlī .... אָהֳלִי ‎ bā-hŏri ...... בָּחֳרִי

Practice.

אֲבִי אָבוּ אֲבִילִי אֲדוֹנִי אֲדֹנִי אֱלֹהֵי אֱלֹהַי אַהֲבָה
אָהֳלִי אַחֲלִי אֲחֻזּוּ אַחֲרִיתִי הֲלוּמֵי הֲלִיכִי הֲגוֹרָה
חֲמִישִׁי עֲבָדַי עֳנִי עֲרִירִי הַאֲזִינִי גְּאָלֻחוּ תְּהִלָּה
אֲהָמָיָה בַּעֲבוּרִי הֶעֱלָה בִּלְעֲדֵי הִפָּרְדִי תֶּאֱהָבוּ יִבְחֲרוּ

Words applicable to the preceding rules : —

my father .. אָבִי ‎ alas ...... אוֹי ‎ an island .. אִי
my God .... אֵלִי ‎ me ... אוֹתִי ‎ where .... אֵי
my brother אָחִי ‎ I .... אֲנִי ‎ or .... אוֹ

HEBREW LANGUAGE. 27

a teacher	מוֹרָה	God	יָהּ	my sister	אֲחוֹתִי
raw	נָא	a dove	יוֹנָה	my house	בֵּיתִי
a prophet	נָבִיא	beauty	יוֹפִי	my son	בְּנִי
comfort	נֶחָמָה	a curtain	יְרִיעָה	come	בֹּא
an ornament	עֲדִי	thus	כֹּה	he came	בָּא
humility	עֲנָוָה	if, for	כִּי	she came	בָּאָה
a corner	פֵּאָה	thus, so	כָּכָה	a kid	גְּדִי
the mouth	פֶּה	a prison	כֶּלֶא	a nation	גּוֹי
here	פֹּה	a vessel	כְּלִי	a valley	גַּיְא
wonder	פֶּלֶא	no, not	לֹא	a bee	דְּבוֹרָה
a gazelle	צְבִי	to him	לוֹ	knowledge	דֵּעָה
thirsty	צָמֵא	to me	לִי	he	הוּא
hard	קָשָׁה	to her	לָהּ	she	הִיא
evil	רָעָה	a lion	לָבִיא	he was	הָיָה
a year	שָׁנָה	the moon	לְבָנָה	this	זֶה, זוּ, זוֹ
a field	שָׂדֶה	a brick	לְבֵנָה	the breast	חָזֶה
a box, ark	תֵּבָה	what	מָה	a seer	חֹזֶה
the Law, instruction	תּוֹרָה	who	מִי	a stork	חֲסִידָה
		a hundred	מֵאָה	a lamb	טָלֶה
		fear	מוֹרָא	a basket	טֶנֶא

§ 4.—COMPOUND SYLLABLES.

1. Syllables terminating in a single consonant at the end of words.

dan	דָּן	bad	בַּד	at	אֶת	ab אַב } a in
ak	אַק	ach	אַךְ	lats	לָץ	tau מַט } what.

pen .. פֶּן	ped .. פֶּד	bed .. בֶּד	eb .. אֶב	}	*e in* met.
red .. רֶד	leg .. לֶג	lech .. לֶךְ	hem .. הֶם		
pin .. פִּן	did .. דִּד	bid .. בִּד	ib .. אִב	}	*i in* pin.
sin .. שִׂן	fin .. פִּן	dim .. דִּם	him .. הִם		
good .. גֻּד	full .. פֻּל	bul .. בֻּל	ub .. אֻב	}	*u in* bull.
lum .. לֻם	pull .. פֻּל	wool .. וֻל	wood .. וֻד		
kom .. קָם	mol .. מָל	son .. שָׂן	ob .. אָב	}	*o in* son.
mon .. מָן	som .. שָׂם	shon .. שָׁן	col .. קָל		
shōre .. שֹׁר	gōre .. גֹּר	bōde .. בֹּד	ōb .. אֹב	}	*o in* no.
cōre .. כֹּר	bōre .. בֹּר	sōle .. סֹל	sōre .. שֹׁר		
moon .. מוּן	cool .. כּוּל	rūle .. רוּל	ūb .. אוּב	}	*u in* rule.
room .. רוּם	doom .. דוּם	loom .. לוּם	noon .. נוּן		
mār .. מָר	bār .. בָּר	wār .. וָר	āb .. אָב	}	*a in* far.
nār .. נָר	fār .. פָּר	cār .. כָּר	pār .. פָּר		
pâle .. פֵּל	dâle .. דֵּל	âle .. אֵל	âb .. אֵב	}	*a in* ale.
dâre .. דֵּר	shâre .. שֵׁר	shâme .. שֵׁם	mâr .. מֵר		
pīl .. פִּיל	dīl .. דִּיל	īg .. אִיג	īb .. אִיב	}	*i in* machine.
sīr .. סִיר	shīr .. שִׁיר	kīr .. קִיר	fīl .. פִּיל		

Practice.

אָב אַב אוּב אוֹב אִיב אֶב אָב אַב

אָב אָב בּוּד בֹּד בִּיג בֶּג בַּג אָב אָב

HEBREW LANGUAGE. 29

בּוּ בַּח בָּח נַב גֵּט גֵּךְ גוֹל גּוּל גַּם נֶם דָּג דִּין
דוֹן דֵּעַ דָע הַס הַצ הֵן הֵיק הָר הֵף הִיף הִיף
וָן וֵשׁ וַשׂ זִיק זֵר זִית זֹאת זָת חוֹק חָק חֵר
טָשׁ טַשׁ יָם יַם כְּנ כַּן כֵּן לָךְ לוּף לוּף מִיץ מִין
מִן גֵּין נָק סִיר סַר עִיר עוֹר פֶּשׁ פָּשׂ צִיר צֵת קַמָ
קָם רַךְ שֵׁנ שׁוֹן שִׁין שָׁף שֵׁף צִין קֵן רִין שָׁת שֵׁת
תָּם תֵּן חֵן תּוּף תִּין תָּר תֵּת מֵת מָת פֵּן סוּף

2. Syllables and words beginning with two consonants and terminating in one.

ḥazir .. חֲזִיר	hălōm .... הֲלוֹם	ĕmeth .. אֱמֶת
b'dil .. בְּדִיל	b'ar ...... בְּאֵר	ḥalōm .. חֲלוֹם
y'min .. יְמִין	z'ab ...... זְאָב	d'rōr .. דְּרוֹר
m'ōd .. מְאֹד	g'dūd .... גְּדוּד	l'ōm .. לְאוֹם
ărafel .. עֲרָפֶל	d'bārim .. דְּבָרִים	n'bi-īm .. נְבִיאִים

Observe.—That in all these cases (except in the words אַףְ, אָתְ, or when the last letter is ךְ: as, אַךְ āch, לְךָ lach, מֶלֶךְ mé-lech) the terminating consonant receives no additional mark.

3. But when a word or syllable terminates in two consonants, then both the terminating consonants receive *shera* (:)

ka'mt ...... קָמְתְּ	ā-cha̱lt .... אָכַלְתְּ	ā-ma̱rt .... אָמַרְתְּ
kō'sht ...... קֹשְׁטְ	nā'rd .... נֵרְדְּ	na̱ft .... נֵפְטְ
hof-ka'dt .. הָפְקַדְתְּ	yā-shan't .. יָשַׁנְתְּ	nir-da̱'mt .. נִרְדַּמְתְּ

4. When the second of the terminating consonants is א, the (:) is omitted: as, חֵטְא hât; when the first is א, the sh'va is omitted in both: as, צֵאת tsât, רֹאשׁ rō'sh.

5. When the terminating consonant happens to be in the middle of the word, which generally takes place after short accented or unaccented vowels, or after long vowels having an accent, then the terminating consonant receives *sh'va* (:)*, as—

סַרְפַּד .... כַּרְמֶל .... אָנוּ ......
אַרְמוֹן .... אַרְגָּמָן . תִּפְקֹד ....
מִשְׁפָּט .. גַּרְזֶן ...... שָׁמַרְתָּ ..
יָכָלְתִּי .. קָטֹנְתִּי .. בָּשְׁתִּ* ....

Observe.—That no long vowel can form a compound syllable unless it have a principal accent. Except at the end of such words as are joined to the following by (-) *makkeph*, when the long vowel receives the secondary accent (׀) *metheg*: as, גָּר־שָׁם Gâr-Shā'm, שָׁת־לִי Shāth-Lī'.

Practice.

אָבִיר בָּרוּךְ דְּבִיר גָּדִיל הֲלֹא וְאֵין חֲלוֹם זָמִיר טָלֶה
יָמִין כָּבוֹד מְאֹד לָבוּשׁ מֶלֶךְ נְאֻם סָתָיו עֲקֹב עָרוּךְ
צָבָא פְּתִיל רָצוֹן קְרָב תְּמוֹל שְׁאוֹל הָלַךְ מָלַךְ גָּדַלְתְּ

HEBREW LANGUAGE.

אָבַלְתְּ גָּלַלְתְּ לָמַדְתְּ נָפַלְתְּ לָבַשְׁתְּ רָדַפְתְּ שָׁאַלְתְּ שָׁמַרְתְּ
אַבְרֵךְ אֶגְרוֹף בַּקְבּוּק גִּזְבָּר כְּרוּב כִּלְאָךְ פַּרְדֵּס מִשְׁגָּב
הַרְבֵּה תַּרְבּוּת

Vocabulary consisting of Words applicable to the preceding Rules.

I.

grace .... חֵן	a pit .... בּוֹר	God ...... אֵל
heat .... חוֹם	a garden .. גַּן	a father .. אָב
warm .... חַם	joy ...... גִּיל	a mother .. אֵם
good .... טוֹב	an uncle .. דּוֹד	a brother .. אָח
a row .... טוּר	a fish .... דָּג	light .. אוֹר
dew ...... טַל	blood .... דָּם	fire ...... אֵשׁ
hand .... יָד	wealth .. הוֹן	a man .. אִישׁ
day ...... יוֹם	a mountain הַר	a nation .. אוֹם
the sea .... יָם	a hook ... וָו	not ...... אַל
a cup .... כּוֹס	a spark .. זִיק	but ...... אַךְ
a bag .... כִּיס	sand .... חוֹל	to ...... אֶל
a rock .... כֵּף	a festival .. חַג	if .... אִם
the heart.. לֵב	a thread .. חוּט	daughter .. בַּת
moist .... לַח	palate .... חֵךְ	a son .... בֵּן

contention	רִיב	skin	עוֹר	bitter	מַר
soft, tender	רַךְ	with	עִם	myrrh	מֹר
evil, bad	רַע	a bird	עוֹף	from	מִן
exalted	רָם	a city	עִיר	a sort, kind	מִין
empty	רֵק	the mouth	פֶּה	a lamp	נֵר
but, only	רַק	pure gold	פָּז	a hawk	נֵץ
a lamb	שֶׂה	a bullock	פַּר	a heap, wall	נֵד
a sack	שַׂק	a flower	צִיץ	a banner	נֵס
a name	שֵׁם	shadow	צֵל	a secret	סוֹד
a song	שִׁיר	the voice	קוֹל	a horse	סוּס
an ox	שׁוֹר	light, easy	קַל	a moth	סָס
six	שֵׁשׁ	a nest	קֵן	a basket	סַל
there	שָׁם	a thorn	קוֹץ	a people	עַם
a tooth	שֵׁן	cold	קוֹר	a cloud	עָב
a drum	תֹּף	straw	קַשׁ	a yoke	עוֹל
a hill, heap	תֵּל	much	רַב	upon, over	עַל

II.

yesterday	תְּמוֹל	a lion	אֲרִי	truth	אֱמֶת
a lord	גְּבִיר	a well	בְּאֵר	a nut	אֱגוֹז
a dream	חֲלוֹם	a wolf	זְאֵב	honey	דְּבַשׁ
a spider	עֲבָבִישׁ	a garment	לְבוּשׁ	a friend	יְדִיד
a fool	אֱוִיל	alone	לְבַד	very	מְאֹד

HEBREW LANGUAGE.

III.

| truth .... קֹשְׁטְ | spikenard נֵרְךְּ | naphtha .. נֶפְטְ |
| a bottle ... נֹאד | the head רֹאשׁ | sin .... חֵטְא |

IV.

a hatchet גַּרְזֶן	a table .... שֻׁלְחָן	a girdle אַבְנֵט
a nob .. כַּפְתּוֹר	a flask .... בַּקְבּוּק	fist .... אֶגְרוֹף
a song .. מִזְמוֹר	a queen .. מַלְכָּה	purple .. אַרְגָּמָן
a writing מִכְתָּב	judgment מִשְׁפָּט	iron .... בַּרְזֶל
a treasurer גִּזְבָּר	a mouse .. עַכְבָּר	a border כַּרְכֹּב
a sceptre שַׁרְבִיט	the ground קַרְקַע	a furnace כִּבְשָׁן

§ 5.—Of Sh'va in the Middle of a Word.

In the preceding section we have shown, that *sh'va* preceded by a short accented or unaccented vowel, or by a long accented vowel is *final*, that is to say, the letter having it terminates the syllables. But when *sh'va* is preceded by a letter having *sh'va*, as בְּסְפְּךָ *cas-pchā*; or by a long vowel not having a principal accent, as יֹלְדָה *yō-l'-dāh*; or when the *sh'va* is under the first of a double letter, and the preceding vowel has *metheg**: as, הַלְלוּ *ha-l'-lū*; in all such cases

---

* When the metheg is omitted, some grammarians consider the sh'va as final, as חִקְקִי.

34   ELEMENTS OF THE

the sh'va is *initial*, or in other words, the letter having it begins the syllable.

Examples.

I.

אִשְׁתְּךָ *ish-t'chā'* thy wife
דַּרְכְּךָ *dar-k'chā'* thy way
חֶלְקְךָ *hel-k'chā'* thy portion
יִלְמְדוּ *yil-m'dū'*
קָדְשְׁךָ *kod-sh'chā'*
תִּפְקְדוּ *tif-k'dū'*

II.

אָמְרָה *ām-rāh* she said
שֹׁמְרֵי *shō-m'rē'* keepers of
שֹׁפְטִים *shō-f'tīm* judges
הָלְכָה *hā-l'chāh* she went
יֵרְדוּ *yē-r'dū'* they shall go down
יִירְשׁוּ *yī-r'shū'* they shall inherit

III.

הִנְנִי *hin-nī'* behold me
חַלְלֵי *chal-lē'* slain of
נָדְדוּ *nād-dū'* they wandered
רַנְּנוּ *ran-n'nū'* sing ye
טַלְלֵי *tal-lē'* dew of
קִלְלַת *kil-lath'* curse of

Observe.—When the letter which ought to have *sh'va initial* is either ח, ה, א, or ע, it receives one of the semi-vowels (ֲ ֱ ֳ) instead of sh'va: as, zar-ăcha' זַרְעֲךָ, ō-hăbī אֹהֲבִי, mâ-ănū מָאֲנוּ, yō-ḥăză-mō יֹאחֲזֵמוֹ. See page 25.

---

* The vowel preceding sh'va initial generally receives ( ) metheg, to show that it forms a simple syllable.

HEBREW LANGUAGE.

Words exemplifying the preceding Rules.

priests	כֹּהֲנִים	thy silver	כַּסְפְּךָ
they said	אָמְרוּ	thy king	מַלְכְּךָ
praise ye	הַלְלוּ	judges	שׁוֹפְטִים
a waste	שְׁמָמָה	thy bread	לַחְמְךָ
they shall fear	יְרָאוּ	thy seed	זַרְעֲךָ
a trumpet	חֲצֹצְרָה	overseers	שׁוֹטְרִים
rulers	מוֹשְׁלִים	shout ye	רַנְּנוּ
a broom	מַטְאֲטֵא	she went	הָלְכָה
your way	דַּרְכְּכֶם	merchants	סֹחֲרִים

§ 6.—DAGESH.

(See p. 6.)

1. Examples of words in which the dot (*dagesh*) in the letters בגד כפת is (*kal*) simple, namely:—

1st. When they begin a word—

grass	דֶּשֶׁא	rain	גֶּשֶׁם	morning	בֹּקֶר
straw	תֶּבֶן	a mule	פֶּרֶד	a dog	כֶּלֶב

Observe.—The *dagesh* is omitted when such words are preceded by others terminating in one of the *quiescent letters* א, ה, ו, י (see p. 21), as תֵּרְאוּ פָנַי, הָיְתָה תֹהוּ, לִי כֹל לֹא בֶן. This rule is, however, subject to many exceptions, which will be noticed in the progress of the work.

2ⁿᵈ· When they begin a syllable in the middle of a word, and are preceded by a *compound syllable* (see p. 21.), as—

מִסְפָּר a number . . גַּרְגַּר a berry . . מַרְדּוּת rebellion
מַלְכָּה a queen . . חֶרְפָּה a reproach . . מַחְתָּה a coal-pan

Observe.—When the letters בנד כפת are preceded by a *simple syllable:* as, אֵבֶל *mourning*, אֹכֶל *food*, אֶבֶן *a stone;* or by *initial sh'va*, as לְבוּשׁ *a garment*, גְּדִי *a kid* (except the words שְׁתַּיִם, שְׁתֵּי); or by a *semi-vowel;* as, מַאֲכָל *food*, אַהֲבָה *love*, the *dagesh* is omitted.

These letters (בנד כפת) may, therefore, be considered as an index by which the nature of a preceding *sh'va* may be determined. If they have *dagesh*, which, according to the above rules indicates that they begin the syllable, then the preceding sh'va must of course be *final:* מִסְפָּר, מַלְכָּה, must therefore be read mis-pā'r, mal-cā, and not, mi-s'pār, ma-l'cā : but if they have no *dagesh*, then the preceding sh'va is *initial:* יָרְדוּ, רָדְפוּ must be read yā-r'dū, rā-d'fū, and not, yār-dū, rād-fū. By the same rule, words like the following: מַלְכֵי לִגְבוּל, בִּגְדֵי, ought to be read ma-l'chū, bi-g'dā, li-g'vūl, and not mal-chā, big-dā, lig-vūl, etc., as some grammarians maintain.

2. Dagesh ḥazak (*strong dagesh*, see page 6) doubles the letter in which it occurs: as, אִכָּר, סֻלָּם, ic-cār, sul-lām.

It is always preceded by a vowel*, and may occur in any letter except א, ה, ח, ע, ר·

---

* In some instances *dagesh ḥazak* occurs at the beginning of words, but then it must be pronounced with the last syllable of the preceding word: as, מֹשֶׁה לֵּאמֹר mōshel-lāmōr.

Examples of words in which the dot (Dagesh) is (Hazak) strong.

an oak	אֵלָה	a burden	מַשָּׂא
a gift	מַתָּנָה	a hut	סֻכָּה
a judge	דַּיָּן	a husbandman	אִכָּר
sabbath	שַׁבָּת	a goblet, bowl	אַגָּן
a blind man	עִוֵּר	a bunch	אֲגֻדָּה
deluge	מַבּוּל	a staff	מַקֵּל
teeth	שִׁנַּיִם	a word	מִלָּה
a window	חַלּוֹן	a ring	טַבַּעַת
a prayer	תְּפִלָּה	a law	חֻקָּה
praise	תְּהִלָּה	a bride	כַּלָּה
a roll, volume	מְגִלָּה	a ladder	סֻלָּם
dread	מְחִתָּה	a sickle	מַגָּל

When ו receives dagesh, it appears similar to the vowel וּ ū; yet it may easily be distinguished from it, as the consonant preceding the *vowel* ū is always without a vowel point: thus, אוּר ūr, שׁוּר shūr, גּוּר gūr; but when the dot represents *dagesh*, the preceding consonant has always a vowel: as, אִוָּה iv-vā′, שִׁוָּה shiv-vā′, עִוֵּר iv-vā′r, קַוָּם kav-vā′m.

Observe.—Consonants having *dagesh hazak* and *sh'va* are pronounced in a similar manner as two consonants, each having sh'va in the middle of a word. (See § 5, p. 33.) דַּבְּרִי is pronounced like דַּבְ־בְּרִי dab-b'ri; פֻּקְּדוּ like פֻּקְ־קְדוּ puk-k'dū; מִנְּשׂוֹא like מִנְ־נְשׂוֹא min-n'sō.

§ 7.—Miscellaneous Remarks.

1. As one of the greatest difficulties with which the learner has to contend, is to determine when sh'va is *initial* and when *final*, we shall collect here the several rules as given in the preceding sections.

Sh'va is Initial—

1ˢᵗ. At the beginning of words: as, בְּנוֹ, בְּלִי. (See chap. II. § 3.)

2ⁿᵈ. When preceded by another sh'va: as, כָּסְפְּךָ cas-p'chā, יִשְׁמְרוּ yish-m'rū'. (See § 5 I.)

3ʳᵈ. When preceded by a long unaccented vowel: as, אָמְרוּ ā-m'rū. (See § 5. II.)

4ᵗʰ. When on the first of a double letter: as, הִנְנִי hi-n'nī. (See § 5 III.)

5ᵗʰ. When followed by either of the letters ד, ג, ב, ת, פ, כ, without dagesh. (See § 6. page 36.)

6ᵗʰ. When under a letter having dagesh: as, דַּבְּרִי dab-brī. (See § 6, 37.)

7ᵗʰ. When preceded by metheg: as, יִשְׁנוּ yi-sh'nū*. (See pp. 22 and 33.)

---

* This might be taken as a general rule; for since *metheg* shows that the vowel to which it is annexed is a simple syllable, it follows that the succeeding letter commences the next syllable, and consequently if it have *sh'va* it must be *initial*. Unfortunately, the punctuators have often omitted this useful mark (ˈ) where they ought to have inserted it, and inserted it where they ought to have

Sh'va is Final—

1st. At the end of words: as, אַתְּ at, קָמְתְּ kamt. (See § 4.)

2nd. When preceded by short vowels not having metheg, as אַרְמוֹן ar-mōn*. (See § 4.)

3rd. When preceded by a long vowel having a principal accent: as, שֹׁבְנָה shō'v-nā*. (See § 4.)

On the Vowels (ָ) and (ׇ).

2. As (ָ) represent *ā long* as well as *o short*, and as (ׇ) is often long although unaccompanied by י, the following rules will be found useful to distinguish them.

(ָ) and (ׇ) are *long* whenever they form simple syllables, accented or unaccented, or compound accented syllables.

(ָ) and (ׇ) are *short* whenever they form compound syllables without having an accent.

Thus, in הָאָדָם—

הָ is a simple syllable because it has a secondary accent, *metheg*.

---

omitted it; and grammarians, relying too much on the correctness of manuscripts or the printed text, have given rules respecting this secondary accent, which have no other foundation than the mistakes of transcribers and printers.

* To these two rules there are several exceptions, which will be noticed in the progress of the work.

אָ is so likewise, as it is not followed by either dagesh or sh'va *final**.

דָּם is a compound syllable, yet (ָ) is long, because it has a principal accent. The word is therefore pronounced hā-ā-dā'm.

The first (.) in וַהֲקִמֹתִי (Gen. vi. 18.) and in יִשְׁמָךְ (Gen. xlviii. 20.) are long, because they have *metheg*. So is likewise the second (.) in תַּנִּינִם (Gen. i. 21), because it forms a compound accented syllable. See the following examples.

שָׁמְרָה	shā-m'rā'	she guarded
קָם	kā'm	he rose
גָּר־שָׁם	gār-shā'm	he dwelt there
חָכְמָה	ḥā-ch'mā	she was wise
רִב	rīv, or rīb	strife, contention
זָכְרָה	zā-ch'rā'	she remembered
יִשְׁנוּ	yī-sh'nū'	they shall sleep
רָנַן	rā-na'n	he shouted, rejoiced

---

* Short (ָ) forms sometimes simple syllables, as in קָדָשִׁים ko-dā-shīm, חָדָשִׁים ḥo-dā-shīm, when the short (ָ) has generally two dots added: thus, קֳדָשִׁים. These are, however, often omitted, and it then requires a knowledge of Etymology to distinguish it from long (ָ). See Etymology and Syntax, page 70, under the form פֹּעַל.

יִרְאוּ . . yī-r'ū' . . . they shall fear

*דָּרְבָן . . dā-r'vā'n . . a goad.

But the first (ָ) and (ָ) in the following words are *short*, because they form compound syllables without having the accent, being followed either by sh'va *final*, *dagesh*, or a terminating consonant.

Examples.

שָׁמְרָה . . shom-rā' . . keep thou

כָּל־בָּשָׂר . . col·bā-sā'r . . all flesh

חָכְמָה . . hoch-mā' . . wisdom

רִבּוֹא . . rib·bō' . . . a myriad

†וַיָּקָם . . vay-yā'-kom . and he rose

---

* *Gesenius*, in his "*Lehrgebäude*," page 43, asserts (without sufficient authority) that the first (ָ) in this word ought to be pronounced short—dŏr·ban; but I have followed *Kimchi* and other eminent grammarians, who consider it as long. *Kimchi*, in treating of this and several other words, such as יָשְׁפֵה (Exod. xxviii. 20), דָּרְבֹנוֹת (Eccles. xii. 13), דָּלְיָו (Num. xxiv. 7), adds:—קבלנו קריאתם בקמץ רחב ולא שמענו ולא ראינו בו מחלוקת: "We have received it as certain, that these words are read with *long kametz*, nor have we seen or heard any dispute on the subject." *Michlol Katon*, page 148.

† In וַיָּקָם the first (ָ) is *long*, because it has the accent, but the second is *short*, as it forms a compound syllable without an accent.

By comparing the words in the tables, the learner will see how very important it is to attend to a correct pronunciation.

זָכְרָה . . zoch-rā' . . *remember thou*
יִשְׁנוּ . . yish-nū' . . *they shall repeat*
רָנִּי . . ron-nī' . . *shout thou*
יִרְאוּ . . yir-ū' . . *they shall see*
קָרְבָּן . . kor-bā'n . . *an offering.*

3. Two dots are often added, by way of distinction, to short (ֳ): as, חֳלִי holi, *sickness*; צֳרִי tso-ri, *balsam*; שִׁבֳּלִים shib-bo-lim, *ears of corn*; חֳדָשִׁים *months*, &c.; but then it is liable to be confounded with (ְ:), one of the substitutes of sh'va (§ 3. II). A little practice, however, and particularly an acquaintance with the structure of the language, will soon remove these apparent difficulties.

4. (ֹ) is often substituted for וֹ, and is then pronounced long; but in such cases it generally has either the accent or metheg: as, גְבֹל g'vū'l, יָשֹׁבוּ yā-shu'-vū, יַכְסֹימוֹ y'chas-yū'mn, גְבֹלְךָ g'vū'-l'chā', לִלְאֹת lū-lā-ō'th.

On the Vowel וֹ ō, *when it is preceded by* שׂ s, *or succeeded by* שׁ sh.

5. It has already been stated that ו is frequently omitted, and the *point* placed above the left of the letter to which it belongs, retained: as, לֹא lō, instead לוֹא; בֹּקֶר bō'ker, instead בּוֹקֶר. It has also been remarked, that a point over the left of שׂ indicates it to be *s*, one over the right, שׁ *sh*. Now to avoid the concurrence of two points, which would happen when

וֹ ō is preceded by שׂ s, as in שׂוֹנֵא sō-nâ, or when וֹ is succeeded by שׁ sh, as in מֹשֶׁה, the וֹ is altogether omitted, and the words are written מֹשֶׁה, שֹׂנֵא. The point performs, therefore, in all such cases, two offices. Thus, in the first example שֹׂנֵא, it indicates the nature of the letter, namely, that it represents s, and not sh, and it supplies at the same time the vowel וֹ; the letter שׂ is, therefore, pronounced so. In the second example, מֹשֶׁה, the point supplies the vowel וֹ belonging to מ, and indicates at the same time that שׁ is sh, and got s.

In the following examples, however, where שׁ is preceded by a letter having either a vowel or sh'va, the point indicates only that שׁ is sh; as, מָשָׁל mā-shā'l, הַמָּשָׁל ham-shâl. Likewise in the following words: שֵׂכֶל sé-chel, מַשְׂכִּיל mas-chi'l, where שׂ has either a vowel or sh'va, the dot indicates only that שׂ represents s.

When שׁ sh is succeeded by (וֹ ō), as in שֹׁפָר shōfâr, מִכְשֹׁל mich-shō'l; or שׂ s is preceded by (וֹ ō), as בֹּשֶׂם bō'sem, שׂ receives in either case two points, yet they may easily by distinguished. For in the first two examples where שׁ begins the word or syllable, the first point can only indicate the nature of the letter, and the second its pronunciation; since שׁ has no other vowel. In the second example, בֹּשֶׂם, the first point must belong to ב, as it has no other vowel, and the second point can only mark the nature of the letter שׂ s, since that consonant has already a vowel.

From the preceding observations it follows:—

1st. That שׁ represents *sh*, and *ō* belonging to the preceding syllable, when the preceding consonant has neither vowel nor sh'va: as, מֹשֵׁל mōshâ'l, הַמֹּשֵׁל ham-mō-shâ'l. (See No. 1.)

2nd. That שׁ represents *sh* only, at the beginning of words, when it must have either (:) or a vowel: as, שְׁלֹום sh'lō'm, שָׁלוֹם shā-lōm; and in the middle and end of words, when the preceding consonant has either a (:) or a vowel: as, מְשֹׁל m'shol, מָשָׁל mā-shā'l. (See No. 2.)

3rd. That שׂ is pronounced *so*, when it has neither sh'va nor a vowel: as, שׂנֵא sōnâ', נָשֹׂא nā-sō'. (See No. 3.)

4th. שׂ represents *s* only, when it has either sh'va: as, שְׂנֹא s'nō, or a vowel: as, שָׂמְתָּ sa'm-tā. (See No 4.)

5th. שׂ represents *s* and the vowel *ō* of the preceding consonant, when it has either a vowel: as, בֹּשֶׂם bō'-sem, or sh'va: as, נִשְׂאִים nō-s"īm; or when it terminates a word: as, תָּפֹשׂ tā-fo's. (See No. 5.)

6th. That שׁ is pronounced *shō* when it begins a word: as, שֹׁפָר shō-fā'r; or a syllable: as, מִכְשֹׁל mich-shō'l, or preceded by (:), as לִשֹׁנִי l'-shō-nī'. (See No. 6.)

	3.		2.		1.
an enemy	שׂנֵא	rule thou	מְשֹׁל	a ruler..	מֹשֵׁל
to carry..	נָשֹׂא	dominion	הַמְשֵׁל	the ruler	הַמֹּשֵׁל

3.	2.	1.
satiety .. שֹׂבַע	a proverb .. מָשָׁל	riches .... עֹשֶׁר
to do, make עָשֹׂה	he enquired דָּרַשׁ	to enquire דְּרֹשׁ
to withhold חֲשֹׂךְ	the third שְׁלִישִׁי	thirty .. שְׁלֹשִׁים
to lay bare חָשֹׂף	he darkened חָשַׁךְ	darkness.. חֹשֶׁךְ

6.	5.	4.
a horn .. שֹׁפָר	spice .... בֹּשֶׂם	he hated .. שָׂנֵא
a bribe .. שֹׁחַד	to lay hold תָּפַשׂ	a prince .. נָשִׂיא
a judge .. שֹׁפֵט	a carrier .. נֹשֵׂא	a field .... שָׂדֶה
a gatekeeper שֹׁעֵר	carriers .. נֹשְׂאִים	a burden.. מַשָּׂא
languages לְשֹׁנוֹת	a maker .. עֹשֶׂה	he withheld חָשַׂךְ
an overseer שֹׁטֵר	to urge .... נָגַשׂ	flesh .... בָּשָׂר

6. הּ, חַ, and עַ terminating a word, are pronounced אַע, אַח, אַהּ: as, מַגְבִּיהַּ mag-bī′ah, not *mag-bī-ha*; רוּחַ rū′ah, not *rū′-ha*; רָקִיעַ rākī′-ang, not *rākī-gna*; רוֹצֵחַ rō-tsâ-ah, not *rō-tsâ-ha**.

Practice.

אֱלוֹהַּ גָּבֹהַּ יַגְבִּיהַּ הִתְמַהְמֵהַּ לוּחַ שִׂיחַ פֹּרֵחַ יָרֵחַ
פָּתַח אֶפְרֹחַ שָׁחוֹחַ גָּבִיעַ רָקִיעַ קָרוּעַ מַזְרִיעַ מַרְצֵעַ
מַלְקוֹחַ צְפַרְדֵּעַ

---

* Some, however, pronounce these words mag-bi-ya, rūvah, raki-ya, rō-tsâh.

7. יְהֹוָה or יְיָ is pronounced אֲדֹנָי .. ădōnāy*

  יֱהֹוִה is pronounced .. אֱלֹהִים .. elō-hī'm*

  יְרוּשָׁלַםִ is pronounced יְרוּשָׁלַיִם .. y'rū-shā-lā'-yim

8. Words consisting of the same consonants, yet differing in sense, in consequence of their having different vowel points.

to learn	לְמֹד	God	אֵל
he learned	לָמַד	to	אֶל
to teach	לַמֵּד	not	אַל
he taught	לִמֵּד	a ram	אַיִל
a brick	לְבֵנָה	strength	אֱיָל
the moon	לְבָנָה	to be willing	אָבֹה
a poplar tree	לִבְנֶה	he would	אָבָה
frankincense	לְבֹנָה	enmity	אֵיבָה
to her son	לִבְנָהּ	a woman	אִשָּׁה
a gate	שַׁעַר	her husband	אִישָׁהּ
hair	שֵׂעָר	the sun	חַמָּה
a garment	שַׂלְמָה	a wall	חוֹמָה
perfect	שְׁלֵמָה	anger	חֵמָה
Solomon	שְׁלֹמֹה	milk	חָלָב
her peace	שְׁלוֹמָהּ	fat	חֵלֶב

* This pronunciation is very ancient, as may be proved from the Septuagint and other ancient books. Many learned Christians, however, pronounce these words Jehovah.

HEBREW LANGUAGE. 47

Reading Lessons.
Genesis, Chap. i.

1 בְּרֵאשִׁית בָּרָא אֱלֹהִים אֵת הַשָּׁמַיִם וְאֵת הָאָרֶץ:
2 וְהָאָרֶץ הָיְתָה תֹהוּ וָבֹהוּ וְחֹשֶׁךְ עַל־פְּנֵי תְהוֹם וְרוּחַ
3 אֱלֹהִים מְרַחֶפֶת עַל־פְּנֵי הַמָּיִם: וַיֹּאמֶר אֱלֹהִים יְהִי אוֹר
4 וַיְהִי־אוֹר: וַיַּרְא אֱלֹהִים אֶת־הָאוֹר כִּי־טוֹב וַיַּבְדֵּל אֱלֹהִים
בֵּין הָאוֹר וּבֵין הַחֹשֶׁךְ:

English Pronunciation.	*Division of Syllables.*
1 B'rā=shī'th¹ bā=rā' ĕlō=hī'm ăth hash=shā=ma'=yim v'ăth² hā=ā'=rets:	בְּרֵא־שִׁית בָּ־רָא אֱ־לֹ־הִים אֵת הַ־שָּׁ־מַיִם* וְאֵת הָ־אָ־רֶץ:
2 V'hā=ā'rets hāy'=thā'thō'=hū vā=bō'=hū v'ḥō'=shech al=p'nā' th'hōm v'rū'=ach ĕlō=hī'm m'ra=he'=feth al=p'nā' ham=mā='yim: Vay³=yō'=mer ĕlō=hī'm y'hī ō'r,	וְ־הָ־אָ־רֶץ הָ־יְ־תָה תֹ־הוּ וָ־בֹ־הוּ וְ־חֹ־שֶׁךְ עַל־פְּ־נֵי תְ־הוֹם וְ־רוּחַ אֱ־לֹ־הִים מְ־רַ־חֶ־פֶת עַל־פְּ־נֵי הַ־מָּ־יִם: וַ־יֹּ־אמֶר אֱ־לֹ־הִים יְ־הִי אוֹר
4 va=y'hī ō'r: vay=ya'r ĕlō=hī'm eth-hā=ō'r kī-tō'b vay=yab=dā'l ĕlō=him bân hā=ō'r ūbâ'n ha=ḥō'=shech.	וַ־יְ־הִי־אוֹר: וַ־יַּ־רְא אֱ־לֹ־הִים אֶת־הָ־אוֹר כִּי־טוֹב וַ־יַּ־בְ־דֵּל אֱ־לֹ־הִים בֵּין הָ־אוֹר וּ־בֵין הַ־חֹ־שֶׁךְ:

---

¹ The Spanish Jews who pronounce (ת) like t, and sh'va initial like *short* (ĕ), would read this word Bĕrâ-sheet; and אֵת *ât*, etc.

² This word is pronounced vĕ-âth or wĕ-ât, not *vâth* nor *wât*.

³ Like *y* in *boy*.

* The two dots after ה etc., are made use of to indicate *dagesh ḥazak*.

ANALYSIS.

Verse 1.

בְּרֵאשִׁית *in* [*the*] *beginning*. The dot in בּ is *dagesh kal* (See pp. 6 & 35). The two dots under it (בְּ) *sh'va initial* (p. 23), and must, therefore, be pronounced in conjunction with the following consonant and vowel בְּרֵ· The two dots under רֵ are the sign of the vowel point *tséré* (p. 15). The א is *mute* (p. 22); the three consonants and vowel points forming together the *simple* syllable (p. 21) בְּרֵא b'râ. The dot upon the right of שׁ shows this letter to be equivalent to *sh* (p. 43). The dot under it (שִׁ) forms with the following י, which is *mute* (p. 22) the long vowel *ḥirik* (p. 15); and the ת is pronounced with it, forming together the *compound syllable* (p. 21) שִׁית· The accent is on the last syllable. בְּ *in*, רֵאשִׁית *beginning*.

בָּרָא *he created*[2]. The (ָ) *kamets*, under בּ and רָ is *long* (p. 39), each forming a *simple syllable* (p. 21). א is *mute* (p. 22). Accent on the last syllable.

אֱלֹהִים *God*[1]. The (ֱ) under א is *a semi-vowel* (p. 25); being a substitute for *sh'va initial*, it must be pronounced in conjunction with the next consonant and vowel, thus אֱלֹ elō. The dot at the left of

---

[2] [1] i. e. God created.

לֹ is the vowel point *ḥōlem* (p. 15). The dot under ה is *long ḥirik* (p. 15), being followed by י which is *mute* (p. 22), and forming a compound syllable with final ם, thus הִים *hī'm*. Accent on the last syllable.

אֵת. The א is equal to *à* (p. 15); ת is pronounced with it. This word is the sign of the objective case.

הַשָּׁמַיִם *the heaven.* (-) under ה is the vowel point *pathaḥ* (p. 15). The dot in the שׁ is *dagesh ḥazak* (p. 36), which, as it doubles the letter in which it occurs, makes שׁ equivalent to שׁשׁ; the first of which is pronounced with the syllable that precedes it, הַשׁ *hash*, and the second is pronounced with its own vowel שָׁ *shā*. מַ *ma'*, is a simple syllable having the accent. י is pronounced like *y* in *yes;* the dot beneath it is *short ḥirik* (p. 15), forming a compound syllable with the ם, thus יִם *yim*. The accent is on the *penultimate*, and the whole word is pronounced *hash-shā-má-yim*. ה is the sign of the article *the*.

וְאֵת. (:) is *sh'va initial* (p. 23). אֵת has already been explained. ו is equivalent to *and*.

הָאָרֶץ *the earth.* (ׇ) under ה and א is long (p. 39), forming each a simple syllable. (ֶ) under ר is the vowel point *segol* (p. 15), forming a compound syllable with ץ *final*. Accent on the penultimate. ה is the sign of the article (*the*). The two dots (׃) after this word, indicate the end of the verse.

Verse 2.

וְהָאָרֶץ *and the earth.* See the preceding word. וֹ *and*, ה *the*, אֶרֶץ *earth.*

הָיְתָה *she was.* The small stroke next to הָ is *metheg* (p. 22), which shows that (ָ) is a long vowel, as short (ַ) never admits *metheg;* this being a simple syllable, the (ְ) under י must be *sh'va initial* (p. 37), belonging to ת. The last ה is *mute* (p. 21). Accent on the last syllable. The word is read *hā-'ythā'* not *hāy-thā'.*

תֹהוּ *without form.* Dagesh kal is omitted in ת, because the preceding word ends in a quiescent letter (p. 35). The point next to ת is the vowel ō, forming the syllable תֹ *thō*. The וּ with the dot is the vowel *shurek ū* (p. 15), forming with the ה the syllable הוּ *hū*. Accent on the penultimate syllable.

וָבֹהוּ *and void.* (ָ) under וֹ is a simple syllable. The dot next to ב is the vowel ō. וֹ *and*, בֹהוּ *void.* Accent on the penultimate syllable.

וְחֹשֶׁךְ *and darkness.* The dot upon שׁ performs two offices; it shows that the preceding ח is pronounced hō, and that שׁ is *sh* and not *s* (p. 43). The two dots ךְ are *sh'va final* (p. 38). Accent on the penultimate; and the word is pronounced *v'hō-shech*. וְ *and*, חֹשֶׁךְ *darkness.*

עַל־ *upon.* A compound monosyllable, joined to the next word by (־) *makkeph* (p. 21), and is therefore unaccented.

פְּנֵי *the face of.* The י is *mute* (p. 23).

תְהוֹם *the deep.* A monosyllable. The *sh'va* is *initial.* ת is without dagesh, because the preceding word ends in a *mute* (p. 35).

וְרוּחַ *and the spirit of.* The (-) under ח is pronounced as if it were under a preceding א (p. 45), *e'rū-ach.* וְ *and* רוּחַ *spirit.*

אֱלֹהִים *God.* This word has already been explained.

מְרַחֶפֶת [was] *hovering.* (:) under מ is *sh'va initial.* (-) under ר is the vowel point *pathah* (p. 15), forming together the simple syllable מְרַ *m'ra.* The three dots under ח and פ are *segol* (p. 15), the first forming the simple syllable חֶ *he,* the second the compound syllable פֶת. Accent on the penultimate.

E

עַל־פְּנֵי (See the preceding page).

הַמָּיִם *the waters*. The dot in מ is *dagesh ḥazak*, and is, therefore, equal to מַמָ, one being pronounced with the preceding syllable, thus הַמ, the other with its own vowel (ָ) which is *long ā*, because it has the accent (p. 39). י sounds like *y* in *yes*. The (ִ) under it is short *i*, forming a compound syllable with *final* ם. The word is pronounced *ham-ma'-yim*. ה *the,* מָיִם *waters*. The (:) indicates the end of the verse.

Verse 3.

וַיֹּאמֶר *And he said*[2]. The dot in י is *dagesh ḥazak*. (See the preceding word.) The dot next to יֹ is the vowel *ō*. The א is *mute*. The accent is on the penultimate syllable. The word is pronounced *vay-yō'-mer*.

אֱלֹהִים *God*[1]. (See verse 1.) i. e. *and God said*.

יְהִי *it shall be*. י sounds like *y* in *yes*. The (:) under it is *sh'va initial*. (ִ) under הִ is *long ī* (p. 39). The second י is *mute*. Pronounced *y'hī* or *ye-hī*.

אוֹר *light*. אוֹ represents the vowel *ō* (p. 15), and is pronounced together with the ר, thus, אוֹר *ō'r*.

וַיְהִי־אוֹר *and it was light*. (׀) next to וַ is *metheg*, and consequently the following (:) is *sh'va initial*.

HEBREW LANGUAGE.

(p. 38.) The small horizontal stroke after the second ׳ is *makkeph* (p. 21), in consequence of which the word is unaccented, and is pronounced with the following word אוֹר, thus *ray'hī-ọ'r*. The (:) after אוֹר indicates the end of the verse.

Verse 4.

וַיַּרְא *and he saw*². The dot in ׳ is *dagesh ḥazak*. (:) under the ר is *sh'va final* (p. 39). א is *mute*. The word is pronounced *vay-ya'r*.

אֱלֹהִים *God*¹. (See verse 1.) i. e. *and God saw*.

אֶת sign of the objective case. (־) after ת is *makkeph*, which joins it to the next word, in consequence of which it is unaccented, and has the short vowel (ֶ *e*) instead of (ֵ *â*). Compare this word with אֵת in verse 1.

הָאוֹר *the light* (see the preceding verse). ה *the*, אוֹר *light*.

כִּי־טוֹב *that* [*it was*] *good*. The dot in כ is *dagesh kal* (p. 35). The dot under it (כִּ) is *long ī*. ׳ is *mute*. (־) is *makkeph*, which is the reason that this word is unaccented. It is pronounced with the following word *tō'b*, which has the accent. כִּי *that*, טוֹב *good*.

וַיַּבְדֵּל *and he divided*². וַיְ (see the word וַיְרָא, verse 4). The (:) under בְּ is *sh'va final*, because the דּ which follows it has *dagesh kal* (p. 36). Accent on the last syllable. Pronounced *ray-yab-dâ'l*.

אֱלֹהִים *God*¹. (See verse 1.) i. e. *and God divided*.

בֵּין *between*. The dot in בּ is *dagesh kal*. The ' is mute.

הָאוֹר *the light*. (See the preceding verse.)

וּבֵין *and between*. ו is pronounced *û*, not *vû* (p. 22). בֵּין (see the same word above). ו *and*, בֵּין *between*.

הַחֹשֶׁךְ *the darkness*. (See verse 2.)

PRACTICE.

(Gen. i.)

⁵ וַיִּקְרָא אֱלֹהִים לָאוֹר יוֹם וְלַחֹשֶׁךְ קָרָא לָיְלָה וַיְהִי־עֶרֶב
⁶ וַיְהִי־בֹקֶר יוֹם אֶחָד ׃ וַיֹּאמֶר אֱלֹהִים יְהִי רָקִיעַ בְּתוֹךְ
⁷ הַמָּיִם וִיהִי מַבְדִּיל בֵּין מַיִם לָמָיִם ׃ וַיַּעַשׂ אֱלֹהִים אֶת־
הָרָקִיעַ וַיַּבְדֵּל בֵּין הַמַּיִם אֲשֶׁר מִתַּחַת לָרָקִיעַ וּבֵין הַמַּיִם
⁸ אֲשֶׁר מֵעַל לָרָקִיעַ וַיְהִי־כֵן ׃ וַיִּקְרָא אֱלֹהִים לָרָקִיעַ שָׁמָיִם
וַיְהִי־עֶרֶב וַיְהִי־בֹקֶר יוֹם שֵׁנִי ׃

HEBREW LANGUAGE.

The same verses divided into Syllables, with the literal translation.

Observe.—The English words connected by hyphens answer to the Hebrew words under which they stand: thus, the words ' *And-he called* ' belong to the single Hebrew word וַיִּקְרָא׳]; the words ' *and-to-the-darkness,*' belong to וְלַחֹ֫שֶׁךְ]. The English words *within crotchets* are not expressed in Hebrew.

The letters ᵃ, ᵇ, ᶜ, &c. refer to the explanatory notes. The figures ¹, ², ³, &c, refer to the order of the Hebrew words. Thus *And¹-he-called¹ God²,* means that *and-he-called* are expressed by the *first* Hebrew word וַיִּקְרָא, and that *God* corresponds with the *second* Hebrew word אֱלֹהִים· *m.l.* stand for *more literal; Heb.* for *Hebrew; m.* for *masculine; f.* for *feminine; p.* for *plural.*

Begin at the right and proceed to the left :—

קָרָא	ᶜוְלַחֹ֫שֶׁךְ	יוֹם	לָאוֹרᵇ	אֱלֹהִיםᵃ	וַיִּקְרָא
he-called	and-to-the-darkness,	day	to-the-light	God²	And¹-he-called¹

אֶחָ֫ד׃	יוֹם	בֹּ֫קֶר	וַיְהִי	עֶ֫רֶבᵐ	וַיְהִיᵈ	לָ֫יְלָה
one.	day	morning	and-he-was	evening	And-he-was	night.

הַמָּ֫יִםʰ	בְּתוֹךְᵍ	רָקִ֫יעַᶠ	יְהִי	אֱלֹהִים	וַיֹּ֫אמֶר
the-waters	in-the-midst-of	an expanse	he shall-be	God²	And¹-*he*-said¹

ᵃ i. e. *And God called.*   ᵇ לְ to the, אוֹר light.   ᶜ וְ and, לְ to the, חֹ֫שֶׁךְ darkness.   ᵈ The Hebrew has no neuter gender. Every substantive, with which the verb, pronoun, &c., must agree, is either *masculine* or *feminine.* The learner need scarcely be reminded that in making a free translation he must either omit the pronouns altogether: as, וַיֹּ֫אמֶר אֱלֹהִים *and God said;* or he must substitute the neuter pronoun [it], as in the word וַיְהִי " and he was," i. e. *and it was.*   ᵉ i. e. *One day.*   ᶠ i. e. An expanse shall be.   ᵍ בְּ in, תוֹךְ midst of.   ʰ the, מַיִם waters.

וַ֫יַּ֫עַשׂ ׃ לַמָּ֫יִם ᵇ בֵּ֣ין מַ֫יִם מַבְדִּ֔יל וַיְהִ֖י
And-he-made .to-the-waters waters between a divider and-he-shall-be

הַמָּ֫יִם בֵּ֣ין וַיַּבְדֵּ֗ל אֶת־הָרָקִ֫יעַ ᶜ אֱלֹהִ֔ים
the-waters between and-he-divided , the-expanse God

הַמָּ֫יִם וּבֵ֣ין ᵉ לָרָקִ֗יעַ מִתַּ֫חַת ᵈ אֲשֶׁ֣ר
the-waters and between to-the-expanse from under [were] which

וַיִּקְרָ֫א ׃ כֵּ֖ן וַיְהִי־ לָרָקִ֫יעַ מֵעַ֫ל ᶠ אֲשֶׁ֖ר
And⁶-he-called⁶ .so and-it-was to-the-expanse from-above [were] which

בֹּ֫קֶר וַיְהִי־ עֶ֫רֶב וַיְהִי־ שָׁמַ֫יִם לָרָקִ֫יעַ אֱלֹהִ֔ים
morning and-he-was evening And-he-was .heavens to-the-expanse God

שֵׁנִ֖י ׃ י֥וֹם
.second ʰ day

The learner may now, by way of practice, proceed to divide the following words into their respective syllables, and to analyze them in the same manner as first four verses, page 47.

PRACTICE.

Gen. i. 9—13.

הַשָּׁמַ֫יִם מִתַּ֫חַת הַמַּ֫יִם יִקָּו֫וּ ᶦ אֱלֹהִ֔ים וַיֹּ֫אמֶר
the-heavens from-under the-waters they-shall-be-assembled God² And¹-he-said¹

וַיְהִי־כֵ֫ן ׃ הַיַּבָּשָׁ֔ה וְתֵרָאֶ֖ה אֶחָ֔ד מָק֣וֹם אֶל־
.so and-it-was , the dry-land ᶦ and-she-shall-be-seen , one ᵏ place to

---

ᵃ *A divider*, or something that shall cause a separation. The meaning of this clause is, that the expanse shall form a separation, &c. ᵇ לְ to the, מַ֫יִם waters. * This word is not expressed in English. ᶜ הַ the, רָקִ֫יעַ expanse. ᵈ מִ from, תַּ֫חַת under. ᵉ לְ to the, רָקִ֫יעַ expanse. ᶠ and, בֵּין between. ᵍ מִ from, עַל above. ʰ *i. e.* The second day. ᶦ Pronounced yik-kā-vū. ᵏ *i. e.* To one place. ᶦ *i. e.* And let the dry land be seen or appear. See note ᵈ, in the preceding page.

HEBREW LANGUAGE.

וַיִּקְרָא אֱלֹהִים לַיַּבָּשָׁה אֶרֶץ וּלְמִקְוֵה ᵃ
And¹-he-called¹ God² to-the-dry-land , earth and-to-the-collection-of

הַמַּיִם קָרָא יַמִּים וַיַּרְא אֱלֹהִים כִּי־ טוֹב :
the-waters he-called , seas and-he-saw God that-[it-was] .good

וַיֹּאמֶר אֱלֹהִים תַּדְשֵׁא הָאָרֶץ דֶּשֶׁא עֵשֶׂב מַזְרִיעַ ᵇ
And-he-said¹ God² she-shall-germinate the-earth grass herb seeding

זֶרַע עֵץ פְּרִי עֹשֶׂה־פְּרִי לְמִינוֹ אֲשֶׁר זַרְעוֹ־בוֹ
seed , tree fruit c producing fruit after-his-kind [hath]-which his-seed in-him

עַל הָאָרֶץ וַיְהִי־ כֵן : וַתּוֹצֵא הָאָרֶץ ᵈ
upon the-earth , and-it-was .so And⁵-she-brought-forth⁵ the-earth⁶

דֶּשֶׁא עֵשֶׂב מַזְרִיעַ זֶרַע לְמִינֵהוּ וְעֵץ עֹשֶׂה־פְּרִי
grass , herb seeding seed after-his-kind and-tree producing fruit

אֲשֶׁר זַרְעוֹ־ בוֹ לְמִינֵהוּ וַיַּרְא אֱלֹהִים כִּי
which [had] his-seed in-him after-his-kind. And⁵-he-saw⁵ God⁶ that-[it was]

טוֹב : וַיְהִי־ עֶרֶב וַיְהִי־ בֹקֶר יוֹם שְׁלִישִׁי :
.good And-he-was evening and-he-was morning day ᵉ third

To render the following Reading Lessons as useful as possible, the Hebrew letters expressing the modification of words are printed in *open letters*, and their corresponding English words and variations in *italics*. By this method, the learner will be enabled to acquire, practically, the import of the *prefixes and affixes*, and to ascertain the precise meaning of the Hebrew words.

ᵃ וְ and, לְ to, מִקְוֵה collection of.   ᵇ *m. l. Causing seed.*
i. e. *Having the property of yielding seed.*   ᶜ i. e. Fruit-trees.
ᵈ i. e. And the earth brought forth.   ᵉ i. e. And it was evening
and it was morning the third day.

(Genesis, xxix. 4—11.)

וַיֹּאמֶר לָהֶם יַעֲקֹב	*And*¹-*he*-said¹ *unto*²-*them*² Jacob^a,
אַחַי מֵאַיִן	*my*-Brethren^b, *from*-whence [are]
אַתֶּם וַיֹּאמְרוּ מֵחָרָן	ye? *And-they*-said, *from*-Haran
אֲנָחְנוּ : וַיֹּאמֶר לָהֶם	we [are]. *And-he*-said to-*them*,
הַיְדַעְתֶּם° אֶת־לָבָן בֶּן־נָחוֹר	know-*ye* Laban [the] son-*of*
וַיֹּאמְרוּ יָדָעְנוּ :	Nahor? *And-they*-said, *we*-know
וַיֹּאמֶר לָהֶם הֲשָׁלוֹם°	*And-he*-said unto-*them*, Is peace
לוֹ וַיֹּאמְרוּ שָׁלוֹם	to *him*^d? *And-they-said*, peace^e:
וְהִנֵּה רָחֵל בִּתּוֹ	*and*-behold, Rachel *his*-daughter
בָּאָה¹ עִם־הַצֹּאן^g :	cometh with *the*-sheep^g.
וַיֹּאמֶר הֵן עוֹד הַיּוֹם	*And-he*-said, Lo, yet *the*-day [is]
גָּדוֹל לֹא־עֵת הֵאָסֵף	great^h [it is] not time *to-be*-gathered
הַמִּקְנֶה הַשְׁקוּ¹ הַצֹּאן	*the*-cattle; water-*ye*¹ *the*-sheep,
וּלְכוּ רְעוּ :	*and-go* [and] pasture.

---

^a *i. e.* And Jacob said unto them. ^b *i. e.* My friends. ^c הֲ in this word, and הֲ in הֲשָׁלוֹם are the signs of interrogation. ^d *i. e.* Is he well? ^e *i. e.* He is well. ^f בָּאָה the accent is on the last syllable, showing it to be the participle feminine, used to indicate the present tense, viz. '*she cometh.*' But בָּאָה in verse 9, has the accent on the *penultimate* syllable, indicating it to be the *past tense*, and it is, therefore, rendered '*she came.*' ^g צֹאן is the name for small cattle, such as sheep, goats, &c. ^h *i. e.* It is yet early in the day. ⁱ *m. l.* Make ye, or *cause ye* the sheep *to* drink.

HEBREW LANGUAGE.

וַיֹּאמְרוּ לֹא נוּכַל	And-they-said, not we-shall-be able[a]
עַד אֲשֶׁר יֵאָסְפוּ	until that they-shall-be-assembled
כָּל־הָעֲדָרִים וְגָלֲלוּ	all the-flocks, and-they-shall-roll[b]
אֶת־הָאֶבֶן מֵעַל פִּי	the-stone from-above [the]-mouth-
הַבְּאֵר וְהִשְׁקִינוּ	of the-well, and-we-shall-water[c]
הַצֹּאן׃	the-sheep.
עוֹדֶנּוּ מְדַבֵּר	While-yet-he [was] speaking
עִמָּם וְרָחֵל ׀ בָּאָה עִם־	with-them[d], and-Rachel came with
הַצֹּאן אֲשֶׁר	the-sheep which [belonged]
לְאָבִיהָ כִּי רֹעָה	to-her-father; for a-shepherdess
הִיא׃ וַיְהִי כַּאֲשֶׁר	she [was]. And-it-was when
רָאָה יַעֲקֹב אֶת־רָחֵל בַּת־	Jacob[e] saw[f] Rachel [the] daughter-
לָבָן אֲחִי	of Laban [the] brother-of
אִמּוֹ וְאֶת־צֹאן	his-mother, and-[the]-sheep-of
לָבָן אֲחִי אִמּוֹ	Laban [the] brother-of his-mother,
וַיִּגַּשׁ יַעֲקֹב	and[g]-he-approached[g] Jacob[g],
וַיָּגֶל אֶת־הָאֶבֶן	and-he-rolled the-stone
מֵעַל פִּי	from-above [the] mouth-of
הַבְּאֵר וַיַּשְׁקְ ׀ אֶת־	the-well, and-he-watered[i] the

[a] *i. e.* We cannot.   [b] *i. e.* And the *shepherds* will roll.   [c] See note[i], p. 58.   [d] *i. e.* During the time he was speaking to them.   [e] See note[f], p. 58.   [f] The feminine of רֹעֶה *a shepherd.*   [g] m. l. As *which he saw Jacob, i. e.* just as Jacob saw Rachel.   [h] *i. e.* And Jacob approached.   [i] See note[i], p. 58. Pronounced *vay-yashk.*

צֹאן לָבָן אֲחִי	sheep-of Laban [the] brother-of
אִמּוֹ : וַיִּשַּׁק־יַעֲקֹב	his-mother. And¹-he-kissed² Jacob³
לְרָחֵל וַיִּשָּׂא	to-Rachel, and-he-lifted-up
אֶת־קֹלוֹ וַיֵּבְךְּᵃ :	his-voice, and-he-wept.
וַיַּגֵּד יַעֲקֹב לְרָחֵל כִּי	And¹-he-told¹ Jacob² to Rachel that
אֲחִי אָבִיהָ הוּא	[the] brotherᵇ-of-her-father he [was],
וְכִי בֶן־רִבְקָה	and-that [the] son of Rebecca
הוּא וַתָּרָןᶜ וַתַּגֵּד	he [was]; and-she-ran and-she-told
לְאָבִיהָ :	[it] to-her-father.

(Genesis, xxxi. 36—43.)

וַיַּעַן יַעֲקֹב וַיֹּאמֶר	And¹-he-answered¹ Jacob² and-said
לְלָבָן מַה־פִּשְׁעִי	to-Laban, What [is] my-trespass?
מַה חַטָּאתִי כִּי	What [is] my-sin? that
דָלַקְתָּ אַחֲרָי :	thou-hast-pursued after-me.
כִּי מִשַּׁשְׁתָּ	[Now] that thou-hast-searched
אֶת־כָּל־כֵּלַי מַה־	all-my-vessels, what
מָּצָאתָ מִכֹּל	hast-thou-found from-all [the]

ᵃ There are three dots in the letter ךְּ. The first is *dagesh*, indicating that ך is pronounced like *ch* in *chord*. The two other dots are *sh'va* final. (See p. 29.) Root בכה to weep.   ᵇ *i.e.* That he was a relative or kinsman.   ᶜ The second (ָ) in this word is *short*, because it forms a *compound unaccented* syllable. (See p. 41.)

HEBREW LANGUAGE. 61

כְּלֵי־בֵיתְךָ שִׂים	vessels-*of thy*-house ? place [it]
כֹּה נֶגֶד אַחָי	here before *my*-brethren
וְאַחֶיךָ	and-*thy*-brethren,
וְיוֹכִיחוּ בֵּין	and-*they-shall*-decide[a] between
שְׁנֵינוּ : זֶה עֶשְׂרִים שָׁנָה	*us*-two. This twenty years[b]
אָנֹכִי עִמָּךְ רְחֵלֶיךָ	I [have been] with-*thee, thy*-ewes
וְעִזֶּיךָ לֹא	and-*thy*-she-goats not
שִׁכֵּלוּ	have cast-their-young
וְאֵילֵי צֹאנְךָ לֹא	and-[the] rams-*of thy*-flock not
אָכָלְתִּי : טְרֵפָה	have *I* eaten. *What-was*-torn [of
לֹא־הֵבֵאתִי	beast[c]] not-*have-I*-brought
אֵלֶיךָ אָנֹכִי	unto-*thee*, [but]-*I*
אֲחַטֶּנָּה[d]	*was-obliged*-to-bear-the-loss[d] ;
מִיָּדִי תְּבַקְשֶׁנָּה	*from-my*-hand *didst-thou*-require-it[e],
גְּנֻבְתִי יוֹם וּגְנֻבְתִי	[whether]stolen *by* day *or*-stolen-*by*
לָיְלָה : הָיִיתִי בַיּוֹם	night. [Where] *I*-was *in-the*-day
אֲכָלַנִי חֹרֶב	consumed-*me* [the] heat[g],
וְקֶרַח בַּלָּיְלָה	and-[the]-frost *in-the*-night,

---

[a] *i. e.* That they may decide.   [b] *Heb.* year.   [c] *m. l.* A torn one, *f.*   [d] *m. l. I-should*-miss-*her, i. e.* I was obliged to account for whatever was torn by beasts.   [e] *m. l. Thou-wouldst seek*-[her], *i. e. the torn* one, ק ought to have had *dagesh.* This and the preceding tense are in Hebrew in the *future* [f]גְנַבְתִּי (׃) in this and the following word, is substituted for (׳), and has, therefore, *metheg* annexed. (See page 42.)   [g] lit. *The dryness*, or the drought.

וַתִּדַּד שְׁנָתִי	and-she[a]-wandered my-sleep
מֵעֵינָי: זֶה־לִּי	from-mine-eyes. This-[is]-to-me
עֶשְׂרִים שָׁנָה בְּבֵיתֶךָ	twenty years[b] in-thy-house[c];
עֲבַדְתִּיךָ אַרְבַּע־עֶשְׂרֵה	I-served-thee fourteen
שָׁנָה בִּשְׁתֵּי בְנֹתֶיךָ	years[b] for-two-of thy-daughters,
וְשֵׁשׁ שָׁנִים בְּצֹאנֶךָ	and-six years for-thy-cattle;
וַתַּחֲלֵף אֶת־מַשְׂכֻּרְתִּי	and-thou-didst-change my-wages
עֲשֶׂרֶת מֹנִים: לוּלֵי אֱלֹהֵי	ten times. Unless [the] God-of
אָבִי אֱלֹהֵי אַבְרָהָם	my-father, [the] God-of Abraham,
וּפַחַד יִצְחָק הָיָה	and [the]-fear[d]-of Isaac, had-been
לִי כִּי עַתָּה רֵיקָם	for-me[e], surely now empty
שִׁלַּחְתָּנִי	thou-wouldest-have-sent-me-away
אֶת־עָנְיִי וְאֶת־יְגִיעַ	my-affliction and-the-labours-of
כַּפַּי רָאָה אֱלֹהִים	my-hands God saw[f],
וַיּוֹכַח אָמֶשׁ:	and-he-decided[g] last-night.
וַיַּעַן לָבָן וַיֹּאמֶר	And-he-answered Laban and-said
אֶל יַעֲקֹב הַבָּנוֹת	unto Jacob,— Thy-daughters [are]
בְּנֹתַי וְהַבָּנִים	my-daughters, and-the-sons [are]
בָּנַי וְהַצֹּאן	my-sons, and the-cattle [are]

---

[a] *i. e.* My sleep wandered, &c. שָׁנָה sleep, being of the feminine gender. [b] *Heb.* year. [c] *i. e.* I have now been twenty years, &c. [d] *i. e.* He whom Isaac reverenced, namely, God. [e] *i. e.* With me. [f] *Heb.* saw God, *i. e.* God saw. [g] Or rebuked.

צֹאנִי וְכֹל אֲשֶׁר־אַתָּה	my-cattle, and-all which thou
רֹאֶה לִי־הוּא	seest, to-me it-[is]ᵃ;
וְלִבְנֹתַי מָה	and-to-my-daughters what
אֶעֱשֶׂה לָאֵלֶּה הַיּוֹם אוֹ	shall-I-do to-these this-day, or
לִבְנֵיהֶן אֲשֶׁר	unto-their-children which
יָלָדוּ :	they-have-born.

Nathan's Parable. (2 Sam. xii. 1—12.)

וַיִּשְׁלַח יְהֹוָה אֶת־נָתָן אֶל־	And¹ the-Lord² sent Nathan to
דָּוִד וַיָּבֹא אֵלָיו	David, and-he-came unto-him,
וַיֹּאמֶר לוֹ שְׁנֵי אֲנָשִׁים הָיוּ	and-he-said to-him. Two men were
בְּעִיר אֶחָתᵇ אֶחָד עָשִׁיר	in¹ one² city¹; one rich,
וְאֶחָד רָאשׁ : לְעָשִׁיר הָיָה ᶜ	and-one poor. To-the rich man wasᶜ
צֹאן וּבָקָר הַרְבֵּה מְאֹד	flocks and-herds much veryᵈ.
וְלָרָשׁ אֵין־כֹּל ᵉ	And-to-the-poor-man nothingᵉ at-
כִּי אִם־כִּבְשָׂה אַחַת קְטַנָּה	all, save one⁴ little⁵ ewe-lamb³,
אֲשֶׁר קָנָה	which [he-had]-bought,
וַיְחַיֶּהָ	and-he-nourished-her,

ᵃ *m. l.* To me, he, *i. e. is mine*, or *belongs to me.*   ᵇ *m. l.* In-the-city one.   ᶜ *i. e.* The rich man had.   ᵈ *i. e.* In great abundance.   ᵉ *i. e.* And the poor man had nothing, &c.

וַתִּגְדַּל עִמּוֹ	*and-she*-grew-up with-*him*,
וְעִם־בָּנָיו יַחְדָּו	*and*-with *his*-children together;
מִפִּתּוֹ ᵃ תֹאכַל ᵇ	*from-his*-morsel *she-used-to* eat,
וּמִכֹּסוֹ	*and-from-his*-cup
תִשְׁתֶּה ᵇ	*she-used-to* drink,
וּבְחֵיקוֹ תִשְׁכָּב ᵇ	*and-in-his*-bosom *she-used-to*-lie,
וַתְּהִי־לוֹ	*and-she*-was to-*him*
כְּבַת: וַיָּבֹא	*as-a*-daughter. And-there-came ᶜ
הֵלֶךְ לָאִישׁ הֶעָשִׁיר	*a*-traveller to ᶜ-the³-rich³-man²,
וַיַּחְמֹל לָקַחַת	*and-he*-had-compassion *to*-take
מִצֹּאנוֹ	*from-his*-[own]-flock
וּמִבְּקָרוֹ	*and-from-his*-[own]-herd
לַעֲשׂוֹת	*to*-make-[a feast]
לָאֹרֵחַ	*to-the*-way-faring-man
הַבָּא לוֹ	*who*-had-come unto-*him*,
וַיִּקַּח אֶת־	*and-he*-took *the*
כִּבְשַׂת הָאִישׁ הָרָאשׁ	lamb-*of the²-poor³-man²*
וַיַּעֲשֶׂהָ לָאִישׁ	*and*-prepared-*it* ᵈ *for-the*-man
הַבָּא אֵלָיו:	*that-had*-come unto-*him*.
וַיִּחַר ᵉ אַף	*And-it*-kindled ᵉ [the]-anger-*of*

ᵃ פַּת a *morsel, bit,* or *piece* of bread.   ᵇ These three verbs are in Hebrew in the *future tense,* a mode of expression generally employed to indicate an action which is frequently or usually done.   ᶜ *Heb.* and-he-came.   ᵈ *m. l.* And he made her, *i. e.* he dressed the lamb.   ᵉ *m. l.* And he kindled ; אַף *anger,* being masculine.

דָּוִד בָּאִישׁ	David *against-the*-man,
מְאֹד וַיֹּאמֶר אֶל	exceedingly, *and-he*-said unto
נָתָן חַי־יְהוָה כִּי	Nathan, [as] *the*-Lord¹-liveth² that
בֶן־מָוֶת הָאִישׁ	a son-*of*-death[a] [is] *the*-man
הָעֹשֶׂה זֹאת׃ וְאֶת־הַכִּבְשָׂה	*that*-doeth this. *And-the*-lamb
יְשַׁלֵּם אַרְבַּעְתָּיִם עֵקֶב אֲשֶׁר	*he-shall*-pay four-*fold*, because
עָשָׂה אֶת־הַדָּבָר הַזֶּה	*he*-did this² thing³,
וְעַל אֲשֶׁר לֹא־חָמָל׃	*and*-because *he-did*⁴ not³ pity⁴.
וַיֹּאמֶר נָתָן אֶל־דָּוִד אַתָּה	*And*¹ Nathan³ said¹ *to*-David. Thou
הָאִישׁ כֹּה־אָמַר	[art] *the*-man. Thus said [the]
יְהוָה אֱלֹהֵי יִשְׂרָאֵל אָנֹכִי	Lord God-*of* Israel, I
מְשַׁחְתִּיךָ לְמֶלֶךְ עַל־	anointed-*thee for-a*-king over
יִשְׂרָאֵל וְאָנֹכִי הִצַּלְתִּיךָ	Israel, *and*-I delivered-*thee*
מִיַּד שָׁאוּל׃	*from the*-hand-*of* Saul.
וָאֶתְּנָה לְךָ אֶת־בֵּית	*And-I*-gave to-*thee the*-house-*of*-
אֲדֹנֶיךָ וְאֶת־נְשֵׁי	*thy*-master[b], *and-the* wives-*of*
אֲדֹנֶיךָ בְּחֵיקֶךָ	*thy*-master *into-thy*-bosom,
וָאֶתְּנָה לְךָ אֶת־בֵּית	*And-I*-gave to-*thee the*-house-*of*
יִשְׂרָאֵל וִיהוּדָה וְאִם־מְעָט	Israel *and*-Judah, *and*-if little[c]
וְאֹסִפָה לְךָ	then-*I-would*-add to-*thee*

---

[a] "A son of death the man," *i. e. the man who did this, deserves death.* [b] *Heb.* masters. The plural of this word being mostly used instead of the singular. [c] *i. e.* If these be too little (few), I would add as many and as many more.

כָּהֵנָה וְכָהֵנָה ׃ מַדּוּעַ	as-they and-as-they[a]. Why
בָּזִיתָ אֶת־דְּבַר	hast-thou despised-the-word-of
יְהֹוָה לַעֲשׂוֹת הָרַע	the-Lord, to-do what-is evil[b]
בְּעֵינָיו אֵת אוּרִיָּה הַחִתִּי	in-his-eyes[c] ? Uriah the-Hittite
הִכִּיתָ בַחֶרֶב	thou-hast-smitten with-the-sword,
וְאֶת־אִשְׁתּוֹ לָקַחְתָּ	and-his-wife thou-hast-taken
לְךָ לְאִשָּׁה וְאֹתוֹ	to-thee for-a-wife, and-him
הָרַגְתָּ בַּחֶרֶב	thou-hast-slain with-the-sword-of
בְּנֵי עַמּוֹן ׃	the-sons-of Ammon.

(Psalm xxiv. 11—15.)

לְכוּ־בָנִים שִׁמְעוּ־לִי	Come-ye children, hearken-ye unto-me:
יִרְאַת יְהֹוָה אֲלַמֶּדְכֶם ׃	[The]-fear-of the-Lord I-will-teach-you.
מִי־הָאִישׁ הֶחָפֵץ חַיִּים	Who [is] the-man that-desireth life,
אֹהֵב יָמִים לִרְאוֹת טוֹב ׃	[that] loveth days to-see-good ?
נְצֹר לְשׁוֹנְךָ מֵרָע	Keep thy-tongue from-evil,
וּשְׂפָתֶיךָ מִדַּבֵּר מִרְמָה ׃	and-thy-lips from-speaking deceit.
סוּר מֵרָע וַעֲשֵׂה־טוֹב	Depart from-evil and-do good,
בַּקֵּשׁ שָׁלוֹם וְרָדְפֵהוּ ׃	seek peace and-pursue-it[k].

---

[a] *i. e.* As many and as many.   * From עשה to do.   [b] Heb. *The evil, i. e.* that which is evil.   [c] *i. e.* In his sight.   [d] *Lit.* go ye.   [e] *Sing.* בֵּן a son, *plu.* בָּנִים sons, or children.   [f] יִרְאָה fear, יִרְאַת fear of.   [g] This word is never used in the singular number.   [h] From ראה to see.   [i] שָׂפָה a lip.   [k] *Heb.* him.

HEBREW LANGUAGE.

(Isaiah lviii. with slight alterations.)

פָּרֹס לָרָעֵב לַחְמֶךָ	Break to-the-hungry thy-bread,
וַעֲנִיִּים מְרוּדִים תָּבִיא בָיִת	and¹-[the] afflicted² poor¹ bring-into [the] house;
כִּי־תִרְאֶהᵃ עָרֹם וְכִסִּיתוֹ	when thou-seest [the]-naked then-cover-him:
וּמִבְּשָׂרְךָ לֹא תִתְעַלָּםᵇ :	and-from-thy-flesh [do] not hide-thyself.
אָז תִּקְרָא וַיהוָֹה יַעֲנֶה	Then shalt-thou-call and-the-Lord will answer;
תְּשַׁוַּע וְיֹאמַר הִנֵּנִי :	thou-shalt-cry, and-he-will-say, Here-I-am.

(Proverbs vii. 1—4.)

בְּנִי שְׁמֹר מִצְוֹתָיᶜ וֶחְיֵה	My-son, keep my-commandments and-live;
וְתוֹרָתִיᵈ כְּאִישׁוֹןᵉ עֵינֶיךָ :	and-my-law as-the apple-of thine-eyes.
קָשְׁרֵם עַל־אֶצְבְּעוֹתֶיךָ	Bind-them upon thy-fingers,
כָּתְבֵם עַל־לוּחַ לִבֶּךָ :	write-them upon the-table-of thine-heart.
אֱמֹר לַחָכְמָה אֲחֹתִיᶠ אָתְּ	Say unto-wisdom, My-sister thou-[art];
וּמוֹדָע לַבִּינָה תִקְרָא :	and-a-friend to-understanding thou-shalt-call ᵍ.

ᵃ m. l. If thou shouldst see.   ᵇ m. l. Not shalt-thou-hide-thyself.
ᶜ Sing. מִצְוָה mits-vāh, a command.   ᵈ תּוֹרָה a law.
ᵉ m. l. The little man; a name given to the apple of the eye from the reflected image it presents to the beholder.   ᶠ אָחוֹת a sister.
ᵍ i. e. Consider understanding as thy friend.

כִּי אֹרֶךְ יָמִים בִּימִינָהּ	For length-*of* days [is] *in-her-*right-hand,
בִּשְׂמֹאולָהּ עֹשֶׁר וְכָבוֹד׃	*in-her-*left-hand riches *and*-honor.
דְּרָכֶיהָ דַרְכֵי נֹעַם	*Her-*ways [are] ways-*of* pleasantness,
וְכָל-נְתִיבוֹתֶיהָ שָׁלוֹם׃	*and*-all *her*-paths [are] peace.

Proverbs vi. 6—11.

לֵךְ אֶל-נְמָלָה עָצֵל	Go to [the] ant, [thou]-sluggard ;
רְאֵה דְרָכֶיהָ וַחֲכָם׃	see *her*-ways, *and-be* wise.
אֲשֶׁר אֵין-לָהּ קָצִין	Which not to-*her*[a] [a] guide,
שֹׁטֵר וּמֹשֵׁל	overseer, *and*-ruler. [Yet]
תָּכִין בַּקַּיִץ לַחְמָהּ	*She*-provideth *in*-summer *her*-meat,
אָגְרָה[b] בַקָּצִיר מַאֲכָלָהּ׃	*she*-gathereth *in*-harvest *her*-food.
עַד-מָתַי עָצֵל תִּשְׁכָּב	How long[c] sluggard ! *wilt-thou-*lie down ?
מָתַי תָּקוּם מִשְּׁנָתֶךָ	when *wilt-thou-*arise *from-thy-*sleep ?
מְעַט שֵׁנוֹת[d] מְעַט תְּנוּמוֹת[e]	[Yet a] little sleep, [a] little slumber,
מְעַט חִבֻּק יָדַיִם לִשְׁכָּב׃	[a] little folding-*of* hands, *to-*lie down,—
וּבָא-כִמְהַלֵּךְ רֵאשֶׁךָ	*And-he-will-*come *like-a-*traveller thy-poverty[f]
וּמַחְסֹרְךָ כְּאִישׁ מָגֵן׃	*and-thy-*want *as-a-*man [with a]-shield[g].

---

[a] Who has neither guide, nor overseer, nor ruler, yet provideth, etc.
[b] *Heb.* She gathered. [c] *Heb.* Until when. [d] שֵׁנָה sleep.
[e] תְּנוּמָה slumber. [f] *i. e.* Thy poverty will come suddenly.
[g] *i. e.* As an armed man.

HEBREW LANGUAGE.

Cant. ii. 10—14.

עָנָה דוֹדִי וְאָמַר לִי	He-called-aloud my-beloved[a] and-said to-me,
קוּמִי לָךְ רַעְיָתִי[c] יָפָתִי וּלְכִי־לָךְ:	Arise[b] my-love, my-beauty, and-come-away[d].
כִּי־הִנֵּה הַסְּתָיו עָבָר	For lo, the-winter hath-passed,
הַגֶּשֶׁם חָלַף הָלַךְ לוֹ:	the-rain hath-flitted-away, he-is-gone[e].
הַנִּצָּנִים נִרְאוּ[f] בָאָרֶץ	The-blossoms have-appeared on-the-earth,
עֵת הַזָּמִיר הִגִּיעַ[g]	the-time-of song* hath-come,
וְקוֹל הַתּוֹר נִשְׁמַע בְּאַרְצֵנוּ:	and-the-voice-of the-turtle hath-been-heard in-our-land :
הַתְּאֵנָה חָנְטָה פַגֶּיהָ	The-fig-tree she-hath-embalmed her-green-figs,
וְהַגְּפָנִים סְמָדַר נָתְנוּ רֵיחַ	and-the-vines. [the] tender-grape, they-have-yielded fragrance.
קוּמִי־לָךְ רַעְיָתִי יָפָתִי וּלְכִי־לָךְ:	Arise my love, my-beauty, and-come-away[d].
יוֹנָתִי בְּחַגְוֵי הַסֶּלַע	My-dove! [who art] in-the-cleft-of the-rock,
הַרְאִינִי[h] אֶת־מַרְאַיִךְ	[O] let-me-see thy-countenance,
הַשְׁמִיעִנִי[i] אֶת קוֹלֵךְ	let-me-hear thy-voice ;
כִּי־קוֹלֵךְ עָרֵב	for sweet[g] [is] thy-voice[f],
וּמַרְאֵךְ[k] נָאוֶה:	and-thy-countenance [is] comely.

---

[a] *i. e.* My beloved exclaimed.   [b] *Heb.* arise to thee (an idiomatic expression).   [c] רַעְיָה *a female friend,* companion.   [d] *Heb.* and go to thee (an idiomatic expression).   [e] *Heb.* he is gone to him, (an idiomatic expression).   [f] *m. l.* Were seen.   * *Heb.* the song.   [g] *m. l.* He has touched, *i. e.* arrived.   [h] *m. l.* Cause me to see.   [i] *m. l.* Cause me to hear.   [k] מַרְאֶה from רָאָה to see.

(Cant. vi. 2—4.)

אֲנִי יְשֵׁנָה וְלִבִּי עֵר	I sleep, but[a]-my-heart waketh:—
קוֹל דּוֹדִי דוֹפֵק	[The]-voice-of my-beloved—he knocketh!
"פִּתְחִי־לִי אֲחוֹתִי	"Open-to-me, my-sister!
רַעְיָתִי יוֹנָתִי תַמָּתִי	my-love, my-dove, my-innocent-one!
שֶׁרֹאשִׁי נִמְלָא־טָל	for-my-head is-filled [with] dew,
קְוֻצּוֹתַי רְסִיסֵי לָיְלָה:"	my-locks [with] the-drops-of-[the]-night."
פָּשַׁטְתִּי אֶת־כֻּתָּנְתִּי	I-have-put-off my-garment
אֵיכָכָה אֶלְבָּשֶׁנָּה	how shall-I-put-it-[b] on?
רָחַצְתִּי אֶת־רַגְלַי	I-have-washed my-feet,
אֵיכָכָה אֲטַנְּפֵם:	how shall-I-defile-them?
דּוֹדִי שָׁלַח יָדוֹ מִן־הַחוֹר	My-beloved put-forth his-hand from the-lattice,
וּמֵעַי הָמוּ עָלָיו:	and-my-bowels yearned[c] for-him.

(*Man's Nothingness.* Job xiv. 1—10.)

אָדָם יְלוּד אִשָּׁה	Man born-of woman
קְצַר יָמִים וּשְׂבַע־רֹגֶז:	[is] short-of-days and-full-of trouble,
כְּצִיץ יָצָא וַיִּמָּל	Like-a-flower he-cometh-forth and-is cut-off;

---

[a] *Heb.* and.   [b] *Heb.* her, because כֻּתֹּנֶת is of the feminine gender.   [c] An expression denoting great compassion.
[d] *Lit.* And saturated, or satiated of.

וַיִּבְרַח כַּצֵּל וְלֹא יַעֲמוֹד׃[a]	and-fleeth like-a-shadow, and[a]-abideth[a]-not[a]
אַף־עַל־זֶה פָּקַחְתָּ עֵינֶיךָ	Even upon him[b] hast-thou-opened thine-eyes?
וְאֹתִי תָבִיא בְמִשְׁפָּט עִמָּךְ׃	And-me wilt-thou-bring in-judgment with-thee?
מִי־יִתֵּן טָהוֹר מִטָּמֵא	Who can-produce[c] clean from-unclean?
לֹא אֶחָד׃	Not one[d].
אִם־חֲרוּצִים יָמָיו	If determined [be] his-days,—
מִסְפַּר־חֳדָשָׁיו אִתָּךְ	[if the] number-of his-months [be] with-thee,—
חֻקָּיו עָשִׂיתָ וְלֹא יַעֲבֹר׃	[if] his-bounds thou-hast-made—which[f] he-cannot-pass:—
שְׁעֵה מֵעָלָיו וְיֶחְדָּל	[Then] turn from-upon-him, and-let-him-cease[g],
עַד־יִרְצֶה כְּשָׂכִיר יוֹמוֹ׃	until he-shall-accomplish, as-a hireling, his-day[h].
כִּי יֵשׁ לָעֵץ תִּקְוָה	For there-is to-the-tree a-hope,
אִם־יִכָּרֵת וְעוֹד יַחֲלִיף	if he-should-be-cut-down, again[i] will-he reproduce[k],
וְיֹנַקְתּוֹ[l] לֹא תֶחְדָּל׃	and-his-suckers-will not-cease[m].

---

[a] m. l. And he shall not stand. [b] Heb. this[m], i. e. upon this being. [c] Heb. shall give, i. e. who can expect purity from impurity. [d] i. e. None. [e] The first (ׇ) is short (ŭ). [f] m. l. And not he shall pass. [g] i. e. And let him cease to suffer. [h] i. e. Until like a hireling he shall have accomplished his task. [i] Heb. And again. [k] Heb. and he will exchange, i. e. produce fresh branches. [l] Sing. יֹנֶקֶת a sucker, יוֹנַקְתּוֹ his sucker. [m] i. e. Will not fail.

אִם־יַזְקִין בָּאָרֶץ שָׁרְשׁוֹ	If *he should-become*-old *in-the-*earth *his-*root^a
וּבֶעָפָר יָמוּת גִּזְעוֹ :	*and-in-the-*dust *should-he-die his-*stem^a.
מֵרֵיחַ מַיִם יַפְרִיחַ	*From-the-*scent-*of* water *he-will-*flourish ;
וְעָשָׂה קָצִיר כְּמוֹ־נָטַע :	*and*-he-will-produce *a*-harvest^b as-*a* plant^c.
וְגֶבֶר ^d יָמוּת וַיֶּחֱלָשׁ	*But-*man dieth *and-*wasteth-away.
וַיִּגְוַע אָדָם ^d וְאַיּוֹ :	*and*¹ man² expireth¹ *and-*where [is] he ?

---

^a *i.e.* Should its root become old,—should its stem die, yet the tree will again revive, etc.   ^b קָצִיר *a harvest*, or according to some, *a cutting*, i. e. *young shoots*.   ^c נֶטַע *a plant*. Thus several of the versions, Jarchi, and other commentators, who consider this word as a *noun*: many grammarians, however, consider it as a *verb*, and then the words כְּמוֹ נָטַע ought to be rendered, '*as when fresh planted.*'   ^d גֶּבֶר, אֱנוֹשׁ, אָדָם.— These words have this in common, that they all signify *man*, yet there is some distinction between them. The first, derived from אֲדָמָה *ground, earth*, is mostly applied to man in general, or mankind, *common, earthly man*. The second, derived from אָנַשׁ, *to be sick, mortal*, includes the idea of *mortality*, i. e. *mortal man*. The third, derived from גָּבַר, *to be strong*, includes the idea of *strength* and *power*. Hence the propriety of these terms in their respective places, and particularly of the word וַיֶּחֱלָשׁ '*and he had become weak.*' The literal sense of this verse is, וְגֶבֶר and *the powerful man dies*, וַיֶּחֱלָשׁ having previously been deprived of his strength.

(*The same sentiments expressed by the inspired Psalmist.*
Psalm ciii. 15—17.)

אֱנוֹשׁ כֶּחָצִיר יָמָיו Man *like*-grass [are] *his*-days;

כְּצִיץ הַשָּׂדֶה כֵּן יָצִיץ: *as-the*-flower-*of the*-field so he-shoots-up[a].

כִּי רוּחַ[b] עָבְרָה־בּוֹ[c] וְאֵינֶנּוּ For [a]-wind passeth over-*him and-he*-exists-not

וְלֹא־יַכִּירֶנּוּ עוֹד מְקוֹמוֹ[c]: *and-it*-shall not know-*him*[c] again his-[own] place.

וְחֶסֶד יְהֹוָה But-[the]-mercy-*of the*-Lord

מֵעוֹלָם וְעַד־עוֹלָם[d] [is]-*for*-ever *and*-ever

עַל יְרֵאָיו upon those-*that*-fear-*him*,

וְצִדְקָתוֹ לִבְנֵי בָנִים: *and-his*-righteousness [extends] *to*-child*ren's* child*ren*.

---

[a] Or flourishes. [b] The primitive meaning of רוּחַ is, *wind*, air in motion, but it is also used to denote *the breath, a breath of air*, the Divine *Spirit* or *Soul*. This clause may, therefore, be rendered either, '*For a breath passes*, *over* (or *through*) *him, and he exists no more, i. e.* a breath of air is sufficient to deprive him of his mortal existence; or, '*For the spirit*,' *i. e.* the Divine Spirit, the soul, etc.

[c] The translators of the established version, having probably adopted the opinion of some interpreters and commentators, that the pronouns refer to צִיץ *flower*, have rendered them by *it*. I have, however, followed *Aben Jachia*, who considers the pronouns as referring to אֱנוֹשׁ *man*. As for the phrase, '*And the place shall not know him again*,' it must in either case be considered as a poetical expression.

[d] *m. l.* From everlasting and until everlasting, *i. e.* the mercy of God abideth for ever, and extends to those who fear him.

(*God known from his works.* Job xii. 7.)

שְׁאַל בְּהֵמוֹת וְתֹרֶךָ	Ask [the] beasts, *and-they¹-will-*teach-*thee:*
וְעוֹף הַשָּׁמַיִם וְיַגֶּד־לָךְ :	*and-*[the] birds-*of the-*heaven, *and-they*ᵇ*-will-*tell thee:
אוֹ שִׂיחַ לָאָרֶץ וְתֹרֶךָ	Or speak *to-the-*earth, *and-she-will-*teach-*thee.*
וִיסַפְּרוּ לְךָ דְּגֵי הַיָּם :	*and they-will-*tell thee *the-*fishes-*of the-*seaᶜ.
מִי לֹא־יָדַע בְּכָל־אֵלֶּה	Who knoweth³ not² *in-*all these⁴
כִּי־יַד־יְהֹוָה עָשְׂתָה זֹּאת :	that *the-*hand-*of-the* Lord hath-done thisᵈ ?
אֲשֶׁר בְּיָדוֹ נֶפֶשׁ כָּל־חָי	*In²-*whose¹-hand² [is] *the-*soul-*of* all-*the-*living
וְרוּחַ כָּל־בְּשַׂר־אִישׁ :	*and-*[the] spirit-*of-*all men ?
הֲלֹא אֹזֶן מִלִּין תִּבְחָן	Doth-not [the]-ear² distinguish¹ words³ ?
וְחֵךְ אֹכֶל יִטְעַם־לוֹ :	*and*[the]-palate [the] food it tastes ?
בִּישִׁישִׁים חָכְמָה	[Is-there-not] wisdom² *in-the-*aged¹
וְאֹרֶךְ יָמִים תְּבוּנָה :	*and* [in] length-*of* days understanding * ?

ᵃ *Heb.* and *she* will teach thee, *i. e.* each of them will teach you. ᵇ *Heb.* and he will tell thee. ᶜ *i. e.* And the fishes of the sea will tell thee. ᵈ *i. e.* Who cannot discern from all these that the power of the Lord has formed them. ᵉ *m. l.* 'And the spirit of all flesh of man;' alluding to the animal spirit—that even this is not the effect of mere organization. ᶠ *m. l.* Shall taste to him, *i. e.* what is agreeable or disagreeable to it. The word הֲלֹא *is it not*, must be understood in this clause as well as in the following. * The words *and whence do they derive it?* must here be understood, and the next verse must be considered as the answer.

HEBREW LANGUAGE. 75

עִמּוֹ הָכְמָה וּגְבוּרָה	With-*him* (God) [*are*]-wisdom *and*-strength
לוֹ עֵצָה וּתְבוּנָה:	To-*him* [belong]-counsel *and*-understanding.

(*God's Omniscience.* Psalm xciv.)

עַד־מָתַי רְשָׁעִים יְהוָה	How-long[a] [shall the] wicked, [O] Lord!
עַד־מָתַי רְשָׁעִים יַעֲלֹזוּ:	How-long[a], [the]-wicked, *shall-they*-triumph?
עַמְּךָ יְהוָה יְדַכְּאוּ	*Thy*-people, Lord, *they*-crush[b];
וְנַחֲלָתְךָ יְעַנּוּ:	*and-thy*-heritage *they*-afflict[b]:
אַלְמָנָה וְגֵר יַהֲרֹגוּ	Widow *and*-stranger *they*-slay[b]
וִיתוֹמִים יְרַצֵּחוּ:	*and*-orphans *they*-murder[b]:
וַיֹּאמְרוּ לֹא יִרְאֶה־יָּהּ	*And*-[yet]-they-say, God [?] shall[a]-not[2]-see[a];
וְלֹא־יָבִין אֱלֹהֵי יַעֲקֹב:	*and*[1]-*he*[2] *shall*[2]-not[1] regard[c] — the God-*of* Jacob[c].
בִּינוּ בֹּעֲרִים בָּעָם	Consider-*ye* brutes, *amongst-the* people,
וּכְסִילִים מָתַי תַּשְׂכִּילוּ:	*and*-[ye] fools, when *will-ye*-be-wise?
הֲנֹטַע אֹזֶן הֲלֹא יִשְׁמָע	*He-that*-planteth [the]-ear *shall-he*-not-hear?
אִם יֹצֵר עַיִן הֲלֹא־יַבִּיט:	Or-*he-that*-formeth [the]-eye *shall*-not-he-see?
הֲיֹסֵר גּוֹיִם הֲלֹא יוֹכִיחַ	*He-that*-chastises nations *shall*[1]-not[2]-*he*[1]-punish[1]?

---

[a] *Heb.* Till when.   [b] The corresponding Hebrew verbs are expressed in the future *shall crush*, they shall or will afflict, etc.   [c] *i. e.* The God of Jacob will not regard.

הַמְלַמֵּד אָדָם דָּעַת ׃ יְהוָה He-*that* teacheth-man knowledge*
—the Lord—

יוֹדֵעַ מַחְשְׁבוֹת אָדָם *he*-knoweth *the*-thoughts *of* man

כִּי־הֵמָּה הָבֶל ׃ although they [are] vain.

(*God's Omnipresence.* Psalm, cxxxix. 7—14.)

אָנָה אֵלֵךְ מֵרוּחֶךָ Whither *shall-I-go from-thy* spirit?

וְאָנָה מִפָּנֶיךָ ᵃ אֶבְרָח ׃ *and-*whither *from-thy-*presence *shall*-I-flee?

אִם־אֶסַּק שָׁמַיִם שָׁם אָתָּה If *I* ascend-*up* [into] heaven there thou [art]

וְאַצִּיעָה שְּׁאוֹל הִנֶּךָּ ׃ *and-should-I-*make *my-*bed [in the] grave behold-*thou-art-*there.

אֶשָּׂא כַנְפֵי־שָׁחַר [if] *I* take the wings-*of* the-dawn

---

* Knowledge, דָּעַת· The Hebrew verse ends with this word, which, as it leaves the sense incomplete, has probably induced the Translators of the *Established Version* to add the words '*shall he not know*' (הֲלֹא יֵדָע). But as there are no such words in the Hebrew text, I have preferred the opinion of *Aben Ezra*, who considers the clause הַמְלַמֵּד אָדָם דָּעַת as connected in sense with the following verse; viz. *He that teaches man knowledge*, namely, *the Lord*, *he knows the thoughts of man*, etc. This rendering is congenial to the whole context. For whereas the *wicked* consider the Deity as too exalted to concern himself about their foolish thoughts and vain actions, the inspired Psalmist declares, that since the Divine Being has bestowed knowledge on (אָדָם) *insignificant man*, he knows likewise his thoughts, although those thoughts are vain. (See *Aben Ezra, Comment.; and Mendelssohn's Translation of the Psalms.*)

ᵃ *From thy face, i. e.* from thy attending presence. The word פָּנִים is never used in the singular number.

HEBREW LANGUAGE. 77

אֶשְׁכְּנָה בְּאַחֲרִית יָם׃	If I dwell *in-the* uttermost-part-*of-the* sea
גַּם־שָׁם יָדְךָ תַנְחֵנִי	Even there *thy*-hand shall-lead-*me*
וְתֹאחֲזֵנִי יְמִינֶךָ׃	*and*[1] *thy*-right-hand[2] *shall*[1]-hold[1]-*me*[1].
וָאֹמַר אַךְ־חֹשֶׁךְ יְשׁוּפֵנִי	*If-I*-say but darkness *shall*-cover-*me*,
וְלַיְלָה אוֹר בַּעֲדֵנִי׃	then [the very] night [is] light about-*me*.
גַּם־חֹשֶׁךְ לֹא־יַחֲשִׁיךְ מִמֶּךָ	Yea, darkness hideth not *from*-thee,[b]
וְלַיְלָה כַּיּוֹם יָאִיר	*and* night giveth-light[3] *as-the-*day[d];
כַּחֲשֵׁיכָה כָּאוֹרָה׃	*like* darkness *like* light[e].
כִּי־אַתָּה קָנִיתָ כִלְיֹתָי	For thou *thou-hast*-formed *my*-reins: [f]
תְּסֻכֵּנִי בְּבֶטֶן אִמִּי׃	*thou-hast*-covered-*me in-the-*womb *of my-*mother.
אוֹדְךָ עַל כִּי נוֹרָאוֹת נִפְלֵיתִי	*I-will-*praise-thee because fearfully distinguished-have-*I*-been.[g]
נִפְלָאִים מַעֲשֶׂיךָ	wonderful *are thy-*works—
וְנַפְשִׁי יֹדַעַת מְאֹד׃	*and-that-my-*soul knoweth [it] well! [h]

---

[a] *Kimchi* renders this word '*shall obscure me*,' from עֶרֶב *the evening*.
[b] Lit. 'Shall not darken,' *hide* or *conceal*.   [c] *Lit.* 'Shall cause light,' *i. e. shine, give light*.   [d] The double comparative indicates that the things compared are both alike.   [e] *i. e.* They are both alike to God.   [f] *Lit.* 'Thou hast possessed,' from קָנָה *to obtain possession*, to become proprietor of a thing.

[g] From פָּלָה to separate, to distinguish by particular regard—alluding to the fearful and wonderful characteristics of man.

[h] *i. e.* Wonderful are all thy works; and that my soul should be capable of knowing and discerning it, is not the least wonderful.

(*True Worship.* Micah vi. 6—8.)

בַּמָּה אֲקַדֵּם יְהֹוָה	*With*-what shall-*I*-come-before the-Lord?
אִכַּף לֵאלֹהֵי מָרוֹםᵃ	shall-*I*-bend to-the-God-of heaven?
הַאֲקַדְּמֶנּוּ בְעוֹלוֹת	Shall-*I*-come-before-him with-burnt-offerings?
בַּעֲגָלִים בְּנֵי שָׁנָהᵇ׃	with-calves-*of a*-year-old?
הֲיִרְצֶה יְהֹוָה בְּאַלְפֵי אֵילִים	*Can-the*-Lord be-pleased with-thousands-*of* rams?
בְּרִבְבוֹתᶜ נַחֲלֵי שָׁמֶן	with-*myriads-of* rivers-*of* oil?
הַאֶתֵּן בְּכוֹרִי פִּשְׁעִי	shall-*I*-give *my* first-born [for] *my*-transgression?
פְּרִי בִטְנִיᵈ חַטַּאת נַפְשִׁי׃	the-fruit-*of my*-body [for the] sin-*of-my*-soul?
הִגִּיד לְךָ אָדָם מַה־טּוֹב	*He-has*-told thee, *O* man! what [is] good;
וּמַה־יְהֹוָה דּוֹרֵשׁ מִמְּךָ	*and*-what requires² the-Lord¹ *from*-thee
כִּי אִם־עֲשׂוֹת מִשְׁפָּטᵉ	but to-do justice,
וְאַהֲבַת חֶסֶדᶠ	*and*-to-love mercy.
וְהַצְנֵעᵍ לֶכֶת עִם אֱלֹהֶיךָ׃	*and*-humbly *to*-walk *with-thy*-God.

ᵃ *The height, i. e.* the heaven. ᵇ *Lit.* Sons of a year; a peculiar way of expressing the age of persons or animals. ᶜ רְבָבָה *a myriad,* ten thousand. ᵈ בֶּטֶן the belly, womb, body. ᵉ *Lit. The* doing of justice. ᶠ *Lit. The* love of mercy. ᵍ The infinitive is here used instead of the adverb.

CHAPTER III.

§ 1.—INTRODUCTORY OBSERVATIONS.

Accents.   טְעָמִים ׳ נְגִינוֹת

1. Accents are peculiar marks or characters placed above, below, at the beginning, or end of words, and in a few instances between them.

No part of Hebrew grammar is attended with greater difficulties than the Accents. Grammarians do not agree concerning either their exact number, names, or powers; and many of the most learned have honestly acknowledged their inability to unravel this complicated system, or to explain satisfactorily, why its authors have employed so many signs, or why they have, in many instances, preferred one set of accents to others of the same value. To give even an abridged statement of the contradictory opinions on this subject, would require more space than my limits would allow, and a minuteness of detail wholly inconsistent with the object of an elementary work. Indeed, most willingly would I have spared the learner the embarrassment arising from the multiplicity of the signs, similarity of the forms, and strangeness of the names of the accents, were it not from their close connection with the vowel points, on which they exercise a considerable influence, and for their great utility in pointing out the relation between words considered as members of a sentence. Nevertheless, instead of perplexing the student with rules that cannot be understood without a thorough acquaintance with the general structure of the language, I shall, for the present, only subjoin a table (to which the learner may now and then refer) containing the forms, position, and names of the accents; and point out their general uses and importance.

2. Table containing the forms, position, and names.

FORMS.	POSITION AND NAMES.	FORMS.	POSITION AND NAMES
	Distinctives.		*Conjunctives.*
1 { ֑ ׃	סִלּוּק ׃ or סוֹף פָּסוּק	֜	מוּנַח or שׁוֹפָר יָשָׁר
1 { ֑	אֶתְנָח , אַתְנַחְתָּא	֤	מַהְפַּךְ , שׁוֹפָר הָפוּךְ
{ ֒	סְגוֹל , שְׁרִי , סְגוֹלְתָּא	֝	קַדְמָא
2 { ֔	זָקֵף קָטוֹן	֨	שׁוֹפָר גַּלְגַּל
{ ֕	זָקֵף גָּדוֹל	֩	תְּלִישָׁא קְטַנָּה†
{ ֖	טִפְּחָה .. טַרְחָא*	֗	מֵרְכָא
{ ֗	רְבִיעִי	֛	מֵרְכָא כְפוּלָה
{ ֘	זַרְקָא	֪	יֶרַח בֶּן יוֹמוֹ
3 { ֙	פַּשְׁטָא .. קֶטֶב		
{ ֚	הֻבִּיר		The following occur only in the Psalms, Proverbs, and Job.
{ ֛	יְתִיב	֥	מַהְפַּךְ עוֹלֶה וְיוֹרֵד
{ ֜	שַׁלְשֶׁלֶת	֦	גֶּרֶשׁ וּרְבִיעַ
4 { ֝	פָּזֵר	֧	טִפְּחָא מַפְסִיק , דְּחִי
{ ֞	קַרְנֵי פָרָה , פָּזֵר גָּדוֹל	֨	זַרְקָא וּמֵרְכָא
{ ֟	תְּלִישָׁא גְדוֹלָה , תַּלְשָׁא	֩	זַרְקָא וּמַהְפַּךְ
{ ֠	גֶּרֶשׁ , אַזְלָא		
{ ֡	גֵּרְשַׁיִם .. שְׁנֵי גְרִישִׁין		To the above may be added פָּקֵף (")., which is placed between two or more words; and (׀) מֶתֶג metheg (see p. 22).
{ ׀	פָּסִיק ׀ ᵃ		

*Placed between words as עָשֹׂה פָלָה (Gen. xvii. 21.) This accent is also called לְנַרְמֵיהּ when it occurs before ־ ֗ as— מַעֲשֹׂר ׀ בְּדָבָר הַזֶּה (Gen. xvii. 25.)

When this mark (׀) is placed at the right of sh'va, as in תְּחִי, it is called גַּעְיָא *gang-ya.*

*There are some instances in which this accent is used as a conjunctive.
† Called also תַּרְכָא, and used sometimes as a distinctive of the 4th class.

§ 2.—Nature, Use, and Importance of the Accents.

1. The Hebrews, like many other ancient nations, were accustomed to accompany their public reading with a kind of song or chant*. The accents were, therefore, to them a species of musical notes by which they regulated the particular modulation of the voice and intonations in reading. Hence the name נְגִינוֹת n'gī-nō'th, from נָגַן, to *play on a musical instrument, to sing* or *chant*.

2. But one of the principal uses of the accents is to point out the syllable on which the stress of the voice is to be laid. In this respect they are similar to our accents in the words *hú́man, humáne, coun'tenance, presúme;* with this difference, that in Hebrew, the accent can only be placed either on the last syllable, termed מִלְרַע *below,* i. e. *last;* as, בְּרֵאשִׁית בָּרָא אֱלֹהִים B'rāshī'th bārā' ĕlōhī'm; or on the one before the last, termed מִלְעֵיל *above,* i. e. *penultimate;* as, שָׁמַיִם shā-mā'-yim, אֶרֶץ ā'-rets, תֹהוּ thō'-hū, בֹהוּ bō'-hū,

---

* This custom, in as far as regards the public reading of particular portions of Scripture, such as the LAW (*Pentateuch*), Haphtoroth (*Sections from the Prophets*), etc. is still retained by the Jews, who accompany the reading of each of these portions by peculiar melodies, regulated and represented by the accents. These melodies being merely national, and having no influence on the sense of Scripture, cannot be of any use to the student.

חֹשֶׁךְ hö'sheeḥ, רוּחַ rū'aḥ, כְּרַחֶפֶת m'ra-ḥé-feth, מַיִם mā'-yim* (see Gen. i. 1—2†).

The necessity of laying a stress on a particular syllable in words consisting of more than one syllable, is obvious; for without it, such words could not be distinguished from monosyllables, and would either have no meaning at all, or a different one from that which the speaker might wish to convey. Thus, for instance, *mánage* would sound like *man age*; *ácorn* like *a corn*. Thus also in Hebrew, זֶרַע zé-ra (*seed*), would sound like זֶה רַע, which would signify, '*this is bad.*' בָּשָׂר bā-sā'r (*flesh*), would sound like בָּא שַׂר which means, '*the prince came.*'

3. In English, the accent frequently distinguishes between nouns and verbs: as, to *contráct*, a *cón'tract*, and often alters the meaning of words, as *désert* (a wilderness), *desért* (merit). The same is the case in Hebrew. Thus, בִּינָה bīnā'h, accented on the ultimate, signifies *understanding*; but the same word accented on the *penultimate*, בִּינָה bī'nāh, signifies *understand thou.* קוּמִי kumī', signifies *my rising*; but קוּמִי kū'mi, signifies *rise thou'*. Thus also בֹּאִי bō-ī', *my coming*, בֹּאִי bō'ī, *come thou'*; בָּנוּ bā'nū, *with us*, בָּנוּ bānū', *they did build*; מָרָה mā'rāh, *she is bitter*, מָרָה mārā'h, *he resisted, rebelled.*

---

* As the translations of these words have already been given in pages 51, 57, etc. it was not thought necessary to repeat them here.

† In order not to distract the attention of the learner, we shall confine our examples, whenever it can conveniently be done, to a few of the first chapters of GENESIS.

The preceding examples sufficiently show the necessity of attending to the situation of the accent. But as the particular rules by which that situation may grammatically be known, cannot be well understood without a previous acquaintance with the general structure of the language, we shall reserve them for their proper places; and notice only the two following:—

4. *First Rule.* All words terminating in a compound syllable (p. 20), formed by a long vowel, have their accents on the last syllable: as, בְּרֵאשִׁית, אֱלֹהִים, וַיַּבְדֵּל, תְּהוֹם (Gen. i. 1—7). Of the same character are the following words: גָּדוֹל *great,* קָטֹן *little,* נָהָר *a river,* זָהָב *gold,* מַהֵר *soon,* בָּרוּךְ *blessed,* לִמּוֹד *to learn,* לוֹמֵד *one that learns,* יַעֲזוֹב *he shall forsake,* תִּמְשֹׁל *thou shalt rule,* בַּכֹּל *over all.* This, of course, comprehends all masculine and feminine plurals: as, מְאֹרֹת *lights,* יָמִים *days.*

This rule is founded on a principle maintained by grammarians: viz. '*That unaccented long vowels cannot form a compound syllable.*' Hence, when, from causes to be hereafter explained, the terminating syllable is deprived of its accent, being joined to the following word by מַקֵּף, or when the accent requires to be removed to the penultimate*, the long vowel is changed, generally into its corresponding short vowel: thus (ָ) into (-), (ֵ) into (ֶ), ׀ into short (ָ), etc.

This will explain to the student why the same word often appears with different vowel points, without changing its signification. Thus, אֵת, וְאֵת (Gen. i. 1.) have (ֵ) under א, because they have the accent, but in verse 4, 7, etc. the same words are without the accent, being joined to the words following them, and are, therefore, pointed

---

* As in וַיֵּשֶׁב from וַיַּקָּב יָשַׁב from סָב, לֵךְ אֱלֹךְ instead לֵךְ אֵלֵךְ. (See page 85.)

אֶת־ and not אֵת. It is the same with the word כֹּל chōl, and כָּל־ chol, *all* (see Gen. i. 30). Also with the word יַעֲזָב־ ya-á-zob, (Gen. ii. 24.) and תִּמְשָׁל tim-shol (Gen. iv. 7.) which otherwise would have been תִּמְשֹׁל*, יַעֲזֹב.

5. Second Rule. All words consisting of, or terminating in, two short vowels, the penultimate of which is neither followed by dagesh nor sh'va final, or, in other words, forming simple syllables (p. 20), have their accent on the *penultimate:* as זֶרַע, תַּחַת, עֶרֶב, מַיִם, מִרְחֶפֶת, שָׁמַיִם, אֶרֶץ, יֶרֶק, נֶפֶשׁ, שָׂרִין, כְּמִשְׁלַת, דֶּשֶׁא (Gen. i.) Of the same nature are the following עַיִן *an eye,* רֶגֶל *the foot,* שְׁנַיִם *two,* שִׁנַּיִם *teeth,* בַּיִת *a house,* שַׁעַר *a gate,* יַיִן *wine,* לַיִל *night,* קַיִץ *summer,* שֶׁבַע *seven.*

This rule is founded on another principle maintained by ancient grammarians: viz. *That short vowels cannot form syllables unless they are followed by dagesh or sh'va final.* Hence, when neither of these take place, the vowels must have either *metheg* or a principal accent; and whereas *metheg* cannot come on the penultimate syllable, unless that syllable be succeeded by sh'va initial, it follows that all such words, to which the preceding rule applies, must have the accent. But this rule, though generally correct, is not without its exceptions.

Observe.—That most of the accents as exhibited in the preceding table, are placed on the syllable on which the stress of the voice is to be laid.

---

* In cases where such changes would operate against some other grammatical law, the long vowel is retained, but receives *metheg*: examples are וְשָׁם־ (Gen. ii. 13. 14.) עֵץ (verse 15.) קֵת־ (iv. 12.) שָׁת־ (iv. 25.) etc.

There are, however, some which are always placed on the first letter of the word: as, תַּלְשָׁא֘, יְ֚תִיב, etc. and others which are always placed on the last letter: as, סֶגּוֹל֒, זַרְקָ֘א, etc. In all such cases, the real place of the accents can only be known from analogy.

קַרְקָ֘א and פָּשְׁטָ֙א have the same shape, but the former is always placed on the tonic syllable, whether ultimate or penultimate, whilst the latter comes on the last syllable; and when analogy requires the accent to be on the penultimate, then the ֙ is repeated: as, תֹּ֨ה֙וּ (Gen. i. 2).

When words have two dissimilar accents, as וּֽלְמ֣וֹעֲדִ֔ים (Gen. i. 15.) the first is considered as *metheg*, and the second as the *principal* accent.

To avoid the concurrence of two principal accents which would happen when words accented on the last syllable are followed by accented monosyllables, or by dissyllables accented on the penultimate, the accent of the first word is frequently removed from the *ultimate* to the *penultimate**: as קָ֥רָא לָ֑יְלָה (Gen. i. 5.) instead of קָרָ֑א; אָחֹ֣תִי אָ֔תְּ (Gen. xii. 13.) instead of אֲחֹתִ֔י; הִפָּ֥רֶד נָ֖א (Gen. xiii. 9.) instead of הִפָּרֵ֖ד, (֔) being changed into (֖). In some cases the first word is deprived of its accent, and joined to the next by (־): as, יְעֹב־אִ֔ישׁ (Gen. ii. 24.) instead of יַעֲזֹ֔ב, (ֹ) being changed into *short* (ŏ); לְךָ־לְךָ֔ (Gen. xii. 1. (instead of לֵ֔ךְ, (֔) being changed into (ְ). See Observation on Rule 1. p. 82.

§ 3.—USE OF THE ACCENTS IN SHOWING THE RELATION OF WORDS CONSIDERED AS MEMBERS OF A SENTENCE.

1. The second use of the accents is to show the relation subsisting between words considered as

---

* This is denominated נָסוֹג אָחוֹר *removed back.*

members of a sentence or period. In this respect they are divided into *conjunctives* and *distinctives* (see the Table). The conjunctives have this in common, that they indicate a close connection between the word accented with either of them, and that which immediately follows it, as may be seen from the following examples: וַיֹּאמֶר אֱלֹהִים *and God said,* יְהִי אוֹר *there shall be light,* וַיְהִי אוֹר *and it was light,* וַיַּרְא אֱלֹהִים *and God saw* (Gen. i).

2. The *distinctives* represent pauses of various degrees, according to the order in which they are classed in the Table.

<small>The precise nature of these pauses cannot exactly be defined, as some of them frequently indicate longer or shorter pauses, according to the places which they occupy in a sentence; but speaking generally, they may, in some respect, be compared to our marks of punctuation; and this in the following manner:—</small>

Those contained in No. 1 (p. 79), represent the greatest pauses, somewhat similar to our Period and Colon.

No. 2. . . . Colon & Semicolon.
No. 3. . . . Semicolon & Comma.
No. 4. . . . Comma & Semicomma.

3. The accents comprehended in No. 1 and 2, are the most important, because they point out the simple sentences of which a compound sentence may happen to consist, as well as the principal members: thus,

סִלּוּק accompanied by (:) marks the end of the verse*, whether the verse contains one or more propositions: as, וַיְהִי־עֶרֶב וַיְהִי־בֹקֶר יוֹם שְׁלִישִׁי׃ And-there-was-evening and-there-was-morning the-third day (Gen. i. 13.) וְנֹחַ מָצָא חֵן בְּעֵינֵי יְהוָה But-Noah found grace in-the-eyes of the Lord (Gen. iv. 8.)

אֶתְנָח (ʌ) marks the next principal division, and generally occurs in verses containing two or more distinct propositions: as, וַיֹּאמֶר אֱלֹהִים יְהִי אוֹר וַיְהִי־אוֹר And-God-said, Let-there-be light; and-there-was light (Gen. i. 3). See also the next verse.

Sometimes, however, (ʌ) is placed only by way of emphasis (see Gen. i. 1), where אֱלֹהִים has the accent, although the verse contains only one proposition.

סְגוֹל (ʌ) marks the next principal division, and generally occurs in verses containing three distinct propositions.

וַיַּעַשׂ אֱלֹהִים אֶת־הָרָקִיעַ וַיַּבְדֵּל בֵּין הַמַּיִם אֲשֶׁר מִתַּחַת לָרָקִיעַ וּבֵין הַמַּיִם אֲשֶׁר מֵעַל לָרָקִיעַ וַיְהִי־כֵן׃

And God made the expanse; and he divided between the waters which were under the expanse, and between the waters which were above the expanse: and it was so (Gen. i. 7).

---

* There are, however, instances in which סלוק marks the end of a verse without the sense being completed (see Gen. xxiii. 17).

It is likewise often placed before a parenthesis (see Gen. i. 28. ii. 23), and has very frequently the force of a comma only. The other four indicate sometimes greater and sometimes lesser divisions, according to their situation, regulated chiefly by the length and shortness of the verse, as the learner may perceive, by perusing the phrases in which they are found*.

The principal distinctive accents, and especially סִלּוּק (׀) and אַתְנָח (֑), in consequence of the pauses which they produce, frequently change sh'va into a vowel, and the short vowels into long ones: as, אֲנִי–אָ֫נִי *I*; אַתָּה–אָ֫תָּה *thou*; יָדְךָ–יָדֶ֫ךָ *thy hand*; אֶרֶץ–אָ֫רֶץ; שָׁמַיִם–שָׁמָ֫יִם; מַיִם–מָ֫יִם (Gen. i).

The preceding observations, it is hoped, will be found sufficient to give the learner a general idea of the Hebrew accents. To enter into further detail on a subject so intricate would be a waste of time and labour. I shall, therefore, conclude this article with a few examples, showing the use of the accents in determining the sense of particular passages.

1. וַיֹּ֫אמֶר יְהוָה (Gen. iv. 6) signifies, 'And the Lord said,' because וַיֹּ֫אמֶר has a conjunctive accent, which shows it to be closely connected with the following word: but the same words, וַיֹּאמַ֫ר יְהוָה (Gen. xxiv. 12) signify, 'And he said, O Lord!'

---

* Thus, Zākaph kātōn upon לִרְקִ֫יעַ represents a greater pause than the same accent upon הַמַּ֫יִם (Gen. i. 7). See also verse 2, Gen i., where this accent on the word וָבֹ֫הוּ is equivalent to our *colon*, but on אֱלֹהִ֫ים in the same verse, it is only equivalent to our *comma*.

because וַיֹּאמֶר* has a distinctive accent, showing it to be disjoined from the following word, and forming a phrase by itself.

2. לֹא אֹכַל (Gen. xxiv. 33) with a conjunctive accent on לֹא, signifies, '*I will not eat;*' but the same words with a distinctive accent on לֹא: thus לֹא אֹכַל, would signify, '*No, I will eat*' (see Gen. xviii. 15, 21. xix. 2).

3. וַיֹּאמֶר עֶבֶד אַבְרָהָם אָנֹכִי (Gen. xxiv. 34) without the accents, might either signify '*And the servant of Abraham said, I am,*' etc. or '*And he said, the servant of Abraham I am,*' i. e. and he (Eleazer) said, I am Abraham's servant. The distinctive accents on וַיֹּאמֶר and on אָנֹכִי show that the last is the true meaning.

4. הַמַּלְאָךְ הַגֹּאֵל might signify, '*the redeeming angel;*' but הַמַּלְאָךְ הַגֹּאֵל אֹתִי† (Gen. xlviii. 16) signifies, '*The angel who redeemed me.*' In the former case, the conjunctive accent on הַמַּלְאָךְ would show it to be closely connected with הַגֹּאֵל, as every qualifying word is with that which it qualifies or defines. In the second example, the accent (֥) shows that הַמַּלְאָךְ is less connected with הַגֹּאֵל than this word is with אֹתִי.

5. וּבְנֵי יַעֲקֹב בָּאוּ מִן הַשָּׂדֶה כְּשָׁמְעָם וַיִּתְעַצְּבוּ הָאֲנָשִׁים (Gen. xxxiv. 7). Whether the word כְּשָׁמְעָם belongs to the preceding or to the following clause, cannot be determined by the text, but the (֥) on this word shows that the authors of the accents had

---

* The (-) under מ is in consequence of the distinctive accent.

† This accent, though placed in the Table amongst the conjunctives, is frequently used as a distinctive, and generally shows that the connection between it and the word which follows it, is not so close as that which subsists between the following and that which comes immediately after it.

considered it as separate from the following clauses*, and that the sense is as given in the Established Version: viz. '*And the sons of Jacob came out of the field when* (or, as soon as) *they heard it: and the men*,' etc.

6. וְהִנֵּה עֲלֵה־זַיִת טָרָף בְּפִיהָ (Gen. viii. 2,) might either signify, '*and behold a torn olive leaf in her mouth;*' or, '*and behold an olive leaf torn* (i. e. plucked off) *with her mouth.*' The distinctive accent (ֽ) on זַיִת and the conjunctive accent (ֽ) on טָרָף show that the second is the true meaning of the text: intimating that it was not a floating leaf torn by the waves, but one *which the dove had plucked off*, and from which circumstance Noah concluded that the waters were abated.

7. Without the accents it would be doubtful whether הַגָּדוֹל (Gen. x. 21) relates to שֵׁם or to יֶפֶת; but the conjunctive accent under יֶפֶת shows that it is closely connected with הַגָּדוֹל, and that אֲחִי יֶפֶת הַגָּדוֹל ought to be rendered '*the brother of Japheth the elder,*' as it is in the *Established Version*; and not '*the elder brother of Japheth,*'† as some translators have rendered it. For were this the meaning of the text, the accents ought to have been thus, אֲחִי יֶפֶת הַגָּדוֹל which, however, is not the case.

---

* In the Jerusalem Talmud (*Tract Avodah Zarah*) this word (כישמעם) is indeed added to the list of words which, according to the Talmudists, אֵין לָהֶם הַכְרָע *have no preponderance*, i. e. *are undeterminable*, as they may belong to either part of a sentence; it is, however, evident from our present system of accentuation, that its authors were of a different opinion.

† Thus *Vater* and other German translators, '*der ältere Bruder des Japhet.*' But as in all doubtful cases the authors of the accents ought to have some weight, I prefer, in this instance, the rendering as given in the Established Version.

HEBREW LANGUAGE. 91

Simple Phrases, in which the PRONOUNS *and the Verb* TO BE *are exemplified.*

אָנֹכִי אָבִיךָ[a][b] וְאַתָּה[m] בְּנִי׃	I-[am] *thy*-father, *and*-thou-[art] *my*-son.
אָנֹכִי אִמֵּךְ[d] וְאַתְּ[f] בִּתִּי׃	I-[am] *thy*-mother, *and*-thou-[art] *my*-daughter.
אֲנִי אָחִיךָ[e] וְאַתְּ אֲחוֹתִי׃	I-[am] *thy*-brother, *and*-thou-[art] *my*-sister.
הוּא אָבִי וְהִיא אִמִּי׃	He-[is] *my*-father, *and*-she-[is] *my*-mother.
הִיא אִמּוֹ וְהוּא בְּנָהּ׃	She-[is] *his*-mother, *and*-he-[is] *her*-son.
אֲנַחְנוּ בָנֶיךָ[m] וְאַתָּה אָבִינוּ׃	We-[are] *thy*-sons, *and*-thou-[art] *our*-father.
אָנוּ אַחֶיךָ[f] וְאַתְּ אֲחוֹתֵנוּ׃	We-[are] *thy*-brothers, *and*-thou-[art] *our*-sister.
אַתֶּם[m] בָּנַי וְאַתֵּן[f] בְּנוֹתַי׃	Ye-[are] *my*-sons, *and* ye-[are] *my*-daughters.
הֵם[m] בָּנָיו וְהֵן[f] בְּנוֹתָיו׃	They-[are] *his*-sons, *and*-they-[are] *his*-daughters.
הֵמָּה[m] בְּנֵיכֶם[m] וְהֵנָּה[f] בְּנוֹתֵיכֶן[f]׃	They-[are] *your*-sons, *and*-they-[are] *your*-daughters.
הִיא אִמְּכֶם[m] וְהוּא אֲבִיכֶם[m]׃	She-[is] *your*-mother, *and*-he-[is] *your* father.

☞ The terminations marked [m] are used when the person or persons addressed, or to whom the possessive pronouns relate, are of the Masculine Gender; those marked [f] are Feminine; and the rest are common to both Genders.

[a] אָב *a father.*   [b] בֵּן *a son.*   [c] אֵם *a mother.*
[d] בַּת *a daughter.*   [e] אָח *a brother.*   [f] אָחוֹת *a sister.*

זֶה ׀ בְּנֵנוּ וְזֹאת׀ בִּתֵּנוּ׃	This-[is] *our*-son, *and*-this-[is] *our*-daughter.
אֵלֶּה בְנֵיהֶם ׀ וְאֵלֶּה אֲחֵיהֶן׃	These-[are] *their*-sons, *and*-these-[are] *their*-brothers.
הוּא אִישׁ וְהִיא אִשָּׁה׃	He-[is a] man, *and*-she-[is a] woman.
אַתָּה וְזֹאת הִיא הָאִשָּׁה׃	Thou-[art] *the*-man. She-[is] *the* woman.
הַנַּעַר הַזֶּה ׀ הַנַּעֲרָה הַזֹּאת׃	This² boy¹. This² girl¹.
זֶה הַנַּעַר ׀ זֹאת הַנַּעֲרָה׃	This-[is] *the*-boy. This-[is] *the*-girl.
הַנְּעָרִים הָאֵלֶּה ׀ הַנְּעָרוֹת הָאֵלֶּה׃	These² boys¹. These² girls¹.
אֵלֶּה הַנְּעָרִים ׀ אֵלֶּה הַנְּעָרוֹת	These-[are] *the*-boys. These-[are] *the*-girls.
זֹאת הָאִשָּׁה וְזֶה בְנָהּ׃	This-[is] *the*-woman, *and*-this-[is] *her*-son.
לֹא זֶה הַדֶּרֶךְ וְלֹא זוֹ הָעִיר׃	This²-[is] not¹ *the*-way, neither-[is] this *the*-city[a].
מִי זֶה ׀ מַה זֶּה׃	Who-[is] this? What-[is] this?
מֶה עָשִׂיתִי לָךְ׃	What *have-I*-done to-*thee?*
מַה זֹּאת ׀ מָה אֵלֶּה׃	What-[is] this? Who-[are] these?
מִי אַתָּה ׀ מַה שְּׁמֶךָ׃	Who-[art] thou? What-[is] *thy*-name?
בַּת מִי אַתְּ׃	Whose daughter-[art] thou?[b]
בֶּן מִי זֶה הָעֶלֶם׃	Whose son-[is] this lad?[c]
הָאִישׁ אֲשֶׁר רָאָה אֹתִי׃	*The*-man who saw me.

---

[a] *m. l.* Not this the way, and not this the city.
[b] *m. l.* Daughter who thou?   [c] *m. l.* Son who this *the*-lad?

הַבַּיִת אֲשֶׁר בָּנָה׃	*The*-house which he-built.
אָנֹכִי נַעַר קָטֹן׃	I-[am a] little³ boy².
אָנֹכִי נַעֲרָה קְטַנָּה׃	I-[am a] little³ girl².
אַתָּה אִישׁ חָכָם׃	Thou-[art a] wise³ man².
הוּא מֶלֶךְ גָּדוֹל׃	He-[is a] great³ king².
הִיא אִשָּׁה חֲכָמָה׃	She-[is a] wise³ woman².
אֲנַחְנוּ רְעֵבִים וּצְמֵאִים׃	We-[are] hungry *and*-thirsty.
קַיִן הָיָה עֹבֵד אֲדָמָה׃	Cain was [a] tiller-*of* [the]-ground.
חַוָּה הָיְתָה אֵם כָּל־חָי׃	Eve was mother-*of* all-living.
גֵּר הָיִיתִי בָּאָרֶץ׃	*I-have*-been[b] [a]-stranger¹ *in-the*-land².
אֵיפֹה הָיִיתָ בְּנִי׃	Where *hast-thou*-been, *my*-son?
אֵיפֹה הָיִיתְ בִּתִּי׃	Where *hast-thou*-been, *my*-daughter?
הָיִינוּ בְּבֵית אָחִינוּ׃	*We-have*-been *in-the*-house *of our*-brother.
הֱיִיתֶם בַּמָּקוֹם הַזֶּה׃	*Ye-have*-been *in²*-*this³*-place².
לֹא הֱיִיתֶן שָׁמָּה׃	*Ye-have²ᶠ* not¹ been³ there.
בָּנָיו וּבְנוֹתָיו הָיוּ פֹה׃	*His*-sons *and-his*-daughters were-here.
יֵשׁ[a] לִי[b] כֶּסֶף׃	There-is to-me silver, *i. e.* I have silver.
—לְךָ[ᵃ] זָהָב׃	—to-*thee* gold, *i.e.* thou hast gold.

---

[a] Strictly speaking, יֵשׁ signifies 'there exists,' and אֵין 'there exists not.'

[b] The dative Pronouns are frequently used to denote possession without the word יֵשׁ.

יֵשׁ לְךָ נְחֹשֶׁת׃	There-is to-*thee* copper, *i.e.* thou hast copper.
— לוֹ בַּרְזֶל׃	—to-*him* iron, *i.e.* he has iron.
— לָהּ בְּדִיל׃	—to-*her* tin, *i.e.* she has tin.
— לָנוּ עֹפֶרֶת׃	—to-*us* lead, *i.e.* we have lead.
— לָכֶם ״ בַּיִת׃	—to-*you* [a]-house, *i.e.* you have a house.
— לָכֶן ׳ בָּתִּים׃	—to-*you* houses, *i.e.* you have houses.
— לָהֶם ״ עֶבֶד׃	—to-*them* [a]-slave, *i.e.* they have a slave.
— לָהֶן ׳ עֲבָדִים׃	—to-*them* slaves, *i.e.* they have slaves,
הֲיֵשׁ לוֹ אָח׃	Is-there to-*him* [a]-brother, *i.e.* has he a brother?
הֲיֵשׁ לוֹ בֵן׃	Is-there to-*him* [a]-son, *i.e.* has he a son?
יֶשׁ־לָנוּ אָב זָקֵן׃	There-is to-*us* an aged[4] father[1], *i.e.* we have an aged father.
יֶשׁ־לִי אֵם זְקֵנָה׃	There-is to-*me* an aged[4] mother[1], *i.e.* I have an aged mother.
אֵין לִי בֵן׃	There-is-not to-*me* [a]-son, *i.e.* I have not a son.
אֵין לָהּ בַּת׃	There-is-not to-*her* [a]-daughter, *i.e.* she has not a daughter.
לוֹ הָיָה בֵן יָחִיד׃	To-*him* was [an]-only[4] son[3], *i.e.* he had an only son.
לָהּ הָיְתָה בַּת יְחִידָה׃	To-*her* was [an]-only[4] daughter[3], *i.e.* she had an only daughter.
בָּנִים רַבִּים הָיוּ לוֹ׃	Many sons were to-*him*, *i.e.* he had many sons.
לֹא הָיוּ לוֹ אַחִים׃	Not[1] to-*him*[2] were[2] brothers, *i.e.* he had no brothers.

HEBREW LANGUAGE.

כֶּרֶם הָיָה לִשְׁלֹמֹה:	[A]-vineyard [there]-was to-Solomon, i.e. Solomon had a vineyard.
שָׂדוֹת וּכְרָמִים יִהְיוּ לָךְ:	Fields and vineyards shall-be to-thee, i. e. thou shalt have fields and vineyards.
לֹא הָיוּ עִמִּי:	They-were[2] not[1] with-me.
אָנֹכִי אֶהְיֶה ᵃ עִמְּךָ:	I-will-be with-thee ᵐ.
אַתָּה תִּהְיֶה ᵇ עִמּוֹ:	Thouᵐ shalt-be with-him.
אַתְּ תִּהְיִי ᵇ עִמָּהּ:	Thouᶠ shalt-be with-her.
הוּא יִהְיֶה עִמָּךְ:	He-shall-be with theeᶠ.
הִיא תִּהְיֶה עִמָּנוּ:	She shall-be with-us.
נַחְנוּ נִהְיֶה יִמָּכֶם:	We shall-be with-youᵐ.
אַתֶּם תִּהְיוּ עִמָּהֶם:	Youᵐ shall-be with-themᵐ.
אַתֵּן תִּהְיֶינָה עִמָּהֶן:	Youᶠ shall-be with-themᶠ.
הֵם יִהְיוּ עִמָּכֶן:	Theyᵐ shall-be with-youᶠ.
הֵן תִּהְיֶינָה אִתָּנוּ:	They shall-be with-us.
בָּרוּךְ תִּהְיֶה:	Blessedᵐ thou-shalt-beᵐ.
בְּרוּכָה תִּהְיֶה:	She-will-be[2] blessed[1]ᶠ.
הוּא יִהְיֶה חָכָם:	He will-be-[a]-wise-[man].
יִהְיוּ כְּמוֹץ לִפְנֵי רוּחַ:	They-shall-be as-chaff before [the]-wind.
נְשֵׁיכֶם ᶜ תִּהְיֶינָה אַלְמָנוֹת ᵈ:	Your-wives shall-be widows.

ᵃ Will or shall be. ᵇ Wilt or shalt be, etc.
ᶜ נָשִׁים women. ᵈ אַלְמָנָה a widow.

בְּנִי הֱיֵה אָב לָאֶבְיוֹנִים׃	My-son be [a]-father to-the-needy.
בִּתִּי הֱיִי[b] אֵם לַעֲנִיִּים׃	My-daughter be [a]-mother to-the-poor.
לָמָּה תִּהְיוּ אַחֲרֹנִים׃	Why will-you-be last.
מִי יוֹדֵעַ הֶחָכָם יִהְיֶה׃	Who knows-[whether]³ he-will-be⁴ wise³.
לֹא תִהְיֶה לוֹ כְּנֹשֶׁה׃	Thou-shalt² not¹ be² unto-him as-a-creditor.
רָבוּעַ יִהְיֶה הַמִּזְבֵּחַ׃	The-altar³ shall-be² square¹.
יִהְיוּ יָמָיו מְעַטִּים׃	His-days² shall-be¹ few³.
לֹא יִהְיוּ כַּאֲבוֹתָם׃	They-shall² not¹ be² as-their-fathers.
יְהוָֹה הָיָה הֹוֶה וְיִהְיֶה׃	The Lord was, is, and-shall-be.

[a] p. m. הֱיוּ be ye.   [b] p. f. הֱיֶינָה be ye.

THE END.

THE

ETYMOLOGY AND SYNTAX

(IN CONTINUATION OF THE ELEMENTS)

OF

THE HEBREW LANGUAGE,

BY HYMAN HURWITZ,

PROFESSOR OF HEBREW IN UNIVERSITY COLLEGE, LONDON, AUTHOR
OF VINDICLE HEBRAICLE, HEBREW TALES, ETC.

Third Edition.—Revised and Enlarged.

LONDON:
PRINTED FOR TAYLOR AND WALTON,
BOOKSELLERS AND PUBLISHERS TO UNIVERSITY COLLEGE,
28, UPPER GOWER STREET.

M DCCC.XLI.

LONDON:
PRINTED BY JOHN WERTHEIMER AND CO.,
CIRCUS PLACE, FINSBURY CIRCUS.

PREFACE.

To enable the learner to read and write the Hebrew Language with comparative ease was the chief object of the First Part of this work. The road to the venerable structure having thus been cleared, the student may now imagine himself standing at its portal, waiting for an introduction to the interior, and a right of admission to the sacred treasures which it contains. To afford him this passport, and, if we may vary the metaphor, to place in his possession the keys by which the several caskets are to be opened, is the aim of the following pages. They unfold the ETYMOLOGY and SYNTAX of the Language.

A mere catalogue of the names of Authors who have written on Hebrew Grammar, with the titles of their works, would occupy no scanty chapter in a Bibliographic Dictionary. To promise therefore any novelty, in respect of the usual forms common to all Grammars, would be both idle and presumptuous. Let it suffice to say, that after a careful perusal of the standard works, the Author ventures to affirm, that nothing of the least apparent practical importance or utility in the volumes of *Ben Gannach, Jarchi, Aben Ezra, M. and D. Kimchi, Abraham de Balmes, Elias Levita, Ben Zeeb, &c., Buxtorf, Glassius, Schultens, Michaëlis, Vater, Gesenius, &c.*, has been overlooked. Neither have any of their decisions been neglected, but after due thought, and from a conviction that they were either erroneous, or foreign from the purpose of the present work. If I might advance any pretension to novelty, it would be in reference to a higher object, to a more permanent interest; namely, that of making a knowledge of the Hebrew Language conducive to a philosophic insight into the structure and essential principles of language universally. Deeply convinced that words are the signs of men's *thoughts*, and not, as grammarians one after the other have agreed to assert, the representatives of *things*, I have omitted no opportunity of impressing this truth on the student's attention; and instead of contenting myself with that artificial classification or arrangement which assists indeed the passive memory, but, when exclusively relied on, tends to depress the higher powers, I have endeavoured to re-infuse into the words the living spirit by which they were once animated; opening out the rich and productive, though comparatively few, sources, from which they are derived, still splitting and ramifying, under the various modifying causes and influences. With this view, I have sought to fix the attention, first, on the primary image, and then on the derivative signification; and to exhibit the influence of the former on the latter, which is too often overlooked by the Translators, and lost in the idiom of a different language. "Accustom yourself," observes the well-known author of the *Aids to Reflection*, " to reflect on the words you use, hear, or read, their birth, derivation and history. For if words are not THINGS, they are LIVING POWERS, by which the things of most importance to mankind are actuated, combined and humanized."* "Horne Tooke entitled his celebrated work, Επεα πτεροεντα, *Winged Words:* or language not only the *vehicle* of thought, but its wheels. The *wheels* of the intellect I admit them to be; but such as Ezekiel beheld in 'the visions of God,' as he sate amongst the captives by the river of Chebar. 'Whithersoever the spirit was to go, the wheels went, and thither was their spirit to go: *for the spirit of the living creatures was in the wheels also.*' "†

In short, throughout the whole work I have designedly addressed myself to the active faculties of the intellect, rather than to the mere memory; yet not on this account neglecting, or less solicitous, to furnish the student with whatever aids may abridge his labour or tend to facilitate his progress.

The Hebrew is generally considered the most simple of all languages. If by simplicity is meant

* Preface p. xi.   † Ibid. pp. vii. viii.

the simplicity of *sentiment* or of *style*, nothing can be more just. In the Sacred Records you find none of those

> ———— swelling epithets thick laid
> As varnish on a harlot's cheek, the rest
> Thin sown with aught of profit or delight.—
>
> In them is *plainest* taught and easiest learnt,
> What makes a nation happy and keeps it so.
> *Paradise Regained.*

But when the term *simplicity* is applied, as it often is, to the words of the language, and when *simple* is opposed to *compound*, nothing can be more erroneous. In point of fact, scarcely can a single sentence be shown, in which the greater part of the words are not compounds, that is, composed of the principal word and of one or more modificatory letters, the relics or abbreviations of other words: and as the latter, though not numerous, are susceptible of various combinations, the same word will often appear under a variety of aspects, to the perplexity of the young student, and, not rarely, even of the advanced scholar. These difficulties I have endeavoured to remove—

1*st.* By explaining the modificatory letters, shewing their derivations, distinct signification, and the manner in which they are either prefixed or affixed to the principal words.

2*nd.* By presenting, throughout the etymological part, the modificatory letters, in a type differing from that of the principal words, by which means the learner may easily find out the root of each.

3rd. By various tables, exhibiting at one view the principal modifications of which each of the essential parts of speech is susceptible.

4th. By short and appropriate exercises.—These, whilst they will in some measure break the tedium more or less inseparable from grammatical studies, may at the same time serve as a criterion by which the student may ascertain his own progress.

In treating of the different parts of speech, Orientalists generally begin with the verb. I have, however, preferred the method adopted in teaching the European languages, as that to which the student may be supposed to be already accustomed. The same consideration has influenced me in the arrangement of the different parts of the verb. Those who are in the habit of teaching the Hebrew language, know how embarrassing it is to the learner to begin to conjugate a verb from what appears to him the wrong end, namely the third person instead of the first. In this work, therefore, the verb has been placed in the order which it occupies in the grammars of modern languages. No inconvenience can possibly arise from these alterations, as the general structure of the language is so fully explained in the introductory chapter to the Etymology.

In what regards the Syntax, the Author hopes that it will be found as plain and as comprehensive as the nature of the subject would admit. The introductory chapter to this part of the work should be read with particular attention, as it contains the principles on which most of the rules are founded.

Though it is highly advisable that the learner should at first confine his reading to the Sacred Records, yet it is desirable that he should, after having made sufficient progress, become acquainted with the uninspired writings of the Hebrews. With this view, several extracts from scarce books are given in the Appendix. A few specimens of translations from various languages have been inserted, to show the capabilities of the language.

Lastly, an Index, containing most of the words explained in this work, has been added; forming an extensive *Vocabulary* of the language, and supplying in some measure, the want of a Dictionary.

On the whole, the Author hopes he may be allowed to say, that by availing himself of the labours of those who have preceded him in the same career, and by the unwearied attention which he has himself bestowed on the subject, he has been able to condense in this volume more useful and interesting information on the Hebrew Language, than is to be found in any similar work of equal extent.

University College, London,
January, 1841.

CONTENTS.

	PAGE.
Nature of Words and their Classification	1 to 5
Derivation	6 ,, 13
Roots	14 ,, 16
Conjugation	17 ,, 18
Form of Words	18 ,, 20
Manner of Forming Substantives from Verbs	20 ,, 28
Inflection and Modification of Words	28 ,, 33
Nouns and their Modifications	33 ,, 35
Prefixes	35 ,, 40
Affixes	41 ,, 43
Gender	44 ,, 47
Number	48 ,, 52
Case	53
Absolute and Constructive State of Words	54 ,, 58
Explanation of Tables, I. II. III. IV.	58 ,, 60
Change of Vowels in the Process of Declension	60 ,, 62
Immutable and Mutable Vowels	62 ,, 63
Classification of Nouns	63 ,, 84
Adjectives and their Variations	85 ,, 87
Comparison of Adjectives	87 ,, 89
Numerals	89 ,, 94
Pronouns	95

CONTENTS.

	PAGE.
Personal Pronouns, Table IX.	96
Demonstrative Pronouns	97 to 98
Relative Pronouns	99
Interrogative Pronouns	100 ,, 103
Primitive and Derivative Verbs	103 ,, 104
Character and Signification of the Several Forms or Branches of the Verb, as *Kal, Niphal, &c.*	104 ,, 109
Moods and Tenses	109 ,, 110
Participles	114 ,, 115
Paradigm of a Perfect Verb, 1st Conjugation, Table X.	115
Remarks and Observations on the same	116 ,, 122
Verbs whose roots contain one of the letters א ה ח ע	122 ,, 128
2nd Conjugation	128 ,, 130
3rd ditto	130 ,, 133
4th ditto	134 ,, 137
5th ditto	137 ,, 142
6th ditto	142 ,, 144
7th ditto	144 ,, 148
The Verb הָיֹה *to be*, and חָיֹה *to live*	148 ,, 150
8th Conjugation	150 ,, 155
Tables, XI. XII. XIII. XIV.	155
Doubly Imperfect Verbs	156 ,, 161
Irregular Verbs	161 ,, 162
Quadriliteral and Pluriliteral Verbs	162 ,, 163
Objective Pronominal Affixes	165 ,, 166
Tables XV. XVI.	166
Separable and Inseparable Particles	167 ,, 173
Introductory Observations on the Syntax, Nature of Prepositions and their Constituent Parts	174 ,, 179
On the Several Kinds of Propositions	180 ,, 186
Subordinate Members of ditto	186 ,, 187
Pleonasms	188
Ellipsis	188
Syntax of the Noun and the Article	189 ,, 193

	PAGE.
Cases	193 to 199
Number	199 „ 201
Repetition of Nouns	201 „ 202
Syntax of Adjectives	202 „ 203
—— of Numerals	203 „ 208
—— of Pronouns	208 „ 212
—— of the Verb היה	212 „ 214
Tenses	215 „ 220
Application of the Tenses	220 „ 227
Moods	227 „ 231
Imperative Mood	231 „ 233
Subjunctive and Potential Moods	233 „ 234
Participles	234 „ 236
Concord of the Verb	236 „ 239
Government of the Verb	239 „ 241
Particles	241 „ 249
Arrangement of Words	249 „ 256

APPENDIX.

I. Folly of Idolatry	259 „ 260
II. Origin of Ditto	260 „ 261
III. Wisdom	262 „ 263
IV. Copy of a Letter from the Roman Senate to the Jews	263 „ 264
V. Ditto from Jonathan the High Priest to the Spartans	265 „ 266
VI. Tales from the Talmud	267 „ 268
VII. Fables	268 „ 269
VIII. Anecdotes	269 „ 270
IX. Moral Maxims	271 „ 272
X. A Metrical Paraphrase of the 8th Psalm	272 „ 274
XI. Truth	274 „ 275
XII. Hope and Fear	275 „ 276
XIII. The Contented Shepherd	276 „ 277

CONTENTS.

		PAGE.		
XIV.	Rules of Life	278		
XV.	The Metamorphosed Physician	279		
XVI.	Philanthropy	280	to	281
XVII.	De Consolatione Philosophiæ	282	,,	283
XVIII.	God Save the King	284	,,	287
XIX.	La Tourterelle, &c.	287		
XX.	Morgen-Gedanken	288	,,	292
XXI.	La Partenza	292	,,	298
XXII.	Sonetto del Marini	298	,,	299
XXIII.	Non Ebur, neque Aureum	300	,,	301
Register of Words.		303	,,	313

ETYMOLOGY.

CHAPTER I.

Introductory Observations.

1. Etymology is that part of grammar which treats of the derivation of words, and of their classification and modifications in connection with their derivation.

Nature of Words and their Classification.

2. Words are articulate sounds which mankind use as signs of mental conceptions and thoughts; and language* is the denomination given to the collective number of words by which human thoughts are conveyed.

3. As the representative of thoughts, language must contain signs corresponding with the various

---

* In Hebrew לָשׁוֹן *tongue*, or שָׂפָה *lip*, these being the chief organs employed in the production of articulate sounds.

species of conceptions which the mind is capable of forming; and since all human beings are similarly organised, and consequently subject to similar impressions,—since they are all endowed with similar intellectual faculties, by which they are enabled not only to notice those impressions and consequent feelings, but likewise to trace them to their correspondents in nature, and thus to become acquainted at once with the phenomena of nature and of their own minds,—in short, since human thoughts differ only in degree, but not in kind, and all languages are only so many different copies taken from the same original, it follows that the words or signs of which languages are constituted must all admit of the same classification; and, consequently, that the Hebrew can have neither fewer nor more essential parts of speech than the English or any other language.

4. The most philosophical classification of words is perhaps the following:—

[*a*]—Such as indicate the *objects* of thoughts, or the *subjects* of discourse. This class comprehends the names of beings with which the mind becomes acquainted through the senses; as, אוֹר *light*, רוּחַ *wind*, אֵשׁ *fire*, עֵץ a *tree*, &c., or by its own intellectual faculties, as אֵל *God*, רוּחַ a *spirit*, מַחֲשָׁבָה *thought, reflection*.

[*b*]—Such as serve to express whatever is affirmed respecting the objects of contemplation. This class comprehends *verbs*, or words denoting action, passion, being, or modes of existence, whether physical or intellectual: as, רָדַף *to pursue,* נִרְדַּף *he or it was pursued,* חָשַׁב *to reflect, think,* &c. הָיָה *to be, to exist,* אָדַם *to be red,* חָכַם *he was wise,* גָּדַל *to be great.*

[*c*]—Such as serve to qualify or to particularise either the subject or the predicate when they happen to be general terms. This class comprehends Adjectives, Adverbs and Definitives.*

[*d*]—Such as serve to indicate the relations of things; or words, in which the expression of general relations has superseded or diverted the attention of the mind from their primary particular meaning—viz., the relation of origin, dependency, cause, purpose, medium, instrumentality, similitude, junction, &c. This class comprehends Prepositions and Conjunctions.

[*e*]—Such as indicate particular affections or emotions, as, joy, sorrow, exultation, surprise, &c.†

---

* It will be shewn in the progress of the work, that the words included in this and in the following class are, in reality, Nouns, or Verbs, used for the particular purposes described; so that, strictly speaking, these two alone are the most essential parts of speech.

† Many grammarians will not allow Interjections to be called a part of speech, considering them as mere instinctive or mechanical ejaculations. That they are so, when uttered under the immediate impulse of passion, cannot be denied; but as they are frequently

6   THE ETYMOLOGY OF

As the student is, however, supposed to be already familiar with the usual grammatical classification, we shall retain it, and distribute the words of the Hebrew language into *Nouns, Adjectives, Pronouns, Verbs, Adverbs, Prepositions, Conjunctions,* and *Interjections.** The introductory notices prefixed, will sufficiently enable the student to distinguish between those which are primitive and essential distinctions, and those which are secondary, and in part technical—*i. e.* belonging to the *art* rather than to the *philosophy* of grammar.

Derivation.

5. In all languages we find clusters of words allied both in sound and in signification; such, for instance, are the following English words:—*love, lover, lovely, loving, loved, beloved, loveliness, &c.; just, justly, justify, justifier, justifiable, justification, &c.;* but, in Hebrew, this has an especial claim on the student's attention: thus—

---

used in representing our own *past* emotions, or those of other persons, and as, in all such cases, they are uttered as deliberately as any other word, I think they are sufficiently entitled to be numbered amongst the parts of speech.

* The early Hebrew Grammarians reckoned only three parts of speech: 1—שֵׁם *the name,* in which they included nouns and adjectives: 2—פַּעַל *the verb:* 3—מִלָּה *the particle,* in which they included the other classes.

THE HEBREW LANGUAGE. 7

רֹאשׁ rōsh, *the head,* the chief and principal part of the body.
רֵאשִׁית rā-shith, *chiefness, principalness, beginning.*
רִאשׁוֹן ri-shōn, *first,* in order or dignity.

מָלַךְ mā-loch, *to reign.*
מֹלֵךְ mō-lech, *one that reigns.*
מָלַךְ mā-lach, *he reigned.*

מֶלֶךְ me-lech, *a king.*
מַלְכָּה mal-cāh, *a queen.*
מַלְכוּת mal-chūth, *a kingdom.*

עָלָה ā-lōh, *to ascend.*
עֹלֶה o-leh, *one that ascends.*
עֹלָה o-lāh, *a burnt offering.*†
עָלָה ā-lāh, *he ascended.*
עָלֶה ā-leh, *a leaf.*
עַל āl, *upon, above.*‡

עֶלְיוֹן el-yōn, *most high.*
מַעֲלֶה ma-àleh, *an ascent, step.**
מַעֲלָה ma-ālāh, *upwards.*
נַעֲלָה na-ālāh, *exalted, raised.*
עֱלִי eli, *a pestle.*
תְּעָלָה §th'-ā-lāh, *a conduit or aqueduct.*

Now it is evident, that in these and similar collections of words, there can be but one primitive, from which the rest are derived. Equally evident is it, that by knowing the sense attached to the primitive, and the manner in which it is varied,

---

* Lit. The place where, or the instruments by which one ascends; also one that causes to ascend.

† *i. e.* What ascends upon the altar.

‡ The words עֹל ōl, *a yoke;* עוֹלֵל o-lāl, *a child;* נַעַל na-àl, *a shoe, sandal;* מַנְעוּל man-ùl, *a lock, bar;* מְעִיל m'il, *an upper garment,* &c., owe probably their origin to the same primitive, although they are placed by lexicographers under different roots.

§ *i. e.* Through which water is made to ascend.

in order to express different objects, or different shades of meaning, together with the various modifications of which each part of speech is susceptible, the labour of learning a language is greatly abridged. Hence the importance of attaining a thorough knowledge of the primitives.

6. As the only purpose of language is to communicate thoughts and judgments (which when clothed in words are called propositions), and as every judgment must contain at least a subject and a predicate, and every proposition, a noun and an attribute*, it follows that these two species of words must have formed the very rudiments of language. But, as if both could not have been invented at the same time, it has been made a question which of the two has a right to claim the priority. Most of the Oriental grammarians have decided in favour of the Verb. Many eminent philologists, however, maintain that the first invented terms were Nouns, because the objects by which men found themselves surrounded, and on many of which their very existence depended, would naturally claim their attention first. This is, indeed, in some respect true; but it proceeds on a mistake, which we have sought to preclude in our

---

* Substantives are often used as predicates; but then they are always accompanied by the verb TO BE, which is, however, seldom expressed in Hebrew, except when past or future time is indicated.

definition of language. Assuming *that words* primarily *correspond to things*, these writers have not perceived that though the things must have existed, and in most instances have been seen, prior to their modes of appearance, as moving, acting, or being acted on, yet by means of the latter only are they first brought into notice, so as to become the distinct objects of human consciousness — that is, *thoughts;* and that words *immediately* refer to our *thoughts* of the things, as images or generalised conceptions, and only by a second reflection to the things themselves. The following consideration will shew this truth in a still clearer point of view :—It will readily be granted that before names could have been assigned to objects, the objects themselves must have been known. Now, as all the knowledge we possibly can have of objects, consists in an acquaintance with their qualities, properties, or modes of existence, which indeed are so many signs by which things are manifested to the mind through the senses (for the substratum which supports the properties, as it is not an an object of sensation, can only be inferred by the mind*); and as all these are *attributes* and not *substances*†, it follows that the mind must have a notion of the attribute, before it can form a distinct conception of the object. It follows further, that in every

---

* See Maimonides' הלכות יסודי התורה.

† See Mr. Coleridge's definition of the word *substance*, in his " Aids to Reflection," Aphorism xii. p. 6.

such conception, the attribute by which the object is distinguished from every other being, must form a part; and, consequently, that the class of words which grammarians denominate *nouns*, must originally have been *verbal* (somewhat like the words called participles), expressive of some property or circumstances by which the named object was characterised. And, indeed, such is still the character of the far greater portion of Hebrew nouns, even of those which designate natural objects : thus—

רָקִיעַ rāki-á, *the firmament*, lit. *the expanse*, or that which is *expanded*.

חַמָּה ham-māh, *the sun**, lit. *the hot one*, as being the source of heat.

חֶרֶס he-res, another name of the *sun*, from its drying and burning power.

לְבָנָה l'bā-nāh, *the moon*†, lit. *the white one*, from its pale light; and from this circumstance several other substances appear to have derived their names : as —

---

* Another name of the sun is שֶׁמֶשׁ shemesh, which is probably a compound; viz. שָׁם אֵשׁ shām âsh, *the distant fire;* and שָׁמַיִם shā-ma-yim; שָׁם מַיִם sham mayim, *the distant water*. (See Jarchi's Comment on Gen. i. 7.)

† The moon is also called יָרֵחַ ya-rá-ah, from its *dilating* and increasing light: hence יֶרַח *a month*;—from which it appears that the Hebrew months were originally *lunar*.

לִבְנֶה lib'neh (λευκη), *the white,* amongst trees (populus alba, *the white poplar*).

לְבֹנָה l'bō-nāh (λιβανος), *the white,* amongst odoriferous gums; frankincense.

לְבָנוֹן l'bānōn (*Lebanon*), *the white mountain;* from its whiteness, being constantly covered with snow.

לְבֵנָה l'bá-nāh, *a brick,* from the white clay of which it is formed.

הֶלְבְּנָה ḥel-b'nāh,* *galbanum, a fragrant gum;* from its cream-like colour.

חַי ḥay†, *f.* חַיָּה ḥa-yāh, *an animal, a living being;* lit. *a breather,* or *a being that breathes;* breathing being the characteristic of animated beings.

עוֹף ōf†, *a bird, fowl;* lit. *the flier,* or that which flies.

שָׂעִיר sā-ïr, *the goat;* lit. *the hairy, the shaggy:* and from the same circumstance—

שְׂעוֹרָה s'ō-rāh (*hordeum*), *barley,* from the roughness of its awn.

שְׂעָרָה or סְעָרָה s'ō-rāh, *a tempest;* & שַׂעַר sā-ar, *horror.*

---

* Most lexicographers place this word under the root חָלָב; it is, however, probable that חָלָב itself received its denomination from its colour. Hence also the Rabbinical חֶלְבּוֹן ḥelbōn (*albumen*), *the white of an egg.*

† These are real Onomatopoeia,—חַי ḥay, imitative of the sound heard in forcibly emitting the breath; עוֹף ōf, that heard in the starting of a bird. Of the same character are the words אֵשׁ ésh, *fire;* אוֹר ōr, *light, fire;* רוּחַ ru-aḥ, *wind;* and many others.

7. This being the case, we can easily comprehend how the same word would be frequently used both as a noun and as a verb: as a *noun*, when it was used as the *subject* of discourse; and as a verb, when it was used as the *predicate*. Thus, the word אוֹר in the following sentence is used as a substantive: as, יְהִי אוֹר *There shall be light*, or *light shall be* (Gen. i. 3); but in the following phrases it is used as a verb: thus, הַבֹּקֶר אוֹר *The morning (was) light* (Gen. xliv. 3.) וְאוֹר לָכֶם *And it will be light unto you* (1 Sam. xxii. 10); אֹרוּ עֵינָי *My eyes have become light* (1 Sam. xiv. 29); i. e. capable of perceiving by means of light. Thus also the before-mentioned word חַי hay, *a living being*, or *a being that breathes*, is used in the following phrases as a verb*: as, וַיְחִי שֶׁלַח *And Salah lived* (Gen. xi. 14); עוֹד יוֹסֵף בְּנִי חָי *My son Joseph liveth still* (Gen. xlv. 21);—and כָּבֵד cā-bád, *the liver* (lit. the *heavy, the weighty*, being the heaviest part of the body in proportion to its bulk) signifies also *it is heavy†* (Gen. xlvii. 4); and *it was heavy* (Gen. xlvii. 13).

---

* It is likewise frequently used as an adjective: as, שׁוֹר חַי *a living ox;* כֶּלֶב חַי *a living dog;* בָּשָׂר חַי *raw flesh;* (*i.e.* in the same state as when living).

† Hence also כֹּבֶד kō-bed, *weight, heaviness;* כְּבֵדוּת k'bá-dūth, *difficulty;* כָּבוֹד kā-bōd, *honour, glory*, literally, *weight, (gravitas);* and כַּבֵּד kab-bád, *to honour;* מְכַבֵּד m'chab-bád, *one that honours;* נִכְבָּד nich-bád, *honourable, one that has become honourable;* מְכֻבָּד m'chu-bád, *one that is honoured;* מַכְבִּיר mach-bīd, *one that causes heaviness, an oppressor;* מִתְכַּבֵּד mith-cab-bád, *one that*

It is moreover frequently used as an adjective: as, מַשָּׂא כָּבֵד *a heavy burden.*

8. In all these examples, it is evident that there is no distinction whatever between the noun and the verb; but even in those where a distinction exists, it is so slight, as clearly to show the common origin of the words: thus—

דְּבֹר dā-bōr, *to speak.*
דֹּבֵר dōbár, *one that speaks, a speaker.*
דָּבַר dā-bar, *he spake,*
דָּבָר dā-bār, *a word,* or *thing.*
אָמֹר ā-mōr, *to say.*
אָמַר ā-mar, *he said.*
אֹמֶר ō-mer, *a saying.*

קָרֹב kā-rōb, *to be nigh, to approach.*

קָרַב kā-rab, *he* or *it came near.*
קָרֹב or קָרוֹב kā-rōb, *one that is nigh, related, a relative, kinsman.*
קֶרֶב ke-reb, *the inner part of the body, the intestines, bowels.*
קָרְבָּן kor-bān, *an offering.*
קְרָב k'rāb, *conflict, battle.*
קִרְבָה kir-bāh, *relationship, approachment.*

9. There are, indeed, many verbs which owe their derivation to nouns: as, for instance, עָפַר* *to throw dust;* עָשֵׁן *to smoke,* from עָשָׁן† *smoke;* מָלַח *to salt,* from מֶלַח *salt;* there are likewise many nouns which

---

honours himself, pretends to be honourable; with their numerous modifications.

* From עָפָר *dust.*

† This word is probably derived from אֵשׁ *fire;* smoke being the sign of fire. מֶלַח *salt,* is probably compounded of מַה *what,* לַח

cannot be referred to verbs, as רֹאשׁ *the head;* רֶגֶל *the foot, leg;* דֶּגֶל *a standard, flag, banner, &c.;* but this does not at all invalidate the preceding arguments; as these words, though now considered as primitives, may owe their origin to verbs which had fallen into disuse*, or to such as have not reached us; for it is not to be supposed that the Hebrews had no other words than those contained in the Sacred Records. Both theory and fact lead me, therefore, to conclude that the Hebrew nouns were originally *verbalia;* and the verbs ought to be considered as the elements of speech, not on account of their priority of invention, but because they generally contain the primary signification of words.

Roots.

10. The part of the verb containing the primary signification which runs through all its branches and derivatives, is the *infinitive mood*†, or the name of the

---

moist, i. e. *that which contracts moisture,* and רֶגֶל and דֶּגֶל are probably derived from one of the several roots which signify to explore, remove, reveal, &c. This is, however, mere conjecture; and indeed we are too far removed from the infancy of language to speak decisively on the origin of words.

* See S. de Sacy's remarks (*Grammaire Arabe,* § 231), on the word بَلَدَ, whose root למד does not occur in Arabic, though it is very frequently used in Hebrew.

† Many Grammarians consider the third person masculine past tense, as the *root;* thus, הָלַךְ *he went,* שָׁמַר *he kept.* But as the

action. It is called by some Hebrew grammarians
מָקוֹר mā-kōr, *the fountain;* by others, שֹׁרֶשׁ shō-resh,
the root, radix. It consists generally of the three

notion expressed by this form of the verb is too complex to be
considered as the primitive, I have preferred the opinion of those
grammarians who regard the infinitive as the root. Thus the
פתח דברי (a grammatical work, generally attributed to D. Kimchi.)
יֵשׁ דבור אחד שהוא שרש לכל אלה החלקים ונקרא מקור לפי
שהוא התחלת הדבור וישרש ההגיון וממנו יוצאות כל הפעולות הנזכרות ,
והיא המחשבה לעשות כשיאמר האדם הנני חושב לבנות בית זה ,
טרם המעשה באה המחשבה לעשות , ועל זה נקרא מקור :

" There is one word which is the root to all these parts (*i.e.* the
past, present, and future tenses, &c.); it is called *mākōr,* the fountain,
because it is the principle of speech, and the root of contemplation.
From it proceed all the before-mentioned parts of the verb. It is
the thought to do a thing. Thus, when a man says, 'Behold, I
intend to build this house,'—the thought *to build* must precede the
deed; and on this account it is called מקור *the fountain.*"

Thus, likewise, *Abraham de Balmis,* in מקנה אברם (Peculium Abræ.)

המקור ישרש כל פעולה וכו' ועל כן כאשר ישאלך מי שירצה איזה שרש
למדתי לא תאמר לָמַד כי אם לָמֹד עין הפעל בחולם :

" The infinitive mood is the root of every action, &c. And therefore, should any one ask you what is the root of למדתי lā-mad-tī
(*I did learn*), do not answer לָמַד lā-mad (*he did learn*), but לָמֹד
lā-mōd (*to learn*)."

The infinitive must not be confounded with the abstract noun,
which is likewise the name of the action : as, אָהֹב *to love,* אַהֲבָה *love;*
שְׂנֹא *to hate,* שִׂנְאָה *hatred.* They are nearly allied in their signification, and are, therefore, often substituted for one another. The
difference between them will be explained in the Syntax.

consonants, forming either monosyllables (when the middle letter happens to be ו or י): as, בּוֹא bō, *to come, to enter;* בִּין bīn, *to understand, perceive;* גּוּר* gūr, *to sojourn:* or dissyllables, as הָלֹךְ hā-lōch, *to walk;* שָׁמֹר shā-mōr, *to keep, to guard;* בָּלַע† *to swallow.*

11. The three consonants of which the primitive is composed, are called *radicals;* whereas those which are added for the purpose of diversification, are termed *serviles.*‡ To distinguish the radicals from each other, we shall call them the 1st, 2nd, and 3rd

---

* Many of the ancient grammarians very justly considered these and similar roots as שְׁנָיִים *bi-literals*, because the middle letter has more the character of a vowel than a consonant, being always quiescent, and often omitted: as גּוּר *to sojourn,* גָּר *he sojourned,* גֵּר *a sojourner, &c.* See Aben Ezra in צָחוֹת and מֹאזְנַיִם; and Abraham de Balmis in *Peculium Abræ,—De Partitione Verborum.*

† Roots consisting of four or more letters are, comparatively speaking, few in number. They are mostly either of foreign origin, as פִּתְגָם *an order, edict;* or compounded, as בְּלִיַּעַל *wicked, worthless,* from בְּלִי *without,* and יַעַל *merit, utility;* עַבְטִיט *thick mud,* from עָב *thick,* and טִיט *mud or clay.*

That many of the tri-literals are, most probably, likewise compounds, appears from several words cited in the preceding notes; numerous other examples of the same kind may be seen in "Vindiciæ Hebraicæ," pp. 42—46.

‡ The serviles consist of the following exclusively:—א ב ה ו י כ ל מ נ ש ת while no letter of the alphabet is excluded from the formation of the *radicals.* We shall distinguish the serviles in most cases by open letters, thus, ב א, &c.

letters of the root. Thus, פ is the first, ע is the second, and ל the third letter of the root פָּעֹל pāōl, *to act;* שׁ the first, ב the second, and ר the third letter of the root שָׁבֹר shā-bor, *to break.*

Conjugations.

12. Primitives may consist of any three letters of the alphabet, but they receive different names, according to the particular consonants of which they are constituted, and form different conjugations.

13. Such as have neither of the following letters—י, נ, א, for their *first* radical, nor ו or י for the *second,* nor א or ה for the third radical, and in which the second and third are not the same letter, are called שְׁלֵמִים *perfect;* because in the various changes which the primitive undergoes, the three consonants remain unaltered: as, זָכֹר *to remember;* זָכַרְתִּי *I remembered;* זִכָּרוֹן *a remembrance.*

These verbs form the first conjugation.

14. Such as have נ for their first radical, are denominated הֲסֵרִים *defectives;* because the נ is dropped in many of the derivatives; as, נָתֹן *to give;* אֶתֵּן (instead of אֶנְתֵּן) *I will give;* מַתָּנָה (instead of מִנְתָּנָה) *a gift.*

These form the second conjugation.

15. Such as have א or י for the first radical: as, אָכֹל *to eat*, יָדַע *to know**; א for the third, as מָצָא *to find*; ה for the third, as פָּדֹה *to redeem*; ו or י for the second letter, as קוּם *to rise*, בִּין *to understand*; are called נָחִים *quiescents*, because these letters are either *mute* or changed into other letters.

These form the third, fourth, fifth, sixth, and seventh Conjugation.

16. Such as have their second and third radicals the same, as מָדַד *to measure*, are called כְּפוּלִים *double*; the middle letter being frequently dropped in the derivatives: as, אָמֹד (instead of אֶמְדֹד) *I will measure*; לָמֹד (instead of לִמְדֹד) *in order to measure*; מִדָּה (instead of מִדְדָה) *a measure*.

These form the eighth Conjugation.

Form of Words.

17. The consonants, together with their appropriate vowel-points, constitute what is denominated the *form* of the primitive; and any alteration made in it, either by the omission or mutation of any of its letters or vowel-points, or by the addition of one or more letters, will necessarily produce a different *form*, indicative of a variation in the signification; as may be seen from the following examples:—

---

* The י is often dropped, as אֵדַע (instead אֵידַע) *I will know*.

Thus, from the infinitive שְׁבֹר shā-bōr, *to break*, (used both as a noun and as a verb), are derived—

1st. The participle active and passive—

שֹׁבֵר shō-bár, *one that breaks.*
שָׁבוּר shābūr, *broken.*

{ Used as nouns and verbs, and forming, with the personal pronouns, the present tense: as אֲנִי שֹׁבֵר *I break.*

2nd. The third person preterite, as—

שָׁבַר shā-bar, *he broke.*

{ From this, the rest of the tense is formed, by *post-fixing* fragments of the pronouns: as, שָׁבַרְתִּי *I broke,* שָׁבַרְתָּ *thou brokest.*

3rd. The imperative, as—

שְׁבֹר sh'bōr, *break thou,* m.

{ From which is formed the future tense, by *prefixing* fragments of the pronouns: as, אֶשְׁבֹּר *I will break,* תִּשְׁבֹּר *thou shalt break.*

4th. Nouns used in this sense only: as, שֶׁבֶר she-ber, *a break, breach, injury;* שִׁבָּרוֹן shib-bā-rōn, *a break, calamity, destruction;* מַשְׁבֵּר mish-bār, *a breaker, wave, billow.*

5th. Other infinitives, which in their turn give birth to nouns, participles, and other parts of the derivative verbs.

18. To understand this thoroughly, the student must bear in mind, that every attribute expressive of transitive action may be considered under various points of view:—

1ˢᵗ· As expressive of simple action :—

אָכֹל to eat,   אָכַל he did eat.

2ⁿᵈ· As expressive of simple passion :—

הֵאָכֵל to be eaten,   נֶאֱכַל he was eaten.

3ʳᵈ· As expressive of intense action :—

אַבֵּל to devour, consume,   אִבֵּל he consumed, devoured.

4ᵗʰ· As expressive of intense passion :—

אֻבַּל to be devoured, consumed,   אֻבַּל he was consumed, &c.

5ᵗʰ· As causing another to act :—

הַאֲכֵל to cause to eat, *i. e.* to feed,   הֶאֱכִיל he fed, &c.

6ᵗʰ· As being made to perform an action :—

הָאֳכַל to be caused to eat, to be fed,   הָאֳכַל he was fed.

7ᵗʰ· Reflex action, or such as is performed by the agent on himself :—

הִתְאַכֵּל to consume, devour one's self,   הִתְאַכֵּל he consumed himself.

The first of these divisions may be called the *primitive*, the other six, *derivative* verbs. Their *technical* names are, 1ˢᵗ, Pa-ăl; 2ⁿᵈ, Niphăl; 3ʳᵈ, Piĕl; 4ᵗʰ, Pū-ăl; 5ᵗʰ, Hiph-ĭl; 6ᵗʰ, Hoph-ăl; 7ᵗʰ, Hith-pa-ăl.

Manner of forming Substantives from Verbs.

19. Substantives are formed from verbs in various ways :—

1ˢᵗ· By changing the vowel-points of the root: as, מֶלֶךְ *a king*, from מָלַךְ *to reign ;* אֹכֶל *food, victuals*, from אָכֹל *to eat.*

2nd. By dropping one of the radicals: as, גַּן *a garden*, from גנן *to shelter;* גֵּר *a stranger*, from גּוּר *to sojourn.*

3rd. By adding one or more of the following letters י, ת, נ, מ, א, ה*, to the root: as, מַאֲכָל *food, provision*, (lit. what is eatable or eaten); מַאֲכֶלֶת *a knife* (lit. an instrument used in eating), from אָכַל; מִקְנֶה *cattle†* (lit. what is purchased, or the medium of purchasing); קָצִיר *harvest*, or *a reaper*, from קָצַר *to reap, cut down.*

4th. By the three preceding methods combined: as, מַתָּנָה *a gift*, from נָתַן *to give;* מִטָּה *a bed*, מַטֶּה *a staff, tribe*, from נָטָה *to stretch out, incline;* תַּכְלִית *the end, completion*, from כָּלָה *to finish, complete.*

---

* These letters may be called the *Formative Letters.*—They are either prefixed, affixed, or inserted in the middle of words, by which a great variety of forms are produced.

† This word, derived from קָנָה *to possess, to purchase, to obtain,* favours the supposition that cattle were in the early ages regarded as the chief measure of value, the same as money in our days. This appears to have been the case during the Trojan war, as is evident from the Iliad, B. VI.—

"For Diomed's brass arms, of mean device,
For which *nine oxen* paid (a vulgar price),
He gave his own of gold divinely wrought,
A hundred beeves the shining purchase bought."

And though silver had already in the time of Abraham become the chief standard of value, yet cattle were equally used as the medium of exchange, even in subsequent times, as appears from Genesis xxxviii. 17, and xxxiii. 19; קְשִׂיטָה being rendered by most of the ancient translators, *lamb.* Thus Sept. *ἀμνων.* Onkelos חוּרְפָן, Vul. agnis.

מִשְׁקָל (mish-kal), WEIGHT OR COMMON MEASURE OF WORDS.

20. To be able to refer words to their roots, and to ascertain the difference between them and their derivatives, a model, pattern, or common measure, with which words in general may be compared, is necessary.

For this purpose, the ancient grammarians selected the word פָּעַל*, and borrowed from it and its derivatives their grammatical terms.

21. Imagining that the essence of the verb consists in action, and the word פָּעַל signifying *to act*, they employed this word to denote the *verb* in general, whether active, passive, or neuter.

22. Considering the 3rd person sing. *m.* preterite,

---

* The middle letter of פעל being one of the gutturals, which are subject to peculiar laws of punctuation, has induced several modern grammarians to substitute the verb פָּקַד or קָטֹל for it. I have, however, retained it, as it is used by all the ancient grammarians; and even the moderns have adopted it, as far as relates to the technical terms *Niphál*, *Piél*, *Puál*, &c. And, indeed, it matters not what word we take as a *common measure*, provided the difference between the *gutturals* and *non-gutturals* be pointed out; which ought to be done in either case.

THE HEBREW LANGUAGE.

as the root of the primitive verb; and the same person of the derivative verbs as the principal words from which their respective tenses, moods, &c. are formed; and these words being, in the verb under consideration, as follows—

1st, פָּעַל Pā-äl, *he acted,*
2nd, נִפְעַל Niph-äl, *he was acted upon,*
3rd, פִּעֵל Pi-êl*, *he acted with intensity, &c.*
4th, פֻּעַל Pu-äl, *he was acted upon with intensity,*
5th, הִפְעִיל Hiph-ïl, *he caused another to act,*
6th, הָפְעַל Hoph-äl, *he was caused by another to act,*
7th, הִתְפַּעַל Hith-pā-äl, *he acted upon himself,—*

they adopted them as technical terms, to indicate the principal branches of the verb in general.

And this is indeed the process of the human mind when it begins to reflect. An impressive, single instance is taken, or rather obtrudes itself on the recollection: it is then discovered that the properties or attributes noticed in this instance, are common characters in a large number of instances: and thus, the individual impression is raised into a general or generic conception; and the word by which it was named, becomes a general term: and general terms applied to the purposes of classification, in the aid or ordonnance of the memory, are technical terms; without which no art nor science can be taught.

---

* When the second radical is a non-guttural, it receives *Dagesh*, (See Part I. 32): as, קִדֵּשׁ *he sanctified;* שֻׁבַּר *he was shattered;* הִתְקַדֵּשׁ *he sanctified himself.*

Thus they denominated all verbs denoting simple actions, *Pa-àl* or קַל *kal* (i. e. *light, simple*), because the root is here found in its simplest form; whereas, the other branches have either an additional letter, or a dagesh in the second letter of the root. Those that denote simple passion, or the passive voice, they called נִפְעַל *Niphàl;* those that denote intense action, they termed פִּעֵל *Pi-el;* and so on with the rest.

23. As the conjugations of verbs are regulated by the letters of which the root consists, and as the root פָּעַל consists of פ *Pe,* ע *Ain,* and ל *Lamed,* they denominated the first letter of every root, פ *Pe;* the second ע *Ain;* and the third ל *Lamed.*

Thus they called the שׁ of שָׁבַר, *Pe;* the בּ *Ain;* and the ר, *Lamed.*

Thus they likewise denominated all verbs having נ for the first radical, as—

נָגַשׁ to approach; נָפַל to fall; (2nd conjugation*)...... פ"נ

Those that have א for the first radical, as—

אָכַל to eat; אָמַר to say; (3rd conjugation)...... פ"א

Those that have י for the first radical, as—

יָשַׁב to sit; יָדַע to know; (4th conjugation)...... פ"י

---

* The first conjugation, as we have already observed (p. 17), they called שְׁלֵמִים; and the 8th, כְּפוּלִים.

Those having ו for the second radical, as—

גּוּר to sojourn;   שׁוּב to return;   (5th conjugation)...... ע"ו

Those having א for the third radical, as—

מָצָא to find;   קָרָא to call;   (6th conjugation)...... ל"א

Those having ה for the third radical, as—

קָנָה to obtain;   רָאָה to see;   (7th conjugation)...... ל"ה

And by this means, they readily distinguished the different conjugations from each other, and ascertained the peculiarities belonging to each.

24. By having thus a standard, or common measure, with which to compare words, we may easily ascertain their general meaning.

Thus, by knowing that פָּעַל is the 3rd person masculine preterite of all active transitive verbs, פּוֹעֵל the active participle, and פָּעוּל the passive participle, we may be certain that שָׁבַר, לָמַד, פָּקַד, are the 3rd person *m.* pret.; that שׁוֹבֵר, לוֹמֵד, פּוֹקֵד, are participles active; and שָׁבוּר, לָמוּד, פָּקוּד, are passive participles. Thus, also, by knowing that the form, which the 3rd person *m.* preterite of instransitive verbs assumes, is mostly פָּעֵל, we may, without hesitation, say that יָבֵשׁ, זָקֵן, &c. are intransitive verbs, and the same will hold good with every other part of the verb.

25. In the same manner the forms of nouns and adjectives may be ascertained by comparing them with a similar form deduced from פָּעַל; and by knowing the grammatical changes of which the *form* is

susceptible, we may at once know the changes which most words, having a similar *form*, must undergo in the process of declension.

Thus, all words consisting of three radicals (of the 1st conjugation, p. 17), having (ָ) for their first and second vowel-points: as, דָּבָר *a word*, חָכָם *a wise man*, זָהָב *gold*, &c. are said to be of מִשְׁקָל (the form) פָּעָל.

Those that have (ָ) for the first, and (ֵ) for the second: as, הָצֵר *a court*, זָקֵן *an old man*, are of the form פָּעֵל.

Those that have (ָ) for the first, and (ִי) for the second vowel-points: as, פָּקִיד *an overseer*, קָצִיר *harvest*, are of the form פָּעִיל.

Those that have (ָ) for the first, and (וֹ) or (וּ) for the second vowel-points: as, אָדוֹן *a lord*, גָּדוֹל *great*, בָּרוּךְ *blessed*, עָצוּם *mighty*, are of the forms פָּעוֹל and פָּעוּל.

All words of the above forms have their accent on the last syllable.

Those that have ‿ for the first, and (ֶ) or (-) for the second vowel-point: as, אֹזֶן *an ear*, שֹׁחַד *a bribe*, are of the form פֹּעֶל.

Those that have (ֶ) or (-) for their first and second vowel-points: as, מֶלֶךְ *a king*, אֶרֶץ *land*, נַעַר* *a boy*, רֶגַע *an instant*; or (ֵ) for the first, and (ֶ) for the

---

* The vowel-point (-) in this and similar words, is substituted for (ֶ), on account of the guttural letter.

second vowel-points: as, סֵפֶר *a book*, &c. are of the form פֵּעֶל and פֶּעַל*.

Words of the last-mentioned forms have their accent on the penultimate.

מִשְׁפָּט *judgment*, from שָׁפַט *to judge*, is of the form מִפְעָל; מ being the formative letter.

מַמְלָכָה *a kingdom*, from מָלַךְ *to reign*, is of the form מִפְעָלָה; מ and ה being the formative letters.

מַטָּע *a plant* (from נָטַע), מַדָּע *knowledge* (from יָדַע *to know*), are of the form מַעַל†; מ being the formative letter, and נ in the first, and י in the second word being dropped.

מַתָּנָה *a gift* (from נָתַן *to give*), is of the form מַעֲלָה†; נ the first radical being dropped, and מ and ה being the formative letters.

גֵּר *a stranger* (from גּוּר *to sojourn*), is of the form פֵּל, the second radical being omitted.

בֵּן *a son*, from בָּנָה, is of the form פֵּע, the third radical being dropped.

צֵל *a shadow*, from צָלַל, is of the form פֵּל; the first of the double letters being dropped.

מְגִלָּה *a roll, volume*, from גָּלַל, is said to be of the form מִפְלָה; מ and ה being the formative letters, and the second radical omitted.

---

* These forms are, by some grammarians, called Segolates.

† The second radical of this and the following form receive Dagesh, to show the absence of the first radical. If we take the verb פָּקַד as the *common measure*, these two forms will be מַקָּד & מַקְּדָה.

The preceding examples, it is hoped, will be deemed sufficient to give the learner a general conception of the formation of nouns, which is all that is aimed at in this chapter. Further information on this intricate subject will be found in Chapter III.

Inflection and Modification of Words.

26. Whoever considers the rapidity of thoughts, will allow that even the most concise language is but a slow instrument for the purpose of communicating them. Attempts have, therefore, been made in all languages, especially in those of ancient date, to shorten the process, by expressing all such general notions as are applicable to whole classes of words— as, for instance, the gender, number, and case of nouns, the moods, tenses, &c. of verbs—by inflections (probably taken from some already existing word), instead of doing it by entire words. The Hebrew is particularly remarkable in this respect; for it not only expresses the before-mentioned grammatical accidents by inflections, but also such words as occur most frequently in discourse; as, for instance, the article, *the;* the conjunction, *and;* the relative, *who, which, that;* the possessive pronoun, *my, thy, his,* &c.; and both the *nominative* and *objective,* when they happen to be pronouns. By this means, whole phrases may be expressed in single words: as, יֶאֱהָבֵנִי *he will love me,* וְיֶאֱהָבְךָ *and he will love thee;* הוֹצֵאתִיךָ *I have caused thee to go forth,* &c.

27. The manner in which this is effected, is no less ingenious than remarkable, and shows, most clearly, that language is neither the result of accident, nor of capricious compact, but the product of mind—of mind fully aware of the object in view, and endeavouring to effect it in the simplest way possible. But before we proceed, it is necessary for the student to know the personal pronouns. These are—

Sing.		Plur.	
אָנֹכִי or *אֲנִי . .	I	אֲנַחְנוּ or אָנוּ §	we
אַתָּה † *m.* אַתְּ *f.*	.... thou	אַתֶּם *m.* אַתֶּן *f.*	.... you
הוּא ‡	he	הֵם or הֵמָּה ...	they, *m.*
הִיא	she	הֵן or הֵנָּה ...	they, *f.*

* This word is considered as a primitive. It is, however, probably derived from אָנָה, or rather עָנָה *to exclaim*, or *to commence a discourse* (א and ע being mutable letters). See Cant. ii. 10; Job iii. 2. It means, literally, *the exclaimer* or *speaker*.

† אַתָּה is evidently derived from אני׳ The dagesh in ת indicates the absence of נ, which is still preserved in some of the dialects: as, אַנְתָּ), اَنْ|. The ת is, perhaps, a contraction of אֵת (sign of the objective). The same observation is applicable to the words אַתְּ, אַתֶּם, אַתֶּן, instead of אַנְתְּ, אַנְתֶּם, אַנְתֶּן.

‡ הוּא is probably derived from the verb הָיָה *to be*, הֹוֶה *one that is* (written sometimes with א), and means, literally, *a being*. It is frequently used instead of the substantive verb.

§ This appears to be the plural of אָנֹכִי, although written with ה.

28. Now, instead of expressing the pronouns by separate words, fragments of the personal pronouns are subjoined to the nouns, and amalgamated with them.

Thus, יָד *a hand,* יָדִי* *my hand* (lit. *hand I,* or belonging to the speaker); יָדְךָ *thy hand* (lit. *hand thou,* or, belonging to the person addressed); יָדוֹ *his hand,* יֶדְכֶם † *your hand,* יָדֵינוּ *our hands,* וְיָדֵנוּ ‡ *and our hands,* &c.

Thus also דָּבָר *a word,* דְּבָרִי *my word,* דְּבָרְךָ *thy word,* דְּבָרוֹ *his word,* דְּבָרָהּ *her word,* דְּבָרֵנוּ *our word,* דִּבְרֵיהֶם &c. See Declension of nouns, Tab. II.

29. *Obs.* 1.—As the accent can come only either on the ultimate or the penultimate syllable, it follows, that when words are thus augmented by additional syllables, the accent must be removed from its original place; and hence, in order to accelerate the pronunciation, a change in the vowel points becomes necessary. Thus, in דָּבָר the accent is upon the syllable בָר; but in דְּבָרִי it is placed upon רִי; the first vowel-point (ָ) is therefore changed into (ְ); and in דִּבְרֵיהֶם,

---

* These terminations, denominated *affixes,* are evidently contractions of the personal pronouns: thus, י, from אֲנִי *I;* ו, from הוּא (still more evident in the word פִּיהוּ *his mouth,* i. e. פִּ *mouth,* הוּא *he;* שָׂדֵהוּ *his field,* i. e. שָׂדֶה *field,* הוּא *he*); נוּ, from אָנוּ *we.*

† ךָ and כֶם. The derivation of these terminations is very uncertain. It is supposed, not without reason, that אָנֹכִי had originally a form for the second person sing. and plur. : as, אכה or אנכה *thou* or אנכם or אכם *you,* from which these fragments were taken.

‡ This letter (ו), used for the conjunction *and,* is evidently a fragment of the noun וָו *a hook, a thing that joins.*

where the accent is removed still further, being placed upon הָ‎, a still greater contraction of the vowel-points takes place*.

30. *Obs.* 2.—Vowel-points which are thus liable to be changed, are called *mutable*. There are, however, many which, as they constitute the characteristic distinction of the words in which they are found, can, on that account, not be changed into any other, and are retained notwithstanding the removal of the accent. They are, for this reason, called *immutable.* Such, for instance, is the וֹ in שֹׁמֵר‎ *a keeper, guard,* it being the characteristic of the active participle. Such also, are all the short vowels followed by dagesh, indicative of their being derived from the derivative verb פִּעֵל‎ (פִּקֵּד‎): as, מַלָּח‎ *a mariner,* סֻלָּם‎ *a ladder;* or from roots whose 2nd and 3rd radicals are the same; תְּהִלָּה‎ *praise,* תְּפִלָּה‎ *prayer,* &c. &c.

31. The definite article is expressed by the prefix הַ†, as הַיָּד‎ *the hand,* and all the cases (except the genitive), are expressed by single letters taken from prepositions: as, לְיָד‎ *to a hand* (לְ‎ being taken from אֶל‎ *to*); מִיָּד‎ *from a hand* (מ‎ being taken from מִן‎ *from*); בְּיָד‎ *with* or *in a hand,* מִיָּדֵינוּ‎ *from our hands,* &c., &c.

32. In the same simple manner are the persons and tenses of the verb indicated. The *past,* by *post-*

---

* Similar contractions, as Gesenius justly remarks, are found in other languages: as, Ἡατηρομου, for Πατηρ ἐμου; *ecca* and *eccum* for *ecce ea* and *ecce cum.*

† This fragment (ה) is probably derived from הֵא‎ *there is,* or הֵן‎ *behold.* Some grammarians suppose it to be taken from the Arabic article; but I see no reason why we should have recourse to the language of Arabia, in cases where we can more easily refer words to their Hebraic origin.

fixing fragments of the pronouns to the verb; and the *future*, by *prefixing* them. Let us take, for instance, the three principal parts of the primitive verb פָּקֹד :—

   Infinitive .... פְּקֹד *to visit.*
   Imperative ...... פְּקֹד *visit thou*, m.
   3rd person *m.* past .. פָּקַד *he visited.*

Now, subjoining to the last תָּ (from אַתָּה *thou*), we have פָּקַדְתָּ *visited thou*, i.e. *thou hast visited;* נוּ (from אָנוּ *we*), we have פָּקַדְנוּ *visited we*, i.e. *we have visited;* תֶּם (from אַתֶּם *ye*), and we have פְּקַדְתֶּם *visited ye*, i.e. *ye have visited;* denoting the past time by the position of the root.

33. Thus, also, by prefixing א (from אֲנִי *I*), to פְּקֹד, we have אֶפְקֹד *I-will-visit;* תִּ (from אַתָּה *thou*), we have תִּפְקֹד *thou-shalt-visit*, &c. &c.; indicating by the prefixes, not only the person, but likewise (by their position), that the time is future. Further, by subjoining other fragments to this, or the past tense, the objective pronouns are likewise indicated: as, אֶפְקְדֵהוּ *I-will-visit-him*, פְּקַדְתִּיהוּ *I-have-visited-him*, פְּקַדְתִּיךָ *I-have-visited-thee*, וְיִפְקְדֵנִי *and-he-will-visit-me*, &c.

It is this which gives the Hebrew language that conciseness for which it is so remarkable, making its words keep pace almost with the thoughts which they represent.

Having thus given a general outline of the structure of the language, we shall proceed to treat, in the following chapters, of each part of speech separately.

CHAPTER II.

Nouns and their Modifications.

34. Nouns are generally distributed into—

I.—Common nouns, or appellatives: as, אִישׁ *a man*, בֵּן *son*.

II.—Proper names: as, יִשְׂרָאֵל *Israel*, אֲרָם *Aram*, יְרוּשָׁלַיִם *Jerusalem*.

35. Proper names, are the names of particular individuals, thus distinguished from others of the same kind. Common names are, on the contrary, the names of *genera* and *species*; and, unless they are accompanied by some restrictive sign or word, denote either the whole species or kind: as, אָדָם וּבְהֵמָה תּוֹשִׁיעַ יְהוָֹה *Lord! thou helpest* man *and* beast (Ps. xxxvi. 6),—or any one of the kind: as, מַכֵּה אָדָם יוּמָת "*He that killeth* a man (*i. e.* any man) *shall be put to death*" (Levit. xxiv. 21). As the Hebrew has no indefinite article, the context alone can show in which of the two senses the noun is to be understood.

36. The restrictive words, by which appellatives are made to express particular individuals, are called *definitives*. Such are, the article *the*; the demonstrative pronouns, *this, that*, &c.; the pronominal adjectives, *my, thy*, &c. The restriction is, however, more frequently

effected by the annexation of another noun, which serves to define that which precedes it: as, בֵּן *son*, בֶּן־מֶלֶךְ *son of a king*, בֶּן־הַמֶּלֶךְ *son of the king*, or *the son of the king*; בֶּן־יִשְׂרָאֵל *Israel's son*, or *the son of Israel*.

37. Nouns are frequently varied or altered, in order to express the different modifications of which they are susceptible. This is done in various ways:—

I.—By altering one or more of the vowel-points: as, בֵּן *son*, בֶּן *son of*, בֶּן־אַבְרָהָם *Abraham's son*, דָּבָר *word*, דְּבַר *word of*, דְּבַר־הַמֶּלֶךְ *the word of the king*.

II.—By adding one or more letters either at the beginning or at the end of the words: as, הַדָּבָר *the word*, וְהַדָּבָר *and the word*, דְּבָרִי *my word*, דִּבְרֵיכֶם *your words*.

38. Letters added at the beginning of words are denominated *Prefixes*; those that are added at the end, are termed *Affixes*.

The Prefixes leave the accent of the words unaltered, and therefore produce no alteration in the vowel-points; but the affixes draw the accent from its original place toward the termination, and therefore produce, generally, a change in the vowel-points. See the preceding examples, and Art. 29.

39. Every word thus varied by additional letters, may in some measure be considered as a compound; and as every compound is best understood by know-

THE HEBREW LANGUAGE.

ing its constituent parts, we think it most advisable to explain the prefixes and affixes before we treat of the general properties of nouns.

PREFIXES.

40. The following are the prefixes of Nouns:—

הַ—with dagesh in the following letter: as, הַנָּהָר, הָ or הֶ without dagesh: as, הָאוֹר, express the definite article *the;* for which reason, this letter (ה) is called the *definite* ה.

Obs. הַ is used before nouns beginning with any letter capable of receiving Dagesh: as, נָהָר *a river*, הַנָּהָר* *the river*.

הָ is used before nouns beginning with either of the letters ר, ע, ה, א†: as, אוֹר *light*, הָאוֹר *the light;* הָר *a mountain*, הָהָר *the mountain;* עֶבֶד *a servant*, הָעֶבֶד *the servant;* רֹאשׁ *head*, הָרֹאשׁ *the head.*

הֶ is used mostly before nouns (not being monosyllables) beginning with ע, ח, or ה, having long unaccented (ָ)

---

* The effect of dagesh after a vowel, is to double the letter in which it is placed.—(See Part I. p. 36) This word must, therefore, be pronounced *han-nā-hā'r*. The dagesh is, however, sometimes omitted: as, הַיְאוֹר *the river*, הַיְלָדִים *the children*.

† As the Gutturals ר, ע, ח, ה, א, cannot easily be pronounced double, the Dagesh would be useless in them; it is, therefore, compensated by changing (ַ) into (ָ) or (ֶ). Before ח, however, the original vowel (ַ) is mostly retained: as, הַחֹשֶׁךְ *the darkness.* Sometimes also, before ה: as, הַהֶבֶל *the vanity.* We also find הַחַי *the living*, and הָחַי and הֶחָי. These deviations are, however, too unimportant to be longer dwelt upon.

THE ETYMOLOGY OF

for their first vowel: as, עָנָן *a cloud*, הֶעָנָן *the cloud*; הֶחָלָב *the milk*; הֶהָרִים *the mountains*.*

הַ or הֲ—without dagesh† in the following letter, indicates interrogation: thus, שֹׁמֵר *a keeper*, הֲשֹׁמֵר *the keeper*, הֲשֹׁמֵר אָחִי אָנֹכִי *the keeper?—the keeper of my brother (am) I?* i. e. *Am I the keeper of my brother?* (Gen. iv. 9.)

Obs.—This is called the interrogative ה. It is used before any word in a state of interrogation: as, לֹא *not*, הֲלֹא *is it not?* יֵשׁ *there is*, הֲיֵשׁ *is there?* [Before the gutturals it takes, mostly, (-): as, אַתָּה *thou*, הַאַתָּה בְנִי *art thou my son?* הַעֵת *is it time?*] before words beginning with any letter having Sh'va; thus, בְּרָכָה *a blessing*, הַבְּרָכָה *the blessing*, הַבְרָכָה *a blessing?*‡

---

* Before participles, ה is often used as a relative pronoun: thus, הַמְלַמֵּד *the teacher*, or *who teaches*; הַהוֹלֵךְ *who* or *which goes?*

† In a few instances we find Dagesh after the interrogative ה: as, הַשְּׁמֵנָה *whether fat?* (Num. xiii.) הַבְּמַחֲנִים *whether in camps?* (ibid.) We likewise find הֶחָזָק *whether strong?* (ibid); but in these cases, the context easily shows that they are interrogatives. In הַדְּרָכַי *whether my ways?* הַיִּיטַב *will it be well?* (cited by some grammarians), it is equally evident that the ה is interrogative; as the definite ה is seldom found before nouns having the pronominal affixes, or before verbs in the past or future tense.

‡ The reason of this change is, lest two initial Sh'vas should come together—thus, הַבְּרָכָה, which is contrary to the genius of the language.

THE HEBREW LANGUAGE. 37

וְ *and* (from וָו *a hook, plug*), is used to express junction, and connection in general: as, זֶרַע וְקָצִיר וְקֹר וָחֹם וְקַיִץ וָחֹרֶף וְיוֹם וָלָיְלָה *Seed-time* and *harvest*, and-*cold*, and-*heat*, and-*summer*, and-*winter*, and-*day*, and-*night*. (Gen. viii. 22.) And with the definite article, וְהַ *and the:* as, לְךָ יְהוָה הַגְּדֻלָּה וְהַגְּבוּרָה וְהַתִּפְאֶרֶת וְהַנֵּצַח וְהַהוֹד *Thine, O Lord,* [*is*] the-*greatness,* and-the-*strength,* and-the-*glory,* and-the-*victory,* and-the-*majesty.* (1 Chron. xxix. 2.)

בְּ *in, with* (probably, from בּוֹא *to enter, to come in*), is used to express the relations denoted by the ablative case, or by the prepositions, *in, with, on, among, at,* &c.: as, בְּאֶרֶץ in-*a-land,* בְּאֶבֶן with-*a-stone,* בְּהַר on-*a-mountain,* בְּיִשְׂרָאֵל amongst-*Israel,* בְּדָבָר in, on, or with *a word or thing.*

כְּ *as* (probably from כֹּה *thus, in this manner;* or from כָּכָה (כָּךְ), *so, thus,*) is used to express comparison and proportion generally, and answers to the words *as, so, according to, about, almost,* &c.: as, כְּאֶרֶץ as-*a-land,* כְּעֶבֶד as-*a-servant,* כְּאֵיפָה about-*an-ephah,* כְּדָבָר as-*a-word.*

לְ *to, for* (from אֶל *to,* is used to express the relations of tendency and purpose, denoted by the dative case, or by the words *to, for in order,* &c.: as, לְאֶרֶץ to-*a-land,* לְדָבָר to or for-*a-thing.*

Obs. 1.—To express the relations denoted by the letters בְּ, כְּ, לְ, definitely, either ה is annexed, as בַּהַדָּבָר in-the-*word*,

THE ETYMOLOGY OF

כַּהַדָּבָר as-the-*word*; or, which is more usual, the ה is omitted, and its vowel-point is placed under those respective letters: thus, בַּדָּבָר in-the-*word*, כַּדָּבָר as-the-*word*, לַדָּבָר to-the-*word**.

2.—When ה occurs before these prefixes, it indicates interrogation: thus, לְהַבֵּן to-the-*son*, הֲלַבֵּן if-to-the-*son*?

---

* The prefixes ל, כ, ב, ו, are frequently added to other words: as, גָּדוֹל וְקָטֹן great and-*small*, אֲנִי וְהוּא I and-*he*, אָכַל וְשָׁתָה he-*eat* and-*drank*, לֶאֱכֹל וְלִשְׁתּוֹת to-*eat* and-*to-drink*, &c. Their proper points are (ְ):—thus, לְ, כְּ, בְּ, וְ. The (ְ) is, however, frequently changed for other vowels, which causes great embarrassment to the young student.—To prevent this, he is requested to attend to the following rules:—

    I. ו is changed into וּ (pronounced אוּ) before words beginning with either of the labials פ, מ, ו, ב; or before words beginning with any letter having Sh'va: as, וּבֶגֶד and-*a-garment*, וּדְבַשׁ and-*honey*.

    II. It is changed into וָ before words having a distinctive accent on the first letter: as, לֶחֶם וָיַיִן bread and-*wine*.

    III. Before words beginning with Sh'va, the letters ל, כ, ב, receive (ִ ִ): as, בִּדְבַר in-the-*word-of*, כִּדְבַר as-the-*word-of*, לִדְבַר to-the-*word-of*. Before the gutturals, definitely, ~~or in pause~~, they follow the same rule as the definite ה. (Art. 40).

    IV. Before words beginning with י, the letters ל, כ, ב, ו, receive (ִ י), י becoming quiescent: as, יְהִי he-shall-*be*, וִיהִי and-he-shall-*be*, יְמֵי days-*of*, בִּימֵי in-the days-*of*, כִּימֵי as-the-days-*of*.

    V. Before the semi-vowels (ֲ) (ֳ) (ֱ), they receive the corresponding short vowels: as, בֶּאֱמֶת truth, וֶאֱמֶת and-*truth*, וַאֲנִי, לַחֲצִי, כַּחֲצִי, בַּחֲצִי, וַחֲצִי half, חֲצִי in-*truth*, &c.:

    VI. Before אֱלֹהִים God, they take (ֵ); א becoming quiescent: thus, וֵאלֹהִים, לֵאלֹהִים, &c.

Likewise לֵאמֹר (*for the purpose of saying*)

לֵאמֹר,

THE HEBREW LANGUAGE.

מְ or מִ*, from מִן *from*, is used to express the relation of *origin, cause:* as, מִגּוֹי from-*a-nation*, מִדְבָר from-*a-thing*, מִדַּבֵּר from-*speaking*, מֵאִישׁ from or out-of-*a-man*, &c.; and with the definite article, מֵה *from-the:* as, מֵהַמִּדְבָּר from-the *desert*.

Obs.—After adjectives, it denotes the comparative degree: as, חָזָק מִצּוּר *stronger-than a-rock*.—(See Adjectives, Art. 87.)

41. To the preceding may be added the particle אֵת or אֶת־, which, though not a prefix, always precedes nouns in a definite state, and is often joined to them in order to express their objective cases: as, '*In the beginning God created* אֵת הַשָּׁמַיִם the *heaven*, כַּבֵּד אֶת־אָבִיךָ וְאֶת־אִמֶּךָ *and the earth*;' '*Honor* thy-*father* and-thy-*mother*;' וַיִּשְׂרָאֵל אָהַב אֶת־ יוֹסֵף '*And-Israel-loved Joseph*.'

VII. Before אֲדֹנָי and its variations, also before יְהוָה they take (-): as, וַיהוָה, לַאדֹנָי וַאדֹנָי; בַּיהוָה, &c. As these changes are chiefly for the sake of euphony, and as they do not affect the signification of words, I deem it unnecessary to enter into further detail.

* מִ before the gutturals.

‡ From this punctuation of the prefixes before the word יְהוָה, it is evident that the word was anciently pronounced אֲדֹנָי. Had it been pronounced *Jehovah*, as some learned men suppose, the points must have been וַיְהוָה, בְּיְהוָה, as the words in No. IV.

THE ETYMOLOGY OF

Exercise.

Translate and analyse the following words:—

*דֶּרֶךְ, וְדֶרֶךְ, בְּדֶרֶךְ, כְּדֶרֶךְ, לְדֶרֶךְ, מִדֶּרֶךְ, הַדֶּרֶךְ,
הַדָּרֶךְ, וְהַדֶּרֶךְ, כְּהַדֶּרֶךְ, בַּהַדֶּרֶךְ, וּבַדֶּרֶךְ, הַבַּדֶּרֶךְ, כְּהַדֶּרֶךְ,
כַּדֶּרֶךְ, מֵהַדֶּרֶךְ, וּמֵהַדֶּרֶךְ, אֶת־הַדֶּרֶךְ׃

†אֶרֶץ, הָאָרֶץ, וְהָאָרֶץ, בְּאֶרֶץ, בָּאָרֶץ, וּבָאָרֶץ, כְּאֶרֶץ,
כָּאָרֶץ, לְאֶרֶץ, וּלְאֶרֶץ, לָאָרֶץ, וְלָאָרֶץ, מֵאֶרֶץ, וּמֵאֶרֶץ,
מֵהָאָרֶץ, אֶת־הָאָרֶץ׃

‡חָכָם, וְחָכָם, הֶחָכָם, כְּהֶחָכָם, לְחָכָם, לֶחָכָם,
מֵחָכָם׃ §חָכְמָה, הַחָכְמָה, וְחָכְמָה, וְהַחָכְמָה, בְּחָכְמָה,
בַּחָכְמָה, לְחָכְמָה, וּלְחָכְמָה, מֵחָכְמָה׃

Render the following into Hebrew:—

A day‖, and a day, as a day, in a day, to a day, and to a day; the day, and the day, as the day, in the day, to the day, from the day, and from the day; from day to day.

A woman¶, to a woman, the woman, to the woman, and to the woman, and a woman, from a woman, from the woman, and from the woman.

~~The~~ slave**, a slave, and the slave, and a slave, a slave? as a slave, as the slave, to a slave, to the slave, from a slave, from the slave, and to the slave.

---

* A way, ~~a road~~. †Land, ~~earth~~. ‡ A wise man. § Wisdom.
‖ יוֹם   ¶ אִשָּׁה   ** עֶבֶד

Affixes.

42. The following are the principal Affixes:—

הָ ...with the accent on the last syllable, is used to denote the feminine gender: as, אִישׁ *a man,* אִשָּׁה *a woman,* נָבִיא *a prophet,* נְבִיאָה *a prophetess;* פּוֹקֵר *a visitor,* פּוֹקְרָה *a female visitor.*

Obs. הָ with the accent on the penultimate, is sometimes used to express tendency towards a place: as, חָרָן *Haran,* חָרָנָה *towards Haran;* נֶגֶב *the south,* נֶגְבָּה *towards the south.* Nouns terminating in ה, change that letter into ת: as, מָרָה *Marah,* מָרָתָה *to Marah.*

הָ without the accent, is likewise added, sometimes, by way of euphony: as, לַיְלָה for לֵיל *night.* In such cases ה is said to be *Paragogic.*

ת ...with the accent on the penultimate, is used to denote the feminine participle: as, שׁוֹפֵט *one that judges, a judge; f.* שׁוֹפֶטֶת: also שׁוֹפְטָה.

ים ...is used to indicate the plural of masculine nouns: as, נְבִיאִים *prophets,* פּוֹקְדִים *visitors,* יוֹם *a day,* יָמִים *days;* שָׁנָה *a year,* שָׁנִים *years.*

ַיִם ...is used to express two of a kind: as, יוֹמַיִם *two days,* שְׁנָתַיִם *two years.*

וֹת ...is used to express the plural feminine: as נַעֲרָה *a girl, a young woman,* נְעָרוֹת *girls;* דֶּלֶת *p.* דְּלָתוֹת *doors.*

THE ETYMOLOGY OF

The following affixes are used to denote the possessive Pronouns :—

		שִׁיר a song, m.	שִׁירָה a song, f.
ִי—my	שִׁירִי my song	שִׁירָתִי my song
ךָ—thy, m.	שִׁירְךָ thy song, m.	שִׁירָתְךָ thy — m.
ךְ—thy, f.	שִׁירֵךְ thy song, f.	שִׁירָתֵךְ thy — f.
וֹ his	שִׁירוֹ his —	שִׁירָתוֹ his — m.
ה—her	שִׁירָהּ her —	שִׁירָתָהּ her —
נוּ—our	שִׁירֵנוּ our —	שִׁירָתֵנוּ our —
כֶם—your	*שִׁירְכֶם your — m.	שִׁירַתְכֶם your — m.
כֶן—your, f.	*שִׁירְכֶן your — f.	שִׁירַתְכֶן your — f.
ם—their, m.	שִׁירָם their — m.	שִׁירָתָם their — m.
ן—their	שִׁירָן their — f.	שִׁירָתָן their —

When the things possessed are plural.

	שִׁירִים songs, m.	שִׁירוֹת songs, f.
ַי—my	שִׁירַי my songs	שִׁירוֹתַי my songs
יךָ—thy, m.	שִׁירֶיךָ thy — m.	שִׁירוֹתֶיךָ thy — m.
יִךְ—thy, f.	שִׁירַיִךְ thy — f.	שִׁירוֹתַיִךְ thy — f.
יו—his	שִׁירָיו his —	שִׁירוֹתָיו his —
יהָ—her	שִׁירֶיהָ her —	שִׁירוֹתֶיהָ her —
ינוּ—our	שִׁירֵינוּ our —	שִׁירוֹתֵינוּ our —
יכֶם—your	*שִׁירֵיכֶם your — m.	שִׁירוֹתֵיכֶם your — m.
יכֶן—your, f.	*שִׁירֵיכֶן your — f.	שִׁירוֹתֵיכֶן your — f.
יהֶם—their, m.	*שִׁירֵיהֶם their — m.	שִׁירוֹתֵיהֶם their — m.
יהֶן—their, f.	*שִׁירֵיהֶן their — f.	שִׁירוֹתֵיהֶן their — f.

* כֶם, כֶן, הֶם, הֶן, are denominated *heavy affixes*, because they always have the accent; the rest are denominated *light affixes*.

שִׁירוֹתָם (m.)

שִׁירוֹתָן (f.)

41. To the preceding affixes may be added, the termination ִ‫י‬, ‫ית‬ ִ and ‫יָה‬, by which patronymics, or nouns denoting extraction, are formed from proper names: as, עִבְרִי a *Hebrew*, f. עִבְרִית, or עִבְרִיָה, from עֵבֶר *Heber;* עַמּוֹנִי *an Ammonite,* f. עַמֹּנִית, from עַמּוֹן *Ammon.*

Exercises.

Add the possessive pronouns to the following nouns: —

תּוֹרָה *a law,* סֻכָּה *a hut,* like שִׁירָה; סוּס *a horse,* גִּבּוֹר *a strong man,* like שִׁיר

Render the following into English: —

גְּמַלִּים*, הַגְּמַלִּים, וְהַגְּמַלִּים, וּבַגְּמַלִּים, לִגְמַלִּים,
לִגְמַלֶּיךָ, גְּמַלֶּיהָ, גְּמַלָּה, וּגְמַלֵיהֶם, וְלִגְמַלֵיהֶם:
מֶלֶךְ†, וּמֶלֶךְ, לְמֶלֶךְ, הַמֶּלֶךְ, וְהַמֶּלֶךְ, הֲמֶלֶךְ,
כְּמֶלֶךְ, מֵהַמֶּלֶךְ, בַּמֶּלֶךְ, לַמֶּלֶךְ, וְלַמֶּלֶךְ, לְהַמֶּלֶךְ, הַכְּמֶלֶךְ,
כְּהַמֶּלֶךְ, מַלְכִּי, בְּמַלְכִּי, מַלְכְּךָ, מַלְכֵּךְ, מַלְכּוֹ, בְּמַלְכּוֹ,
מַלְכָּה, וּלְמַלְכָּה, מַלְכָּם, בְּמַלְכָּם, וּמְלָכִים, הַמְּלָכִים,
בַּמְּלָכִים, לַמְּלָכִים, וְהַמְּלָכִים, מְלָכֵינוּ, לִמְלָכֵינוּ, מַלְכֵיכֶם,
מְלָכֶיהָ, מַלְכֵיהֶם, וּמַלְכֵיהֶם, מַלְכָּה‡, וְהַמַּלְכָּה, מַלְכוּת,
לְמַלְכוּת:
מַלְכוּת§, מַלְכוּתְךָ, בְּמַלְכוּתוֹ, וּמַלְכוּתָהּ, לְמַלְכוּתָהּ,

---

*Camels. † A king. ‡ A queen. § A ~~kingdom~~ reign.

44   THE ETYMOLOGY OF

מַלְכוּתָם, בְּמַלְכוּתָם: מַמְלָכָה*, וּמַמְלָכָה, וְהַמַּמְלָכָה,
בְּמַמְלָכָה, בַּמַּמְלָכָה, וּמִמַּמְלָכָה, מַמְלַכְתִּי, כְּמַלְכֻתְךָ,
מַמְלַכְתֵּנוּ, מַמְלָכוֹת, וְהַמַּמְלָכוֹת:

GENDER.

42. There are two genders, the masculine and the feminine. Of the masculine are—

1st. Names of males and their functions: as, שֵׁם *Shem*, אָב *a father*, כֹּהֵן *a priest*.

2nd. Names of nations, rivers, and mountains: as, עַם *a people*, כְּנַעַן *Canaan*, נָהָר *a river*, יַרְדֵּן *the Jordan*, כַּרְמֶל *Carmel* סִינַי *Sinai*†.

---

* Kingdom.

† To consider inanimate objects, or their names, as masculine or as feminine, appears very irrational; and yet, if we except the English language, the absurdity of thus making a distinction where nature has made none, and where none can be required, prevails in almost all languages. To account for this anomaly, some authors have supposed, that in the infant state of the world, mankind actually imagined that all objects of nature were animated, and consequently attributed to them sexual distinction; considering those objects which manifest themselves by their power and activity — as, for instance, the Wind, the Sun, &c.— as masculine; and, on the contrary, those that appeared of a passive nature — as, for instance, the Earth, the Moon, &c. — as feminine. Others suppose, that the framers of language were guided by some subtle kind of reasoning, which discovers, even in inanimate objects, something

3rd. Names of seasons and months: as, אָבִיב *the Spring*, חֹרֶף *Winter*, נִיסָן *Nisan*.

4th. Names of metals: as, זָהָב *gold*, כֶּסֶף *silver*. Except נְחֹשֶׁת *copper*, which is used in both genders, and עֹפֶרֶת *lead*, which is supposed to be feminine.

---

analogous to sex. These explanations are, however, not at all satisfactory; for independent of the absurdity of supposing the framers of language to have been so subjected to the fancy as not to distinguish between a real animal and a block of wood, or that they should have possessed such refined notions as to discover the most distant analogies, there is this objection, — that, on either supposition, the different names belonging to the same object must have retained the same gender: but this is contrary to fact. Thus, for instance, of the two names יָרֵחַ, לְבָנָה, given to the *Moon*; the first is masculine, and the second, *feminine*; and of the three denominations of the *Sun*, שֶׁמֶשׁ, חֶרֶס, חַמָּה, the first is feminine; the second, masculine; and the third, of both genders. The real cause of the before-mentioned anomaly, as it regards the Hebrew, appears to me this:—that in the infancy of language, especially amongst a pastoral people, which the Hebrews were, the chief subjects of discourse were unavoidably persons and domesticated animals. In these, they observed the natural distinction of sex, which they endeavoured to indicate in their language; and they did it in a very simple way: viz., by adding ה—a mere breathing and certainly the softest and most delicate of consonantal sounds— to the masculine: thus, יֶלֶד *a child, boy*, יַלְדָּה *a girl;* נַעַר *a lad, youth,* נַעֲרָה *a lass, maiden;* שָׂעִיר *a he-goat,* שְׂעִירָה *a she-goat;* כֶּבֶשׂ *a lamb,* כִּבְשָׂה *a ewe-lamb;* &c. &c. Animals which did not often come under view, or in which the distinction of sex was not obvious, were left undistinguished, and their names were used in either gender, just as the fancy of the speaker happened to suggest

43. Of the feminine are —

1st. Names of females and their functions: as, שָׂרָה Sarah, צִלָּה Zillah, אֵם a mother.

2nd. Names of countries and cities: as, אַשּׁוּר Assyria, יְרוּשָׁלַיִם Jerusalem.

3rd. Names of the double members of the human body*: as, אֹזֶן ear, רֶגֶל foot.

4th. Names having the following terminations:—

ָה, as בְּרָכָה a blessing; or יָה, as, עִבְרִיָּה a Hebrew woman.

ֶת, as אֹמֶנֶת a nurse, קְטֹרֶת incense, תִּפְאֶרֶת glory, אֱמֶת truth.

ַת, as קַדַּחַת a burning, a fever, נַחַת quietness, pleasure,

ִית, as רֵאשִׁית beginning, תַּבְנִית form, pattern, עִבְרִית a Hebrew woman.

וּת, as מַלְכוּת a kingdom; or וֹת, as אָחוֹת a sister.

---

at the moment; and hence the origin of the epicene. It was the same with the names of inanimate objects. They were used indiscriminately in either gender; or, as *Aben-Ezra* has expressed it, in his usual laconic style, כָּל שֶׁאֵין בּוֹ רוּחַ חַיִּים זָכְרֵהוּ וְנַקְּבֵהוּ "*Whatever has no life*, male *it* or female *it*." This promiscuous use of the gender, probably prevailed during the infancy of language and for a long period after it. But when the language became fixed by writing, and especially by authoritative books which served as models to subsequent writers, the gender of nouns became, in some measure, likewise fixed. And thus it is, that what in its origin was a matter of indifference, became, in the course of time, a law, from which we cannot now deviate, without being guilty (in the eyes of the half-learned, at least,) of a grammatical impropriety.

* Except יָד *a hand*, עַיִן *an eye*, which are used in both genders.

44. Many nouns are used in both genders, and are therefore said to be of the *common gender:* as, רוּחַ *the wind,* אֵשׁ *fire,* מַחֲנֶה *a camp.*

Amongst these may be numbered the *Epicene:* as, גָּמָל *a camel,* דֹּב *a bear,* יוֹנָה *a dove,* חֲסִידָה *a stork,* male or female.

Exercise.

[Render the following into Hebrew:—

As my songs, *m.* And from thy *f.* songs, *f.* Their *m.* songs *m.* and her song. My camel and his camels. To her camels. And to her camels. And from the king and queen. To her kings and to the queen. To her king and to the queen. From their kings and from the queen. As my king and as your kings. And to the queens. My kingdom and thy kingdom. Her kingdom and his kingdom. From kingdom to kingdom. Our kingdom and the kingdoms. And in my law. As their laws. And from thy law. As my hut. And from thy huts. And to the strong man.]

Formation of Feminine Nouns.

45. Feminine Nouns, as has already been observed (p. 41), are formed by adding ָה or ֶת to the masculine: as, מֶלֶךְ *a king,* מַלְכָּה *a queen;* גָּדוֹל *great,* m. גְּדוֹלָה f.; אוֹמֵן *an educator, foster-father,* אֹמֶנֶת *a foster-mother, a nurse;* פּוֹקֵד *a visitor,* פּוֹקְדָה or פּוֹקֶדֶת f.*

---

* Some receive Dagesh in the last radical: as, אָדֹם *m. red,* f. אֲדֻמָּה; קָטֹן *m. small, little,* f. קְטַנָּה.

Obs. 1.—Masculine nouns terminating in הֶ, form their feminine by changing (v) into (v): as רֹעֶה *a shepherd,* רֹעָה *a shepherdess**.

2.—Those that terminate in ח or ע, receive חַ־ instead חֶ־: as, שׁוֹמֵעַ *a hearer, f.* שׁוֹמַעַת or שׁוֹמְעָה; בֹּרֵחַ *one that runs from danger, f.* בֹּרַחַת†.

3.—Many nouns express their gender by different words: as, אָב *father,* אֵם *mother;* חֲמוֹר *a he-ass,* אָתוֹן *a she-ass;* חָתָן *a bridegroom,* כַּלָּה *a bride;* עֶבֶד *m. a servant, f.* שִׁפְחָה *a bond-maid*‡.

4.—The feminine of אָח *a brother,* is אָחוֹת *sister;* of בֵּן *a son,* בַּת *a daughter;* חָם *a father-in-law,* חָמוֹת *a mother-in-law.*

Number.

46. Hebrew nouns admit of three numbers; the Singular, Plural, and Dual.

Formation of the Plural Number Masculine.

Masculine nouns form their plural mostly by adding ים־§ to the singular: as, מֶלֶךְ *a king,* מְלָכִים *kings.*—(Vide Affixes, p. 41.)

---

* In some of the derivative verbs, the ה is changed into יחַ־ (See Verbs).

† Those that terminate in א, receive only an additional ת: as, נֹשֵׂא *m. a carrier, f.* נֹשֵׂאת or נֹשְׂאָה.

‡ In these and similar words, it will be found that the masculine nouns express functions and attributes peculiar to males, and the feminine such as are peculiar to females.

§ The י is often omitted; especially when the singular terminates in י: as, גּוֹי *a nation,* גּוֹיִם (instead of גּוֹיִים) *nations;* לֵוִי (instead of לְוִיִּי) *a Levite,* לְוִים (instead of לְוִיִּים) *Levites;* ו is likewise frequently omitted: as, אוֹת *a sign, p.* אֹתֹת instead of אוֹתוֹת.

¶ Also מַלְכִין, which is, however, a *Chaldaism*, and ought, therefore, to be considered as an exception.

Formation of the Plural Number Feminine.

47. Feminine nouns form their plural, by adding וֹת to the singular: as, בְּאֵר *a well*, בְּאֵרוֹת—(Vide p. 41.)

Obs. 1.—Those that terminate in הָ֖ or ת, change these terminations into וֹת: as, נַעֲרָה *a girl*, נְעָרוֹת *girls*; בְּתוּלָה *a virgin*, בְּתוּלוֹת *virgins*; אִגֶּרֶת *a letter*, אִגְּרוֹת *letters*; טַבַּעַת *a ring*, טַבָּעוֹת *rings*; כְּתֹנֶת *a coat, tunick*, כֻּתֳּנוֹת *tunicks*. Some, however, retain the ת: as, דֶּלֶת *a door*, דְּלָתוֹת *doors*; קֶשֶׁת *a bow*, קְשָׁתוֹת *bows*; חֲנִית *lance*, חֲנִיתוֹת *lances*.

Obs. 2.—Those which terminate in יָה or ־ִית change these terminations into יּוֹת: as, נָכְרִיָּה *a strange woman*, נָכְרִיּוֹת *strange women*; עִבְרִית *a Hebrew woman*, p. עִבְרִיּוֹת.

3.—Those that terminate in וּת, change (ו) into (ִ), and add יּוֹת: as, מַלְכוּת *a kingdom*, מַלְכֻיּוֹת *kingdoms*.

4.—Many masculine nouns take וֹת for their plural: as, אָב *a father*, אָבוֹת *fathers*; כִּסֵּא *a seat, throne*, p. כִּסְאוֹת; and many nouns feminine take ־ִים for their plural: as אֶבֶן *a stone*, p. אֲבָנִים; שְׂעֹרָה *barley*, p. שְׂעֹרִים.

5.—Some nouns take indiscriminately either the masculine or feminine plural *: thus, דּוֹר *a generation*, p. דּוֹרִים or דּוֹרוֹת; שָׁנָה *a year*, p. שָׁנִים or שָׁנוֹת; חַלּוֹן *a window*, p. חַלּוֹנִים or חַלּוֹנוֹת†.

6.—The names of liquids, seasons, metals‡, and some collectives, are always used in the singular number: as, זָהָב *gold*, כֶּסֶף *silver*, יַיִן *wine*, שֶׁמֶן *oil*; אָבִיב *spring*, חֹרֶף *winter*, חוֹל *sand*, אָבָק *dust*.

---

* See Note, p. 44.

† Also חַלּוֹנִי, which ought to be considered as an exception.

‡ The names of liquids and metals are sometimes found in the plural: but then the word must be considered as expressive of different sorts.

To the preceding may be added abstract terms and proper names, which, from the nature of their signification, do not admit of the plural: as, אַהֲבָה *love**, שִׂנְאָה *hatred*, &c.

7.— Some are used in the plural only: as חַיִּים *life*, רַחֲמִים *mercy*, פָּנִים *the visage, face*, כְּלָיוֹת *reins*, אֲרָוֹת *stables*.

Obs. 8.— The following are rather irregular in the formation of their plural: as, בַּת (instead בְּנָה or בְּנַת) *a daughter*, p. בָּנוֹת; אָחוֹת *a sister*, p. אֲחָיוֹת; שׁוֹר *an ox*, p. שְׁוָרִים; שׁוּק *an open place, a market*, p. שְׁוָקִים; אִישׁ *a man*. p. אִישִׁים, but more frequently אֲנָשִׁים; אִשָּׁה *a woman*, p. אִשּׁוֹת, but more frequently נָשִׁים.

Dual.

41. The dual expresses two of a kind; and is formed by adding ־ַיִם to the singular, whether it be masculine or feminine: as, יוֹם *day*, יָמִים *days*, יוֹמַיִם *two days*; אֶלֶף *a thousand*, אֲלָפִים *thousands*, אַלְפַּיִם *two thousands*; נַעַל *a shoe*, נְעָלוֹת or נְעָלִים *shoes*, נַעֲלַיִם *a pair of shoes*; דֶּלֶת *a door or gate*, דְּלָתוֹת *gates*, דְּלָתַיִם *double doors*.

Obs. 1.— Nouns terminating in ־ָה, change this letter into ת: as, שָׁנָה *a year*, שְׁנָתַיִם *two years*; מֵאָה *a hundred*, מָאתַיִם *two hundred*.

2.— Things that are double by nature or art, are used in the

---

* Some of these are found in the plural; but then they must, like the preceding, be understood as expressive of different kinds: thus חָכְמוֹת *wisdoms*, i. e. *the sciences*; תְּבוּנוֹת *understandings*, i. e. *different objects or degrees of understanding*.

dual instead of the plural: as עַיִן an eye, עֵינַיִם eyes;* יָד hand, יָדַיִם hands; רֶגֶל foot, רַגְלַיִם feet; שָׂפָה lip, שְׂפָתַיִם lips; אֹזֶן ear, אָזְנַיִם ears.

Obs. 3.—מֹאזְנַיִם a pair of scales, a balance; מֶלְקָחַיִם pincers, tongs; רֵחַיִם a hand mill (consisting of two stones), admit not of the singular number.†

4.—The following, and a few other nouns, form their dual by adding ־ִים to the plural: thus, חוֹמָה a wall, חוֹמוֹת f. walls, חֹמֹתַיִם double walls; רְבּוֹא a myriad, רִבֹּאוֹת myriads, רִבֹּתַיִם two myriads.

Exercise.

Give the signification of the following, and form their feminine gender:—

בּוֹרֵחַ, שׁוֹמֵעַ, נָבִיא, גָּדוֹל, אָדֹם, רֹעֶה, שׁוֹפֵט, מֶלֶךְ,

אִישׁ, חָתָן, עֶבֶד, אָח, בֵּן, נָכְרִי, עִבְרִי, יֶלֶד, כֶּבֶשׂ

Give the signification and form the plural of the following:—

פּוֹקֵד, נָבִיא, גָּמָל, שִׁיר, סוּס, גִּבּוֹר, שִׁירָה, דּוֹר,

בְּאֵר, נַעֲרָה, טַבַּעַת, חֲנִית, קֶשֶׁת, כַּף, חַלּוֹן, בַּת, שׁוֹר,

שׁוּק, אָחוֹת

---

* Some of these are found in the plural number; but then they have mostly different significations: thus, עֲיָנוֹת springs, fountains; יָדוֹת tenons, portions; רְגָלִים times; as שָׁלֹשׁ רְגָלִים three times (lit. steps); &c.

† To the above may be added, מַיִם water, שָׁמַיִם heaven, which occur always in the dual form.

THE ETYMOLOGY OF

Give the signification and form the dual of the following:—

יוֹם, אֶלֶף, נַעַל, דֶּלֶת, רֶגֶל, יָד, אֹזֶן, מֵאָה, שָׁנָה, שָׂפָה,
חוֹמָה, רִבּוֹא.

Render the following into English:—

תְּנָה¹ בְּנִי² לִבְּךָ³ לִי וְעֵינֶיךָ⁴ דְּרָכַי⁵ תִּצֹּרְנָה⁶ : אַל־
תֵּלֵךְ⁷ בְּדֶרֶךְ⁵ חַטָּאִים⁸ , מְנַע⁹ רַגְלְךָ¹⁰ מִנְּתִיבָתָם" , כִּי¹²
רַגְלֵיהֶם לָרַע¹³ יָרוּצוּ¹⁴ : כַּבֵּד¹⁵ אֶת־יְיָ מֵהוֹנֶךָ¹⁶ , וּמֵרֵאשִׁית¹⁷
כָּל־תְּבוּאָתֶךָ¹⁸ : כַּבֵּד אֶת־אָבִיךָ¹⁹ וְאֶת־אִמֶּךָ²⁰ ; לֵךְ²¹ אֶל־
נְמָלָה²² עָצֵל²³ , רְאֵה²⁴ דְרָכֶיהָ וַחֲכָם²⁵ : אֲשֶׁר־אֵין־לָהּ²⁶
קָצִין²⁷ שֹׁטֵר²⁸ וּמֹשֵׁל²⁹ תָּכִין³⁰ בַּקַּיִץ³¹ לַחְמָהּ³² אָגְרָה³³
בַקָּצִיר³⁴ מַאֲכָלָהּ³⁵ : אָמַר³⁶ עָצֵל †אֲרִי³⁷ בַּחוּץ³⁸ , שַׁחַל³⁹
בַּדְּרָךְ , בָּרְחֹבוֹת⁴⁰ אֵרָצֵחַ⁴¹ :

¹ Give. ² בֵּן Son, *p.* בָּנִים. ³ לֵב Heart. ⁴ עַיִן Eye. ⁵ דֶּרֶךְ Way. ⁶ They shall observe. ⁷ Go not. * Insert *of.* ⁸ Sinner. ⁹ Withhold. ¹⁰ רֶגֶל Foot. ¹¹ A path. ¹² For. ¹³ Evil. ¹⁴ They run. ¹⁵ Honor. ¹⁶ הוֹן Wealth. ¹⁷ First, chief. ¹⁸ תְּבוּאָה Produce. ¹⁹ אָב Father. ²⁰ אֵם Mother. ²¹ Go. ²² Ant. ²³ Sluggard. ²⁴ See. ²⁵ And be wise. ²⁶ Which not to her, *i. e.* who has neither. ²⁷ Chief. ²⁸ Overseer. ²⁹ Ruler. ³⁰ She provideth. ³¹ Summer. ³² לֶחֶם Bread, provision. ³³ She gathereth. ³⁴ Harvest. ³⁵ Food. ³⁶ The sluggard says. † There is. ³⁷ A lion. ³⁸ Without, street. ³⁹ An old lion. ⁴⁰ A wide place, a market. ⁴¹ I shall be slain.

הַבָּנוֹת¹ , בְּנֹתַי , וְהַבָּנִים * בָּנַי , וְהַצֹּאן² , צֹאנִי , וְלִבְנֹתַי
מַה־אֶעֱשֶׂה³ , אוֹ לִבְנֵיהֶן : אֶת־בְּנֹתָם נִקַּח⁴ לָנוּ וְאֶת־

בְּנֹתֵינוּ נִתֵּן לָהֶם ׃ בְּנֹתֵיכֶם תִּתְּנוּ לָנוּ וְאֶת בְּנוֹתֵינוּ תִּקְחוּ
לָכֶם ׃ בִּנְעָרֵינוּ וּבִזְקֵנֵינוּ בְּבָנֵינוּ וּבִבְנוֹתֵינוּ בְּצֹאנֵנוּ
וּבִבְקָרֵינוּ נֵלֵךְ ׃ לֹא־תַעֲשֶׂה־כָּל־מְלָאכָה אַתָּה וּבִנְךָ
וּבִתֶּךָ עַבְדְּךָ וַאֲמָתֶךָ וּבְהֶמְתֶּךָ וְגֵרְךָ אֲשֶׁר
בִּשְׁעָרֶיךָ ׃ לֵךְ מֵאַרְצְךָ וּמִמּוֹלַדְתְּךָ וּמִבֵּית אָבִיךָ אֶל־
הָאָרֶץ אֲשֶׁר־אַרְאֶךָּ ׃ אֶל אַרְצִי וְאֶל מוֹלַדְתִּי תֵּלֵךְ
וְלָקַחְתָּ אִשָּׁה לִבְנִי מִמִּשְׁפַּחְתִּי וּמִבֵּית אָבִי ׃

[1] בַּת a daughter, p. בָּנוֹת.   * Are.   [2] Cattle, sheep.   [3] What shall I do?   [4] We will take.   [5] We will give.   [6] Ye shall give.   [7] Ye shall take.   [8] נַעַר A boy, youth, p. נְעָרִים.   [9] זָקֵן! An old man, p. זְקֵנִים.   [10] בָּקָר Horned cattle.   [11] We must go.   [12] Ye shall not do any work.   [13] עֶבֶד A servant, slave.   [14] אָמָה A female slave.   [15] בְּהֵמָה or בְּהֵמֹת cattle.   [16] A stranger.   [17] Who is.   [18] שַׁעַר A gate, p. שְׁעָרִים.   [19] Go.   [20] אֶרֶץ Land, country.   [21] Birth-place.   [22] Which I will show thee.   [23] Thou shalt go and take.   [24] מִשְׁפָּחָה A family.   [25] בַּיִת A house, בֵּית house of.

CASE.

49. Most of the relations denoted in Latin, Greek, and other languages, by *cases*, are expressed in Hebrew by the prefixes מ, ל, כ, ב, and by the particle אֵת (Art. 40, 41), or by the prepositions אֶל *to*, מִן *from*. (See Declension of Nouns, Table I.)

50. The relations denoted by the Genitive are indicated by the mere position of the words, or by some slight alteration in them, as will be shown presently.

Absolute and Constructive state of Words.

51. A word is said to be in an *absolute state* when it requires no other word to define it: as, עֶבֶד, *a servant, slave*, p. עֲבָדִים; דָּבָר *a word*, p. דְּבָרִים; כְּלִי or כֶּלִי *a vessel*, p. כֵּלִים.

52. A word is said to be in a *state of construction*, when it requires another word to define or to limit its signification: such, for instance, are the first words in the following examples:—

עֶבֶד אַבְרָהָם . . *servant of Abraham*, or *Abraham's servant*,
עַבְדֵי אַבְרָהָם . . *servants of Abraham*,
דְּבַר הַמֶּלֶךְ . . *the word of the king*,
דְּבַר שֶׁקֶר . . *a word of falsehood*, i. e. *a false word**,
דִּבְרֵי אֱמֶת . . *words of truth*, or *true words*,
כְּלִי בַרְזֶל . . *a vessel of iron*, or *an iron vessel*,
כְּלֵי כֶסֶף . . *vessels of silver*, or *silver vessels*.

53. In all these instances, it is the first word that undergoes the change, *if any* (just the reverse of what takes place in other languages), and it is therefore said to be in a *state of construction*. To understand this more clearly, the student is requested to bear in mind the remark made in Art. 36; namely—that one of the methods by which *general terms* are made to express particular objects or individuals, is, to place one or more words after the noun whose signification is to be

---

* These examples show clearly the origin of *Adjectives*.

limited. By way of further illustration, let us take the general term עֶבֶד in the following sentence:— בִּדְבָרִים לֹא יִוָּסֶר עָבֶד ' *A servant will not be corrected by words*' (Prov. xxix.) Here עֶבֶד is used indefinitely, and means any servant; but as the sense is complete, the word עֶבֶד is said to be in an *independent* or in an *absolute state**; but in the phrase וַיֹּאמֶר עֶבֶד אַבְרָהָם ' *And* [the] *servant-of Abraham* (or *Abraham's servant*) *said*,' עֶבֶד is used in a restrictive sense; and as it depends on the following word אַבְרָהָם which defines and limits it, it is said to be in a *state of construction* or *dependence**. Thus, also, in the phrase לִרְחֹץ רַגְלֵי עַבְדֵי אֲדֹנִי ' *To wash* [the] *feet-of* [the] *servants-of my lord*,' רַגְלֵי *feet of*, and עַבְדֵי *servants of*, are in a state of *dependence* or *construction:* the absolute state of the first, being עֲבָדִים *servants*, and of the second, רַגְלַיִם *feet*.

54. The noun which is put in a state of construction, must precede that which defines or qualifies it: thus, מוּסַר אָב *a father's instruction* (not אָב מוּסַר); בֵּית הַמֶּלֶךְ *the king's house* (not הַמֶּלֶךְ בֵּית).

55. The definite ה, when required, is placed before the definite word, but not before the word in

---

* This state of the noun is denominated by Hebrew grammarians, נִפְרָד *separated;* whereas, the constructive or dependent is called נִסְמָךְ or סָמוּךְ *approached.* It would, perhaps, be better to name the first, the *independent* state, and the second, the *dependent* state. However, for the sake of convenience, we shall *sometimes* denominate the first, the *Nominative;* and the second, the *Genitive*.

construction; because this is already defined by the word which follows it: thus, as in the preceding example, הַבַּיִת מֶלֶךְ (but not הַבַּיִת הַמֶּלֶךְ, nor בֵּית הַמֶּלֶךְ).

56. As both words present only one precise conception, they are, in some respects, considered as a compound word; and for this reason, the first is often joined to the second, by מַקֵּף, and then loses its principal accent: as, גַּן a garden. גַּן־עֵדֶן [the] garden of Eden, מֶלֶךְ־סְדֹם king of Sodom.

57. To facilitate still further the pronunciation, the first word is often abridged by rejecting or contracting one or more of its vowel-points: as,—

בַּיִת a house,   בֵּית house of,   בֵּית תְּפִלָּה house of prayer,
יָד a hand,   יַד hand of,   יַד הַמֶּלֶךְ the hand of the king.

58. Nouns terminating in ה ָ, change this termination into ת ַ: as, שִׁירָה a song, שִׁירַת דּוֹדִי the song of my beloved, תּוֹרָה a law, תּוֹרַת מֹשֶׁה the law of Moses.

. Those that terminate in ה ֶ, retain the ה, but change (ֶ) into (ְ): as, מַחֲנֶה a camp, מַחֲנֵה יִשְׂרָאֵל Israel's camp, מִקְנֶה cattle*, מִקְנֵה אֲבִיכֶם the cattle of your father.

59. The following have their *absolute* and *constructive state* singular alike :—

---

* But the genitive of מִקְנֶה *a purchase,* is מִקְנַת.

When the ה is merely added for the sake of euphony, it is rejected in the genitive: as, לַיְלָה *night,* לֵיל *night of.*

1st. All names whose vowels are immutable (see Ch. III.): as, שִׁיר *a song*, עִיר *a city*, בְּרִית *a covenant*, סוּס *a horse*, רוּחַ *the wind*, קוֹל *voice*, גֵּר *a stranger, sojourner*, אָסִיר *a prisoner*, תַּלְמִיד *a disciple*, כֹּהֵן *a priest*, אֹיֵב *an enemy*, &c.

2nd. All nouns of the following forms—[*a*] פֹּעַל: as, אֹזֶן *ear*, חֹדֶשׁ *a month*, שֹׁחַד *a bribe*, &c. [*b*] פֶּעַל as, מֶלֶךְ *a king*, חֶסֶד *mercy*, נַעַר *a boy*, שַׁחַר *the dawn*, &c. [*c*] פֵּעֶל: as, סֵפֶר *a book*, אֵפֶר *ashes*.

3rd. All feminine nouns having the following terminations—ת ָ, וּת, ת ְ, ִית: as, עֲטֶרֶת *a crown*, כְּתֹנֶת *an under-garment*, יְדִידוּת *friendship*, תּוֹלַעַת *a worm*, רֵאשִׁית *beginning*.

60. The plural and dual terminations, ִים and ַיִם are changed into ֵי: as, דְּבָרִים *words*, דִּבְרֵי הָאִישׁ *the-words-of-the-man*; נָשִׁים *women, wives*, נְשֵׁי הַמֶּלֶךְ *the king's wives*; עֵינַיִם *eyes*, עֵינֵי הָאֲנָשִׁים *the-eyes-of-the-men*.

61. The plural termination וֹת remains unchanged, but the preceding vowels suffer a slight alteration: as, אָבוֹת *fathers*, אֲבוֹת אֲבוֹתֶיךָ *thy fathers' fathers;* בְּרָכוֹת *blessings*, בִּרְכוֹת שָׁמַיִם *blessings of heaven*.

Exercise.

Render the following into Hebrew—

The king of Israel. The law of God. The words of my Lord. The house of my fathers. The song of Moses. The way of sinners. A word of truth. The eyes of the woman. The hands of my sister. The vessels of the house. The blessings of thy father. The sons of my friend. The first of all thy produce. Your father's cattle. The king's camp.

The annexed Tables will enable the student to see the principal modifications of nouns at one view.

Explanation of the Tables.

TABLE I.—The Roman letters in the first column are abbreviations for Nominative, Dative, Objective, Ablative, Comparative, Conjunction.

The second and third columns contain the prefixes and their powers, as used indefinitely or definitely.

The fourth column contains a noun of the singular number with the prefixes, used indefinitely.

The fifth column contains a noun in a state of construction.

The sixth column contains a noun plural with the prefixes, used indefinitely.

The seventh column contains the same noun with the prefixes, used in a state of construction.

The eighth column contains a noun of the singular number with the prefixes, used definitely.

The ninth column contains a noun plural with the prefixes, used definitely.

TABLE II.— No. 1. contains the pronominal affixes, and their powers.

No. 2. contains a noun masculine, with the pronominal affixes.

No. 3. a noun feminine terminating in הָ with the affixes.

62. *Obs.*—Each of the nouns contained in the tables, may be further varied by the prefixes: as לִדְבָרִי *to my word;* objective אֶת־דְּבָרִי

I.

	3. DEF	2. IND.	1.
דְּבָרִים,	הַ the.	¹ a	N.
דְּבָרִים	לַ, to the.	² לְ to a	D.
דְּבָרִים	אֶת or the.	¹ a	Ac.
דְּבָרִים	מֵהַ from the.	³ מִ from a	} Ab.
דְּבָרִים,	בַּ in the.	בְּ with a	
דְּבָרִים,	כַּ as the.	כְּ as a	Com.
וְהַדְּבָרִים	and the.	וְ and	Con.

II.

their			1.	
־ם		דְּבָרִי	דָּבָר } 2.	a word.
־ם ⁶		דְּבָרַי	דְּבָרִים	words.
־ם		תּוֹרָתִי	תּוֹרָה } 3.	a law.
־ם		תּוֹרוֹתַי	תּוֹרוֹת	laws.

III.

	פֹּקְדִי	פּוֹקֵד)	a visiter.
־ם	פֹּקְדִי	פּוֹקְדִים } 1.	visiters.
־ם	אֲהוּבִי	אָהוּב)	beloved.
־ם	פָּקְדִי	פָּקַד 2.	visiting.

them	me.		
־ם	עִמִּי	עִם	with.
־ם	עָלַי	עַל +	upon.

⁵ Or דְּבָרְךָ. תַּחְתִּי for תַּחַת
חוּ ; as, אוֹרֵהוּ for אוֹרוֹ. Job xxv. 3.   ⁷ Or פְּקָדֻהוּ. ¹⁰ Or פְּקָדֻהוּ.

אֶל   עָלַי

DECLENSION OF A SUBSTANTIVE.—TABLE I.

9. the words.	8. the word.	7. words of	6. words	5. word of.	4. a word.	3. Der	2. Ind.	1.
וְדְבָרִים	הַדָּבָר	דִּבְרֵי	דְּבָרִים	דְּבַר	דָּבָר	ךָ, הַ, הָ the.	־ a	N.
לַדְּבָרִים	לַדָּבָר	לְדִבְרֵי	לַדְּבָרִים	לִדְבַר	לְדָבָר	לַ, לָ to the	לְ to a	D.
אֶת הַדְּבָרִים	אֶת הַדָּבָר	אֶת־דִּבְרֵי	דְּבָרִים (אֶת)	אֶת־דְּבַר	דָּבָר	אֵת or אֶת the.	־ a	Ac.
מֵהַדְּבָרִים	מֵהַדָּבָר	מִדִּבְרֵי	מִדְּבָרִים	מִדְּבַר	מִדָּבָר	מֵהַ, מֵהָ, מִן from the.	מִ from a	} Ab.
וּבַדְּבָרִים	בַּדָּבָר	בְּדִבְרֵי	בִּדְבָרִים	בִּדְבַר	וּבְדָבָר	בַּ, בָּ in the.	בְּ with a	
כַּדְּבָרִים	כַּדָּבָר	כְּדִבְרֵי	כִּדְבָרִים	כִּדְבַר	כְּדָבָר	כַּ, כָּ as the.	כְּ as a	Com.
וְהַדְּבָרִים	וְהַדָּבָר	וְדִבְרֵי	וְדְבָרִים	וּדְבַר	וְדָבָר	וְהַ, וְהָ and the	וְ and	Con.

WITH THE PRONOMINAL AFFIXES.—TABLE II.

Dr m.s. ...... m. p. ...... f. p.	־כֶם m. p. ־כֶן f. p.	נוּ	הֶם m. ... ־הֶן f. the	כֶם m. p. כֶן f. p.	כָ m. s. כְ f. s. the	־י m. s. m. p.		
דְּבָרֶהֶם	דְּבַרְכֶם	דְּבָרֵנוּ	דְּבָרוֹ	דְּבָרִי	דְּבָרְךָ	דְּבָרִי	דָּבָר	a word.
דְּבָרֵיהֶם	דִּבְרֵיכֶם	דְּבָרֵינוּ	דְּבָרָיו	דְּבָרֶיהָ	דְּבָרֶיךָ	דְּבָרַי	דְּבָרִים	2. words.
תּוֹרָתָם	תּוֹרַתְכֶם	תּוֹרָתֵנוּ	תּוֹרָתוֹ	תּוֹרָתָהּ	תּוֹרָתְךָ	תּוֹרָתִי	תּוֹרָה	a law.
תּוֹרוֹתָם	תּוֹרוֹתֵיכֶם	תּוֹרוֹתֵינוּ	תּוֹרוֹתָיו	תּוֹרוֹתֶיהָ	תּוֹרוֹתֶיךָ	תּוֹרוֹתַי	תּוֹרוֹת	3. Laws.

INFINITIVES AND PARTICIPLES. TABLE III.

פָּקְדָם	פָּקֶדְכֶם	פָּקְדֵנוּ	פָּקְדוֹ	פָּקְדָהּ	פָּקְדְךָ	פָּקְדִי	פֹּקֵד	a visiter.
פֹּקְדֵיהֶם	פֹּקְדֵיכֶם	פֹּקְדֵינוּ	פֹּקְדָיו	פֹּקְדֶיהָ	פֹּקְדֶיךָ	פֹּקְדַי	פֹּקְדִים	1. visiters.
אֲהוּבָם	אֲהוּבְכֶם	אֲהוּבֵנוּ	אֲהוּבוֹ	אֲהוּבָהּ	אֲהוּבְךָ	אֲהוּבִי	אָהוּב	beloved.
פָּקְדָם	פָּקְדְכֶם	פָּקְדֵנוּ	פָּקְדָהּ	פָּקְדָהּ	פָּקְדְךָ	פָּקְדִי	פָּקֹד	2. visiting.

PREPOSITIONS.—TABLE IV.

them m.	m. f.	you. m.	us.	her.	him.	thee f.	thee m.	me.	
עִמָּם		עִמָּכֶם	עִמָּנוּ	עִמָּהּ	עִמּוֹ	עִמָּךְ	עִמְּךָ	עִמִּי	with.
עֲלֵיהֶם		עֲלֵיכֶם	עָלֵינוּ	עָלֶיהָ	עָלָיו	עָלַיִךְ	עָלֶיךָ	עָלַי	upon.

[1] Not expressed. [2] Or אֶל to. [3] מִן from. [4] Sometimes with בְּ as תַּחְתֵּי for תַּחְתַּי [5] Or דָּבָר especially in pause. [6] In a a few instances with ה as אֹהֳלֹה Gen. ix. 21. or with חוּ as אֵידוֹ for אֵידוֹ Job xxv. 3. [7] The י is sometimes omitted. [8] In poetry מוֹ as גְּדֵיהֶם for גְּדוֹתֵימוֹ (.) פְּקֻדָּה the אֶל אֵלַי אֵלֶיךָ אֵלַיִךְ אֵלָיו אֵלֶיהָ אֵלֵינוּ אֲלֵיכֶם, אֲלֵיכֶן אֲלֵיהֶם, אֲלֵיהֶן.

my word, מִדְּבָרִי *from my word,* וּדְבָרִי *and my word,* &c. וְלִדְבָרוֹ *and to his word;* כִּדְבָרִי *as my words,* כִּדְבָרֶיהָ *as her words,* וּדְבָרֶיךָ *and thy words f.;* וּמִדִּבְרֵיהֶם *and from their words,* &c.: בְּתוֹרָתִי *in my law,* וְתוֹרֹתַי *and my laws,* בְּתוֹרֹתָיו *in his laws,* וּבְתוֹרָתְךָ *and in thy law,* &c.

TABLE III.—No. 1. contains an example of a Participle Active and Passive, with the pronominal affixes.

Obs.—Participles being frequently used as nouns, are varied like them: as, שׁוֹמֵר *a keeper, guardian,* שׁוֹמֵר הַכֵּלִים *the keeper of the vessels,* הַשֹּׁמְרִים *the keepers,* שֹׁמְרֵי הַבַּיִת *the keepers of the house,* וּלְשֹׁמְרֵי תוֹרָתִי *and to the keepers of my law,* or *to those who keep my law.*

No. 2. contains an example of an Infinitive mood with the pronominal affixes: as, פָּקֹד *to visit,* פָּקְדִי *my visiting,* פָּקְדְךָ *thy visiting,* &c.; שָׁמֹר *to keep, to guard,* שָׁמְרִי *my keeping,* or *guarding.*

63. *Obs* 1.—Infinitives, from the nature of their signification, do not admit of all the variation of nouns. They may, however, receive the prefixes מ, ל, ב, בְּ; as, בִּפְקוֹד *in visiting,* כִּפְקֹד *as visiting,* לִפְקֹד *for visiting,* or *to visit,* i. e. *for the purpose of visiting;* מִפְּקֹד *from visiting;* and also the pronominal affixes בְּפָקְדִי *in my visiting,* i. e. *being engaged in the act;* כְּפָקְדִי *as my visiting,* לְפָקְדוֹ *to his visiting,* מִפָּקְדוֹ *from, by,* or *because of his visiting,* בְּפָקְדְךָ *in thy visiting,* &c.

2.—In the latter case, the pronominal affixes have sometimes an objective signification: לְשָׁמְרוֹ *to keep him;* לְעָבְדָהּ וּלְשָׁמְרָהּ *to cultivate her, and to keep her.* (Gen. ii. 15.)

TABLE IV. contains examples of Prepositions (originally nouns) with the pronominal affixes.

64. *Obs.*—Some Prepositions take the pronominal affixes of the singular number: as, לִי *to me,* לְךָ *to thee;* others, those of the plural number: as, אֶל *to,* אֵלַי *to me,* אֵלֶיךָ *to thee.*

60 THE ETYMOLOGY OF

The student may, by way of exercise, decline the following words: אוֹר *light*, עֵד *a witness*, like שִׁיר (p. 42). Thus, אוֹרִי, עֵדִי·; תְּפִלָּה *a prayer*, like שִׁירָה (ibid). Thus, תְּפִלָּתִי—לְבָב *the heart*, like דָּבָר;—אוֹרָה *light*, like תּוֹרָה;—שׁוֹמֵר *a keeper*, like פּוֹקֵד; — פָּקוּד *one that is visited*, like אָהוּב;—שָׁמוֹר *to keep*, like פָּקֹד·.

65. From the preceding rules and observations, it is evident that the modification of nouns are principally expressed by prefixes and affixes. As these are common to all nouns, it follows that, strictly speaking, there cannot be more than one declension. However, as several of the vowel-points are subject to a variety of changes in the process of declension, a further classification is necessary in order to ascertain the principles upon which those changes are founded, and the rules by which they are regulated. This will form the subject of the following chapter, to which, such students as are desirous of having some information on this part of grammar, are referred. Those, however, who are contented with a general knowledge of the language, may pass on at once to the 4th chapter.

CHAPTER III.

ON THE CHANGES WHICH SOME OF THE VOWELS UNDERGO IN THE PROCESS OF DECLENSION.

Introductory Remarks.

66. It has already been remarked, (Art. 29—30), that in consequence of the removal of the accent—which *frequently* takes place when nouns are put in a state of construction, and *always* when they are augmented by the affixes — such of the vowels as are not characteristic of grammatical distinctions are often changed for others, or entirely omitted; by which means the words

are abridged, and their pronunciation facilitated. These changes depend chiefly on the grammatical forms * of the words and their Etymology (though often on *usage* only†) and cannot well be ascertained without classification. The method which the ancient grammarians adopted was this:—they enumerated all or most of the forms of which the nouns of the language were susceptible, and specified under each form the changes to which its vowel-points were subject, together with such words as deviated from the general rule: and thus they exhibited the Etymology and the change of the vowels at the same time. As the forms of words are, however, so very numerous as almost to overburden the memory, modern grammarians‡ have endeavoured to abridge the labour, by distributing

---

* By the grammatical form is meant, that form which a word is said to have according to its Etymology. Thus, the words עֵד *a witness*, שֵׁם *a name*, and, צֵל *shadow*, have apparently the same form; yet, the grammatical form of the first is פֵּל, (Art. 25, p. 27,) the (ּ) of which is immutable, and it is therefore inflected thus, עֵד, עֵדִי, עֵדִים, עֵדֵי, &c. The second, derived from a verb whose third radical is ה, and which is here omitted, is said to be of the form פַּע; the (ּ) being mutable, it is inflected thus: שֵׁם, שְׁמִי, שֵׁמוֹת, שְׁמוֹת, &c. The third, derived from a verb whose second and third radicals are alike, and one of which is omitted, is said to be of the form פַּ–ל. The (ּ) is likewise mutable, and the second letter receives *Dagesh* on being augmented: thus, צֵל, צִלִּי, צִלְּךָ.

† Thus, זְאֵב and פְּאֵר have the same grammatical form (פְּעֵל), yet the first retains (ּ) thus, זְאֵבִי, זְאֵבֵי; but the second changes (:), into (-), and (ּ) into (ֲ) in the genitive plural: thus, פַּאֲרֵי. Thus, likewise, דָּבָר and גְּמָל are both of the form (פָּעָל), yet the former is inflected, דְּבָר, דְּבָרִי, דְּבָרִים, &c., but the latter, גְּמָל, גְּמַלִּי, גְּמַלִּים, &c. Hence the difficulty of giving general rules that shall not be liable to several exceptions.

‡ *J. S. Vater* was the first who adopted this arrangement, which has been much improved by *Gesenius* and other grammarians.

the nouns according as their vowels are either *immutable*, *mutable*, or of a *mixed character*. The chief objection against this arrangement, is that before the student can know whether a vowel is mutable or not, he must often have recourse to the Etymology of the word; and as this cannot well be ascertained without some knowledge of the grammatical forms, he is left to mere conjecture, and the classification becomes almost useless. This inconvenience we have endeavoured to remove in the following Tables, by adding the grammatical form to each division, and by specifying the chief forms belonging to each class, together with most of their exceptions.

The following rules and observations will, it is presumed, facilitate the acquisition of this difficult and, to beginners, embarrassing part of grammar.

Immutable and Mutable Vowels.

67. Immutable are—

1st.—All long vowels followed by either of the quiescent letters, א, י, ו: as, (אָ־) in תָּא *a chamber*, רָאשׁ* *a poor man*; (־ִי), in רִישׁ *poverty*, בֵּין *between*; (־ִי), in כִּיס *a purse, bag*†; (ו), in גּוּר‡ *a whelp*; and (וֹ) or (ֹ־) not followed by (ּ) or (-), as בּוֹס§ *a cup*, כֹּהֵן *a priest, minister*.

---

* This word is sometimes written without א: thus, רָשׁ; but this makes no difference, the vowel being equally immutable.

† Except some words of the form (פְּעִי): as, גְּדִי *a kid*, אֲרִי *a lion*, which change (־ִי) into (ָ) or into (ֵ); thus גְּדָיִים, אֲרָיִים· (פְּעִי); as חֳלִי *sickness*, חָלָיוֹ· (פְּעִי): as, מְרִי *rebellion*, מְרָיִם·

‡ ו is sometimes changed into (וֹ); as, שָׁבוּעַ *a week* p. שָׁבֻעוֹת; מַלְכוּת *kingdom*, p. מַלְכִיּוֹת·

§ ו is sometimes changed into (וֹ) followed by Dagesh: as אָדוֹם *red*, f. אֲדֻמָּה p. אֲדֻמִּים· עָרוֹם *naked*, forms its plural עֲרֻמִּים· This is an anomaly, having *dagesh* after a long vowel, which is contrary to rule.

CLASSIFICATION OF NOUNS.—TABLE V.

Class	f.	their, m.	f.	your, m.	our.	her.	his.	thy, f.	thy, m.	my.	Gen.	Absolute state.	Form.
I.	1 1	אוֹרָם אוֹרֵיהֶם	1 1	אוֹרְכֶם אוֹרֵיכֶם	אוֹרֵנוּ אוֹרֵינוּ	אוֹרָהּ אוֹרֶיהָ	אוֹרוֹ אוֹרָיו	אוֹרֵךְ אוֹרַיִךְ	אוֹרְךָ אוֹרֶיךָ	אוֹרִי אוֹרַי	אוֹר אוֹרֵי	אוֹר p. אוֹרִים	light.	פּוֹר
	1 1	צִדְקָם צִדְקֵיהֶם	1 1	צִדְקְכֶם צִדְקֵיכֶם	צִדְקֵנוּ צִדְקֵינוּ	צִדְקָהּ צִדְקֶיהָ	צִדְקוֹ צִדְקָיו	צִדְקֵךְ צִדְקַיִךְ	צִדְקְךָ צִדְקֶיךָ	צִדְקִי צִדְקַי	צֶדֶק צִדְקֵי	צֶדֶק p. צַדִּיקִים	a just man.	פֶּצֶל
II.	1 1	דָּמָם דְּמֵיהֶם	1 1	דִּמְכֶם דְּמֵיכֶם	דָּמֵנוּ דָּמֵינוּ	דָּמָהּ דָּמֶיהָ	דָּמוֹ דָּמָיו	דָּמֵךְ דָּמַיִךְ	דָּמְךָ דָּמֶיךָ	דָּמִי דָּמַי	דַּם דְּמֵי	דָּם p. דָּמִים	blood.	פַּל
	1 1	שׁוּעָלָם שׁוּעֲלֵיהֶם	1 1	שׁוּעַלְכֶם שׁוּעֲלֵיכֶם	שׁוּעָלֵנוּ שׁוּעָלֵינוּ	שׁוּעָלָהּ שׁוּעָלֶיהָ	שׁוּעָלוֹ שׁוּעָלָיו	שׁוּעָלֵךְ שׁוּעָלַיִךְ	שׁוּעָלְךָ שׁוּעָלֶיךָ	שׁוּעָלִי שׁוּעָלַי	שׁוּעַל שׁוּעֲלֵי	שׁוּעָל p. שׁוּעָלִים	a fox.	פּוֹעָל
III.	1 1	קְצִירָם קְצִירֵיהֶם	1 1	קְצִירְכֶם קְצִירֵיכֶם	קְצִירֵנוּ קְצִירֵינוּ	קְצִירָהּ קְצִירֶיהָ	קְצִירוֹ קְצִירָיו	קְצִירֵךְ קְצִירַיִךְ	קְצִירְךָ קְצִירֶיךָ	קְצִירִי קְצִירַי	קְצִיר קְצִירֵי	קָצִיר p. קְצִירִים	harvest *	פָּצִיל
	1 1	מְלִיצָם מְלִיצֵיהֶם	1 1	מְלִיצְכֶם מְלִיצֵיכֶם	מְלִיצֵנוּ מְלִיצֵינוּ	מְלִיצָהּ מְלִיצֶיהָ	מְלִיצוֹ מְלִיצָיו	מְלִיצֵךְ מְלִיצַיִךְ	מְלִיצְךָ מְלִיצֶיךָ	מְלִיצִי מְלִיצַי	מֵלִיץ מְלִיצֵי	מֵלִיץ p. מְלִיצִים	an interpreter	מְפִיל
IV.	1 1	דְּבָרָם דִּבְרֵיהֶם	1 1	דְּבַרְכֶם דִּבְרֵיכֶם	דְּבָרֵנוּ דְּבָרֵינוּ	דְּבָרָהּ דְּבָרֶיהָ	דְּבָרוֹ דְּבָרָיו	דְּבָרֵךְ דְּבָרַיִךְ	דְּבָרְךָ דְּבָרֶיךָ	דְּבָרִי דְּבָרַי	דְּבַר דִּבְרֵי	דָּבָר p. דְּבָרִים	a word.	פָּעָל
V.	1 1	זְקֵנָם זִקְנֵיהֶם	1 1	זְקַנְכֶם זִקְנֵיכֶם	זְקֵנֵנוּ זְקֵנֵינוּ	זְקֵנָהּ זְקֵנֶיהָ	זְקֵנוֹ זְקֵנָיו	זְקֵנֵךְ זְקֵנַיִךְ	זְקֵנְךָ זְקֵנֶיךָ	זְקֵנִי זְקֵנַי	זְקַן זִקְנֵי	זָקֵן p. זְקֵנִים	an old man.	פָּעֵל
VI.	1 1	דַּרְכָּם דַּרְכֵיהֶם	1 1	דַּרְכְּכֶם דַּרְכֵיכֶם	דַּרְכֵּנוּ דְּרָכֵינוּ	דַּרְכָּהּ דְּרָכֶיהָ	דַּרְכּוֹ דְּרָכָיו	דַּרְכֵּךְ דְּרָכַיִךְ	דַּרְכְּךָ דְּרָכֶיךָ	דַּרְכִּי דְּרָכַי	דֶּרֶךְ דַּרְכֵּי	דֶּרֶךְ p. דְּרָכִים	a way	פֶּעֶל
	1 1	נַעֲרָם נַעֲרֵיהֶם	1 1	נַעַרְכֶם נַעֲרֵיכֶם	נַעֲרֵנוּ נְעָרֵינוּ	נַעֲרָהּ נְעָרֶיהָ	נַעֲרוֹ נְעָרָיו	נַעֲרֵךְ נְעָרַיִךְ	נַעַרְךָ נְעָרֶיךָ	נַעֲרִי נְעָרַי	נַעַר נַעֲרֵי	נַעַר p. נְעָרִים	a boy.	Hed.

The accent is on the last syllable, except before the affixes כִי, יִי, ךִי, הִי, כֶם, כֶן, where it is on the penultimate.   * Or a reaper.

CLASSIFICATION OF NOUNS.—TABLE VI.

Class.			their, m.		your, m.	our.	her.	his.	thy, f.	thy, m.	my.	s.	Absolute State.	
VI. CONTINUED	{	s. p.	כְּפָרָם כְּפָרִים	{	כְּפַרְכֶם כְּפָרֵיכֶם	כְּפָרֵנוּ כְּפָרֵינוּ	כְּפָרָהּ כְּפָרֶיהָ	כְּפָרוֹ כְּפָרָיו	כְּפָרֵךְ כְּפָרַיִךְ	כְּפָרְךָ כְּפָרֶיךָ	כְּפָרִי כְּפָרַי	כְּפַר כְּפָרֵי	כָּפָר s. כְּפָרִים p.	a lamb פער
	{	s. p.	קָדְשָׁם קָדְשֵׁיהֶם	{	קָדְשְׁכֶם קָדְשֵׁיכֶם	קָדְשֵׁנוּ קָדְשֵׁינוּ	קָדְשָׁהּ קָדְשֶׁיהָ	קָדְשׁוֹ קָדְשָׁיו	קָדְשֵׁךְ קָדְשַׁיִךְ	קָדְשְׁךָ קָדְשֶׁיךָ	קָדְשִׁי קָדָשַׁי	קֹדֶשׁ קָדְשֵׁי	קֹדֶשׁ s. קָדָשִׁים p.	a month
	{	s. p.	אֵילָם אֵילֵיהֶם	{	אֵילְכֶם אֵילֵיכֶם	אֵילֵנוּ אֵילֵינוּ	אֵילָהּ אֵילֶיהָ	אֵילוֹ אֵילָיו	אֵילֵךְ אֵילַיִךְ	אֵילְךָ אֵילֶיךָ	אֵילִי אֵילַי	אֵיל אֵילֵי	אַיִל s. אֵילִים p.	a ram פיל
	{	s. p.	מוֹתָם מוֹתֵיהֶם	{	מוֹתְכֶם מוֹתֵיכֶם	מוֹתֵנוּ מוֹתֵינוּ	מוֹתָהּ מוֹתֶיהָ	מוֹתוֹ מוֹתָיו	מוֹתֵךְ מוֹתַיִךְ	מוֹתְךָ מוֹתֶיךָ	מוֹתִי מוֹתַי	מוֹת מוֹתֵי	מָוֶת s. מוֹתִים p.	death פעל
	{	s. p.	חֶלְיָם חֳלָיֵיהֶם	{	חֶלְיְכֶם חֳלָיֵיכֶם	חָלְיֵנוּ חֳלָיֵינוּ	חָלְיָהּ חֳלָיֶיהָ	חָלְיוֹ חֳלָיָיו	חָלְיֵךְ חֳלָיַיִךְ	חָלְיְךָ חֳלָיֶיךָ	חָלְיִי חֳלָיַי	חֳלִי חֳלָיֵי	חֳלִי s. חֳלָיִים p.	sickness סיני
	{	s. p.	כֶּלְיָם כְּלֵיהֶם	{	כֶּלְיְכֶם כְּלֵיכֶם	כֶּלְיֵנוּ כֵּלֵינוּ	כֶּלְיָהּ כֵּלֶיהָ	כֶּלְיוֹ כֵּלָיו	כֶּלְיֵךְ כֵּלַיִךְ	כֶּלְיְךָ כֵּלֶיךָ	כֶּלְיִי כֵּלַי	כְּלִי כְּלֵי	כְּלִי s. כֵּלִים p.	a vessel סיני
VII.	{	s. p.	שְׁמָם שְׁמוֹתָם	{	שִׁמְכֶם שְׁמוֹתֵיכֶם	שְׁמֵנוּ שְׁמוֹתֵינוּ	שְׁמָהּ שְׁמוֹתֶיהָ	שְׁמוֹ שְׁמוֹתָיו	שְׁמֵךְ שְׁמוֹתַיִךְ	שִׁמְךָ שְׁמוֹתֶיךָ	שְׁמִי שְׁמוֹתַי	שֵׁם שְׁמוֹת	שֵׁם s. שֵׁמוֹת p.	a name פע
	{	s. p.	אוֹיְבָם אוֹיְבֵיהֶם	{	אוֹיִבְכֶם אוֹיְבֵיכֶם	אוֹיְבֵנוּ אוֹיְבֵינוּ	אוֹיַבְתָּהּ אוֹיְבֶיהָ	אוֹיְבוֹ אוֹיְבָיו	אוֹיַבְתֵּךְ אוֹיְבַיִךְ	אוֹיִבְךָ אוֹיְבֶיךָ	אוֹיְבִי אוֹיְבַי	אוֹיֵב אוֹיְבֵי	אוֹיֵב s. אוֹיְבִים p.	an enemy מועל
VIII.	{	s. p.	חִצָּם חִצֵּיהֶם	{	חֶצְכֶם חִצֵּיכֶם	חִצֵּנוּ חִצֵּינוּ	חִצָּהּ חִצֶּיהָ	חִצּוֹ חִצָּיו	חִצֵּךְ חִצַּיִךְ	חִצְּךָ חִצֶּיךָ	חִצִּי חִצַּי	חֵץ חִצֵּי	חֵץ s. חִצִּים p.	an arrow פע
	{	s. p.	גְּמַלָּם גְּמַלֵּיהֶם	{	גְּמַלְּכֶם גְּמַלֵּיכֶם	גְּמַלֵּנוּ גְּמַלֵּינוּ	גְּמַלָּהּ גְּמַלֶּיהָ	גְּמַלּוֹ גְּמַלָּיו	גְּמַלֵּךְ גְּמַלַּיִךְ	גְּמַלְּךָ גְּמַלֶּיךָ	גְּמַלִּי גְּמַלַּי	גְּמַל גְּמַלֵּי	גָּמָל s. גְּמַלִּים p.	a camel. מנעל

* Or חֳרָשִׁים   † In pause כְּלִי חֳלִי   ‡ Or חֳלִים

CLASSIFICATION OF NOUNS.—TABLE VII.

Class	f.	their, m.	f.	your, m.	our.	her.	his.	thy, f.	thy, m.	my.	Gen.	Absolute state.	Form.
VIII.	1	סַלָּם		סַלְּכֶם	סַלֵּנוּ	סַלָּהּ	סַלּוֹ	סַלֵּךְ	סַלְּךָ	סַלִּי	סַל	סַל a basket	פַּל
	†	סַלֵּיהֶם		סַלֵּיכֶם	סַלֵּינוּ	סַלֶּיהָ	סַלָּיו	סַלַּיִךְ	סַלֶּיךָ	סַלַּי	סַלֵּי	p. סַלִּים	
	1	חֻקָּם		חֻקְּכֶם	חֻקֵּנוּ	חֻקָּהּ	חֻקּוֹ	חֻקֵּךְ	חֻקְּךָ	חֻקִּי	חָק־	חֹק a law.	פֹּל
	†	חֻקֵּיהֶם		חֻקֵּיכֶם	חֻקֵּינוּ	חֻקֶּיהָ	חֻקָּיו	חֻקַּיִךְ	חֻקֶּיךָ	חֻקַּי	חֻקֵּי	p. חֻקִּים	
	1	קָנָם		קָנְכֶם	קָנֵנוּ	קָנָהּ	קָנֵהוּ	קָנֵךְ	קָנְךָ	קָנִי	קְנֵה־	קָנֶה a reed.*	פָּעָה
	†	קְנֵיהֶם		קְנֵיכֶם	קָנֵינוּ	קָנֶיהָ	קָנָיו	קָנַיִךְ	קָנֶיךָ	קָנַי	קְנֵי	p. קָנִים	
IX.	1	רֹעָם		רְעֲכֶם	רֹעֵנוּ	רֹעָהּ	רֹעֵהוּ	רֹעֵךְ	רֹעֲךָ	רֹעִי	רֹעֵה	רֹעֶה a shepherd	פֹּעֶה
	1	רֹעֵיהֶם		רֹעֵיכֶם	רֹעֵינוּ	רֹעֶיהָ	רֹעָיו	רֹעַיִךְ	רוֹעֶיךָ	רֹעַי	רֹעֵי	p. רֹעִים	
	1	מַעֲשָׂם		מַעֲשֵׂכֶם	מַעֲשֵׂנוּ	מַעֲשֵׂהוּ	מַעֲשֵׂהוּ	מַעֲשֵׂךְ	מַעֲשְׂךָ	מַעֲשִׂי	מַעֲשֵׂה	מַעֲשֶׂה work.	מִפְעֶה
	.	מַעֲשֵׂיהֶם		מַעֲשֵׂיכֶם	מַעֲשֵׂינוּ	מַעֲשֶׂיהָ	מַעֲשָׂיו	מַעֲשַׂיִךְ	מַעֲשֶׂיךָ	מַעֲשַׂי	מַעֲשֵׂי	p. מַעֲשִׂים	
	.	מְגִלָּתָם		מְגִלַּתְכֶם	מְגִלָּתֵנוּ	מְגִלָּתָהּ	מְגִלָּתוֹ	מְגִלָּתֵךְ	מְגִלָּתְךָ	מְגִלָּתִי	מְגִלַּת־	מְגִלָּה a literature.	מִפְעֻלָּה
	.	מְגִלּוֹתֵיהֶם		מְגִלּוֹתֵיכֶם	מְגִלּוֹתֵינוּ	מְגִלּוֹתֶיהָ	מְגִלּוֹתָיו	מְגִלּוֹתַיִךְ	מְגִלּוֹתֶיךָ	מְגִלּוֹתַי	מְגִלּוֹת	p. מְגִלּוֹת	
X.	1	תּוֹרָתָם	;	תּוֹרַתְכֶם	תּוֹרָתֵנוּ	תּוֹרָתָהּ	תּוֹרָתוֹ	תּוֹרָתֵךְ	תּוֹרָתְךָ	תּוֹרָתִי	תּוֹרַת	תּוֹרָה a law.	חוֹעָה
	1	תּוֹרוֹתֵיהֶם	;	תּוֹרוֹתֵיכֶם	תּוֹרוֹתֵינוּ	תּוֹרוֹתֶיהָ	תּוֹרוֹתָיו	תּוֹרוֹתַיִךְ	תּוֹרוֹתֶיךָ	תּוֹרוֹתַי	תּוֹרוֹת	p. תּוֹרוֹת	
XI.	1	שְׁנָתָם	;	שְׁנַתְכֶם	שְׁנָתֵנוּ	שְׁנָתָהּ	שְׁנָתוֹ	שְׁנָתֵךְ	שְׁנָתְךָ	שְׁנָתִי	שְׁנַת	שָׁנָה a year.	פָּעָה
	1	שְׁנוֹתֵיהֶם	;	שְׁנוֹתֵיכֶם	שְׁנוֹתֵינוּ	שְׁנוֹתֶיהָ	שְׁנוֹתָיו	שְׁנוֹתַיִךְ	שְׁנוֹתֶיךָ	שְׁנוֹתַי	שְׁנוֹת	p. שָׁנוֹת	
	1	בִּרְכָתָם	;	בִּרְכַתְכֶם	בִּרְכָתֵנוּ	בִּרְכָתָהּ	בִּרְכָתוֹ	בִּרְכָתֵךְ	בִּרְכָתְךָ	בִּרְכָתִי	בִּרְכַת	בְּרָכָה a blessing.	פִּעְלָה
	1	בִּרְכוֹתֵיהֶם	;	בִּרְכוֹתֵיכֶם	בִּרְכוֹתֵינוּ	בִּרְכוֹתֶיהָ	בִּרְכוֹתָיו	בִּרְכוֹתַיִךְ	בִּרְכוֹתֶיךָ	בִּרְכוֹתַי	בִּרְכוֹת	p. בְּרָכוֹת	
XII.	1	מַלְכָּתָם	;	מַלְכַּתְכֶם	מַלְכָּתֵנוּ	מַלְכָּתָהּ	מַלְכָּתוֹ	מַלְכָּתֵךְ	מַלְכָּתְךָ	מַלְכָּתִי	מַלְכַּת	מַלְכָּה a queen.	פִּעְלָה
	1	מַלְכוֹתֵיהֶם	;	מַלְכוֹתֵיכֶם	מַלְכוֹתֵינוּ	מַלְכוֹתֶיהָ	מַלְכוֹתָיו	מַלְכוֹתַיִךְ	מַלְכוֹתֶיךָ	מַלְכוֹתַי	מַלְכוֹת	p. מְלָכוֹת	

* Or a branch of a candlestick.   † Or חָגִי   ‡ Or עֶדְשִׁים

CLASSIFICATION OF NOUNS.—TABLE VIII.

Class	f.	their, m.	f.	your, m.	our	her	his	thy, f	thy, m.	my.	Gen.	Absolute state.		Form.
XII	1	נַעֲרָתָם	1	נַעֲרַתְכֶם	נַעֲרָתֵנוּ	נַעֲרָתָהּ	נַעֲרָתוֹ	נַעֲרָתֵךְ	נַעֲרָתְךָ	נַעֲרָתִי	נַעֲרַת	נַעֲרָה	a girl	סֶגלוֹת
	1	נַעֲרוֹתָם	1	נַעֲרוֹתֵיכֶם	נַעֲרוֹתֵינוּ	נַעֲרוֹתֶיהָ	נַעֲרוֹתָיו	נַעֲרוֹתַיִךְ	נַעֲרוֹתֶיךָ	נַעֲרוֹתַי	נַעֲרוֹת	נְעָרוֹת	p.	
	1	שִׁפְחָתָם	1	שִׁפְחַתְכֶם	שִׁפְחָתֵנוּ	שִׁפְחָתָהּ	שִׁפְחָתוֹ	שִׁפְחָתֵךְ	שִׁפְחָתְךָ	שִׁפְחָתִי	שִׁפְחַת	שִׁפְחָה	a bondmaid.	Ibid.
	1	שִׁפְחוֹתָם	1	שִׁפְחוֹתֵיכֶם	שִׁפְחוֹתֵינוּ	שִׁפְחוֹתֶיהָ	שִׁפְחוֹתָיו	שִׁפְחוֹתַיִךְ	שִׁפְחוֹתֶיךָ	שִׁפְחוֹתַי	שִׁפְחוֹת	שְׁפָחוֹת	p.	
	1	חָכְמָתָם	1	חָכְמַתְכֶם	חָכְמָתֵנוּ	חָכְמָתָהּ	חָכְמָתוֹ	חָכְמָתֵךְ	חָכְמָתְךָ	חָכְמָתִי	חָכְמַת	חָכְמָה	wisdom	פְּעלָה
	1	חָכְמוֹתָם	1	חָכְמוֹתֵיכֶם	חָכְמוֹתֵינוּ	חָכְמוֹתֶיהָ	חָכְמוֹתָיו	חָכְמוֹתַיִךְ	חָכְמוֹתֶיךָ	חָכְמוֹתַי	חָכְמוֹת	חָכְמוֹת	p.	
XIII	1	עֲטֶרֶתָם	1	עֲטֶרְתְּכֶם	עֲטֶרְתֵּנוּ	עֲטֶרְתָּהּ	עֲטֶרְתּוֹ	עֲטֶרְתֵּךְ	עֲטֶרְתְּךָ	עֲטֶרְתִּי	עֲטֶרֶת	עֲטָרָה	a crown	פֶּגלה
	1	עַטְרוֹתָם	1	עַטְרוֹתֵיכֶם	עַטְרוֹתֵינוּ	עַטְרוֹתֶיהָ	עַטְרוֹתָיו	עַטְרוֹתַיִךְ	עַטְרוֹתֶיךָ	עַטְרוֹתַי	עַטְרוֹת	עֲטָרוֹת	p.	
	1	טַבַּעְתָּם	1	טַבַּעְתְּכֶם	טַבַּעְתֵּנוּ	טַבַּעְתָּהּ	טַבַּעְתּוֹ	טַבַּעְתֵּךְ	טַבַּעְתְּךָ	טַבַּעְתִּי	טַבַּעַת	טַבַּעַת	a ring	פֶּגלת
	1	טַבְּעוֹתָם	1	טַבְּעוֹתֵיכֶם	טַבְּעוֹתֵינוּ	טַבְּעוֹתֶיהָ	טַבְּעוֹתָיו	טַבְּעוֹתַיִךְ	טַבְּעוֹתֶיךָ	טַבְּעוֹתַי	טַבְּעוֹת	טַבָּעוֹת	p.	
IRREGULAR	1	אֲבִיהֶם	1	אֲבִיכֶם	אָבִינוּ	אָבִיהָ	אָבִיו רו	אָבִיךְ	אָבִיךָ	אָבִי	אֲבִי	אָב	a father	
	1	אֲבוֹתָם	1	אֲבוֹתֵיכֶם	אֲבוֹתֵינוּ	אֲבוֹתֶיהָ	אֲבוֹתָיו	אֲבוֹתַיִךְ	אֲבוֹתֶיךָ	אֲבוֹתַי	אֲבוֹת	אָבוֹת	p.	
	1	אֲחִיהֶם	1	אֲחִיכֶם	אָחִינוּ	אָחִיהָ	אָחִיו רו	אָחִיךְ	אָחִיךָ	אָחִי	אֲחִי	אָח	a brother.	
	1	אֲחֵיהֶם	1	אֲחֵיכֶם	אַחֵינוּ	אַחֶיהָ	אֶחָיו	אַחַיִךְ	אַחֶיךָ	אַחַי	אֲחֵי	אַחִים	p.	
	1	אֲחוֹתָם	1	אֲחוֹתְכֶם	אֲחוֹתֵנוּ	אֲחוֹתָהּ	אֲחוֹתוֹ	אֲחוֹתֵךְ	אֲחוֹתְךָ	אֲחוֹתִי	אֲחוֹת	אָחוֹת	a sister.	
	1	אַחְיוֹתָם	1	אַחְיוֹתֵיכֶם	אַחְיוֹתֵינוּ	אַחְיוֹתֶיהָ	אַחְיוֹתָיו	אַחְיוֹתַיִךְ	אַחְיוֹתֶיךָ	אַחְיוֹתַי	אַחְיוֹת	אֲחָיוֹת	p.	
	1	בִּתָּם	1	בִּתְּכֶם	בִּתֵּנוּ	בִּתָּהּ	בִּתּוֹ	בִּתֵּךְ	בִּתְּךָ	בִּתִּי	בַּת	בַּת	a daughter.	
	1	בְּנוֹתָם	1	בְּנוֹתֵיכֶם	בְּנוֹתֵינוּ	בְּנוֹתֶיהָ	בְּנוֹתָיו	בְּנוֹתַיִךְ	בְּנוֹתֶיךָ	בְּנוֹתַי	בְּנוֹת	בָּנוֹת	p.	
	1	פִּיהֶם	1	פִּיכֶם	פִּינוּ	פִּיהָ	פִּיו	פִּיךְ	פִּיךָ	פִּי	פִּי	פֶּה	mouth	
	1	שֶׂהָם	1	שֶׂיְכֶם	שֵׂינוּ	שֶׂיהָ	שֵׂיוּ	שֵׂיךְ	שֶׂיךָ	שֵׂי	שֵׂה	שֶׂה	a lamb	

THE HEBREW LANGUAGE.

Observe.—(ָ) and (ֵ) are likewise immutable when they are either a compensation for *Dagesh*: as the first (ָ) in חָרָשׁ (instead of חַרָּשׁ), *an artist;* the first (ֵ) in חֵרֵשׁ (instead of חִרֵּשׁ) *a deaf person;* or in words derived from verbs of the 5th Conjugation (ע'ו): as, זָר *a stranger, p.* זָרִים, *f.* זָרָה, &c. עֵד *a witness, p.* עֵדִים, *f.* עֵדָה :—and from the 8th Conjugation (כְּפוּלִים): as, מָגֵן *a shield, p.* מָגִנִּים.

2nd.—All short vowels followed by a letter having *dagesh** : as, כַּלָּה *a bride,* אִכָּר *a husbandman,* סֻלָּם *a ladder,* &c.—(See Part I. page 35).

3rd.—All short vowels followed by a letter having *Sh'va final*† : as, קָרְבָּן *an offering,* שֻׁלְחָן *a table,* especially when the first letter is formative : as, מִשְׁפָּט *judgment,* אֶזְרָח *a native.*

4th.—As the change of vowels does not extend beyond the penultimate, it follows that the *antepenultimate* is immutable‡. The first vowel of the following and similar word will therefore be retained : as הֵרָיוֹן *conception,* מִשְׁפָּחָה *a family,* נֶחָמָה *consolation,* בֶּהָלָה *terror,* זִכָּרוֹן *remembrance,* &c.

5th.—*Sh'va* at the commencement of words is always retained, except in words of the form (פְּעָלָה); as, בְּרָכָה *a blessing,* where it is changed into (.): (See class XI.)—and in the form (פְּעִי), where it is changed into (.) or (ֶ).

Obs.—Vowels not included in the preceding rules are mostly mutable.

Classification of Nouns.

68. Nouns may be distributed into thirteen Classes.—(See the annexed Tables.)

---

* Except אִכָּר, from which we find אֲכָרָה and אֲכָרִיָּה.

† Except the forms פְּעָלָה and פְּעֻלָּה: as, שִׁפְחָה *a handmaid,* מַלְכָּה *a queen,* נַעֲרָה *a young woman,* which change their short vowels into (:): thus, נְעָרוֹת, מַלְכוֹת, שְׁפָחוֹת.

‡ Except בַּהֶרֶת *a bright spot, p.* בֶּהָרוֹת; חִזָּיוֹן *a vision, gen.* חֶזְיוֹן p. חֶזְיוֹנוֹת; מֶרְכָּבָה *a chariot, gen.* מִרְכֶּבֶת p. מִרְכָּבוֹת.

1.

69. The first Class comprehends monosyllables and dissyllables whose vowels are *immutable:* as, אוֹר *light,* קוֹל *the voice,* צַדִּיק *a just man.*

The words belonging to this class have, of course, their absolute state and their genitive alike, and retain their vowel-points before all the pronominal affixes. (See Paradigm No. 1.)

Words of the following grammatical form belong to this class:—

(פָּל)—as, זָר *a stranger,* (lit. separated) רָם *exalted, superior,* שָׁר *a singer,* שַׂר *or* שַׂר *a prince,* צָר *or* *צַר *an oppressor.*

(פֵּעָל †) and (פָּל)—as, זֵר *a wreath, border,* גֵּר *a sojourner,* נֵר *a lamp;* שְׁאֵר *a relation,* כְּאֵב *pain.*

(פָּעִיל) and (פִּיל‡)—as, כִּיס *a purse,* מִין *a sort, species,* קִיר *a wall;* גְּבִיר *a master,* שְׁבִיל *a path.*

(פֹּעֹל) and (פּוֹל §)—as, אוֹר *light,* עוֹר *skin,* ‖ כֹּחַ *strength;* חֲמוֹר *an ass,* שְׂאֹר *leaven.*

---

* The genitive singular of these words is שַׂר and צַר·· Of the former we find likewise שַׂרְכֶם *your prince;* otherwise they retain (ָ): thus שָׂרַי, שָׂרִים, שָׂרֵי, שָׂרֵיהֶם, &c., צָרַי, צָרֵיהֶם, &c.

† Except פְּאֵר, which has already been noticed.

‡ Except עִיר *a city,* p. עָרָיו, עָרַי, עָרֵי, עָרִים·

§ Except יוֹם *a day,* p. יָמִים *or* יָמוֹת; *gen.* p. יְמֵי *or* יְמוֹת, — יְמֵי, יְמֵיהֶם, יְמֵיכֶם, &c.; *dual,* יוֹמַיִם·—Except likewise, שׁוֹר *an ox,* p. שְׁוָרִים; חוֹחַ *a thorn,* חוֹחִים *or* חֲוָחִים·

‖ See the second Note in the following page.

THE HEBREW LANGUAGE. 65

לוּחַ† *a* the wind, רוּחַ† *a* whelp, גוּר as,—(*פוּל and פָּעוּל) table, board; גְבוּל *a* boundary, לְבוּשׁ *a* garment.

עָרִין (for עָרִיץ) *a* אַדִיר mighty, (פָּעִיל, פָּעוּל,‡ פָּעִיל)—as, tyrant; גִבּוֹר *a* hero, שִׁכּוֹר *a* drunkard; עַמוּד *a* pillar. תַנוּר *an oven*.

שִׁלְטוֹן might, פַּעֲמוֹן *a* bell; (פַּעֲלוֹן, פִּעָלוֹן, פְּעָלוֹן)—as, power; חֶסְרוֹן want, אֶבְיוֹן *a* poor, needy person.

(מַפְעִיל, מַפְעוּל) מַשְׁחִית *a* destroyer; מַטְמוֹן *a* treasure; (מִפְעוּל, מִפְעוֹל) מַלְבּוּשׁ *a* garment; מִזְמוֹר *a* song.

(אֶפְעוּל, תַפְעִיל) אֶגְרוֹף the fist, אֶפְרוֹחַ *a* chick; תַלְמִיד (תַפְעוּל) *a* disciple; תַעֲנוּג pleasure.

(פְּעָלִית---וּת) אַחֲרִית end, מַלְכוּת kingdom; שְׁאֵרִית *a* (פְּעָלִית) remnant; רֵאשִׁית (for רִאשִׁית) beginning.

To the preceding may be added many words of the following forms:—(פָּלוֹן): as, חַלוֹן *a* window.—Root, חָלַל. (פָּעוּת):

---

* Except שׁוּק *a* market, p. שְׁוָקִים; דּוּד *a* kettle p. דְּוָדִים.

† The vowel under ח is denominated פַּתַח גְנוּבָה *Furtive Pathach.*
It is dropped in the process of declension: as, כֹּחֲךָ, בֹּחִי.

‡ Except צִפּוֹר *a* bird, p. צִפֳּרִים.

§ p. מַלְכֻיוֹת. Thus also from תַּחְתִּית the nether, or lower part, p. תַּחְתִּיוֹת.

as, גָּלוּת captivity: Root, גָּלָה.—(פְּעוּת): as, כְּסוּת a covering, garment.—(פְּעִית): as, חֲנִית * a lance. (מוֹעָא): as, מוֹצָא an outlet, or going out: Root, יָצָא; מוֹרָא fear,†—(מַעָא): as, מַשָּׂא a burden: Root, נָשָׂא.—(מִפְעָא): as, מִקְרָא a convocation.—(תִּיעוֹל): as, תִּירוֹשׁ new wine.—(עֲלָעָל): as, צֶאֱצָא production, issue: Root, יָצָא.

Obs.—Most words of the form פְּעָל, as יְקָר honour, respect, ‡ כְּתָב a writing, retain (ָ) in the genitive singular, and in the absolute plural: as, עֲנָק a neck-chain, p. עֲנָקִים; some, however, take (ַ) in the genitive singular, and dagesh on being inflected; thus, זְמַן time, season; gen. זְמַן, זְמַנִּי, זְמַנִּים, p. זְמַנִּים. Many words of the form פְּעָל receive likewise dagesh: as, הֲדַס a myrtle, p. הֲדַסִּים; מְעַט little, p. מְעַטִּים few; אֲגַם a pond, p. אֲגַמִּים. Sometimes, however, dagesh is omitted: as, אֲגַמֵי, אֲגַמֵיהֶם. From דְּבַשׁ honey, we find דִּבְשִׁי.

II.

69. The second class comprehends monosyllables having mutable (ָ): as, דָּם blood, derived from verbs of the 7th conjugation (לה), and dissyllables which have a similar vowel for their *ultimate*, and an immutable vowel for their *penultimate*: as, אוֹצָר a treasure, מוּסָר correction.

---

* *Plural* חֲנִיתִים or חֲנִיתוֹת, חֲנִיתוֹתֵיהֶם.

† Yet, of this we find מֹרָאֲכֶם.

‡ The only inflections with which this word (כְּתָב) is found in Scripture, are כְּתָבָהּ and כְּתָבָם; but in the later writings, we find it inflected in the following manner:—כְּתָב, *gen.* כְּתָב or כְּתַב— כְּתָבִים, כְּתָבֵי, כְּתָבֵיהֶם, &c. כְּתָבִי, &c.

Obs.—The change consists in this.—1st, (ָ) is changed mostly into (־) in the genitive singular and before the heavy affixes: as, דָּם, *gen.* דַּם, דִּמְכֶם, (for דִּמְכֶם); אוֹצָר, *gen.* אוֹצַר, אוֹצַרְכֶם, &c. 2nd, In the genitive plural, and before the heavy affixes, (ָ) is entirely omitted (Sh'va being substituted for it): thus, *p.* דָּמִים, *gen.* דְּמֵי, דְּמֵיהֶם, &c.; *p.* אוֹצָרוֹת, *gen.* אוֹצְרוֹת, אוֹצְרוֹתֵיהֶם. (See Paradigms, No. II.)

Words of the following form belong to this Class:—

(פֵּעַ) as, יָד* *a hand*, דָּג *a fish*.—(פִּיעֵל, פּוֹעַל, פּוֹעֵל†) as, הֵיכָל *a palace,* עוּגָב *a musical instrument, a harp,* כּוֹכָב *a star.* (פֵּעַל, פֵּעָל, פָּעֵל): as, גַּנָּב *a thief*, כִּכָּר *a talent,* סֻלָּם *a ladder.* (פִּעָלוֹן, פִּעָלָן, פִּעָלוֹן): as, כִּבְשָׁן *a furnace,* קָרְבָּן *an offering,* שֻׁלְחָן *a table.*—(מִפְעָל, אֶפְעָל, מָפָל): as, מָסָךְ *a curtain, covering,* אֶזְרָח *a native,* מִשְׁכָּן *a tabernacle, a dwelling-place,* מִשְׁפָּט *judgment.*—(מֶעַל, מוֹעַל, תּוֹעָל‡): as, מַסָּע *a removing, march,* מוֹסָד *a foundation,* תּוֹשָׁב *a sojourner.*

III.

71. The third Class comprehends words which have a mutable (ָ) or (ֵ) in their penultimate, and

---

* From יָד we find יָדְךָ, יֶדְכֶם *your hand.*

† Several words of this and the following forms take *dagesh*: as, אוֹפָן *a wheel,* שׁוֹשָׁן *a rose,* מִשְׂגָּב *a high place, a place of refuge,* *p.* אוֹפַנִּים, שׁוֹשַׁנִּים, מִשְׂגַּבֵּי, &c. These belong to the eighth class.

‡ Some words of these and the preceding forms retain (ָ) in the genitive plural, &c.; others reject it: as, מַטָּע *a plant;* מִטְּעֵי; מַסְעֵי, מַסָּע; תּוֹשָׁבֵי, תּוֹשָׁב, &c.

an immutable vowel in their ultimate syllable: as, קָצִיר *harvest*, מֵלִין *an interpreter*, בָּרוּךְ *blessed*, עִצָּבוֹן *pain, labour*.

The change consists in substituting (:) for (ָ) and (ֵ); thus, קָצִיר, *gen.* קְצִיר, קְצִירִי &c.; *מֵלִין, מְלִיצֵי, מְלִיצָךְ, &c. עִצָּבוֹן, *gen.* עִצְּבוֹן, עִצְּבוֹנֶךָ, עִצְּבוֹנִי, &c.—

Observe.—As two Sh'vas cannot begin a word, it follows that in words wherein (ְ) is preceded by (:); as, רְעָבוֹן *hunger*, פְּרָזוֹן *an unwalled town*, the (:) must be changed into a vowel; and hence from the first we have in the genitive רַעֲבוֹן, and from the second פְּרָזוֹנוֹ *his*, &c.

Words of the following forms belong to this class:—

(פָּעִיל † פָּעוּל ‡ פָּעוּל, פְּעוּל) as, נָדִיב *a generous, liberal man;* אָדוֹן *a master, lord;* בָּרוּךְ *blessed;* אָמוּן *faithful.*

(פְּעָלוֹן, פִּעָלוֹן) as, זִכָּרוֹן פְּרָזוֹן *a remembrance.*

(פָּלוֹן, פָּעוֹן) as, שָׂשׂוֹן *joy;* יָגוֹן *sorrow.* (מָפוֹל): as, מָקוֹם *a place;* (מַפְעִיל): as, מֵבִין *an intelligent man,* מֵלִין *an interpreter.*

---

* (ֵ) is, however, retained in the genitive singular: as, מֵלִין, *gen.* מֵלִיץ.

† Except שָׁלִישׁ *an officer* (perhaps of the third rank), and שָׁבוּעַ *a week*, which retain (ָ): thus, שָׁלִישִׁים, שָׁבוּעוֹת; to distinguish them from שְׁלִישִׁים *the third time,* שְׁבוּעוֹת *oaths.*

‡ A few words of this form, as טָהוֹר *pure,* גָּדוֹל *great,* change וֹ into short (ָ) on being joined to another word by Makkeph: thus, גְּדָל־, טְהָר־. Several words of this form take *dagesh*, and change (וֹ) into (ֻ): as, אָדוֹם *red, p.* אֲדֻמִּים: עָרוֹם *naked,* עֲרֻמִּים.

IV.

72. The fourth Class comprehends all dissyllables having (ֶָ) or (ֵָ) for their vowels: as, דָּבָר *a word*, לֵבָב *the heart*.

The change consists, 1st — in substituting (:) for the *penultimate* (ָ) or (ֵ), and in changing (ָ) *ultimate* into (-) in the genitive singular, and before the affixes כֶם, ךָ : thus, דְּבַר, דְּבָרְךָ, דִּבְרְכֶם, &c.; דְּבָרְךָ, דְּבָרִי, &c.; דְּבָרִים, &c.—2nd. In the genitive plural and before the heavy affixes, penultimate (ָ) or (ֵ) are changed mostly into (.), more rarely into (-)*; and ultimate (ָ) into (:); thus, דִּבְרֵי, דִּבְרֵיכֶם, דִּבְרֵיכֶן, דִּבְרֵיהֶם, דִּבְרֵיהֶן.

Words of the following forms belong to this class:—

(פָּעָל)†—as, זָהָב *gold*, חָכָם *a wise man*, נָהָר *a river*, בָּשָׂר *flesh*.

(פֵּעָל)—as, שֵׂעָר *a hair*, עֵנָב *a grape*, צֵלָע *a rib*, עָנָף *a twig*, &c.

V.

73. The fifth Class comprehends dissyllables having mutable (ֵ) for their *ultimate*, and mutable (ָ) for their *penultimate*: as, זָקֵן *an old man*.

The vowels are subject to the same changes as those of the preceding class. To this class belong all words of the form (פָּעֵל):

---

* Thus חָכָם *a wise man*, gen. חֲכַם, p. חֲכָמִים, gen. p. חַכְמֵי; כָּנָף *a wing*, dual and p. כְּנָפַיִם, gen. p. כַּנְפֵי.

† Some words of this form take *dagesh*: as, גָּמָל *a camel*, שָׁפָן *the rabbit, jerboa*, קָטָן *little*: thus, גְּמַל, גְּמַלִּי, גְּמַלְּךָ, גְּמַלִּים, &c. They belong, of course, to the 8th class. חָלָב *milk*, has its genitive singular חֲלֵב; לְבָן *white*, לְבִי.

as, חָצֵר *a court,* כָּבֵד *the liver,* קָצֵר *short,* יָתֵד *a plug, nail,* &c.; (פֵּעָא)*: as, טָמֵא *unclean,* מָלֵא *full,* &c.

Obs. — יָרֵךְ *the thigh,* כָּתֵף *the shoulder,* גָּדֵר *a hedge,* גָּזֵל *plunder, robbery,* from their *gen. s.* thus—כָּתֵף, יָרֵךְ, גָּזֵל *or* גְּזֵל, גָּדֵר *or* גְּדֵר.

VI.

74. The sixth Class comprehends all dissyllables which have their accent on the penultimate: as, דֶּרֶךְ *a way* or *road,* שַׁעַר *a gate,* סֵפֶר *a book,* חֹדֶשׁ *a month,* לַיִל *night,* אָוֶן *iniquity, vanity.*

Words of this class have their genitive and absolute state singular alike; except those of the form פֵּעֶל (as מָוֶת *death*), which drop (ּ), and change (ָ) into (ּ—) in their genitive singular, and retain (ּ—) in their inflections: thus, מוֹת, מוֹתִי, מוֹתוֹ, &c. And those of the form פֵּיִל, (as אַיִל *a ram,*) which drop the (.), and change (-) into (..) in the genitive singular; retaining (..) in their inflections; thus, אֵיל, אֵילִי, אֵילְךָ, &c. From עָוֶל *wrong, injustice,* we find, however, *gen.* עֲוָל instead of עוֹל; עֲוָלוֹ instead of עוֹלוֹ, *f.* עוֹלָה; but *p.* עוֹלוֹת.

Words of the following forms belong to this class:

(פֶּעֶל, פֵּעֶל)— as, מֶלֶךְ *a king,* נַעַר *a boy,* בֶּגֶד *a garment,* סֵפֶר *a book,* חֵלֶק *a portion.*

---

* These, however, retain (..) in their genitive singular and plural. Thus, טָמֵא, *gen. s.* טְמֵא, *gen. p.* טְמֵאֵי. Likewise, עָקֵב *the heel, gen. s.* עֲקֵב (but *gen. p.* עִקְבֵי), יָשֵׁן *a sleeper, gen. p.* יְשֵׁנֵי, שָׂמֵחַ, *gen. p.* שְׂמֵחֵי, &c.

THE HEBREW LANGUAGE. 71

The vowels are subject to the following changes:—

(ָ) ultimate is changed into (ְ) before the affixes of the singular, in the genitive plural, and before the heavy affixes: as, מֶלֶךְ, מַלְכֵי, מַלְכֵּי, מַלְכִּיבֶם, מַלְכְּכֶם, &c.; בֶּגֶד, בִּגְדִי, &c. But in the absolute state plural, and before the light affixes, it is changed into (ְ): as, מְלָכִים kings, מְלָכַי my kings, בְּגָדִים garments, בְּגָדַי.

(ֶ) penultimate is changed mostly into (-), but sometimes into (.) before the affixes of the singular, in the genitive plural, and its heavy affixes. Thus, מַ of מֶלֶךְ, and בִּ of בֶּגֶד, are changed into מַ and בִּ; as, מַלְכִּי, בִּגְדִי*, בִּגְדֵיהֶם; but in the plural, and its light affixes, it is changed into (ְ); as, מְלָכִים, &c.

(ָ) penultimate is mostly changed into (.) or (ֶ); as, סֵפֶר, סִפְרִי, סִפְרֵי; חֵלֶק, חֶלְקִי. &c. In the plural it follows the same rule as penultimate (ֶ); thus, סְפָרִים, סִפְרֵי, &c. סִפְרֵיהֶם, &c.

(פָּעֵל)—as, אֹזֶן an ear, חֹדֶשׁ a month, קֹדֶשׁ holiness, רֹחַב breadth, אֹרֶךְ length.

The vowel point (ָ) is changed into short (ֶ), and (ֶ) follows the same rule as in the preceding forms. Thus, חֳדָשִׁים, חָדְשִׁי, חֳדָשִׁים, חָדְשֵׁי.

---

* Some words retain the (ֶ); as, חֶלְדִי, גֶּנְדִּי, גֶּנֶר, &c.; חָלְדִי, חֶלְדִי. Others take either (.) or (-) in the genitive plural; as, יֶלֶד a child, gen. p. יֶלְדֵי or יַלְדֵי.

† The word פֹּעַל work (action), changes (ָ) into (ֶ). It is thus inflected.— פֹּעַל, gen. פֹּעַל, פָּעֳלִי, פָּעֳלְךָ, &c., פָּעָלְכֶם, &c.; plural, פְּעָלִים, פָּעֳלֵי, פָּעֳלֵיכֶם: אֹהֶל a tent, is declined in the same manner. אָהֳלוֹ, אָהֳלְךָ or אָהֳלֶךָ, &c.; But plural אֹהָלִים, אָהֳלֶיךָ; אָהֳלָיו; gen. p. אָהֳלֵי, אָהֳלֵיכֶם, &c.; תֹּאַר a form, תָּאֳרוֹ or תָּאָרוֹ. From קֹמֶץ a handful, we find קֻמְצוֹ; גֹּדֶל greatness, גָּדְלוֹ.

‡ Many words of this form have their plural like those of the preceding form; as, בֹּקֶר, בְּקָרִים; רֹתֶם, רְתָמִים, &c.: בֹּהֶן, נֹגַהּ, נֹכַח from their plural, בְּהוֹנוֹת, נְגֹהוֹת, נְכֹחוֹת.

72   THE ETYMOLOGY OF

(פָּעֵל פִּיעֵל,)—as, עָוֶל *wrong, injustice,* תָּוֶךְ *the middle,* מָוֶת *death;* ‎*זַיִת *an olive,* לַיִל *night,* יַיִן *wine,* עַיִן *an eye.*

The changes of the vowel-points of these forms have already been explained.

(פְּעִי†)—as, פְּרִי *fruit,* גְּדִי *a kid,* אֲרִי *a lion,* ‡ לְחִי *cheek, jaw-bone,* כְּלִי *a vessel.*

(:) is changed into (.) or (ָ); and (.) into (:), in the singular: as, פְּרִי, פֶּרְיָךְ, &c.; כְּלִי, כֶּלְיָה.   In the plural most of them retain (:), and change (.) into (ָ); thus, גְּדָיִים, § אֲרָיִים, or אֲרָיוֹת, *gen. pl.* גְּדָיֵי, &c.—כְּלִי changes (:) into (..), and retains (.); thus, כֵּלִים *gen. pl.* כְּלֵי, בְּלִי, בֶּלְיָה, בְּלָיוּ, &c.; כְּלֵיכֶם, &c.

(פְּעִי)—as, חֳלִי ‖ *sickness,* עֳנִי *affliction,* צֳרִי or צֳרִי *balm,* חֳרִי *burning, anger.*

---

* *Gen. s.* זַיִת—זֵיתִי &c. *p.* זֵיתִים. עַיִן *gen.* עֵין—עֵינִי &c. *p. (dual)* עֵינַיִם *gen.* עֵינֵי—עֵינֶיךָ, עֵינַי, &c. But עֲיָנוֹת, signifies *springs, fountains,* and its genitive is עֵינוֹת. Thus likewise, מַעְיָן *a spring, well, p.* מַעְיָנוֹת or מַעְיָנִים, *gen. p.* מַעְיְנֵי and מַעְיָנוֹת. Several other words of this form have their plural in this manner: as, חַיִל *a host,* חֲיָלִים; עַיִר *a young ass,* עֲיָרִים.—בַּיִת *a house,* forms its plural בָּתִּים, and retains the long (ָ) and dagesh through the plural inflections: thus, *gen.* בָּתֵּי—בָּתֶּיךָ, בָּתַּי, &c.; contrary to general analogy.

† Most words of this form change (:) into (ָ) in pause: thus, פֶּרִי, גֶּדִי, לֶחִי.

‡ The plural (dual) of לְחִי is לְחָיַיִם, *gen.* לְחָיֵי.

§ A few words of this form change ׳ into א in the plural: as, חֲלִי *a ring, p.* חֲלָאִים; פֶּתִי *a simpleton, p.* פְּתָיִים or פְּתָאִים; צְבִי *a gazelle: p.* צְבָיִים or צְבָאִים. *f.* צְבִיָּה *p.* צְבָאוֹת.

‖ In pause צֳרִי, עֳנִי, חֳלִי.

VII.

75. The seventh Class comprehends all words having (ָ) mutable for their ultimate, and an immutable vowel for their penultimate: as מֹשֵׁל *a ruler, regent,* חֹתֵן *a father in law,* אֹהֵב *a lover,* שֹׂנֵא *a hater, enemy,* כִּסֵּא *a covered seat, a throne,* סוֹחֵר *a merchant,* מַקֵּל *a staff,* אֹיֵב *an enemy.* Likewise some of the monosyllables derived from the ל״ה : as, שֵׁם *a name.*

(ָ) is mostly changed into (ְ); as, אוֹיְבִי, אוֹיְבִים, אוֹיְבֵי, מַקְלִי, מַקְלוֹת, חֹתְנוֹ, &c.; or into (ֲ) when the middle letter is a guttural: as, אֲהֲבִי, אֲהֲבוֹ, &c.; סוֹחֲרִים, סוֹחֲרֵי, &c. Before ךָ, כֶם; and כֶן, it is changed mostly into (ְ); as, חֹתֶנְךָ, מַקֶּלְךָ, מַקֶּלְכֶם, sometimes into (ֶ); as, אוֹיִבְךָ; אוֹיִבְכֶם; שִׁמְךָ, שִׁמְכֶן; and into (ֱ) when the 2nd or 3rd radical is a guttural: as, אֱהַבְךָ, אֱהַבְכֶם, שְׂנֵאוּךָ, &c.

In the genitive singular (ָ) is mostly retained, though in some instances it is changed into (ֶ); as, מִזְבֵּחַ *an altar, gen.* מִזְבַּח, מַקֵּל, *gen.* מַקֵּל *or* מַקֶּל.

Words of the following form belong to this class:—

(פֹּעֵל, פּוֹעֵל)—as, פּוֹקֵד *a visitor,* כֹּהֵן *a priest,* עֹרֵב *a raven,* אוֹרֵב *an ambush;* עִוֵּר *a blind man,* עִלֵּג *a stammerer,* אִלֵּם *a dumb person.*

(מַפְעֵל, מִפְעֵל)—as, מַסְמֵר *a nail,* מַכְתֵּשׁ *a mortar,* מַפְתֵּחַ *a key,* מַעֲשֵׂר *a tenth part, tithes;* מִסְכֵּן *a poor man.*

74   THE ETYMOLOGY OF

as, מוֹפֵת (מוֹעֵל פֵּע) a wonder, מוֹעֵד an appointed time, a festival, מוֹקֵשׁ a snare; * שֵׁם a name, בֵּן a son, † עֵץ a tree.

VIII.

76. The eighth Class comprehends all words which double their last letter by *dagesh* on being augmented: as, גַּן a garden, גַּנִּי my garden; לֵב the heart, לִבִּי my heart; חֹק a law, statute, חֻקִּי my statute; גָּמָל a camel, גְּמַלִּי my camel, גְּמַלְּךָ thy camel, &c.

The vowel which precedes *dagesh* becomes immutable, and is therefore, in most cases, retained through all the inflections.

Words of the following forms (derived from roots which have the second and third radical the same) belong to this class.

(פֵּל ‡)—as, סַל a basket, כַּד a pail, bucket, יָם or יַם the sea, עַם or עָם a people, רַךְ soft, tender, דַּל a poor man.

These retain (־) in the genitive singular and in the inflection §.

―――――――――――――――――

* With Makkeph.—שֶׁם־, בֶּן־. The plural of this word (בֵּן) is בָּנִים, *gen. p.* בְּנֵי—בָּנֶיךָ, בְּנֵיכֶם, &c.

† עֵץ and a few others of this form retain (ֵ) through their inflections, except in the genitive plural and the heavy affixes: thus, עֵצִי, עֵצְךָ, &c. *p.* עֵצִים, עֲצֵי, עֲצֵיךָ, *gen. p.* עֲצֵי, עֲצֵיכֶם, &c.

‡ Many words of this form have (ָ) or (־) in their absolute state: as, עַם or עָם; generally (ָ) in pause; as, דַּל, דָּל; גַּל, *a heap*, גָּל; but always (־) in the genitive and the inflections.

§ Except צַד *the side*, פַּת *a small piece, morsel*, סַף *the threshold*, which take (·) in the inflections: thus, צִדִּי, פִּתִּי, צִדְּךָ, פִּתִּים. From

(פֵּל)—as, שֵׁן *a tooth,* צֵל *a shadow,* לֵב *the heart,* קֵץ *end,* חֵךְ *the palate,* אֵשׁ *fire.*

These retain generally (ֵ) in the genitive singular*, but change it into (ְ) in the inflection: as, שְׁנִי, שְׁנוֹ, *p.* שְׁנַיִם†, שְׁנֵי, שְׁנֵי, שְׁנֵיךָ, &c.

(פֹּל)—as, עוֹל *a yoke,* חֹק *a decree,* כֹּל *all, the whole,* עֹז *might, power, strength,* תֹּף *a drum,* תֹּם *innocence.*

Some of these retain ֹ in the genitive: as, עֹל *gen.* עֹל; others change it into short (ָ) with Makkeph: as, כָּל־, חָק.

Before the inflections, (ֹ) is mostly changed into (וֹ): as, עֹל, עָלְךָ, though sometimes into short (ָ): as, עָזִּי; especially before ךָ and כֶם; as, חֹק, חֻקִּי, חֻקְּךָ, חֻקְּכֶם; עֹז, עֻזִּי, עֻזְּךָ or עוּזְךָ.

(מִפְעָל, מִפְעוֹל)—as, מָעוֹז *a place of strength, a fort,* מָעֻזִּי, מָעוֹז or מָעוּז; מָעֻזְּכֶם; מָגֵן *a shield,* מָגִנִּי, *p.* מָגִנֵּי, מָגִנִּים, (ָ) being here immutable.

Many contracted words derived from roots whose second letter is נ, as אַף *face, countenance, anger,* (from אָנַף *to breathe through the nose, to snort*), and בַּת *a daughter* (from בְּנַת feminine of בֵּן *a son*), belong to this class, and are inflected in a similar manner: thus, אַפִּי, אַפְּךָ, אַפּוֹ; *plural,* (dual) אַפַּיִם, *g. p.* אַפֵּי, אַפֶּיךָ, &c. בִּתִּי, בִּתְּךָ, &c. *p.* בָּנוֹת *gen. p.* בְּנוֹת, בְּנוֹתַי, בְּנוֹתֶיךָ,

---

הַר *a mountain,* we have in the plural הָרִים, *gen. p.* הָרֵי, הָרַי, &c. (ָ) being a compensation for *dagesh.* Thus likewise, בַּר, *pure, selected,* בָּרִים, בָּרֵי, &c.

* Except a few which take (ְ) with Makkeph: as, לֶב־, שֶׁן־.

† But שְׁנַיִם signifies *two;* and שָׁנִים *years,* שְׁנֵי *my years,* שְׁנֶיךָ *thy years.* Several words of this form change (ֵ) into (ִ): as כֵּן *a stand, basis,* כַּנּוֹ; קֵן *a nest,* with Makkeph קָן־; but in other respects regular קִנִּי, &c. From אֵשׁ *fire,* we have אִשּׁוֹ, אִשְּׁים and אִשְּׁכֶם instead of אִשְׁכֶם.

בְּנוֹתֶיךָ, &c. Many words of other forms receiving *dagesh* on being augmented, belong likewise to this class: as, גָּמָל *a camel,* וְכָן׳ *time,* שַׁבָּת *the day of rest, the sabbath,* עָנִי *a poor (humble) man, &c.* Most of these have already been noticed in the preceding notes.

IX.

77. The ninth Class comprehends all words terminating in ־ֶה; as, שָׂדֶה *a field,* רֹעֶה * *a shepherd,* יָפֶה *beautiful, handsome,* מַחֲנֶה *a camp,* רֹאֶה *a seer,* מַרְאֶה *appearance, colour, vision,* מַעֲשֶׂה *work.*

1. ־ֶה is changed into ־ֵה in the genitive singular: as, רֹעֵה *gen.*; שָׂדֶה, *gen.* שְׂדֵה.

2. Before the inflections it is dropped: as, רֹעִי, רֹעֵי, רֹעִים, &c. שָׂדוֹת, *gen. p.* שְׂדוֹת; שְׂדוֹתַי, *or p.* שָׂדַי, שָׂדְךָ, שָׂדֵךְ, &c. שָׂדִים (by analogy), *gen. p.* שָׂדַי, שָׂדְיָ, שָׂדֶיךָ, שָׂדֵינוּ, &c.

3. Before the affix of the third person masculine singular, ה is mostly retained†: as, שָׂדֵהוּ, מַעֲשֵׂהוּ, מַרְאֵהוּ, &c.—Third person *f. s.* מַעֲשָׂהּ, מַרְאָהּ or מַעֲשֶׂהָ, or מַרְאֶהָ.‡

---

* Words comprehended in this class, are derived from roots whose third radical is ה; they form their feminine by changing (ֶ) into (ָ): as, רֹעָה *a shepherdess;* m. יָפֶה, *f.* יָפָה; עֹלָה *one that ascends, f.* עֹלָה. Except בֹּכֶה *one who weeps, weeping,* צֹפֶה *one who watches, a watchman,* and a few others which form their feminine בֹּכִיָּה, צֹפִיָּה.

† This is likewise the case with some nouns not terminating in ה: as, פִּלֶגֶשׁ *a concubine,* פִּלַגְשֵׁהוּ; יָד *a hand,* יָדֵהוּ.

‡ *Aben Ezra* (in צחות) asserts, indeed, that this form (מַעֲשֶׂהָ) is inadmissible: I have, however, followed *Kimchi*, who justifies its usage.

Words of the following form belong to this class:—

קָנֶה (פָּעָה, פֶּעָה, פּוֹעָה)—as, חָזֶה, *the breast,* p. חָזוֹת; קָנֶה *a reed, a sconce,* p. קָנִים or קָנוֹת; עָלֶה *a leaf,* p. עָלִים; גֵּאֶה *arrogant,* p. גֵּאִים; *רֵעֶה a friend, companion,* p. רֵעִים; קֹנֶה *a purchaser,* p. קֹנִים.

מִשְׁנֶה (מִפְעָה, מַפְעָה)—as, מִקְנֶה p. מִקְנִים; מִשְׁנֶה *second in rank, double,* p. מִשְׁנִים; מַחֲנֶה p. מַחֲנוֹת *dual* מַחֲנָיִם. (מָעָה)—as, מַטֶּה *a staff, branch, tribe,* p. מַטִּים or מַטּוֹת; מַכֶּה *one that strikes,* p. מַכִּים, &c.

78. The following four Classes comprehend nouns feminine terminating in ־ָה, ־ֶת, ־ַת.

Those that terminate in ־ָה have this in common:—

1st.—That they change ־ָה into ־ַת in the genitive singular, and before בֶּם, בֶּן.

2nd.—That they retain ת and ־ in the rest of the inflections of the singular number.

3rd.—That they form their plural by changing ־ָה into וֹת, which termination is retained through all the plural inflections.

For the changes to which nouns terminating in ת are subject, see remarks on Class XIII.

X.

79. The tenth Class comprehends all nouns terminating in ־ָה, preceded by an immutable vowel: as, גְּבוּרָה *strength,* תְּחִנָּה *a prayer, supplication.*

---

* רֵעֶה, מִשְׁנֶה, and מִקְרֶה, retain (־) in the genitive singular.

Excepting the genitive singular, and before בֶּם and בֶּן, as already noticed in the preceding observation, both vowels are retained. The plural is formed by וֹת, and the absolute state plural and its genitive are the same. Thus, גְּבוּרָה, gen. גְּבוּרַת—גְּבוּרָתִי; p. גְּבוּרוֹת gen. גְּבוּרוֹתַי—גְּבוּרוֹת, &c.

Words of the following forms belong to this class:—

(פְּעִילָה, פְּעוּלָה, פְּעִילָה)— as, אֲכִילָה *a meal;* עֲבוֹדָה *service, labour;* גְּדֻלָּה or גְּדוּלָה *greatness, joy.*

(פְּעוּלָה, פְּעִילָה)—as, חַבּוּרָה *a bruise,* בִּכּוּרָה *an early fig.*

(פָּלָה, פֵּילָה, פִּילָה)— as, צָרָה *distress, anguish,* קָמָה *standing corn;* שֵׂיבָה *old age,* צֵידָה *provision;* בִּינָה *understanding.*

(פָּלָה, פֻּלָּה, פִּלָּה)— as, כַּלָּה *a bride;* מִדָּה *a measure;* סֻכָּה *a hut, tabernacle,* חֻקָּה *a law.*

(תִּפְלָה, מִפְלָה)—as, תְּפִלָּה *a prayer,* תְּהִלָּה *praise;* מְגִלָּה *a roll, volume.*

(מֵעָה, תּוֹעָה)—as, מַכָּה *a smiting, wound,* מַסָּה *a tempting, temptation;* תּוֹרָה *a law, instruction,* תּוֹדָה *an acknowledgment, thanks.*

XI.

80. The eleventh class comprehends nouns having the same termination as the preceding, viz. ־ָה, but preceded by mutable (ָ) or (ֵ): as, שָׁנָה *a year,* שֵׁנָה *sleep.*

THE HEBREW LANGUAGE. 79

‐ָה ultimate has already been explained; and (ָ) or (ֳ) penultimate are changed into (ְ), except in the plural absolute. Thus, שָׁנָה, *gen.* שְׁנַת, שְׁנָתִי, &c. Plural שָׁנוֹת, *gen.* שְׁנוֹת שְׁנוֹתַי, &c.

Obs.—Words having (ָ ָ) for their vowels, preceded by (ְ), change (ְ) into (.) or (-): as, בְּרָכָה *a blessing, gen.* בִּרְכַּת, בִּרְכָתִי, בִּרְכָתְךָ. &c., *p.* בְּרָכוֹת, *gen.* בִּרְכוֹת בִּרְכוֹתַי. See the examples under the form פְּעָלָה.

Words of the following forms belong to this class:—

(פֶּעָה, פָּעָה)—as, שָׁנָה *a year,* יָפָה *fair, beautiful,* מָנָה* *a portion,* שָׂפָה † *lip;* פֵּאָה *a corner,* מֵאָה ‡ *a hundred.*

(עֲלָה, מוֹעֲלָה-ע)—as, עֵצָה *advice, counsel,* שֵׁנָה *sleep,* חֵמָה *anger;* מוֹרָשָׁה *an inheritance,* מוֹעֵצָה *a device.*

(פְּעָלָה, פֶּעְלָה)§—as, נְדָבָה *a free gift, gen.* נִדְבַת; צְדָקָה *righteousness, gen.* צִדְקַת; גְּעָרָה *a rebuke, gen.* גַּעֲרַת; קְעָרָה *a dish, gen.* קַעֲרַת; חֲרָדָה ‖ *terror, gen.* חֶרְדַת; נְבֵלָה *a carcase, gen.* נִבְלַת.

---

* מְנוּחָיהּ (Est. ii. 9.) is a deviation from the rule.

† *p.* שְׂפָתוֹת or (dual) שְׂפָתַיִם, *gen. p.* שִׂפְתוֹת or שִׂפְתֵי; אָלָה *an oath,* retains the first (ָ); thus, *gen.* אָלַת, אָלָתִי, &c.

‡ *p.* מֵאוֹת, dual מָאתַיִם, instead of מְאָתַיִם.

§ Most words of this form retain (ֲ) in the genitive: as, אֲבֵדָה, *gen.* אֲבֵדַת—אֲבֵדָתִי; בְּהֵמָה *cattle,* has its genitive בֶּהֱמַת—בֶּהֱמָתִי; עֲטָרָה *a crown, gen.* עֲטֶרֶת; מַצֵּבָה, *gen.* מַצֶּבֶת. (See observation on Class XIII.)

‖ *p.* קְעָרוֹת, *gen.* קַעֲרוֹת. קְעָרוֹתָיו (Exod. xxv.) is a deviation from the general rule. Several words of these forms retain (ְ) in the genitive: as, מְעָרָה *a cave, gen.* מְעָרַת; תְּעָלָה *an aqueduct, gen.* תְּעָלַת.

XII.

81. The twelfth Class comprehends feminine nouns chiefly derived from words of the forms פֶּעַל, פֵּעֶל and פְּעֵל; as, for instance, מַלְכָּה *a queen*, from מֶלֶךְ *a king*; נַעֲרָה *a young woman, a girl*, from נַעַר *a boy*; עֶזְרָה *aid, assistance*, from עֵזֶר *an aid, help*; סִתְרָה *a hiding-place, shelter*, from סֵתֶר *a secret place, shelter, protection*; חָרְבָה *a waste, ruin*, from חֹרֶב *dryness desolation*.

קָה has already been explained. The short vowels (-) (ִ) (.) and (ָ) with the following (:) are retained, except before the absolute state plural, where the short vowels are changed into (:), and the (:) of the second letter into (ָ).—Thus מַלְכָּה, *p*. מְלָכוֹת; שִׂמְלָה, *p*. שְׂמָלוֹת; חֶרְפָּה, *p*. חֲרָפוֹת; חָרְבָה *p*. חֳרָבוֹת; נַעֲרָה, *p*. נְעָרוֹת.

Words of the following forms belong to this Class:—

שַׁלְמָה *a young woman*, עַלְמָה —as, (פָּעֳלָה, פְּעֵלָה, פַּעֲלָה)
שִׂמְחָה *a robe, garment*; שִׂמְלָה and, (פְּעֵלָה)
יַלְדָּה *a girl*, כִּבְשָׂה or, כַּבְשָׂה *a ewe-lamb*, אַהֲבָה *love*, joy,
שִׁפְחָה *a bondmaid*; חֶרְפָּה *a reproach*; חָרְבָה *a ruin, desolation*, חָכְמָה *wisdom*; עָרְמָה *cunningness*.

XIII.

82. The thirteenth Class comprehends feminine nouns terminating in ־ַת, ־ֵת, ־ֶת, ־ָת, or ־ְת, as, גְּבֶרֶת *a mistress*, כְּתֹנֶת* *a coat*, טַבַּעַת *a ring*.

---

* This word has several other forms. (See Kimchi in שרשים).

The Genitive and Absolute state singular are the same: as, גְּבֶרֶת g. גְּבֶרֶת. — On being augmented by the pronominal affixes, ת receives *dagesh*, the last vowel is changed into (:) and the penultimate (ָ) is either retained, as בְּהֶמַת *cattle*, בְּהֶמְתִּי, בְּהֶמְתְּךָ, or it is changed into (-) or (.) as מִשְׁמַרְתִּי *keeping, trust*; גִּבְרֶת—גִּבְרְתִּי. Penultimate ָ is mostly changed into short (ִ); as, קְטֹרֶת *incense*, קְטָרְתִּי.*

Obs.—Most Nouns belonging to this class have two forms for their absolute state: as, גְּבֶרֶת and גְּבִירָה — בְּהֵמָה and בְּהֵמָה—מִלְחֶמֶת and מִלְחָמָה *war,* — מַצֶּבֶת and מַצֵּבָה *a pillar*, תּוֹלַעַת and תּוֹלֵעָה *a worm* (in the same manner as the participles פֹּקֶדֶת and פֹּקְדָה). Now, the singular is regulated by the first form (terminating in ת ֶ) as already described; but the plural is regulated by the termination ה ָ, and hence the plural of גְּבֶרֶת is גְּבִירוֹת—גְּבִירוֹתַי, &c., without *dagesh* (from גְּבִירָה). Thus likewise from מִלְחֶמֶת—מִלְחָמָה; but *p.* מִלְחָמוֹת—מִלְחֲמוֹתַי (from מִלְחָמָה). From מַצֵּבוֹת—מַצֵּבֹת, but *p.* מַצְּבֹתַי—מַצְּבֶת.

Words of the following forms belong to this Class:—

† ;עֲטֶרֶת, גְּבֶרֶת, as — (פֹּעֶלֶת, פֹּעֶלֶת, פֹּעֶלֶת, פֹּעֶלֶת) הְכֵלֶת *blue, or sky-coloured;* כֹּתֶרֶת *a crown, chapiter;* נְחֹשֶׁת *copper*, יְכֹלֶת *ability,* תּוֹלַעַת *a worm,* (פֹּעֶלֶת, פֹּעֶלֶת, פֹּעֶלֶת)—as, אַדֶּרֶת *a mantle,* קַדַּחַת *a fever;* ‡אִגֶּרֶת *a letter,;* כַּפֹּרֶת *a covering, the mercy seat,* כֻּסֶּמֶת *spelt,* (lit. *the shorn*), שִׁבֹּלֶת § *an ear of corn.*

---

* But from נְחֹשֶׁת we have נְחָשְׁתִּי, נְחָשְׁתְּךָ. From מַשְׂכֹּרֶת *hire,* we have מַשְׂכָּרְתִּי.

† *p.* עֲטָרוֹת (from עֲטָרָה) *g.* עַטְרוֹת.   ‡ אִגְּרוֹת.
§ *p.* שִׁבֳּלֵי, *g.* שִׁבֳּלִים.

מִלְחָמָה or מִלְחֶמֶת —as, (מִפְעָלָה or מִפְעֶלֶת, מִפְעָלֶת) מִשְׁקֶלֶת rule, dominion, מֶמְשָׁלָה a family, †מִשְׁפָּחָה war,

תִּפְאֶרֶת or תִּפְאָרָה —as, (תִּפְעָלָה or תִּפְעֶלֶת, אִפְעֶלֶת) glory, splendour; אַמְתַּחַת a sack.

שָׁבַת staying, sitting, (עֶלֶת —as, תּוֹעֶלֶת, מוֹעֶלֶת) שִׁבְתִּי my sitting, תּוֹחֶלֶת hope, מוֹלֶדֶת birth-place, native-place.

To the above class belong אִשָּׁת g. אֵשֶׁת or אִשָּׁה —אִשְׁתִּי, אִשְׁתְּךָ p. אִשּׁוֹת, or more usually נָשִׁים, g. p. נְשֵׁי־נָשֵׁי —נְשֵׁי־אֱמֶת truth, (for אֱמֶנֶת), is thus inflected אֲמִתִּי, אֲמִתְּךָ, אֲמִתּוֹ, &c.

Exercise.

In translating the following exercises, the student must insert the words is, ARE, &c., where he finds the asterisks* : as,—

כָּל־יְמֵי עָנִי¹ רָעִים, וְטוֹב לֵב² מִשְׁתֶּה תָמִיד

All the days of the afflicted man ARE *evil, and (but) a cheerful heart* is *a continual feast.*

שְׁמַע¹ בְּנִי² מוּסַר² אָבִיךָ, וְאַל־תִּטּוֹשׁ³ תּוֹרַת אִמֶּךָ:
יִרְאַת⁴ יְיָ* רֵאשִׁית⁵ דָּעַת⁶: מָוֶת⁷ וְחַיִּים* בְּיַד⁸ לָשׁוֹן⁹:

¹ Hear בְּן. ‡ ² Instruction. ³ Do not forsake. ⁴ Fear. ⁵ Beginning, or chief. ⁶ Knowledge. ⁷ Death. ⁸ Hand, power. ⁹ Tongue.

---

† Or מִשְׁפַּחַת, p. מִשְׁפָּחוֹת, g. p. מִשְׁפְּחוֹת.

‡ For the signification of the untranslated words, see the *Index of Words* at the end of the work.

THE HEBREW LANGUAGE. 83

הוֹן¹⁰ עָשִׁיר¹¹ קִרְיַת¹² עֹז¹³, מְחִתַּת¹⁴ דַלִּים¹⁵ רֵישָׁם¹⁶ : גַּם¹⁷
לְרֵעֵהוּ¹⁸ יִשָּׂנֵא¹⁹ רָשׁ²⁰, וְאֹהֲבֵי²¹ עָשִׁיר רַבִּים²² : כָּל־אֲחֵי רָשׁ
שְׂנֵאֻהוּ²³, וְדַל מֵרֵעֵהוּ יִפָּרֵד²⁴ : רֵעֲךָ וְרֵעַ אָבִיךָ אַל־תַּעֲזֹב²⁵,
וּבֵית אָחִיךָ אַל־תָּבוֹא²⁶ בְּיוֹם אֵידֶךָ²⁷ : שׁוֹט²⁸ לַסּוּס,
מֶתֶג²⁹ לַחֲמוֹר, וְשֵׁבֶט³⁰ לְגֵו³¹ כְּסִילִים³² : עֲטֶרֶת³³ זְקֵנִים
בְּנֵי בָנִים, וְתִפְאֶרֶת³⁴ בָּנִים אֲבוֹתָם³⁵ : עֲטֶרֶת תִּפְאֶרֶת
שֵׂיבָה³⁶, בְּדֶרֶךְ צְדָקָה³⁷ תִּמָּצֵא³⁸ : זֶבַח³⁹ רְשָׁעִים⁴⁰ תּוֹעֲבַת
יְיָ, וּתְפִלַּת⁴² יְשָׁרִים⁴³ רְצוֹנוֹ⁴⁴ : מַקְרִיב⁴⁵ זֶבַח מְחִיל⁴⁶ דַּלִּים
זוֹבֵחַ⁴⁷ בֵּן לְעֵינֵי⁴⁸ אָבִיו : זִבְחֵי צַדִּיקִים שַׁוְעַת⁴⁹ פִּיהֶם
וְקוֹל⁵⁰ רִנָּתָם⁵¹ יְבַקַּע⁵² שָׁמָיִם : בּוֹנֶה⁵³ בֵּיתוֹ בְּחֵיל זָרִים⁵⁴
כּוֹנֵס⁵⁵ אֲבָנִים⁵⁶ לְקִבְרוֹ⁵⁷ :

---

¹⁰ Wealth. ¹¹ The rich *man*.* ¹² City. ¹³ Strength. ¹⁴ Dread, destruction. ¹⁵ A poor *man*. ¹⁶ Poverty. ¹⁷ Likewise, even. ¹⁸ Neighbour, *friend*. ¹⁹ Is-hated. ²⁰ A poor *man*. ²¹ A lover, friend. ²² Many. ²³ Hate-him.† ²⁴ Is-separated. ²⁵ Do-not forsake. ²⁶ Do-not-come. ²⁷ Calamity. ²⁸ A whip. ²⁹ A bridle. ³⁰ A rod. ³¹ Body, back. ³² A fool. ³³ A crown. ³⁴ Glory. ³⁵ Parents. ³⁶ Old age. ³⁷ Righteousness. ³⁸ She-(it) will-be-found. ³⁹ Sacrifice. ⁴⁰ רָשָׁע a wicked man. ⁴¹ Abomination. ⁴² Prayer. ⁴³ יָשָׁר a *straight*, upright man. ⁴⁴ רָצוֹן will, delight, favor. ⁴⁵ He-that-offers. ⁴⁶ חַיִל wealth, substance, goods. ⁴⁷ *Is like one* that slays. ⁴⁸ Before-the-eyes-of, in-the-presence-of. ⁴⁹ Cry, supplication. ⁵⁰ Sound. ⁵¹ Song, prayer. ⁵² Cleaves, *penetrates*. ⁵³ He-that-builds. ⁵⁴ A stranger. ⁵⁵ Gathers. ⁵⁶ A stone. ⁵⁷ A grave.

---

* The words in *Italics* are not expressed in Hebrew.

† The words connected by *Hyphens* are expressed by one Hebrew word.

A virtuous woman [woman[1]-of virtue[2]] *is a* crown[3] to [of]-her husband,[4] but-[and]-as-rottenness[5] in his bones,[6] *is* one-that-causes-shame.[7]

House[8] and-wealth[9] *are the* inheritance[10]-of fathers[11], but-[and] from-the-Lord *is a* prudent[12]woman [woman prudent].

The way[13]-of *a*-fool[14] *is* right[15] in-his-*own*-eyes;[16] but-[*and*] *the*-wise-*man*[17] hearkens[18] unto counsel.[19]

The light[20]-of *the* eyes rejoices[21] *the* heart;[22] and-a-good-report[23] [*and-report good*] fattens[24] *the* bone.

In-*the*-light[25]-of *the* king's countenance [*face-of the*[26] *king*[27]] *is* life;[28] and-his-favour[29] *is as*-a-cloud[30]-of the latter-rain.[31]

The wrath[32]-of *a* king *is as* messengers[33]-of death: but [*and*] a wise man [a man wise[34]] will-pacify-it[35] [her].

The grave[36] and-destruction[37] *are* before[38] the Lord, how-much-more[39]-*then* the hearts-of *the* children[40]-of men? [*man*[41]].

אִשָּׁה [1] חַיִל [2] עֲטֶרֶת [3] בַּעֲלִי [4] רָקָב [5] עֶצֶם [6] עַצְמוֹת [7] p. מְבִישָׁה [8] בַּיִת [9] הוֹן
נַחֲלָה [10] אָב [11] מַשְׂכֶּלֶת [12] — [13] דֶּרֶךְ [14] אֱוִיל [15] יָשָׁר [16] עַיִן [17] חָכָם [18] שׁוֹמֵעַ [19]
עֵצָה [20] מָאוֹר [21] — [22] לֵב [23] יְשַׂמַּח [24] שְׁמוּעָה טוֹבָה [25] תְּדַשֵּׁן [26] אוֹר [27] פָּנִים
מֶלֶךְ [28] חַיִּים [29] רָצוֹן [30] עָב [31] מַלְקוֹשׁ [32] — [33] חֵמָה [34] מַלְאָךְ [35] p. מַלְאָכִים [36] אִישׁ חָכָם
יְכַפְּרֶנָּה [37] — [38] שְׁאוֹל [39] אֲבַדּוֹן [40] נֶגֶד [41] כִּי אַף [42] בֵּן [43] p. בָּנִים [44] אָדָם

CHAPTER IV.

Adjectives.

83. Adjectives are attributes expressive of the properties of nouns, conjointly with which they form either the subject, or some other part of a proposition: as—

מַעֲנֶה רַּךְ יָשִׁיב חֵמָה ׃ A soft *answer turneth away wrath.*

שְׁמוּעָה טוֹבָה תְּדַשֶּׁן עָצֶם ׃ A good *report maketh the bone fat.*

אֲרִי נֹהֵם וְדֹב שׁוֹקֵק As a roaring *lion, and* a greedy *bear, so is*

מוֹשֵׁל רָשָׁע עַל עַם דָּל ׃ A wicked *ruler over* a poor *people.*

84. As qualifying words, adjectives are placed after their respective nouns: thus, אִישׁ טוֹב *a man good*, i. e. *a good man;* but not טוֹב אִישׁ.

85. Adjectives agree with their nouns in gender and number :* thus—

---

* Adjectives, considered as mere attributes, cannot, strictly speaking, admit of either *gender* or *number;* but being in their origin, *nouns* or *participles,* in which sense they are still frequently used, the distinction of gender and number became necessary; and it was retained, even where they were used merely as qualifying words.

THE ETYMOLOGY OF

אִישׁ טוֹב *a good man*   אֲנָשִׁים טוֹבִים *good men*
אִשָּׁה טוֹבָה *a good woman*   נָשִׁים טוֹבוֹת *good women.*

86. Further, when the noun is in a definite state, that is, where the noun has the definite ה, or any of the pronominal affixes,* the adjective receives the definite ה; otherwise, the attribute ceases to be the qualifying word, and becomes the predicate of the noun which it accompanies.

Examples.

הָאִישׁ הַטּוֹב *the good man*
הָאִשָּׁה הַטּוֹבָה *the good woman*
הָאֲנָשִׁים הַטּוֹבִים *the good men*
הַנָּשִׁים הַטּוֹבוֹת *the good women*
בְּנִי הַקָּטָן *my little son*
בִּתְּךָ הַקְּטַנָּה *thy little daughter*
בָּנָיו הַקְּטַנִּים *his little sons*
בְּנוֹתֵיכֶם הַקְּטַנּוֹת *your little daughters*

הָאִישׁ טוֹב *the man is good*
הָאִשָּׁה טוֹבָה *the woman is good*
הָאֲנָשִׁים טוֹבִים *the men are good*
הַנָּשִׁים טוֹבוֹת *the women are good*

---

* Or with proper names, which are in their nature definite: thus שִׁמְעוֹן הַצַּדִּיק *the just Simeon* or *Simeon the just;* whereas שִׁמְעוֹן צַדִּיק signifies *Simeon is just.*

בְּנִי קָטֹן my son is *little*
בִּתְּךָ קְטַנָּה thy daughter is *little*
בָּנָיו קְטַנִּים his sons are *little*
בְּנוֹתֵיכֶם קְטַנּוֹת your daughters are *little*.

Comparison of Adjectives.

87. The degrees of comparison are expressed by prefixing to the noun, with which any thing is compared, the letters כ *as*, מ *from*, (*than*), and ב *in*, *amongst*; the adjective not being subject to any change, except to indicate the gender and number of the noun compared.

כ indicates equality : as—

גָּדוֹל כַּיָּם *great* As *the sea.*

מ or מִן indicates superiority : as—

גָּדוֹל מֵהַיָּם *great from the sea,* i. e. *greater than the sea.*

ב the superlative : as—

הַגָּדוֹל בָּאֲנָשִׁים *the great amongst men,* i. e. *the greatest of men.*

Additional Examples.

מִי זֹאת הַנִּשְׁקָפָה כְּמוֹ־שָׁחַר *Who* (is) *this that-looketh-forth as-the-dawn,*

יָפָה כַלְּבָנָה בָּרָה כַּחַמָּה *fair as-the-moon, pure as-the-sun.*

טוֹב חַסְדְּךָ מֵחַיִּים *Better* (is) *thy mercy than life.*

לֹא טוֹב אָנֹכִי מֵאֲבוֹתַי *I am not better than my ancestors.*

קַלִּים הָיוּ רֹדְפֵינוּ מִנִּשְׁרֵי שָׁמָיִם   *Our pursuers were swifter* than *the eagles of heaven.*

הִנֵּה אַלְפִּי הַדַּל בִּמְנַשֶּׁה   *Behold my thousand* (i. e. *my family*) [*is*] *the poorest* among *Manasseh;*

וְאָנֹכִי הַצָּעִיר בְּבֵית אָבִי   and *I* [am] *the* least *in my father's house.*

There are several other methods of indicating the *superlative*, for which the student is referred to the Syntax.

Exercise.

מֶלֶךְ¹, גָּדוֹל², הַמֶּלֶךְ, הַגָּדוֹל, הַמֶּלֶךְ גָּדוֹל*, הַמֶּלֶךְ הַגָּדוֹל,
גָּדוֹל² מְלָכִים גְּדוֹלִים, הַמְּלָכִים, גְּדוֹלִים*, הַמְּלָכִים הַגְּדוֹלִים,
עִיר³ גְּדֻלָה וַחֲזָקָה⁴, הָעִיר הַגְּדֻלָה וְהַחֲזָקָה, הָעִיר* גְּדוֹלָה
וַחֲזָקָה, עָרִים גְּדֹלוֹת, הֶעָרִים הַגְּדֹלוֹת, הֶעָרִים* גְּדֹלוֹת,
מָתוֹק⁵ בִּדְבַשׁ⁶, מָתוֹק מִדְּבַשׁ, מַר⁷ מִמָּוֶת⁸, מָרָה כַּלַּעֲנָה⁹,
חָלָק¹⁰ מִשֶּׁמֶן¹¹, הַגָּדוֹל בַּמְּלָכִים, הַקָּטֹן בָּאֲנָשִׁים, הַגִּבּוֹר¹²
בַּגִּבּוֹרִים, הֶחָכָם¹³ בַּחֲכָמִים:

¹ A king. ² Great. * Insert the copula is or are according as the noun is singular or plural. ³ עִיר a city, *p.* עָרִים. ⁴ חָזָק strong. ⁵ Sweet. ⁶ Honey. ⁷ Bitter. ⁸ Death. ⁹ Wormwood. ¹⁰ Smooth. ¹¹ Oil. ¹² Strong, mighty. ¹³ Wise.

מָתוֹק* הָאוֹר¹ וְטוֹב² לָעֵינַיִם³: מְתוּקָה⁴ שְׁנַת⁵
הָעֹבֵד⁵, כְּשׁוֹשַׁנָּה⁶ בֵּין⁷ הַחוֹחִים⁸, כֵּן⁹ רַעְיָתִי¹⁰ בֵּין

¹ Light. ² Good. ³ עַיִן eye. ⁴ שֵׁנָה sleep. ⁵ A labourer. ⁶ A rose. ⁷ Amongst. ⁸ חוֹחַ a thorn. ⁹ So. ¹⁰ רֹעָה a shepherdess.

THE HEBREW LANGUAGE.

הַבָּנוֹת ": כְּהֻמִין "² * לַשִּׁנַיִם "³ * וּבֶעָשָׁן "⁴ * לָעֵינַיִם כֵּן * הֶעָצֵל "⁵
לְשֹׁלְחָיו "⁶ : חֵלֶק מִשֶּׁמֶן "⁷ חִכּוֹ "⁷ * וְאַחֲרִיתָהּ "⁸ * מָרָה כַלַּעֲנָה :
עֵז "⁹ בָּמָּוֶת * אַהֲבָה ²⁰ קָשָׁה ²¹ מִשְׁאוֹל ²² * קִנְאָה ²³ * מַה ²⁴*
עַז מֵאֲרִי ²⁵ וּמַה מָּתוֹק מִדְּבָשׁ : טוֹב אַחֲרִית דָּבָר
מֵרֵאשִׁיתוֹ ²⁶ : טוֹבָה חָכְמָה ²⁷ מִגְּבוּרָה ²⁸ : טוֹב ²⁹ כֶּלֶב חַי
מֵאַרְיֵה מֵת : הָאָדָם ³⁰ הַגָּדוֹל בָּעֲנָקִים ³¹ , הִיא הָיְתָה ³²
יָפָה ³³ בַּנָּשִׁים וְהַנָּאוָה ³⁴ בַּבָּנוֹת :

¹¹ בַּת a daughter. p. בָּנוֹת. ¹² Vinegar. ¹³ שֵׁן a tooth. ¹⁴ Smoke.
¹⁵ Sluggard. ¹⁶ To those that send him. ¹⁷ חֵךְ the palate, gums.
¹⁸ End. ¹⁹ Strong, bold. ²⁰ Love. ²¹ Hard. ²² The grave. ²³ Jealousy.
²⁴ What. ²⁵ A lion. ²⁶ Beginning. ²⁷ Wisdom. ²⁸ Strength.
²⁹ A dog. ³⁰ Man. ³¹ A giant. ³² Was. ³³ Fair, beautiful.
³⁴ Comely, agreeable.

NUMERALS.

88. Numerals are generally divided into—

1st.—*Cardinals;* as,* אֶחָד *m.*, אַחַת *f.*, one,† שְׁלֹשָׁה *m.*
שָׁלֹשׁ *f. three.*

2nd.—*Ordinals:* as, רִאשׁוֹן *m.* רִאשׁוֹנָה *f. first*
שֵׁנִי, *m.* שֵׁנִית *second; and.*

3rd.—*Fractional:* as, חֲצִי *half,* שְׁלִישִׁית *a third part.*

---

* In Ezek. xviii. and xxxiii. we find the words אָח and חַד used for אֶחָד.

† It is very remarkable that (ָה) which is generally the characteristic of the feminine, becomes the sign of the masculine in the *numerals* from three to ten; the feminine being indicated by dropping the ָה. The only rational explanation that can be given of this peculiarity, is, that numerals, being in their nature abstract terms,

Cardinal Numbers.

89. Cardinal numbers, from one to twenty, admit of gender: as, אִישׁ אֶחָד *one man;* אִשָּׁה אַחַת *one woman;* אַחַד עָשָׂר בָּנִים *eleven sons,* אַחַת עֶשְׂרֵה בָּנוֹת *eleven daughters;* but above twenty they are common to both genders.

Further, from one to six inclusive, they assume frequently a constructive form * (which does not however alter their signification): as, אֶחָד *one,* אַחַד עָשָׂר *eleven;* שְׁנַיִם *two,* שְׁנַיִם עֵדִים or שְׁנֵי עֵדִים *two witnesses;* שָׁלֹשׁ *three,* שְׁלֹשׁ עֶשְׂרֵה *thirteen,* שְׁלֹשׁ מֵאוֹת *three hundred.*

---

have, like most other abstract nouns, originally received the same termination: as, for instance, חָכְמָה *wisdom,* גְּבוּרָה *strength,* תְּבוּנָה *understanding.* And however strange it may appear, that the *abstract* should have preceded the *concrete,* yet, that this was actually the process in the formation of language, may be proved by more arguments than one. Be this as it may, certain it is that the gender of numerals is an unnecessary incumbrance on language. That it may be dispensed with, without occasioning the least ambiguity, is evident from its extending only to numerals under *twenty.* Still more evident is it from the English language, which, in this respect, is the most rational of any language with which I am acquainted.

* This *form* appears similar to the *genitive* form of nouns; it does not, however, express the same relation. Except the words אַחַד and אַחַת, which are sometimes used in the genitive; as אַחַד הֶהָרִים *one-of the mountains;* אַחַת עָרֶיךָ *one-of thy cities.* But even these cease to be *genitives* when followed by מ; as, אַחַד מִבָּנָיו *one of his sons;* אַחַת מֵעֵינֶיךָ *one of thine eyes,* *of* being expressed by מ, which literally means *from,* and not by the *form* of the *numeral.*

90. Cardinal numbers from one to ten.

	Fem.		Mas.			
	Const.	Absolute.	Const.	Absolute.		
One	אַחַת	אֶחָת	אַחַד	אֶחָד†	1	א*
Two	שְׁתֵּי or שְׁתֵּים	שְׁתַּיִם	שְׁנֵי or שְׁנֵים	שְׁנַיִם	2	ב
Three	שְׁלֹשׁ	שָׁלֹשׁ	שְׁלֹשֶׁת‡	שְׁלֹשָׁה	3	ג
Four	—	אַרְבַּע	אַרְבַּעַת	אַרְבָּעָה	4	ד
Five	חֲמֵשׁ	חָמֵשׁ	חֲמֵשֶׁת	חֲמִשָּׁה	5	ה
Six	שֵׁשׁ	שֵׁשׁ	שֵׁשֶׁת	שִׁשָּׁה	6	ו
Seven	שְׁבַע	שֶׁבַע	שִׁבְעַת	שִׁבְעָה	7	ז
Eight	—	שְׁמֹנֶה	שְׁמוֹנַת	שְׁמֹנָה	8	ח
Nine	תְּשַׁע	תֵּשַׁע	תִּשְׁעַת	תִּשְׁעָה	9	ט
Ten	—	עֶשֶׂר	עֲשֶׂרֶת	עֲשָׂרָה	10	י

* The *letters* are used as *numerals* in the printed Hebrew Bibles, to mark the Chapters and Verses: and by the *Masoretical* and *Rabbinical* writers for various other purposes; but they are never used in the sacred text. The following are a few specimens of this species of notation. Number of verses contained—

In Genesis   אך לד = 1000 + 500 + 30 + 4 = 1534
   Exodus   ארט = 1000 + 200 + 9   = 1209
   Leviticus   נטף = 50 + 9 + 800   = 859
   Numbers   ארפח = 1000 + 200 + 80 + 8 = 1288
   Deuteronomy   הנן = 5 + 50 + 900   = 955

† אֶחָד and עֲשָׂרָה admit of the plural: as, אֲחָדִים *units*, עֲשָׂרוֹת *tens, decades*.

‡ Many Grammarians consider the numerals having the termination (ת) as nouns denoting a collection of units: as, for instance, שְׁלֹשֶׁת יָמִים a *triad* of days, or a period of time consisting of

Ten to twenty.

	Mas.	Fem.		
Eleven	——	אַחַד עָשָׂר*	אַחַת עֶשְׂרֵה	11	יא
Twelve	——	שְׁנֵים עָשָׂר	שְׁתֵּים עֶשְׂרֵה	12	יב
Thirteen	——	שְׁלֹשָׁה עָשָׂר	שְׁלֹשׁ עֶשְׂרֵה	13	יג
Fourteen	——	אַרְבָּעָה עָשָׂר	אַרְבַּע עֶשְׂרֵה	14	יד
Fifteen	——	חֲמִשָּׁה עָשָׂר	חָמֵשׁ עֶשְׂרֵה	15	טו
Sixteen	——	שִׁשָּׁה עָשָׂר	שֵׁשׁ עֶשְׂרֵה	16	טז
Seventeen	——	שִׁבְעָה עָשָׂר	שְׁבַע עֶשְׂרֵה	17	יז
Eighteen	——	שְׁמֹנָה עָשָׂר	שְׁמֹנֶה עֶשְׂרֵה	18	יח
Nineteen	——	תִּשְׁעָה עָשָׂר	תְּשַׁע עֶשְׂרֵה	19	יט

Twenty and upwards.

Twenty.............................	עֶשְׂרִים	כ
Twenty-one..................	אֶחָד וְעֶשְׂרִים	כא
Twenty-two.................	שְׁנַיִם וְעֶשְׂרִים	כב
Twenty-three..............	שְׁלֹשָׁה וְעֶשְׂרִים	כג
Thirty...........................	שְׁלֹשִׁים	ל
Forty............................	אַרְבָּעִים	מ

---

three days, עֲשֶׂרֶת אֲנָשִׁים, a *decade* of men. This distinction appears to me merely imaginary, as I really can discover no difference of meaning between שְׁמֹנַת עָשָׂר אֶלֶף and שְׁמֹנָה עָשָׂר אֶלֶף. (Judg. xx. 25—44.) Or between וְלַנְּקֵבָה עֲשֶׂרֶת שְׁקָלִים and וְלַנְּקֵבָה עֲשָׂרָה שְׁקָלִים (Lev. xxvii. 5—7.)

*Or עַשְׁתֵּי עֶשְׂרֵה, עַשְׁתֵּי עָשָׂר.

THE HEBREW LANGUAGE.

Fifty	חֲמִשִּׁים	נ
Sixty	שִׁשִּׁים	ס
Seventy	שִׁבְעִים	ע
Eighty	שְׁמֹנִים	פ
Ninety	תִּשְׁעִים	צ
Hundred	מֵאָה cons. מְאַת	ק
Two Hundred	מָאתַיִם or שְׁנֵי מֵאוֹת	ר
Three Hundred	שְׁלֹשׁ מֵאוֹת	ש
Four Hundred	אַרְבַּע מֵאוֹת	ת
Five Hundred	חֲמֵשׁ מֵאוֹת	ך
Six Hundred	שֵׁשׁ מֵאוֹת	ם
Seven Hundred	שְׁבַע מֵאוֹת	ן
Eight Hundred	שְׁמֹנֶה מֵאוֹת	ף
Nine Hundred	תְּשַׁע מֵאוֹת	ץ
A Thousand	אֶלֶף	א
Two Thousand	אַלְפַּיִם · שְׁנֵי אֲלָפִים	ב
Three Thousand	שְׁלֹשֶׁת אֲלָפִים	ג
Ten Thousand	רִבּוֹא · עֲשֶׂרֶת אֲלָפִים	י
Twenty Thousand	רִבּוֹאתַיִם	כ
Thirty Thousand	שְׁלֹשׁ רִבּוֹא	
Hundred Thousand	מְאַת אֶלֶף	
Two Millions	עֶשְׂרִים מֵאוֹת אֶלֶף	

Ordinal Numbers.

91. The following are the Ordinal Numbers:

First............	רִאשׁוֹנָה............	רִאשׁוֹן
Second............	שֵׁנִית............	שֵׁנִי
Third............	שְׁלִישִׁית............	שְׁלִישִׁי
Fourth............	רְבִיעִית............	רְבִיעִי
Fifth............	חֲמִישִׁית............	חֲמִישִׁי
Sixth............	שִׁשִּׁית............	שִׁשִּׁי
Seventh............	שְׁבִיעִית............	שְׁבִיעִי
Eighth............	שְׁמִינִית............	שְׁמִינִי
Ninth............	תְּשִׁיעִית............	תְּשִׁיעִי
Tenth............	עֲשִׂירִית............	עֲשִׂירִי

Obs. 1.—The *Ordinals* are formed from their *Cardinals*, in the same manner as *Patronymics* are formed from *Proper Names**. Thus, from שְׁנַיִם *two,*—שֵׁנִי, שֵׁנִית *second.* From שֵׁשׁ *six,*—שִׁשִּׁי שִׁשִּׁית *sixth.* The rest take an additional י between the second and third radical: as, from שָׁלֹשׁ *three, m.* שְׁלִישִׁי. *f.* שְׁלִישִׁית. Except רִאשׁוֹן, derived from רֹאשׁ *the head, chief.*

2.—Above ten, the cardinal numbers are used to express the ordinals: but then the number always follows the noun, or the noun is repeated:—Thus, שְׁנֵים עָשָׂר יוֹם *twelve days,* but יוֹם הַשְּׁנֵים עָשָׂר יוֹם or הַשְּׁנַיִם עָשָׂר *the twelfth day,* חֲמִשִּׁים שָׁנָה *fifty years;* but שְׁנַת הַחֲמִשִּׁים or שָׁנָה הַחֲמִשִּׁים *the fiftieth year.*

Even from one to ten, the cardinals are often used for the ordinals: as, בִּשְׁנַת אַרְבַּע *in the year four,* בִּשְׁנַת שֶׁבַע *in the year seven, i. e. in the fourth, seventh, year.*†

---

* As from מִצְרִי,—מִצְרַיִם, and מִצְרִית·

† In such cases the numeral is always followed by ל: as, בֶּעָשׂוֹר לַחֹדֶשׁ *in the tenth day of the month.*

Fractional Numbers.

92. The Fractional numbers are, חֵצִי *m.*, מֶחֱצָה *f.* *a half, gen.* חֲצִי *m.* מֶחֱצַת or מַחֲצִית *f.* The rest of the *fractional* numbers are indicated by placing the feminine *ordinals* before the noun: thus, שְׁלִישִׁית הַשָּׁנָה *the third (part) of a year;* whereas, שָׁנָה הַשְּׁלִישִׁית signifies, *the third year.* In some cases the noun is omitted: as, ' And ye shall give חֲמִישִׁית *a fifth unto Pharaoh.*'— (Gen. xlvii. 24.)

The student may, by way of exercise, translate the fifth chapter of Genesis, verses 3—39; or chapter xi. verses 19—26, which contain most of the cardinal numbers.

CHAPTER V.

Pronouns.

93. Pronouns are generally divided into Personal, Demonstrative, Relative, and Interrogative.

94. Personal pronouns are declined in the same manner as nouns; namely, by means of prepositions or their fragments, which are added to the terminations of the pronouns: thus, the preposition, אֶל *to,* and the termination י (from אֲנִי *I*), form אֵלִי; or still further abridged, לִי *to* or *for me;* and with נוּ (from אָנוּ *we,* לָנוּ *to us.* Thus likewise מִן *from,* and י, forms מִנִּי or מִמֶּנִּי *from me.* (See the following Table.)

Personal Pronouns.—Table IX.

	3rd Person.		2nd Person.		1st Person. אֲנִי*		
							Singular.
She	הִיא	Thou m.	אַתָּה	I	אָנֹכִי[1]	Nom.
To her	לָהּ	To thee	לְךָ	To, or for me	לִי[3]	Dat.
Her	אֹתָהּ	Thee	אֹתְךָ	Me	אֹתִי[9]	Obj.
From her	מִמֶּנָּה	From thee	מִמְּךָ	From me	מִמֶּנִּי[5]	Abl.
On her	עָלֶיהָ	In, or on thee	בְּךָ	In or on me	בִּי[6]	Abl.
As she	כָּמוֹהָ	As thou	כָּמוֹךָ	As I	כָּמוֹנִי[9]	Comp.
							Plural.
They	הֵם	You	אַתֶּם[11]	We	אֲנַחְנוּ[10]	Nom.
To them	לָהֶם[13]	To you	לָכֶם	To, or for us	לָנוּ	Dat.
Them	אֹתָם[15]	You	אֶתְכֶם	Us	אֹתָנוּ	Obj.
From them	מֵהֶם[17]	From you	מִכֶּם	From us	מִמֶּנּוּ	Abl.
On them	עֲלֵיהֶם[18]	On you	עֲלֵיכֶם	On us	עָלֵינוּ	Abl.
As they	כָּהֵם[20]	As you	כָּכֶם	As we	כָּמוֹנוּ[19]	Comp.

[1] Likewise, אֲנִי. [2] In pause, הִיא. [3] In pause, לִי. [4] In pause, אֹתִי, likewise, אֹתָנוּ. [5] Or מִמֶּנִּי. [6] In pause, בִּי. [7] Or מִמֶּנָּה. [8] In pause, בָּהּ. [9] Or כָּמֹנִי. [10] Likewise, אֲנַחְנוּ. [11] Or אַתֵּן f. [12] Or לָכֶן. [13] Or לָמוֹ. [14] Or אֶתְהֶן, or אֶתְכֶן. [15] Or אֹתָן. [16] Or מִכֶּן. [17] Or מֵהֶן. [18] Or עֲלֵיהֶן. [19] Or כָּמֹנוּ f. כָּהֵן. [20] Or כָּהֶם.

* In compliance with custom, I have denominated לְ, אֶת, בְּ, by the usual technical terms, Dative, Objective, &c ; but the student will readily perceive, that these words, except that they express the same relations denoted by *cases* in other languages, have little else in common ; and if it be correct to denominate prepositions inflected by pronominal affixes, *cases*, then we shall have in Hebrew as many cases of pronouns as there are prepositions in the language.

95. Each of the preceding pronouns may be further varied :—

1st.—By the conjunctive וְ *and:* as, וַאֲנִי *and I*, &c. וְלִי *and unto me*, וּמִמֶּנָּה *and from her*, וְאוֹתִי *and me*, וּבָהֶם *and on or amongst them.*

2nd.—By the interrogative הֲ: as, הַאַתָּה בְּנִי *art-thou my son?* הֲמִמֶּנִּי יִפָּלֵא כָּל־דָּבָר *if-for-us thou*, i. e. *art thou for us?* הֲלָנוּ אַתָּה *if-from-me can be difficult any thing*, i. e. *is their any thing too difficult for me?*

3rd.—By שׁ (from אֲשֶׁר) *that, which:* as, שֶׁאֲנִי *that I*, שֶׁהֵם *that they*, שֶׁלִּי *that which belongs to me*, שֶׁלְּךָ *that which belongs to thee.*

Obs.—שֶׁלִּי, שֶׁלְּךָ, &c. are considered, by some Grammarians, as possessive pronouns, corresponding with *my, thy, &c.* or with *mine, thine,* &c. They are, however, seldom used (except by Rabbinical writers) in either of these senses, and are evidently compounded of שׁ and the dative pronouns, in the same manner as the Chaldaic and Syriac דִּילִי, דִּילָךְ, ܕܝܠܝ, ܕܝܠܟ, are compounded of דִּי *which,* לִי *to me,* &c.

The manner in which the Hebrew expresses the relative possessive pronouns, *my, thy, his,* &c., is, by adding the pronominal affixes to the substantive, as has already been explained in the preceding pages; whilst the absolute possessive, *mine, thine, his, &c.,* are expressed by the dative pronouns, לִי *to me,* לְךָ *to thee,* &c.: as, לִי כָּל־הָאָרֶץ ' Mine *is the whole earth,*' (Exod. xix. 5.) לוֹ יִהְיֶה ' *To him it shall be,* i. e. his, (Levit. viii. 8—9.) לְךָ שָׁמַיִם אַף לְךָ אָרֶץ ' Thine are the *heavens,* thine *also is the earth,* (Psalm xcix. 11.) דּוֹדִי לִי וַאֲנִי לוֹ ' *My beloved is* mine, *and I am* his, (Cant. ii. 16).

The pronouns הוּא, הִיא, הֵם, הֵן, are sometimes used as demonstratives. (See the following section).

Demonstrative Pronouns.

96. The following are the Demonstrative Pronouns:

זֶה, rarely, זוּ, *m.* זֹאת, rarely זוֹ, *f.* —— —— This

הַלָּזֶה, *m.* הַלֵּזוּ *f.* —— הַלָּז *Com.* That yonder

אֵלֶּה, rarely אֵל. —— —— These *or* those

They are declined thus :—

These אֵלֶּה	This זֹאת	This זֶה	Nom.
To these לְאֵלֶּה	To this לְזֹאת	To this לְזֶה	Dative.
These אֶת־אֵלֶּה	This אֶת־זֹאת	This אֶת־זֶה	Ob.
From these מֵאֵלֶּה	From this מִזֹּאת	From this מִזֶּה	Ab.
With these בְּאֵלֶּה	With this בְּזֹאת	In this בָּזֶה	
As these כְּאֵלֶּה	As this כְּזֹאת	As this כָּזֶה	Com.

97. הוּא and הִיא are frequently used for the demonstrative pronoun, *that*; and הֵם and הֵן for *those*; but they cannot, like the preceding, receive any of the prefixes (except הַ). The rest of the prefixes, when required, are added to the noun: as, הָאִישׁ הַהוּא *that man*, מִן הָאִישׁ הַהוּא *from that man*, בָּאִישׁ הַהוּא *on* or *against that man*.

98. Demonstrative pronouns, like other definitives and adjectives, follow the nouns to which they belong: as—

הָאִישׁ הַזֶּה *this man*		הָאִישׁ הַהוּא *that man*	
הָאִשָּׁה הַזֹּאת *this woman*		הָאִשָּׁה הַהִיא *that woman*	
הָאֲנָשִׁים הָאֵלֶּה *these men*		הָאֲנָשִׁים הָהֵם *those men*	
הַנָּשִׁים הָאֵלֶּה *these women*		הַנָּשִׁים הָהֵן׃ *those women.*	

But when the pronouns precede their substantives, the הַ is omitted, and the verb, *to be*, is understood: as, זֶה הָאִישׁ *This is the man*, הוּא הַדָּבָר *That is the thing*, הִיא הָאִשָּׁה *That is the woman*, אֵלֶּה הָאֲנָשִׁים *These are the men*, וְאֵלֶּה שְׁמוֹת בְּנֵי יִשְׂרָאֵל *And-these are the-names-of the-sons-of Israel.*

Relative Pronouns.

99. The relative pronoun אֲשֶׁר (as a prefix שֶׁ), *who, which, that, what,* is indeclinable; the gender, number and case being indicated by the variation of the noun, or some other word in the sentence.

Examples.

יְהוָֹה אֲשֶׁר דִּבֶּר לִי *The-Lord* WHO *spake to me.* (Gen. xxiv. 17.)

אִישׁ אֲשֶׁר אִמּוֹ *A man* WHO HIS *mother,* i. e. *a man* whose *mother.*

הַנַּעֲרָה אֲשֶׁר אֹמַר אֵלֶיהָ *The damsel* WHO *I shall say* TO HER i. e. *the damsel to* whom *I shall say.*

הָאָרֶץ אֲשֶׁר יָצָאתָ מִשָּׁם *The-land* WHICH *thou-didst go-out* FROM *there,* i. e. *the land* from which or whence *thou camest.* (Gen. xxiv. 5.)

הָאָרֶץ אֲשֶׁר אַתָּה שֹׁכֵב עָלֶיהָ *The land* WHICH *thou liest* UPON *her,* i. e. upon which *thou liest* (Gen. xxviii. 13).

אִישׁ אֲשֶׁר רוּחַ אֱלֹהִים בּוֹ *A-man* WHO *the-spirit-of God* IN-HIM, i. e. in whom *the spirit of God is.* (Gen. xli. 38.)

In elliptical phrases, however, where the antecedent is omitted, the relative admits of the prefixes מ, ל, כ, ב; as, כַּאֲשֶׁר, בַּאֲשֶׁר. (See Syntax.)

100. Before verbs, and especially before participles, the definite הַ is frequently used instead of the relative: as, הַסֹּבֵב *which compasses* (Gen. ii. 10), הַהֹלֵךְ *which goeth* (Gen. ii. 14), הַהֹלֵךְ *who went* (Gen. xiii. 5), Lit. *the compasser, the goer.*

Interrogative Pronouns.

101. The interrogative pronouns are מִי *who?* מָה מֶה* *what? how?* as, מִי אַתָּה *who art thou?* מִי הָאִישׁ הַזֶּה *who is this man?* מִי אַתְּ בִּתִּי *who art thou, my daughter?* מָה אֹמַר *what shall I say?* מַה שְּׁמוֹ *what is his name?* מַה טּוֹב *how good!* מַה נּוֹרָא *how awful!*

Obs.—מִי is applied to persons, מָה to things: מִי הוּא signifies *who is he?* מִי הִיא *who is she?* But מַה הוּא (*what he*), מַה־הִיא (*what she*), signify *what is* IT? The same מִי אֵלֶּה *who are these (persons)?* but מָה אֵלֶּה *what are these (things).*

מִי is thus declined:—מִי *who,* לְמִי *to whom* or *whose,* אֶת־מִי *whom,* מִמִּי *from whom,* בְּמִי *with* or *through whom.*

The manner in which the adjective pronouns, *each, every, any, one, none, all, such,* &c., are expressed, will be explained in the Syntax.

---

* מָה generally before words beginning with ח or ע (excepting in seven places, according to the *Masorah,* where it is sometimes מֶה or מַה); מֶה before those which begin with א, ה, or ר, except before הוּא and הִיא, where it is always מַה.

THE HEBREW LANGUAGE.

Exercise.

גֵּר אָנֹכִי ¹ עִמָּכֶם ׃ אָנֹכִי ² בִּנְךָ ³ ׃ מִי ⁴ אַתָּה בְּנִי ⁵ ׃
מִי ⁶ אַתְּ בִּתִּי ⁷ ׃ בֶּן־אַבְרָהָם אָנִי ⁸ ׃ בַּת בְּתוּאֵל אָנֹכִי ׃
אֲנִי ⁹ יוֹסֵף אֲחִיכֶם אֲשֶׁר מְכַרְתֶּם ¹⁰ אֹתִי מִצְרָיְמָה ׃ אִמְרִי
אֲחֹתִי ¹¹ אָתְּ ׃ הוּא אָמַר לִי אֲחֹתִי הִיא וְהִיא אָמְרָה ¹²
אָחִי הוּא ׃ אֶת־אַחַי אָנֹכִי מְבַקֵּשׁ ¹³ הַגִּידָה ¹⁴ לִי אֵיפֹה
הֵם רֹעִים ¹⁵ ׃ וַיֹּאמֶר ¹⁶ אֲלֵיהֶם מְרַגְּלִים ¹⁷ אַתֶּם ׃ וַיֹּאמְרוּ ¹⁸
אֵלָיו לֹא ¹⁹ אֲדֹנִי ²⁰ כֻּלָּנוּ ²¹ בְּנֵי אִישׁ אֶחָד נָחְנוּ ²² בָּנִים ²³
אֲנַחְנוּ ׃ שְׁנֵים עָשָׂר עֲבָדֶיךָ ²⁴ אַחִים אֲנַחְנוּ בְּנֵי אִישׁ
אֶחָד בְּאֶרֶץ כְּנָעַן ׃ לְמִי אַתָּה וְאָנָה תֵלֵךְ וּלְמִי אֵלֶּה
לְפָנֶיךָ ²⁵ ׃ הַשְׁלִיכוּ ²⁶ אֹתוֹ אֶל הַבּוֹר הַזֶּה אֲשֶׁר בַּמִּדְבָּר וְיָד
אַל־תִּשְׁלְחוּ ²⁷ בּוֹ ׃

¹ בֵּן. ² First-born. ³ בַּת. ⁴ אָח a brother. ⁵ Ye have sold.
⁶ מִצְרַיִם Egypt. ⁷ Say. ⁸ אָחוֹת a sister. ⁹ He said. ¹⁰ She said.
¹¹ Seeking. ¹² Tell. ¹³ Pasturing. ¹⁴ And he said. ¹⁵ מְרַגֵּל a spy.
¹⁶ And they said. ¹⁷ No. ¹⁸ אָדוֹן a lord. ¹⁹ כֹּל all. ²⁰ בֵּן honest,
upright. ²¹ עֶבֶד. ²² Before thee. ²³ Cast ye. ²⁴ Ye shall not *send*,
i. e. *lay*.

לָמָּה רִמִּיתֶם ¹ אֹתָנוּ לֵאמֹר ² רְחוֹקִים ³ אֲנַחְנוּ מִכֶּם
מְאֹד ⁴ וְאַתֶּם בְּקִרְבֵּנוּ ⁵ יֹשְׁבִים ⁶ ׃ הִנֵּה ⁷ אָנֹכִי בָּא ⁸ אֶל בְּנֵי
יִשְׂרָאֵל וְאָמַרְתִּי ⁹ לָהֶם אֱלֹהֵי ¹⁰ אֲבוֹתֵיכֶם ¹¹ שְׁלָחַנִי ¹² אֲלֵיכֶם

¹ Have ye deceived. ² Saying. ³ רָחוֹק distant. ⁴ Very. ⁵ קֶרֶב
midst. ⁶ יֹשֵׁב one that sits, dwells. ⁷ Behold. ⁸ Come. ⁹ And
I say. ¹⁰ The-God-of. ¹¹ אָבוֹת fathers. ¹² He-has-sent-me.

וַאֲמָרוּ"¹³ לִי מַה"· שְׁמוֹ"¹⁴· מָה אֹמַר"¹⁵ אֲלֵיהֶם: מַה"· זֹאת עָשָׂה"
אֱלֹהִים לָנוּ : מֶה"· הַמַּעֲשֶׂה"¹⁷ הַזֶּה אֲשֶׁר עֲשִׂיתֶם"¹⁸ : אַתֶּם
יְדַעְתֶּן"¹⁹ כִּי²⁰ בְּכָל־כֹּחִי"²¹ עָבַדְתִּי"²² אֶת־אֲבִיכֶן"²³ וַאֲבִיכֶן
הֵתֵל"²⁴ בִּי : הִנֵּה לִי שְׁתֵּי בָנוֹת אוֹצִיאָה"²⁵ אֶתְהֶן אֲלֵיכֶם
אֵינֶנּוּ גָדוֹל בַּבַּיִת הַזֶּה מִמֶּנִּי וְלֹא־חָשַׂךְ"²⁶ מִמֶּנִּי מְאוּמָה"²⁷
כִּי־אִם"²⁸ אוֹתָךְ : בְּזֹאת נֵאוֹת"²⁹ לָכֶם אִם תִּהְיוּ כָמוֹנוּ :
גוּר"³⁰ בָּאָרֶץ הַזֹּאת : אֶרֶץ אֲשֶׁר אֲבָנֶיהָ"³¹ בַרְזֶל :

¹³ And-they-shall-say. ¹⁴ שֵׁם a name. ¹⁵ Shall I say. ¹⁶ Did. ¹⁷ Deed.
¹⁸ Ye have done. ¹⁹ Know. ²⁰ That. ²¹ כֹּחַ strength. ²² I-have-served.
²³ אָב ²⁴ He has deceived (deceit accompanied with derision).
²⁵ I-will bring out. ²⁶ He did not withhold. ²⁷ Any thing. ²⁸ But.
²⁹ We will consent. ³⁰ Dwell. ³¹ אֶבֶן

I *am* thy*-father, and-thou* *art* my-daughter.†
She *is* my-mother, and-these *are* her-children. This
is my little son, and-this *is* my little daughter. He
loved¹ her more-than-all² his-children. They are my
father's brothers, and she is my sister. Is this your
little brother who called³ me? Is this the little girl
who said⁴ that⁵ her father loved her more than all his
daughters? This *is* not the city,* nor is this the
house,ᵐ which I have built.⁶ Who *art* thou, my son?
and what is thy name? Who *art* thou, my-dauhtger?

בָּנִיתִי ⁶ כִּי ⁵ אָמְרָה ⁴ קָרָא ³ מִכָּל ² אָהַב ¹

---

† The Hebrew of most of the phrases contained in this exercise
will be found, with very slight alterations, in the first part of this
work, pp. 87 – 89.

and-what *is* thy-name? He *is a* wise man and a great king. She *is* fairer[7] than-her-sister, and the most comely[8] amongst daughters. His little brother will-be greater[9]-than-he. Whose *art* thou,[m] and whither goest[10]-thou, and whose *are* these before[11]-thee? Whither is thy[f] beloved [12] gone [went[13]], O *thou* fairest of women! whither did thy beloved turn[14] that-we-may-seek-him[15] with thee.[16]

הָלַךְ [13]   דּוֹר [12]   לְפָנֶיךָ [11]   תֵּלֵךְ [10]   יִגְדַּל [9]   נָאוָה [8]   יָפָה [7]
פָּנָה [14]   וּנְבַקְשֶׁנּוּ [15]   עִם [16]

CHAPTER VI.

Verbs.

102. Verbs are either Primitive or Derivative, (art. 18, page 20.) Perfect or Imperfect,* (art. 13—16.) Primitive verbs are either transitive, intransitive, or neuter. Derivative verbs are either active, passive, or reflective.

Primitive transitive verbs admit of seven principal forms, divisions, or branches†, denominated—
1, קַל or פָּעַל; 2, נִפְעַל; 3, פִּעֵל; 4, פֻּעַל; 5, הִפְעִיל; 6, הָפְעַל; 7, הִתְפַּעֵל. (Art. 18.)

---

* All verbs not included in the first conjugation, (Art. 13.) are called *imperfect*.

† The want of a technical term to designate these variations collectively, is particularly felt in treating of this part of Hebrew

Obs 1.— Intransitive verbs do not, of course, admit of all the preceding forms ; nor, indeed, do all transitive verbs,— some being used in one form only, others in several, and few in all.

2.—The first of these forms, קַל, is appropriated to primitive verbs, the rest to the derivatives.

3.— קַל, פָּעֵל and הִפְעִיל, are called *active forms*, because they are mostly used in an active sense. נִפְעַל, פֻּעַל, and הָפְעַל, are denominated *passive forms*, and הִתְפָּעֵל, the *reflective form.* *

4.—These several forms or branches may be considered as so many separate verbs, each of which admits of mood, tense, person, &c,; they are all derived from one and the same root, which mostly consists of three letters, denominated *radicals.* †
(Art. 18.)

Character and Signification of the several Forms or Branches.

103. קַל or פָּעַל expresses simple action, (transitive or intransitive,) *being* or *a state of being* ; as,

---

Grammar. The name בִּנְיָנִים *buildings*, used by the ancient Grammarians, would sound rather awkwardly in English ; still more objectionable are the modern denominations, *voices, conjugations,* &c. as they are apt to mislead the student. For want of a more suitable term, we shall denominate them *forms* or *branches*.

* Some verbs admit of several other *forms*, denominated פְּעַלְעַל, פְּעַלְעֵל, הִתְפָּעֵל, פִּלְפֵּל, &c. but as these occur very rarely, it was not thought necessary to enumerate them.

† Letters added to the root for the purpose of modification are, by way of distinction, denominated *serviles*. (See Note p.16.) Those that are added to some part of the verb by way of euphony or emphasis, are called *Paragogic*. They are ה, ו, י, מ, נ, and, in a few instances, א.

פָּקַד to visit,* פָּקַד he visited; הָיָה to be, הָיָה he was; חָלָה to be sick, חָלָה he was sick.

104. נִפְעַל expresses the *passive* of the preceding *form*. Its characteristic is the *prefix* (נ): as, נִכְסוֹף to be desirous; נִפְקַד he was visited. This letter is, however, dropped, and its omission indicated by *dagesh* in the first letter of the root, whenever it is preceded by another *servile*: as, הִפָּקֵד (for הִנְפָּקֵד) to be visited; אֶשָּׁבֵר (for אֶנְשָׁבֵר) *I shall be broken.*

Obs. 1.—When the first radical happens to be a *guttural*, the *dagesh* is compensated by placing a long vowel under the preceding servile: as, הֵאָכֵל *to be eaten.*

2.—Neuter verbs cannot, strictly speaking, admit of a passive; there are, nevertheless, many verbs of this description found in the passive form; but then they generally indicate a transition from one state into another: as from הָיָה *he existed,* נִהְיָה *he became, was brought into existence, it happened.* From חָלָה *to be sick,* נֶחֱלָה *he became sick.*

3.—Some verbs of this form have apparently a reflective signification: as, וָאֵחָבֵא and *I hid myself* (Gen. iii. 18.), הִפָּרֵד *separate thyself,* (Gen. xiii. 13.), הֵאָסְפוּ *gather yourselves together,*

---

* The primary signification of this verb (פָּקַד) is to view anything with the mental eye, to bear it in mind, have a regard for it; and hence its secondary meaning:—to visit, inspect, examine, review, muster, number, to appoint a person as an inspector, to intrust a person with any thing; in which senses we find this verb used in its several branches, in various parts of *Scripture.* For the sake of convenience, however, we shall render it by *to visit.*

(Gen. xlix. 1.); but even these indicate rather an abstaining from action than reflex action, and may, in most cases, be rendered in the passive*: thus, וָאֵחָבֵא and *I remained hidden*, (*I hid myself*, would be וָאֶתְחַבֵּא), as in Gen. iii. 8, וַיִּתְחַבֵּא *and he hid himself*); הִפָּרֵד *be separated*, i. e. *do not follow me*; הִשָּׁמֶר *take heed, beware*, i. e. *abstain from doing* (Gen. xxxi. 24); הֵאָסְפוּ *remain assembled*.

4.—A few words of this form are apparently used in an active sense: as, נִשְׁבַּע *he swore*, נִלְחַם *he fought*, נֶאֱנַח *he sighed*; but they do not entirely lose their passive signification; for, he that swears, is at the same time sworn, *i. e.* made to do so by some authority; and he that fights, is at the same time fought. נֶאֱנַח means literally *he became eased*, the physical effect of sighing.

105. פִּעֵל has generally a transitive signification†, and indicates mostly intense action and energy; but sometimes it has a frequentative or a causative meaning. Its characteristic is *dagesh* in the second letter of the root; as—

---

* *Ewald* in his "*Kritische Grammatik der Hebraische Sprache*," Art. 103, maintains that the primary signification of this *form* is reflective. But in adopting this opinion, the learned author appears to me to have made the *exceptions* the *rule*, and the rule the exception; as, for every single instance where this form denotes reflex action, there are hundreds where it cannot be rendered otherwise than in a passive sense. Thus — Gen. ii. 4, בְּהִבָּרְאָם; ii. 23, יִקָּרֵא; iii. 4, וְנִפְקְחוּ; 7, וַתִּפָּקַחְנָה; iv. 18, וַיִּוָּלֵד; v. 2, הִבָּרְאָם; vi. 21, יֵאָכֵל; vii. 11, נִבְקְעוּ, נִפְתָּחוּ; 22, וַיִּמַּח; viii. 2, וַיִּסָּכְרוּ, וַיִּכָּלֵא; 5, נִרְאוּ; ix. ibid. יִפָּרֶת, וְנִרְאֲתָה; x. 9, יֵאָמַר, &c.

† In a few instances it is used intransitively, without losing its signification of intensity; as, מִהַר *he hastened*; צָמַח *it sprouted, grew*; צִצָּה *it grew rapidly, abundantly*.

Kal.		Piel.	
שָׁבַר	to break.	שִׁבַּר	to break in pieces, to shatter.
אָבַד	to be lost, to perish.	אִבֵּד	to destroy, to ruin.
רָדַף	to pursue.	רִדֵּף	to pursue continually, to prosecute.
כָּתַב	to write.	כִּתֵּב	to write often, repeatedly.*
חָזַק	he was strong.	חִזֵּק	he made strong, he strengthened, fortified.
לָמַד	to learn.	לִמֵּד	he made another learn, i. e. he taught.

Thus likewise שָׁכַח *he forgot,* שִׁכַּח *he caused to forget, brought into oblivion;* טָהַר *he was clean, pure,* טִהַר *he made clean, purified ;* טָמֵא† *he was unclean,* טִמֵּא *he made unclean, defiled.*

106. פִּעֵל is the passive of the preceding: its characteristic is *dagesh* in the second radical, and (ִ) under the first: as, שֻׁבַּר *he was shattered;* לֻמַּד *he was taught.*

---

* Hence it often denotes habitual action; thus, כּוֹתֵב *one that writes;* but כַּתָּב *one that is accustomed to write,* i. e. *a writer by profession:* רוֹצֵחַ *one that kills;* but מְרַצֵּחַ *one that has committed the action repeatedly, an assassin.*

† These two verbs, and a few others are, in some instances, used in a particular sense: as, וְטִהֲרוֹ הַכֹּהֵן *And the priest shall make him clean,* i. e. *he shall pronounce him clean* (Levit. xiii. 28); וְטִמְּאוֹ אֹתוֹ *and he shall make him unclean,* i. e. *he shall pronounce him unclean* (Levit. xiii. 3). The same is the case with some verbs in Hiphil: as, וְהִצְדִּיקוּ אֶת הַצַּדִּיק *And they shall justify the righteous* (Deut. xxv. 1), i. e. *declare him just.* In a few instances, we find verbs of this form (*Piel*) have an opposite signification to what they have in קַל: as, סָקַל *to stone,* סִקֵּל *to remove stones.*

Obs.—When the second radical happens to be one of the letters ר, ע, ח, ה, א, the *dagesh* is compensated by lengthening the preceding vowel: as, בָּאֵר (for בּאֵר) *to explain* ; בֵּאֵר (for בּאֵר) *he explained* ; בֵּרַךְ (for בּרַךְ) *he blessed* ; בֹּרַךְ (for בּרַךְ) *he was blessed.**

107. הִפְעִיל has mostly a causative signification; its characteristic is the prefix ה, the second radical having (–) or (י–): as, הַפְקֵד or הַפְקִיד *to cause another to visit*; הֶאֱכִיל *he caused another to eat*, i.e. *he fed*, or *provided him with food;* הִבְעִיר *he caused another to burn.*†

108. הֻפְעַל is the passive of the preceding: its characteristic is the prefix ה with short (–) or (ֻ): as, הֻפְקַד *he was caused to visit;* הֻשְׁכַּב *he was caused to lie down.*

---

* This compensation does not, however, always take place: as, וַיִּנְאַץ *he vexed,* נָהַג *he led,* טִהַר *he purified,* פִּחֵשׁ *he denied,* בִּעֵר *he kindled.*

† There is, in some instances, a distinction between the use of the verb in Piel and Hiphil: as, KAL, בָּעַר *to burn, to be on fire;* Piel, בִּעֵר *to make burn, to kindle, to set on fire,* הִבְעִיר *to cause to burn,* i.e. to cause something to burn another object (See Gen. iii. 2, 3.— xxxv. 3, Jud. xv.) In many instances, however, the two forms have the same sense.

Many verbs have a different signification in the different forms: as, פָּתַח *to open,* פִּתַּח *to open with force; hence to engrave:* וַיִּבְרַךְ (Kal) signifies *and he kneeled,* from בֶּרֶךְ *the knee;* וַיַּבְרֵךְ (Hip.) *he caused to kneel* (See Gen. xxiv. 'And he made the camels to kneel') : but וַיְבָרֶךְ (Piel) signifies *he blessed.*

109. הִתְפָּעֵל has mostly a reflective signification :* its characteristic is the prefix הִת added to the form Piel: as, הִתְפַּקֵּד *to visit* or *to inspect one's self*; הִתְנַפֵּל *he threw himself* (from נָפֹל *to fall*); הִתְגַּלָּה *he uncovered himself*. It often signifies mere *pretension*, or a feigning to be what, in fact, one is not: as, הִתְחַלָּה *to pretend to be sick*; הִתְעַשֵּׁר *he pretended to be rich, acted the rich man*, or *boasted to be such*.

Obs.—The derivative verbs are nevertheless frequently used in other senses. (See the notes.)

Moods and Tenses.

110. The primitive as well as the derivative verbs admit of three moods, namely, the *Infinitive*, the *Imperative*†, and the *Indicative*.

---

* Some verbs of this form (Hiph.) have a neuter signification, others denote intensity: as, יַלְבִּינוּ *they shall become white*; יַאְדִּימוּ *they shall become red*; הִשְׁלִיךְ *he threw down, cast away*, הִשְׁכִּים *he rose early, i.e.* with eagerness, or before the usual time.

Several verbs of this form denote *continuance* or *repetition*, others have nearly the same signification as in קַל: as, הִתְפַּלֵּל *he prayed earnestly, devoutly;* הִתְהַלֵּךְ *he walked continually*, or *he walked by his own effort, unassisted;* הִתְאַבֵּל *he mourned greatly;* הִתְאַנַּף *he was angry.*

† Except the derivative verbs, Puàl, Hophàl, and Hithpaél, which being passive verbs, admit not the imperative. Niphàl, though likewise passive, admits this mood, but then it has either a reflective meaning, or it must be taken in the sense of *abstaining from action*. (See Obs. 3, p. 105.)

Each of the three active forms admits of two participles*; one *active* the other *passive* (varied by gender and number): the rest of the forms have one participle only.

111. The form of the infinitives of primitive verbs is mostly פָּקֹד, called the *absolute*, or פְּקֹד, denominated the *constructive* form.

112. From this infinitive, the infinitives of the derivative verbs are formed, as has already been explained in the preceding pages. (See Table X.)

113. Infinitives are, in their nature, abstract nouns†, and as such, they admit of the prefixes, בְּ, כְּ, מִ, לְ: as, פְּקֹד or פָּקֹד *to visit*, בִּפְקֹד *in visiting*, כִּפְקֹד *as visiting*, לִפְקֹד *to visit*, or *for the purpose of visiting*, מִפְּקֹד *from visiting*, בְּהִפָּקֵד *in being visited*, כְּהִפָּקֵד *as being visited*, &c. The infinitives of the rest of the derivative verbs are inflected in the same manner. (See Table X.)

114. The imperative mood admits only the second person masculine and feminine, singular and plural.

---

* Except neuter verbs. (See Obs. 4, p. 117.)
† For the same reason they admit the pronominal *affixes*. (See Table III.)

The second persons *m.* of the imperatives are formed from their respective infinitives, from which they either do not differ at all, or in a very slight degree.

The second person feminine receives ׳ in addition to the masculine; the second person *m. p.* וּ; the second person *f. p.* נָה. Thus—

Infinitive (KAL)   Infinitive (NIPHAL.)
פָּקֹד or פְּקֹד   הִפָּקֵד
Imperative.   Imperative.

פְּקֹד	*visit thou,*	*m. s.*	הִפָּקֵד	*be visited,*	*m. s.*
פִּקְדִי		*f. s.*	הִפָּקְדִי		*f. s.*
פִּקְדוּ	*visit ye,*	*m. p.*	הִפָּקְדוּ	*be ye visited,*	*m. p.*
פְּקֹדְנָה		*f. p.*	הִפָּקַרְנָה		*f. p.*

(See Table X.)

115. The indicative mood admits only of two tenses; the *past* and the *future*.

The third person *m. s.* of the past is formed from the infinitive, mostly by a slight change in the vowel point: as—

        Infinitive.   3rd *person.*

Kal   פָּקֹד .... פָּקַד
Piel   פַּקֵּד .... פִּקֵּד
Pual   פֻּקַּד .... פֻּקַּד
Hiphïl   הַפְקֵד .... הִפְקִיד

The third person of *Hophál* and *Hithpaël* are formed in the same manner. (See Table X.) In Niphál the ה is rejected, and the characteristic נ retained: thus, from הִפָּקֵד (for הִנְפָקֵד) *to be visited,* נִפְקַד *he was visited.*

116. The rest of the persons are formed from the third person *m.*, by subjoining to it the letters תִּי *I ;* תָּ *thou, m. ;* תְּ *thou, f. ;* הָ—* *she ;* נוּ *we ;* תֶּם *you, m. ;* תֶּן *you, f. ;* וּ for both genders, *they.* (See Table X.)

117. The future tenses are formed by prefixing to the *imperative* the following letters, ת, נ, י, א : thus— imp. פְּקֹד—*future,* אֶפְקֹד *I shall visit ;* תִּפְקֹד *thou shalt visit,* תִּפְקְדִי *thou shalt visit, f. ;* יִפְקְדוּ *they shall visit, m.,* &c.

118. In the same manner are the future tenses of derivative verbs formed; except the future of Niphál, which rejects the ה of the imperative. (See Table X.)

---

* (הָ—) The student need scarcely be reminded that this is the feminine termination of *nouns* and *participles ;* and hence we may infer that both the third person masculine, as well as the feminine, were originally participles of the past tense: thus, פָּקַד *one that* did *visit,* פָּקְדָה *a female* that *did visit.* Professor Lee, in his elaborate work on the Hebrew Language (Art. 152 and 195), supposes that they were originally *nouns ;* this is very probable, especially if we admit that nouns were originally *verbalia.* (See Art. 6, p. 10.)

119. The *future* tenses with the prefix וּ and *dagesh* in the following letter*, or וָ (before א), are often used to express the *past*; as, תִּפְקֹד *thou* shalt *visit*, וְתִפְקֹד *and thou* hast *visited*, אֶפְקֹד *I* shall *visit*, וָאֶפְקֹד *and I* did *visit*; יֹאמַר *he* shall *say*, וַיֹּאמֶר *and he said*; נֵלֵךְ *we* shall *go*, וַיֵּלֶךְ *and he went*.

Obs. 1.—This prefix (וּ or וָ) is denominated by Grammarians וָ *conversive*†, because it changes the tense from future into past. But וּ (with sh'va) before future tenses, is merely *copulative*: as, וְאֶפְקֹד *and I shall visit*; וְיֹאמַר *and he shall say*.

2.—Words thus converted from the future into the past by the prefix וּ,‡ having any but a principal distinctive accent on the last syllable, have their accent removed from the *ultimate* to the *penultimate*, and the last long vowel changed into a short one, provided the third radical is not א, and the *penultimate* is a simple syllable, not

---

* Except where the prefix is י with sh'va: as, יְהִי, יְדַבֵּר, &c., when the dagesh is omitted: thus, וִיהִי, וִידַבֵּר, &c. Except, likewise, when the prefix is א, as אֹכִיר, אֵלֵךְ, אֶפְקֹד, where the dagesh is compensated by the long vowel under the וָ: thus, וָאֹמַר, וָאֵלֶךְ, &c.

† I have, for the sake of distinction, retained this technical term, though it is evident that the ו never loses its copulative power even when it is said to be conversive. The fact is, that this letter always retains its primitive signification, namely, *junction*; but it not only joins words and phrases, but likewise the *time* and other circumstances. That its influence is not confined to the past and future only, but that it extends likewise to the present tense, and to the several moods, might easily be proved by numerous examples, were this the proper place to enter into such a disquisition.

‡ The prefix וּ has no influence on the accent. (See the examples in the first note.)

followed by sh'va: thus, וַיֹּאמֶר, וַיֵּשֶׁב, וַיָּקָם, וַיָּסֹב, וַיִּפְגַּע, — וַיֹּאמֶר, וַיִּיקַץ, וַיָּקָם, וַיָּשׁוּב, וַיִּיקַם, וַיֵּשֶׁב. But if the preceding conditions be wanting, the accent is not removed; hence we have וַיֹּאמֶר, וַיָּמוֹת, וַיְדַבֵּר, וַיִּקְרָא, וַיִּגַּשׁ, וַיֶּאֱהַב, &c. The accent is likewise retained in verbs of the fourth conjugation, having chirik instead of (ּ) in the future: as, וַיִּישַׁן, וַיִּיקַץ.

120. The past tense, with the prefix וֹ or וּ, expresses *future* time when preceded by a verb in the *future*, or by an imperative: as, פָּקַדְתִּי *I have visited*, וּפָקַדְתִּי *and I shall visit*; אָמַרְתָּ *thou hast said*, וְאָמַרְתָּ *and thou shalt say**; הָיָה *he or it was*, וְהָיָה *and he or it shall be*; אָמַר *he said*, וְאָמַר *and he shall say*.

Obs. 1.—This וֹ is likewise denominated *conversive*. But when a past tense, having וֹ prefixed, is preceded by another past tense, the וֹ is in that case merely *copulative*, and the verb retains its past signification: as, קָרָא וְאָמַר *he called and said*.

2.—These rules, which will be more fully explained in the *Syntax*, are equally applicable to the tenses of the derivative verbs.

121. The active participle of the primitive verb (קַל), is formed mostly by inserting וֹ (or its vowel point†) between the *first* and *second* radical: as,

---

* In such cases the accent of the first and second person singular is removed to the ultimate syllable. (See the above examples.) Except verbs whose third radical is a quiescent letter: as, וְרָאִיתִי, וּמָצָאתָ.

† Except verbs of the fifth, and some of the eighth conjugations.

THE HEBREW LANGUAGE. 115

פּוֹקֵד or פֹּקֵד *one that visits*, and the passive participle, by inserting וּ between the *second* and *third* radical: as, פָּקוּד.

122. The participles of the derivative verbs are mostly formed by the prefixes נ, מְ, מַ, מִ, מִת*, or by a change in the vowel points.

Obs.—Participles being in their nature *nouns*, are varied like them by *gender* and *number* (see the following Table), and by the pronominal affixes. (Table III.) They are inserted amongst the verbs, because they supply the present tense, for which the Hebrew has no particular *form :* as, *m.* אֲנִי פֹּקֵד—*f.* אֲנִי פֹּקֶדֶת *I am visiting*, or *I visit.* (See page 117.)

123. To conjugate a verb, is to express all the modifications of which it is susceptible. As these modifications are chiefly indicated by prefixes and affixes, and as these are common to all verbs, there can, strictly speaking, be only one conjugation; nevertheless, as the vowel-points and some of the letters constituting the root are subject to various changes, verbs have been distributed by most Grammarians into eight classes or conjugations (Art. 12), the first of which comprehends *perfect verbs* (Art. 13), the rest comprehend *imperfect verbs* (Art. 14—16).

The annexed table contains a model of a *perfect verb*.

---

* These letters are probably fragments of the words מִי *who*, or מָה *what*.

124. *Remarks and Observations on the preceding Verb.*

Obs. 1.—The *dagesh*, in the first radical beginning a word or syllable, as פָּקֹד, פָּקַדְתִּי, &c. הִתְפַּקֵּד, &c., is used only in roots beginning with either of the letters ב ג ד כ פ ת, but not in those beginning with any other letter: as, הִתְלַפֵּד, לְמַדְתִּי, לְמֹד.

2.—The accent is on the second radical when the same has a vowel, but when it has (:) the accent is placed on the next vowel; except the terminations ־ֶם, ־ֶן, which always take the accent, notwithstanding the second radical has a vowel. Except likewise the plural terminations of the participles.

Kal.

3.—פָּקֹד—The *forms* of the infinitive of *Kal* are either (פָּעֹל): as, פָּקֹד *to visit* שָׁכֹב *to lie down;* or (פְּעֹל): as, פְּקֹד; or (פְּעַל): as, *יְשָׁכַב.

The first is denominated the *absolute form,* and is chiefly used by way of emphasis, before and after other verbs: as. פָּקֹד יִפְקֹד אֶתְכֶם *visiting, he will visit you,* i. e. *he will surely visit you.* (Gen. 1. 24.)

The second and third are denominated the *constructive forms,* and are chiefly used with the letters, מ, ל, כ, ב, : as, בִּפְקֹד *in visiting,* בִּפְקֹד, &c. (See the preceding Table.) בִּשְׁכַב *in lying down,* בִּשְׁכַב, לִשְׁכַב.†

Before מַקֵּף, (ֹ) is changed into short (ָ): as, מְשֹׁל, cons. מְשָׁל-, *to rule,* מְשָׁל-בָּנוּ *to rule over us.* This rule is equally applicable to all words terminating in (ֹ): as תִּמְשֹׁל, אֶמְשֹׁל, with מַקֵּף, תִּמְשָׁל-, אֶמְשָׁל-, &c. (See Part I. p. 79.)

---

* The following *forms* occur sometimes, בְּשֵׁל *to boil;* גְּדֵל *to be great;* לְיִרְאָה *to fear;* לְאַהֲבָה *to love;* לְקָרְבָה *to approach.* But the first two are probably *adjectives,* and the latter *abstract nouns,* used instead of the regular infinitives.

† The *constructive form* is often used without the letters מ, ל, כ, ב. (See Syntax.)

Obs. 4. — Participles, as has already been observed, supply the present tense: as, אַתָּה עוֹמֵד *m.* אֲנִי לוֹמֵד, *m.* אֲנִי לוֹמֶדֶת, *f.* *I learn ;** אַתְּ עוֹמֶדֶת *f. thou standest ;* הוּא יוֹשֵׁב *he sits,* הִיא יוֹשֶׁבֶת *she sits ;* אֲנוּ הֹלְכִים *m.* אָנוּ הֹלְכוֹת *we walk,* &c. אֲנִי קֹרֵא *I call,* אֲנִי קְרוּא *I am called, invited.*

Verbs which imply neither action nor passion admit neither active nor passive participles, the noun adjective being used like other nouns in conjunction with the personal pronouns in the present tense (the verb *to be* being understood). Thus, as we say אֲנִי אָדָם *I* am *a man,* הוּא מֶלֶךְ *he is a king ,* אֲנַחְנוּ אֲנָשִׁים *we* are *men,* so likewise אֲנִי חָכָם (not חוֹכֵם) *I* am *wise,* הוּא חָכָם *he is wise,* הֵמָּה חֲכָמִים *they* are *wise ;* אֲנִי אָדֹם *I* am *red ;* אַתָּה גָּדוֹל *thou* art *great,* הַמְּלָאכָה גְדֹלָה *the work* is *great ;* רְעֵבִים אֲנַחְנוּ *we* are *hungry.*

Additional Examples.

דּוֹדִי צַח וְאָדוֹם *My beloved* is *white and ruddy.* (Cant. v. 10.)

שְׁחוֹרָה אֲנִי וְנָאוָה *I* am *black, and (yet) comely.* (Ibid. i. 5.)

יָדְעוּ כִּי רְעֵבִים אֲנַחְנוּ *They know that we* are *hungry.* (2 Kings vii. 12.)

הָעָם רָעֵב וְעָיֵף וְצָמֵא *The people* are *hungry, and-weary, and-thirsty.* (2 Sam. xvii. 29.)

Obs. 5. — פָּקַד — This is by some grammarians called the *root.* It has either (-) for the second vowel, as the word under consideration,

---

* *Lit.* I am a learner, or I am learning. In a few instances we find the active participle takes (ֹ֒) instead (ֹ֒): as, תּוֹמִיךְ (Ps. xvi. 5.) יוֹסִיף (Isa. xxix. 14.) or (-) : as אֹבַד A few also are found with ה (Paragogic): as, בֹּעֵרָה (Hos. vii. 4.) Or with י (Paragogic) : as, שֹׁכְנִי (Deut. iii. 3.)

and then it is said to be of the *form* פָּעַל, which is chiefly appropriated for active verbs. Or it has (ִ) or (ַ) for the second vowel, and then it is said to be of the form פָּעֵל, and פָּעַל: as, חָפֵץ *he was willing*, זָקֵן *he was old*; יָכֹל *he was able*, קָטֹן *he was little.**

Obs. 6.—Verbs of the *form* פָּעֵל express their different persons in the same manner as פָּעַל (פָּקַד): thus, חָפֵץ, חָפַצְתִּי, חָפְצָה, &c.† (not חָפֵצְתִּי). But those of the form פָּעֹל, retain (ֹ) in all cases where those of the form פָּעַל have (-). Except in the second person plural, where they change (ֹ) into short (ָ): thus, יָכֹל, יָכֹלְתִּי, יָכְלָה, יָכֹל, יָכְלוּ, יְכָלְתֶּם ‡, יְכָלְתֶּן ‡, יָכֹלְנוּ ‡, &c. *Future* אוּכַל *I shall be able*, תּוּכַל, &c.

The three forms occur in the 35th verse of the 40th chapter of Exodus:—

וְלֹא־יָכֹל מֹשֶׁה לָבוֹא אֶל־אֹהֶל מוֹעֵד כִּי־שָׁכַן עָלָיו הֶעָנָן וּכְבוֹד יְהוָה מָלֵא אֶת־הַמִּשְׁכָּן:

And Moses was *not able to enter into the tent of the congregation, because the cloud* rested *thereon, and the glory of the Lord* filled *the Tabernacle.*

---

* Verbs of this form have, (of course,) their infinitives, participles m., and third persons the same.

† In pause, (see Part I. p. 84.) חָפֵץ, חָפְצָה, חָפְצוּ; יָכֹל, יָכְלָה, יָכְלוּ; whereas those of the form פָּעַל change (-) and (:) into long (ָ) as אָמַר *he said*, אָמְרָה, אָמְרוּ.

‡ This change is founded on the rule given in Part I. p. 79, namely, that unaccented long vowels cannot form a compound syllable without an accent; and, as in the instances before us, the vowel (ֹ) cannot retain the accent, on account of the terminations תֶּם, תֶּן (see p. 116), it follows, that the vowel must be changed into its corresponding (ָ): thus, יְכָלְתֶּם, יְכָלְתֶּן. For the same reason is (ֹ) in יָכֹלְתִּי, יָכֹלְתָּ, changed into short (ָ) when they occur with ו *conversive*: thus, וָיְכָלְתָּ, וָיְכָלְתִּי.

Obs. 7.—פָּקַרְתִּי—Verbs, whose third radical is ת, drop this letter before the affixes תִּי, תָּ, תְּ, תֶּם, and תֶּן: as, כָּרֹת *to cut*, כָּרַת *he cut*, כָּרַתִּי, כָּרַתָּ, כָּרַתְּ, כְּרַתֶּם, כְּרַתֶּן (not כָּרַתְתִּי, כָּרַתְתָּ). The same in the derivative verbs הִכְרַתִּי (not הִכְרַתְתִּי), נִכְרַתִּי, &c.

8.—The verb נָתַן *to give*, נָתַן *he gave*, follows the same rule dropping the second נ: as, נָתַתִּי *I gave*, נָתַתָּ, נָתַתְּ, נָתַתֶּם, נָתַתֶּן (not נָתַנְתִּי, &c.); נ is likewise dropped before the affixes נוּ, נָה: as, נָתַנּוּ (for נָתַנְנוּ) *we gave*; הַאֲזֵנָּה (for הַאֲזֵנְנָה) *listen ye*.

9.—פָּקַרְתָּה—Sometimes with an additional ה (Paragogic): as, זָמַנְתָּה (Josh. xiii. 11), נָפַלְתָּה (2 Kings xiv. 10).

10.—פָּקַרְתְּ—The first (:) is changed into (-) when the third radical is ע: as, יָשַׁעְתְּ.

11.—פָּקְרָה—In a few instances with ת: as, אָזְלַת (Deut. xxxii), נִפְלָאת (Psalm cxviii), and with א*: as, גָּבְהָא (Ezek. xxxi).

12.—פְּקֹד—Some verbs (mostly intransitives) take (-) instead of (ֹ) for their second vowel in the imperative and future: as, קְרַב *come near*, *approach*, fut. אֶקְרַב; שְׁכַב *lie down*, fut. אֶשְׁכַּב; especially when the second radical is a guttural, or the third ח or ע: as, שְׁאַל *ask*, שַׁאֲלִי, שַׁאֲלוּ, fut. אֶשְׁאַל; צְעַק *cry*, fut. אֶצְעַק; שְׁלַח *send*, אֶשְׁלַח; שְׁמַע *hear*, אֶשְׁמַע· Some take an additional ה (Paragogic), with short (ָ) or (ֶ) for their first vowel: as, שָׁמְרָה for שְׁמֹר, קָרְבָה for קְרַב, שָׁלְחָה for שְׁלַח; שָׁמְעָה, and in pause, שָׁמֵעָה for שְׁמַע· Some few take short (ָ) in the second person: as, מָלְכִי *reign thou*, f.—חָרְבִי, in pause חָרֳבִי *be dry*, f.—חָרְבוּ m. p. *be ye dry*, *desolate*.

13.—פְּקֹדְנָה—ה is sometimes dropped, and the vowel placed under the final ן: as, קְרֶאןָ *call ye*, שְׁמַעְןָ *hear ye*, (instead קְרֶאנָה, שְׁמַעְנָה). So likewise the third person p. f. fut. תִּהְיֶיןָ for תִּהְיֶינָה *they shall be*.

---

* In a few instances we find the third person plural m. with א; as, הָלְכוּא *they went* (Josh. x.), אָבוּא *they were willing*; for הָלְכוּ, אָבוּ·

Obs. 14.—אֶפְקֹד—Sometimes with an additional ה; as, אֶשְׁמְרָה *I will keep,* אֶשְׁלְחָה *I will send;* for אֶשְׁמֹר, אֶשְׁלַח. So likewise with some of the other persons: as, יָחִישָׁה *let him hasten,* for יָחִישׁ; נִשְׁלְחָה for נִשְׁלַח.

15.—תִּפְקְדוּ, יִפְקְדוּ—Sometimes with ן (Paragogic): as, תִּשְׁמְעוּן, יִשְׁמְעוּן* for תִּשְׁמְעוּ, יִשְׁמְעוּ.

Niphal.

16.—*Inf.* הִפָּקֵד—Or with (ִ): as, הֵאָכֵל. (Lev. vii. 18.)

When the ה is preceded by the prefixes ל, ב, it is sometimes omitted, and its vowel-point is placed under those letters: as, בַּעֲטֹף for בְּהֵעָטֹף (Lam. ii.) לֵעָנוֹת for לְהֵעָנוֹת (Ex. x). The same in Hiphil, לְהַשְׁמִיעַ for לְיַשְׁמִיעַ.

17.—*Part.* נִפְקָד—With (ׇ) to distinguish it from the third person *m.* of the past, which has always (-); except in pause, when the distinction is lost. But the feminine participle נִפְקָדָה is distinguished from the third person נִפְקָדָה (in pause), by the position of the accent.

Obs. — This participle indicates that the action is in progress, but the passive participle of KAL indicates that the action is completed; thus—

הַשַּׁעַר נִסְגָּר *the gate is shutting.*
הַשַּׁעַר סָגוּר *the gate is shut.*

18.—נִפְקַד—In a few instances with ו: as, נֶהְפּוֹךְ (Est. ix. 1.) נִמּוֹל (Gen. xviii. 27.)

19.—*Imp.* הִפָּקֵד—The accent is sometimes moved back to the penultimate, which circumstance necessarily produces a change in the vowel from *long* to *short:* as, הִפָּרֵד, תִּשָּׁבֵר or יִשָּׁבֶר. (See Part I. p. 81.)

20.—אֶפָּקֵד—See the preceding remark. The א has some-

---

* Seldom with the second person *f.*: as, תִּדְבָּקִין, תַּעֲשִׂין (Ruth) for תַּעֲשִׂי, תִּדְבָּקִי.

times (.): as, אֶשְׁבַּע (Gen. xxi. 24.) אִמָּלֵט; and with an additional ה: as, אִמָּלְטָה (Gen. xix. 20).

Obs. 21.—יִפְקֹד.—With conversive ו sometimes with (-): as, וַיִּגְמַל (Gen. xxi. 8); and with (ֶ) when the accent is on the penultimate: as, וַיֹּאמֶר (Gen. xxv. 9).

22.—תִּפְקֹדְנָה—Sometimes with (-): as, תִּזְכֹּרְנָה.

Piel.

23. —*Inf.* פַּקֵּד—In some instances with (ָ): as, רַפֹּא (Exod. xxi) יַסּוֹר (Ps. cxviii).

24.—פִּקֵּד—Sometimes with (-): as, אִבַּד *he destroyed*, especially when the 3rd radical is ה, or ע, or ר: as, שִׁלַּח *he sent away*, גִּדַּע *he cut off*, שִׁבַּר *he broke in pieces*; and sometimes with (ֵ): as, דִּבֶּר or דִּבֵּר *he spoke*.

Puäl.

25.—פֻּקַּד—In a few instances with short (ַ) instead of (ֻ): as, פָּרַת (Ezek. xiv. 4).

Hiphïl.

26.—*Inf.* הַפְקִיד or הַפְקֵד—and in a few instances with (-) for the last vowel: as, הַפְצֵר (1 Sam. xv).

27.—*Part. Pas.* מַפְקִיד—or with short (ִ) instead of (ִי): as, כָּשׁוֹר, מָשְׁחָת.

28.—*Fut.* אַפְקִיד—instead of אֲהַפְקִיד, the ה being omitted, and its vowel placed under the prefixes. In a few instances we find the ה retained: as, יְהוֹשִׁיעַ (Ps. cxvi.) יְהֵלִילוּ (Is. lii.) instead יוֹשִׁיעַ, יֵילִילוּ.

29.—יַפְקִיד.—Sometimes with (-): as, יַבְטַח, and sometimes with (ֵ): as, יִכְרֵת; especially with conversive ו: as, וַיַּבְדֵּל.

Hophäl.

30.—*Past* הָפְקַד or הָפְקַר—with short (ַ) through the whole branch, unless when followed by (ִ) in which case the first (ַ) becomes long: as, הָחֳרַב, הָעֳמַדְתָּ, הָעֳמַד, fut. אֶעֳמַד, &c.

Obs. 31.—*Part.* הַפְקֵד or הָפְקָד—The same (*Past*) הָפְקַדְתִּי or הָפְקַדְתָּ, &c. (*Fut.*) אָפְקַד or אֻפְקַד, &c.

32.—הִתְפַּקֵּד*—or with (-) for the last vowel: as, הִתְחַזֵּק he strengthened himself, appeared firm, or he took courage. This derivative verb is formed by adding הִת to the derivative verb *Piël*, the punctuation of which has already been explained: observe, however,—

1st. When the first radical is שׁ or ס, these letters exchange place with ת: thus, הִשְׁתַּבַּח *he praised or glorified himself*, (for הִתְשַׁבַּח); הִסְתַּתֵּר *he hid himself* (for הִתְסַתֵּר).

2nd. When the first radical is צ, the ת is changed into ט, and transposed as before: thus, הִצְטַדֵּק *he justified himself* (for הִתְצַדֵּק).

3rd. In a few instances we find the ת omitted: as, מְשַׁהֵר (Lev. xiv.) for מִתְטַהֵר; יְטַמָּא (Lev. xxi.) for יִתְטַמָּא.

Verbs whose Roots contain one of the Gutturals.

Verbs of this description differ in some respect from the model פָּקַד, as will be explained presently.

I. *First Radical,* ע, ח, ה, א.

125. When the first radical happens to be either of these letters it receives -: or ־: (and in Hophal ־:) in every instance where the *first radical* of פָּקַד, or of any other perfect verb, would receive *Sh'va* (:)—

---

* The passive of this form is הִתְפָּעַל (Hothpaël): as, לֹא הָתְפָּקְדוּ (Num. i. 47.) 'They were not caused to be numbered,' *i. e.* they were not caused (ordered) to muster themselves. This form is, however, very seldom used.

Thus, עָמֹד *to stand*, אָסֹף *to gather*, have their *Inf. cons.* and *Imp.* עָמֹד, אֱסֹף (not עָמֹד, אֲסֹף),—עֲמֹדְנָה (not עֲמֹדְנָה).

Obs. 1.—In such cases, the serviles preceding these letters take the corresponding short vowels for their vowel-points: as, בֶּאֱסֹף *in gathering*, לֶאֱסֹף, &c.—בַּעֲמֹד *in standing*, לַעֲמֹד, &c. (not בֶּעֱמֹד). And hence their futures will be*—

אֶאֱסֹף תֶּאֱסֹף תַּאַסְפִּי† יַאֲסֹף &c. נֶאֱסֹף תַּאַסְפוּ תֶּאֱסֹפְנָה
אֶעֱמֹד תַּעֲמֹד תַּעַמְדִי יַעֲמֹד &c. נַעֲמֹד תַּעַמְדוּ תַּעֲמֹדְנָה

The same in Niphal: as, נֶאֱסַף *he was gathered*, נֶאֶסְפָה, נֶאֶסְפוּ, &c.—נֶעֱמַד, נֶעֶמְדָה, נֶעֶמְדוּ, נֶעֱמַדְתָּ, &c. And in Hiphil—Inf. הַעֲמִיד, Imp. הַעֲמֵד or הַעֲמֵד, Fut. אַעֲמִיד, תַּעֲמִיד, תַּעֲמִידִי, &c. Hophal—Inf. הָעֳמַד, past tense, הָעֳמַד, הָעָמְדָה, הָעֳמַדְתִּי, &c. Fut. אָעֳמַד, תָּעֳמַד, תָּעָמְדִי, תָּעֳמַד, &c.

2.—Piel, Pual, and Hithpael are conjugated regularly, like the similar derivative verbs of פָּקֹד.

3.—The *dagesh*, which these letters do not admit, is compen-

---

* In all instances marked thus *, the verb פָּקֹד would receive two *sh'vas*: as, תִּפְקְדִי, תִּפְקְדוּ, נִפְקְדוּ, &c., the second of which is initial. Now, if the semi-vowels which are in their nature substitutes for *sh'va* initial (Part I. p. 23) were to be retained, two *initial sh'vas* would necessarily come together: as, תְּאַסְפִּי or תְּאַסְפוּ, which is contrary to the genius of the language; the semi-vowel is therefore changed into a short vowel. Sometimes, however, the semi-vowel is retained, and the second *sh'va* changed into a vowel: as, תֶּאֱהָבוּ *ye shall love*. Some verbs retain simple *sh'va* notwithstanding the guttural: as from חָמֹד *to desire*, יַחְמֹד; תַּחְמֹד, נֶחְמָד, &c., and from חָסֵר *to want*, יַחְסְרוּ, יֶחְסַר. Especially the verbs הָיָה *to be*, חָיָה *to live*: as, תִּהְיֶה, אֶהְיֶה,—תִּחְיֶה, אֶחְיֶה, &c.

† Or, תֶּאֶסְפִּי.

sated by lengthening the vowel of the prefix. Thus, מֵאָסֹף *from gathering*, instead of מְאָסֹף (compare מִפְּקֹד). הֵאָסֵף *to be gathered*, אֵאָסֵף *I shall be gathered*, יֵאָסֵף *he shall be gathered*, &c. (compare אֶפְקֹד, הֻפְקַד, &c.).

The last rule is equally applicable to verbs whose first radical is (ר): as, רְדֹף *to pursue*, מֵרְדֹף *from pursuing*, אֵרְדֹף *I shall be pursued*.

II. *Second Radical*, ע, ח, ה, א.

126. When the second radical happens to be either of these letters, then the infinitive follows the general rule: as, בָּחֹר *to choose*, בִּבְחֹר *in choosing*, לִבְחֹר, &c. But the imperative and future take (-ַ) instead of (-ֹ): as, בְּחַר *choose thou*, m., Fut. אֶבְחַר,* תִּבְחַר, &c.

Further, the guttural takes (-ֲ) whenever the second radical (ק) of פָּקַד would receive (ְ); as, בַּחֲרִי *choose thou*, בַּחֲרוּ, &c. Past בָּחֲרָה, בָּחֲרוּ. Fut. תִּבְחֲרִי, תִּבְחֲרוּ, יִבְחֲרוּ.—Niphal, נִבְחֲרָה, נִבְחֲרוּ. Imp. הִבָּחֲרִי, הִבָּחֲרוּ. Fut. תִּבָּחֲרִי, תִּבָּחֲרוּ, יִבָּחֲרוּ. Thus likewise זְעַק *to cry, to call aloud*, Imp. זְעַק, זַעֲקִי—בָּעַר *he burnt*, בַּעֲרָה, בַּעֲרוּ.

In *Piël, Puäl*, and *Hithpaël*, the dagesh (which these letters and the letter ר will not admit), is mostly compensated by lengthening the vowel of the first radical†: as, בֵּעֵר *to kindle, set on fire*, (for

---

* A few verbs of this description retain (-ֹ): as, יִנְהֹם, אֶזְעֹם, תִּמְעֹל.

† There are, however, some verbs where the *dagesh* is not compensated: as, נִאֵץ *he vexed*, נִחַם *he comforted, he consoled*, &c.

בֵּעֵר). Thus, likewise, בָּרוֹךְ *to bless.*—Piél., Inf. בָּרֵךְ (for בָּרַךְ).
Part. act. מְבָרֵךְ, מְבָרְכָה, מְבָרֶכֶת, &c. Part. pass. מְבֹרָךְ, &c. Imp.
בָּרֵךְ, בָּרְכִי, &c. Fut. אֲבָרֵךְ, תְּבָרֵךְ, &c. Past tense, בֵּרַכְתָּ, בֵּרַכְתִּי, &c.
Puál, Inf. בֹּרַךְ (for בָּרַךְ) *to be blessed;* Part. בֹּרָךְ, &c. Past tense,
בֹּרַכְתָּ, בֹּרַכְתִּי, &c., Fut. אֲבֹרַךְ, תְּבֹרַךְ, &c. Hithpaél, הִתְבָּרֵךְ, Part.
מִתְבָּרֵךְ, &c.

III. *Third Radical,* ח *or* ע.

127. When the third radical happens to be one of these letters, an additional (-) denominated פַּתַּח גְּנוּבָה *Pathah Furtivum,* is added to them whenever they terminate a word, and are preceded by the vowels (וֹ) (וּ), ('ִ-), or (ּ·): as, שָׁמוֹעַ *to hear,* בִּשְׁמֹעַ *in hearing,* בִּשְׁמֵעַ, &c. Part. act. שֹׁמֵעַ*, *f.* שֹׁמַעַת; Part. pass. שָׁמוּעַ. Niphál, הִשָּׁמַע (abridged הִשָּׁמֵעַ) *to be heard;* Fut. אֶשָּׁמַע·† Hiphíl, הִשְׁמִיעַ or הִשְׁמֵעַ; Imp. הַשְׁמַע, &c. הַשְׁמַעְנָה, &c. Part. מַשְׁמִיעַ, &c. Past tense, הִשְׁמִיעַ &c., הִשְׁמַעַתְּ; Fut. אַשְׁמִיעַ, &c. תִּשְׁמַעְנָה‡, &c.

The (:) of the second person feminine, and (ִ-) of the imperative and future, and (ּ·) of the other parts of the verb, are changed into (-): as, שָׁמַעַתְּ (for שְׁמַעְתְּ); נִשְׁמַעַתְּ (for נִשְׁמַעְתְּ); שְׁמַע, שָׁמַעְנָה (for שְׁמַעְנָה); אֶשְׁמַע (for אֶשְׁמֹעַ). Niphál, Imp. הִשָּׁמַע (for הִשָּׁמֵעַ). Piél, שַׁמַּע (for שַׁמֵּעַ) &c.

---

* (ִ-) is sometimes omitted: as, רֹקַע for רֹקֵעַ.

† Or with (ּ·): as, אִשָּׁבַע *I shall* or *will swear,* תִּשָּׁבַע, &c.

‡ Or abridged תַּשְׁמַע for תַּשְׁמִיעַ—יַבְטַח for יַבְטִיחַ *he shall cause to trust, inspire confidence.*

לָמַדְתִּי¹ חָכְמָה וָדַעַת׃ לִמַּדְתִּי אֶתְכֶם חֻקִּים² וּמִשְׁפָּטִים
טוֹבִים׃ לִמֵּד דַּעַת אֶת־הָעָם׃ לֹא לָמַד צֶדֶק³׃ לָמְדָה
לְשׁוֹן⁴ הָעָם׃ לִמַּדְתָּם דַּרְכֵּי⁵ הַגּוֹיִם׃ צֶדֶק לָמְדוּ יֹשְׁבֵי־
תֵבֵל⁶׃ לִמְּדוּ לְשׁוֹנָם דַּבֶּר⁷ שֶׁקֶר׃ אָנֹכִי לוֹמֵד לְשׁוֹן עִבְרִי⁸׃
וְהִיא לוֹמֶדֶת לְשׁוֹן כַּשְׂדִּים⁹׃ הוּא מְלַמֵּד אֹתָנוּ תּוֹרַת
אֱלֹהִים׃ הִיא מְלַמֶּדֶת אֹתִי לַעֲשׂוֹת¹⁰ הַטּוֹב וְהַיָּשָׁר¹¹׃
לִמּוּד טֶרֶם¹² תִּלְמַד׃ אֲלַמֵּד חֻקֶּיךָ׃ הֲבִינֵנִי¹³ וְאֶלְמְדָה
מִצְוֺתֶיךָ¹⁴׃ אֲלַמְּדָה פֹשְׁעִים¹⁵ דְּרָכֶיךָ׃ לִמְדוּ הֵיטֵב׃ לָמְדוּ
בְנֵיכֶם חָכְמָה׃ לַמְּדֵנָה בְנוֹתֵיכֶם דַּבֶּר אֱמֶת׃ לֹא יִלְמְדוּ
עוֹד מִלְחָמָה׃ לְמַעַן¹⁶ אֲשֶׁר לֹא־יְלַמְּדוּ אֶתְכֶם לַעֲשׂוֹת
כְּכֹל תּוֹעֲבֹתָם¹⁷ אֲשֶׁר עָשׂוּ¹⁸ לֵאלֹהֵיהֶם׃ שְׁמַע יִשְׂרָאֵל
אֶת־הַחֻקִּים וְאֶת־הַמִּשְׁפָּטִים אֲשֶׁר אָנֹכִי דֹבֵר¹⁹ בְּאָזְנֵיכֶם²⁰
הַיּוֹם²¹ וּלְמַדְתֶּם אֹתָם׃ הַקְהֵל²² אֶת־הָעָם וְאַשְׁמִעֵם אֹתָם
אֶת־דְּבָרָי אֲשֶׁר יִלְמְדוּן לְיִרְאָה²³ אֹתִי וְאֶת־בְּנֵיהֶם
יְלַמֵּדוּן׃ הֲמָלֹךְ²⁴ תִּמְלֹךְ עָלֵינוּ אִם מָשׁוֹל²⁵ תִּמְשֹׁל בָּנוּ׃

¹ לָמוֹד to learn, *Pi.* לַמֵּד to teach. ² חֹק. ³ Righteousness. ⁴ לָשׁוֹן language. ⁵ דֶּרֶךְ. ⁶ The inhabitants of the world. ⁷ *Pi.* to speak. ⁸ Hebrew. ⁹ Chaldeans. ¹⁰ To do. ¹¹ Straight, right. ¹² Before. ¹³ Cause me to understand. "We shall use this sign to indicate that the letter over which it is placed is Paragogic; that the verb after which it is placed is to be understood in a converted time. ¹⁴ מִצְוָה. ¹⁵ פָּשַׁע to transgress. ¹⁶ In order. ¹⁷ תּוֹעֵבָה. ¹⁸ They did. ¹⁹ דָּבַר to say, speak. ²⁰ אֹזֶן. ²¹ This day, to-day. ²² *Hip.* to cause to come together, to assemble. ²³ To fear. ²⁴ מָלַךְ to reign, in *Hip.* to cause to reign, to appoint any one as king, *Hop.* to be appointed king. ²⁵ מָשַׁל to rule, govern.

THE HEBREW LANGUAGE.   127

לֹא אֶמְשֹׁל אֲנִי בָּכֶם וְלֹא יִמְשֹׁל בְּנִי בָּכֶם: אֹתִי מָאָסוּ[26]
מִמְּלֹךְ עֲלֵיהֶם: אַמְלִיךְ עֲלֵיכֶם מֶלֶךְ: אַתָּה הִמְלַכְתָּ אֶת
עַבְדְּךָ: אֲדֹנֵינוּ[27] הַמֶּלֶךְ דָּוִד הִמְלִיךְ אֶת שְׁלֹמֹה: הָמְלַךְ
עַל מַלְכוּת[28] בַּשָּׂדִים:

[26] מָאַס to despise. [27] אָדוֹן a lord. [28] Kingdom, realm.

שָׁמַעְתִּי אֶת אָבִיךָ מְדַבֵּר אֶל אָחִיךָ: כֵּן[1] בְּנוֹת צְלָפְחָד
דֹּבְרֹת: כֵּן בְּנֵי יוֹסֵף דֹּבְרִים: עוֹד הֵם מְדַבְּרִים וַאֲנִי
אֶשְׁמָע: שִׁמְעָה כִּי פָקַד יְיָ אֶת עַמּוֹ לָתֵת[2] לָהֶם לָחֶם:
הִנֵּה[3] בְּנֵי יִשְׂרָאֵל לֹא שָׁמְעוּ אֵלַי וְאֵיךְ[4] יִשְׁמָעֵנִי פַרְעֹה[5]:
וַקּוֹל נִשְׁמַע הַבַּיִת[6] פַּרְעֹה: דִּבְרֵי חֲכָמִים בְּנַחַת[7] נִשְׁמָעִים:
קוֹל כִּנּוֹרֶיךָ לֹא יִשָּׁמַע עוֹד[9]: תִּשְׁמַע זַעֲקָה[10] מִבָּתֵּיהֶם:
מִי הִשְׁמִיעַ זֹאת מִקֶּדֶם[11]: מִשָּׁמַיִם הִשְׁמַעְתָּ דִין[12]: הִנֵּה
עַל הֶהָרִים רַגְלֵי מְבַשֵּׂר[13] מַשְׁמִיעַ שָׁלוֹם[14]: שְׁמוּעָה[15]
שָׁמַעְנוּ מֵאֵת יְיָ וְצִיר[16] בַּגּוֹיִם שֻׁלָּח[17]: הֵן בַּעֲוֹנֹתֵיכֶם[18]
נִמְכַּרְתֶּם[19] וּבְפִשְׁעֵיכֶם[20] שֻׁלְּחָה אִמְּכֶם: רַק[21] לֹא הָיָה
כְאַחְאָב[22] אֲשֶׁר הִתְמַכֵּר לַעֲשׂוֹת הָרַע בְּעֵינֵי יְיָ: אֶת בְּנֵיהֶם
וְאֶת בְּנוֹתֵיהֶם הֶעֱבִירוּ[23] בָאֵשׁ וַיִּתְמַכְּרוּ לַעֲשׂוֹת הָרַע

[1] Justly, right. [2] To give. [3] Behold. [4] How. [5] Pharaoh. [6] בַּיִת
[7] Ease, quietness. [8] A harp. [9] Again, any more. [10] A cry, lamentation. [11] Before, formerly. [12] Judgment. [13] בִּשֵּׂר Pi. to bring joyful tidings. [14] Peace. [15] What is heard, a report. [16] A messenger. [17] Pu. was sent. [18] עָוֹן sin. [19] מָכַר to sell, נִמְכַּר he was sold, הִתְמַכֵּר he sold himself, or offered himself for sale. [20] פֶּשַׁע a transgression. [21] But. [22] Ahab. [23] עָבַר to pass, הֶעֱבִיר he made

THE ETYMOLOGY OF

בְּעֵינֵי יְיָ לְהַכְעִיסוֹ²⁴ : וְהִתְמַכַּרְתֶּם²⁵ שָׁם לְאֹיְבֶיךָ²⁵ לַעֲבָדִים
וְלִשְׁפָחוֹת²⁶ וְאֵין קֹנֶה²⁷ : בָּרוּךְ²⁹ תִּהְיֶה²⁸ מִכָּל־הָעַמִּים : בְּרוּכָה
אַתְּ לַיְיָ בִּתִּי : בְּרָכִים אַתֶּם לַיְיָ : אֵלֶּה יַעַמְדוּ³⁰ לְבָרֵךְ³¹ אֶת
הָעָם : בָּרֵךְ אֶת־עַמְּךָ יִשְׂרָאֵל : בָּרְכִי נַפְשִׁי³² אֶת יְיָ : בָּרְכוּ
עַמִּים אֱלֹהֵינוּ : אֲבָרְכָה אֶת יְיָ בְּכָל־עֵת³³ : מִן הַיּוֹם
הַזֶּה אֲבָרֵךְ אֹתוֹ : כֹּה³⁴ תְבָרְכוּ אֶת־בְּנֵי יִשְׂרָאֵל : אֶת־אֲשֶׁר
תְּבָרֵךְ מְבֹרָךְ : טוֹב עַיִן³⁵ הוּא יְבֹרָךְ³⁵ : תְּבוֹרַךְ מִנָּשִׁים יָעֵל³⁶ :
הִנֵּה בֵרַכְתִּי אֹתָם ; מַעֲשֵׂה³⁷ יָדָיו בֵּרַכְתָּ : בֵּרְכָנוּ אֶתְכֶם
בְּשֵׁם יְיָ : מְבָרֵךְ רֵעֵהוּ בְּקוֹל גָּדוֹל : הַמִּתְבָּרֵךְ³⁸ בָּאָרֶץ
יִתְבָּרֵךְ בֵּאלֹהֵי אָמֵן³⁹ : הִתְבָּרֵךְ בִּלְבָבוֹ⁴⁰ : וְהִתְבָּרְכוּ
בְזַרְעֲךָ⁴¹ כֹּל גּוֹיֵי הָאָרֶץ : וְיִתְבָּרְכוּ בוֹ כָּל־גּוֹיִם :

²⁴ פָּעַם to be vexed, לְהַכְעִיסוֹ Hip. to make him vexed. ²⁵ אֹיֵב An enemy. ²⁶ עָבַד ²⁷ שִׁפְחָה ²⁸ And no purchaser. ²⁹ Blessed (*kal*). ³⁰ עָמַד to stand. ³¹ To bless. ³² נֶפֶשׁ ³³ At all times. ³⁴ Thus. ³⁵ Good of eye, *i. e.* one that is kind, generous. ³⁶ *Jael*. ³⁷ The work of. ³⁸ He that blesses himself. ³⁹ Truth. ⁴⁰ לֵב ⁴¹ זֶרַע seed, offspring.

2nd Conjugation.

128. The second Conjugation comprehends all verbs whose first radical is נ: as, נָגַשׁ *to approach*, *Inf. cons.* נְגֹשׁ or גֶּשֶׁת.

The נ is dropped in every situation where the first radical of פָּקַד (or of any other perfect verb) receives (:)*, the defect being indicated by *dagesh* in the 2nd radical, whenever it

---

* Except the persons which receive the affixes תֶּן, תֶּם, and some in the passive participles.

is preceded by a *servile* having a vowel: as, גַּשׁ for נְגַשׁ (compare פְּקֹד); אֶגַּשׁ for אֶנְגַּשׁ (compare אֶפְקֹד). But in every situation where the first radical of פָּקַד has a vowel, the נ is retained, and the verb is inflected like פָּקַד: as, נָגַשׁ, נָגַשְׁתִּי (compare פָּקַדְתִּי).

Hence we have *Inf. cons.* (of *Kal*), גֶּשֶׁת* *in approaching*, מִגֶּשֶׁת, לָגֶשֶׁת, בְּגֶשֶׁת.

Imp. גַּשׁ or גְּשָׁה†, גְּשִׁי‡, גְּשׁוּ, גֵּשְׁנָה. *Future,* אֶגַּשׁ, תִּגַּשׁ, תִּגְּשִׁי, &c.

Niphal.

Part. נִגָּשׁ (for נִנְגָּשׁ). *Past tense,* נִגַּשְׁתִּי (for נִנְגַּשְׁתִּי).

Hiphil.

Inf. and *Imp.* הַגֵּשׁ, הַגִּישׁ (for הַנְגִּישׁ, &c.) *Part. act.* מַגִּישׁ. *Part. Pas.* מֻגָּשׁ. *Past tense,* הִגַּשְׁתִּי. *Fut.* אַגִּישׁ, &c.

Hophal.

Inf. הֻגַּשׁ (for הֻנְגַּשׁ). *Past tense,* הֻגַּשְׁתִּי. *Fut.* אֻגַּשׁ, &c.

---

* Some verbs of this conjugation retain the נ in the *Inf. Cons.*, and in the *Imp.*: as, נָפֹל *to fall*, בִּנְפֹל כִּנְפֹל לִנְפֹל. *Imp.* נְפֹל, נִפְלוּ;—but *Fut.* אֶפֹּל, תִּפֹּל.

Some few retain נ likewise in the future: as, נָצֹר *to keep*, יִנְצֹר or יִצֹּר; especially when the second radical happens to be a guttural: as, יִנְאַק *he shall cry*, יִנְעַם *he shall be pleasant, agreeable*: and in Hiphil הִנְחִיל *he has caused to inherit*, הִנְחַלְתִּי, &c., fut. אַנְחִיל, תַּנְחִיל, &c.

† Hence with מקף, גֶּשׁ־: with paragogic ה, גְּשָׁה.

‡ Or with (ִ), גְּשִׁי גְּשׁוּ &c.

All the other parts of the verb are conjugated like פָּקַד :— thus, *Past tense of* Kal, נָגַשְׁתִּי, נָגַשְׁתָּ, &c. *Part. act.* נוֹגֵשׁ. *Part. pas.* נָגוּשׁ, &c.—*Inf. Imp.* and *Fut.* of Niphal, הִנָּגֵשׁ, אֶנָּגֵשׁ, &c. And so likewise the whole of Piel, Pual, and Hithpael: as, נִגֵּשׁ, נֻגַּשׁ, הִתְנַגֵּשׁ.

129. The verb נָתַן *to give*, drops, in some instances, the second, and in others the first נ:—thus, *Inf. cons.* נָתֹן or תֵּת for תֶּנֶת. בְּנָתֹן or בְּתֵת *in giving*, לָתֵת, &c. *Imp.* תֵּן, תְּנִי, &c. *Fut.* אֶתֵּן, תִּתֵּן, &c. (for אֶנְתֵּן, &c. *Past tense*, נָתַתִּי, נָתַתָּ (for נָתַנְתִּי, &c.) Niphal, *Inf.* הִנָּתֵן or הִנָּתוֹן. *Imp.* הִנָּתֵן. *Fut.* אֶנָּתֵן. *Part.* נִתָּן. *Past,* נִתַּן, נִתַּתִּי, &c.

130. The verb לָקַח *to take*, is conjugated in the same manner: thus, *Inf. cons.* קַחַת *to take*, בְּקַחַת *in taking*, לָקַחַת, &c. *Imp.* קַח or לְקַח—קְחִי or לְקְחִי, &c. *Fut.* אֶקַּח, תִּקַּח (for אֶלְקַח). *Past tense*, לָקַחְתִּי. Niphal, הִלָּקַח. *Past tense*, נִלְקַחְתִּי or נִלְקַחְתִּי, &c.

3rd Conjugation.

131. The third Conjugation comprehends all verbs having א for their first radical: as, אָכַל *to eat,* אָסַף *to gather, assemble.*

This letter (א), being a guttural, will of course, follow the rules laid down in (Art. 125), that is, it will receive one of the semivowels where the first radical of פָּקַד receives (:), and the *dagesh*, which it does not admit, will be compensated by lengthening the vowel of the prefix.

THE HEBREW LANGUAGE.

132. In the first person future of KAL, the (א) is either rejected or retained. In the first case, the prefixes, נ, ת, י, א, receive (–ָ): as, אֹכַל (for אֶאֱכֹל)* *I will or shall eat.* †תֹּאכַל, נֹאכַל, יֹאכַל, תֹּאכְלִי, &c. In the second case, the prefixes נ, ת, י, א, receive (–ֶ): as, אֶאֱסֹף *I will gather,* תֶּאֱסֹף, נֶאֱסֹף, יֶאֱסֹף, ‡תֶּאַסְפִי. (See Obs. 1. Art. 125.)

Obs.—The verbs אָבַד *to be lost, to perish,* אָבָה *to be willing, to consent,* אָמַר *to say,* אָפָה *to bake,* form their future like אָכַל: thus, אֹבֶה, תֹּאמַר, אֹמַר; תֹּאבַד, אֹבַד, תֹּאפֶה, אֹפֶה, &c. But the verbs אָהֵב *to love,* אָחַז *to seize, to lay hold of,* אָצַר *to treasure up,* אָסַף *to gather, collect, &c.,* retain mostly the א and the (–ֶ), though they sometimes reject it, and take (–ָ) or (–ֶ): as, אֶאֱסֹף or אֶסְפָּה (Micah vii.) or יַאֲסוֹף or יֹסֵף (2 Sam. vi.) אֵהַב or אֹהַב *I will love,* יֶאֱהַב, תֶּאֱהַב, &c. תֹּאחֵז, אֹחֵז or תֶּאֱחֹז. Some take (–ֻ); as, אָזַל *to go away,* Fut. אֵזֶל, תֵּזֶל, &c.—אָחַר *to tarry,* Fut. יֶאֱחַר, תֵּחַר.—אָתָה *to come,* Fut. אֶאֱתֶה, אֶתֶה or יֶאֱתֶה.

In every other respect, these verbs are conjugated like those of the first conjugation.

---

* The א is frequently rejected in the other persons: as, תֹּחֵז (2 Sam. xx.) for תֶּאֱחֵז: תֹּמְרוּ (2 Sam. xix.) for תֹּאמְרוּ; תֹּבָא (Prov. i.) for תֹּאבֶה; and אִין (Job xxxii.) for אַיִן, וָאֶבְדְּךָ (Ezek. xxvii.) וָאַאַבֶּדְךָ. But these ought rather to be considered as anomalies.

† In pause, sometimes with (–ֹ)—תֹּאמַר, נֹאבַל, תֹּאבַל.

‡ See note p. 122.

K

Exercise.

וַיֹּאמֶר אֵלָיו אָבִיו גְּשׁוּ וּשְׁקָה לִּי בְּנִי וַיִּגַּשׁ
וַיִּשַּׁק לוֹ: וַיִּקְרָא דָוִד לְאַחַד מֵהַנְּעָרִים וַיֹּאמֶר גַּשׁ
פְּגַע בּוֹ: וַיֹּאמֶר לְכָל־הָעָם גְּשׁוּ אֵלַי וַיִּגְּשׁוּ אֵלָיו
כָל־הָעָם: וַתִּגַּשְׁןָ הַשְּׁפָחוֹת הֵנָּה וְיַלְדֵיהֶן וַתִּשְׁתַּחֲוֶיןָ גַּם
לֵאָה וִילָדֶיהָ וְאַחַר נִגַּשׁ יוֹסֵף וְרָחֵל: לְעֵת
הָאֹכֶל גּשִׁי הֲלֹם וְאָכַלְתְּ מִן הַלֶּחֶם וְטָבַלְתְּ
פִּתֵּךְ בַּחֹמֶץ: וַיֹּאמֶר הַגִּשָׁה לִּי וְאֹכְלָה מִצֵּיד בְּנִי
וַיַּגֶּשׁ־לוֹ וַיֹּאכַל: יָדָיו לֹא־אֲסֻרוֹת וְרַגְלֶיךָ לֹא
לִנְחֻשְׁתַּיִם הֻגָּשׁוּ: כִּנְפוֹל לִפְנֵי בְּנֵי עַוְלָה נָפָלְתָּ:
וַיַּחֲלֹם וְהִנֵּה סֻלָּם מֻצָּב אַרְצָה וְרֹאשׁוֹ מַגִּיעַ
הַשָּׁמָיְמָה: וְהִנֵּה יְהֹוָה נִצָּב עָלָיו: הָאִשָּׁה אֲשֶׁר
נָתַתָּה עִמָּדִי הִיא נָתְנָה לִּי מִן הָעֵץ וָאֹכֵל:
מִפְּרִי עֵץ־הַגָּן נֹאכֵל וּמִפְּרִי הָעֵץ אֲשֶׁר בְּתוֹךְ־הַגָּן
אָמַר אֱלֹהִים לֹא תֹאכְלוּ מִמֶּנּוּ וְלֹא תִגְּעוּ בּוֹ: תֶּן־

[1] נָגַשׁ to approach, to draw near. [2] נָשַׁק to kiss. [3] And he called. [4] David. [5] פָּגַע to meet, to slay. [6] A people. [7] שִׁפְחָה a maid-servant. [8] יֶלֶד a child. [9] Leah. [10] Afterwards. [11] Joseph. [12] Rachel. [13] At the time. [14] Food, meal. [15] Hither. [16] אָכַל to eat. [17] Bread. [18] טָבַל to dip. [19] פַּת a morsel, crumb. [20] Vinegar. [21] Game, venison. [22] אָסַר to bind. [23] Fetters, chains. [24] נָפַל to fall. [25] חָלַם to dream. [26] A ladder. [27] נָצַב to stand. [28] נָגַע to touch, reach. [29] Stood. [30] נָתַן to give. [31] With me. [32] A tree. [33] Fruit. [34] A garden. [35] תָּוֶךְ the middle. [36] נָגַע.

THE HEBREW LANGUAGE. 133

לִי הַנֶּפֶשׁ[37] וְהָרְכֻשׁ[38] קַח[39] לָךְ : וַיִּקַּח בֶּן־בָּקָר[40] רַךְ[41]
וָטוֹב וַיִּתֵּן אֶל הַנַּעַר : וַתֹּאמֶר הָאִשָּׁה הַזֹּאת אָמְרָה
אֵלַי תְּנִי אֶת־בְּנֵךְ וְנֹאכַל אֹתוֹ הַיּוֹם[42] וְאֶת־בְּנִי נֹאכַל
מָחָר[43] : נִטְעוּ[44] גַּנּוֹת וְאִכְלוּ אֶת־פִּרְיָנוֹ[45], קְחוּ לִבְנֵיכֶם
נָשִׁים[46] וְאֶת־בְּנוֹתֵיכֶם תְּנוּ לַאֲנָשִׁים : הַחָכְמָה[47] וְהַמַּדָּע[48]
נָתוּן לָךְ וְעֹשֶׁר[49] וְכָבוֹד[50] אֶתֶּן־לָךְ : תֶּבֶן[51] אֵין גִּתָּן
לַעֲבָדֶיךָ[52] וּלְבֵנִים[53] אֹמְרִים לָנוּ עֲשׂוּ[54] וְהִנֵּה עֲבָדֶיךָ
מֻכִּים[55] : לְכוּ[56] עִבְדוּ[57] וְתֶבֶן לֹא־יִנָּתֵן לָכֶם, וְתֹכֶן[58] לְבֵנִים
תִּתֵּנוּ : נִתְּנָה לְךָ גַּם אֶת־זֹאת; הִיא לֹא נִתְּנָה לוֹ לְאִשָּׁה :
הִנָּתֹן תִּנָּתֵן הָעִיר[59] הַזֹּאת בְּיַד מֶלֶךְ בָּבֶל[60] : יִתֶּן לָנוּ
שִׁבְעָה אֲנָשִׁים מִבָּנָיו : דָּרְכוּ[61] קַשְׁתָּם[62] לְהַפִּיל[63] עָנִי[64]
וְאֶבְיוֹן[65] : לְכוּ וְנַפִּילָה גוֹרָלוֹת ׳ וַיַּפִּלוּ גוֹרָלֹת, וַיִּפֹּל
הַגּוֹרָל עַל יוֹנָה[67] : הוּא הִפִּיל לָהֶן גּוֹרָל : רַבִּים חֲלָלִים[68]
הִפִּילָה : גּוֹרָלְךָ תַּפִּיל בְּתוֹכֵנוּ : עַצְלָה[69] תַּפִּיל תַּרְדֵּמָה[70] :
וָאֶתְנַפַּל[71] לִפְנֵי יְהֹוָה אֶת־אַרְבָּעִים הַיּוֹם וְאֶת־אַרְבָּעִים
הַלַּיְלָה[72] אֲשֶׁר הִתְנַפָּלְתִּי :

---

[37] The persons. [38] Wealth, goods. [39] לקח to take. [40] A calf. [41] Tender.
[42] To-day. [43] To-morrow. [44] נטע to plant. [45] Their fruit. [46] Wives.
[47] Wisdom. [48] Knowledge. [49] Riches. [50] Honor. [51] Straw.
[52] עבד a servant. [53] Bricks. [54] Make. [55] נכה to strike, smite, beat.
[56] Go. [57] עבד to serve, to labor. [58] The number, quantity. [59] The
city. [60] Babel. [61] דרך קשת to bend or stretch the bow. [62] קשת.
[63] To cause to fall, to throw down. [64] The poor. [65] The needy.
[66] Lot. [67] Jonah. [68] Slain. [69] Sloth. [70] Deep sleep. [71] התנפל to
throw one's self down. [72] ליל night.

4th Conjugation.

133. The fourth Conjugation comprehends all verbs whose first radical is ׳: as, יָשַׁב *to sit*, יָרֹד *to go down*, יָנַק *to suck*.

The ׳ is either retained without losing its consonantal sound, as in the preceding examples; or it is *quiescent*, and the preceding vowel lengthened : as, אֵשֵׁב *I shall* or *will sit :* or it is entirely dropped : as, שֵׁב *sit*, דַּע *know ;* or it is changed into וֹ, pronounced or quiescent : as, הִוָּדַע *to be known*, הִוָּשֵׁב *to be inhabited ;* הוֹדִיעַ *he made known*, הוֹשִׁיב *he caused to sit, he made* or *caused to be inhabited.*

Kal.

The *Inf. abs.* is regular; as, יָשֹׁב *to sit*, יָרֹעַ *to know*, &c.

The *Inf. cons.* drops ׳, and receives ת; as, שֶׁבֶת; and with the letters מ, ל, כ, ב. מִשֶּׁבֶת, לָשֶׁבֶת, כְּשֶׁבֶת, בְּשֶׁבֶת, לָדַעַת.*

The *Participles* are regular: as, יֹשֵׁב, יוֹשְׁבָה, or יוֹשֶׁבֶת, יוֹשְׁבִים, יוֹשְׁבוֹת. *Part. pas.* יָשׁוּב, יְשׁוּבָה, &c. The *Past* tense is likewise regular ; as, יָשַׁב *he did sit*, יָשְׁבָה, יָשַׁבְתִּי, &c.

---

* דַּעַת on account of the guttural. ה is sometimes substituted for ת : as, לְדֵעָה (for לָדַעַת) מֹרְדָה (for מֹרְדַת) Some few have their *Inf. Cons.* without either ת or ה; as, בִּיבֹשׁ *in drying*, from יָבֵשׁ; לְסֹד from יָסַד *to lay the foundation*, לִישֹׁן from יָשֵׁן *to sleep*, לְרֹא from יָרֵא *to fear*.

The *Imp.* drops mostly the י: as, שֵׁב *sit*, שְׁבִי; שְׁבוּ, שְׁבֶנָה.

The *Future* follows the *Imperative.* The letters נ, ת, י, א, receive mostly the vowel (..) or (–ֵ): as, אֵשֵׁב *I shall or will sit*, תֵּשֵׁב, תֵּשְׁבִי or אִינַק, תִּינַק, תִּינְקִי *I shall suck*, †.

Niphal.

In נִפְעַל, the י is changed into וֹ, which is either pronounced or quiescent. Thus, *Inf.* הִוָּשֵׁב (for הִיָּשֵׁב) *to be inhabited*, כְּהִוָּשֵׁב, בְּהִוָּשֵׁב, &c. The *Imp.* is the same: thus, הִוָּשֵׁב, הִוָּשְׁבִי, הִוָּשְׁבוּ, הִוָּשֵׁבְנָה. The *Future* is אִוָּשֵׁב, תִּוָּשֵׁב, תִּוָּשְׁבִי,‡ &c.

The *Participles* are נוֹשָׁב, נוֹשָׁבָה or נוֹשֶׁבֶת, &c. The *Past tense* is נוֹשַׁב, נוֹשָׁבָה, נוֹשַׁבְתִּי, &c.

Piël, Puäl, and Hithpaël

Are regular: as, יִשֵּׁב *he settled, placed,* יֻשַּׁב, הִתְיַשֵּׁב§; and from יָלַד *to bring forth,* יִלֵּד *he assisted in bringing forth.*‖

---

* Sometimes with an additional ה: as, שָׁבָה *sit*, רְדָה *descend.* In a few instances we find the י retained in the *Imperative:* as, יְצֹק *pour out,* (Ezek. xxiv. 3.)

† Sometimes without י: as, רַשׁ for יִירַשׁ (Gen. xxii.) *he will inherit.*

‡ From יָרֹה *to throw, to shoot,* we have יָרָה Exod. ix. (instead of יִוָּרֶה.)

§ Some few verbs have ו instead of י in *Hithp.*: as, הִתְוַדַּע *he made himself known.* הִתְוַדָּה *he confessed.*

‖ Hence מְיַלֶּדֶת *a midwife.*

Part. מְיַלֵּד,—יָלַד *he was born;*—הִתְיַלֵּד *he traced his birth, entered his name in the family register.*

Hiphil.

In הִפְעִיל, י *is mostly changed into* ו: *thus, Inf.* הוֹשִׁיב *to cause to sit,* בְּהוֹשִׁיב, לְהוֹשִׁיב—*Imp.* הוֹשֵׁב, הוֹשִׁיבִי—*Fut.* תּוֹשִׁיב, אוֹשִׁיב—*Part. act.* מוֹשִׁיב,—מוֹשִׁיבָה—*Part. pas.* מוּשָׁב, &c.—*Past tense,* הוֹשִׁיב, הוֹשִׁיבָה, הוֹשַׁבְתִּי.

Some, however, retain י: as from יָטַב *to be good.* Hiphil, הֵיטִיב or הֵיטִיב *to make good, to do well.*—*Imp.* הֵיטֵב, הֵיטִיבִי, &c.—*Fut.* אֵיטִיב or אֵיטִיב, תֵּיטִיב, &c.—*Part.* מֵיטִיב, &c.— *Past tense* הֵיטִיב, הֵיטִיבָה, הֵיטַבְתִּי, &c. The same from יָנַק *to suck,* הֵינִיק *he caused to suck,* הֵינַקְתִּי.—*Part.* מֵינִיק, מֵינִיקָה. *Imp.* הֵינִיק, הֵינִיקִי.—*Fut.* אֵינִיק, תֵּינִיק, &c.*

Hophal.

In הָפְעַל, י *is changed into* ו: *thus, Inf.* הוּשַׁב.—*Part.* הוּשָׁב.—*Past. tense,* הוּשַׁב, הוּשַׁבְתִּי.—*Fut.* אוּשַׁב, &c.

Obs.—The following verbs supply the omission of י by dagesh,† like verbs of the second conjugation:—

---

* Some of the modern Grammarians suppose that those which have ו in Hiphil, had originally ו for their first radical, as in Arabic: thus, ورد ولد‎ ورك‎, &c. There is, however, not a single example in Hebrew of a verb beginning with וֹ.

† They are therefore denominated חַסְרֵי פ״י deficient in י.

יָצַג, Hiphil, הִצִּיג *he placed ;* יָצַע *to spread out,* Hiphil, הַצִּיעַ; יָצַק *to pour out,* Fut. (Kal) אֶצּוֹק; יָצַר *to form,* Fut. אֶצֹּר, יָצַר; יָצַת *to burn, set on fire,* Niphál, נִצַּת; Hiphil הִצִּית*.

5th Conjugation.

134. The fifth Conjugation comprehends all verbs whose second radical is ו or י: as, קוֹם or קוּם *to rise,* שׁוּב *to return,* בִּין† *to understand,* רוֹב or רִיב *to contend, dispute.*

These letters are generally quiescent, but sometimes they are omitted.‡

---

* To these, some Grammarians add יָצַב *to place. Niphal,* נִצָּב, נִצַּבְתָּ. *Hiphil,* הִצִּיב fut. אַצִּיב: נָח *Hiphil,* הִנִּיחַ *he left alone.* It is, however, very probable that these are derived from verbs whose first radical is נ.

† When ו or י retain their consonantal sound, as in אָיַב *to hate,* גָּוַע *to expire,* they are conjugated like the perfect verb. Thus, אָיַבְתִּי *I hated,* גָּוַעְתִּי *I expired.* Fut. אֶגְוַע, &c.

‡ Most of the early grammarians maintained that the second radical of these and similar verbs is ו; that בִּין, רִיב, שִׂים, &c. are *infinitives* of *Hiphil,* written without ה, *i. e.* for הָבִין, הָרִיב, &c.; and that אָבִין, תָּבִין, אָרִיב, &c. are the futures of *Hiphil.* But as these verbs have mostly the same signification as those of קַל, and as the י is evidently a radical in some parts of the verb, as, בִּינוֹתִי *I have understood, searched,* רִיבֹת *thou didst contend,* I think the moderns are sufficiently justified in considering י as the second radical; or, which is still more probable, that these verbs were written with either י or ו׃

Kal.

The *Infinitive absolute* has mostly וֹ, though sometimes וּ, or ‎ָ ‎ for its vowel; as in the preceding examples.

The *Infinitive cons.* has mostly וּ, more rarely וֹ or ִי for its vowel: as, בְּשׁוּב *in returning*, לָשׁוּב, מָשׁוּב.—מוֹת *to die*, בָּמוֹת, בָּמוֹת, לָמוּת—לָרִיב *to contend*.

The *Imperative* and the *Passive participle* are mostly like the *Inf. cons.*: thus, קוּם, *קוּמִי, קוּמוּ, קֹמְנָה.—*Part. pas.* קוּמוֹת ‡,קוּמִים, קוּמָה †,קוּם. And from בִּין, *Imp.* בִּין, בִּינִי, בִּינוּ, &c.

The *Future* follows the *Imperative;* and its prefixes א י ת נ, have long (ָ): thus, אָקוּם *I will rise*, תָּקוּם, תָּקוּמִי, &c. And from בִּין, אָבִין, תָּבִין, תָּבִינִי.‖

The *third persons m. Past tense*, have either (ָ) or (ֵ) or וֹ for their vowels: thus—

קָם *he rose*, קָמָה *f.* קָמוּ *p.* and the other persons—קָמוּ, קַמְתְּ, קַמְתָּ, קַמְנוּ, קַמְתֶּם, קַמְתֶּן, קָמְתִּי.

מֵת *he died*, מֵתָה *f.* מֵתוּ *p.* and the other persons—מֵתִי, מַתְּ, מַתָּ, מַתְנוּ, מַתֶּם, מַתֶּן.

---

* And with paragogic ה: as, קוּמָה, בִּינָה. But the noun בִּינָה *understanding*, has the accent on the last syllable.

† Sometimes with (ֹ): as from בּוֹשׁ *to be ashamed;* Part. בּוֹשָׁה &c.; and from טוֹב *to be good*, טוֹבָה, טוֹבִים, &c.

‡ We have likewise קוֹמִים. (2 Kings xvi. 7.)

‖ According to the early grammarians, the future would be אָבוּן, תָּבוּן, which is, however, not used. *Past tense*, בַּנְתִּי or בִּינוֹתִי, בַּנְתָּ, בָּן, בָּנָה, בַּנּוּ, בַּנְתֶּם, בָּנוּ.

בּוֹשׁ *he was ashamed,* בָּשָׁה *f.* בּשׁ *p.* and the other persons—
בָּשְׁתֶּן, *בָּשְׁתָּ,* בֹּשְׁתְּ, בֹּשְׁנוּ, בָּשְׁתֶּם, בֹּשְׁתִּי.
The *Active Participle* is the same as the *third person m.*:
thus, קָם *one that rises,* קָמָה†, קָמִים, קָמוֹת.—מֵת *one that is
dead,* מֵתָה, מֵתִים, מֵתוֹת.—בּוֹשׁ *one that feels ashamed,*
בּוֹשָׁה, בּוֹשִׁים, בּוֹשׁוֹת.

Niphal.

The *Infinitive* is הָקוֹם, הִבּוֹן, and with ב, כ, ל, מ, בְּהָקוֹם,
מֵהָקוֹם, לְהָקוֹם, בְּהָקוֹם.

The *Imperative* is the same, הֵקוֹם, הֵקוֹמִי, הֵקוֹמוּ, הֵקוֹמְנָה.

The *Future* is אֶקּוֹם, תִּקּוֹם, תִּקּוֹמִי.

The *Participles,* נָקוֹם. &c., נָבוֹן, נְבוֹנָה, נְבוֹנִים, נְבוֹנוֹת.

The *Past tense* is נְקוֹמֹתִי······נָקוֹמוּ, נְקוֹמָה, נָקוֹם,
נְקוֹמֹת, &c.

Piël and Puäl.

פִּעֵל and פֻּעַל double the last radical. Thus, *Inf.*
קוֹמֵם‡ *to raise up, re-establish.—Imp.* the same.—*Fut.*

---

* With short ָ, because קָם and קַם have the accent. (See Part I.
p. 79.)

† The *participle feminine* has the accent on the last syllable.
and is thus distinguished from the third person *f.* past, which has
always the accent on the *penultimate.*

‡ Or like the perfect verb: thus, קִים *to establish, confirm, perform,* קִים *he established, performed;* especially in Rabbinical
Hebrew, קִימְתִּי, קִימְתָּ, &c.

אֲקוֹמֵם.—*Part. act.* מְקוֹמֵם, &c.—*Part. pas.* מְקוֹמָם, &c.—*Past tense,* קוֹמֵם, קוֹמְמָה, קוֹמְמוּ,—קוֹמַמְתִּי, קוֹמַמְתְּ, &c.

Puäl is conjugated in the same manner, with this difference, that it takes (-) where *Piël* has (..): thus, *Inf.* קוֹמַם.—*Fut.* אֲקוֹמַם.—*Past tense,* קוֹמַם, &c.* The other parts of *Puäl* are like *Piël*, and can only be distinguished by the context.

Hiphil.

Inf. הָקֵם or הָקִים *to raise, to cause to stand, establish,* בְּהָקִים, לְהָקִים, &c.—*Imp.* הָקֵם, הָקִימִי, הָקִימוּ, הָקֵמְנָה.—*Fut.* אָקִים, תָּקִים, תְּקִימִי†, &c.—*Part. act.* מֵקִים, מְקִימָה, &c.‡—*Part. pas.* מוּקָם, מוּקָמָה, &c.—*Past tense* הֵקִים, הֵקִימָה, הֵקִימוּ – הֲקִימוֹת, הֲקִימוֹתִי, &c., or הֲקַמְתִּי, הֲקַמְתָּ, &c.

Hophal.

Hophal takes וּ for the first radical: thus, *Inf.* הוּקַם.—*Fut.* אוּקַם, &c.—*Part.* הוּקָם, &c.—*Past tense,* הוּקַם, הוּקְמָה, הוּקַמְתָּ, הוּקַמְתִּי—הוּקְמוּ, &c.

---

* Participle, קוֹמָם, קוֹמָמִים, קוֹמָמָה, קוֹמָמוֹת.

† Or with (..): as, אָפֵר *I will frustrate, annul,* יָפֵר; or with (-), when the third radical is a guttural: as, אָרַע *I will ill-treat, cause evil.*

‡ Or with (..): as, מֵפֵר; and with (-): as, מֵרַע.

§ Or with (-): as, הֵפֵר, הֵרַע.

Hithpael is formed by adding its characteristic letters to Piel: thus, הִתְקוֹמֵם *he aroused himself, opposed himself*; *Imp.* הִתְקוֹמֵם, הִתְקוֹמְמִי, &c.

Exercise.

יָרַד¹ יָרְדְנוּ לִשְׁבָּר־אֹכֶל² : וַיֹּאמֶר לֹא נוּכַל³
לָרֶדֶת אִם־יֵשׁ אָחִינוּ הַקָּטֹן אִתָּנוּ וְיָרַדְנוּ : הִנֵּה עַם
יוֹרֵד מֵרָאשֵׁי⁴ הֶהָרִים : הֵמָּה יֹרְדִים מִקְצֵה⁵ הָעִיר :
רַגְלֶיהָ יֹרְדוֹת מָוֶת : בְּתוֹךְ עַמִּי אָנֹכִי יֹשָׁבֶת⁶ : דּוֹדִי
יָרַד לְגַנּוֹ : אֶל גִּנַּת־אֱגוֹז⁷ יָרַדְתִּי : יָרְדוּ בִמְצוֹלֹת⁸ כְּמוֹ
אָבֶן : אֵשׁ יָרְדָה מֵהַשָּׁמַיִם : קוּם רֵד מַהֵר מִזֶּה : רְדִי
וּשְׁבִי עַל עָפָר⁹ בַּת־בָּבֶל : אָנֹכִי אֵרֵד עִמָּךְ : לֹא יֵרֵד
בְּנִי עִמָּכֶם : הֲיָדוֹעַ¹⁰ נֵדַע כִּי יֹאמַר הוֹרִידוּ אֶת־
אֲחִיכֶם : יוֹסֵף הוּרַד מִצְרַיְמָה : אַךְ אֶל שְׁאוֹל¹¹ תּוּרָד :
שׁוּב¹² וְשֵׁב עִם הַמֶּלֶךְ : שֻׁבְנָה בְנֹתַי לָמָּה תֵלַכְנָה¹³
עִמִּי : שְׁבוּ פֹה עַד אֲשֶׁר נָשׁוּב : אַתָּה יָדַעְתָּ שִׁבְתִּי
וְקוּמִי : אֲדֹנִי יֵדַע כִּי הַיְלָדִים¹⁴ רַכִּים¹⁵ : הַחַיִּים¹⁶

¹ To go down, to descend. ² To purchase food. ³ Root, יכל, to be able. ⁴ רֹאשׁ head, top. ⁵ קָצֶה the end, extremity. ⁶ יָשַׁב to sit. ⁷ Nut. ⁸ מְצוּלָה the depth. ⁹ Dust. ¹⁰ יָדוֹעַ to know. ¹¹ The grave. ¹² To return. ¹³ ילך to go. ¹⁴ ילד a child. ¹⁵ רַךְ tender, young. ¹⁶ The living.

142 THE ETYMOLOGY OF

יוֹדְעִים שָׂמֻתוּ[17] : אָבֵן[18] נוֹדַע הַדָּבָר : אַל־יִוָּדַע כִּי בָאָה
הָאִשָּׁה : אַל־תּוֹדְעִי לָאִישׁ[20] : וַיֻּגַּד הַדָּבָר לְמָרְדֳּכַי[21] :
אֶת־מִשְׁפָּטִי[22] הוֹדַעְתִּי אוֹתָם : אַחֲרֵי הוֹדִיעַ אֱלֹהִים
אוֹתְךָ אֶת־כָּל־זֹאת אֵין[23] נָבוֹן וְחָכָם כָּמוֹךָ : אוֹדִיעַ
אֱמוּנָתְךָ[24] בְּפִי : רֹב[25] שָׁנִים יוֹדִיעוּ חָכְמָה : בַּמַּרְאָה[26]
אֵלָיו אֶתְוַדָּע : לֹא עָמַד[27] אִישׁ אִתּוֹ בְּהִתְוַדַּע יוֹסֵף אֶל
אֶחָיו : אָבִינוּ מֵת[28] בַּמִּדְבָּר : אֶל אֲשֶׁר תֵּלְכִי אֵלֵךְ וּבַאֲשֶׁר
תָּלִינִי[29] אָלִין : בַּאֲשֶׁר תָּמוּתִי אָמוּת וְשָׁם אֶקָּבֵר[30] : אָנֹכִי
מֵתִי אֶת־מָשִׁיחַ[31] יְהוָֹה : עֲמָד־נָא עָלַי וּמֹתְתֵנִי : רָעָה[32]
תְּמוֹתֵת רָשָׁע[33] : אֶת בְּנֵיהֶם לֹא הֵמִית : אַתֶּם הֲמִתֶּם
אֶת־עַם יְהוָֹה : אֶת־שְׁנֵי בְנֵי תָּמִית : הֲמָה הֻמְתוּ בִּימֵי
קָצִיר[34] : מָחָר[35] אַתָּה מוּמָת : לֹא יוּמְתוּ אָבוֹת[36] עַל
בָּנִים : מִפְּנֵי שֵׂיבָה[37] תָּקוּם : מַמְלַכְתְּךָ[38] לֹא־תָקוּם :
מֵקִים מֵעָפָר דָּל[39] : נָבִיא[40] אָקִים לָהֶם : וַיָּקָם מֶלֶךְ
חָדָשׁ[41] : וַיָּקָם עַל־סֶלַע[42] רַגְלַי[43] :

[17] מוּת to die. [18] Truly. [19] Came. [20] To any one. [21] Mordecai.
[22] Judgment. [23] Root, בִּין to understand. [24] אֱמוּנָה truth. [25] Multitude. [26] A vision. [27] To stand. [28] Died. [29] לוּן to lodge, remain during night. [30] קבר to bury. [31] The anointed. [32] Evil. [33] The wicked. [34] Harvest. [35] To-morrow. [36] Parents. [37] Old age.
[38] מַמְלֶכֶת kingdom. [39] Poor, indigent. [40] A prophet. [41] New.
[42] A rock. [43] רֶגֶל foot.

6th Conjugation.

128. The sixth Conjugation comprehends all

verbs whose third radical is א: as, מָצָא *to find*, קָרָא *to call*.

They are thus conjugated:—

Kal.

Inf. מְצֹא, מָצֹא* *to find*, הִמָּצֵא *in finding*, לִמְצֹא, &c.—
Imp. מְצָא, מִצְאִי, מִצְאוּ, מְצֶאנָה.†—*Fut.* אֶמְצָא, תִּמְצָא,
תִּמְצְאִי, &c.—*Part. act.* מוֹצֵא, מוֹצְאָה or מוֹצֵאת, מוֹצְאִים,
מוֹצְאוֹת.—*Part. pas.* מָצוּא, מְצוּאָה, מְצוּאִים, מְצוּאוֹת.—
Past tense, מָצָאת, מָצָאתָ, מָצָאתִי—מָצְאוּ, מָצְאָה, ‡מָצָא, &c.

Niphal.

Inf. and *Imp.* הִמָּצֵא, &c.—*Fut.* אֶמָּצֵא, &c.—*Part.* נִמְצָא,
&c.—*Past tense,* נִמְצָא, נִמְצְאָה, &c., נִמְצֵאתָ, נִמְצֵאת,
נִמְצֵאתִי, &c.

———

* Sometimes with ה: as, קָרָא *to call*, קָרָאת; מָלֵא *to be full*, מָלְאַת.
† ה is sometimes omitted: as, מְצֶאןָ.
‡ Some verbs (chiefly *intransitives*) have (ֵ) instead of (ָ) for the second radical: as, מָלֵא *he was full*, מָלְאָה—מָלְאוּ, מָלֵאתָ, מָלֵאת, &c. In such cases, the participle active of *Kal* has the same form as the third person *m. past.* Thus, מָלֵא—whence מְלֵאָה, מְלֵאוֹת, מְלֵאִים. Thus likewise טָמֵא *he is unclean*, or *one that is unclean*, טְמֵאָה, טְמֵאִים, טְמֵאוֹת—צָמֵא *he is thirsty*, or *one that is thirsty*, צְמֵאָה, צְמֵאִים, צְמֵאוֹת.

Piël.

Inf. and *Imp.* מַצֵּא.—*Fut.* אֲמַצֵּא, &c.—*Part. act.* מְמַצֵּא, &c.—*Part. pas.* מְמֻצָּא, &c.—*Past tense,* מִצֵּא, &c.

Puäl.

Inf. מֻצָּא.—*Fut.* אֲמֻצָּא, &c.—*Part.* מֻצָּא, &c.—*Past tense* מֻצָּא, &c.—מֻצֵּאת, מֻצֵּאתָ, מֻצֵּאתִי,—&c.

Hiphil.

Inf. הַמְצִיא.—*Imp.* הַמְצֵא, &c.—*Fut.* אַמְצִיא, &c.—*Part. act.* מַמְצִיא.—*Part. pas.* מֻמְצָא, &c.—*Past tense,* הִמְצִיא, הִמְצִיאָה, &c.—הִמְצֵאתִי, הִמְצֵאתָ, הִמְצֵאת, &c.

Hophäl.

הָמְצָא or הֻמְצָא in the same manner as הָפְקַד or הֻפְקַד.

Hithpaël,

הִתְמַצֵּא, &c. like הִתְפַּקֵּד.

7th CONJUGATION.

136. The Seventh Conjugation comprehends all

verbs whose third radical is ה without, *mappik*,*
(Part I. p. 21) ; as, גָּלָה *to reveal*, בָּכָה *to weep*.

The letter is changed into ת or י, or it is omitted.

Kal.

Inf. abs. גָּלֹה *to reveal*.†—*Inf. cons.* גְּלוֹת, בִּגְלוֹת, בִּגְלוֹת,
&c.—*Imp.* גְּלֵה, גְּלִי, גְּלוּ, גְּלֶינָה.—*Fut.* אֶגְלֶה, תִּגְלֶה ‡, תִּגְלִי,
יִגְלֶה, &c.—*Part. act.* גֹּלֶה, גֹּלָה § גֹּלִים, גֹּלוֹת.—*Part. pas.*

---

* Verbs having הּ (with *mappik*) for the third radical, are conjugated like perfect verbs: thus, גָּבַהְתִּי *I was high*, (not גָּבִיתִי), גָּבַהּ· *Part.* גָּבֹהַּ, גְּבוֹהִים· *Fut.* אֶגְבַּהּ· (the ה retaining the *mappik* in all parts of the verb wherein it forms the last letter).

† In a few instances with ו׃ as, קָנוֹ *to purchase* (2 Sam. xxiv. 24), instead of קָנָה ; עָשׂוֹ *to do* (Gen. xxxi. 38), for לַעֲשׂוֹת.

‡ The prefixes ן, ת, י have mostly (ֶ) or (ֱ) when the first radical is a guttural: as, תַּעֲלֶה *thou shalt ascend*, יַעֲלֶה; תַּחֲנֶה *thou shalt encamp*, תֶּחֱזֶה *thou shalt see*. The ה is sometimes dropped: as, יַעַל *he shall ascend* (for יַעֲלֶה); יַעַשׂ *he shall do* (for יַעֲשֶׂה); especially with *conversive* (ו): as, וַיַּעַל *and he ascended*; וַיַּעַשׂ *and he did*; וַנֵּפֶן *and we turned*. And when the second radical happens to be either of the letters ת, ק, פ, כ, ט, ד, ב, both receive (ִ): as, וַיִּשְׁבְּ *and he captured*, וַיֵּבְךְּ *and he wept*.

§ Instead גֹּלְהָ.—In some instances י is substituted for the third radical (ה): as, בֹּכִיָּה *one that weeps, f.*, so likewise in the past tense, חָסָיָה *she trusted* (for חָסְתָה); חָסָיוּ *they trusted* (for חָסוּ). And in the future, יִשְׁלָיוּ *they shall be tranquil*; especially with a Paragogic letter: as, אֶהֱמָיָה *I shall roar, be disquieted*, (for אֶהֱמֶה); יֶהֱמָיוּן (for יֶהֱמוּ).

THE ETYMOLOGY OF

*גָּלוּ, גָּלְתָה, גָּלָה, גְּלוּיִם, גְּלוּיָה, גְּלוּיוֹת.—Past tense, גָּלוּי, &c. גָּלִיתִי, גָּלִיתָ.

Niphal.

Inf. abs. הִגָּלֹה.—Cons. בְּהִגָּלוֹת, הִגָּלוֹת, &c.—Imp. הִגָּלֵה, &c.—Fut. אֶגָּלֶה, תִּגָּלֶה, תִּגָּלִי, הִגָּלוּ, הִגָּלֶינָה.—Part. נִגְלֶה, נִגְלָה, &c.—Past tense, נִגְלְתָה, נִגְלוּ—נִגְלֵיתִי, נִגְלֵית, &c.

Piël.

Inf. גַּלֹּה or גַּלּוֹת.—Imp. גַּלֵּה, &c.—Fut. אֲגַלֶּה†, &c.—Part. act. מְגַלֶּה, &c.—Part. pas. מְגֻלֶּה, &c.—Past tense, גִּלָּה, גִּלְּתָה, &c.—גִּלִּיתִי, &c.

Puäl.

Inf. גֻּלֹּה, גֻּלּוֹת.—Fut. אֲגֻלֶּה.—Part. גֻּלֶּה.—Past tense, גֻּלָּה, גֻּלְּתָה, &c.—גֻּלֵּיתִי, &c.

Hiphil.

Inf. הַגְלֵה, הַגְלוֹת.—Imp. הַגְלֵה‡, &c.—Fut. אַגְלֶה,

---

* גָּלוּ with the accent on the last syllable: whereas verbs of the fifth conjugation have their accent on the *penultimate*, as, קָמוּ, *they stood up.*—שָׁבוּ (from שׁוּב) signifies, *they returned;* but שָׁבוּ (from שָׁבָה) signifies, *they captured, took prisoners.*

† And without ה: as, יְצַו *he shall command* (for יְצַוֶּה).

‡ The ה is sometimes dropped: as, הַעַל *bring up* (for הַעֲלֵה).

מִגְלָה, &c.—*Part. pas.* מָגְלָה.—*Part. act.* יַגְלֶה, תַגְלֶה, &c.
Past tense, הִגְלֵיתִי—הִגְלָה, הִגְלְתָה, הִגְלָה or הִגְלוּ, &c.
הִגְלִינוּ.

Hophal.

Takes (ָ) for the first vowel, and the radical ה follows the same rule as in the preceding branches: thus, הָגְלֵיתִי, הָגְלֵיתָ, &c. תָּגְלֶה, אָגְלֶה, &c.

Hithpaël.

הִתְגַּלָּה, אֶתְגַּלֶּה, &c., הִתְגַּלֵּיתָ, וְהִתְגַּלֵּיתִי, &c.

137. The verbs הָיָה *to be,* חָיָה *to live,* belong to this conjugation; but they deviate in some measure from the preceding rules, as may be seen from the following examples:—

Inf. abs. הָיֹה *to be.*—*Inf. cons.* הֱיוֹת, בִּהְיוֹת *in being,* מִהְיוֹת, לִהְיוֹת.

Imp. הֱיֵה *be thou, m.,* הֱיִי or הֲיִי *f.,* הֱיוּ *p. m.,* הֱיֶינָה *f.*
Fut. אֶהְיֶה or אֱהִי *I shall or will be;* תִּהְיֶה or תְּהִי; *f.* תִּהְיֶה or תְּהִי; יִהְיֶה or יְהִי; נִהְיֶה or נְהִי; תִּהְיוּ, תִּהְיֶינָה *f.* תְּהִיֶן or תִּהְיֶינָה *f.,* יִהְיוּ.

---

* And with *conversive* וַ-יֶּגֶל: וַיֶּפֶן *and he caused to turn;* וַיַּרְא (2 Kings ii.) *and he caused to see,* i. e. *he shewed.*

L.

148   THE ETYMOLOGY OF

Part. m. הֹוֶה or הָוֶה, f. הֹוָה or הָיָה, p. הֹוִים*, f. הֹוֹת*.

Past tense, הָיִיתִי, הָיִיתָ, הָיִיתְ f. הָיָה, הָיְתָה f. הָיִינוּ, הָיוּ f. הֱיִיתֶן, הֱיִיתֶם.

In *Niphal* we find some of the persons of the past tense only: thus, נִהְיֵיתִי *I have become*, נִהְיֵיתָ, נִהְיָה; and by *analogy*, נִהְיֵינוּ, נִהְיֵיתֶם, נִהְיֵיתֶן, נִהְיוּ.

Infinitive Absolute חָיֹה *to live*.

Kal.

Imp. חֲיֵה, חֲיִי, חֲיוּ, חֲיֶינָה.—*Fut.* אֶחְיֶה, תִּחְיֶה, תִּחְיִי, יִחְיֶה or יְחִי, תְּחִי, נִחְיֶה, &c.—*Part.* חַי, חַיָּה, חַיִּים, חַיּוֹת.—*Past tense*, חָיִיתִי, חָיִיתָ, חָיִיתְ, חָיָה, חָיְתָה, חָיִינוּ, חֲיִיתֶם, חֲיִיתֶן, חָיוּ.

Niphal not used.

Piël.

Inf. חַיֵּה *to preserve, sustain life*, חַיּוֹת, לְחַיּוֹת.—*Imp.* חַיֵּה, חַיִּי, חַיּוּ, חַיֶּינָה.—*Fut.* אֲחַיֶּה, תְּחַיֶּה, תְּחַיִּי, יְחַיֶּה, נְחַיֶּה.—*Part.* מְחַיֶּה, תְּחַיֶּינָה, יְחַיּוּ, תְּחַיּוּ, &c. Past tense, חִיִּיתִי, חִיִּיתָ, חִיִּיתְ, חִיָּה, חִיִּינוּ, חִיִּיתֶם, חִיִּיתֶן, חִיּוּ.

Hiphïl.

Inf. הַחֲיֵה *to cause to live, restore life, revive*, לְהַחֲיוֹת.—*Imp.* הַחֲיֵה, &c.—*Past tense*, הֶחֱיֵיתִי, הֶחֱיֵיתָ, הֶחֱיֵיתְ, הֶחֱיָה, הֶחֱיְתָה, &c.

---

* Or הֱיוֹת—הֹיִים.

Exercise.

בְּטֶרֶם ֫ יֵדַע הַנַּעַר קְרֹא ֫ אָבִי וְאִמִּי : מָה הַדָּבָר
הַזֶּה עָשִׂיתָ לָּנוּ לְבִלְתִּי קְרֹאות לָנוּ : קוֹל קוֹרֵא
בַּמִּדְבָּר פַּנּוּ ֫ דֶרֶךְ : גַּם לְיַחַד אֲנִי קָרוּא ֫ לָהּ עִם
הַמֶּלֶךְ : יִקְרָא לַנַּעֲרָה וְיִשְׁאָלָה ֫ אֶת־פִּיהָ : שִׁמְךָ עָלֵינוּ
נִקְרָא : אֲנִי לֹא נִקְרֵאתִי לָבוֹא ֫ אֶל הַמֶּלֶךְ זֶה שְׁלוֹשִׁים
יוֹם : הֲלֹא הַחָכְמָה תִקְרָא וּתְבוּנָה תִתֵּן קוֹלָהּ : אָז
תִקְרָא וַיהוָֹה ֫ יַעֲנֶה ֫ : לָזֹאת יִקָּרֵא אִשָּׁה : אַשְׁרֵי אָדָם
מָצָא חָכְמָה : גַּם צִפּוֹר ֫ מָצְאָה ֫ בַיִת : דְּבַשׁ ֫ מָצָאתָ
אֱכֹל דַּיֶּךָּ ֫ : לֵךְ מְצָא אֶת־הַחִצִּים : עִם אֲשֶׁר תִּמְצָא
אֶת־אֱלֹהֶיךָ לֹא יִחְיֶה : תִּמְצָא שִׁפְחָתְךָ ֫ חֵן בְּעֵינֶיךָ ֫ :
אִם הִמָּצֵא תִמָּצֵא בְיָדוֹ הַגְּנֵבָה ֫ שְׁנַיִם ֫ יְשַׁלֵּם ֫ :
וּלְבַדַּתְּ ֫ בָּבֶל וְאַתְּ לֹא יָדַעַתְּ, נִמְצֵאת וְגַם נִתְפַּשְׂתְּ ֫ :
שְׂפָתָיו ֫ מָלְאוּ זַעַם ֫ : יְמִינָם ֫ מָלְאָה שֹּׁחַד ֫ : מָלֵא
קַרְנְךָ ֫ שֶׁמֶן : נִמְלָא בָתֵּינוּ ֫ שָׁלָל ֫ : מָלֵא בָתֵּיהֶם כָּל־
טוּב ֫ : חָטָא ֫ וְהֶחֱטִיא אֶת־יִשְׂרָאֵל : גַּם אוֹתוֹ הֶחֱטִיאוּ
הַנָּשִׁים הַנָּכְרִיּוֹת ֫ : לֹא יֵשְׁבוּ בְאַרְצְךָ פֶּן יַחֲטִיאוּ אֹתְךָ

[1] Before. [2] R. קרא. [3] R. עשׂה to do. [4] Not. [5] R. פנה to turn, Pi. to clear away. [6] Called, invited. [7] שׁאל to ask. [8] To come. [9] ענה to answer. [10] A bird. [11] Honey. [12] דַי sufficient, enough. [13] עין. [14] Theft. [15] To pay. [16] לכד to catch. [17] תפשׂ to lay hold of. [18] שָׂפָה lip. [19] Anger. [20] The right hand. [21] A bribe. [22] קֶרֶן a horn. [23] בַּיִת. [24] Spoil, plunder. [25] Goods, riches. [26] To sin. [27] Strange.

לִי : רְאֵה²⁸ זֶה מָצָאתִי : רָאֹה רָאִיתִי אֶת־עֳנִי עַמִּי :
דְּעִי וּרְאִי מַה תַּעֲשִׂי²⁹ : צְאֶינָה³⁰ וּרְאֶינָה בְּנוֹת צִיּוֹן :
אֹזֶן שֹׁמַעַת וְעַיִן רֹאָה יְהוָה עָשָׂה גַּם־שְׁנֵיהֶם³¹ : מָה
רָאִיתָ כִּי עָשִׂיתָ אֶת־הַדָּבָר הַזֶּה : רָאֹה כִּי לֹא גְעֶשְׂתָה
עֲצָתוֹ³² : עַתָּה תִרְאֶה אֲשֶׁר אֶעֱשֶׂה לָהֶם : עֵינַי עִוְרִים³³
תִרְאֶינָה : בְּאוֹרְךָ נִרְאֶה אוֹר : אֱלֹהֵי אֲבוֹתֵיכֶם גְּרָאָה
אֵלָי : הַיּוֹם אֵרָאֶה אֵלָיו : מַעֲשִׂים³⁴ אֲשֶׁר לֹא יֵעָשׂוּ
עֲשִׂיתָן עִמָּדִי : הִנֵּה הֶרְאָה אֱלֹהִים אֹתִי גַּם אֶת־זַרְעֶךָ
אֹתָהּ הָרְאֵיתָ לָדַעַת : אֶת־אוֹיְבֵיהֶם כִּסָּה³⁵ הַיָּם : כְּלִמָּה³⁶
כִסְּתָה פָנָי : אֶרֶץ אַל תְּכַסִּי דָמִי : בַּחֹשֶׁךְ שְׁמוֹ יְכֻסֶּה :
הַזְּקֵנִים³⁷ מְכֻסִּים בַּשַּׂקִּים³⁸ : הַבְּהֵמָה הַבָּקָר וְהַצֹּאן אַל־
יִטְעֲמוּ³⁹ מְאוּמָה⁴⁰ , אַל־יִרְעוּ⁴¹ וּמַיִם אַל־יִשְׁתּוּ⁴² וְיִתְכַּסּוּ
שַׂקִּים וְיִקְרְאוּ אֶל־אֱלֹהִים בְּחָזְקָה⁴³ וְיָשֻׁבוּ⁴⁴ אִישׁ⁴⁵ מִדַּרְכּוֹ
הָרָעָה :

²⁸ רָאָה to see. ²⁹ עָשָׂה to do. ³⁰ יָצָא to go out. ³¹ Both. ³² עֵצָה advice. ³³ עִוֵּר a blind man. ³⁴ מַעֲשֶׂה work, deed. ³⁵ כָּסָה to cover. ³⁶ Shame. ³⁷ זָקֵן an old man. ³⁸ A sack, sack-cloth. ³⁹ טָעַם to taste. ⁴⁰ Any-thing. ⁴¹ רָעָה to feed. ⁴² שָׁתָה to drink. ⁴³ With force, vehemently. ⁴⁴ שׁוּב to return. ⁴⁵ Each.

8th Conjugation.

138. The Eighth Conjugation comprehends verbs whose second and third radical are the same; as, מָדַד *to measure*, סָבַב *to surround*.

THE HEBREW LANGUAGE.

The second radical is mostly dropped, and its vowel transferred to the first radical. The deficiency of the second is indicated by *dagesh* in the third radical, in all cases where it has a vowel. In many parts of the verb, however, the second radical is retained, and conjugated like the perfect verb פָּקַד.

Kal.

Inf. abs. סָבֹב or סֹב *to turn about, surround.*—*Inf. cons.* סֹב, סֹבִּי*, סֹבּוּ,—*Imp.* מָסֹב.—לִסְבֹּב, לָסֹב or סֹב, בְּסֹב, בְּסֹב,
אָסֹב‡, תָּסֹב, תָּסֹבִּי, יָסֹב, תָּסֹב, וְסֹב, תָּסֹבּוּ,—*Fut.* תְּסֻבֶּינָה†.—*Part. act.* סַב, סַבָּה, סַבִּים, יָסֹבּוּ, תְּסֻבֶּינָה§.—סוּבְבָה, סוֹבֵב, or like the perfect verb, סַבּוֹת; or סוּבָבָה, סוּבָבִים,
סוּבָבוֹת.—*Part. pas.* סָבוּב, סְבוּבָה, סְבוּבִים,
סְבוּבוֹת.—*Past tense,* סַב‖, סַבָּה, סַבּוּ—סַבּוֹתִי; סַבּוֹתָ, סַבּוֹת,
סַבֹּתֶן, סַבֹּתֶם, סַבֹּנוּ.

- - -

* Sometimes with short (ˇ): as, רָנִּי *sing* or *exult thou, f.* (Isa. liv. 1.) רָנּוּ *m. pl.*

† The long vowel (ֹ) is changed into (ׇ) because a long vowel cannot form a compound syllable without the accent; and as the accent can never come on the *ante-penultimate,* the long vowel must necessarily be changed. (See Part I. p. 79.)

‡ The prefixes ב, ת, י, א, have long (ˉ), except the second and third persons *f. pl.*

§ (ֹ) is changed into (ׇ) for the reason stated before. For the same reason is (ֹ) changed into short (ˇ), with *conversive* ו: as, יָסֹב *he shall surround,* וַיָּקָב *and he surrounded,* וַיָּקָב.

‖ Or סָבַב, like the perfect verb. In the same manner. זַמִּי *he imagined, intended,* זָמְמָה, זָמְמָה.

Niphal.

Inf. הִסֵּב*, בְּהִסֹּב, &c.—*Imp.* הִסֹּב or הִסֵּב, הִסַּבִּי, הִסַּבּוּ, הִסַּבֶּינָה.—*Fut.* אֶסַּב†, תִּסַּב, תִּסַּבִּי, יִסַּב, &c.—*Part.* נָסָב or נָסֵב, נְסַבָּה, נְסַבִּים, &c.—*Past tense,* נָסַב or נִגְסַב‡, or נָסַבָּה, נְסַבְּתָּ, נְסַבְּתִּי—נָסַבּוּ, נְסֵבָּה, &c.

Piël, Puäl, and Hithpaël

Are conjugated either like perfect verbs, as, סַבֵּב to bring about, to cause;§ הַלֵּל to praise, קַלֵּל to curse, הִלֵּל he praised, הֻלַּל he was praised, הֻלַּלְתִּי I was praised, &c. הִתְהַלֵּל he praised himself, boasted.—*Part.* מְהַלֵּל, מְהַלֵּל, מִתְהַלֵּל &c.—*Imp.* הַלֵּל, הַלְּלִי, הַלְּלוּ‖&c. הִתְהַלֵּל, הִתְהַלְּלִי, &c., and *Fut.* אֲהַלֵּל, אֱהַלֵּל, אֶתְהַלֵּל, &c. Or they are conjugated like verbs of the fifth conjugation (ע"ו). Thus *Inf.* סוֹבֵב to go about, encompass; הוֹלֵל to make foolish, frantic, to act without reason.—*Imp.* סוֹבֵב, סוֹבְבִי, &c.—*Fut.* אֲסוֹבֵב, &c.—*Part. act.* מְסוֹבֵב, &c.—*Part. pas.* מְסוֹבָב.—

---

* Or with (..); as, הֻמַּים to be melted.

† Or with (ִ) אֶתֹּם I shall be finished, completed, תִּתֹּם, יִתֹּם; or with (-): as, יִמַּד he shall be measured. In a few instances without dagesh; as, אֵקַל I shall be light, i. e. not esteemed, תֵּקַל.

‡ Sometimes with וֹ: as, נָגוֹל he was rolled, נָגֹלּוּ they were rolled together.

§ Hence the Rabbinical, סִבָּה a cause.

‖ Hence *Hallelujah*, הַלְלוּיָהּ i. e. Praise ye the Lord.

Past tense, סוֹבַב, סוֹבְבָה, סוֹבְבוּ—סוֹבַבְתִּי, &c.—Puʼal,
Inf. סוֹבָב.—*Fut.* אֲסֻבַּב.—*Past tense,* סוֹבַב, סוֹבַבְתִּי, &c.—
Hithpaʼel, וְהִסְתּוֹבֵב; or from גָּלַל—הִתְגּוֹלֵל *he rolled himself.*

Hiphil.

הָסֵב.—*Imp.* הָסֵב, הָסֵבִּי, &c.—*Fut.* אָסֵב, תָּסֵב, תָּסֵבִּי,
&c.—*Part. act.* מֵסֵב, מְסִבָּה, &c.—*Part. pas.* מוּסָב, מוּסַבָּה,
&c.—*Past tense,* הֵסֵב,* הֵסֵבוּ—הֲסִבּוֹתִי, הֲסִבָּה, הֲסִבַּת, &c.

Hophal.

Inf. הוּסַב.—*Fut.* אוּסַב, תּוּסַב, תּוּסַבִּי, &c.—*Part.* הוּסָב,
הוּסַבָּה, &c.—*Past tense,* הוּסַב, הוּסַבָּה, הוּסַבּוּ—הוּסַבְתִּי,
הוּסַבְתָּ, &c.

Exercise.

רַב־לָכֶם סֹב אֶת־הָהָר הַזֶּה : עִבְרוּ וְסֹבּוּ אֶת־הָעִיר :
בַּיּוֹם הַשְּׁבִיעִי תָּסֹבּוּ אֶת־הָעִיר שֶׁבַע פְּעָמִים : לֹא נָסֹב
עַד בֹּאוּ פֹה : סַבֹּתֶם אֶת־הַמָּקוֹם : וַיַּסֵב אֶת־הַר־שֵׂעִיר
יָמִים רַבִּים[2] : אֲנִי הוֹלֵךְ לָמֹד[3] אֶרֶץ־יְרוּשָׁלַיִם[5] לִרְאוֹת

[1] Much, enough. [2] Seven times. [3] Many. [4] מדד to measure; in *Hith.* to stretch one's self. [5] Jerusalem.

---

* Or with (-̣): as, הֵקֵל *he caused to be light,* הֵמֵר *he made bitter.*

כַּמָּה אָרְכָּהּ וְכַמָּה רָחְבָּהּ ׃ מִן הַמִּדָּה הַזֹּאת תָּמוּד ׃
סָבַב אֶל רוּחַ הַיָּם מָדַד חֲמֵשׁ מֵאוֹת קָנִים ׃ וַיַּגֵּד אֶת
הַשַּׁעַר ׃ הַיּוֹם גַּלּוֹתִי֙ אֶת־חֶרְפַּת מִצְרַיִם מֵעֲלֵיכֶם ׃ גֹּלּוּ
אֲבָנִים גְּדֹלִים עַל פִּי הַמְּעָרָה ׃ נָסַבּוּ בָּתֵּיהֶם לַאֲחֵרִים
וְנָגֹלּוּ בַסֵּפֶר הַשָּׁמַיִם וְכָל צְבָאָם יִבּוֹל֙ בִּנְבֹל עָלֶה
מִגֶּפֶן ׃ כְּחוֹל הַיָּם אֲשֶׁר לֹא יִמַּד וְלֹא יִסָּפֵר֙ ׃ אִם
יִמַּדּוּ שָׁמַיִם מִלְמַעְלָה וְיֵחָקְרוּ֙[10] מוֹסְדֵי־אֶרֶץ--לְמָטָּה גַּם
אֲנִי אֶמְאַס֙[11] בְּכָל־זֶרַע יִשְׂרָאֵל ׃ שֶׁבַע פְּעָמִים בַּיּוֹם הִלַּלְתִּי֙[12]
אוֹתָךְ ׃ בֵּאלֹהִים הִלַּלְנוּ כָּל־הַיּוֹם ׃ הַלְלִי אֱלֹהַיִךְ צִיּוֹן ׃
אֲהַלְלָה שֵׁם אֱלֹהִים בְּשִׁיר ׃ לֹא הַמֵּתִים֙[13] יְהַלְלוּ יָהּ ׃
לְפִי שִׂכְלוֹ֙[14] יְהֻלַּל אִישׁ ׃ כָּל־הַנְּשָׁמָה֙[15] תְּהַלֵּל יָהּ ׃ רַנִּי֙[16]
וְשִׂמְחִי בַת צִיּוֹן ׃ רָנּוּ שָׁמַיִם וְגִילִי֙[17] אָרֶץ ׃ הָקִיצוּ֙[18] וְרַנְּנוּ
שֹׁכְנֵי֙[19] עָפָר֙[20] ׃ בְּהַנְיָח אַלְבִּישׁ֙[21] יֶשַׁע֙[22] וַחֲסִידֶיהָ֙[23] רַנֵּן
יְרַנֵּנוּ ׃ אָז יְדַלֵּג֙[24] כָּאַיָּל פִּסֵּחַ֙[25] וְתָרֹן לְשׁוֹן אִלֵּם֙[26] תְּרַנֵּן
לְשׁוֹנִי צִדְקֶךָ ׃ תְּרַנֶּנָה שְׂפָתַי ׃ בַּכְּרָמִים֙[27] לֹא יְרֻנָּן ׃
מוֹצָאֵי בֹקֶר וָעֶרֶב תַּרְנִין ׃ לֵב אַלְמָנָה אַרְנִן ׃ הִנֵּה

[6] גלל to roll, roll away, remove, in *Hith.* to roll one's self, to wallow. [7] נבל to wither, waste. [8] The vine. [9] ספר to number. [10] חקר to search. [11] מאס to despise. [12] הלל to praise; in *Hith.* to praise one's self, to boast. [13] A dead person. [14] Sense, understanding. [15] Soul. [16] רנן to shout, to sing. [17] גיל to rejoice. [18] Awake. [19] שכן one that dwells. [20] Dust. [21] לבש to dress, to clothe. [22] Salvation. [23] A pious man. [24] דלג to jump. [25] The lame. [26] Dumb. [27] כרם a vineyard.

TABLE XI.

Exhibiting all the Infinitive and Imperative Moods of the Perfect and Imperfect Verbs, Primitive as well as Derivative, at one view.

INFINITIVE MOODS.

פְּעוּלִים Eighth Conjugation.	נְחִי ל״ה Seventh Conjugation.	נְחִי ל״א Sixth Conjugation.	נְחִי ע״ו Fifth Conjugation.	נְחִי פ״י Fourth Conjugation.	נְחִי פ״א Third Conjugation.	הַכֵּרִים Second Conjugation.	שְׁלֵמִים First Conjugation.	
סָבֹב וּ סַב בֹּסֹב &c.	גְּלֹה גְּלוֹת הַגְלוֹת &c.	מְצֹא וּקְצֹא &c.	קוּם וּקוּם &c.	יָשֹׁב שֶׁבֶת וּשְׁבַת &c.	אָכֹל הָאָכֹל &c.	נָגֹשׁ נֶשֶׁת הִנָּגֵשׁ &c.	לְמֹד יְמֹד וּלְמֹד &c.	Kal.
רֹקַב רֹסַב בְּרֹקַב &c.	נִגְלֹה הִנָּגְלוֹת &c.	הִמָּצֵא בְּהִמָּצֵא &c.	הִקּוֹם בְּהִקּוֹם &c.	הִיָּשֵׁב וְהִנָּשֵׁב &c.	הֵאָכֵל וְהֵאָכֵל &c.	וְנִגֹּשׁ הִנָּגֵשׁ &c.	וְנִלְמַד הִלָּמֵד &c.	Niph.
סֹבֵב הַסֹּבֵב &c.	גַּלֹּה גַּלּוֹת וְגַלּוֹת &c.	מַצֵּא הִמַּצֵּא &c.	קוֹמֵם הְקוֹמֵם &c.	יַשֵּׁב הַיָּשֵׁב &c.	אַכֵּל הָאַכֵּל &c.	נַגֵּשׁ הִנַּגֵּשׁ &c.	לַמֵּד הְלַמֵּד &c.	Pi.
סֹבַּב הַסֹּבַּב &c.	גֻּלֹּה גֻּלּוֹת הֻגְלוֹת &c.	מֻצֵּא הֻמְצֵא &c.	קוֹמֵי הֻקוֹמֵי &c.	יֻשַּׁב הֻיָּשֵּׁב &c.	אֻכַּל רֻאֲכַל &c.	נֻגַּשׁ הֻנְגַּשׁ &c.	לֻמַּד הֻלְמַד &c.	Pu.
הָסֵב הַסָּב &c.	הַעֲלֹה עֲלוֹת הַגְלוֹת &c.	הַמְצִיא הַמְצִיא &c.	הָקֵם וּהְקֵם &c.	הוֹשִׁיב יֹשֵׁב הֹשֵׁב &c.	הַאֲכִיל הַאֲכֵל &c.	וַיֵּגֶשׁ הַגִּישׁ &c.	וַיַּלְמֵד הַלְמֵד &c.	Hiph.
הוּסַב בְּהוּסַב &c.	הָגְלֹה הָגְלוֹת &c.	וַיֻּמְצָא הָמְצָא &c.	הוּקַם הָקֵם &c.	הוּשַׁב וְהוּשַׁב &c.	הָאֳכַל וְהֻאֱכַל &c.	וַיֻּגַּשׁ בְּהֻגַּשׁ &c.	וַיֻּלְמַד הָלְמַד &c.	Hoph.
וְהִתְיָה וְהִתְעַלּוֹת הַסְתֹּבֵב הִסְתַּחֲבֵב &c.	וְהִתְחַמֵּא וְהִתְחַמֵּא הִתְחַמְּאוֹת &c.	הִתְקוֹמֵם בְּהִתְקוֹמֵם &c.	וַיִּתְיַשֵּׁב הִתְיַצֵּב &c.	וְנֶאֱכַל בְּהִתְאַכֵּל &c.	הִתְנַגֵּשׁ בְּהִתְנַגֵּשׁ &c.	וַיִּתְחַמֵּד בְּהִתְלַמֵּד &c.	Hith.

IMPERATIVE MOODS.

סֹב סֹבִּי סֹבוּ סְבֶינָה	גְּלֵה גְּלִי גְּלוּ גְּלֵינָה	כְּצָא מִצְאִי מִצְאוּ מְצֶאנָה	קוּם קוּמִי קוּמוּ קֹמְנָה	שֵׁב שְׁבִי שְׁבוּ שְׁבֶנָה	אֱכֹל אִכְלִי אִכְלוּ אֲכֹלְנָה	גַּשׁ גְּשִׁי גְשׁוּ גְּשֶׁנָה	לְמֹד לִמְדִי לִמְדוּ לְמֹדְנָה	Kal.
הִסַּב וְהִסַּבִּי הִסַּבוּ וְשִׁבִּינָה	הִגָּלֶה הִגָּלִי הִגָּלוּ הִגָּלֶינָה	הִמָּצֵא הִמָּצְאִי הִמָּצְאוּ הִמָּצֶאנָה	וַיָּקֹם הִקּוֹמִי הִקּוֹמוּ הִקּוֹמֶנָה	הִוָּשֵׁב הִוָּשְׁבִי הִוָּשְׁבוּ הִוָּשַׁבְנָה	הֵאָכֵל הֵאָכְרִי הֵאָכְרוּ הֵאָכְרֶנָה	הִנָּגֵשׁ הִנָּגְשִׁי הִנָּגְשׁוּ הִנָּגַשְׁנָה	הִלָּמֵד וְהִלָּמְדִי הִלָּמְדוּ הִלָּמַדְנָה	Niph.
סוֹבֵב סוֹבְבִי סוֹבְבוּ סוֹבַבְנָה	גַּלֵּה גַּלִּי גַּלּוּ גַּלֵּינָה	מַצֵּא מַצְּאִי מַצְּאוּ מַצֶּאנָה	קוֹמֵם קוֹמְמִי קוֹמְמוּ קוֹמֵמְנָה	יַשֵּׁב יַשְּׁבִי יַשְּׁבוּ יַשְׁבְּנָה	אַכֵּל אַכְּלִי אַכְּלוּ אַכֵּלְנָה	נַגֵּשׁ נַגְּשִׁי נַגְּשׁוּ נַגֵּשְׁנָה	לַמֵּד לַמְּדִי לַמְּדוּ לְמֵּדְנָה	Piel.
הָסֵב הָסֵבִּי הָסֵבוּ הַסִּבֶּנָה	הַעֲלֵה וְגַלִּי הַגְלִי הַמְצִיאִנָה	הַמְצֵא הַמְצִיאִי הַמְצִיאוּ הַמְצֶאנָה	הָקֵם הָקִימִי הָקִימוּ הֲקֵמְנָה	הוֹשֵׁב הוֹשִׁיבִי הוֹשִׁיבוּ הוֹשֵׁבְנָה	הַאֲכֵל הַאֲכִירִי הַאֲכִילוּ הַאֲכִילֶנָה	הַגֵּשׁ הַגִּישִׁי הַגִּישׁוּ הַגֵּשְׁנָה	הַלְמֵד הַלְמִדִי הַלְמִידוּ הַלְמֵדְנָה	Hiph.
הִסְתּוֹבֵב הִסְתַּחְבְּכִי הִסְתַּחְבְבוּ הִסְתַּחְבְּנָה	הִתְחַמֵּא הִתְחַמַּאי הִתְחַמְּאוּ הִתְחַמַּאנָה	הִתְקוֹמֵם הִתְקוֹמְמִי הִתְקוֹמְמוּ הִתְקוֹמֵמְנָה	הִתְיַשֵּׁב הִתְיַשְּׁבִי הִתְיַשְּׁבוּ הִתְיַשֵּׁבְנָה	הִתְאַכֵּל הִתְאַכְּלִי הִתְאַכְּלוּ הִתְאַכֵּלְנָה	הִתְנַגֵּשׁ הִתְנַגְּשִׁי הִתְנַגְּשׁוּ הִתְנַגֵּשְׁנָה	הִתְלַמֵּד הִתְלַמְּדִי הִתְלַמְּדוּ הִתְלַמֵּדְנָה	Hith.

* מִגֶּשֶׁת לְגֶשֶׁת כְּנֶשֶׁת בְּנִשְׁחָ. The rest of the infinitives are varied in the same manner; thus, מִלְּמֹד לִלְמֹד כַּלְמֹד בִּלְמֹד &c. וּבֶאֱכֹל הֶאָכֹל &c.

TABLE XII.

Exhibiting the Future Tenses of all the Perfect and Imperfect, Verbs Primitive as well as Derivative, at one view.

עָתִיד Future.	שְׁלֵמִים First Conjugation.	הכרים Second Conjugation.	נֶחֱיִ פ"א Third Conjugation.	נֶחֱיִ פ"י Fourth Conjugation.	נֶחֱיִ ע"ו Fifth Conjugation.	נֶחֱיִ ל"א Sixth Conjugation.	נֶחֱיִ ל"ה Seventh Conjugation.	הכפולים Eighth Conjugation.
I	אֶלְמַד	Fem.	אֹכַל	אוֹשֵׁב	אָקוּם	אֶמְצָא	אֶגְלֶה	אֶסּוֹב
Thou	תִּלְמַד	תִּלְמְדִי	תֹּאכַל, אָכְלִי	תֵּשֵׁב, שְׁבִי	תָּקוּם, קוּמִי	תִּמְצָא, צְאִי	תִּגְלֶה, גְּלִי	תָּסוֹב, סֹבִּי
He	יִלְמַד		יֹאכַל	יֵשֵׁב	יָקוּם	יִמְצָא	יִגְלֶה	יָסֹב
She	תִּלְמַד		תֹּאכַל	תֵּשֵׁב	תָּקוּם	תִּמְצָא	תִּגְלֶה	תָּסֹב
We	נִלְמַד		נֹאכַל	נֵשֵׁב	נָקוּם	נִמְצָא	נִגְלֶה	נָסֹב
You	תִּלְמְדוּ, קֹדְנָה	תִּגְלֶינָה	תֹּאכְלוּ, אֲכַלְנָה	תֵּשְׁבוּ, שֵׁבְנָה	תָּקוּמוּ, קֻמְנָה	תִּמְצְאוּ, צֶאנָה	תִּגְלוּ, גְּלֶינָה	תָּסֹבּוּ, סֻבֶּינָה
They	יִלְמְדוּ		יֹאכְלוּ	יֵשְׁבוּ	יָקוּמוּ	יִמְצְאוּ	יִגְלוּ	יָסֹבּוּ
I	אֶלְמַד	Fem.	אֹכַל	אוֹשֵׁב	אָקִים		אַגְלֶה	אָסֵב
Thou	תִּלְמַד, מְדִי	תַּגְנִיס	תַּאֲכִיל, אָכִלִי	תּוֹשִׁיב, שִׁיבִי	תָּקִים, קִימִי		תַּגְלֶה, גְלִי	תָּסֵב, סֵבִּי
He	יַלְמַד	יַגְנִיס	יַאֲכִיל	יוֹשִׁיב	יָקִים		יַגְלֶה	יָסֵב
She	תַּלְמַד	תַּגְנִיס	תַּאֲכִיל	תּוֹשִׁיב	תָּקִים		תַּגְלֶה	תָּסֵב
We	נַלְמַד	נַגְנִיס	נַאֲכִיל	נוֹשִׁיב	נָקִים		נַגְלֶה	נָסֵב
You	תַּלְמְדוּ, מֵדְנָה	תַּגְנִיסוּ	תַּאֲכִילוּ, אָכֵלְנָה	תּוֹשִׁיבוּ, שֵׁבְנָה	תָּקִימוּ, קְמֵנָה		תַּגְלוּ, גְּלֶינָה	תָּסֵבּוּ, סֻבֶּינָה
They	יַלְמְדוּ		יַאֲכִילוּ	יוֹשִׁיבוּ	יָקִימוּ		יַגְלוּ	יָסֵבּוּ
I	אֲלֻמַּד	Fem.	אֻכַּל	אוּשַׁב	אוּקַם	אֻמְצָא	אֲגֻלֶּה	אוּסַב
Thou	תְּלֻמַּד, מְדִי	תְּגֻנַּס	תֻּאֲכַל, אֻכְּלִי	תּוּשַׁב, שְׁבִי	תּוּקַם, קוּמִי		תְּגֻלֶּה, גְּלִי	תּוּסַב, סֹבִּי
He	יְלֻמַּד	יְגֻנַּס	יֻאֲכַל	יוּשַׁב	יוּקַם		יְגֻלֶּה	יוּסַב
She	תְּלֻמַּד	תְּגֻנַּס	תֻּאֲכַל	תּוּשַׁב	תּוּקַם		תְּגֻלֶּה	תּוּסַב
We	נְלֻמַּד	נְגֻנַּס	נֻאֲכַל	נוּשַׁב	נוּקַם		נְגֻלֶּה	נוּסַב
You	תְּלֻמְּדוּ, מֵדְנָה	תְּגֻנְסוּ	תֻּאֲכְלוּ, אֲכַלְנָה	תּוּשְׁבוּ, שֵׁבְנָה	תּוּקְמוּ, קֻמְנָה		תְּגֻלּוּ, גְּלֶינָה	תּוּסַבּוּ, סֻבֶּינָה
They	יְלֻמְּדוּ		יֻאֲכְלוּ	יוּשְׁבוּ	יוּקְמוּ		יְגֻלּוּ	יוּסַבּוּ
I	אַלְמִיד	Fem.	אַאֲכִיל	אוּשִׁיב	אָקִים	אַמְצִיא	אַגְלֶה	אַסֵב
Thou	תַּלְמִיד, דִי	תַּגְנִישׁ	תַּאֲכִיל, אָכִלִי	תּוֹשִׁיב, שִׁיבִי	תָּקִים, קִימִי	תַּמְצִיא, צְאִי	תַּגְלֶה, גְּלִי	תָּסֵב, סֵבִּי
He	יַלְמִיד	חַיִם	יַאֲכִיל	יוֹשִׁיב	יָקִים	יַמְצִיא	יַגְלֶה	יַסֵב
She	תַּלְמִיד	תַּגְנִיס	תַּאֲכִיל	תּוֹשִׁיב	תָּקִים	תַּמְצִיא	תַּגְלֶה	תַּסֵב
We	נַלְמִיד	נַגְנִיס	נַאֲכִיל	נוֹשִׁיב	נָקִים	נַמְצִיא	נַגְלֶה	נַסֵב
You	תַּלְמִידוּ, מֵדְנָה	תַּגְנִישׁוּ	תַּאֲכִילוּ, אֲכַלְנָה	תּוֹשִׁיבוּ, שֵׁבְנָה	תָּקִימוּ, קֻמְנָה	תַּמְצִיאוּ, צֶאנָה	תַּגְלוּ, גְּלֶינָה	תָּסֵבּוּ, סֻבֶּינָה
They	יַלְמִידוּ		יַאֲכִילוּ	יוֹשִׁיבוּ	יָקִימוּ	יַמְצִיאוּ	יַגְלוּ	יָסֵבּוּ
I	אָלְמַד	Fem.	אָאֳכַל	אוּשַׁב	אוּקַם	אָמְצָא	אָגְלֶה	אוּסַב
Thou	תָּלְמַד	תָּגְנַס, דִי	תָּאֳכַל, אָכְלִי	תּוּשַׁב, שְׁבִי	תּוּקַם, קוּמִי	תָּמְצָא, צְאִי	תָּגְלֶה	תּוּסַב
He	יָלְמַד	יָגְנַס	יָאֳכַל	יוּשַׁב	יוּקַם	יָמְצָא	יָגְלֶה	יוּסַב
She	תָּלְמַד	תָּגְנַס	תָּאֳכַל	תּוּשַׁב	תּוּקַם	תָּמְצָא	תָּגְלֶה	תּוּסַב
We	נָלְמַד	נָגְנַס	נָאֳכַל	נוּשַׁב	נוּקַם	נָמְצָא	נָגְלֶה	נוּסַב
You	תָּלְמְדוּ, קֵדְנָה		תָּאֳכְלוּ, אֲכַלְנָה	תּוּשְׁבוּ, שֵׁבְנָה	תּוּקְמוּ, קֻמְנָה	תָּמְצְאוּ, צֶאנָה	תָּגְלוּ, גְּלֶינָה	תּוּסַבּוּ, סֻבֶּינָה
They	יָלְמְדוּ		יָאֳכְלוּ	יוּשְׁבוּ	יוּקְמוּ	יָמְצְאוּ	יָגְלוּ	יוּסַבּוּ
I	אֶתְלַמַּד	Fem.	אֶתְנַגֵּשׁ	אֶתְאַכֵּל	אֶתְיַשֵּׁב	אֶתְקוֹמֵם	אֶתְמַצֵּא	אֶתְגַּלֶּה	אֶסְתּוֹבֵב
Thou	תִּתְלַמַּד, דִי	תִּתְנַגְּשִׁי	תִּתְאַכֵּל, אָכְּלִי	תִּתְיַשֵּׁב, שְׁבִי	תִּתְקוֹמֵם, מִי	תִּתְמַצֵּא, צְאִי	תִּתְגַּלֶּה, גְּלִי	תִּסְתּוֹבֵב
He	יִתְלַמַּד	יִתְנַגֵּשׁ	יִתְאַכֵּל	יִתְיַשֵּׁב	יִתְקוֹמֵם	יִתְמַצֵּא	יִתְגַּלֶּה	יִסְתּוֹבֵב
She	תִּתְלַמַּד	תִּתְנַגֵּשׁ	תִּתְאַכֵּל	תִּתְיַשֵּׁב	תִּתְקוֹמֵם	תִּתְמַצֵּא	תִּתְגַּלֶּה	תִּסְתּוֹבֵב
We	נִתְלַמַּד	נִתְנַגֵּשׁ	נִתְאַכֵּל	נִתְיַשֵּׁב	נִתְקוֹמֵם	נִתְמַצֵּא	נִתְגַּלֶּה	נִסְתּוֹבֵב
You	תִּתְלַמְּדוּ, לְמֵדְנָה	תִּתְנַגְּשׁוּ, גַּשְׁנָה	תִּתְאַכְּלוּ, כַּלְנָה	תִּתְיַשְּׁבוּ, שַׁבְנָה	תִּתְקוֹמְמוּ, מֵמְנָה	תִּתְמַצְּאוּ, צֶאנָה	תִּתְגַּלּוּ, גַּלֶּינָה	תִּסְתּוֹבְבוּ, בַבְנָה
They	יִתְלַמְּדוּ		יִתְנַגְּשׁוּ	יִתְאַכְּלוּ	יִתְיַשְּׁבוּ	יִתְקוֹמְמוּ	יִתְמַצְּאוּ	יִתְגַּלּוּ	יִסְתּוֹבְבוּ

TABLE XIII.

Exhibiting the Participles of all the Perfect and Imperfect Verbs, Primitive as well as Derivative, at one view.

כפולים Eighth Conjugation	נחי ל״ה Seventh Conjugation	נחי ל״א Sixth Conjugation	נחי ע״ו Fifth Conjugation	נחי פ״י Fourth Conjugation	נחי פ״א Third Conjugation	חסרים Second Conjugation	שלמים First Conjugation	בינוני Participle	
סָב	נוֹלֶה	מוֹצֵא	קָם	יוֹשֵׁב	אוֹכֵל	נוֹגֵשׂ	לוֹמֵד		
סַבָּה	נוֹלָה	מוֹצְאָה	קָמָה	יוֹשְׁבָה	אוֹכְלָה	נוֹגְשָׂה	לוֹמְדָה	Act.	
—	—	מוֹצְאוֹת	—	יוֹשֶׁבֶת	אוֹכֶלֶת	נוֹגֶשֶׂת	לוֹמֶדֶת		
סַבִּים	נוֹלִים	מוֹצְאִים	קָמִים	יוֹשְׁבִים	אוֹכְלִים	נוֹגְשִׂים	לוֹמְדִים		Kal.
סַבּוֹת	נוֹלוֹת	מוֹצְאוֹת	קָמוֹת	יוֹשְׁבוֹת	אוֹכְלוֹת	נוֹגְשׂוֹת	לוֹמְדוֹת		
סָבוּב	גָלוּי	צָווּא	קוּם	יָבוּךְ	אָכוּר	נָגוּשׂ	לָמוּר		
סְבוּבָה	גְלוּיָה	מְצוּאָה	קוּמָה	יְסוּבָּה	אֲכוּלָה	נְגוּשָׂה	לְמוּדָה	Pas.	
סְבוּבִים	גְלוּיִים	מְצוּאִים	קוּמִים	יְסוּבִים	אֲכוּרִים	נְגוּשִׂים	לְמוּדִים		
סְבוּבוֹת	גְלוּיוֹת	מְצוּאוֹת	קוּמוֹת	יְסוּבוֹת	אֲכוּרוֹת	נְגוּשׂוֹת	לְמוּדוֹת		
נָקֹב	נִגְלֶה	נִמְצָא	נָקוֹם	נוֹשָׁב	נֶאֱכָל	נִגָּשׂ	נִלְמָד		
נִסַּבָּה	נִגְלָה	נִמְצָאָה	נָקֳמָה	נוֹשְׁבָה	נֶאֶכְלָה	נִגְּשָׂה	נִלְמָדָה		
—	נִגְלֵית	נִמְצֵאת	נְקוֹמַת	נוֹשֶׁבֶת	נֶאֱכֶלֶת	נִגֶּשֶׁת	נִלְמֶדֶת		Niphal.
נְסַבִּים	נִגְלִים	נִמְצָאִים	נְקוֹמִים	נוֹשְׁבִים	נֶאֱכָלִים	נִגָּשִׂים	נִלְמָדִים		
נְסַבּוֹת	נִגְלוֹת	נִמְצָאוֹת	נְקוֹמוֹת	נוֹשְׁבוֹת	נֶאֱכָלוֹת	נִגָּשׂוֹת	נִלְמָדוֹת		
מְסוֹבֵב	מְגַלֶּה	מְמַצֵּא	מְקוֹמֵם	מְיַשֵּׁב	מְאַכֵּל	מְנַגֵּשׂ	מְלַמֵּד		
מְסוֹבְבָה	מְגַלָּה	מְמַצְּאָה	לְקוֹמְמָה	מְיַשְּׁבָה	מְאַכְּלָה	מְנַגְּשָׂה	מְלַמְּדָה	Act.	
מְסוֹבֶבֶת	—	מְמַצֵּאת	מְקוֹמֶמֶת	מְיַשֶּׁבֶת	מְאַכֶּלֶת	מְנַגֶּשֶׁת	מְלַמֶּדֶת		Piel
מְסוֹבְבִים	מְגַלִּים	מְמַצְּאִים	מְקוֹמְמִים	מְיַשְּׁבִים	מְאַכְּלִים	מְנַגְּשִׂים	מְלַמְּדִים		
מְסוֹבְבוֹת	מְגַלּוֹת	מְמַצְּאוֹת	מְקוֹמְמוֹת	מְיַשְּׁבוֹת	מְאַכְּלוֹת	מְנַגְּשׂוֹת	מְלַמְּדוֹת		
מְסוֹבָב	מְגֻלֶּה	יְמֻצָּא	מְקוֹמָם	מְיֻשָּׁב	מְאֻכָּל	מְנֻגָּשׂ	מְלֻמָּד		
מְסוֹבָבָה	מְגֻלָּה	מְמֻצָּאָה	מְקוֹמָה	מְיֻשָּׁה	מְאֻכָּלָה	מְנֻגָּשָׂה	מְלֻמָּדָה	Pas.	
מְסוֹבֶבֶת	—	מְמֻצֵּאת	מְקוֹמֶמֶת	מְיֻשֶּׁבֶת	מְאֻכֶּלֶת	מְנֻגֶּשֶׁת	מְלֻמֶּדֶת		
מְסוֹבָבִים	מְגֻלִּים	מְמֻצָּאִים	מְקוֹמָמִים	מְיֻשָּׁבִים	מְאֻכָּלִים	מְנֻגָּשִׂים	מְלֻמָּדִים		
מְסוֹבָבוֹת	מְגֻלּוֹת	מְמֻצָּאוֹת	מְקוֹמָמוֹת	מְיֻשָּׁבוֹת	מְאֻכָּלוֹת	מְנֻגָּשׂוֹת	מְלֻמָּדוֹת		
סוּבַּב	גֻּלָּה	קוּצָּא	קוּקָם	יֻשָּׁב	אֻכַּל	נֻגַּשׂ	לֻמַּד		
סוּבְּבָה	גֻּלָּה	קוּצְּאָה	קוֹמְמָה	יֻשְּׁבָה	אֻכְּלָה	נֻגְּשָׂה	לֻמְּדָה		
סוּבְּבִים	גֻּלִּים	קוּצְּאִים	קוֹמְמִים	יֻשְּׁבוּ	אֻכְּלִים	נֻגְּשִׂים	לֻמְּדִים		Pual.
סוּבְּבוֹת	גֻּלּוֹת	קוּצְּאוֹת	מוּעֲשׂוּן	יֻשְּׁבוֹת	אֻכְּלוֹת	נֻגְּשׂוֹת	לֻמְּדוֹת		
מֵסֵב	מַגְלֶה	מַמְצִיא	מֵקִים	מוֹשִׁיב	מַאֲכִיל	מַגִּישׂ	מַלְמִיד		
מְסִבָּה	מַגְלָה	מַמְצִיאָה	הְקִימָה	מוֹשִׁיבָה	מַאֲכִילָה	מַגִּישָׁה	מַלְמִידָה		
—	—	מַמְצֵאת	מוֹשִׁיבַת	מַאֲכֶלֶת	מַאֲכִילָה	מַגֶּשֶׁת	מַלְמֶדֶת	Act.	
מְסִבִּים	מַגְלִים	מַמְצִיאִים	מְקִימִים	מוֹשִׁיבִים	מַאֲכִילִים	מַגִּישִׂים	מַלְמִידִים		Hiphil.
מְסִבּוֹת	מַגְלוֹת	מַמְצִיאוֹת	מְקִימוֹת	מוֹשִׁיבוֹת	מַאֲכִילוֹת	מַגִּישׂוֹת	מַלְמִידוֹת		
מוּסָב	מֻגְלֶה	מֻמְצָא	מוּקָם	מוּשָׁב	מָאֳכָל	הֻגַּשׂ	מֻלְמָד		
מוּסַבָּה	מֻגְלָה	מֻמְצָאָה	הֻקְמָה	מוּשְׁבָה	מָאֳכָלָה	מֻגְּשָׂה	מֻלְמָדָה	Pas.	
—	—	מֻמְצֵאת	—	מוּשֶׁבֶת	מָאֳכֶלֶת	מֻגֶּשֶׁת	מֻלְמֶדֶת		
מוּסַבִּים	מֻגְלִים	מֻמְצָאִים	מֻקְמִים	מוּשָׁבִים	מָאֳכָלִים	מֻגָּשִׂים	מֻלְמָדִים		
מוּסַבּוֹת	מֻגְלוֹת	מֻמְצָאוֹת	מֻקְמוֹת	מוּשָׁבוֹת	מָאֳכָלוֹת	מֻגָּשׂוֹת	מֻלְמָדוֹת		
הוּסַב	הָגְלָה	הֻמְצָא	הוּקַם	הוּשָׁב	הָאֳכַל	הֻגַּשׂ	הֻלְמַד		
הוּסַבָּה	הָגְלָה	הֻמְצְאָה	הוּקְמָה	הוּשְׁבָה	הָאֳכְלָה	הֻגְּשָׁה	הֻלְמְדָה		Hophal
הוּסַבִּים	הָגְלִים	הֻמְצָאִים	הוּקְמִים	הוּשְׁבִים	הָאֳכָלִים	הֻגָּשִׂים	הֻלְמָדִים		
הוּסַבּוֹת	הָגְלוֹת	הֻמְצָאוֹת	הוּקְמוֹת	הוּשְׁבוֹת	הָאֳכָלוֹת	הֻגָּשׂוֹת	הֻלְמָדוֹת		
מִסְתּוֹבֵב	מִתְגַּלֶּה	מִתְקוֹמֵא	מִתְקוֹמֵם	מִתְיַשֵּׁב	מִתְאַכֵּל	מִתְנַגֵּשׂ	מִתְלַמֵּד		
מִסְתּוֹבְבָה	מִתְגַּלָּה	מִתְקוֹמְאָה	מִתְקוֹמְמָה	מִתְיַשְּׁבָה	מִתְאַכְּלָה	מִתְנַגְּשָׂה	מִתְלַמְּדָה		Hithpael.
מִסְתּוֹבֶבֶת	מִתְגַּלֵּית	—	מִתְקוֹמֶמֶת	מִתְיַשֶּׁבֶת	מִתְאַכֶּלֶת	מִתְנַגֶּשֶׁת	מִתְלַמֶּדֶת		
מִסְתּוֹבְבִים	מִתְגַּלִּים	מִתְקוֹמְאִים	מִתְקוֹמְמִים	מִתְיַשְּׁבִים	מִתְאַכְּלִים	מִתְנַגְּשִׂים	מִתְלַמְּדִים		
מִסְתּוֹבְבוֹת	מִתְגַּלּוֹת	מִתְקוֹמְאוֹת	מִתְקוֹמְמוֹת	מִתְיַשְּׁבוֹת	מִתְאַכְּלוֹת	מִתְנַגְּשׂוֹת	מִתְלַמְּדוֹת		

TABLE XIV.
Exhibiting the Past Tenses of all the Perfect and Imperfect, Verbs Primitive as well as Derivative, at one view.

כפולים Eighth Conjugation	נחי ל״ה Seventh Conjugation	נחי ל״א Sixth Conjugation	נחי ע״ו Fifth Conjugation	נחי פ״י Fourth Conjugation	נחי א״א Third Conjugation	חסרים Second Conjugation	שלמים First Conjugation	
כַּבֹּתִי	גָּלִיתִי	מָצָאתִי	קַמְתִּי	יָשַׁבְתִּי	אָכַלְתִּי	נָגַשְׁתִּי	לָמַדְתִּי	I
סַבּוֹתָ .ת	גָּלִיתָ .ת	מָצָאתָ .ת	קַמְתָּ .ת	יָשַׁבְתָּ .ת	אָכַלְתָּ .ת	נָגַשְׁתָּ .ת	לָמַדְתָּ .ת	Thou
סַב	גָּלָה	מָצָא	קָם	יָשַׁב	אָכַל	נָגַשׁ	לָמַד	He	Kal
סַבָּה	גָּלְתָה	מָצְאָה	קָמָה	יָשְׁבָה	אָכְלָה	נָגְשָׁה	לָמְדָה	She
סַבּוּנוּ	גָּלִינוּ	מָצָאנוּ	קַמְנוּ	יָשַׁבְנוּ	אָכַלְנוּ	נָגַשְׁנוּ	לָמַדְנוּ	We
סַבּוֹתֶם .ן	גְּלִיתֶם .ן	מְצָאתֶם .ן	קַמְתֶּם .ן	יְשַׁבְתֶּם .ן	אֲכַלְתֶּם .ן	נְגַשְׁתֶּם .ן	לְמַדְתֶּם .ן	You
סַבּוּ	גָּלוּ	מָצְאוּ	קָמוּ	יָשְׁבוּ	אָכְלוּ	נָגְשׁוּ	לָמְדוּ	They
וְנִסְבּוֹתִי	נִגְלֵיתִי	נִמְצֵאתִי	נְקוּמֹתִי	נוֹשַׁבְתִּי	נֶאֱכַלְתִּי	נִגַּשְׁתִּי	וְלִלְמַדְתִּי	I
וְנִסַבֹּת .ת	נִגְלֵיתָ .ת	נִמְצֵאתָ .ת	נְקוּמֹתָ .ת	נוֹשַׁבְתָּ .ת	נֶאֱכַלְתָּ .ת	נִגַּשְׁתָּ .ת	וְלִלְמַדְתָּ .ת	Thou
וְנָסַב	נִגְלָה	נִמְצָא	נָקוֹם	נוֹשַׁב	נֶאֱכַל	נִגַּשׁ	וְלִלְמַד	He
וְנָסַבָּה	נִגְלְתָה	נִמְצְאָה	נְקוּמָה	נוֹשְׁבָה	נֶאֶכְלָה	נִגְּשָׁה	וְלִלְמְדָה	She	Niphal
וְנָסַבּוּנוּ	נִגְלִינוּ	נִמְצֵאנוּ	נְקוּמֹנוּ	נוֹשַׁבְנוּ	נֶאֱכַלְנוּ	נִגַּשְׁנוּ	וְלִלְמַדְנוּ	We
וְנָסַבּוֹתֶם .ן	נִגְלֵיתֶם .ן	נִמְצֵאתֶם .ן	נְקוּמֹתֶם .ן	נוֹשַׁבְתֶּם .ן	נֶאֱכַלְתֶּם .ן	נִגַּשְׁתֶּם .ן	וְלִלְמַדְתֶּם .ן	You
וְנָסַבּוּ	נִגְלוּ	נִמְצְאוּ	נְקוּמוּ	נוֹשְׁבוּ	נֶאֶכְלוּ	נִגְּשׁוּ	וְלִלְמְדוּ	They
סוֹבַבְתִּי	גִּלִּיתִי	מִצֵּאתִי	קוֹמַמְתִּי	יִשַּׁבְתִּי	אִכַּלְתִּי	נִגַּשְׁתִּי	לִמַּדְתִּי	I
סוֹבַבְתָּ .ת	גִּלִּיתָ .ת	מִצֵּאתָ .ת	קוֹמַמְתָּ .ת	יִשַּׁבְתָּ .ת	אִכַּלְתָּ .ת	נִגַּשְׁתָּ .ת	לִמַּדְתָּ .ת	Thou
סוֹבֵב	גִּלָּה	מִצֵּא	קוֹמֵם	יִשֵּׁב	אִכֵּל	נִגֵּשׁ	לִמֵּד	He
סוֹבְבָה	גִּלְּתָה	מִצְּאָה	קוֹמְמָה	יִשְּׁבָה	אִכְּלָה	נִגְּשָׁה	לִמְּדָה	She	Pael
סוֹבַבְנוּ	גִּלִּינוּ	מִצֵּאנוּ	קוֹמַמְנוּ	יִשַּׁבְנוּ	אִכַּלְנוּ	נִגַּשְׁנוּ	לִמַּדְנוּ	We
סוֹבַבְתֶּם .ן	גִּלִּיתֶם .ן	מִצֵּאתֶם .ן	קוֹמַמְתֶּם .ן	יִשַּׁבְתֶּם .ן	אִכַּלְתֶּם .ן	נִגַּשְׁתֶּם .ן	לִמַּדְתֶּם .ן	You
סוֹבְבוּ	גִּלּוּ	מִצְּאוּ	קוֹמְמוּ	יִשְּׁבוּ	אִכְּלוּ	נִגְּשׁוּ	לִמְּדוּ	They
סוֹבַבְתִּי	גֻּלֵּיתִי	מֻצֵּאתִי	קוֹמַמְתִּי	יֻשַּׁבְתִּי	אֻכַּלְתִּי	נֻגַּשְׁתִּי	לֻמַּדְתִּי	I
סוֹבַבְתָּ .ת	גֻּלֵּיתָ .ת	מֻצֵּאתָ .ת	קוֹמַמְתָּ .ת	יֻשַּׁבְתָּ .ת	אֻכַּלְתָּ .ת	נֻגַּשְׁתָּ .ת	לֻמַּדְתָּ .ת	Thou
סוֹבַב	גֻּלָּה	מֻצָּא	קוֹמַם	יֻשַּׁב	אֻכַּל	נֻגַּשׁ	לֻמַּד	He
סוֹבְבָה	גֻּלְּתָה	מֻצְּאָה	קוֹמְמָה	יֻשְּׁבָה	אֻכְּלָה	נֻגְּשָׁה	לֻמְּדָה	She	Pual
סוֹבַבְנוּ	גֻּלֵּינוּ	מֻצֵּאנוּ	קוֹמַמְנוּ	יֻשַּׁבְנוּ	אֻכַּלְנוּ	נֻגַּשְׁנוּ	לֻמַּדְנוּ	We
סוֹבַבְתֶּם .ן	גֻּלֵּיתֶם .ן	מֻצֵּאתֶם .ן	קוֹמַמְתֶּם .ן	יֻשַּׁבְתֶּם .ן	אֻכַּלְתֶּם .ן	נֻגַּשְׁתֶּם .ן	לֻמַּדְתֶּם .ן	You
סוֹבְבוּ	גֻּלּוּ	מֻצְּאוּ	קוֹמְמוּ	יֻשְּׁבוּ	אֻכְּלוּ	נֻגְּשׁוּ	לֻמְּדוּ	They
וַהֲסִבּוֹתִי	וְגִלִּיתִי	וְהִמְצֵאתִי	וַהֲקִימוֹתִי	וְהוֹשַׁבְתִּי	וְהַאֲכַלְתִּי	וְהִגַּשְׁתִּי	וְהִלְמַדְתִּי	I
וַהֲסִבֹּת .ת	וְהִגְלֵיתָ .ת	וְהִמְצֵאתָ .ת	וַהֲקִימוֹתָ .ת	וְהוֹשַׁבְתָּ .ת	וְהַאֲכַלְתָּ .ת	וְהִגַּשְׁתָּ .ת	וְהִלְמַדְתָּ .ת	Thou
וְהֵסֵב	הִגְלָה	הִמְצִיא	הֵקִים	הוֹשִׁיב	הֶאֱכִיל	הִגִּישׁ	הִלְמִיד	He
וַהֲסִבָּה	הִגְלְתָה	הִמְצִיאָה	הֵקִימָה	הוֹשִׁיבָה	הֶאֱכִילָה	הִגִּישָׁה	הִלְמִידָה	She	Hiphil
וַהֲסִבּוֹנוּ	וְהִגְלִינוּ	וְהִמְצֵאנוּ	וַהֲקִימוֹנוּ	וְהוֹשַׁבְנוּ	וְהַאֲכַלְנוּ	וְהִגַּשְׁנוּ	וְהִלְמַדְנוּ	We
וַהֲסִבּוֹתֶם .ן	וְהִגְלֵיתֶם .ן	וְהִמְצֵאתֶם .ן	וַהֲקִימוֹתֶם .ן	וְהוֹשַׁבְתֶּם .ן	וְהַאֲכַלְתֶּם .ן	וְהִגַּשְׁתֶּם .ן	וְהִלְמַדְתֶּם .ן	You
וְהֵסֵבּוּ	הִגְלוּ	הִמְצִיאוּ	הֵקִימוּ	הוֹשִׁיבוּ	הֶאֱכִילוּ	הִגִּישׁוּ	הִלְמִידוּ	They
וְהוּסַבּוֹתִי	הָגְלֵיתִי	הֻמְצֵאתִי	וְהוּקַמְתִּי	וְהוּשַׁבְתִּי	וְהָאֳכַלְתִּי	וְהֻגַּשְׁתִּי	וְהָלְמַדְתִּי	I
וְהוּסַבֹּת .ת	וְהָגְלֵיתָ .ת	הֻמְצֵאתָ .ת	וְהוּקַמְתָּ .ת	וְהוּשַׁבְתָּ .ת	וְהָאֳכַלְתָּ .ת	וְהֻגַּשְׁתָּ .ת	וְהָלְמַדְתָּ .ת	Thou
הוּסַב	הָגְלָה	הֻמְצָא	הוּקַם	הוּשַׁב	הָאֳכַל	הֻגַּשׁ	הָלְמַד	He
הוּסַבָּה	הָגְלְתָה	הֻמְצְאָה	הוּקְמָה	הוּשְׁבָה	הָאֳכְלָה	הֻגְּשָׁה	הָלְמְדָה	She	Huphal
וְהוּסַבּוֹנוּ	וְהָגְלֵינוּ	הֻמְצֵאנוּ	וְהוּקַמְנוּ	וְהוּשַׁבְנוּ	וְהָאֳכַלְנוּ	וְהֻגַּשְׁנוּ	וְהָלְמַדְנוּ	We
וְהוּסַבּוֹתֶם .ן	וְהָגְלֵיתֶם .ן	הֻמְצֵאתֶם .ן	וְהוּקַמְתֶּם .ן	וְהוּשַׁבְתֶּם .ן	וְהָאֳכַלְתֶּם .ן	וְהֻגַּשְׁתֶּם .ן	וְהָלְמַדְתֶּם .ן	You
וְהוּסַבּוּ	הָגְלוּ	הֻמְצְאוּ	הוּקְמוּ	הוּשְׁבוּ	הָאֳכְלוּ	הֻגְּשׁוּ	הָלְמְדוּ	They
וְהִסְתּוֹבַבְתִּי	וְהִתְגַּלֵּיתִי	הִתְמַצֵּאתִי	וְהִתְקוֹמַמְתִּי	וְהִתְיַשַּׁבְתִּי	וְהִתְאַכַּלְתִּי	וְהִתְנַגַּשְׁתִּי	וְהִתְלַמַּדְתִּי	I
וְהִסְתּוֹבַבְתָּ .ת	וְהִתְגַּלִּיתָ .ת	הִתְמַצֵּאתָ .ת	וְהִתְקוֹמַמְתָּ .ת	וְהִתְיַשַּׁבְתָּ .ת	וְהִתְאַכַּלְתָּ .ת	וְהִתְנַגַּשְׁתָּ .ת	וְהִתְלַמַּדְתָּ .ת	Thou
וְהִסְתּוֹבֵב	הִתְגַּלָּה	הִתְמַצֵּא	הִתְקוֹמֵם	הִתְיַשֵּׁב	הִתְאַכֵּל	הִתְנַגֵּשׁ	הִתְלַמֵּד	He
וְהִסְתּוֹבְבָה	וְהִתְגַּלְּתָה	הִתְמַצְּאָה	הִתְקוֹמְמָה	הִתְיַשְּׁבָה	הִתְאַכְּלָה	הִתְנַגְּשָׁה	הִתְלַמְּדָה	She	Hithpael
וְהִסְתּוֹבַבְנוּ	וְהִתְגַּלִּינוּ	הִתְמַצֵּאנוּ	וְהִתְקוֹמַמְנוּ	וְהִתְיַשַּׁבְנוּ	וְהִתְאַכַּלְנוּ	וְהִתְנַגַּשְׁנוּ	וְהִתְלַמַּדְנוּ	We
וְהִסְתּוֹבַבְתֶּם .ן	וְהִתְגַּלִּיתֶם .ן	הִתְמַצֵּאתֶם .ן	וְהִתְקוֹמַמְתֶּם .ן	וְהִתְיַשַּׁבְתֶּם .ן	וְהִתְאַכַּלְתֶּם .ן	וְהִתְנַגַּשְׁתֶּם .ן	וְהִתְלַמַּדְתֶּם .ן	You
וְהִסְתּוֹבְבוּ	הִתְגַּלּוּ	הִתְמַצְּאוּ	הִתְקוֹמְמוּ	הִתְיַשְּׁבוּ	הִתְאַכְּלוּ	הִתְנַגְּשׁוּ	וְהִתְלַמְּדוּ	They

THE HEBREW LANGUAGE. 155

יָדִי עִמָּךְ לְהָשֵׁב אֵלֶיךָ אֶת־כָּל יִשְׂרָאֵל : אַתָּה הֲסִבֹּתָ
אֶת־לִבָּם : הָסֵבִּי עֵינַיִךְ מִנֶּגְדִּי : וַיֵּשֶׁב ° אֱלֹהִים אֶת־הָעָם :
אַל תִּתְהַלֵּל בְּיוֹם מָחָר כִּי לֹא תֵדַע מַה יֵּלֶד יוֹם : בְּרוֹב
עֲשָׂרָם יִתְהַלָּלוּ : אַל יִתְהַלֵּל חָכָם בְּחָכְמָתוֹ וְאַל יִתְהַלֵּל
הַגִּבּוֹר בִּגְבוּרָתוֹ אַל יִתְהַלֵּל עָשִׁיר בְּעָשְׁרוֹ כִּי אִם־בְּזֹאת
יִתְהַלֵּל הַמִּתְהַלֵּל הַשְׂכֵּל[28] וְיָדֹעַ אֹתִי : וַיִּתְמֹדֵד° עַל
הַיֶּלֶד שָׁלֹשׁ פְּעָמִים : וַעֲמָשָׂא[29] מְגֻלָּל בַּדָּם בְּתוֹךְ
הַמְסִלָּה[30]° : וַיִּרְאוּ° הָאֲנָשִׁים כִּי הוּבְאוּ בֵּית יוֹסֵף וַיֹּאמְרוּ°
עַל־דְּבַר[31] הַכֶּסֶף הַשָּׁב בְּאַמְתְּחֹתֵינוּ[32] בַּתְּחִלָּה[33] אֲנַחְנוּ
מוּבָאִים לְהִתְגֹּלֵל עָלֵינוּ וּלְהִתְנַפֵּל עָלֵינוּ וְלָקַחַת אֹתָנוּ
לַעֲבָדִים וְאֶת־חֲמֹרֵינוּ :

[28] To understand, to contemplate. [29] And Amasa. [30] A way, highway. [31] On account of. [32] אַמְתַּחַת a sack. [33] At first.

The accompanying Tables, containing paradigms of the verbs of the several conjugations, are so constructed, that the student may at one view see the distinguishing characteristic of each conjugation and its several branches.

Table XI. contains all the Infinitive and Imperative Moods of the eight conjugations.

Table XII. contains all the Future Tenses.

Table XIII. contains all the Participles.

Table XIV. contains all the Past Tenses.

CHAPTER VII.

Doubly Imperfect Verbs.

139. From the preceding exposition of the Hebrew verbs, it appears that the differences between the perfect and imperfect verbs, arise from the latter having either (נ), or one of the *quiescents* י, ו, ה, א, as a constituent part of their *roots*. But the root may have both נ and one of the *quiescents*, at the same time, as radicals—as, for instance, נָשָׂא *to bear, to carry, to lift up;* נָטֹה *to stretch out, bend, incline ;*—or it may have two *quiescents :* as, אָבֹה *to be willing, to consent ;* יָצָא *to issue, to go out ;* יָרֵא *to fear ;* יָרֹה *to throw, to dart ;* בּוֹא *to come.* In such cases, the verbs are said to be doubly imperfect; and they will be subject, at the same time, to the rules specified under the several conjugations to which each letter has a reference.

Thus, for instance, the נ of נָשָׂא will be regulated by the rules laid down under the second conjugation (p. 127), and we shall have for the future אֶשָּׂא (for אֶנְשָׂא), and א will be regulated by the rules laid down under the sixth conjugation (p. 142); and hence אֶשָּׂא, with (ָ) under the second radical, instead of אֶשַּׂא or אֶשָּׁא. Thus, likewise, the א of אָבֹה will follow the rules of the third conjugation, and we shall, therefore, have in the future אֹבֶה *I shall be willing,* תֹּאבֶה, &c.; whilst the ה will follow the rules of the seventh conjugation; and we shall have in the past tense, אָבִיתָ, אָבִיתִי, in the same manner as from גָּלֹה, גָּלִיתִי, גָּלִיתָ, &c. This will appear still more clear from the following examples, in which the leading words of the several verbs are given, leaving it to the student to fill up the rest by way of exercise.

THE HEBREW LANGUAGE.

140. First radical נ, and third א : as, נָשָׂא *to carry*.

Kal.

Inf. abs. נָשֹׂא.—*Cons.* נְשֹׂא or שְׂאֵת, בִּשְׂאֵת, לָשֵׂאת, &c.— *Imp.* שָׂא, שְׂאִי, &c.—*Fut.* יִשָּׂא, &c.—*Part. act.* נֹשֵׂא, &c. *Part. pas.* נָשׂוּא.—*Past tense,* נָשָׂא, &c. נָשָׂאתִי.

Niphal.

Inf. הִנָּשֵׂא *to be carried,* בְּהִנָּשֵׂא, &c.—*Imp.* הִנָּשֵׂא, &c.— *Fut.* אֶנָּשֵׂא, &c.—*Part.* נִשָּׂא, נִשָּׂאָה, &c.—*Past tense,* נִשָּׂא, נִשְּׂאָה, נִשֵּׂאתִי, &c.

Piël.

Inf. נַשֵּׂא *to exalt,* בְּנַשֵּׂא, &c.—*Imp.* נַשֵּׂא, &c.—*Fut.* אֲנַשֵּׂא. *Part. act.* מְנַשֵּׂא.—*Part. pas.* מְנֻשָּׂא.—*Past tense,* נִשֵּׂא— נִשֵּׂאתִי, &c.

Puäl.

Inf. נֻשָּׂא.—*Fut.* אֲנֻשָּׂא.—*Part.* נֻשָּׂא.—*Past tense,* נֻשָּׂא, נֻשֵּׂאתִי, &c.

Hiphil.

Inf. הַשִּׂיא or הַשֵּׂא *to cause to bear.*—*Imp.* הַשֵּׂא.—*Fut.* אַשִּׂיא.—*Part. act.* מַשִּׂיא.—*Part. pas.* מֻשָּׂא.—*Past tense,* הִשִּׂיא—הִשֵּׂאת, הִשֵּׂאתָ, הִשֵּׂאתִי, &c.

Hophal.

Inf. הֻשָּׂא.—*Fut.* אֻשָּׂא.—*Part.* הֻשָּׂא.—*Past tense,* הֻשָּׂא, הֻשְּׂאָה—הֻשֵּׂאתִי.

Hithpaël.

Inf. הִתְנַשֵּׂא *to exalt one's self.*—*Imp.* הִתְנַשֵּׂא.—*Fut.* אֶתְנַשֵּׂא.—*Part.* מִתְנַשֵּׂא.—*Past tense,* הִתְנַשֵּׂא—הִתְנַשֵּׂאתִי.

141. First radical נ, and third ה: as, נטה *to incline, to stretch out.*

Kal.

Inf. נְטוֹת, נְטוֹת, בִּנְטוֹת.—*Imp.* נְטֵה, *f.* נְטִי.—*Fut.* אֶטֶּה or אַט.—*Part. act.* נוֹטֶה, *f.* נוֹטִיָּה.—*Part. pas.* נָטוּי, *f.* נְטוּיָה.—*Past tense,* נָטָה, נָטְתָה—נָטִיתִי.

Niphál.

Inf. הִנָּטֵה—הִנָּטוֹת.—*Imp.* הִנָּטֵה.— *Fut.* אֶנָּטֶה.— *Part.* נִטֶּה, *f.* נִטָּה.— *Past tense,* נִטָּה, נִטְּתָה—נִטֵּיתִי.

Piél.

Inf. נַטּוֹת—נַטֵּה.*—*Imp.* נַטֵּה.—*Fut.* אֲנַטֶּה.—*Part. act.* מְנַטֶּה.—*Part. pas.* מְנֻטֶּה.—*Past tense,* נִטָּה, נִטְּתָה—נִטֵּיתִי.

Puál and Hithpaël

Need no further explanation, as the former is formed by substituting (ֻ) for the first short vowel of Piél; and the latter, by prefixing הִת &c. before Piél, as before directed.

Hiphíl.

Inf. הַטֵּה, הַטּוֹת, בְּהַטּוֹת.—*Imp.* הַט or הַטֵּה, *f.* הַטִּי. *Fut.* גַּט or נַטֶּה, יַט, or יַטֶּה, תַּטִּי, תַּטֶּה or אַט, אַטֶּה

---

* As לִנְטוֹת—נְטוֹת.

הֵטוּ, &c.—*Part. act.* מַטֶּה.—*Part. pas.* מֻטֶּה. - *Past tense,* הִטֵּיתִי–הִטָּה, הִטְּתָה, &c.

Hophál.

Takes (ָ) instead of (-) and (.) : as, *Fut.* יֻטֶּה.—*Past tense,* הֻטֵּיתִי–הֻטָּה.

142. First radical א, and third ה : as, אָפָה *to bake.*

Kal.

Inf. אֲפוֹת–אֲפֹה, הֵאָפוֹת.—*Imp.* אֱפֵה, *f.* אֱפִי.—*Fut.* אֹפֶה, תֹּאפֶה, *f.* תֹּאפִי.—*Part. act.* אֹפֶה, *f.* אֹפָה.—*Part. pas.* אָפוּי, *f.* אֲפוּיָה.—*Past tense,* אָפִיתִי–אָפָה, אָפְתָה.

Niphál.

Inf. הֵאָפֶה *to be baked,* הֵאָפוֹת, הֵהָאָפוֹת.—*Imp.* אֵאָפֶה. *Part.* נֶאֱפֶה.—*Past tense,* נֶאֱפָה, &c.

143. First radical י, and third א : as, יָצָא *to go out,* יָרֵא *to fear.*

Kal.

Inf. צֵאת–צֵאת, בְּצֵאת; יִרְא–יִרְא.—*Imp.* צֵא, *f.* צְאִי, יְרָא, *f.* יִרְאִי.—*Fut.* אֵצֵא, תֵּצֵא, אִירָא, תִּירָא.—*Part. act.* יֹצֵא, יָרֵא or יָרֵאת—יָרֵא (like מָלֵא) יְרֵאָה.—*Part. pas.* יָרוּא, יְרוּאָה.—*Past tense,* יָצָא, יֵרֵא; יָצָאתִי–יָצְאָה יָרֵאתִי.

Niphál.

Inf. הִוָּרֵא *to be feared.*—*Imp.* הִוָּרֵא.—*Fut.* אִוָּרֵא, תִּוָּרֵא. *Part.* נוֹרָא, נוֹרָאָה.—*Past tense,* נוֹרָא—נוֹרֵאתִי.

Hiphil.

Inf. הוֹצִיא *to cause to come out, to bring out,* לְהוֹצִיא.—
Imp. הוֹצֵא, הוֹצִיאִי.—*Fut.* אוֹצִיא.—*Part. act.* מוֹצִיא.—
Part. pas. מוּצָא.—*Past tense,* הוֹצִיא—הוֹצֵאתִי.

Hophál.

הוּצָא.—*Fut.* אוּצָא.—*Past tense,* הוּצָא—הוּצֵאתִי.

144. First radical י, and third ה: as, יָרָה *to throw, to shoot.*

Kal.

Inf. אִירָה.—*Fut.* יְרִי *f.* יְרִי.—*Imp.* יְרֵה, יְרוֹת-יָרֹה.—*Part. act.* יֹרֶה, *f.* יֹרָה.—*Part. pas.* יָרוּי, *f.* יְרוּיָה.—*Past tense,* יָרָה, יָרְתָה—יָרִיתִי.

Niphál.

Inf. אִוָּרֶה or.—*Fut.* הִיָּרֶה or הִוָּרֵה.—*Imp.* הִוָּרֵה, הִוָּרוֹת.—*Part. act.* נוֹרֶה, *f.* נוֹרָה.—*Part. pas.* נוֹרָה—נוֹרֵיתִי.

Hiphil.

Inf. הוֹרָה *to throw, shew, instruct,* הוֹרוֹת, בְּהוֹרוֹת.—*Imp.* הוֹרֵה, *f.* הוֹרִי.—*Fut.* אוֹרֶה*.—*Part. act.* מוֹרֶה.—*Part. pas.* מוֹרָה.—*Past tense,* הוֹרָה, הוֹרְתָה—הוֹרֵיתִי†.

---

* And without ה—אוֹר, תּוֹר, &c.; hence וַיֹּר *and he shot* (2 Kings xiii. 17).

† Piel would, by analogy, be יָרָה, יָרוֹת, as we find from יָדָה *to throw,* יַדּוּ, יַדּוֹת; and Hith. הִתְוָדָה similar to הִתְוַדָּה *he confessed.*

145. Second radical ו, and third א: as, בוֹא *to come*.

Kal.

Inf. בּוֹא—בְּבוֹא.—*Imp.* בּוֹא, *f.* בְּאִי—*Fut.* אָבוֹא, תָּבֹא.
Part. בָּא, בָּאָה.—*Past tense,* בָּא, בָּאָה-בָּאתִי-בָּאתָ, בָּאת.

Hiphil.

Inf. הָבֵא or הָבִיא *to cause to come, i. e. to bring,* בְּהָבִיא.
Imp. הָבֵא or הָבִיא.—*Fut.* אָבִיא.—*Part. act.* מֵבִיא.—*Part. pas.* מוּבָא.—*Past tense,* הֵבִיא, הֵבִיאָה—הֲבֵאתִי or הֲבִיאוֹתִי.

Hophal.

Inf. הוּבָא.—*Fut.* אוּבָא, תּוּבָא, תּוּבְאִי.—*Past tense,* הוּבָאת, הוּבֵאתָ, הוּבֵאתִי—הוּבְאָה, הוּבָא.

Irregular Verbs.

146. Irregular verbs are such as do not form their several forms from the same root; as, for instance, הָלַכְתִּי *I went,* הוֹלֵךְ *one that goes,* are formed from the root הָלַךְ. The same is the case with the whole of Niphal, Piël, and Hithpaël: as, נֶהֱלַכְתִּי *I passed away;* הִלַּכְתִּי *I have walked frequently;* הִתְהַלַּכְתִּי, &c. But the *Imperative* and *Future* of Kal, and the whole of Hiphil are formed as if the root was יָלַךְ: thus, לֵךְ *m.,* לְכִי *f. go,* אֵלֵךְ *I will go,* תֵּלֵךְ, תֵּלְכִי, &c. הוֹלִיךְ *he made go, i. e. he led.*—Fut. אוֹלִיךְ, תּוֹלִיךְ, &c.—Part. מוֹלִיךְ, &c.

The same remark will apply to several other verbs: as, טוֹב *to be good.*—*Part.* טוֹב, טוֹבָה, &c.—*Past tense,* טוֹבְתָּ, טוֹבְתִּי (like verbs of the fifth conjugation), the root is therefore said to be טוֹב. But the *future* is אִישַׁב, תֵּימַב; and Hiphil, אִישִׁיב, הֵישִׁיב (like verbs of the fourth conjugation), the root is therefore said to be יָטַב.

Thus, likewise, from the root יָגֹר *to fear*, (fourth conjugation), we have יָגֹרְתִּי *I feared*, יָגֹרְתָּ, &c.; but *Imp.* גוּר.—*Fut.* אָגוּר, תָּגוּר, &c. from גוּר (fifth conjugation).

From יָכֹל *to be able,* we have יָכֹלְתִּי *I was able ;* but *future,* אוּכַל *I shall be able,* תּוּכַל, &c.; which is the future of *Hophal,* and means, lit. *I shall be made able,* or *I shall be enabled.*

From שָׁתֹה *to drink,* we have שָׁתִיתִי *I drank,* אֶשְׁתֶּה *I shall drink.* But Hiphil is formed from שָׁקֹה: thus, הִשְׁקָה *he caused to drink,* אַשְׁקֶה *I shall make drink* (not אַשְׁתֶּה הִשְׁתָּה*).

Quadriliteral and Pluriliteral Verbs.

147. Verbs whose roots consist of four letters, are denominated *Quadriliterals;* those that consist of more than four letters, are denominated *Pluriliterals:* as, †כִּלְכֵּל *to support, maintain;* מָהְמֵהַּ ‡ *to linger, delay;* סְחַרְחֹר *to turn about, to flutter, palpitate.*

These are, strictly speaking, derivative verbs, and are found only in פִּעֵל, פָּעַל and הִתְפָּעֵל. They are inflected in the

---

* To the above may be added, what are by Grammarians called *mixed forms:* as, for instance, יֵרְדּוֹף (Psalm viii. 6) in which the first and third vowel shews the word to be in KAL; but the second vowel and the *dagesh* are the signs of PIEL.

† Derived from כּוּל *to contain, comprehend, sustain.*

‡ Used only in *Hith.:* לְהִתְמַהְמֵהַּ *to stay* (Exod. xiii.), probably compounded of מָה *what;* indicative of *delay, lingering.*

THE HEBREW LANGUAGE.

same manner as other verbs: thus, *Inf.* and *Imp.* בַּלְכֵּל. *Fut.* אֲבַלְכֵּל.—*Part. act.* מְבַלְכֵּל.—*Part. pas.* מְבֻלְכָּל.—*Past tense,* בֻּלְכַּלְתִּי. Pual, בֻּלְכַּל *to be supported, maintained,* &c.; and Hithpael (by analogy) הִתְבַּלְכֵּל, &c.

In the same manner, we have from שַׁעֲשַׁע *to delight, take pleasure.* Hithpael, הִשְׁתַּעֲשַׁעְתִּי *I have amused myself, took delight in:* and from הָמָה, הִתְמַהְמָנוּ.

Exercise.

וַיַּרְא[1] יוֹסֵף אֶת־אֶחָיו וַיַּכִּרֵ[2] אֹתָם וַיִּתְנַכֵּר אֲלֵיהֶם
וַיְדַבֵּר אִתָּם קָשׁוֹת[3] וַיֹּאמֶר אֲלֵהֶם מֵאַיִן בָּאתֶם וַיֹּאמְרוּ
מֵאֶרֶץ כְּנַעַן לִשְׁבָּר־אֹכֶל[4] : וַיַּכֵּר יוֹסֵף אֶת־אֶחָיו וְהֵם לֹא
הִכִּרֻהוּ : וַיִּזְכֹּר[6] יוֹסֵף אֶת הַחֲלֹמוֹת אֲשֶׁר חָלַם[7]
לָהֶם וַיֹּאמֶר לָהֶם מְרַגְּלִים[8] אַתֶּם לִרְאוֹת אֶת־עֶרְוַת[10]
הָאָרֶץ בָּאתֶם : וַיֹּאמְרוּ אֵלָיו לֹא אֲדֹנִי וַעֲבָדֶיךָ בָּאוּ
לִשְׁבָּר־אֹכֶל : וַיֹּאמֶר אֲלֵיהֶם יוֹסֵף שִׁלְחוּ[11] מִכֶּם אֶחָד
וְיִקַּח[12] אֶת־אֲחִיכֶם וְאַתֶּם הֵאָסְרוּ[13] וְיִבָּחֲנוּ[14] דִבְרֵיכֶם הָאֱמֶת

[1] Instead of וַיִּרְאֶה,—Root רָאָה [2] Root נָכַר, Hip. הִכִּר *to recognize.*—Hith. *to make one's self appear a stranger, to feign or to pretend not to know.* [3] קָשֶׁה *hard, rough.* [4] To purchase, chiefly food or corn; hence שֶׁבֶר and בַּר *corn.* [5] Food, from אָכַל. [6] זָכַר *to remember.* [7] He dreamed, hence חֲלוֹם *a dream.* [8] מְרַגֵּל *a spy,* from רָגַל *to travel about on foot, to explore,* originally derived from רֶגֶל *the foot.* [9] Root רָאָה. [10] The nakedness. [11] Root, שָׁלַח *to send.* [12] Root, לָקַח. [13] Root, אָסַר *to bind.* [14] Root, בָּחַן.

164 THE ETYMOLOGY OF

אִתְּכֶם : וַיֶּאֱסֹף[15] אֹתָם אֶל מִשְׁמָר[16] שְׁלֹשֶׁת יָמִים : וַיֹּאמֶר
אֲלֵיהֶם בַּיּוֹם הַשְּׁלִישִׁי זֹאת עֲשׂוּ[17] וִחְיוּ[18] אֶת הָאֱלֹהִים אֲנִי
יָרֵא[19] : אִם בֵּנִים[20] אַתֶּם אֲחִיכֶם אֶחָד יֵאָסֵר בְּבֵית מִשְׁמַרְכֶם
וְאַתֶּם לְכוּ[21] הָבִיאוּ שֶׁבֶר רַעֲבוֹן[22] בָּתֵּיכֶם : וְאֶת־אֲחִיכֶם
הַקָּטֹן תָּבִיאוּ אֵלַי וְיֵאָמְנוּ[23] דִבְרֵיכֶם וְלֹא תָמוּתוּ וַיַּעֲשׂוּ
כֵן : וַיֹּאמְרוּ אִישׁ אֶל אָחִיו אֲבָל[24] אֲשֵׁמִים[25] אֲנַחְנוּ עַל
אָחִינוּ אֲשֶׁר רָאִינוּ[26] צָרַת[27] נַפְשׁוֹ בְּהִתְחַנְנוֹ[28] אֵלֵינוּ וְלֹא
שָׁמָעְנוּ עַל־כֵּן בָּאָה אֵלֵינוּ הַצָּרָה הַזֹּאת : וַיַּעַן[29] רְאוּבֵן
אֹתָם לֵאמֹר הֲלֹא אָמַרְתִּי אֲלֵיכֶם לֵאמֹר אַל תֶּחֶטְאוּ[30]
בַיֶּלֶד וְלֹא שְׁמַעְתֶּם וְגַם־דָּמוֹ הִנֵּה נִדְרָשׁ[31] : וְהֵם לֹא יָדְעוּ
כִּי שֹׁמֵעַ יוֹסֵף כִּי הַמֵּלִיץ[32] בֵּינֹתָם : וַיִּסֹּב[33] מֵעֲלֵיהֶם וַיֵּבְךְּ[34]
וַיָּשָׁב[35] אֲלֵיהֶם וַיְדַבֵּר אֲלֵיהֶם וַיִּקַּח מֵאִתָּם אֶת־שִׁמְעוֹן
וַיֶּאֱסֹר אֹתוֹ לְעֵינֵיהֶם : וַיְצַו[36] יוֹסֵף וַיְמַלְאוּ[37] אֶת־כְּלֵיהֶם
בָּר וּלְהָשִׁיב כַּסְפֵּיהֶם אִישׁ אֶל שַׂקּוֹ[38] וְלָתֵת[39] לָהֶם צֵדָה[40]
לַדָּרֶךְ : וַיִּשְׂאוּ[41] אֶת שִׁבְרָם עַל חֲמֹרֵיהֶם וַיֵּלְכוּ מִשָּׁם :

to try, to prove. [15] Root אָסֹף. [16] A prison, from שָׁמֹר *to guard.* [17] Root, עָשֹׂה. [18] Root חָיֹה. [19] Root, יָרֵא *to fear.* [20] בֵּן *right, honest.* [21] Root, לֵךְ. [22] Hunger. [23] And they shall be verified. [24] But verily. [25] אָשֵׁם *to be guilty.* [26] Root, רָאֹה. [27] צָרָה *anguish.* [28] Root, חָנָן; in Hith. *to beseech, entreat.* [29] Root, עָנֹה *to exclaim, answer.* [30] חָטָא *to sin.* [31] דָּרֹשׁ *to require.* [32] An interpreter. [33] Root סָבַב. [34] Root, בָּכֹה *to weep.* [35] Root, שׁוּב *to return.* [36] Root, צָוֹה *to command.* [37] Root, מָלֵא *to fill.* [38] שַׂק *a sack.* [39] Root, תֵּת—נָתֹן. [40] Provision, from צוּד *to hunt.* [41] Root, נָשֹׂא.

Objective Pronominal Affixes.

148. The objective pronouns *me* אֹתִי, *thee* אֹתְךָ, אֹתָךְ..., *him* אֹתוֹ, *her* אֹתָהּ, &c. (see Table IX.), are very frequently expressed by fragments subjoined to the different parts of the *Imperative Mood, Past* and *Future tenses* of verbs transitive: as, פָּקְדֵנִי *visit*-me, בָּרְכֵנִי *bless*-me, for פְּקֹד *visit,* אֹתִי *me;* בָּרֵךְ *bless,* אֹתִי *me.*—פְּקָדַנִי *he-visited* me, בֵּרְכַנִי *he-blessed* me, for פָּקַד *he visited* אֹתִי me, אֹתִי, בֵּרֵךְ—פְּקַדְתִּיךָ *I-have-visited-*thee, for פָּקַדְתִּי אֹתְךָ—אֶפְקְדוֹ or אֶפְקְדֵהוּ *I-shall-visit-*him, for אֶפְקֹד אֹתוֹ.

The following are the terminations by which the objective pronouns are indicated.—

נִי *me,*   ךָ *thee,* m.   ךְ *thee,* f.   וֹ or הוּ *him,*   ה or הָ *her.*
נוּ *us,*   כֶם *you,* m.   כֶן *you,* f.   ם *them,* m.   ן *them,* f*.

149. The manner in which these are affixed to verbs, and the changes to which the vowel-points of the latter are subject in consequence of the augmentation, are exhibited in the following Tables.

Obs.—The affixes of the Infinitives and Participles will be found in Table III. p. 56.

---

* These terminations are denominated objective pronominal affixes, to distinguish them from the similar affixes which are added to nouns, participles, and infinitives, to denote the pronouns, *my, thy, his, &c.* (see Table II. III.); and from the terminations תִּי, תָּ, תְּ, &c., which are used to indicate the *personal pronouns, I, thou, &c.*

Exercise.

אָהַבְתִּי¹ אֶתְכֶם אָמַר² יְהוָה, וַאֲמַרְתֶּם בַּמָּה אֲהַבְתָּנוּ :
אֵיךְ³ תֹּאמַר אֲהַבְתִּיךְ וְלִבְּךָ אֵין אִתִּי : וַתֹּאמֶר אֵשֶׁת
שִׁמְשׁוֹן אֵלָיו, רַק שְׂנֵאתַנִי⁴, וְלֹא אֲהַבְתָּנִי : יָקַרְתָּ⁵ בְּעֵינַי
נִכְבַּדְתָּ,⁶ וַאֲנִי אֲהַבְתִּיךָ : כַּלָּתֵךְ⁷ אֲשֶׁר אֲהֵבַתֶךְ יְלָדַתּוּ⁸ :
וַיִּקְרָא אֶת שְׁמוֹ שְׁלֹמֹה, וַיהוָה אֲהֵבוֹ : עַתָּה יֶאֱהָבַנִי
אִישִׁי⁹ : וַיָּבֹא דָּוִד אֶל שָׁאוּל, וַיַּעֲמֹד לְפָנָיו, וַיֶּאֱהָבֵהוּ
מְאֹד : וַיִּקַּח אֶת רִבְקָה, וַתְּהִי לוֹ לְאִשָּׁה, וַיֶּאֱהָבֶהָ :
וַיִּשְׂנָאֶהָ אַמְנוֹן שִׂנְאָה גְדוֹלָה מְאֹד, כִּי גְדוֹלָה הַשִּׂנְאָה
אֲשֶׁר שְׂנֵאָהּ מֵאַהֲבָה אֲשֶׁר אֲהֵבָהּ : הֲלֹא¹⁰ מְשַׂנְאֶיךָ יְהוָה
אֶשְׂנָא, תַּכְלִית¹¹ שִׂנְאָה שְׂנֵאתִים : רָאֹה אֹיְבַי כִּי רַבּוּ,¹²
וְשִׂנְאַת חָמָס¹³ שְׂנֵאוּנִי : כָּל־אֲחֵי רָשׁ שְׂנֵאֻהוּ : בְּנֵי קְנֵה
חָכְמָה, אַל תַּעַזְבָהּ¹⁴ וְתִשְׁמְרֶךָ¹⁵ אֱהָבֶהָ וְתִצְּרֶךָ,¹⁶ תְּכַבְּדְךָ¹⁷
כִּי תְחַבְּקֶנָּה¹⁸ : אִם רָעֵב שֹׂנַאֲךָ הַאֲכִילֵהוּ לָחֶם, וְאִם צָמֵא
הַשְׁקֵהוּ¹⁹ מָיִם : אַל תּוֹכַח²⁰ לֵץ פֶּן יִשְׂנָאֶךָ, הוֹכַח לְחָכָם
וְיֶאֱהָבֶךָ :

---

¹ אָהֵב *to love.* ² אָמַר *to say.* ³ How. ⁴ שָׂנֵא *to hate.* ⁵ To be rare, esteemed. ⁶ Thou art honorable. ⁷ כַּלָּה *a daughter-in-law.* ⁸ יָלַד *to bring forth, to bear children.* ⁹ My husband. ¹⁰ Is it not, behold. ¹¹ The end, extremity of. ¹² They are many. ¹³ Violence. ¹⁴ To forsake. ¹⁵ To keep, preserve. ¹⁶ נָצַר *to guard, watch.* ¹⁷ כָּבֵד to honor. ¹⁸ חָבַק *to embrace.* ¹⁹ שָׁקָה Hip. *to make drink.* ²⁰ יָכַח *to reprove.*

CHAPTER VIII.

Particles.

150. Under this *term*, the ancient grammarians comprehended all such words as are used for the purpose of defining, explaining, or modifying either the principal parts, or the whole of a sentence, and of showing the relation and connection between its several members; and hence they justly extended this denomination even to the *Article* and the *Pronouns*. Modern grammarians, however, have limited this term to ADVERBS, PREPOSITIONS, CONJUNCTIONS, and INTERJECTIONS; and in this restricted sense we shall henceforth use it.

151. Particles are divided into *Inseparable* and *Separable*—

The *Inseparable* are parts of words attached to others, with which they are incorporated: such are the ה and מ in אַרְצָה towards-*the-land*, מֵאֶרֶץ from-*the-land*;—the ו and ל in וְלָאָרֶץ and-to-*the-land*. (See Prefixes, pp. 37—39.)

152. The *Separable* consist of entire words: as, עַתָּה *now*, הַיּוֹם *to-day*, יוֹמָם *during the day*, לְפָנִים *formerly*, לִפְנֵי *before*, מִפְּנֵי *because*, עַל *upon*, כֵּן *so*, אֵין *not*, הֵיטֵב *well*, מְהֵרָה, מַהֵר *soon, quickly*, מַדּוּעַ *wherefore*, הֵן *behold*, הָבָה *come! go to!*

153. Many particles admit of the pronominal affixes (page 58). These must be rendered either by the Personal, Possessive, or Objective Pronouns, according as the idiom of the English language may require it: thus—

אֵין *not*, אֵינֶנִּי *not* I, or *I am not*, אֵינְךָ *not* THOU, or *thou-art-not;*

יֵשׁ *there-exists*, יֶשְׁךָ THOU-*existest*, or *thou-art;* יֶשְׁנוּ HE-*exists*, or *he is.*

אַיֵּה, אֵי *where, in what place?* אַיּוֹ *where-is*-HE? אַיָּם *where-are-they?*

בִּגְלַל *on account, for the sake,* בִּגְלָלִי *for*-MY-*sake;* בִּגְלָלֵךְ *f. for*-THY-*sake,* בִּגְלַלְכֶם *for*-YOUR-*sake.* (See Art. 28.)

זוּלָתִי *besides, except,* זוּלָתִי *besides-*ME; זוּלָתְךָ *besides, or except-*THEE.

לִפְנֵי *before,* לְפָנַי *before-*ME, לְפָנֶיךָ *before-*THEE; לְפָנָיו *before-*HIM.

154. Most of the particles are either nouns in their *absolute* or *constructive* state, adjectives, pronouns, or verbs*, used for the purpose of modification. Many of them are compounded of several

---

* I do not wish to be understood as if I meant to intimate that particles might not, in their turn, have given birth to other words: on the contrary, I think it highly probable that several *adjectives, nouns,* and even *verbs* owe their origin to them. Thus, כָּלָא *to be full,* מָלֵא *full,* are probably compounded of מַה *what,* לֹא *not,* i.e. what will not contain more; קָאֵן *to refuse,* from מָר and אֵין *not;* הֹוָה *calamity,* from הוֹי *alas! wo!* פּוּן *to be distracted, to be in a wavering, uncertain state of mind,* from פֶּן *perhaps* (itself derived from פָּנָה *to turn*). See *Aben Ezra* in צָחוֹת, and *Kimchi* in שְׁרָשִׁים on the word אָפוּנָה. (Psalm lxxxviii. 15.)

words; others are abbreviated or elliptical expressions, or exclamations, used for the purpose of soliciting attention: thus—

עַתָּה is evidently derived from עֵת *time*, and means *present time*; and hence, *now*.

לְפָנִים is evidently the noun פָּנִים (*the face, countenance, front*), in its *absolute* state, with the prefix לְ; and means, literally, *to-the-face*, and hence, *formerly, forwards*.

לִפְנֵי is the same noun, in its constructive state, with the prefix לְ; and means, literally, *to-the-face-of*, and hence *before*.

מִפְּנֵי is the same noun, with the prefix מִ, and means, literally, *from-the-face-of*, or from that which is *before, in front*; and as every cause necessarily precedes the effect, this word came to signify *cause* or *because*. From the same source are derived, מִלִּפְנֵי (compounded of מִן־אֶל־פְּנֵי) *away from, from-the-presence-of*; עַל־פְּנֵי *upon-the-surface-of*, &c.

הַיּוֹם *to-day*, is the noun יוֹם with the definite ה; lit. *this day*; and *יוֹמָם *by day, during the day*, is evidently derived from the same noun.

עַל *upon*, is derived from עָלָה† *to ascend*. From the same root are derived מַעֲלָה *upwards*, מִמַּעַל *from-above*, &c.

כֵּן *so*, is derived from the verb כּוּן the primary signification of which is, *to adapt, to adjust*; and hence, *to prepare, to establish, to fashion*. From כֵּן are formed אָכֵן *it is so, truly, behold*, לָכֵן *therefore*, עַל־כֵּן *upon this, hence*‡.

---

* Several other *adverbs* have this termination: as, רֵיקָם *with-empty-hands* (from רִיק *emptiness, vacuity*).—חִנָּם *gratuitously, without cause* (from חֵן *grace, favour*).—This termination, is, however, not peculiar to *adverbs*, as several nouns have the same: thus, סֻלָּם *a ladder*, עוֹלָם *eternity*.

† *Kimchi* derives this particle from the noun עַל *the upper part*, which, however, is itself derived from עָלָה.

‡ For further explanation of this particle, see Vindiciæ Hebraicæ, page 52.

אֵין is the constructive *form* of אַיִן, which signifies *non-existence, not extant*. Its antithesis is יֵשׁ, which means, *actual existence, real being*; and hence, יֵשׁ* *there-is-in-being, extant, there exists*.

הֵיטֵב *well*, is the infinitive (Hiph.) of the verb יָטַב *to be good*, and means, literally, *to-make-good*.

מַהֵר *soon, quickly*, is the infinitive or imperative of מָהֹר *to hasten*.

הָבָה *go to!* is a derivative from יָהַב *to give, yield*.

אֵיפֹה *where*, is compounded of אֵי, a particle of interrogation, and פֹּה *here*; and אֵיכָה, אֵיכָה *how*, of אֵי, and כֹּה *thus*.

מַדּוּעַ is compounded of מָה *what*, and יָדוּעַ, (or, according to Kimchi, from מָה and עֵד) literally, *what is known?* what is the motive or impelling cause? From מָה comes likewise לָמָּה, literally, *to what*, i.e. *for what purpose?* and בַּמָּה *how many? how long?* literally, *as-what*, i.e. *as what number? as what time?*

בָּזֶה *here*, מִזֶּה *hence*, are compounded of the demonstrative זֶה *this*, and the separable particles בְּ and מִ, lit. *in this, from-this*: the word *place* being understood.

155. There are, indeed, many particles—as, for instance, לֹא *not*, הֵן, הִנֵּה *behold!* מָתַי *when*, אִם *if, provided*, &c.—whose etymology is less obvious; for which reason, it may be supposed, they have been considered by some grammarians as *primitives*. It is, however, very probable, that even these are derivatives. Thus, לֹא is probably derived from לָאָה *to be weary, to be exhausted, to labour in vain;* and hence

---

* In Chaldaic אִית, Syriac ܐܝܬ, Arabic اِيش. In these languages it is used negatively לָית, לֵית (compounded of לָא and אִית) *there is not*. In Hebrew, however, we find it only once (Psalm cxxxv.) used in combination with the negative particle אֵין (Psalm cxxxv. 17); and then it is a pleonasm, as אֵין already expresses the notion of non-existence.

THE HEBREW LANGUAGE.   171

הָלְאָה *beyond, far off, out of reach.* הֵא, הִנֵּה, הֵן, are probably mere exclamations for the purpose of soliciting attention; מָתַי *when, at what time?* appears to be a compound of מָה *what,* and עֵת *time;* and אִם *if* (if needs we must have a *triliteral* for a root) is, perhaps, derived from אָמַם *to be attached, related, connected*.*

156. The great influence which these words have in discourse, as well as their frequent occurrence, renders it highly desirable that the student should become familiar with their *general* signification. For this purpose the following list, containing most of the particles not already noticed is here subjoined:—

---

* The primary signification of the primitive from which this and several other words are derived, appears to be *correlativeness*, or the reciprocal relations between distinct objects, neither of which could exist in a perfect state, or, in some instances, even be conceived without the other: as, for example, אֵם *the female parent, the mother;* אֱמֶת *the truth,* i. e. the exact conformity of human conceptions with the real nature of things, and between our thoughts and words or actions. And hence the secondary meaning of *union, attachment, accompaniment, integrity, completeness, perfection,* &c., as found in the following words, אֻמָּה, לְאֹם, אוֹם *a nation, kingdom,* עַם *a people;* עֲמִית *an associate neighbour;* עֻמַּת *corresponding;* לְעֻמַּת *towards, opposite;* תָּאַם *to entwine,* תְּאֹמִים *twins,* אֹמֵן *a foster-father,* אֹמֶנֶת *a foster-mother,* תָּם *innocent, complete, upright,* תָּמִים *perfect;* אֱמוּנָה, אָמֵן *faith, confidence, adherence.* Hence, likewise, the particle עִם *with* (accompaniment), and אִם *if* (attach, or add, as a condition). Thus, אִם תֵּלְכִי עִמִּי וְהָלָכְתִּי *if thou wilt go with me, then will I go, i. e.* attach as a condition of my going, that thou go with me; or the condition on which my going depends, is thy accompanying me.

אֲבָל	but, yet, nevertheless, indeed.	אָן, אָנָה	whither.
אֲבוֹי		אָנָּא, נָא, בִּי	pray, particles of entreaty.
אוֹי, אוֹיָה, הוֹי	ah! woe! alas!	אַף, גַּם	also, even, likewise.
אֲהָהּ, יָהּ		אַף־כִּי	how much more, how much less.
אוֹ, אוֹ־אוֹ	or, or—either	אֶפֶס	except, only.
אוּלַי	perhaps, suppose.	אֵצֶל	near, close by.
אוּלָם	surely, verily.	אֶתְמוֹל	yesterday.
אָז, אֲזַי	then, at that time.	תְּמוֹל	
אָחוֹר	back, backward, behind.	אֵת	sign of the objective me, אוֹתִי, אוֹתָךְ &c.
אֲחֹרַנִּית	backwards.	אֵת, אִתִּי	with, with me.
אַחַר	after, behind, beyond.	בִּגְלַל	on account of, for the sake.
אַחֲרֵי		בַּעֲבוּר	
אַט, לְאַט	slowly, softly.	בֵּין	between.
אֵי, אַיֵּה, אֵיפֹה	where, where now?	בְּלִי	not, without.
אֵיכָה, אֵיכֹה	how, in what manner?	בִּלְתִּי	unless, without, not.
אֵיכָכָה, אֵיךְ		בִּלְעֲדֵי	save, besides.
אִין, אַל, לֹא	no, not.	דַּי	enough.
בַּל, בְּלִי		הֶאָח	aha! exultation.
אֵיפֹא	now, then.	הֲלוֹם	hither, here.
אַךְ, רַק	only, scarcely, but.	הַרְבֵּה	much.
אִלּוּ	if.	חוּץ	besides, without.
אַלְלַי	woe to me!	טֶרֶם	not yet, before.
אִם	if, when.	יַחַד, יַחְדָּו	together, united.
אִם־לֹא	if not, unless.	כֹּה, כָּכָה	thus, so.
אָמְנָם	truly.	כִּי	when, if, for, that, because, but.
אֶמֶשׁ	last night.		

כְּמוֹ	as, thereabouts.	עַד עֲדֵי	until, till.
לְבַד	alone, only, besides.	עוֹד	again.
לוּ	would! I wish, perhaps.	עַד־אָנָה עַד־מָתַי	how long.
לוּלֵא	were it not.		
לְמַעַן	in order.	עַד הֵנָּה	until now.
מְאֹד	very.	עִמָּדִי	with me.
מֵאָז	since.	עֵקֶב	because.
מֵאַיִן	whence.	פֹּה	here.
מִבַּיִת	within.	פֶּה אֶחָד	unanimously.
מִחוּץ	without, externally.	פַּעַם	once.
מוּל, נֹכַח	over, against, towards.	פַּעֲמַיִם	twice.
		פִּתְאוֹם	suddenly.
מָחָר, מָחֳרָת	to-morrow.	רֵיקָם	emptily.
מַטָּה	below, downwards.	שִׁלְשׁוֹם	the day before yesterday.
מִלְּמַטָּה	beneath.		
מְעַט	a little, few.	שָׁם שָׁמָּה	there, thither.
מְעַט מִזְעֵיר	very little.	תַּחַת	beneath, instead.
נֶגֶד לְעֻמַּת	before, opposite.	תָּמִיד	constantly, always.
סָבִיב	round about.		

SYNTAX.

CHAPTER I.

INTRODUCTORY OBSERVATIONS.

157. Syntax is that part of Grammar which treats of the significance of the inflections of words combined with their relative positions.

By the method adopted in the preceding part of this work, many of the syntactical rules have necessarily been anticipated. These we shall here collect, and add such as have not already been noticed. But before we proceed, we think it advisable to make some general remarks on the nature of propositions and their constituent parts.

158. A proposition is an assemblage of words or oral signs, representing a judgment of the mind.

159. As every judgment necessarily includes two conceptions, one of which is affirmed or denied of the other, it follows that every proposition must have two terms, one answering to that conception which is the primary object of the mind's contemplation, and

SYNTAX OF THE HEBREW LANGUAGE. 175

which is denominated the SUBJECT*, the other corresponding with that which the mind judges to be or not to be congruous with the *subject*. The second term is denominated the PREDICATE or *attribute*. Further, as in every judgment there necessarily must be an act of the mind which decides whether the two conceptions *are* or *are not* congruous, every proposition ought to have a word or sign to indicate this mental decision. This word or sign is denominated the COPULA.

Obs. 1.—But though every proposition necessarily consists of these three parts, yet it is not alike needful that each part should be expressed by a separate word; for as we shall presently see, when the *predicate* is a verb, the copula is in all languages included in it, and when the *subject* happens to be a *pronoun* and the *predicate* a *verb*, the three parts may, in Hebrew, be expressed in a single word.

Obs. 2.—The grammatical term for the *subject* is the *Nominative*. When the predicate implies action, the *subject* or nominative is likewise called the *agent*.

160. In the following propositions—'God is omnipotent.' 'Water is a fluid.' 'This water is hot.' 'This water is not cold.'—The words *God*, *water*, are the *subjects; omnipotent, fluid, hot, cold*, are the *predicates;* and IS, the *copula*.

---

* The subject is denominated in Hebrew, נושׂא *the carrier* or *bearer*, because it supports, as it were, the other parts of the proposition; the *predicate* is denominated נישׂא that which is *carried* or *borne*.

161. *Obs.* 1.—The 1*st* and 2*nd* propositions in the preceding examples are denominated *Absolute propositions,* because the properties expressed by the predicates are essential to their respective subjects, and belong to them under every possible condition. Such propositions can have no reference to time; their *copulas* are therefore merely assertory. But the 3*rd* and 4*th* examples are denominated *Contingent propositions,* because the qualities denoted by the predicates are not essential to the subjects, and may exist conjointly with them at particular times, and not at others; and hence in all such propositions the *copula* must express the time, as,—The water *is* hot, *was* hot, *will be* cold, &c.

162. *Obs.* 2.—In English, as well as in most languages, the copula is generally represented by some part of the verb '*to be*'*. This is likewise mostly the case in Hebrew, in propositions which refer to *past* or *future* time: as, הָיִיתִי מֶלֶךְ (ᴬ) *I was a king,* אֶהְיֶה גָּדוֹל (ᴮ) *I shall be great.* But in all *absolute* propositions, or in *contingent* propositions which refer to present time, the *copula* is omitted, and inferred from the juxtaposition of the words: as, אֱלֹהִים צַדִּיק (ᶜ) *God* (is†) *just.*—הָאִישׁ גָּדוֹל (ᴰ) *The man* (is) *great.* אַתָּה קָדוֹשׁ (ᴱ) *Thou* (art) *holy:*—or the pronouns הוּא, הִיא, הֵמָּה, הֵנָּה, are used to represent the copula: as, יְהוָֹה הוּא אֱלֹהִים (ꜰ) *The Lord is God,*—יִרְאַת יְהוָֹה הִיא חָכְמָה (ᴳ) *The fear of the Lord is wisdom.*

Words employed to express the Subject.

163. The subject may be a *Noun* (as in Prop. c. D. F.); or a *Pronoun,* the substitute of a noun (as

---

* This verb is often used to express simple existence: as, *God is,* in which case it is itself the predicate.

† The words *within* crotchets are not expressed in Hebrew.

in Prop. E.); or an *Adjective*, or an *Infinitive*. (See Prop. II. and I. Art. 164.)

164. As every conception implies an existence, real or imaginary, it would follow that the subject and the predicate, each of which represent an existence (Art. 159.), ought to be *nouns* or names of existences; nevertheless, as each being may be distinguished from every other by some quality, property or circumstance, it is often sufficient to express the quality, property, &c., without mentioning the noun to which they belong; and hence an adjective may often be used as the subject or as the predicate: thus, חָכָם יָרֵא וְסָר מֵרָע (ⁿ) *A wise (man) feareth, and departeth from evil*, lit. A wise (man is) a fearer and departer from evil. Further, as the mind is able, by the faculty of abstraction, to view a quality, &c., without reference to the particular object to which it may belong, an *Abstract noun* or an *Infinitive* (*name of an action*) may be used as the subject, or as the predicate*: thus, יִרְאַת יְהֹוָה הִיא חָכְמָה וְסוּר מֵרָע בִּינָה *The fear of the Lord is wisdom; and to depart from evil (is) understanding.*

Words used for the Predicate.

165. The Predicate may be a *Noun* (as in Prop. A. Art. 162.):—an *Adjective* (as in Prop. B. Art. 162.): or a *Verb*, in which last case the *copula* is, even in English, included in the predicate: thus, אַבְרָהָם עָמַד *Abraham stood*, עָמַרְתִּי *I stood;* which expressions are equivalent to אַבְרָהָם הָיָה עוֹמֵד *Abraham was standing*, הָיִיתִי עוֹמֵד *I was standing.*

---

* Hence we see the reason why, in such instances, the Hebrew adjectives must be varied by gender and number: thus, חֲכָמָה, חֲכָמִים. (See adjectives, Art. 85.)

Thus likewise 'I walk,' 'He writes,' 'She writes,' may be resolved into 'I am walking,' 'He is writing,' &c.

166. *Obs.* 1.—As the Hebrew verb has no form to express time present, the participle (a noun) must be used as the predicate, in all such instances: Thus אֲנִי הוֹלֵךְ, הוּא כּוֹתֵב, הִיא כּוֹתֶבֶת, Lit. *I am a walker. He is a writer,* &c. (See Art. 17, 124.)

167. *Obs.* 2. The past and future tenses of the Hebrew verb being so constructed as to include the personal pronouns, (see verbs) all propositions in which the subject is a *pronoun*, and the predicate a *verb*, may be expressed by a single word; as, יָשַׁב *He dwelt*, אֵשֵׁב *I shall dwell.* But the unavoidable consequence of this construction of the verb is, that when the subject is a noun, or a distinct pronoun, and the predicate a verb, there will, apparently, be two subjects, one represented by the noun or the distinct pronoun, and the other by the pronoun inherent in the form of the verb: thus, אַבְרָהָם יָשַׁב *Abraham he dwelt.*—אֲנִי יָשַׁבְתִּי *I I-dwelt.** שָׂרָה צָחֲקָה *Sarah she-laughed.* However, as the two subjects refer to the same thing, they must be considered as in *Apposition;* and in translating such phrases into English, the pronoun must be omitted: thus, וַיֹּאמֶר אֱלֹהִים *And God said,* (not, and he said God, nor, and he God said.)

168. *Obs.* 3.—The verbal form can, in English, be used only where the predicate implies *action, passion,* or their contraries, want of action or passion, or a state of being, dependent in some measure on the will or inherent power of the subject: as, *I walk, run, suffer, sit,* &c.; but when the predicate expresses *quality* or

---

* Sometimes, however, the distinct pronouns are purposely introduced for the sake of emphasis.

quantity (coming under the predicaments *how*, and *how much*), the predicate can only be formed by an *adjective* accompanied by the *copula*: as, *I am, was, shall be wise, little, great*, &c. In Hebrew, however, the predicate may assume a verbal form, although it expresses the notions of quality or quantity: as, חָלִיתִי *I was sick*, יֶחְכַּם *he shall be wise*, יִגְדַּל *he shall be great*. Or it may, as in English, be formed by an adjective and the *copula*: thus, הָיִיתִי חוֹלֶה *I was sick*, יִהְיֶה חָכָם *he shall be wise*.

169. *Obs. 4.*—When the predicate is a *verb*, the proposition may, for the sake of distinction, be denominated *verbal*; but when the predicate is a *noun* or an *adjective*, the proposition may be termed *nominal*. Such propositions occur very frequently in Hebrew: as, לֵץ הַיַּיִן הֹמֶה שֵׁכָר *Wine* (*is a*) *mocker, strong drink* (*is a*) *blusterer* (Prov. xx. 1); אֵשֶׁת חַיִל עֲטֶרֶת בַּעְלָהּ *a virtuous woman* (*is a*) *crown of* [to] *her husband* (Prov. xii. 4).

Concord between the Subject and its Predicate.

170. The predicate must agree with the subject in *gender* and *number*, and (if a verb) in *person*. There are, however, several exceptions to this rule, which will be noticed hereafter.

Obs.—When the predicate is a noun (Art. 165), it must, even in English, agree, in some instances in gender, and always in number; as, *he is a prince, she is a princess, they are princes*, &c. But when the predicate is an adjective, the agreement is entirely neglected: as, *he is wise, she is wise*, &c. In Hebrew, however, the predicate must always agree with its subject; and it would be as improper to say הָאֲנָשִׁים גָּדוֹל or הָאִשָּׁה גָּדוֹל as it would be to say הָאִשָּׁה מֶלֶךְ or הָאֲנָשִׁים מֶלֶךְ. (See Art. 85.)

Of the several kinds of Propositions.

171. Propositions may be distributed into *General, Indefinite, Particular, Simple, Compound, Incomplex,* and *Complex.*

172. A *General* proposition is that which has a general term, representing a whole class of beings for its *subject:* as, אָדָם לְעָמָל יוּלָּד *man is born unto trouble.*

173. An *Indefinite* proposition is that which has an indefinite noun for its subject: as, בָּא אָדָם *a man came,* אֲנָשִׁים בָּאוּ *men came.*

Obs.—As the Hebrew has no indefinite article, the context alone can decide whether a proposition is *general* or only *indefinite* (see Art. 35). In some instances, however, the word אֶחָד *m.* אַחַת *f. one,* is used for the indefinite article: as, נָבִיא אֶחָד זָקֵן *an old prophet* (2 Kings xiii. 11); אִשָּׁה אַחַת *one woman* (2 Kings iv. 1); lit. *one old prophet, one woman.**

174. A *Particular* proposition is that in which the subject is a term relating to a particular individual, or to particular individuals. Such terms are the personal and demonstrative pronouns, proper names, and common nouns whose general signification is restricted by some definite term.

---

* Hence the origin of the indefinite article, *a, an;* German, *ein, eine;* French, *un, une.*

175. A *Simple* proposition is that which has only *one* subject and *one* predicate. (See the preceding examples.)

176. A *Compound* proposition is that which has *several* subjects or several predicates, or both: as, אַבְרָהָם וְשָׂרָה זְקֵנִים *Abraham and Sarah* (*were*) *old* (Gen. xviii); וְהָאָרֶץ הָיְתָה תֹהוּ וָבֹהוּ *and the earth was formless and void* (Gen. i. 2); וַתַּעַן רָחֵל וְלֵאָה וַתֹּאמַרְנָה *and Rachel and Leah answered and said* (Gen. xxvi. 14); וּמִצְרַיִם אָדָם וְלֹא אֵל וְסוּסֵיהֶם בָּשָׂר וְלֹא רוּחַ *and the Egyptians* (*are*) *men, and not God; and their horses* (*are*) *flesh, and not spirit* (Isa. xxxi. 3).

177. *Obs.*—In compound propositions there is generally an ellipsis either of one of the *subjects* or of one of the *predicates:* thus, the first example is equivalent to 'Abraham was *old*,' and 'Sarah was *old*;' and the second, to 'The *earth* was *formless*,' and 'The *earth* was *void*.' The same is the case with the other examples.

178. An *Incomplex* proposition is that in which the subject and the predicate are each expressed by a single word, as הוּא מֶלֶךְ *he* (*is a*) *king;* הַמֶּלֶךְ חָכָם *the king* (*is*) *wise*.

179. A *Complex* proposition is that in which either the subject or the predicate, or both, are expressed by several words, some of which serve to explain, define, or qualify the leading words: as—

182   THE SYNTAX OF

(A) אֲנִי חֹתֶנְךָ יִתְרוֹ בָּא   I thy-father-in-law Jethro (am) coming.

(B) זֶה דָּוִד הַמֶּלֶךְ   This (is) David the-king.

(C) מַלְכֵי יִשְׂרָאֵל הֵם מַלְכֵי חֶסֶד   (The) kings-of Israel are kings of mercy.*

(D) נַעֲמָן שַׂר צְבָא מֶלֶךְ אֲרָם הָיָה אִישׁ גָּדוֹל   Naaman, captain-of (the) host-of (the) king-of Syria, was a great man.

(E) הָאִישׁ אֲשֶׁר נִמְצָא הַגָּבִיעַ בְּיָדוֹ הוּא יִהְיֶה עָבֶד   The man in whose-hand the cup was found, he shall be a slave.

180. *Obs.* 1.—The several words forming a complex term may be either so many names for the *same* object, which is thus, as it were, presented, for the sake of distinction, under different points of view: such, for instance, are the several words, *I, thy-father-in-law, Jethro,* (the subject of Prop. A.) and the words *David the king,* (the predicate of Prop. B.): or the several words may be names of *different* objects, between which there may subsist one of those numerous relations denoted in many languages by the *genitive* case, and by the *possessive case*,† or the preposition *of* in English; such, for instance, are the words which represent the *subject* and *predicate* of Prop. C. Now, when the first happens to take place, the several words are said to be in *apposition,* and must *agree* in case, that is, they must be in the same *case* in which the leading word happens to be. But when the second happens to take place, one of the words is said to *govern* the other in the *genitive;* and in Hebrew, the word which is *defined* must be in a state of *construction* (Art. 52), to distinguish it from the *defining* word or words: thus, מַלְכֵי (not מְלָכִים).

---

* *i. e.* Merciful kings.

† It is almost needless to observe that *possession* is but one of the numerous relations denoted by this case.

The student will likewise observe that this mode of *construction* is often used, where, in English, we should use an adjective (epithet) as the qualifying word: thus, מַלְכֵי חֶסֶד *kings of mercy*, instead of *merciful kings*.

181. *Obs.* 2.—In Prop. D. the words representing the subject are of a mixed nature, and one of those representing the predicate is an adjective (epithet).

182. *Obs.* 3.—In Prop. E. the leading word הָאִישׁ is defined by a proposition. In such cases the leading word must be followed by the relative אֲשֶׁר, or by its equivalents הַ, שֶׁ (Art. 95, 100).

183. *Obs.* 4.—In all complex propositions, a distinction may be made between the *grammatical* and the *logical* subject. Thus, the grammatical subject, or the *Nominative* of the last example (Prop. E.) is, *the man*. But the logical subject is, *the man in whose hand the cup was found*. The remark is equally applicable to the *predicate*.

184. From the preceding observations, it appears that when two or more words come together, they may form either an *entire* proposition, or only a part of one. Now, as the *copula* is frequently omitted, the student may often be at a loss to distinguish between the one and the other. The following considerations will, however, remove every difficulty.

The several words are either all *indefinite*; or they are all *definite*; or some are *indefinite*, and others *definite*.

RULE I.—When the words are all *indefinite*, or all *definite* (without the copula), they form only a part of the proposition: thus—

All Indefinite.

אִשָּׁה אַלְמָנָה   *A woman a widow,* i. e. *a widow woman.*
אִישׁ טוֹב   *A man good,* i. e. *a good man.*
אֶרֶץ טוֹבָה וּרְחָבָה   *A land good and extensive,* i. e. *a good and extensive land.*

All Definite.

הָאִשָּׁה הָאַלְמָנָה   *The woman the widow,* i. e. *the widow woman.**
הָאִישׁ הַטּוֹב   *The man the good,* i. e. *the good man.*
הָאָרֶץ הַטּוֹבָה וְהָרְחָבָה   *The land the good and the extensive,* i. e. *the good and the extensive land.*
שְׁלֹמֹה הַמֶּלֶךְ   *Solomon the king.*
הָאִישׁ הַזֶּה   *The man the this,* i. e. *this man.*
הָאֲנָשִׁים הָאֵלֶּה   *The men the these,* i. e. *these men.*
הָאִישׁ הַהוֹלֵךְ   *The man the goer,* i. e. *the man that goes.*

RULE II.—But when one of the words is *definite*, and the other *indefinite*, then the definite term, whether simple or complex, is the *subject*, and the indefinite term is the *predicate;* thus—

הָאִשָּׁה אַלְמָנָה *   *The woman (is a) widow.*
הָאִישׁ טוֹב or טוֹב הָאִישׁ   *The man (is) good,* or *good is the man.*
הָאָרֶץ טוֹבָה וּרְחָבָה   *The land (is) good and extensive.*
זֶה הָאִישׁ   *This (is) the man* †.
אֵלֶּה הָאֲנָשִׁים   *These (are) the men.*
הָאִישׁ הוֹלֵךְ   *The man goes.*

---

* See the several examples—Art. 86, 98, 101, and the exercises which accompany them.

† When the subject is a pronoun, the predicate may be either *definite* or *indefinite:* as, אַתָּה אִישׁ *thou (art a) man,* אַתָּה הָאִישׁ *thou (art) the man,* מִי הָאִישׁ *who (is) the man,* מָה אֱנוֹשׁ *what (is) man?*

Rule III.—In case two definite terms are to form a proposition, the copula must be inserted: thus,— וְחָם הוּא אֲבִי כְנָעַן and *Ham* was *the father of Canaan** (Gen. ix. 18); וְהַלֻּחוֹת מַעֲשֵׂה אֱלֹהִים הֵמָּה וְהַמִּכְתָּב מִכְתַּב אֱלֹהִים הוּא and *the tables* were (*the*) *work of God, and the writing* was (*the*) *writing of God*† (Ex. xxxii. 16).

185. Propositions are likewise divided into *Affirmative* and *Negative*.

An *Affirmative* proposition is that in which the *copula*, whether expressed or understood, is not affected by a *negative* particle‡, as in most of the preceding examples.

---

* Compare the phrase חָם אֲבִי כְנָעַן *Ham the father of Canaan*, in verse 22, where it forms only a part of a sentence.

† The copula is, however, even in such cases, omitted, when no ambiguity can arise from the omission: as, הַקּוֹל קוֹל יַעֲקֹב *the voice is* (*the*) *voice of Jacob;* הַבָּנוֹת בְּנֹתַי *the daughters* (*are*) *my daughters.* It is likewise frequently omitted in the poetical books of Scripture, where the style is intentionally concise and elliptical.

‡ A proposition may contain one or more *negatives*, and yet be affirmative, provided the negative does not affect the *copula*. Thus, *Blessed* (*is*) *the man that walketh not in the counsel of the ungodly, nor standeth in the way of sinners,* &c. &c. (Ps. i. 1, 2), is an affirmative proposition; being equivalent to, *The man who walketh not in the counsel of,* &c., &c., is *blessed*.

186. A *Negative* proposition is that in which the *copula* is affected by one of the negative particles, אֵין, לֹא, אַל, בַּל, בִּלְתִּי.

187. *Obs.*—These particles are not synonymous, though they all express *negation*.

אֵין indicates the non-existence of the *subject*, and is therefore chiefly used before nouns and participles, and in combination with the personal pronouns: thus, אֵין יוֹסֵף בַּבּוֹר *Joseph was not in the pit* (Gen. xxxvii. 29), lit. *Joseph existed not*, &c.; הַיֶּלֶד אֵינֶנּוּ *the child is not* (Gen. xxx.), lit. *the child, he exists not,* or *is not here*; אֵינֶנִּי נֹתֵן לָכֶם תֶּבֶן *I will not give you straw* (Ex. v. 10), lit. *I am not a giver of straw to you.*

לֹא indicates the non-existence of the *predicate*, and is therefore chiefly used before verbs in the *past* and *future :* as, לֹא נָתַן *he gave not,* לֹא יִתֵּן *he shall not give;* thus, אַתָּה אָדָם וְלֹא אֵל signifies, *thou art a man, and not a god;* whereas וְאֵין אֵל would signify, *and there is no god.*

בַּל has the same signification as לֹא, but is chiefly used in poetry.

אַל is chiefly used for exhorting, entreating, and wishing; and is therefore only used before verbs in the *future.*

בִּלְתִּי is chiefly used before *infinitives.*

Subordinate Members of a Proposition.

188. The words explained in the preceding pages, belong either to the *subject* or to the *predicate*, of which they form a constituent part. But a proposition may contain several other words, which, though they form neither a part of the one, nor of the other, are yet necessary to complete the sense*: such, for instance, are the words אֶת־כָּל־אֶחָיו, and בַּחֶרֶב, in the following sentence, וַיַּהֲרוֹג אֶת־כָּל־אֶחָיו בַּחֶרֶב *and he slew all his brethren with the sword.* Such likewise are the words לְאִשָּׁה—לָאִישׁ הַזֶּה—אֶת־בִּתִּי in the following verse—אֶת־בִּתִּי נָתַתִּי לָאִישׁ הַזֶּה לְאִשָּׁה *I gave my daughter to this man for a wife.* These are generally denominated the *complements* or the subordinate parts of a proposition; and, like the principal parts, they may either be *definite* or *indefinite*, *complex* or *incomplex*.

189. *Obs.* 1.—The subordinate members are, in some languages, distinguished from the more essential parts by particular terminations (cases). In Hebrew, they are indicated by the prefixes ב כ ל מ and by the particle אֶת (Art. 40, 41). Or, as in English, by prepositions.

190. *Obs.* 2.—The subordinate parts are chiefly *regulated* by the nature of the predicate and its signification. For when the predicate is an active transitive verb, it must be accompanied by a word or words on which the action falls (the objective את); and when it denotes causative action (Hiphil), it often requires two objective cases. If it signify *giving, delivering, restoring, &c.,* it will require both an objective and a dative case (ל or אֶל). If it imply *motion,* the place where the motion begins, or from which it originates (מִן or מ) and where it terminates (ל or אֶל or עַד) must often be expressed.

---

* This will generally be the case when the judgment or affirmation of the mind respects an event, incident, or contingent act; or briefly, in narrative sentences.

191. *Obs.* 3.—Sometimes we wish to express the *instrument* with which (בְּ), the purpose for which (לְ), or the *place* and *time in* which (בְּ) the action is performed, or the intention and remission of the action or attribute (ADVERBS), and so on with regard to a variety of other circumstances, all of which must be considered as so many subordinate parts of a proposition.

192. *Obs.* 4.—Amongst these, may likewise be reckoned all words and phrases which are apparently superfluous (PLEONASMS), but which are introduced either for the purpose of additional explanation, emphasis, or amplification: as, וַתִּרְאֵהוּ אֶת־הַיֶּלֶד *and-she-saw him, the child,* i. e. *and she saw it,* namely, *the child,* (Ex. ii. 6); אָנֹכִי אָנֹכִי הוּא מְנַחֶמְכֶם *I, I am your comforter,* i. e. *I, even I, am,* &c. (Isa. li. 12); רָנִּי עֲקָרָה לֹא יָלָדָה *sing, O barren! who never bore* (Isa. liv. 1); וְשַׂמְתִּי עֵינִי עֲלֵיהֶם לְרָעָה וְלֹא לְטוֹבָה *and-I-will-set mine eye against them for evil,* and not for good (Amos ix. 4).

193. *Obs.* 5.—The reverse of this grammatical figure is ELLIPSIS, by which some word or phrase is omitted, which must, however, be supplied by the reader, in order to complete the *regular* or full construction*. Of the omission of the *copula* we have already given numerous examples. The following are examples of the omission of other words; יָרֵא לֵאמֹר אִשְׁתִּי—פֶּן יַהַרְגֻנִי אַנְשֵׁי הַמָּקוֹם *he feared to-say—my-sister—lest-the-men-of the-place should-kill-me* (Gen. xxvi. 7), where the words הִיא *she-is,* and כִּי אָמַר *for-he-said,* must be supplied: עֵינַיִךְ יוֹנִים *thine eyes (are)—doves,* supply the word

---

* This species of *ellipsis* must not be confounded with the *ellipsis* of *parallelism*, and which may, by way of distinction, be called *metrical ellipsis*. The latter is entirely artificial, and consists in omitting in every alternate line a corresponding word or phrase used in the first line. We have a perfect specimen of this species of poetical composition in the hundred and fourteenth Psalm: but this is not the place to enlarge on such a subject.

עֵינֵי *eyes-of* (Cant. i. 15); וְאִישׁ־נַּפְנוֹ וְאִישׁ־תְּאֵנָתוֹ—*cat-ye each—his-vine, and-each—his fig-tree, &c.*, supply the word פְּרִי *the fruit of* (2 Kings xviii. 31); כָּזֹה—עָשִׂיתָ *what (is) this (that) thou-hast-done*, supply אֲשֶׁר (Gen. iii. 13); שְׁבִי אַלְמָנָה בֵית אָבִיךְ (Gen. xxviii.), supply (בְּ) בְּבֵית *in the house of;* וְאֵת שָׂדַי וִיבָרְכֶךָ (Gen. xliv. 25), supply (מִ) וּמֵאֵת *and from;* אֵלָיו פִּי קָרָאתִי (Ps. lxvi. 17), supply (בְּ) בְּפִי *with my mouth;* אֲגַם מָיִם (Ps. cxiv. 8), supply (לְ) לַאֲגַם *into a pool-of.*

The student will do well to impress the preceding remarks on his mind, as many apparent obscurities and anomalies are entirely owing to the *omission* of some word or inflection*, which may, however, be easily supplied by the context.

CHAPTER II.

SYNTAX OF THE NOUN.

194. The definite הַ (p. 35), is used like *the* in English, to direct the attention to a particular individual, or to particular individuals, known either by their universality, or pre-eminence, as having been previously mentioned, or as described by some circumstance: as, הַשָּׁמַיִם *the heaven,* הָאוֹר *the light* (Gen. i.); הַמִּקְדָּשׁ *the sanctuary* (Lev. xii. 4); הָאָדָם אֲשֶׁר יָצָר *the man whom he had formed* (Gen. ii. 8).

195. The article is omitted:—1st, before proper nouns:—2nd, before nouns in a state of construc-

---

* See Kimchi's MICHLOL, pp. 57, 58.

tion* (See Art. 55):—3rd, before nouns having any of the possessive pronominal affixes† (p. 42); because, as in all these cases the noun is already known to refer to particular individuals, the article would be superfluous.

196. *Obs.* 1.—Some proper names of countries, cities, &c., do, however, sometimes take the article: as, הַגִּלְעָד *the Gilead*‡,

---

* There are apparently some exceptions to this rule; as, for instance, הָאֹהֱלָה שָׂרָה *into the tent of Sarah* (Gen. xxiv. 67); הָאֵל בֵּית־אֵל *the God of Beth-el* (Gen. xxxi. 13); הָאָרוֹן הַבְּרִית *the ark of the covenant* (Jos. iii. 14):—but these are elliptical expressions, in which the real noun in *construction* is omitted: thus, הָאֹהֱלָה אֹהֶל שָׂרָה *into the tent*, namely, (*the*) *tent of Sarah*, הָאֵל בֵּית אֵל *the God*, namely, (*the*) *God of Bethel*.

† בְּתוֹךְ הָאֹהָלִי (Jos. vii. 21), הָרוֹתֶיהָ (2 Kings xv. 16), and a few others are exceptions.

‡ Most of the proper names were originally *historical*, or commemorative: as, גַּלְעֵד GALEED, i. e. *heap of witness*, from גַּל *a heap, a mound*, and עֵד *a witness*; מִצְפֶּה MIZPEH, i. e. *a watching-place*, from צָפָה *to look out, to watch* (See Gen. xxxi. 47, 48, 49); גִּלְגָּל GILGAL, from גָּלַל *to roll away, remove* (Jos. v. 9): or they were *epithetical*, i. e. expressive of some distinguishing quality: as, לְבָנוֹן *the white mountain;* רָמָה *the high city* or *place*. In either case they include *a common name*; and hence we see the reason why they are sometimes used *with*, and sometimes without the article, according as they refer to the place alone, or in combination with the circumstance from which the name is derived. In most cases, however, the common name is omitted: thus, הַגִּלְעָד for אֶרֶץ הַגִּלְעָד or אֶרֶץ גִּלְעָד, in the same manner as we say 'The Thames,' for 'The *River* Thames.'

הַגִּלְגָּל *the Gilgal,* הַלְּבָנוֹן *the Lebanon,* הַיַּרְדֵּן *the Jordan*.* (See the Notes.)

197. *Obs.* 2.—The article is used, though omitted in English, when the noun stands for the whole species or kind: as, הָאָדָם יִרְאֶה לַעֵינָיִם† *man looks to the eyes*† (1 Sam. xvi. 7), Hebrew, *the man.*

198. It is likewise used occasionally before nouns in the *vocative:* as, הַאֲזִינוּ הַשָּׁמַיִם *give ear, O ye heavens!* lit. *give ye ear, the heavens!*

199. It is placed before *adjectives* and *demonstrative pronouns,* to distinguish the *epithet* and *definite* from the predicate (see Art. 86, 98, 184); and before participles not having any of the possessive pronominal affixes, instead of the relative pronoun (Art. 100).

200. When, therefore, a participle has the definite הַ and a pronominal affix, the latter must be rendered in English by the corresponding objective pronoun: thus, הַמַּעַלְךָ *who caused* THEE *to go up* (Deut. xx. 1); הַמַּעֲלָם *who caused* THEM *to go up?* (Is. lxiii. 11).

Repetition of the Article.

201. The article must be repeated before every noun‡ belonging to the same part of a proposition: thus, אֵלֶּה הַחֻקִּים וְהַמִּשְׁפָּטִים וְהַתּוֹרוֹת *these are*

---

* This word (יַרְדֵּן) is generally derived from יָרֹד, *to descend;* but it is probably a compound of יְאֹר *river,* and דָּן *Dan,* the name of a place near its source.

† *i. e.* On the outward appearance.

‡ Except where the noun is already defined (Art. 193). See the words אוֹצַר בֵּית יהוה and וּכְלֵי הַנְּחֹשֶׁת in the next page.

the statutes and judgments and laws (Levit. xxvi. 46), HEBREW, *the* judgments and *the* laws*.

רַק הַכֶּסֶף וְהַזָּהָב וּכְלֵי הַנְּחֹשֶׁת וְהַבַּרְזֶל נָתְנוּ אוֹצַר בֵּית יְהוָה (Josh. vi. 24.) ׃

הַמַּסֹּת הַגְּדֹלֹת אֲשֶׁר רָאוּ עֵינֶיךָ וְהָאֹתֹת וְהַמֹּפְתִים וְהַיָּד הַחֲזָקָה וְהַזְּרֹעַ הַנְּטוּיָה (Deut. vii. 19.) ׃

202. This rule is equally applicable to the *prefixes* and *affixes*; and it matters not whether some of the nouns are in construction or in apposition: thus—

וַיִּקַּח אַבְרָהָם אֶת־יִשְׁמָעֵאל בְּנוֹ וְאֵת כָּל־יְלִידֵי בֵיתוֹ וְאֵת כָּל־מִקְנַת כַּסְפּוֹ
And Abraham took Ishmael his son, and all that were born in his house, and all that were bought with his money, &c. (Gen. xvii. 23).

Obs.—When the first of several terms in *apposition* is a *proper name*, the prefix, &c., is placed before the first, and omitted before the rest, as in the preceding example, אֶת־יִשְׁמָעֵאל בְּנוֹ. But when the *proper name* stands after the other terms, then the prefix, &c., must be repeated before each of the terms: thus, אֶת־בְּנוֹ אֶת־יִשְׁמָעֵאל *his son, namely, Ishmael;* לַאדֹנִי לְעֵשָׂו to *my lord, to Esau* (Gen. xxxii. 5); קַח־נָא אֶת־בִּנְךָ אֶת־יְחִידְךָ—אֶת־יִצְחָק (Gen. xxii. 2).

Additional Examples.

לֶךְ־לְךָ מֵאַרְצְךָ וּמִמּוֹלַדְתְּךָ וּמִבֵּית אָבִיךָ ׃ (Gen. xii. 1.)

וְאַבְרָם כָּבֵד מְאֹד בַּמִּקְנֶה בַּכֶּסֶף וּבַזָּהָב ׃ (Gen. xiii. 2.)

אֶת־הַמִּשְׁכָּן אֶת־אָהֳלוֹ וְאֶת־מִכְסֵהוּ אֶת־קְרָסָיו † וְאֶת־

---

* The untranslated verses are inserted by way of exercise.

† The particle אֵת is, however, sometimes omitted: especially

(Ex. xxxv. 11.) : קְרָשָׁיו אֶת־בְּרִיחָיו אֶת־עַמֻּדָיו וְאֶת־אֲדָנָיו
נָטָה אֶת־יָדְךָ בְּמַטְּךָ עַל־הַנְּהָרוֹת עַל־הַיְאֹרִים וְעַל
הָאֲגַמִּים : וְכָרוּ הַצְפַרְדְּעִים מִמְּךָ וּמִבָּתֶּיךָ וּמֵעֲבָדֶיךָ
וּמֵעַמֶּךָ : (Ex. viii. 1–7.) וְגַם נְתַתִּיו לַלֵּוִי וְלַגֵּר לַיָּתוֹם
וְלָאַלְמָנָה : (Deut. xxiv. 2.)

CASE.

203. The *Nominative* may be known, as in other languages, by its being the *subject* of the proposition.

Obs. 1.—When the *predicate* is a passive verb, the *objective* is sometimes used instead of the *nominative:* as, וַיּוּשַׁב אֵת מֹשֶׁה *and Moses was brought back* (Ex. x. 8); יֻתַּן אֵת הָאָרֶץ *let this land be given* (Num. xxxii. 5); because, though the words מֹשֶׁה and הָאָרֶץ are the *subjects*, they are nevertheless the *objects* of the several actions.

204. *Obs. 2.*—The nominative is often found as if it were detached from the rest of the sentence; in which case it is called the *Nominative Absolute:* as, אִישׁ זְרוֹעַ לוֹ הָאָרֶץ *the man of power, to him belongs the earth* (Job xxii. 8), i.e. *as to the mighty man, his is the earth;* קַיִץ וָחֹרֶף אַתָּה יְצַרְתָּם *as to summer and winter, thou hast made them* (Ps. lxxiv. 17).

205. The *Genitive* is indicated by placing the

---

where no ambiguity can arise from the omission. Compare the above-cited passage with קרסיו קרשיו בריחיו, &c. (Ex. xxxix. 33). Compare, likewise, Lev. xi. 13, with Deut. xiv. 12.

noun which is defined* in a state of construction (Art. 51, 61).

The *defined word* may be denominated the *antecedent*†, and the defining term the *consequent*.

Thus, in the following examples, בַּת מֶלֶךְ (*a*) *daughter of* (*a*) *king*, בֶּן הַמֶּלֶךְ (*the*) *son of the king*, אֵימַת מֶלֶךְ (*the*) *terror of* (*a*) *king*‡, מַלְכֵי עַמִּים *kings of nations*, זֵר זָהָב *a border-of gold*,

---

* We have already observed (Art. 36, 53) that the vague signification of common nouns is often defined by adding to them another word (or words) expressive of the *material* of which they are formed: as, קַעֲרַת כֶּסֶף (*a*) *dish of silver*, i. e. *a silver dish* ; כְּלֵי בַרְזֶל *vessels of iron*, i. e. *iron vessels*—or the use for which they are intended; as, כְּלֵי מִלְחָמָה *instruments of war*, בֵּית תְּפִלָּה *a house of prayer* ;—or by mentioning the person to whom they belong; as, בֵּית הַמֶּלֶךְ (*the*) *house of the king*, אֹהֶל יַעֲקֹב (*the*) *tent of Jacob* ;—or the object of which they form a part : as, רֹאשׁ הָהָר *the top of the mountain* ; פִּי הַבְּאֵר *the mouth of the well* ; and, in short, by adding a word expressive of any of those numerous relations which subsist between objects—as *cause* and *effect*, *agent* and *patient*, the *whole* and its *parts*, &c., &c., and vice versa. Now, in all such cases, the word which is defined must be placed before that which is to define it.

† The Antecedent is denominated by Hebrew Grammarians, נִסְמָךְ or סָמוּךְ, i. e. *that which is supported*; the Consequent is termed סוֹמֵךְ *the supporter*.

‡ This mode of expression is, in most languages, liable to ambiguity ; for *the terror of the king*, may either mean the terror with which he is affected, or the terror with which he inspires others. It is the same with respect to the possessive affixes : מוֹרַאֲכֶם *your fear* (Gen. ix. 2), signifies the fear which others will have for you, and is therefore properly rendered in the Established Version, *the fear of you :* but the same word in Isaiah viii. 13, signifies *the Being*

i. e. *a golden border,*—the words בַּת, בֶּן, אֵימַת, מַלְכֵי, and זֵר, are the *antecedents,* and מֶלֶךְ, הַמֶּלֶךְ, עַמִּים, and זָהָב are the *consequents.*

206. The antecedent must be an *indefinite** term; and therefore it cannot be a *pronoun,* nor a *proper name,* nor a noun having the definite ה (Art. 194) or a pronominal affix. When therefore a pronominal affix is required, it must be added to the *consequent:* thus, בֶּן בִּנְךָ (*the*) *son-of thy-son,* עַבְדֵי אֲדֹנֶיךָ (*the*) *servants-of thy-master,* כְּלֵי מִלְחַמְתּוֹ (*the*) *instruments-of his war* (for, *his instruments of war*), הַר קָדְשִׁי (*the*) *mountain-of my-holiness* (for, *my holy mountain*†).

207. The *antecedent* may be an adjective, the substantive being understood (Art. 164): as יְפֵה תֹאַר *m.* יְפַת תֹּאַר *f. beautiful of form,* i. e. *one of beautiful form.* טוֹבַת מַרְאֶה *good of appearance,* i. e. *of good appearance,*

---

whom you ought to fear. Thus likewise מוֹרָאִי *my fear* may signify the fear with which I am affected; but מוֹרָאִי in Malachi i. 6, signifies the fear (*reverence*) due to me. The context will, however, generally show in what sense the words are to be understood.

* Because if it were definite it would require no further definition.

† It is in this manner that the Hebrew often uses *nouns* instead of adjectives. When, however, a real adjective is used, the pronominal affix must be added to the noun, as בִּתִּי הַקְּטַנָּה *my-daughter the-little,* i. e. *my little daughter.*

גְּדָל כֹּחַ *great of strength*, i. e. *of great strength:* or a participle, as שְׁבוּרֵי לֵב (*the*) *broken-of-heart*, i. e. *the broken-hearted;* יֹשְׁבֵי חֹשֶׁךְ (*the*) *sitters of darkness*, i. e. *those that sit (dwell) in darkness;* רֹדְפֵי צֶדֶק (*the*) *pursuers* (*followers*) *of righteousness*, i. e. *those that follow righteousness;* מְבַקְשֵׁי יְהֹוָה (*the*) *seekers of the Lord*, i. e. *those that seek the Lord**: or it may be an infinitive: as, עֲשׂוֹת מִשְׁפָּט *to-do justice*, i. e. (*the*) *doing of justice;* שֶׁבֶת אַחִים (*the*) *sitting of brothers*, i. e. *when brothers sit;* בְּצֵאת הַשָּׁנָה *in-*(*the*)-*going out-of the year*, i. e. *at the end of the year*.

208. The *consequent* may consist of any word capable of defining the *antecedent;* it may therefore be a demonstrative pronoun; as עֹשֵׂה־אֵלֶּה (*the*) *doer of these* (*things*) i. e. *whoever does so.* (Ps. xv. 5):—or it may be a relative pronoun (Art. 182) expressed or understood; as מְקוֹם אֲשֶׁר יוֹסֵף אָסוּר שָׁם (*the*) *place where Joseph was bound* (Gen. xl. 3); שְׂפַת [אֲשֶׁר] לֹא יָדַעְתִּי *a language* (*which*) *I know not* (Ps. lxxxi. 5).

209. The consequent is sometimes preceded by a preposition: as, הוֹלְכֵי עַל דֶּרֶךְ (*the*) *walkers-of upon the way*, i. e. *those that walk on the way;* כְּשִׂמְחַת בַּקָּצִיר *as joy-of in harvest*, i. e. *as the joy of*

---

* From the numerous examples given above, it is evident that the state of construction cannot always be expressed in English by the possessive case, or by the preposition *of*. In translating such phrases, recourse must therefore be had to such turns of expression as are agréeable to the idiom of the language.

(*men*) *in harvest.* But such phrases are either elliptical, as in the last example; or they are idiomatic expressions, in which the state of construction is used for the *absolute state,* merely to facilitate the pronunciation of the complex terms. Of the same character are the following words, נְהַר פְּרָת *the river (of) Euphrates;* כְּיֵין הַטּוֹב *as wine that is good* (Cant. viii), i. e. *as good wine;* נִטְעֵי נַעֲמָנִים *pleasant plants* (Isa. xvii. 10).

210. The *absolute state* is sometimes used instead of the *constructive*: as, טוּרִים אָבֶן (Exod. xxviii. 17) for טוּרֵי אָבֶן *rows of stone* *; אֲמָרִים אֱמֶת (Prov. xx. 21) for אִמְרֵי אֱמֶת *words of truth.*

211. Several words in construction may follow each other: as, לֵב רָאשֵׁי עַם הָאָרֶץ (*the*) *heart-of* (*the*) *chiefs-of* (*the*) *people-of the land,* רוּחַ כָּל־בְּשַׂר־אִישׁ *the spirit-of* (*the*) *whole-of* (*the*) *flesh-of man* (Job xii), i. e. *the spirit of every living being.* In such cases, each of the intermediate terms is *consequent* and *antecedent* at the same time; *consequent* to the preceding word, and *antecedent* to that which comes after it: thus, in the first example, the word רָאשֵׁי is the consequent of לֵב, and the antecedent of עַם; and עַם is the consequent of רָאשֵׁי and the antecedent of הָאָרֶץ. — וְאֵלֶּה יְמֵי שְׁנֵי־חַיֵּי אַבְרָהָם (Gen. xxv. 6); גִּבּוֹרֵי חַיִל מְלֶאכֶת עֲבוֹדַת בֵּית־הָאֱלֹהִים (1 Chron. ix. 13).

---

* Some grammarians think that words of this description are in *apposition,* similar to nouns denoting weight, measure, time, &c., as, כִּכָּרִים כֶּסֶף *two talents (of) silver;* אֵיפָה שְׂעֹרִים *an ephah (of) barley;*—others are of opinion that they are elliptical, the real *consequent* being omitted; thus, אמרים אמרי אמת *words,* namely, *words of truth,* &c., in the same manner as we find that the *antecedent* is sometimes omitted: thus, חֲמֻדוֹת אָתָּה (Dan. ix) for אִישׁ חֲמֻדוֹת.

212. A noun in a state of construction, followed by the same noun in the plural, is often used to express the superlative degree: thus, מֶלֶךְ מְלָכִים *King of kings*, i. e. *the greatest of kings*; עֶבֶד עֲבָדִים *a slave of slaves*, i. e. *the most abject of slaves*; קֹדֶשׁ הַקֳּדָשִׁים (Exod. xxvii. 34); שְׁמֵי הַשָּׁמַיִם (1 Kings viii. 28).

Dative.

213. The dative case is indicated by the prefix לְ or by the preposition אֶל (Art. 40. p. 37).

214. The sign of the dative is often used instead of the genitive to express the relation of property or possession: as, רָאִיתִי בֵּן לְיִשַׁי (1 Sam. xvi. 18) *I have seen a son (belonging) to Jesse*, i. e. *Jesse's son*; מִזְמוֹר לְדָוִד *a Psalm to David*, i. e. *of David*. The לְ is frequently preceded by אֲשֶׁר: as, וְרָחֵל בָּאָה עִם הַצֹּאן אֲשֶׁר לְאָבִיהָ (Gen. xxix. 9); *and Rachel came with the sheep which (belonged) to her father*, i. e. *with her father's sheep*; פֶּתַח הַבַּיִת לֶאֱלִישָׁע (2 Kings v. 9); אַפִּיר הָרֹעִים אֲשֶׁר לְשָׁאוּל (1 Sam. xxi. 8).

Objective Case.

215. The *objective* is indicated by the particle אֵת or אֶת־ (Art. 41): but it is used only when the noun is in a definite state*; and even then it is frequently omitted. When this takes place, or when the noun is used indefinitely, the objective may be known by its

---

* By *the definite state* is meant, when the noun has the definite ה, or one of the possessive pronominal affixes; or when it is in a state of construction, or when it is a proper name.

position after the verb*, which is either expressed or understood ; as בֶּן יְכַבֵּד אָב וְעֶבֶד אֲדֹנָיו (Mal. i. 6.).

Ablative and Vocative Case.

216. The *Ablative* case is indicated by the prefixes, בְּ *in, with,* &c. מ or מִן *from* (Art. 40).

217. The Hebrew has no particular form for the *Vocative* ; but it may easily be known by the general sense of the sentence :—

Compare הַיָּם רָאָה וַיָּנֹס Ps. civ. 3. with v. 5. of the same chapter, מַה לְךָ הַיָּם כִּי תָנוּס.

Number.

218. Generic terms of the singular number are often used to express the entire species ; as :—

---

* In the *inverted* style, where both the nominative and objective are often placed before or after the verb, they may be distinguished from each other by the agreement of the verb with the former. Thus, in the following example, כָּבוֹד חֲכָמִים יִנְחָלוּ (Prov. iii. 35), though both the objective and nominative *precede* the verb, yet it is evident that חֲכָמִים *wise* (*men*), which is in the plural, must be the nominative, because the verb יִנְחָלוּ *they inherit,* agrees with it; and כָּבוֹד must be the *objective ;* for were it the nominative, the verb must have been in the singular, יִנְחַל. So likewise in the following verse, תְּמוֹתֵת רָשָׁע רָעָה (Ps. xxxiv.) though both the nominative and objective follow the verb, yet it is evident that רָעָה *evil, f.* must be the nominative, because the verb תְּמוֹתֵת *she slays,* which is likewise feminine, agrees with it ; whereas רָשָׁע being masculine, would require the verb יְמוֹתֵת.

מֵהָעוֹף לְמִינֵהוּ (Gen. vi. 20) *of the fowl after his kind*, i. e. *of fowls after their kind; and I have* שׁוֹר וַחֲמוֹר צֹאן וְעֶבֶד וְשִׁפְחָה *an ox, and an ass, and sheep, and a man servant, and a female servant* (Gen. xxxii. 5), i. e. *oxen, asses*, &c.

This is especially the case with patronymics; as, הָאֱמֹרִי *the Amorite*, הַכְּנַעֲנִי *the Canaanite*, i. e. *the Amorites, the Canaanites;* וַיַּרְא יִשְׂרָאֵל *and Israel saw*, i. e. *and the Israelites saw*.

219. Nouns which occur only in the plural or dual form (Art. 47): as, פָּנִים, חַיִּים, מַיִם*, drop the מ in the genitive, and take the plural pronominal affixes (p. 42), even when they are used in the sense of the singular: thus, פָּנִים *the countenance, face, or faces*, gen. פְּנֵי הַכְּרוּבִים *the faces of the cherubim;* פְּנֵי הַכְּרוּב *the face of the cherub;* פְּנֵי (not פָּנַי) *my face*, פָּנֶיךָ *thy face*, &c., חַיִּים *life*, g. חַיֵּי *the life of*, חַיַּי (not חַיִּי) *my life*, חַיָּיו *his life*, &c.†

220. The plural of nouns expressing dignity and majesty is generally used instead of the singular; thus:—

אָדוֹן, p. אֲדֹנִים‡ *Lord;* אָדוֹן, p. אֲדֹנָי *Lord-of;* אֲדֹנִי *my lord* (to

---

* The genitive of מַיִם *water* or *waters*, is מֵי or מֵימֵי ; but the second מ must be retained when the word is used with pronominal affixes: thus, מֵימַי מֵימֶיךָ מֵימֵי.

† Words of this description have their adjectives, pronouns, and verbs mostly in the plural: as, מַיִם קְדוֹשִׁים *holy water;* פָּנִים זֹעֲמִים *an angry countenance;* הֵמָּה מֵי מְרִיבָה ; וַיֵּצְאוּ מַיִם רַבִּים (Num. xx. 11); (Num. xx. 13). The agreement in such instances is merely *formal*. Sometimes, however, they have their adjectives, verbs, &c., in the singular number. (See Num. xix. 13; 1 Sam. iv. 16; Isa. xxx. 20).

‡ This is denominated *pluralis excellentiæ*, because it does not actually indicate plurality, but great dignity: so, likewise, בֹּרְאֶיךָ

distinguish it from אֲדֹנִי Lord, applied only to the *Divine Being*); אֲדֹנַי *my Lords*. The rest of the plural affixes are used for the singular: as, אֲדֹנֶיךָ *thy Lord* (not אֲדֹנְךָ); אֲדֹנָיו *his Lord* (not אֲדֹנוֹ), אֲדֹנֵינוּ, &c.; בַּעַל *a master, superior, possessor,* בְּעָלָיו *his master;* בְּעָלֶיהָ *her master*.

The words אֱלֹהִים, אֱלֹהֵי, אֱלֹהֶיךָ, אֱלֹהֵינוּ, &c., though they have plural terminations, are often used with verbs, pronouns, &c., of the singular number, and must be rendered in the singular, when applied to the *Divine Being*: as, בָּרָא אֱלֹהִים *God created,* הוּא אֱלֹהֶיךָ *he is thy God*†. But when these words are applied to heathen deities, they may be rendered either in the singular or plural number, according as they refer to one of those false gods, or to more than one: thus, כְּמוֹשׁ אֱלֹהֶיךָ (Judg. xi. 24) *Chemosh thy God*; אֱלֹהֶיךָ (Gen. xxxi. 32) *thy Gods*. In the latter case, the adjectives, verbs, &c., are always expressed in the plural: as, אֱלֹהִים אֲחֵרִים *strange Gods;* אֵלֶּה אֱלֹהֶיךָ יִשְׂרָאֵל—אֱלֹהִים אֲשֶׁר יֵלְכוּ (Exod. xxxii. i. 4).

Repetition of Nouns.

221. The same noun is sometimes repeated:—

1*st.*—To indicate emphasis and effect: as, צֶדֶק צֶדֶק תִּרְדֹּף (Deut. xvi. 20) *justice, justice thou shalt follow,* i. e. *let it be thy*

---

thy Creator; עֹשֶׂיךָ *thy Maker;* these are, however, very seldom used in this form.

* But בַּעֲלִי *my husband, master;* בַּעְלָהּ *her husband,* are used in the singular.

† There are indeed examples where אלהים occurs with plural verbs and plural adjectives, &c., but even then it is generally accompanied by some word indicating unity: thus, in Gen. i. 26. xi. 7., the verbs נֵרְדָה נַעֲשֶׂה are *plural,* yet the verbs וַיֵּרֶד וַיֹּאמֶר are in the *singular.* In Josh. xxiv. 19. though the adjective קְדֹשִׁים is in the *plural,* the accompanying pronoun הוּא is in the *singular.*

constant aim; אַבְשָׁלוֹם בְּנִי בְנִי (2 Sam. xviii. 33) *O Absalom, my son, my son!*—אֶרֶץ אֶרֶץ אֶרֶץ (Jer. xxii. 29) *O earth, earth, earth, hear the word of the Lord!*

2nd.—To indicate multitude: וְעֵמֶק הַשִּׂדִּים בֶּאֱרֹת בֶּאֱרֹת חֵמָר (Gen. xiv. 10). *and the vale of Siddim (was) pits, pits, slime,* i. e. *full of slime pits;* חֳמָרִים חֳמָרִים (Exod. viii. 10) *heaps, heaps,* i. e. *a great many heaps.*

3rd.—To denote distribution: as בַּבֹּקֶר בַּבֹּקֶר (Exod. xxxii. 3) *in the morning, in the morning,* i. e. *every morning;* יוֹם יוֹם *day, day,* i. e. *every day,* or *daily.*

4th.—To denote diversity; in which case, the second noun takes (וְ); as (Deut. xxv. 13) *thou shalt not have in thy bag* אֶבֶן וָאָבֶן *a stone and a stone,* i. e. *divers weights;* בְּלֵב וָלֵב יְדַבֵּרוּ (Isa. xii. 3) *with heart and heart they speak,* i. e. *they speak with duplicity.*

CHAPTER III.

ADJECTIVES.

222. Adjectives are used either as qualifying words (Art. 83, 84), or as predicates (Art. 86).

In either case, they generally agree with their substantives in gender and number (Art. 86).

223. Adjectives are frequently used without their substantives: as, חָכָם *a wise,* (*man*) חֲכָמִים *wise* (*men*), חֲכָמוֹת *wise* (*women*), רַכָּה *a tender* (*woman*), &c.

224. In such cases, the adjective assumes the character of a noun, and is often susceptible of the same variations: חַכְמֵי הַגּוֹיִם

the wise-(men) of nations, חֲכָמָיו *his wise-(men),* חֲכָמֶיךָ *thy wise-(men),* גְּדֹלָיו *his great-(men),* גְּדֹלֶיהָ *her great (men).*

Degrees of Comparison.

225. Having already described (Art. 87) how the several degrees of comparison are expressed, we have only to add the following observations:—

1st.—that reciprocal comparison is denoted by the repetition of the כ, before the compared words: thus הָעָם כַּכֹּהֵן signifies, *the people are like the priest,* but כָּעָם כַּכֹּהֵן signifies, *the people are like the priest, and the priest is like the people.*

2nd.—That the superlative is often indicated—(A) by repeating the adjective: as עָמֹק עָמֹק *deep, deep, i. e. very deep;* רַע רַע יֹאמַר הַקּוֹנֶה (Prov. xx. 14) *bad, bad, says the buyer, i. e. the buyer says (before the purchase is made) it is very bad:*—(B) by adding the word מְאֹד *might, strength, very,* or מְאֹד מְאֹד *very, very, i. e. exceedingly good:*—(c) By adding one of the names of God—עִיר גְּדוֹלָה לֵאלֹהִים *a city great to God, i. e. a very great city;* הַרְרֵי אֵל *mountains of God*;* אַרְזֵי אֵל *cedars of God, i. e. the highest mountains, the loftiest cedars*†*;*—(D) by the repetition of the noun (See Art. 212)‡; מֶלֶךְ מְלָכִים *King of kings,* עֶבֶד עֲבָדִים *slave of slaves.*

NUMERALS.

226. אֶחָד and אַחַת are always placed after the

---

* Intensity is often denoted in the same manner: as שַׁלְהֶבֶתְיָה *a flame of God, i. e. a vehement flame;* מַאְפֵּלְיָה *a darkness of God, i. e. very great darkness.*

† The positive, in a state of construction, or with the article, is sometimes used for the superlative: as, קְטוֹן בָּנָיו *the least of his children,* וְדָוִד הוּא הַקָּטֹן *and David was the smallest.*

‡ In such cases the noun must be in the plural.

name of the thing numbered, and take the definite ה when the noun is used definitely: as, קֶרֶשׁ אֶחָד *one board*, הַקֶּרֶשׁ הָאֶחָד *the one board;* מַחֲנֶה אַחַת *one camp*, הַמַּחֲנֶה הָאַחַת *the one camp.*

227. The rest of the cardinal numbers mostly precede their nouns, and never take the definite ה, except as explained hereafter: thus שְׁנֵי אֲנָשִׁים or שְׁנַיִם אֲנָשִׁים *two men*, שְׁנֵי הָאֲנָשִׁים or הָאֲנָשִׁים שְׁנַיִם *the two men;* עֶשְׂרִים קְרָשִׁים *twenty boards*, עֶשְׂרִים הַקְּרָשִׁים *the twenty boards.* (See Exod. xl. 12, 18; xli. 4, 7, 20, 24, 26, 27.)

Obs. 1.—The numerals are placed generally after the nouns when several things are specified and enumerated: as, (Gen. xxxii. 13—15) *and he took of that which came to his hand* מִנְחָה *a present*, &c. (consisting of) עִזִּים מָאתַיִם *she-goats, two hundred,* וּתְיָשִׁים עֶשְׂרִים *and he-goats, twenty;* רְחֵלִים מָאתַיִם *ewes, two hundred,* וְאֵילִים עֶשְׂרִים *and rams, twenty,* &c. &c. (see likewise Num. vii. 13—88; xxvii. xxix. xxxi. 21—45)*: or when the numeral is the predicate: as, עַמּוּדֵיהֶם עֶשְׂרִים וְאַדְנֵיהֶם עֶשְׂרִים (Exod. xxxviii. 10) *their pillars (were) twenty, and their sockets (were) twenty.*

2.—The numerals receive the definite article when they refer to a number previously mentioned, or otherwise known, especially when the noun is omitted†: as, הָאַרְבָּעִים *the forty,* הָעֶשְׂרִים, הָעֲשָׂרָה (Gen. xviii. 29, 32), אַרְבָּעָה מְלָכִים אֶת־הַחֲמִשָּׁה (Gen. xiv. 9), הָאֶחָד (Gen. xix. 9; xlii. 27).

---

* In such cases, the article is sometimes repeated before each of the numerals: as, הַשְּׁלֹשָׁה וְהַשִּׁבְעִים וְהַמָּאתַיִם (Num. iii. 46).

† In the composite numbers from 11 to 20, we find the definite sometimes before the *decimal* or before the noun: thus, אֶל שְׁנֵים אֶת שְׁתֵּים עֶשְׂרֵה הָאֲבָנִים–הֶעָשׂוֹר אִישׁ (Josh. iv. 4. 20).

THE HEBREW LANGUAGE. 205

Obs. 3.—The cardinal numbers from 2 to 10 require plural nouns with which the numerals must agree in gender: as, שְׁנֵי or שְׁנַיִם בָּנִים *two sons;* שְׁתֵּי or שְׁתַּיִם בָּנוֹת *two daughters;* שִׁבְעָה נְעָרִים *seven boys,* שֶׁבַע נְעָרוֹת *seven girls,* עֲשָׂרָה יָמִים *ten days,* עֶשֶׂר נָשִׁים *ten women**.

4.—Above ten the name of the thing numbered may be either in the singular or plural: as, אַחַד עָשָׂר יוֹם *eleven day,* i. e. *days* (Deut. i. 2); אַחַד עָשָׂר כּוֹכָבִים *eleven stars* (Gen. xxxvii. 8)†; אַחַת עֶשְׂרֵה שָׁנָה *eleven years;* אַחַת עֶשְׂרֵה עָרִים *thirteen cities,* שְׁלֹשׁ עֶשְׂרֵה עִיר or שְׁלֹשׁ עֶשְׂרֵה עָרִים *thirteen cities;* עֶשְׂרִים קֶרֶשׁ or עֶשְׂרִים קְרָשִׁים *twenty boards;* מֵאָה אַמָּה or מֵאָה אַמּוֹת *a hundred cubits;* אֶלֶף אִישׁ *a thousand men;* אֶלֶף פָּרָשִׁים *a thousand horsemen.*

5.—From eleven to twenty, the less number must precede the greater, without an intervening (וְ). (See Cardinal Numbers, p. 91). But from twenty and above, it is immaterial which comes first, but the וְ must be added: thus, אֶחָד וְעֶשְׂרִים or עֶשְׂרִים וְאֶחָד *one-and-twenty.*

6.—מֵאָה *a hundred* (cons. מְאַת, p. מֵאוֹת, dual, מָאתַיִם *two hundred*), though of the common gender, requires, on account of its feminine termination, the units which precede its plural (מֵאוֹת), to be of the cons. fem.: thus, שְׁלֹשׁ מֵאוֹת *three hundred* (not

---

* The agreement in gender takes place equally from ten to twenty: as, חֲמִשָּׁה עָשָׂר בָּנִים *fifteen sons;* חֲמִשָּׁה עָשָׂר בָּנוֹת *fifteen daughters.* But the numerals from twenty and above are common to both genders; the units, however, which are joined to them follow the genders of the noun: thus, אַרְבָּעִים וּשְׁנַיִם אִישׁ, אַרְבָּעִים וּשְׁתַּיִם עִיר.

† In this respect we must be guided by scriptural usage: for though we find אֶלֶף אִישׁ, אַחַד עָשָׂר יוֹם, yet it would not be correct to say אֶלֶף בֵּן, or אַחַד עָשָׂר כּוֹכָב.

שֵׁשׁ מֵאוֹת *אֶלֶף (יְשֹׁלֶשֶׁת מֵאוֹת nor שְׁלִישָׁה nor שָׁלִישׁ *אֶלֶף); *שֵׁשׁ מֵאוֹת* six hundred thousand (not שִׁשָּׁה).

Obs. 7.—אֶלֶף *a thousand* (plural, אֲלָפִים *thousands*); dual, אַלְפַּיִם *two thousands* (cons. אַלְפֵי); though it is common to both genders, yet being considered as of the masculine gender, requires the plural termination ־ים, and the cons. *m.* units, from 3000 to 10,000 both inclusive: as, שְׁלֹשֶׁת אֲלָפִים *three thousands*†; עֲשֶׂרֶת אֲלָפִים *ten thousands;* but above that number, אֶלֶף is used instead of אֲלָפִים: thus, שְׁנֵי עָשָׂר אֶלֶף or שְׁנַיִם־עָשָׂר אֶלֶף *twelve thousand;* שִׁשָּׁה עָשָׂר אֶלֶף *sixteen thousand;* שְׁנַיִם וְעֶשְׂרִים אֶלֶף or עֶשְׂרִים וּשְׁנַיִם אֶלֶף *twenty-two thousand.*

8.—The word אֶלֶף is sometimes repeated: as, שֵׁשׁ מֵאוֹת אֶלֶף וְשִׁבְעִים אֶלֶף וַחֲמֵשֶׁת אֲלָפִים *six hundred and seventy-five thousand.* This is likewise the case with the word שָׁנָה: as, מֵאָה שָׁנָה וְעֶשְׂרִים שָׁנָה וְשֶׁבַע שָׁנִים *one hundred year, and twenty year, and seven years,* i. e. *one hundred and twenty-seven years.*

9.—Some of the cardinal numbers take the pronominal affixes: as, בֵּין שְׁנֵינוּ (Gen. xxxi. 37) *betwixt us two* (both); וַיִּהְיוּ שְׁנֵיהֶם עֲרוּמִּים (Gen. ii. 25) *and they were both naked;* הִכָּה שָׁאוּל בַּאֲלָפָיו וְדָוִד (Num. xii. 4) *ye three;* שְׁלָשְׁתְּכֶם בְּרִבְבוֹתָיו (1 Sam. xviii. 3) *Saul hath slain his thousands, and David his ten thousands.*

---

* Particular attention must be paid to the insertion or the omission of וֹ: thus, for instance, in the above number, if a וֹ were added to אֶלֶף, thus שֵׁשׁ מֵאוֹת וְאֶלֶף the number would stand for 600 + 1000 = 1600. It would amount to the same were we to reverse the order and insert וֹ, thus אֶלֶף וְשֵׁשׁ מֵאוֹת; but, שֵׁשׁ מֵאוֹת אֶלֶף without וֹ, stands for 600 × 1000 = 600,000. Thus likewise מָאתַיִם אֶלֶף is *two hundred thousand;* but כָּאתַיִם וְאֶלֶף or אֶלֶף וּמָאתַיִם is *one thousand two hundred.*

† There are a few exceptions to these rules, especially in the later Hebrew.

THE HEBREW LANGUAGE.   207

Obs. 10—Several of the numerals (besides שְׁנַיִם and שִׁתַּיִם), have a dual form, to express the addition of the same quantity: as, אַרְבָּעְתַּיִם *fourfold*, שִׁבְעָתַיִם *sevenfold*.

11.—When the cardinal numbers are used distributively, they are repeated without the conjunctive וְ: as, שְׁנַיִם שְׁנַיִם *two two*, i. e. *two and two*, or *by twos*; שִׁבְעָה שִׁבְעָה *seven seven*, i. e. *by sevens*.

12.—The cardinal numbers are sometimes used to express the adverbs פַּעַם *once*, פַּעֲמַיִם *twice*, &c.: as, לֹא אַחַת וְלֹא שְׁתָּיִם (2 Kings vi. 10) *not once, nor twice**; שִׁבְעִים וְשִׁבְעָה (Gen. iv. 24) *seven and seventy fold, or times*.

228. The ordinal numbers extend only to ten. Above this number, the cardinals are used to express them. (Art. 91. p. 93).

229. Like other adjectives, they follow their nouns, with which they *agree* in gender†, and they take the definite ה when the noun is used definitely: thus, בֵּן שֵׁנִי *a second son*; הַחֹדֶשׁ הַשֵּׁנִי *the second month*;

---

* These adverbs are, however, more generally expressed by the word פַּעַם *once*, פְּעָמַיִם *twice*, שָׁלֹשׁ פְּעָמִים or שָׁלֹשׁ רְגָלִים *three times*, אֶלֶף פְּעָמִים *a thousand times*, שֶׁבַע שָׁנִים שֶׁבַע פְּעָמִים *seven years seven times*, i. e. *forty-nine years*: or by מֹנִים (from מָנָה *to number*) עֲשֶׂרֶת מֹנִים, *ten times*.

† The ordinals רִאשׁוֹן, רִאשֹׁנָה, agree likewise in number: as, הַיָּמִים הָרִאשֹׁנִים *the first days*, הַצָּרוֹת הָרִאשֹׁנוֹת *the first* (*former*) *troubles*; אֶת שֶׁבַע הַפָּרוֹת הָרִאשֹׁנוֹת הַבְּרִיאוֹת *the first seven fat kine*.

בַּשָּׁנָה הַשְּׁלִישִׁית בַּחֹדֶשׁ הַשְּׁלִישִׁי *in the third month*; in the third year.†*

230. The cardinals אֶחָת, אֶחָד are frequently used for the ordinals רִאשׁוֹן, רִאשֹׁנָה, and the noun is sometimes omitted: as, בְּאֶחָד לַחֹדֶשׁ (Gen. viii. 5) *on the first (day) of the month*, lit. *in one (day) to the month;* וַיְהִי בְּאַחַת וְשֵׁשׁ־מֵאוֹת שָׁנָה בָּרִאשׁוֹן בְּאֶחָד לַחֹדֶשׁ (Gen. viii. 13) *and it came to pass in the six hundredth and first year, in the first (month), the first (day) of the month:* so likewise בָּעֲשִׂירִי (ibid. v. 5) *in the tenth (month).*

CHAPTER IV.

PRONOUNS.

231. The distinct pronouns, as well as the pronominal affixes, are often introduced for the sake of emphasis, explanation, &c., (Art. 192) together with the nouns for which they stand: as, הִנֵּה יָלְדָה מִלְכָּה גַם הִיא בָּנִים (Gen. xxii. 20) *behold Milcha, she has also born children;* וּמֵעֵץ הַדַּעַת טוֹב וָרָע לֹא תֹאכַל מִמֶּנּוּ (Gen. ii. 17) *and of the tree of knowledge of good and evil, thou shalt not eat of it;* יְבִיאֶהָ אֵת תְּרוּמַת יְהוָה (Exod. xxxv. 5) lit. *he shall bring her (it) the offering*

---

* שְׁלִישִׁית הַשָּׁנָה, signifies *the third part of a year* (Art. 92).

† Some of the ordinals are used in the plural, the noun being omitted: as, שְׁנַיִם (for שְׁנֵי) *second (stories);* שְׁלִישִׁים (for שְׁלִישִׁיִּים) *third (stories).* (See Gen. vi. 15.)

of the Lord, i. e. *he shall bring it*, namely, *the offering of the Lord*.

232. For the same purpose, or by way of antithesis, are the distinct pronouns introduced, together with the verbs in which they are included: as, (Gen. xxi. 24) *and Abraham said* אָנֹכִי אִשָּׁבֵעַ *I-will-swear*, lit. *I, I-will-swear;* אַתָּה תִבְחַר וְלֹא אָנִי (Job xxxiv. 33), lit. *thou, thou-shalt choose but not I;* הֵמָּה יֹאבֵדוּ וְאַתָּה תַעֲמֹד (Ps. cii. 27), lit. *they, they-shall-perish, but thou, thou shalt endure*.

Obs.—The distinct pronoun thus repeated, must be in the nominative, in whatever case the other pronouns may happen to be: as, גַּם הוּא יֻלַּד־בֵּן וּלְשֵׁת (Gen. iv. 26) *and to Seth, to him also* (Heb *he—not* לוֹ) *there was born a son;* בָּרֲכֵנִי גַם אָנִי אָבִי (Gen. xxvii. 38) *bless me, even me* (Heb. *even I*, not אֹתִי) *O my father!*—יְהוּדָה אַתָּה יוֹדוּךָ אַחֶיךָ (Gen. xlix. 8) lit. *Judah, thou, they-shall praise thee, thy brethren*, i. e. *but thou, O Judah! thy brethren shall praise thee*, this being the antithesis of *Cursed be their anger*, in the preceding verse.

233. When a pronoun is the subject of a sentence, and the predicate is either a noun, adjective, or participle (not a verb), it includes the *copula:* as, אֲנִי יְהוָֹה *I (am) the Lord;* עֵירֹם אַתָּה *thou art naked*. (See Art. 162.)

234. The nominative pronouns of the third person are often used as demonstrative pronouns (Art. 97, 98). They are likewise used for the word *same:* as, הוּא הַסֹּבֵב (Gen. ii. 13) *the same that compasseth;* הִיא הָאִשָּׁה (Gen. xxiv. 44) *the same is the woman;* הֵמָּה הַגִּבֹּרִים (Gen. vi. 4).

235. The objective pronominal affixes can, strictly speaking, be only joined to transitive verbs; nevertheless we find some instances in which they are found with intransitive verbs: as, לֹא יְגֻרְךָ רָע *evil cannot dwell (with) thee* (Ps. v. 4); וַיִּזְעָקוּךְ *and-they-cried (to) thee* (Neh. ix. 28); נְתַתָּנִי *thou hast given (to) me* (Josh. xv. 19); יְצָאוּנִי *they are gone (from) me* (Jer. x. 20).

236. The relative pronoun אֲשֶׁר is not susceptible of any variation (Art. 99). It admits, however, of the prefixes מ, ל, כ, ב, namely, when the antecedent is omitted; as in the following examples:—

(Gen. xxi. 17.) כִּי שָׁמַע אֱלֹהִים אֶת קוֹל הַנַּעַר בַּאֲשֶׁר הוּא שָׁם

For God has heard the voice of the lad in which *he is there*, i. e. *in the* place *in which*, &c.

(Gen. xxvii. 4.) עֲשֵׂה לִי מַטְעַמִּים כַּאֲשֶׁר אָהַבְתִּי

Make unto me savoury meat as which *I love*, i. e. *such* (savoury meat) *as that, &c.*

(Gen. xliii. 16.) וַיֹּאמֶר לַאֲשֶׁר עַל בֵּיתוֹ

And he said to-who was (appointed) over his house, i. e. *to the* man *who was appointed, or to the ruler who, &c.*

(Ruth ii. 9.) וְשָׁתִית מֵאֲשֶׁר יִשְׁאֲבוּן הַנְּעָרִים

And thou shalt drink from which, i. e. *from (the water which) the young men will draw.*

237. The relative is sometimes omitted: as, בְּאֶרֶץ לֹא לָהֶם (Gen. xv. 13) *in a land* which (*belongs*) *not to them.* (See Art. 193.)

238. The adjective pronouns, *each, every, either, any, one, none, one another, whoever,* &c. &c., for which the Hebrew has no distinct words, are chiefly expressed by the repetition of the noun (Art. 221), or by periphrastic expressions, consisting of the words אִישׁ *man,* כֹּל *all,* דָּבָר *a thing,* in combination with some word or phrase (see the following examples).

וַיִּתֵּן אִישׁ בִּתְרוֹ לִקְרַאת רֵעֵהוּ (Gen. xv. 10.)
And he placed each *piece** one against another†.

וַיִּקְחוּ—אִישׁ חַרְבּוֹ (Gen. xxxiv. 25.)
And they took each *his sword.*

שְׁבוּ אִישׁ תַּחְתָּיו אַל יֵצֵא אִישׁ מִמְּקֹמוֹ (Exod. xvi. 29.)
Abide ye every man *in his place,* let no man ‡ *go out of his place.*

וְאִישׁ לֹא יַעֲלֶה עִמָּךְ וְגַם אִישׁ אַל יֵרָא (Exod. xxxiv. 3.)
And no man *shall come up with thee,* neither let any man *be seen.*

הוֹצִיאוּ כָל־אִישׁ מֵעָלָי (Gen. xlv. 1.)
Cause every one *to go out from me.*

אִישׁ מִמֶּנּוּ—לֹא יִכְלֶה (Gen. xxiii. 6.)
None *of us shall withhold* §.

אִישׁ אֲשֶׁר יִרְקַח כָּמֹהוּ (Exod. xxx. 33.)
Whosoever ‖ *compoundeth* any *like it.*

לֹא רָאוּ אִישׁ אֶת־אָחִיו וְלֹא קָמוּ אִישׁ מִתַּחְתָּיו (Exod. x. 24.)
They saw not one *another¶,* neither rose any one *from his place.*

---

* lit. His piece. † lit. His neighbour. ‡ lit. Let not any man go out. § lit. A man of us shall not. ‖ lit. Any man who shall, &c.
¶ lit. They saw not a man his brother. Feminine אִשָּׁה אֶל אֲחוֹתָהּ (Gen. xxvi. 3).

כָּל־הֹרֵג קַיִן (Gen. iv. 15.)
Whosoever *slays Cain*,
לֹא תַעֲשֶׂה כָל־מְלָאכָה *(Exod. xx. 10.)
Thou shalt not do any *work*.
אֵין כֹּל *nothing*; לֹא דָבָר *nothing*; כָּל דָּבָר *every thing*; *nothing whatever*.

239. The reflex pronouns, *myself, thyself, &c.*, are mostly expressed by the form *Hithpael*. Sometimes, however, they are indicated by the word נֶפֶשׁ *soul*, עֶצֶם *bone, substance*, or by some other word indicative of a part of the human body: as, אֹהֵב נַפְשׁוֹ *he that loves himself*; קָמוּ עַל נַפְשָׁם *they had decreed for themselves*; בְּעֶצֶם הַיּוֹם הַזֶּה *in the selfsame day*; וַתִּצְחַק שָׂרָה בְּקִרְבָּהּ *and Sarah laughed within herself.*

Obs.—In a few instances we find the *objective* pronouns used instead of the reflex: thus, וַיִּרְעוּ הָרֹעִים אוֹתָם *and the shepherds fed themselves* (Ezek. xxxiv. 5); וַיִּרְאוּ שֹׁטְרֵי בְנֵי יִשְׂרָאֵל אֹתָם בְּרָע (Exod. v. 19).

CHAPTER V.

VERBS.

The verb הָיָה is used:—

1st.—To express absolute existence: as, יְהוָה הָיָה הֹוֶה וְיִהְיֶה *the Lord was, is, and shall be.*

---

* But לֹא תַעֲשֶׂה כָּל־הַמְּלָאכָה would signify *thou shalt not do the whole of the work*, and would imply that part of it might be done.

2nd.—To represent the copula in propositions relating to *past* and *future* time (Art. 162, 168).

3rd.—To denote past or future* possession; in which case it is accompanied by the dative pronouns, or by the sign of the dative ל, and is then equivalent to the English verb *to have:* as, בָּנִים רַבִּים הָיוּ לוֹ *many sons were to him*, i. e. *he had many children;* זֵתִים יִהְיוּ לְךָ *olive trees shall be to thee*, i. e. *thou shalt* or *wilt have;* כֶּרֶם הָיָה לִשְׁלֹמֹה *Solomon had a vineyard* †.

4th.—To mark transition from one state or condition into another· as, יְהִי לְתַנִּין *it shall become a serpent;* וַיְהִי לְתַנִּין *and it became a serpent* (Exod. vii. 9, 10); הָיְתָה לָמַס *she has become tributary*‡ (Lam. i. 1); בִּסְפֵּךְ הָיָה לְסִגִּים : אֵיכָה הָיְתָה לְזוֹנָה קִרְיָה נֶאֱמָנָה (Isa. i).

240. *Obs.* 1.—With participles, it is mostly used to indicate past or future continued action: as, יוֹסֵף הָיָה רֹעֶה (Gen. xxxvii. 2)

---

* Present possession is commonly indicated by the dative pronouns, the copula being omitted: as, הִנֵּה־נָא לִי שְׁתֵּי בָנוֹת *behold now, I have two daughters;* כֹּל אֲשֶׁר לְךָ *whatsoever thou hast* (Gen. xix. 8, 12): or by יֵשׁ, as, יֶשׁ־לִי רָב (Gen. xxxiii.) *I have enough;* הֲיֵשׁ לָכֶם אָב אוֹ אָח : יֶשׁ־לָנוּ אָב זָקֵן (Gen. xliv). See the various examples in Part I. p. 94.

† Sometimes, however, the verb is omitted: as, וְלָהּ שִׁפְחָה מִצְרִית *and she had an Egyptian handmaid* (Gen. xvi. 1).

‡ The ל is omitted when the noun has the prefix כ: as, הָיְתָה כְּאַלְמָנָה (Lam. i. 1) *she is become as a widow;* הֵן הָאָדָם הָיָה כְּאַחַד מִמֶּנּוּ (Gen. iii. 22).

וּבְנֵיכֶם יִהְיוּ רֹעִים בַּמִּדְבָּר אַרְבָּעִים שָׁנָה ;.Joseph was feeding the flock, &c (Num. xiv. 22) and your children shall be feeding (wandering) in the wilderness forty years; הַבָּקָר הָיוּ חֹרְשׁוֹת (Job i. 14) the oxen were ploughing*: וּמִשָּׁרֵת הָיָה רֹעֶה אֶת צֹאן יִתְרוֹ חֹתְנוֹ (Exod. iii. 1): וַיְהִי שָׁאוּל אֹיֵב אֶת־דָּוִד כָּל־הַיָּמִים (1 Sam. xviii. 29).

241. *Obs.* 2.—Before infinitives having the prefix ל, it has the same force as the adverb *about*, indicating any approaching event: as, וַיְהִי הַשֶּׁמֶשׁ לָבוֹא (Gen. xv. 12) *and the sun was about to go down*, i. e. *and it was about the time when the sun was going down*; וַיְהִי הַשַּׁעַר לִסְגֹּר (Josh. ii. 5) *and it was about the shutting of the gate*, or *when the gate was to be shut*†.

242. *Obs.* 3.—Lastly, it is often used impersonally, at the introduction of a narrative, or in the middle of a discourse; and must then be rendered by *it happened, it shall happen, it came to pass*, &c.: as, וַיְהִי מִקֵּץ יָמִים (Gen. iv. 3) *and it came to pass after some days that*, &c.: וְהָיָה כִּי יִרְאוּ אֹתָךְ הַמִּצְרִים (Gen. xii. 12) *and it shall come to pass, when the Egyptians shall see thee, that*, &c.: וְהָיָה הַנַּעֲרָה אֲשֶׁר אֹמַר אֵלֶיהָ (Gen. v. 14): וַיְהִי כְּבֹא אַבְרָם (Gen. xxiv. 14).

---

* The verb הָיָה is, however, frequently omitted: as, וְרוּחַ אֱלֹהִים מְרַחֶפֶת (Gen. i. 1) *and the spirit of God* הָיְתָה *was moving* (brooding): וְהוּא יֹשֵׁב פֶּתַח־הָאֹהֶל (Gen. xviii. 1) for וְהוּא הָיָה יֹשֵׁב: וְרִבְקָה אֹהֶבֶת אֶת־יַעֲקֹב (Ibid. 10) for וְשָׂרָה הָיְתָה שֹׁמַעַת: וְשָׂרָה שֹׁמַעַת (Gen. xxv. 28).

† Various idiomatic expressions, which cannot be rendered literally into English, are formed by this verb and the infinitive: as, וְהָיָה לֶאֱכֹל (Deut. xxxi. 7) *and I will hide my face from them* and *they shall be devoured*, lit. *and he shall be to eat*, i. e. *he shall be an object of prey to any one*.

Tenses.

Present Tense.

243. Hebrew verbs have no form whereby *present time* can be indicated. The progress of an action at the time of speaking can, therefore, only be inferred from the juxtaposition of the participles (verbal nouns* or names of the *agents* and *patients*), with their respective *subjects*, in the same manner as is done in *nominal propositions* (Art. 169) relating to present time: thus, אֲנִי אֹהֵב *I (am) loving*, or *I love*, אַתָּה אָהוּב *thou (art) loved ;* אַבְרָהָם הוֹלֵךְ *Abraham (is) walking.* (See Art. 124. Obs. 4).

244. *Obs.*—In the same manner as nominal propositions may be expressed in the *past* and in the *future* by the aid of the verb הָיָה *to be* (Art. 162); so likewise may *verbal* propositions: as, יוֹסֵף הָיָה רֹעֶה (Gen. xxvii. 2) *Joseph* WAS FEEDING; אִישׁ הָיָה עֹמֵד אֶצְלִי (Ez. xliii. 6) *a man* WAS STANDING *near me;* יְהֹוָה יִהְיֶה שֹׁמֵעַ (Jud. xi. 14) *the Lord* SHALL BE HEARING (See Art. 240).

---

* Hence it is that these words are varied by gender, even when they are used to express the first person of the present tense: as, אֲנִי אֹהֵב *m.*, אֲנִי אֹהֶבֶת *f. I love :* whereas no such distinction is made in the *past* and *future* tenses, אֶאֱהֹב, אָהַבְתִּי, אֶפְקֹד, פָּקַדְתִּי, being common to both *genders*. Hence, likewise, the reason why, in the present tense, the *subject* and *predicate* must be expressed in separate words; whereas in the *past* and *future* tenses, they are expressed in one word, when the subject happens to be a *pronoun*.

245. But the verb *to be* is often omitted*, especially when the time may be known from the context, or from some word which marks the time: as, (Gen. i. 2) *and the earth* הָיְתָה *was without form and void; and darkness (was) upon the face of the deep; and the spirit of God* מְרַחֶפֶת *(was) brooding upon,* &c.; וְהוּא יֹשֵׁב (Gen. xviii. 1) *and he (was) sitting;* וְהוּא עֹמֵד (Ibid.) *and he (was) standing;* מָחָר אָנֹכִי נִצָּב (Exod. xvii. 9) *to-morrow I shall be standing;* הִנְנִי מֵבִיא מָחָר אַרְבֶּה (Exod. x. 5).

Past and Future Tenses.

246. The *past* and *future* tenses are indicated by the form of the verb. The past by the *affixes*, the future by *prefixes* (Art. 116—117): as, לָמַדְתִּי, אֶלְמֹד.

But either of these tenses having the prefix ו *and*, which shows that they are connected with a preceding verb, must be construed in the same time (and frequently in the same mood) in which the preceding verb happens to be: thus, אָמַר *he said,* וַיִּקְרָא וַיֹּאמַר *he called and said;* but, preceded by a *future*, it must be rendered in the future; as in Gen. xlvi. 33, *and it shall come to pass* כִּי יִקְרָא אֲלֵיכֶם פַּרְעֹה וְאָמַר *when Pharaoh* SHALL CALL *you, and* SHALL SAY†; thus

---

* Many grammarians, not attending to this circumstance, have been led into the erroneous opinion that participles are capable of representing all the tenses. Nothing is, however, more common in Hebrew than the ellipsis of the verb *to be*.

† The principle upon which this and the following rules are founded, appears to be this—*that the conjunction* ו *joins the same moods and tenses;* nor will this appear so strange, when it is

likewise, אָמַרְתָּ *thou didst say;* וְדִבַּרְתָּ וְאָמַרְתָּ *thou hast spoken and said;* but דַּבֵּר * וְאָמַרְתָּ *speak, and say;* תְּדַבֵּר וְאָמַרְתָּ *thou shalt speak, and shalt say.*

247. *Obs.* 1.—The ו receives in both cases (ִ), (ְ), or *shurek* for its vowel-point†. It is the same with the *future tense*: thus, יֹאמְרוּ signifies *they shall* or *will say*; וְיֹאמְרוּ (Deut. xxxii. 7) *ask*.. and they *will say*, but בָּאוּ־וַיֹּאמְרוּ (Exod. v. 1) signifies, *they came and* SAID; וָאֹמַר (Ezek. iii. 15) *and I shall say,* but פָּקַדְתִּי וְאָמַר (Ex. iii. 16, 17) signifies, *I have visited and I* HAVE SAID; יֹאמַר *he shall say,* וַיֹּאמֶר *and he* SAID‡. (See Art. 119.)

248. *Obs.* 2.—When a future is thus used to express past time, the prefix ו has always the vowel point (-) with dagesh in the following letter, or (ָ) when the following letter does not admit dagesh

---

considered that the ו often supplies the place of *subjects, predicates,* and even *negative particles,* when either of them have been mentioned in a preceding member of a sentence.

* In such cases, the accent of the first and second person singular is removed to the ultimate syllable: as, וְדִבַּרְתִּי־דִּבַּרְתִּי; except verbs whose third radical is a quiescent letter: as, רָאִיתִי, וּמָצָאתָ

† Except when the accent happens to come immediately after ו: וָחָי which may be rendered, *and he shall live,* or *he did live* (see Num. xxi. 8, 9).

‡ The accent is, in such cases, removed to the *penultimate,* provided neither *dagesh kazak,* nor *sh'ra* final succeeds such vowel, and the word is not in pause; otherwise the accent retains its place: as, וַיֹּאמֶר, וַיִּגַּשׁ, וַיִּשְׁמֹר· It is owing to the removal of the accent that the final long vowel of verbs is sometimes changed into a short vowel: thus, יָקוּם, יָשׁוּב, יָסוֹב—וַיָּקָם, וַיָּשָׁב, וַיָּסָב: and for the same reason the radical ה of verbs of the Sixth Conjugation is dropped: thus, יִבְנֶה—יִרְאֶה· וַיִּבֶן, וַיַּרְא·

(see the preceding examples); whereas the conjunctive ו has always (:), (.), or *shurek* for its vowel point (see note, p. 38).

249. *Obs.* 3.—This tense is often found at the beginning of chapters and books (as in Gen. ii. vi. vii. Levit. i. &c.), where, of course, no other verb can precede it; but this occurs only in historical narratives, which necessarily refer to past time, and where no mistake can possibly arise. Besides, the vowel of the ו fully indicates, in all such instances, that the verb must be construed in the past.

250. *Obs.* 4.—These converted tenses are never used unless preceded by the prefix ו; in every other instance, the *simple past* and the *simple future* are used.

251. *Obs.* 5.—Hence it is that in the converted tenses the verbs must precede their subjects: as, וַיֹּאמֶר אֱלֹהִים (Gen. i. 3) *and he said God*, i.e. *and God said*; וְאָמַר פַּרְעֹה (Exod. xiv. 3) *and he shall say, Pharaoh*, i.e. *and Pharaoh shall say*; וְאָמַר הַכֹּהֵן; וְאָמְרָה הָאִשָּׁה (Num. v.): but the simple tenses may have their subjects *before* or *after* them: thus, בָּרָא אֱלֹהִים (Gen. i. 1) *he created*, namely, *God*, i.e. *God created;* וְהָאָרֶץ הָיְתָה (Ibid. 2) *and the earth was;* מַלְאָכִי יֵלֵךְ לְפָנֶיךָ (Exod. xxxiii. 23) or מַלְאָכִי יֵלֵךְ לְפָנֶיךָ (Exod. xxxii. 34) *mine angel shall go before thee.*

252. *Obs.* 6.—There is no difference whatever in point of signification between the simple and converted tenses. Those that represent the past are used for the *Imperfect, Perfect,* and *Pluperfect.* אָמַר may, therefore, be rendered—*he said, he* HAS *said, he* HAD *said:* so likewise וַיֹּאמֶר* may be rendered—*and he* SAID,

---

* The predominant sense of this converted tense is that of the *Imperfect.* It is mostly used in narratives, for which reason it is denominated by some grammarians, the *historical tense.*

and he HAS *said, and he* HAD *said.* The context alone can determine in which of these three senses either of the verbs are used. It is the same with the future tenses: as, יֹאמַר *he shall say,* וַיֹּאמֶר *and he shall say ;* יְהִי *they shall be,* וְהָיוּ *and they shall be.* (See Art. 255).

253. *Obs.* 7.—When the same verb occurs twice in the same sentence*, and the clauses are in opposition, the first takes commonly the converted form, and the second the simple form: as, וַיִּקְרָא אֱלֹהִים לָאוֹר יוֹם וְלַחֹשֶׁךְ קָרָא לָיְלָה (Gen. i. 5, 8, 10); וַיְהִי הֶבֶל רֹעֵה צֹאן וְקַיִן הָיָה עֹבֵד אֲדָמָה (Gen. iv. 2); see *v.* 3—4, 4—5, of the same chapter, and xi. 3, xxxv. 19, &c. FUTURE, וַאֲכַלְתֶּם בְּשַׂר בְּנֵיכֶם וּבְשַׂר בְּנֹתֵיכֶם תֹּאכֵלוּ (Lev. xxvi. 29); וְהָיְתָה אַרְצְכֶם שְׁמָמָה וְעָרֵיכֶם יִהְיוּ חָרְבָּה (Ibid. 33.—See likewise *v.* 42, and Num. v. 17.—Deut. xxviii. 12, 13).

254. The following passages in which the same verbs are construed differently, according as they are preceded by a *past* or by a *future* tense, are inserted here for the purpose of still further elucidating the preceding remarks respecting the tenses.

Examples of verbs of the past with the prefix ו retaining their past signification, in consequence of their being preceded by a simple past tense.

past. *past.*
אִישׁ הָיָה בְּאֶרֶץ עוּץ וְהָיָה
(Job i. 1.)

Examples of verbs assuming a future signification in consequence of being preceded by a simple future or by an imperative.

fut.
וְלֹא יִקָּרֵא עוֹד
c. fut.
אֶת־שִׁמְךָ אַבְרָם וְהָיָה שִׁמְךָ
(Gen. xvii. 5.)

c. fut. *imp.*
וְהָיָה .... קַח לְךָ
(Gen. vi. 21.)

---

* Or even in two consecutive verses, as in Gen. iv. 4, 5.

THE SYNTAX OF

past. *past.* נָשָׂא אֱוִיל מְרֹדַךְ וַיֹּאכַל לֶחֶם (2 Kings xxv. 27, 29.)	*c. fut.* *fut.* יִשָּׂא פַרְעֹה וְתָלָה וְאָכַל הָעוֹף (Gen. xl. 19.)
	subjunc. *subjunc.* פֶּן יִשְׁלַח יָדוֹ וְלָקַח וְאָכַל (Gen. iii. 22.)
past. *past.* וַיַּעֲקֹב שָׁמַע......וְהֶחֱרִישׁ (Gen. xxxiv. 5.)	וְאִשָּׁה כִּי תִדֹּר וְשָׁמַע וְהֶחֱרִישׁ (Num. xxx. 5, 4.)

Examples of future verbs assuming a past signification, in consequence of being preceded by a simple past tense.

Examples of verbs in the future having the prefix ו, and yet retaining their future signification, on account of being preceded by a simple future or an imperative.

c. past. *c. past.* *past.* אִישׁ רִיב הָיִיתִי וָאֶזְעַק וָאֶרְאֶה (Judg. xii. 2—4.)	*fut.* *fut.* אֵרֲדָה־נָּא וְאֶרְאֶה (Gen. xviii. 21.)
c. past. *c. past.* *past.* יָשַׁבְתִּי וָאֶבְכֶּה וָאֶתְאַבְּלָה וָאֱהִי צָם * וּמִתְפַּלֵּל (Neh. i. 4—5.)	*fut.* *fut.* *imp.* הַרְפֵּה מִמֶּנִּי וְאֵלְכָה וְאֶבְכֶּה (Judg. xi. 37.)
c. past. c. past. c. past. c. past. past. נָשָׂא וַיַּעַל וַיָּנַח וַיָּכֶם וַתֶּחְשַׁךְ וַיֹּאכַל (Exod. x. 14, 15.)	*fut.* *fut.* *imp.* נְטֵה יָדְךָ...וְיַעַל...וְיֹאכַל... (Exod. x. 12.)

Use and Application of the Tenses.

255. The predominant use of the Tenses is the same in Hebrew as in other languages, viz.—

---

* It has already been observed that the participle with the verb *to be* expresses continued or repeated action.

† For וָאֱהִי מִתְפַּלֵּל. as nothing is more common in Hebrew than the ellipsis of the verb הָיָה.

The PRESENT indicates the conjoined existence of the *subject* and *predicate* at the time of speaking, and, of course, that the action is in a progressive state*: as, מָה הַדָּבָר הַזֶּה אֲשֶׁר אַתָּה עֹשֶׂה לָעָם מַדּוּעַ אַתָּה יֹשֵׁב לְבַדֶּךָ (Exod. xviii. 14) *What (is) this thing that thou* doest (*art doing*) *to the people? Why* sittest *thou* (*art thou sitting*) *alone?*—אֲדֹנִי יֹדֵעַ כִּי הַיְלָדִים רַכִּים (Gen. xxiii. 13) *My lord* knoweth *that the children are* tender (*young*);—תֶּבֶן אֵין נִתָּן לַעֲבָדֶיךָ וּלְבֵנִים אֹמְרִים לָנוּ עֲשׂוּ וְהִנֵּה עֲבָדֶיךָ מֻכִּים (Exod. v. 16).

The PAST Tenses are used to represent the conjoint existence of the *subject* and *predicate* at a time prior to that of speaking, without expressing whether the time is completely past, and the action is completely finished or not, nor whether it has any reference to another point of time specified in the sentence; these must be inferred from the context†: as, וַיהוָֹה פָּקַד אֶת־שָׂרָה כַּאֲשֶׁר אָמָר וַיַּעַשׂ יְהוָֹה לְשָׂרָה כַּאֲשֶׁר דִּבֵּר (Gen. xxi. 1) *And the Lord* visited *Sarah as he* had said, *and the Lord* did *unto Sarah as he* had spoken;

---

* This appears to be the characteristic of the active participles, and therefore all the tenses which are compounded of them, whether the verb *to be* is *expressed* or *understood*, indicate the action in a state of progress.

† The want of distinct forms for the *subdivisions* of the *past*, occasions no difficulty whatever; for the same circumstances which, in other languages, induce a writer or speaker to make use of either of the subdivisions, easily show in what sense the Hebrew *past* is to be understood.

פָּקַד יְהֹוָה צְבָאוֹת אֶת־עֶדְרוֹ (Zech. x. 3) *The Lord of hosts* hath visited *his flock;* כִּי שָׁמְעָה בִּשְׂדֵה מוֹאָב כִּי פָקַד יְהֹוָה אֶת־עַמּוֹ (Ruth i. 6) *For she* had heard *in the field* (country) *of Moab, that the Lord* had visited *his people.*

The FUTURE is used to indicate the conjoint existence of the *subject* and *predicate* in a time subsequent to that of speaking*: as, גֵּר יִהְיֶה זַרְעֲךָ (Gen. xv. 13) *thy seed* will be *a stranger;* וְאַתָּה תָּבוֹא אֶל־אֲבֹתֶיךָ בְּשָׁלוֹם תִּקָּבֵר בְּשֵׂיבָה טוֹבָה (Gen. xv. 15) *and thou* shalt come *to thy fathers in peace, thou* shalt be buried *in a good old age;* וְהָיָה מִקֵּץ שִׁבְעִים שָׁנָה יִפְקֹד יְהֹוָה אֶת־צֹר (Isa. xxiii. 17) *and it* shall come *to pass after the end of seventy years, that the Lord* will visit *Tyre;* אָמַר אוֹיֵב אֶרְדֹּף אַשִּׂיג אֲחַלֵּק שָׁלָל תִּמְלָאֵמוֹ נַפְשִׁי אָרִיק חַרְבִּי תּוֹרִישֵׁמוֹ יָדִי *the enemy said, I will pursue, I will overtake, I will divide the spoil: my desire shall be satisfied upon them†; I will draw my sword, my hand shall destroy them‡* (Exod. xv. 9).

---

* Some grammarians consider this tense as an *aorist*, others as a *present tense:* but though this form of the verb is used in some instances to express *present* time, yet there can be no doubt that its *predominant* use is to express future time. It has, therefore, very justly been considered by the ancient grammarians, as well as by *Gesenius*, as a future tense.

† Literally, *my soul shall be full of them:* i. e. *my soul shall be satiated with vengeance.*

‡ We have here a beautiful specimen of the *figure* which rhetoricians call *asyndeton.* The inspired poet, by omitting the conjunctive

256. The Hebrews use their present tense where in English we commonly use the imperfect:

1st.—In imagery, or in the recital of dreams and visions, when the narrator represents a past occurrence, in the same manner as he, or the person of whom he speaks, originally saw it, and as if it were still present to him. Such recitals are generally introduced by the word וְהִנֵּה *and behold*, being an invitation to the hearer to place himself in the same situation: as, וַיַּחֲלֹם וְהִנֵּה סֻלָּם מֻצָּב אַרְצָה וְרֹאשׁוֹ מַגִּיעַ הַשָּׁמָיְמָה וְהִנֵּה מַלְאֲכֵי אֱלֹהִים עֹלִים וְיֹרְדִים בּוֹ (Gen. xxviii. 12) lit. *And he dreamed, and behold, a ladder* placed *upon the earth, and its top* reaching *towards heaven; and behold, angels of God* ascending *and* descending *upon it.* (See also Gen. xl. xli.)

וְהִנֵּה יְהוָֹה עֹבֵר וְרוּחַ גְּדוֹלָה וְחָזָק מְפָרֵק הָרִים וּמְשַׁבֵּר סְלָעִים לִפְנֵי יְהוָֹה : לֹא בָרוּחַ יְהוָֹה וְאַחַר הָרוּחַ רַעַשׁ לֹא בָרַעַשׁ יְהוָֹה : וְאַחַר הָרַעַשׁ אֵשׁ לֹא בָאֵשׁ יְהוָֹה וְאַחַר הָאֵשׁ קוֹל דְּמָמָה דַקָּה : וַיְהִי כִּשְׁמֹעַ אֵלִיָּהוּ וַיָּלֶט פָּנָיו בְּאַדַּרְתּוֹ : (1 Kings xix. 11—13.) lit. *And behold, the Lord* passing *by, and a great and strong wind* disjoining *mountains, and* shivering *rocks before the Lord; not in the wind* (is) *the Lord; and after the wind an earthquake; not in the earthquake* (is) *the Lord: and after the earthquake a fire; not in the fire* (is) *the Lord; and after the fire a still soft voice*. And when Elijah heard it, he wrapped his face in his mantle, &c.*

ן before each verb, marks not only the vehemence of the passion with which the Egyptians were animated, but likewise the ease and the rapidity with which they imagined they could satisfy their thirst of vengeance. (Compare Cæsar's *reni, vidi, vici.*) Nor is the next passage less beautiful: נָשַׁפְתָּ בְרוּחֲךָ כִּסָּמוֹ יָם *a breath of air from the Lord was sufficient to blast all these towering hopes, and to annihilate the proud boasters.*

* It was the voice of Mercy,—the gentle voice of Truth which is never heard amidst destroying elements. Well might the holy

257. *2nd.*—When a whole phrase is used as explanatory of a preceding verb, or as its objective case, and the phrase indicates an action or event, or circumstance which existed at a time contemporary with that which is denoted by the preceding verb: as, (Gen. iii. 7) וַיֵּדְעוּ *and they knew* (not כִּי עֲרוּמִים הָיוּ *that they were naked*), but כִּי עֲרוּמִים הֵם *that they are naked**, because that which they *knew* was not their *past condition*, but their condition at the time when they attained this knowledge†; וַתֵּרֶא כִּי מִתְאַמֶּצֶת הִיא לָלֶכֶת (Ruth i. 18) lit. *And she saw that she is persisting to go;* וַיַּרְא יַעֲקֹב כִּי יֶשׁ־שֶׁבֶר בְּמִצְרַיִם (Gen. xlii. 1) lit. *and Jacob saw that there is corn, &c.* So likewise, וַיַּרְא וְהִנֵּה שְׁלֹשָׁה אֲנָשִׁים נִצָּבִים עָלָיו (Gen. xviii. 1) *And he saw, and behold, three men are standing by him* (not *stood*), because the two circumstances happened at the same time.

258. The *Present* Tense is used in Hebrew, in some cases where we use in English the future: viz.

---

prophet, contrasting his own burning zeal with the soothing voice of Divine Mercy, "*hide his face in a mantle.*" The sublimity of this passage, and the moral truths to be drawn from it, need scarcely be pointed out to the student.

* Accustomed as we are in modern language to relate all past events in the historical tense, such phraseology appears very strange: it is nevertheless very correct in a logical point of view.

† When the attained knowlege is of any thing *past* or *future*, then these respective tenses are used: as, וַיֵּדַע נֹחַ כִּי קַלּוּ הַמַּיִם (Gen. viii. 11); וַיֵּדַע אוֹנָן כִּי לֹא (Gen. ix. 24); וַיֵּדַע אֵת אֲשֶׁר עָשָׂה לוֹ בְּנוֹ הַקָּטָן לֹא יִהְיֶה (Gen. xxxviii. 9).

‡ The word יֵשׁ is never employed in the past, yet, for the reason before stated, the authors of the Established Version have rendered it by the imperfect *was*. In the next verse, however, שָׁמַעְתִּי כִּי יֶשׁ־שֶׁבֶר בְּמִצְרַיִם which they justly considered as a quotation, they have preserved its original meaning: thus, *I have heard that there is*, &c.

when the future event is fast approaching, and is certain to occur; or where the future time is marked by some other word or phrase: thus, כִּי מַשְׁחִיתִים אֲנַחְנוּ (Gen. xix. 13) *For we will destroy*, Heb. *for we are destroying—are about to destroy ;* כִּי לְיָמִים עוֹד שִׁבְעָה אָנֹכִי מַמְטִיר (Gen. vii. 4) *For yet seven days, and I will cause it to rain*, Heb. *I cause it to rain*, the time being already specified by כִּי לְיָמִים עוֹד שִׁבְעָה.

259. *Obs.*—We sometimes make use of the present tense in English not exactly to denote the present moment, but as a general expression: as when we say, *I love my country, he loves his children*, &c. In such cases, the Hebrew uses mostly the *past tense*, though sometimes the *future* or *present :* thus, (Exod. xxi. 5) *Should the servant say, I love my master*, &c. Heb. אָהַבְתִּי *I have loved ;* (Gen. xxxi. 6) *and ye know that with all my power*, &c. Heb. יְדַעְתֶּן *ye have known ;* (Gen. xxvii. 2) *behold now, I am old, I know not,* &c. Heb. לֹא יָדַעְתִּי—זָקַנְתִּי; (1 Kings iii. 7) *I know not how to go out, or to come in,* Heb. לֹא אֵדַע fut.

260. Events that occur *frequently*, and *habitual* actions, are generally expressed in Hebrew by the future tense, though in English we use in such cases the past: thus, (Gen. ii. 6) *But a mist went up*, Heb. וְאֵד יַעֲלֶה *and a mist shall go up*, i.e. *a mist continued to ascend repeatedly, often ;* (Num. ix. 16) *So it was always, the cloud covered it,* &c. Heb. כֵּן יִהְיֶה *so it used to be,* יְכַסֶּנּוּ הֶעָנָן *the cloud used to cover it.* In the same sense ought all the verbs that occur in Num. ix. 16—23 (such as יַחֲנוּ, יִסְעוּ, &c) to be

understood. So likewise (Job i. 5) *thus did Job*, Heb. יַעֲשֶׂה *he continued to do, did so repeatedly*.

261. The *future* is likewise sometimes used for the *past*, or the *present*, after the words אָז *then*, טֶרֶם *not yet*: as, אָז יָשִׁיר (Exod. xv.) *then sang Moses, &c.*; טֶרֶם אֲכַלֶּה (Gen xxiv.) *before I had finished;* טֶרֶם תִּירָאוּן (Exod. ix. 33) *ye do not fear*.*

262. Absolute propositions and general truths, which are in most languages expressed in the *present* tense, may in Hebrew be announced in any of the tenses; it being well understood that such propositions not being subject to time, the verbs which they contain can only be *assertory;* and therefore whatever *form* the verbs contained in such sentences may happen to have, they must, when translated into English, be expressed in the *present* tense: thus, דּוֹר הֹלֵךְ וְדוֹר בָּא וְהָאָרֶץ לְעוֹלָם עֹמָדֶת (Ecc. i. 4) *A generation* passeth *away, and a generation* cometh; *but the earth* abideth *for ever*.

In this sentence the *predicates* being all expressed by *participles*, must of course be rendered in English in the present tense. But the predicates of the two following propositions: וְזָרַח הַשֶּׁמֶשׁ וּבָא הַשָּׁמֶשׁ (v.5) though the verbs are in the *past*, must nevertheless be rendered in the *present;* viz. *the sun* riseth, *and the sun* setteth—because the propositions express a natural phenomenon which occurs repeatedly

---

* Sometimes after מָה *what*, מֵאַיִן *whence*: as, מַה תְּבַקֵּשׁ *What seekest thou?* מֵאַיִן תָּבוֹא *Whence comest thou?*

and constantly. In the same sense must the propositions contained in the *eighth verse* be understood, although the verbs תִּמָּלֵא, יוּכַל, תִּשְׂבַּע כָּל־הַדְּבָרִים יְגֵעִים לֹא־יוּכַל are future forms: thus, אִישׁ לְדַבֵּר לֹא־תִשְׂבַּע עַיִן לִרְאוֹת וְלֹא־תִמָּלֵא אֹזֶן מִשְּׁמֹעַ *All things are labouring*, man cannot utter it†; the eye is never satisfied‡ with seeing, nor the ear filled§ with hearing.*

By way of further illustration, we refer the student to the first Psalm, where he will find four verbs in the *past,* עָמָד, יָשַׁב, הָיָה, הָלָךְ; eight in the *future,* יֶהְגֶּה, יִתֵּן, יִבּוֹל, יַעֲשֶׂה, יַצְלִיחַ, יָקוּמוּ, תֹּאבֵד; one *active* and one *passive* participle, יוֹדֵעַ, שָׁתוּל, all which must, for the reasons, before stated, be rendered in the present.

Moods.

Infinitive Mood.

263. Infinitives considered as nouns (Art. 113.) may be used :—

1st. As the subjects of a proposition (Art. 163).

Thus, לֹא טוֹב הֱיוֹת הָאָדָם לְבַדּוֹ (Gen. ii. 18) lit. *the being of the man alone (is) not good,* i. e. *to be alone without the intended aid is a condition not fit for man;* עֲשֹׂה צְדָקָה וּמִשְׁפָּט נִבְחָר לַיהֹוָה מִזָּבַח (Prov. xxi. 3).

2nd. As the *complement* of other verbs by which they are governed, or as their objective cases :—

Thus, לֹא אוּכַל לַעֲשׂוֹת דָּבָר (Gen. xix. 22) *I am not able to do any thing;* מֵאֵן בִּלְעָם הֲלֹךְ עִמָּנוּ (Num. xxii. 14) *Balaam refused*

---

* *i. e.* In a state of activity. † *i. e.* He cannot describe it.
‡ *i. e.* Not satiated. § *i. e.* It becomes not weary.

to go with us*; לֹא אֵדַע צֵאת וָבֹא (1 Kings iii. 7) *I know not to go out and to come in*, i. e. *the going out nor the coming in;* מֵאֲנָה הִנָּחֵם נַפְשִׁי (Ps. lxxvii. 3) *my soul refused to be comforted.*

3rd. As the *antecedent* or *consequent* of a noun:—

Thus, לִפְנֵי מְלָךְ־מֶלֶךְ לִבְנֵי יִשְׂרָאֵל (Gen. xxxvi. 31) lit. *before the reigning of a king to (over) the children of Israel;* בְּיוֹם אֲכָלְךָ מִמֶּנּוּ (Gen. ii. 16) *in the day of thy eating thereof;* מִשְּׁנַת הִמָּכְרוֹ (Lev. xxv. 50) *from the year of his being sold.*

264. Like substantives, they admit of the pronominal affixes, and may be the objects of comparison:—

Thus, אַתָּה יָדַעְתָּ שִׁבְתִּי וְקוּמִי (Ps. cxxxix. 2) *thou knowest my sitting and my rising;* וְשִׁבְתְּךָ וְצֵאתְךָ וּבוֹאֲךָ יָדַעְתִּי וְאֵת הִתְרַגֶּזְךָ אֵלָי (Isa. xxxvii. 28); טוֹב תִּתִּי אוֹתָהּ לָךְ מִתִּתִּי אוֹתָהּ לְאִישׁ אַחֵר (Gen. xxix. 19) lit. *better (is) my giving her unto thee than my giving her unto another man;* טוֹב לָנוּ עֲבֹד אֶת־מִצְרַיִם מִמֻּתֵנוּ בַּמִּדְבָּר (Exod. xiv. 11).

265. They likewise admit the prefixes בְּ, כְּ, לְ, מִ, and other prepositions to mark several relations:—

לְ to complete the sense of a preceding verb: as, כִּי הֵחֵל הָאָדָם לָרֹב (Gen. vi. 1) *when men began to multiply;* כִּלָּה לְדַבֵּר (Gen. xxiv. 14) *he finished to speak,* i. e. *he had finished,* or *he had done speaking;*

---

* In such cases the infinitive constructive, with or without לְ, is mostly used, though sometimes the infinitive absolute: as, (Isa. xlii. 24) וְלֹא אָבוּ בִּדְרָכָיו הָלוֹךְ. A finite verb is sometimes used instead of the infinitive: as, אֵיכָכָה אוּכַל וְרָאִיתִי (Esth. viii.) for אוּכַל לִרְאוֹת.

כִּלָּה לִשְׁתּוֹת *he had done drinking;*—or to mark the purpose of a preceding verb: as, וַיֵּצְאוּ לָלֶכֶת (Gen. xii. 5) *and they went forth to go,* i. e. *with the intention of going into the land, &c.;* וָאֵרֵד לְהַצִּילוֹ (Exod. iii. 8) *and I came down to deliver him.*

266. With ב or כ they are used to indicate the coincidence of two actions or events in point of time; that is, that one action or event *did* or *will* occur at or about the same time when another *did* or *will* take place: thus, בְּבֹאִי מִפַּדָּן מֵתָה עָלַי רָחֵל (Gen. xlviii. 7) *in my coming from Padan, Rachel died by me, &c.,* i. e. *Rachel died at the time of my coming (or when I came) from Padan;* אֶלְעַג בְּבֹא פַחְדְּכֶם (Prov. i. 26) *I will mock in the coming of your fear,* i. e. *whenever that shall happen;* בְּבוֹא רָשָׁע בָּא גַם בּוּז (Ibid. xviii. 3) *in the coming of the wicked, cometh also contempt,* i. e. *when the wicked cometh, there cometh likewise contempt;* רְאוּ כְּבֹא הַמַּלְאָךְ סִגְרוּ הַדֶּלֶת (2 Kings vi. 32) *look, at the coming of the messenger, shut the door,* i. e. *as soon as he shall arrive.* So likewise (2 Kings x. 2) וַיְהִי כְּבֹא הַסֵּפֶר הַזֶּה אֲלֵיכֶם וּרְאִיתֶם וְשַׂמְתֶּם; but, כְּבֹא הַסֵּפֶר אֲלֵיהֶם וַיִּקְחוּ (Ibid. 7) *and it came to pass on the coming of the letter to them, and they took,* i. e. *when the letter came, then they took, &c.;* וַיְהִי כְהוֹצִיאָם אֹתָם הַחוּצָה וַיֹּאמֶר (Gen. xix. 17); וַיְהִי כְּשַׁחַת אֱלֹהִים—וַיִּזְכֹּר (Ibid. 29).

267. With מ, they are used like nouns in the ablative*: as, וַיָּשֻׁבוּ מִתּוּר הָאָרֶץ (Num. xiii. 25) *and they returned from searching of the land;* מִשּׁוּט בָּאָרֶץ וּמֵהִתְהַלֵּךְ בָּהּ (Job i. 7) *from going to and fro on the earth, and from walking up and down in it.*

268. Sometimes, however, the מ is used in a negative sense thus, (Gen. xxvii. 1) *and his eyes were dim* מֵרְאֹת *from seeing,*

---

* Or as a sign of the comparative, which has already been explained.

i. e. *so that he could not see;* סָגַר כָּל־בַּיִת מִבּוֹא (Isa. xxiv. 10) *every house is shut up from entering,* i. e. *so that none can enter;* הֻשָּׁמֶר לְךָ מִדַּבֵּר עִם יַעֲקֹב מִטּוֹב וְעַד רָע (Gen. xxxi. 29)*.

269. The infinitive absolute (Art. 111) is used before or after *finite verbs,* to indicate *energy, intensity,* or *emphasis,* and must frequently be rendered in English by the adverbs, *surely, certainly, continually, greatly, indeed, &c.*

270. Thus, מוֹת תָּמוּת (Gen. ii. 17) *dying, thou shalt die,* i. e. *thou shalt surely die;* הַרְבָּה אַרְבֶּה (Ibid. iii. 16) *I will greatly encrease;* הָיוֹ יִהְיֶה (Ibid. xviii. 18) *he will assuredly be;* הֲמָלֹךְ תִּמְלֹךְ עָלֵינוּ (Ibid. xxxvii. 8) *shalt thou indeed reign over us?* וַיֵּצֵא יָצוֹא וָשׁוֹב (Ibid. viii. 8) *and he went out going and returning,* i. e. *repeatedly going to and fro, &c.;* וְעַתָּה הָלֹךְ הָלַכְתָּ כִּי נִכְסֹף נִכְסַפְתָּה (Ibid. xxxi. 30).

271. The infinitive absolute is sometimes used for finite verbs, especially for the imperative: as, כִּי צֻמְתֶּם וְסָפוֹד (Zech. vii. 5) *when ye fasted and mourned;* וְכָתוֹב וְחָתוֹם (Jer. xxxii. 44) *and they shall write, and they shall seal;* זָכוֹר אֶת יוֹם הַשַּׁבָּת (Exod. xx. 8) *remember the Sabbath day;* שָׁמוֹעַ בֵּין אֲחֵיכֶם (Deut. i. 16) אוֹ מָכֹר לְנָכְרִי (Ibid. xiv. 21)†.

272. The infinitive absolute is sometimes used as a noun: as, אָלֹה וְכַחֵשׁ וְרָצֹחַ וְגָנֹב וְנָאֹף (Hos. iv. 2) lit. *to swear, and to*

---

* In all the above cases, the infinitive constructive is mostly used.

† It is highly probable that in most of these cases there is an ellipsis of the finite verb: thus, זָכוֹר תִּזְכּוֹר; וְסָפוֹד סָפְדָתֶם; מָכוֹר תִּמְכֹּר, &c.

lie, and to murder, and to steal, &c., break out in abundance: i. e. Imprecation, and murder, and theft, and adultery, overspread the land.

273. Infinitives are sometimes used as *adverbs:* as, (Exod. xxx. 36) *and thou shalt beat (pound) some of it* הָדֵק *very small:* (Deut. xiii. 14) *Thou shalt enquire, and make search, and ask* הֵיטֵב *well, diligently.*

274. This is likewise the case with *finite verbs*, followed by an infinitive, or by a finite verb: as, (Gen. xxvii. 20) *how is it that* מִהַרְתָּ לִמְצֹא *thou hast found so quickly,* lit. *thou hast hastened to find;* (Exod. ii. 18) *how is it that* בָּא הַיּוֹם מִהַרְתֶּן *ye are come so soon to day,* lit. *ye have hastened to come:* הִרְבְּתָה לְהִתְפַּלֵּל (1 Sam. i. 12) *she encreased to pray,* i. e. *she prayed much, continued to pray:* אַל תַּרְבּוּ תְדַבְּרוּ (1 Sam. ii. 3) *do not encrease, do not speak,* i.e. *do not speak continually.*

275. This is especially the case with the verbs יָסַף *to add, to encrease,* שׁוּב *to return:* as, וַתֹּסֶף לָלֶדֶת (Gen. iv. 2) *and she brought forth again,* lit. *and she encreased to bring forth:* וְלֹא יָסְפָה שׁוּב (Gen. viii. 12) *and she did not again return:* וַיָּשָׁב יִצְחָק וַיַּחְפֹּר (Ibid. xxvi. 18) *and Isaac dug again,* lit. *and he returned and he dug:* וַיָּשָׁב וַיִּשְׁלַח אֵלָיו (2 Kings i. 2): וַיֹּסֶף אַבְרָהָם וַיִּקַּח אִשָּׁה (Gen xxv. 1).

Imperative Mood.

276. The Imperative is used in Hebrew, as in other languages, for commanding, entreating, &c.

It admits only of the second person singular and plural, *m.* and *f.** and is used only affirmatively.

Prohibitions and admonitions are expressed by the future, accompanied by the negative particles לֹא, אַל: as, לֹא תֹאכַל (Gen. ii. 17) *thou shalt not eat;* אַל תִּשְׁלַח יָדְךָ אֶל הַנַּעַר *lay not thine hand upon the lad;* וְאַל תַּעַשׂ לוֹ מְאוּמָה (Gen. xxii. 12).

277. *Obs.* 1.—אַל is mostly used when a wish is expressed, in which case it is generally followed by נָא†: as, אַל נָא תַעֲבֹר (Gen. xviii. 3) *do not pass, I pray:*—or in expression of encouragement, admonition, and advice: as, אַל תִּירָא אַבְרָם (Gen. xv. 1) *fear not Abraham;* אַל תֵּלֵךְ (Prov. i. 15); אַל תְּדַבֵּר (Ibid).

278. *Obs.* 2.—A future preceded by an imperative is often used as an imperative: as, לֵךְ וְאָסַפְתָּ (Exod. iii. 16).

279. *Obs.* 3.—The imperative is sometimes used for the future: as, Gen. xx. 7. *and he shall pray for thee,* וֶחְיֵה *and live,* i. e.

---

* When an imperative sense for the first and third persons is required, the future is used: as, אָרוּצָה or אֶרְצֶה (with paragogic ה) *let me run* (2 Sam. xviii. 22, 23); יְהִי *there shall be,* or *let there be;* יֵלְכוּ *let them go,* or *they shall go.* But these and similar expressions are often merely declarative, intimating neither a command nor even a wish: as, יְהִי שְׁמוֹ לְעוֹלָם (Ps. lxxii. 17) *his name will be for ever;* יֵלְכוּ לְבַקֵּשׁ אֶת־יְהוָה (Hos. v. 6) *they will go to seek the Lord.* In this sense ought the several verbs in the thirty-fifth Psalm, verses 4, 5, 6, and in several other places, to be understood.

† This particle is likewise used for the same purpose in affirmative phrases: as, יֻקַּח נָא מְעַט מַיִם (Gen. xviii. 4) *let a little water be taken;* סוּרוּ נָא (Ibid. xix. 2).

and thou shalt live; וְאֶת עֵשָׂו וָחָי (Ibid. xlii. 18); וּמֵת...וְהֵאָסֵף (Deut. xxxii. 50).

Subjunctive and Potential Moods.

280. The several Moods denominated by Grammarians, Subjunctive, Potential, Optative, &c., are indicated in Hebrew by the particles פֶּן, אִם, כִּי, אוּלַי, אִלּוּ, לוּ, לוּלֵי, or לוּלֵא, or by the phrase מִי יִתֵּן*, expressive of contingency, conditionality, possibility, wish, &c., the verb retaining the same form which it has in the indicative:—

Thus, פֶּן *lest;* (Gen. iii. 22) פֶּן יִשְׁלַח יָדוֹ וְלָקַח...וְאָכַל *lest he put forth his hand and take...and eat,* &c.; פֶּן תְּמֻתוּן (Ibid. 3).

אִם *if, provided;* (Gen. xviii. 26) אִם אֶמְצָא בִסְדֹם...וְנָשָׂאתִי *if I find in Sodom....then will I spare,* &c. (Gen. xxxii. 9); אִם יָבוֹא עֵשָׂו אֶל...וְהִכָּהוּ...וְהָיָה *if Esau come to....and smite it, then,* &c. (See Exod. xxi.)

כִּי *if, that;* (Exod. xxi. 7) וְכִי יִמְכֹּר אִישׁ אֶת בִּתּוֹ *and if a man sell his daughter,* &c.; (Gen. xxxviii. 16) *what wilt thou give me,* כִּי תָבֹא אֵלָי *that thou mayest come,* &c.; (Exod. iii. 11) *who am I,* כִּי אֵלֵךְ *that I should go...* וְכִי אוֹצִיא *and that I should bring forth,* &c. (Judg. ix. 28) מִי אֲבִימֶלֶךְ...כִּי נַעַבְדֶנּוּ.

אוּלַי *peradventure, perhaps;* (Gen. xviii. 24) אוּלַי יֵשׁ חֲמִשִּׁים צַדִּיקִם בְּתוֹךְ הָעִיר *peradventure there be fifty righteous within the city;* (Lam. iii. 29) אוּלַי יֵשׁ תִּקְוָה.

---

* Likewise by אֲשֶׁר *that* (Gen. xi. 7); לְמַעַן *in order that* (Gen. xxvii. 25); בַּעֲבוּר *that* (Gen. xxvii. 4). The *Optative* is frequently indicated by the particle נָא: as, יִגְמָר־נָא רַע רְשָׁעִים (Ps. vii. 10) *O that the wickedness of the wicked might come to an end!* These moods must, however, often be inferred from the context.

אִלּוּ *though, if;* (Ecc. vi. 6) וְאִלּוּ חָיָה אֶלֶף שָׁנִים פַּעֲמַיִם *and though he live twice a thousand years, &c.;* (Esth. vii. 4) וְאִלּוּ לַעֲבָדִים וְלִשְׁפָחוֹת נִמְכַּרְנוּ הֶחֱרַשְׁתִּי.

לוּ *O that, would;* (Gen. xvii. 18) לוּ יִשְׁמָעֵאל יִחְיֶה לְפָנֶיךָ *O that Ishmael might live before thee!* (Gen. xxx. 34) לוּ יְהִי כִדְבָרֶיךָ *would it might be according to thy words.*

לוּלֵי אֱלֹהֵי or לוּלֵא *were it not, except;* (Gen. xxxi. 42) לוּלֵי אֱלֹהֵי אָבִי .... הָיָה לִי כִּי עַתָּה רֵיקָם שִׁלַּחְתָּנִי *except that the God of my father .... had been with me, thou hadst sent me away now empty;* (Judg. xiv. 18) לוּלֵא חֲרַשְׁתֶּם בְּעֶגְלָתִי לֹא מְצָאתֶם חִידָתִי.

מִי יִתֵּן *who would give, grant, would, O that:* as, מִי יִתֵּן מוּתֵנוּ בְּאֶרֶץ מִצְרַיִם (Exod. xvi. 3) *would (to God) we had died .... in the land of Egypt;* מִי יִתֵּן כָל־עַם יְהֹוָה נְבִיאִים (Num. xi. 29) *would (to God) that all the Lord's people were prophets;* בַּבֹּקֶר תֹּאמַר מִי יִתֵּן עֶרֶב וּבָעֶרֶב תֹּאמַר מִי יִתֵּן בֹּקֶר (Deut. xxviii. 67).

PARTICIPLES.

281. Participles are used in Hebrew as nouns (Art. 122, 207), as Adjectives (Art. 83), and as verbs (Art. 245); and follow, according to the sense in which they are employed, the rules of these respective parts of speech.

282. They are often used in a very unlimited sense; in which case, the pronouns, *whoso, whoever, he that,* &c., though not expressed, must be supplied: as—

אֹהֵב מוּסָר אֹהֵב דָּעַת (Prov. xii. 1.)
וְשׂוֹנֵא תוֹכַחַת בָּעַר׃

Whoso loveth instruction, loveth knowledge; but he that hateth reproof (is) a brute; lit. *a lover of wisdom (is) a lover of knowledge; and, &c.*

עֹבֵד אַדְמָתוֹ יִשְׂבַּע לָחֶם (Prov. xii. 11.)
He that tilleth his land shall be satisfied with bread.

אַשְׁרֵי אָדָם שֹׁמֵעַ לִי·····כִּי מֹצְאִי מָצָא חַיִּים······וְחֹטְאִי חֹמֵס נַפְשׁוֹ (Ibid. viii. 34—36.)
Blessed (is the) man who hearkeneth unto me, &c. . . . . For whoso findeth me, findeth life, &c. . . . . But he that misseth me, wrongeth his soul.

מְשַׁמְּרִים הַבְלֵי שָׁוְא חַסְדָּם יַעֲזֹבוּ (Jonah ii. 9.)
They that observe lying vanities, forsake their own mercy.

283. This is likewise often the case even when the particle has the prefix ה, especially when it is preceded by כָּל, or by the same *finite* verb* : as, כָּל הַשֹּׁמֵעַ (Gen. xxi. 7) *whoever shall hear it ;* (2 Sam. xvii. 9) וְשָׁמַע הַשֹּׁמֵעַ, lit. *and he shall hear the hearer,* &c., i. e. *whosoever shall hear ;* כִּי יִפֹּל הַנֹּפֵל (Deut. xxii. 8).

284. Participles are sometimes used as the objects of preceding verbs : as, שָׁמַעְתִּי אֹמְרִים נֵלְכָה (Gen. xxxvii. 17) *I have heard them say, Let us go,* &c. ; (Gen. xxvii. 6) *and Rebekah spake unto Jacob her son* לֵאמֹר† *saying,* מְדַבֵּר אֶת־אָבִיךָ הִנֵּה שָׁמַעְתִּי

---

* Or when followed by the same finite verb : as, (Ezek. iii. 27) הַשֹּׁמֵעַ יִשְׁמָע.

† The word לֵאמֹר (inf. cons. of אָמֹר) so often used in Scripture, is generally introduced before a quotation. In the instance before us it is used twice. By the first, the sacred writer indicates that

אֶל עֵשָׂו אָחִיךָ לֵאמֹר: הָבִיאָה לִּי צַיִד *behold I heard thy father speak unto Esau thy brother, saying, Bring me venison,* &c.

Concord of the Verb with the Nominative.

285. The verb generally agrees with its *nominative* or *subject* in number, gender, and person: except—

1st.—The *pluralis excellentiæ*, which mostly, but not always, takes a verb in the singular: as, (Gen. i. 1)) בָּרָא אֱלֹהִים; (Exod. xxi. 4) אִם אֲדֹנָיו יִתֶּן־לוֹ; (Ibid. 29) *וְגַם בְּעָלָיו יוּמָת; (Gen. xx. 13) הִתְעוּ אֹתִי אֱלֹהִים (See Art. 220.)

2nd.—When the verb *precedes* its subject, in which case the verb may or may not agree with it†: as, (Gen. i. 14) יְהִי מְאֹרֹת, where

---

the words following it are the very words spoken by Rebekah, including the second לֵאמֹר, by which she introduces the words of Isaac, or at least their general sense, namely, הָבִיאָה לִּי צַיִד.

* In these instances, the agreement is logical, *i. e.* according to the signification; but in the last example, the agreement is merely *formal*.

† Verbs, considered as mere attributes, cannot, strictly speaking, admit either of *number, gender,* or *person;* these can only belong to the *pronouns*, which are included in the form of the verb. Now, we can easily suppose that the mind of the *speaker* may, in some instances, be chiefly directed to the attribute, without immediately thinking of the particular subject or subjects to which the attribute may happen to belong (as is the case when verbs are used impersonally); the subject being introduced, as it were, by a sort of afterthought, and of course, as merely explanatory; and hence the reason why in such instances the *concord* is disregarded.

the *verb* is singular masculine, and the *noun* plural feminine ; (Num. ix. 6) וַיְהִי אֲנָשִׁים, here the verb is in the singular, and the noun is in the plural ; (Gen. ix. 23) וַיִּקַּח שֵׁם וָיֶפֶת, here we have two nouns connected by a copulative, yet the verb is in the singular ; (Job xlii. 15) וְלֹא נִמְצָא נָשִׁים יָפוֹת.

3rd.—When the subject is *complex* (Art. 180), and one of the terms (the *consequent*) happens to be *plural*, then the verb is sometimes put in the *plural*, although the leading word (the *antecedent*) is in the singular : as, (Gen. iv. 10) קוֹל דְּמֵי אָחִיךָ צֹעֲקִים ; (1 Sam. ii. 4) וּמִסְפָּר יָמָיו רַבִּים ; (Job xxxviii. 21) קֶשֶׁת גִּבּוֹרִים חַתִּים.

4th.—When a plural noun is used distributively : as, יוּמָת····מְחַלְלֶיהָ (Ex. xxxi. 14) lit. *her profaners......he shall die,* i. e. *every one that profanes it (the Sabbath), shall die ;* (Gen. xlix. 22) בָּנוֹת צָעֲדָה ; (Prov. iii. 18) וְתֹמְכֶיהָ מְאֻשָּׁר.

5th.—Sometimes when the apparent subject is a nominative absolute (Art. 204) : as, וּזְרֹעוֹת יְתוֹמִים יְדֻכָּא (Job xxii. 9) *and (as to the arms) of the orphans, it is broken ;* (Hab. i. 16) וּמַאֲכָלוֹ בְּרִאָה.

6th.—When the verb היה is used as a connecting verb, it may agree either with the *subject* or the *predicate :* as, (Gen. i. 11) נְקֻדִים יִהְיֶה שְׂכָרֶךָ ; (Gen. xxxi. 8) וְהָאָרֶץ הָיְתָה תֹהוּ וָבֹהוּ· The concord is, however, often entirely disregarded* : as, (Gen. xli. 53)·····שְׁנֵי עֶשְׂרֹנִים יִהְיֶה ; (Levit. xxiv. 5) שֶׁבַע שְׁנֵי הָרָעָב אֲשֶׁר הָיָה הַחַלָּה הָאֶחָת.

---

* This is likewise often the case when a pronoun is used as the *copula :* as, (Lev. xxv.) כִּי בָתֵּי עָרֵי הַלְוִיִּם הִיא אֲחֻזָּתָם ; (Josh. xiii. 14) אִשֵּׁי יְהוָֹה·····הוּא נַחֲלָתוֹ ; (Jer. x. 3) כִּי חֻקּוֹת הָעַמִּים הֶבֶל הוּא· The reason of this is evident, as the *copula* cannot, strictly speaking, be effected by *gender* or *number.* Several apparent anomalies may be attributed to the omission of some word : as, (1 Sam. xxv. 27) שִׁפְחָתְךָ····הֵבִיא אֲשֶׁר הַבְּרָכָה הַזֹּאת, where the word נַעַר is probably omitted. There are, however, many discordances that cannot be thus explained.

286. When several *subjects* of different genders*, having the same predicate or verb, are connected, and the predicate is in the plural, then the masculine plural is used: as, (Gen xviii. 11) וְאַבְרָהָם וְשָׂרָה (not רֹאוֹת) וּמָנוֹחַ וְאִשְׁתּוֹ רֹאִים (Jud. xiii. 19) ; זְקֵנִים.

But the *verb* or *predicate* may be in the singular, in which case either the masculine or the feminine may be used: as, (Gen. xxiv. 55) וַתְּדַבֵּר מִרְיָם וְאַהֲרֹן (Num. xii.) ; (Exod. xxi. 4) שֶׁמֶן וּקְטֹרֶת יְשַׂמַּח לֵב (Prov. xxvii. 9) ; הָאִשָּׁה וִילָדֶיהָ תִּהְיֶה לַאדֹנֶיהָ (1 Kings xvii. 15) וַתֹּאכַל הִיא וָהוּא.

287. When the subject is a Noun of the *common gender*, the verb may be in either gender: as, (Levit. iv. 2) נֶפֶשׁ כִּי תֶחֱטָא ... וְעָשְׂתָה ; (Is. xxxiii. 9) אָבַל אֻמְלְלָה אָרֶץ.

288. When the subject is a collective noun, the verb may be either in the singular or plural: as, וַיִּרֶב הָעָם וַיַּעַצְמוּ (Exod. i. 20).

289. When the subject is indefinite, as when we say *some one did so and so*, the Hebrew makes use of the verb of the third person: as, עַל כֵּן קָרָא שְׁמוֹ בָּבֶל (Gen. xi. 9) *therefore was the name of the city*

---

* When the several subjects consist of pronouns of different persons, the verbs must then agree with that which is, in the language of grammarians, the most noble; that is, the 1st person has the preference over the other two, and the 2nd over the 3rd: as, לְכָה נִכְרְתָה בְרִית אֲנִי וָאַתָּה (Gen. xxxi. 44) ; (2 Sam. xix. 30) אַתָּה וְצִיבָא תַּחְלְקוּ אֶת־הַשָּׂדֶה.

called Babel, Heb. *therefore he called*, i. e. *some one**;
וַיֹּאמֶר לְיוֹסֵף (Gen. xlviii. 1) *and one told Joseph;*
וַיֻּגַּד לְיַעֲקֹב (Ibid. 2): or by the passive verb: as,
וַיֻּגַּד לְאַבְרָהָם (Gen. xxii. 20) *and it was told Abraham,*
i. e. *some one told him.*

Obs. 1.—The third person of the verb is likewise used when the subject or cause is unknown, and where, in English, the neuter pronoun is used: as, וַיֵּצֶר־לוֹ (Gen. xxxii. 8) *and it grieved him;* צַר לִי *it grieves me;* וַיְהִי הַגֶּשֶׁם lit. *and he was the rain*, i. e. *it rained;* וַיְהִי קוֹלוֹת וּבְרָקִים *and there was thunder and lightning*, i. e. *it thundered and lightened.*

Obs. 2.—The third person is sometimes used instead of the second or first, and nouns instead of pronouns, in addressing a superior: thus, פַּרְעֹה קָצַף עַל עֲבָדָיו (Gen. xli. 10) *Pharaoh was wroth with his servants,* for יְדַבֶּר־נָא עַבְדְּךָ דָבָר בְּאָזְנֵי אֲדֹנִי—;אַתָּה קָצַפְתָּ עַל עֲבָדֶיךָ (Gen. xliv. 18) for אֲדֹנִי שָׁאַל אֶת־עֲבָדָיו;—אֲדַבְּרָה־נָּא דָבָר בְּאָזְנֶיךָ for אַתָּה שָׁאַלְתָּ אֹתָנוּ (See likewise Gen. xix. 19; xxxiii. 13, 14)†.

Government of Verbs.

290. Active transitive verbs‡ govern the objective case: as, וְיִשְׂרָאֵל אָהַב אֶת יוֹסֵף (Gen. xxxvii. 3) *and Israel loved Joseph;* שָׁמַרְתִּי פִקּוּדֶיךָ וְעֵדֹתֶיךָ (Ps. cxix. 168) *I have kept thy precepts and thy testimonies.*

---

* This corresponds with the German *man*, and the French *on*.

† Thus we see that the language of politeness, or rather of abject humility, was early in vogue amongst mankind.

‡ Many verbs are used both *intransitively* and *transitively*: as, וְאִישׁ יִשְׂרָאֵל הָפַךְ (Judg. xx. 41) *and the men of Israel turned;* הָפַךְ לִבָּם לִשְׂנֹא עַמּוֹ (Ps. cv. 25) *he turned their hearts to hate his people;* הָפַךְ אֶת מֵימֵיהֶם לְדָם (Ibid. 29).

291. Some verbs govern two objective cases: as, שְׁאַל־נָא אֶת־הַכֹּהֲנִים תּוֹרָה (Hag. ii. 11) *ask the priests (concerning) the law;* אֲלַמְּדָה פֹשְׁעִים דְּרָכֶיךָ (Ps. li. 15) *I will teach transgressors thy way.*

292. This is especially the case with verbs in *Hiphil*: as, לְהַעֲבִיר אֶת־הַמֶּלֶךְ אֶת־הַיַּרְדֵּן (2 Sam. xix. 16) *to make the king pass over the Jordan;* וְהַעֲבַדְתִּיךָ אֶת־אֹיְבֶיךָ (Jer. xvii. 4) *and I will cause thee to serve thine enemies*.*

293. The student will recollect that when we speak of *cases* in Hebrew, nothing is meant but the signs† (prefixes or prepositions) which are added to the subordinate member of a sentence (Art. 188), in order to distinguish them from the more essential parts. Now, what particular prefix or preposition these subordinate members or complements require, must depend, as has already been observed (Art. 190), on the signification of the verb, and on the intention of the speaker; and this intention can often only be known from the particular prefix or preposition which accompanies the *complement*, and by which the signification of the verb is frequently varied. Thus the verb עָבַד construed with אֵת signifies *to labour, to cultivate, to serve;* but with בְּ it signifies, *to impose labour:* שָׁעָה construed with אֶל signifies *to attend to, to regard;* but with

---

* Generally verbs, &c., which are transitive in קַל, become doubly transitive in פִּעֵל: as, לָמַד (Is. xxvi. 10) *he learned;* לִמֵּד (Ecc. xii. 9) *he caused to learn,* or *he taught.*

† But these signs are sometimes omitted (Art. 215), in which case the connection is said to be *immediate*. The complement of a verb may be the name of the action (Art. 263), and then it is said, in the language of grammarians, to be governed in the *infinitive mood*.

מ or מִן it signifies *to turn away, disregard;* שָׁאַל אֶת־ is *to ask,* שָׁאַל־בְּ *to consult,* מֵעִם or מִן שָׁאַל *to request,* שָׁאֲל־לְ *to inquire.*

Miscellaneous Remarks.

294. The words קוּם *to rise,* נָשָׂא *to lift up, to raise,* פָּנָה *to turn,* and a few others, are often used pleonastically before other verbs: as, וַיָּקָם וַיֵּלֶךְ *and he rose and went;* וַיִּשָּׂא עֵינָיו וַיַּרְא *and he lifted up his eyes and saw;* וַיִּפֶן וַיֵּצֵא *and he turned and went out;* וַיִּשָּׂא אֶת רַגְלָיו וַיֵּלֶךְ.

295. Nouns derived from the same root with the verb are often added to it pleonastically: as, וַיִּדַּר יַעֲקֹב נֶדֶר *and Jacob vowed a vow;* בָּכוּ בְכִי גָדוֹל *they wept a great weeping*;* חֲלוֹם חָלַמְתִּי (Gen. xli. 15); וַיֶּחֱרַד יִצְחָק חֲרָדָה גְדֹלָה (Gen. xxvii. 33).

CHAPTER VI.

PARTICLES.

Adverbs.

296. The modifications of attributes, which in many languages are expressed by adverbs, are indicated in Hebrew in various ways:—

---

* Some grammarians suppose that this mode of expression denotes *emphasis,* but it appears to mark the almost child-like simplicity of the early ages, rather than any thing else.

242   THE SYNTAX OF

1st. By the repetition of the *noun* or *adjective* (Art. 221, 225).—2nd. By the *infinitive absolute* (Art. 269, 270).—3rd. By a *finite* verb, in conjunction with an *infinitive constructive* or with another *finite* verb. (Art. 273, 275).—4th. By *abstract nouns* or other words* used adverbially: as, (Exod. xii. 11) *and ye shall eat it* בְּחִפָּזוֹן *with hastiness*, i. e. *in haste*, or *hastily;* (Ibid. xiv. 25) *and they drove them* (*the chariots*) בִּכְבֵדֻת *with heaviness*, i. e. *heavily;* (Judg. viii. 1) *and they contended with him* בְּחָזְקָה *with vehemence*, or *vehemently*.

297. *Obs.*—Some of these words are never used in an adverbial sense without some of the prefixes מ, ל, כ, ב, as in the preceding examples: others are always used without prefixes: as, (Josh. ii. 1) חֶרֶשׁ *secretly* (from חֵרֵשׁ *deaf*); חִנָּם *gratuitously;* (Lam. i. 9) פְּלָאִים *wonders*, i. e. *wonderfully*. Some, again, are used indiscriminately with or without prefixes: as, בֶּטַח (Deut. xii. 10); לָבֶטַח (Lev. xxv. 19); *in safety, securely;* while others are used in different senses, according as they *have* or *have not* any of the prefixes: as, לְבַד *alone, only, separately*, but מִלְּבַד† *besides, except;* מָתַי *when*, but לְמָתַי *for when, for what period of time;* אַיִן cons. אֵין *non-existence, nothing*, לְאַיִן *into nothing*, כְּאַיִן *as nothing;* but, מֵאַיִן signifies *whence*, and מֵאֵין *without*, or rather *from want of existence*, or *because there existed not;* (See Is. v. 9; 1. 2); and

---

* See Art. 154.

† As מִלְּבַד הָרָעָב הָרִאשׁוֹן (Gen. xxvi. 1) *besides the first famine*. But the מ is often prefixed before the noun: as, לְבַד מִטַּף (Exod. xii. 37) *besides children;* which is the same as מִלְּבַד הַטַּף.

בְּאֵין *without*, i. e. *where there exists not*, or in the *non-existence* (see Prov. v. 23, xi. 14), לֹא *not*, בְּלֹא *without**.

298. הֲלֹא *is it not?* is mostly used in indirect assertions, when the inquirer knows that the answer must be in the affirmative. It is therefore often equivalent to a positive assertion†, and may be rendered by *behold:* as, הֲלֹא אַחֶיךָ רֹעִים בִּשְׁכֶם (Gen. xxxvii. 13) *Do not thy brethren pasture in Shechem?* i. e. *they do pasture, &c.;*

---

* The distinction between אַיִן and אֵין, and between these and לֹא, &c., has already been pointed out in Art. 154, 187. Nevertheless, as it is important for the student to have a clear view of the subject, we shall repeat our former remarks, and elucidate them by examples.

אַיִן is a noun, and signifies *non-existence, nothing.* It is opposed to יֵשׁ, which signifies *real* being. אַיִן is used in the *absolute state*, but אֵין when in construction with other words. Thus, *absolute state*, הֲיֵשׁ יְהוָֹה בְּקִרְבֵּנוּ אִם אָיִן (Exod. xvii. 7) *Is the Lord amongst us or not?* lit. *Is the Lord in existence? &c.* or *Is he not in existence amongst us?* Cons. אֵין בַּיִת אֲשֶׁר אֵין שָׁם מֵת (Exod. xii. 30) *there was not a house where there was not one dead,* lit. *there was no house in existence where there was not a dead person in existence.* Both אַיִן and אֵין indicate the non-existence of the *subject,* whereas לֹא indicates the non-existence of the *predicate* or *attribute* (see the examples in Art. 187). The affirmative answer to the question הֲיֵשׁ פֹּה אִישׁ (Jud. iv. 20) *is there any man here?* or הֲיֵשׁ בָּזֶה הָרֹאֶה (1 Sam. ix. 11) *is the seer here?* is יֵשׁ *there exists.* The negative answer is אַיִן *there exists not.* But the affirmative answer to הָרָאֹה אַתָּה *seest thou?* or הֲרָאִיתָ *hast thou seen?* is כֵּן *so, yes,* or רָאִיתִי—רֹאֶה אָנֹכִי; and the negative answer is לֹא. אֵין כֹּל signifies *nothing whatever,* excluding the whole as well as the parts: but לֹא כֹל signifies *not all,* excluding the whole but not all the parts.

† A negative is often implied in affirmative interrogations: as, (Ezek. xviii. 23) הֶחָפֹץ אֶחְפֹּץ מוֹת רָשָׁע *do I then desire the death of the wicked?* which is equivalent to *I do not desire, &c.*

הֲלֹא הֵמָּה בְּעֵבֶר הַיַּרְדֵּן (Deut. xi. 30) *Are they not on the other side Jordan?* i. e. *Behold they are,* &c.

299. Two negatives are not, in Hebrew, equivalent to an affirmative, but only strengthen the negation: as, הֲמִבְּלִי אֵין קְבָרִים בְּמִצְרַיִם (Exod. xiv. 11).

300. Negatives are sometimes added to nouns, adjectives, &c., to denote *privation*: as, אֵין־מִסְפָּר *innumerable*, אֵין־נָכוֹן *unprepared*; אֵין־אוֹנִים *powerless, impotent*; לֹא־כֹחַ *strengthless*; לֹא־חָכָם *unwise*; לֹא בָנִים *childless*; בֹּקֶר לֹא עָבוֹת *a cloudless morning*; לֹא־יוֹעִיל *useless, profitless*; לֹא־אֵל *not-a-God,* i. e. *an idol*; לֹא־עָם *not a nation,* i. e. *a lawless horde**; בְּלִי־שֵׁם *without a name,* i. e. *infamous*; בִּלְתִּי סָרָה *irremovable*†; אַל־מָוֶת *immortality*‡.

301. The negatives are sometimes omitted, and must be supplied by the reader: as, (1 Sam. ii. 3) אַל תַּרְבּוּ תְדַבְּרוּ גְבֹהָה גְבֹהָה יֵצֵא; (Ps. ix. 19) כִּי לֹא לָנֶצַח יִשָּׁכַח אֶבְיוֹן תִּקְוַת, supply עָתָק מִפִּיכֶם; עֲנִיִּים־תֹּאבַד לָעַד, supply לֹא.

This is especially the case when two negative propositions are joined together by וְ, when both the *negative* as well as the *predicate* of the second proposition are often omitted: as, (Ps. i. 5) עַל־כֵּן לֹא־יָקֻמוּ רְשָׁעִים בַּמִּשְׁפָּט וְחַטָּאִים־בַּעֲדַת צַדִּיקִים, supply לֹא יָקֻמוּ, or render the וְ by *nor*.

The repetition of adverbs denotes intensity: as, (Deut. xxviii. 43) *the stranger that is amongst thee shall get up above thee,* מַעְלָה מָּעְלָה *upwards upwards,* i. e. *very high; and thou shalt come down* מַטָּה מָטָּה *low low,* i. e. *very low.*

---

* Thus, (Deut. xxii. 21) הֵם קִנְאוּנִי בְלֹא־אֵל....וַאֲנִי אַקְנִיאֵם בְּלֹא־עָם.
† (Is. xiv. 6) מַכַּת בִּלְתִּי סָרָה.
‡ (Prov. xii. 28) בְּאֹרַח צְדָקָה חַיִּים וְדֶרֶךְ נְתִיבָה אַל־מָוֶת.

General Remarks on the Particles.

302. Particles (originally nouns or verbs, Art. 154) are used in Hebrew, as in other languages, not only in various senses, but for various purposes. The same word being often employed as an *adverb*, *preposition*, or *conjunction** : thus, עַל *upon, over, for, because*, &c. ; תַּחַת *below, beneath, under, instead, because;* בִּלְתִּי (probably from בָּלָה *to waste away*) *not, without, except, unless,* &c.

303. *Obs.* 1.—The student must, however, not suppose that these words have really so many different significations; for on strict examination it will be found, that however variously the Hebrew particles may be applied, they never lose their primary signification. But in translating them into modern languages, their force cannot always be given by one and the same word. This is owing to various causes, but chiefly to this—That most of the Hebrew particles are the signs of *general relations* as well as of their various *grades*, or, if I may be allowed the expression, of their *subordinate relations*. Now, the Sacred Writers often use a particle expressive of a general relation, leaving the *subordinate* to be inferred from the *context ;* but in modern languages, these subordinate relations must be expressed by distinct words. Thus, for instance, אֶל, לְ (probably from אָלָה *to tend, extend*) denotes *tendency* in general; but whether this *tendency* is to produce a union of contact, or merely an approximation, or whether it imports the final result of an action, is not expressed

---

* There are, however, many particles which are never used but as *adverbs:* as, פֹּה *here,* שָׁם *there:* or as prepositions; as, בֵּין *between :* or as conjunctions only ; as, אַף *but,* וְ *and*.

by the *particle*, but must be inferred from the context. Hence the reason why it cannot always be rendered by *to*, but occasionally by *at, near, by, for, that, &c.*

It is the same with the inseparable particle ו (from וָו *a hook*); it indicates the general relation of *connection*, but whether this connection is *copulative, adversative, concessive, &c.*, must often be inferred from the context*. Nor is this so difficult as it may at first appear. No attentive reader can for a moment doubt that the ו in וְאֵת הָאָרֶץ (Gen. i. 1) means *and*, showing that the verb בָּרָא refers to הָאָרֶץ as well as to הַשָּׁמַיִם; nor that the ו in וְקַיִן הָיָה (Gen. iv. 2) or in וְאֶל קַיִן (Ibid. 5) ought to be rendered *but*, because the propositions to which these words belong, stand in disjunctive *opposition* to those which immediately precede them; nor that the ו in וְאֵימִנָה and in וְאַשְׂמְאִילָה (Gen. xiii. 9) must be rendered by *then*, because these propositions are the *respondents* or *consequents* to their respective *antecedents*—אִם הַשְּׂמֹאל *if thou wilt take the left;* וְאִם הַיָּמִין *and if thou wilt take the right:* nor that ו in וְלֹא תִגְּעוּ (Gen. iii. 3) must be rendered by *neither*, because it is preceded by the negative proposition לֹא תֹאכְלוּ *ye shall not eat*, and is not in opposition to it. Equally evident is it that the ו in וְאִמּוֹ (Exod. xxi. 17) must be rendered by *or*, as it cannot be supposed that the culprit should go unpunished unless he commit the offence against both parents; in this instance the ו shews that וּמְקַלֵּל refers to אִמּוֹ as well as to אָבִי· These examples, I hope, will tend to remove the erroneous opinion, that the Hebrew particles have such a multiplicity of meanings, and that the single ו has seventy-four different significations!

304. *Obs.* 2.—Many particles appear to be synonymous, but there is generally some shade of difference in their meaning; nor can

---

* That the frequent use of this particle instead of those which express its subordinate relations does not arise from a want of adequate terms, is fully shown in Vindiciæ Hebraicæ, p. 157—163.

they always be indiscriminately used: thus, both אֶל and לְ, are the signs of the dative. But לְ is frequently used before the infinitive mood, to show the *purpose*: as וַיֵּשֶׁב־לֶאֱכֹל *and he sat down to eat*: and before nouns, to indicate the ultimate object: as, וְהָיוּ לְאֹתֹת *and they shall be for signs*. In neither of these cases could אֶל be used; דִּבֶּר־אֵלַי signifies *he spoke unto me*, but דִּבֶּר־לִי (the verb not being accompanied by an objective case) signifies either *he spoke concerning me*, or, as it is often properly rendered in the Established Version, *he promised me*; דִּבֶּר לָכֶם (Deut. i. 11) *he has promised you*; שָׁלַח אֶל נָשָׁי signifies *he sent* TO *my wives*; but, שָׁלַח לְנָשַׁי signifies, *he sent* FOR *my wives*; (see 1 Kings xx. 7) שָׁלַח אֵלַי לְנָשַׁי וּלְבָנַי וּלְכַסְפִּי.

305. Thus, likewise, בִּגְלַל (lit. *in rolling*) from גָּלַל *to roll*, בַּעֲבוּר (lit. *in passing*) from עָבַר *to pass*, refer to the *principal* person for whose *sake* any thing is done, to distinguish him from the person who receives the benefit, &c., not for his own merit, but for that of another. But בִּגְלַל is used only before nouns, whilst בַּעֲבוּר is used before nouns as well as before verbs, and is sometimes equivalent to לְמַעַן (lit. *to answer*) *that, so that*, indicative of the final cause. Thus (Gen. xxxix. 5) *the Lord blessed the Egyptian's house* בִּגְלַל יוֹסֵף *for Joseph's sake;* (Gen. xxx. 27) *the Lord has blessed me* בִּגְלָלֶךָ *for thy sake;* (Gen. viii. 21) בַּעֲבוּר הָאָדָם *for man's sake;* (Gen. xxvii. 4) בַּעֲבוּר תְּבָרֶכְךָ נַפְשִׁי *that my soul may bless thee*. (See Exod. ix. 16).

306. *Obs.* 3.—The remarks contained in Art. 297, may be applied to particles in general :—

Thus, אֶל is never used with a prefix, nor with a preposition preceding it, though it may be used with a preposition following it: as, אֶל־אַחֲרַי *to behind me*, אֶל בֵּין *to between**, אֶל תּוֹךְ *to the midst of*,

---

* These apparent *double prepositions* cannot always be translated literally. Expressions like these, *to behind me, to between me*,

into; whereas אוֹדוֹת *concerning, on account of,* is never used without the particle עַל preceding it: as, עַל אֹדוֹת בְּנוֹ *concerning,* or *because of his son;* עַל אֹדוֹת הַבְּאֵר *concerning,* or *an account of the well* (Gen. xxi).

עַל (from עָלָה *to ascend) upon, above;* מֵעַל *from above,* or *above* (the force of מ being lost in the translation); but מַעַל *above* (lit. *what is above),* though derived from the same root, never occurs without the prefix מ; thus, מִמַּעַל *from above,* or *above;* and מַעֲלָה with local ה, though likewise derived from the same root, is used without the prefix מ; as מַעֲלָה *upwards.*—Sometimes with ל, לְמַעְלָה and with מ and ל, מִלְמַעְלָה.

Thus likewise בִּגְלַל, בְּעֲבוּר, בִּלְתִּי, never occur without בּ, though this letter is, in the two first words, *servile.* Further, בִּגְלַל admits neither a prefix nor a preceding nor following particle. בְּעֲבוּר is sometimes used with ל to mark the final end or purpose; whereas בִּלְתִּי admits both prefixes as well as particles: thus, לְבִלְתִּי שְׁמֹר *(for) not to keep,* מִבִּלְתִּי יְכֹלֶת *from defect of power, from inability,* בִּלְתִּי־אִם *unless, except,* עַד בִּלְתִּי שָׁמַיִם *until the defect of the heavens,* or *until the heavens be no more.* A knowledge of these distinctions can only be acquired by practice.

---

sound very awkwardly to our ears, and so they would to an oriental ear, if these terms were considered exclusively as prepositions— but this usage is perfectly correct in the Hebrew; because most of the prepositions being, in their origin, *nouns,* are often used as such: thus, אַחַר *the* hinder *part, the space* behind; תּוֹךְ the *middle* of; (from תָּוֶךְ *the middle),* בֵּין *the* intermediate *space,* plu. בֵּינוֹת *the intermediate spaces.* Hence the propriety of such expressions, מִלִּפְנֵי מִלְמַעְלָה, לְמַעְלָה, מֵעַל, אֶל מִבֵּין, אֶל־בֵּין, מִבֵּין, מֵאַחֲרֵי, אֶל אַחֲרֵי. But we could not say לִלְפְנֵי, nor אֶל לִפְנֵי because the ל in לִפְנֵי already expresses the relation denoted by the dative, and means literally, *towards* the place where the face is.

307. Several particles, when in construction, require the sign of the *dative* after them: as, * מִבֵּית לַפָּרֹכֶת *within the vail,* lit. *from within to the vail.* i. e. *with reference to it;* מִחוּץ לָעִיר *without the city;* מִמַּעַל לָעֵצִים *upon the wood,* lit. *from above, with reference to the wood;* סָבִיב לַמִּשְׁכָּן וְלַמִּזְבֵּחַ *round about the tabernacle and the altar;* אוֹי לָהֶם *woe unto them!* הֲלִילָה לִי אֲלְלַי לִי *woe unto me!* lit. *lamentation to me! far be it from me! God forbid!* lit. *a profanation be it to me, unbecoming.*

308. *Obs.*—When the particle בֵּין *between,* relates to several objects included in a noun plural, it is placed in immediate construction with that noun: as, בֵּין הַגְּזָרִים *between the pieces,* בֵּין עֵינֶיךָ *between thine eyes†*. But when it relates to two distinct nouns, whether the same or different, then the particle must either be repeated before each of the nouns: as, בֵּין הָאוֹר וּבֵין הַחֹשֶׁךְ (Gen. i. 4) *between the light and between the darkness;* ... בֵּין הַמַּיִם וּבֵין הַמָּיִם (Ibid. 7): or בֵּין is placed before the first noun, and the second receives the prefix לְ; as, בֵּין מַיִם לָמָיִם (Ibid. 6); בֵּין אוֹר לַחֹשֶׁךְ (see Levit. xi. 47; Deut. xvii. 8).

Arrangement of Words.

309. As the most essential parts of speech have in Hebrew their peculiar *forms,* and most of the

---

* Derived from בַּיִת *a house,* itself probably derived from בּוֹא *to come in, to enter.*

† When בֵּין refers to several objects included in the same noun, it is often rendered by *among;* as, בֵּין אַחִים (Prov. vi. 19) *among brethren.*

modifications are indicated by *inflections*, there can be little difficulty in distinguishing the *subject* from the *predicate*, and the principal members from the subordinate parts, whatever situation they may happen to occupy in a sentence. The words may therefore be disposed in almost any order, without occasioning the least confusion or ambiguity.

Thus, even the mere *tyro* may know by barely looking at the form of the two following words אָכַל לֶחֶם that the first is a *finite verb* including the pronoun *he*, and that the second is a *noun*. Further, as אָכַל includes the *subject* as well as the *predicate*, לֶחֶם must be the *objective*, whether it is placed after the verb—thus אָכַל לֶחֶם; or before it—thus לֶחֶם אָכַל.

Thus likewise the words of the following simple sentence, יִשְׂרָאֵל אָהַב אֶת־יוֹסֵף (*Israel loved Joseph*) may receive any arrangement of which they are susceptible without altering the sense :—

I.	יִשְׂרָאֵל אָהַב אֶת־יוֹסֵף	IV.	יִשְׂרָאֵל אֶת־יוֹסֵף אָהַב
II.	אֶת־יוֹסֵף אָהַב יִשְׂרָאֵל	V.	אָהַב אֶת־יוֹסֵף יִשְׂרָאֵל
III.	אֶת־יוֹסֵף יִשְׂרָאֵל אָהַב	VI.	אָהַב יִשְׂרָאֵל אֶת־יוֹסֵף

or VII. וַיֶּאֱהַב יִשְׂרָאֵל אֶת־יוֹסֵף with ו conversive.

The reason of this is obvious. The *verb* being known by its *form*, and the *objective* by the particle אֶת, there remains only the word יִשְׂרָאֵל which must be the *nominative*; and as the words are thus distinctly marked, it matters not what place they occupy.

310. But though, owing to the reason just stated, great latitude is allowed in the arrangement of words, it must not be supposed that they are placed

at random; on the contrary, their proper disposition appears to depend on one principle, viz., that the speaker will naturally express that *first* which strikes his mind most forcibly, and to which he wishes most to draw the attention of his *hearers*.—The more important words will therefore take precedence of those that are less important*.

311. Hence it is that in Hebrew the *qualifying* word must *follow* the words *qualified*, and the *defining* words must be placed after those which are *defined :* thus, בֵּן חָכָם (not חָכָם בֵּן) *a wise son;* יוֹם שֵׁנִי (not שֵׁנִי יוֹם) *second day;* בַּת מֶלֶךְ (not מֶלֶךְ בַּת) *a king's daughter;* הָאִישׁ הַזֶּה (not הַזֶּה הָאִישׁ) *this man.* See Art. 54, 84, 91, 98, 184.

312. Hence it is, likewise, that in common discourse the words follow mostly the natural train of thoughts, that is to say, the *subject*

---

* The order of words in the first verse of the Book of Genesis, may perhaps appear an exception to the general rule, as it begins with a word apparently the least impressive: thus, בְּרֵאשִׁית בָּרָא אֱלֹהִים אֵת הַשָּׁמַיִם וְאֵת הָאָרֶץ. But it is highly probable that the Inspired Penman, by adopting this arrangement in preference to the many which he might have chosen, intended to impress on our minds *first*—that this world had *a beginning*, in contradiction to those who maintained its *eternity:* *secondly*—that it was not the production of *chance*, but a *creation*, a calling into existence by the *Divine Will;* and having thus taught us these important truths, he introduces the Divine Agent, אֱלֹהִים *the Almighty Being*, the Author of all the powers —and last of all, the objective cases—אֶת־הַשָּׁמַיִם וְאֶת־הָאָרֶץ.

or *nominative* is placed *first*, then the *verb* or *predicate*, then the *objective*, or any other subordinate member* : as in the arrangement marked I.

313. But in historic narratives where *actions* and *events* are of greater importance than the *agents*, the *verb* is mostly placed first†, then the *nominative*, then the subordinate members, and last of all, the minor circumstances: as in the arrangement marked VI. VII. The intermediate arrangements marked II. III. IV. V. are used *ad libitum*, according as the speaker attaches more or less importance to either of the words; the most emphatic being generally placed first in order.

314. By way of illustration, let us compare the two following sentences:—

---

* All words and phrases which are introduced to define or to explain the *nominative* or any of the subordinate numbers, are placed immediately after the word which they are to explain: as, הָאִשָּׁה—אֲשֶׁר נָתַתָּה עִמָּדִי—הִיא | נָתְנָה | לִי | מִן־הָעֵץ (Gen. iii. 12); יְהוָֹה—אֱלֹהֵי הַשָּׁמַיִם אֲשֶׁר לְקָחַנִי מִבֵּית אָבִי וּמֵאֶרֶץ מוֹלַדְתִּי וַאֲשֶׁר דִּבֶּר־לִי וַאֲשֶׁר נִשְׁבַּע־לִי לֵאמֹר לְזַרְעֲךָ אֶתֵּן אֶת־הָאָרֶץ הַזֹּאת— הוּא | בָּנָה | אֶת־שַׁעַר בֵּית־*הוּא | יִשְׁלַח | מַלְאָכוֹ | לְפָנֶיךָ (Gen. xxiv. 7); יְהוָה הָעֶלְיוֹן (2 Kings xv. 35).

When the nominative is thus separated from the verb by explanatory circumstances, the personal pronoun corresponding with the nominative is introduced to recall, as it were, the subject; as in the preceding examples. See likewise Deut. i. 30, 36, 38, 39.

† Except when the clauses stand in opposition. .

I.—בְּחֵיקֶךָ | שִׁפְחָתִי | נָתַתִּי | אָנֹכִי· (Gen. xvi. 5.)
I have given my maid into thy bosom.

II.—לְאִשָּׁה | הַזֶּה | לָאִישׁ | נָתַתִּי | אֶת בִּתִּי· (Deut. xxii. 16.)
Lit. *My daughter I gave unto this man for a wife.*

In the first example, the *nominative* אָנֹכִי is placed emphatically (as it is already included in the finite verb נָתַתִּי) *first*; then comes the *verb*, then the *objective*, &c. In the second example, the order is reversed. The objective case is placed first, then the verb including the nominative, then the subordinate members. And why? Because in the first, we have the venerable mistress aware of her importance, which she finds abated by circumstances arising from her *own condescension*, to which she particularly wishes to draw her husband's attention. She, therefore, begins with the *Ego* אָנֹכִי ; 'It was *I*, the mistress of the house, who have condescendingly placed this ungrateful bondwoman in thy bosom.' But in the second example, we have the tender *father*, indignant at the offered insult, pleading the cause of *his child*. He therefore omits the אָנֹכִי, as if he scarcely thought of himself, and begins his address to the judges with אֶת בִּתִּי *my daughter*, as the object nearest his heart.

315. In the following verse, אֶת־יְהוָֹה אֱלֹהֶיךָ תִּירָא וְאֹתוֹ תַעֲבֹד וּבִשְׁמוֹ תִּשָּׁבֵעַ (Deut. vi. 13), we have all the complimentary words placed before their respective verbs and nominatives, because the emphasis rests upon them. Reverse the order, and arrange the words as they are in the translation—אתה תירא את יהוה אלהיך ואתו תעבד, &c., or—וְעֲבֹד אֹתוֹ יְרָא אֶת יהוה אלהיך, &c., and the energy is entirely lost.

316. It is the same with adverbs and other words expressive of mere circumstances, such as חִנָּם, פִּתְאֹם, עַתָּה, רֵיקָם, &c. In ordinary discourse they mostly follow the verb: as, וַיֵּצְאָה הַנָּם (Ex. xxi. 11); וַיֹּאמֶר יְהוָה פִּתְאֹם (Deut. xv. 13); לֹא תְשַׁלְּחֶנּוּ רֵיקָם (Num. xii. 4). But when any particular stress is to be laid upon them, they precede the verb: as, כִּי־עַתָּה רֵיקָם שִׁלַּחְתָּנִי (Gen. xxxi.

42); עַל־כֵּן פִּתְאֹם יָבוֹא אֵידוֹ (Prov. vi. 15). Nay, they are often placed with great propriety at the very beginning of a sentence: as, פִּתְאֹם נָפְלָה בָבֶל (Jer. li. 8). Because the prophet wished to draw attention to the *suddenness* of the destruction of Babylon, so unexpected at the time when she was still flourishing and great.

So likewise, פִּתְאֹם יָבוֹא אֶל־הֵיכָלוֹ הָאָדוֹן אֲשֶׁר אַתֶּם מְבַקְשִׁים (Mal. iii. 1); חִנָּם נִמְכַּרְתֶּם (Is. lii. 3); הַחִנָּם יָרֵא אִיּוֹב אֶת יְהוָֹה (Job i. 9). In all these instances, the adverbs stand first, because they are the most emphatic. Place them in any other part of the sentence, and the effect is lost, as it is indeed in every translation which cannot adopt the same arrangement.

317. But though numerous additional examples might be produced from every part of Scripture, to show that the Sacred Writers paid great attention to the disposition of their words, yet we must not carry this principle too far, by requiring, in every instance, a reason for the particular arrangement which they thought proper to use. This would be as absurd, as to demand why an author does not always use the same identical words to express the same sentiment. On this subject, I cannot do better than recommend to the student's attention the judicious observations of the greatest Hebrew scholar that ever lived, *Aben Ezra*. His words are:—

דַּע כִּי הַמִּלּוֹת הֵם כְּגוּפוֹת וְהַטְּעָמִים הֵם כִּנְשָׁמוֹת וְהַגּוּף
לַנְּשָׁמָה כְּמוֹ כְּלִי: עַל כֵּן מִשְׁפַּט כָּל־הַחֲכָמִים בְּכָל־לָשׁוֹן
שֶׁיִּשְׁמְרוּ הַטְּעָמִים וְאֵינָם חוֹשְׁשִׁין לְשִׁנּוּי הַמִּלּוֹת אַחַר שֶׁהֵם
שָׁוִים בְּטַעֲמָם:

'*Know that words are like bodies, and the senses* (meanings) are like souls; and that the body is a mere instrument (organ) to the soul.*

---

* It is very remarkable that a man so learned as *John Buxtorf*, should have misinterpreted both these passages. Nor is it less remarkable, that of the numerous authors who have profited by his

Hence the practice of all wise men, in every language, to take care of the sense, but they are not solicitous about the change of words, as long as they express the same meaning.' He then cites numerous examples, to show that the Sacred Writer often uses various expressions to convey the same thought; and adds, that no sensible man will require a reason why an author uses sometimes a pleonastic expression, and at other times an elliptical phrase, or why he writes at one time a word מָלֵא *full* (*i. e.* expressing the quiescent letters א ו י), and at other times חָסֵר *deficient;* as for instance, why the word עוֹלָם is sometimes written with the ו, and at other times עֹלָם without it, when, in point of fact, there is no impropriety in either.

Further, in his comment on the word לֵאמֹר (Deut. v. 5) which appears out of its proper position, and speaking of the variations in some of the expressions of the Decalogue, as recited in *Exodus* and in *Deuteronomy*, he says—

אַל תָּשִׂים לֵב אֶל הַמִּלּוֹת כִּי הֵם כְּגוּפוֹת וְהַטְּעָמִים ׃ הֵם כְּרוּחוֹת ׃ וְהַבּוֹרֵת בִּשְׁנֵי כֵלִים זֶה כְּמוֹ זֶה בְּמַעֲשֶׂה מַעֲשֶׂה אֶחָד הוּא ׃

'*Do not be too anxious about the words, for they are like bodies, and the senses (meanings) are like spirits: and he that cuts with either of two instruments, each of which is calculated to produce the same effect,*

---

labours, none should have noticed the mistake. Speaking of the importance of the Hebrew accents (in his Thes. Gram. Ling. Sanctæ, p. 599), he cites the preceding quotations from Aben Ezra's work, and renders the first thus—'*Scito dictiones esse quasi corpora, & accentus* (!) *quasi animas,*' &c. The second he renders thus—'*Ne apponas animum ad dictiones: illæ enim sunt instar corporum, & accentus* (!) *sicut spiritus sive animæ,* &c. What probably misled the learned author is, that the word טְעָמִים is frequently used by Rabbinical writers for *accents*. But that Aben Ezra does not use the word in this sense, is clear enough.

doeth, in fact, the same work.' In short, he strongly recommends to those who study the sacred volume, to look to the spirit, rather than to the *mere letter*.

318. The negative particles, being considered as mere *exponents* or *indices*, are placed immediately* before their respective verbs: as, אַל תֵּלֵךְ, לֹא אָכַל, בַּל חָלִיתִי.

319. For the same reason most of the conjunctions, especially those which indicate the modes of thought, are placed at the beginning of their respective phrases or sentences: as, כִּי תִקְנֶה עֶבֶד עִבְרִי (Ex. xxi. 2); אִם אֲדֹנָיו יִתֶּן־לוֹ אִשָּׁה (Ibid.); אַךְ אִם יוֹם אוֹ יוֹמַיִם יַעֲמֹד לֹא (Ibid.); גַּם כִּי פַסְפּוֹ הוּא (Ibid.) See the examples in Art. 280.

320. For a similar reason, are all words which have the sign of interrogation (הֲ), as well as interrogative pronouns and adverbs, placed at the beginning of interrogative phrases and sentences: as, הֲמָלֹךְ תִּמְלֹךְ עָלֵינוּ אִם מָשׁוֹל תִּמְשֹׁל בָּנוּ (Gen. iv. 9); הֲיֹאמַר אָחִי אָנֹכִי (Gen. xxxviii. 8); מַה תִּתֶּן־לִי (Gen. xii. 19); לָמָּה אָמַרְתָּ אֲחֹתִי הִיא (Gen. xv. 2); אַיֵּה שָׂרָה אִשְׁתֶּךָ (Gen. xviii.); מִי הָאִישׁ הַלָּזֶה (Gen. xxiv.).

321. In a few instances we find the nouns placed, by way of *emphasis*, before the interrogative: as, אֲבוֹתֵיכֶם אַיֵּה הֵם וְהַנְּבִיאִים הַלְעוֹלָם יִחְיוּ (Zech. i. 5); *your fathers where are they? and the prophets will they live for ever?*

---

* Sometimes, however, the particle is separated from the verb by an intervening word: as, לֹא לִבִּי הָלַךְ (2 Kings v. 26); אַל בְּאַפְּךָ תוֹכִיחֵנִי וְאַל בַּחֲמָתְךָ תְיַסְּרֵנִי (Ps. vi. 5).

APPENDIX.

EXTRACTS
FROM
SCARCE HEBREW BOOKS.

I.

Folly of Idolatry.

From the 13th Chapter of Wisdom of Solomon, *v.* 1—10.

אָמְנָם כֵּן הוּא אַךְ לַהֶבֶל דָּמוּ בְּנֵי אָדָם אֲשֶׁר אֵין בָּם
דַּעַת אֱלֹהִים, כִּי אֵינָם יוֹדְעִים אֶת יְיָ וְטוּבוֹ לְנֶגֶד עֵינֵיהֶם ·
לֹא הִכִּירוּ אֶת הַיּוֹצֵר, וְאִם הִבִּיטוּ אֶל מַעֲשָׂיו : וַיְהִי
לְהֵפֶךְ, כִּי אָמְרוּ אֵשׁ אוֹ רוּחַ אוֹ סַעַר אוֹ חוּג הַכֹּכָבִים אוֹ
מַיִם שׁוֹטְפִים אוֹ מְאוֹרוֹת הַשָּׁמַיִם הֵם הָאֱלֹהִים הַמּוֹשְׁלִים
בָּאָרֶץ : וְאִם תִּפְאֶרֶת וּדְבָרִים אֵלּוּ הִשִּׂיאָם לְהַאֲמִין כִּי
אֱלֹהִים הֵם, אֵיךְ לֹא הֵבִינוּ מַה רָם אֲשֶׁר מִמַּעַל לָהֶם
אֲדוֹן הַתִּפְאֶרֶת אֲשֶׁר עָשָׂם : וְאִם עַל כֹּחָם וּגְבוּרָתָם
תָּמָהוּ מַדּוּעַ לֹא הִשְׂכִּילוּ מַה־רַב כֹּחַ יוֹצְרָם : כִּי
בְהִתְמַשֵּׁל הַיּוֹצֵר אֶל מַעֲשָׂיו מִכֹּחַ כֻּלָּם וּמִתִּפְאַרְתָּם יֵרָאֶה
דְּמוּת כְּבוֹדוֹ : וּפֶן תֹּאמַר לֹא יֶאְשְׁמוּ עַל זֹאת כִּי אֶת
יְיָ בִּקְּשׁוּ וְלֹא בָא עַד תְּכוּנָתוֹ חָפְצוּ וַיִּכָּשֵׁלוּ : כִּי עֹדָם

תָּרִים בְּמִפְעֲלוֹתָיו נִלְכְּדוּ לְמַרְאֵה עֵינֵיהֶם כִּי טוֹבִים הָיוּ
כָּל הַדְּבָרִים אֲשֶׁר רָאוּ : לֹא כֵן הוּא וְלֹא יְכֻפַּר לָהֶם
הַדָּבָר הַזֶּה : כִּי אִם יָסְפוּ דַעַת וַיָּבִינוּ מוֹסְדוֹת הָאָרֶץ,
עַל מֶה לֹא הִשִּׂיגוּ חִישׁ מַהֵר אֶת־אֲדוֹן כָּל הַמַּעֲשִׂים
הָאֵלֶּה : וְאֵלֶּה נְבָזִים כֻּלָּם אֲשֶׁר קָרְאוּ בְּשֵׁם אֱלֹהִים לְכָל־
מַעֲשֵׂה יְדֵי אָדָם זָהָב וָכֶסֶף הֲעָשׂוּי בְּכָל מְלֶאכֶת מַעֲשֶׂה
תַּבְנִית כָּל חַיָּה וָאֶבֶן דּוּמָם אֲשֶׁר פִּסְלוּ קַדְמוֹנִים, וַיְשִׂימוּ
בְּסָלָם בִּדְבָרִים מֵתִים :

II.

ORIGIN OF IDOLATRY.

Chap. xiv. v. 15—31.

אָב מִתְעַצֵּב עַל בְּנוֹ אֲשֶׁר מֵת פִּתְאוֹם בְּלֹא
עִתּוֹ עָשָׂה אֶת תַּבְנִיתוֹ וַיַּעַשׂ לֵאלֹהָיו אָדָם מֵת
וַיְצַו לְאַנְשֵׁי בֵיתוֹ לִזְבּוֹחַ לוֹ וּלְעָבְדוֹ : וּבְרוֹב הַיָּמִים
הִתְחַזֵּק הַמִּנְהָג הָרָע הַזֶּה וַיְשִׂימוּ אוֹתוֹ הַמְּלָכִים לְחוֹק
וַיְצַוּוּ לְכַבֵּד אֶת הַפְּסִילִים : כִּי הָאֲנָשִׁים אֲשֶׁר נָרוּ בְּאֶרֶץ
רְחוֹקָה וְלֹא יָכְלוּ לְכַבֵּד אֶת־פְּנֵי הַמֶּלֶךְ וַיַּעֲשׂוּ פֶסֶל
כְּתַבְנִית הַמֶּלֶךְ הַחַי אֲשֶׁר עָבְדוּ לְהַחֲנִיפוֹ בְּאַהֲבָתָם
מֵרָחוֹק כְּמִקָּרוֹב : וְגַם גַּאֲוַת הֶחָרָשׁ אִמְּצָה אֶת־לְבַב
הָאֱוִילִים לַעֲבוֹד אֶת הָעֲבוֹדָה הַזֹּאת : אוּלַי כְּנֶגְמַת

הֶחָרָשׁ הָיְתָה לִמְצוֹא חֵן בְּעֵינֵי הַמֶּלֶךְ וַיִּתְאַמֵּץ לַעֲשׂוֹת תֹּאַר הַתַּבְנִית שָׁלֵם כִּתְאָרוֹ: וּלְבַב דַּלַּת הָעָם אֲשֶׁר נִפְתָּה מֵיוֹפִי הַמְּלָאכָה נָתְנוּ אֱלוֹהַּ הוֹד לַאֲשֶׁר כִּבְּדוּ לְפָנִים כְּאָדָם: וַיְהִי זֹאת כְּמוֹקֵשׁ לְרַגְלֵי בְנֵי אָדָם כִּי מְכוֹבָד עוֹל וּמֵאַכְזָרִיּוֹת הַמּוֹשְׁלִים בָּם קָרְאוּ בְּשָׁמוֹת לָעֵצִים וְלָאֲבָנִים לֹא יִקְרָא בָהֶם כָּל יְצוּר: וַיְהִי נָקֵל בְּעֵינֵיהֶם כִּי חָדְלוּ לָדַעַת אֶת־הָאֱלֹהִים אֲבָל כַּאֲשֶׁר רָגְשׁוּ לָלֶכֶת בְּאִוַּלְתָּם קָרְאוּ לָרָעוֹת הַגְּדוֹלוֹת בְּשֵׁם הַשָּׁלֵם: כִּי כָכָה יַעַבְדוּם זוֹבְחִים אֶת בְּנֵיהֶם אוֹ זוֹלְלִים וְסוֹבְאִים בְּהוֹלֵלוֹת נָכְרִיָּה: לֹא שָׁמְרוּ דֶרֶךְ הַחַיִּים וְלֹא נָשְׂאוּ לָהֶם נָשִׁים כַּמִּשְׁפָּט אַךְ זֶה מְרַצֵּחַ רֵעֵהוּ בְּעָרְמָה וְזֶה יִנְאַף אֶת אֵשֶׁת עֲמִיתוֹ לְהַאֲדִיב נַפְשׁוֹ: הַכֹּל חֻבַּר יַחְדָּו בְּאִוַּלְתָּם דָּם וָרֶצַח גֶּזֶל וּמִרְמָה מַשְׁחָת וּמֶרֶד מְהוּמָה וְאָלָה וְלִצְרוֹר לַאֲנָשִׁים טוֹבִים: נְבָלָה וְהַכְאֵב לֵב גַּם לָקַחַת הַנָּשִׁים בְּחָזְקָה גַּם נִאוּף גַּם זְנוּת כָּל אֵלֶּה נָהֲגוּ בֵּינֵיהֶם: כִּי עֲבוֹדַת הָאֱלִילִים רֵאשִׁית וְתַכְלִית כָּל־רָע: בְּחַגֵּיהֶם מִשְׁתַּכְּרִים מִתְנַבְּאִים סָרָה נֹהֲגִים בְּדֶרֶךְ רָע וְנִשְׁבָּעִים לַשָּׁקֶר: כִּי בַּעֲבוּר יַאֲמִינוּ בָּאֱלִילִים אֲשֶׁר אֵין בָּהֶם רוּחַ חַיִּים לֹא יָגוֹרוּ מֵרָע בְּהִשָּׁבְעָם בָּם לַשָּׁקֶר: וְעַל שְׁתֵּיהֶן יִשָּׁפְטוּ בְּצֶדֶק עַל חָשְׁבָם רָע עַל יְיָ וְעַל הִשָּׁבְעָם בְּמִרְמָה לַשֶּׁקֶר לְהַבְזוֹת כָּל־קֹדֶשׁ: לֹא בְכֹחַ אֵלֶּה אֲשֶׁר יִשָּׁבְעוּ בָּם אֲבָל נִקְמַת צֶדֶק הַמִּתְנַקֶּמֶת בְּיוֹם מִשְׁפָּט מֵרְשָׁעִים תַּעֲשֶׂה זֹאת:

III.

WISDOM.

The 24th Chapter of Ecclesiasticus*.

הַחָכְמָה תְּהַלֵּל נַפְשָׁהּ וּבְקֶרֶב עַם אֱלֹהִים תִּתְפָּאֵר: בַּעֲדַת אֵל תִּפְתַּח פִּיהָ וּבְתוֹךְ עַמּוֹ תִּתְהַדָּר: כִּי מִפִּי עֶלְיוֹן יָצָאָה וְכָעֲרָפֶל כִּסְּתָה אָרֶץ: אָנֹכִי בִּמְרוֹם עֶלְיוֹן מִשְׁכָּנִי וְכִסְאִי בְּעַמּוּד הֶעָנָן: בַּשָּׁמַיִם עִמּוֹ הָיִיתִי וּבְמַעֲמַקֵּי תְהוֹמוֹת שָׁם אָנִי: בְּמַעֲיָנוֹת נִכְבַּדֵּי מַיִם וּבְמוֹסְדוֹת תֵּבֵל הָלַכְתִּי וּבְכָל עַם וָאֹם שָׁלָטְתִּי: בְּכָל אֵלֶּה מְנוּחָה בִּקַּשְׁתִּי וְאַיֵּה אֵיפֹה מְקוֹם מְנוּחָתִי: אָז פָּקַד עָלַי יוֹצֵר כֹּל וְאֵל עוֹשֵׂנִי אָמַר לִי בְּיַעֲקֹב תִּשְׁכֹּן וּבְיִשְׂרָאֵל תִּשְׁתָּרֵר: מֵרֹאשׁ קַדְמֵי תֵבֵל נִבְרֵאתִי וּלְעוֹלְמֵי עַד לֹא יָסוּף זִכְרִי: בְּמִשְׁכַּן קָדְשׁוֹ לְפָנָיו עֲבַדְתִּי וְשָׁם בְּצִיּוֹן אִתּוֹ קַמְתִּי: קִרְיָה אֲהוּבַת אֲבוֹתַי נַחְתִּי וִירוּשָׁלַיִם עִיר מֶמְשַׁלְתִּי: רְבִיתִי בְּעַם סְגֻלַּת יְיָ בְּיִשְׂרָאֵל חֶבֶל נַחֲלָתוֹ: גָּדַלְתִּי בְּאַרְזֵי בַלְּבָנוֹן כְּעֵץ זַיִת בִּשְׂנִיר וְחֶרְמוֹן: כַּתֹּמֶר בְּעֵין גֶּדִי כַּשּׁוֹשַׁנָּה בְּעֵמֶק יְרִיחוֹ: כְּזַיִת הִרְחִיבוּ דָלִיּוֹתַי וּכְעֵץ עַל פַּלְגֵי מַיִם פּוּרוֹתָי: כְּקִנָּמוֹן וּבַשָּׂמִים רֹאשׁ בְּשָׂמַי וּכְמָר דְּרוֹר נָתַתִּי רֵיחִי: כִּלְבוֹנָה וְחֶלְבְּנָה וַאֲהָלִים וָצֳרִי, כַּשֶּׁמֶן הַטּוֹב רֵיחִי: כְּאֵלָה הִכוּ שָׁרָשַׁי וַעֲנָפַי שֶׁבַח וִיקָר: כְּהַדְרַת גֶּפֶן שָׂפְרָתִי וּפְרָחַי פִּרְחֵי הוֹד וְהָדָר: שְׂעוּ אֵלַי

---

* Translated by Ben-Zeeb.

מְשַׁחֲרַי וּמִפִּרְיֵי הַטּוֹב תִּתְעַנָּגוּ : כִּי מָתוֹק מְצוּף לְקָחִי
וּמִנֹּפֶת אֲמָרִי : אוֹכְלַי עוֹד יִרְעָבוּן וְשׁוֹתַי יָשׁוּבוּ יִצְמָאוּן לִי
שִׁימֵעַ לִי לֹא יִפּוֹל וְעוֹשֵׂה דְבָרַי לֹא יִכָּשֵׁל : כָּל אֵלֶּה
בְּסֵפֶר בְּרִית יְיָ כְּתוּבִים : תּוֹרָה צִוָּה לָנוּ מֹשֶׁה מוֹרָשָׁה
קְהִלַּת יַעֲקֹב : מָלְאָה חָכְמָה כַּפִּישׁוֹן וְכַנְּהַר חִדֶּקֶל בִּימֵי
הָאָבִיב : מַטִּיפָה שֵׂכֶל כִּנְהַר פְּרָת וְכַיַּרְדֵּן בִּימֵי הַקָּצִיר :
מַבִּיעָה לֶקַח כַּיְאוֹר וְכַגִּיחוֹן בִּימֵי הַבָּצִיר : לֹא נָמְרוּ
קַדְמוֹנִים הַחָכְמָה וְהָאַחֲרוֹנִים לֹא יַשִּׂיגוּהָ : כִּי רְחָבָה הִיא
מִנִּי יָם וַעֲמוּקָה מִתְּהוֹם רַבָּה : אַף אָנִי כַּנָּהָר מַשְׁקֶה
וְכִבְרֵכַת מַיִם עֲלֵי גַן יָרָק : אָמַרְתִּי אַשְׁקֶה גַנִּי וְאַרְוֶה
עֲרוּגַת מַטָּעַי : וְהִנֵּה הָיִיתִי לִתְעָלָה וּמִתְעָלָה לְנַחַל
וּמִנַּחַל לְנָהָר וּמִנָּהָר לְיָם : עוֹד יָאִירוּ קַרְנֵי הוֹד אֲמָרַי
כַּשַּׁחַר וְיָפוּצוּ גוֹיֵי לְקָחִי עַל כָּל אֲפָסִים : עוֹד כִּנְבוּאַת יְיָ
אַטִּיף מִלָּתִי וְלִקְחִי אָקִים לְדוֹר אַחֲרוֹן :

IV.

Copy of the first Letter which the Roman Senate sent to the Jews.

Maccab*. Chap. viii. v. 22—37.

וְזֹאת מִשְׁנֶה הַסֵּפֶר אֲשֶׁר כָּתְבוּ עַל לֻחוֹת נְחֹשֶׁת
וַיִּשְׁלָחוּ אֹתוֹ יְרוּשָׁלַיְמָה לִהְיוֹת לָהֶם לְזֵכֶר הַבְּרִית :

---

* Translated into Hebrew by Dr. S. I. Fränkel. The whole of the *Apocrypha* has been translated by this learned man into pure Hebrew, and may be had at Messrs. Taylor and Walton's, Upper Gower Street.

יְצַו יְיָ אֶת־בִּרְכָתוֹ שָׁלוֹם לְעַם רוֹמָא וּלְעַם יְהוּדָה גַּם בַּיָּם וְגַם בַּיַּבָּשָׁה וְחֶרֶב לֹא־תַעֲבֹר בְּאַרְצָם עַד עוֹלָם: אוּלָם כִּי־תִקְרֶה מִלְחָמָה בְּרוֹמָא אוֹ בְּכָל־אֶרֶץ מֶמְשַׁלְתָּם אוֹ בְּבַעֲלֵי בְרִיתָם עוֹד יַעְזְרוּ אוֹתָם הַיְהוּדִים בֶּאֱמֶת וּבְתָמִים כְּפִי עִנְיַן הַדָּבָר: וְלֹא וְכַלְכְּלוּ אֶת־אוֹיְבֵי רוֹמָא לֹא־בְצֵידָה וְלֹא־בְנֶשֶׁק לֹא־בְכֶסֶף וְלֹא־בָאֳנִיּוֹת בִּרְצוֹן הָרוֹמָאִים: כָּל־אֵלֶּה יִשְׁמְרוּ לַעֲשׂוֹת בְּלִי קַחַת דָּבָר בִּמְחִירָם:

וְכִי תִקְרֶה מִלְחָמָה בְּאֶרֶץ הַיְהוּדִים יָבֹאוּ אַנְשֵׁי רוֹמָא לְעָזְרָתָם בֶּאֱמֶת וּבְתָמִים כְּפִי עִנְיַן הַדָּבָר: וְנָתֹן לֹא־יִתְּנוּ לְאוֹיְבֵי הַיְהוּדִים לֹא־אֹכֶל וְלֹא־נֶשֶׁק לֹא־כֶסֶף וְלֹא־אֳנִיּוֹת כִּי זֶה רְצוֹן הָרוֹמָאִים וְאֶת־אֵלֶּה יִשְׁמְרוּ לַעֲשׂוֹת בְּלִי־מַעַל וּמִרְמָה: עַל־פִּי הַדְּבָרִים הָאֵלֶּה הֻקַּם הַבְּרִית בֵּין בְּנֵי־רוֹמָא וּבֵין הַיְהוּדִים: וְכִי יַעֲלֶה עַל־לֵב שְׁנֵיהֶם לְהוֹסִיף עַל־אֵלֶּה אוֹ לִגְרֹעַ מֵהֶם כְּחֶפְצָם יַעֲשׂוֹ וְכָל־אֲשֶׁר יוֹסִיפוּ אוֹ יִגְרְעוּ יָקוּם:

וְעַל־אוֹדוֹת דֵּימֵיטְרִיּוֹס אֲשֶׁר עָשַׁק אֶת־הַיְהוּדִים כָּתְבוּ לוֹ לֵאמֹר: מַה־לְּךָ כִּי־תִסְתּוֹלֵל בַּיְּהוּדִים וְהֵם אַחֵינוּ וְאַנְשֵׁי בְרִיתֵינוּ: וְהָיָה כִּי־יָשׁוּבוּ אֵלֵינוּ לִצְעֹק עָלֶיךָ בֹּא נָבֹא לְעֶזְרָתָם וְנִלְחַמָה־בָךְ בַּיָּם וּבַיַּבָּשָׁה:

V.

Copy of a Letter which Jonathan the High-Priest wrote to the Spartans.

1 Maccab. chap. xii. v. 6—24.

וְזֹאת מִשְׁנֵה הַסֵּפֶר אֲשֶׁר שָׁלַח יוֹנָתָן לְיוֹשְׁבֵי אַשְׁפַּרְתָּא:
יוֹנָתָן הַכֹּהֵן הַגָּדוֹל וְזִקְנֵי הָעָם וְהַכֹּהֲנִים וְכָל־עַם־הַיְּהוּדִים לְאַחֵיהֶם אַנְשֵׁי אַשְׁפַּרְתָּא שָׁלוֹם:
הִנֵּה זֶה יָמִים רַבִּים וְאַרְיֻוֶשׁ מַלְכְּכֶם שָׁלַח סְפָרִים אֶל־חוֹנִיוֹ כֹּהֵן הַגָּדוֹל לֵאמֹר כִּי אֲנָשִׁים אַחִים אֲנַחְנוּ כַּכָּתוּב בְּמִשְׁנֵה הַסֵּפֶר אֲשֶׁר מִתָּחַת: וְחוֹנִיוֹ שָׂמַח לִקְרַאת הַצִּיר אֲשֶׁר שָׁלַח וַיִּקַּח אֶת סֵפֶר הַבְּרִית וְהָאַהֲבָה מִיָּדוֹ: וְעַתָּה אִם־אָמְנָם לֹא־חָסַרְנוּ דָבָר וְתוֹרַת יְיָ אֲשֶׁר בְּיָדֵינוּ לְתַנְחוּמִים לָנוּ: לֹא חָדַלְנוּ מִשְׁלֹחַ לָכֶם אֶת־מַלְאָכֵינוּ אֵלֶּה לְחַדֵּשׁ וּלְחַזֵּק אֶת בְּרִית הָאַהֲבָה וְהָאַחֲוָה עִמָּכֶם פֶּן־נֵחָשֵׁב כְּזָרִים בְּעֵינֵיכֶם כִּי אָרְכוּ הַיָּמִים אֲשֶׁר שְׁלַחְתֶּם לָנוּ: לָכֵן דְּעִי־נָא כִּי כָל־שַׁבָּת וּמוֹעֵד אֲשֶׁר נַקְרִיב בָּהֶם קָרְבָּן לֵאלֹהִים וְנִזְכַּרְתֶּם נֵּס־אַתֶּם עַל־עֹלוֹתֵינוּ וּבִתְפִלָּתֵינוּ כַּאֲשֶׁר יָאוֹת לְהַעְתִּיר אֶל־יְיָ בְּעַד שְׁלוֹם הָאַחִים: כִּי בִּשְׁלוֹמָם וּבִכְבוֹדָם יָגֵל וְיִשְׂמַח לִבֵּנוּ: וְאַף כִּי צָרוֹת רַבּוֹת וְרָעוֹת עָבְרוּ עַל־נַפְשֵׁנוּ כִּי נִלְחַמְנוּ עִם כָּל־

הַמְּלָכִים מִסָּבִיב אֲשֶׁר קָמוּ עָלֵינוּ לְהַשְׁחִיתֵנוּ: לֹא עָלָה
עַל־לִבֵּנוּ לְהוֹגִיעַ אֶתְכֶם אוֹ אֶת־בַּעֲלֵי בְּרִיתֵנוּ לְבַקֵּשׁ
עֶזְרָה מִיָּדָם בַּמִּלְחָמוֹת הָאֵלֶּה: כִּי יְיָ אֱלֹהִים הָיָה בְּעוֹזְרֵינוּ
וְהִצִּילָנוּ מִכַּף צָרֵינוּ וַיַּכְנִיעֵם לְפָנֵינוּ: אוּלָם בִּשְׁלֹחַ כָּעֵת
אֶת־מַלְאָכֵינוּ אֶת־נוּמֶנְיוֹס בֶּן־אַנְטִיוֹכוֹס וְאֶת־אַנְטִיפַּטְרוֹס
בֶּן־יֵשׁוּעַ לְאַחֵינוּ בְּנֵי־רוֹמָא לְחַדֵּשׁ אֶת־בְּרִית הָאַהֲבָה
הַנּוֹשֶׁנֶת עִמָּהֶם: הִפְקַדְנוּ אוֹתָם לָלֶכֶת גַּם אֲלֵיכֶם לִשְׁאֹל
לִשְׁלוֹמְכֶם וְלָתֵת אֶת־הַסֵּפֶר הַזֶּה בְּיֶדְכֶם וּלְחַדֵּשׁ אֶת־
בְּרִיתֵנוּ אִתְּכֶם · וְאִם יִיטַב בְּעֵינֵיכֶם תָּשִׁיבוּ אֹתָנוּ דָּבָר:
וְזֹאת מִשְׁנֵה הַסֵּפֶר אֲשֶׁר שָׁלַח אַרְיָוֶשׁ לְחוֹנִיּוֹ:

אַרְיָוֶשׁ מֶלֶךְ אַשְׁפַּרְתָּא לְחוֹנִיּוֹ כֹּהֵן הַגָּדוֹל שָׁלוֹם:

מָצָאנוּ כָּתוּב בְּדִבְרֵי הַיָּמִים כִּי יֹשְׁבֵי אַשְׁפַּרְתָּא
וְהַיְּהוּדִים אֲנָשִׁים אַחִים הֵמָּה וְאַבְרָהָם אָב לִשְׁנֵיהֶם ·
וְעַתָּה כִּי־יָדַעְנוּ זֹאת הוֹאִילוּ־נָא וְכִתְבוּ לָנוּ הַשָּׁלוֹם
לָכֶם וְגַם אֲנַחְנוּ נִכְתֹּב לָכֶם: גּוֹרָל אֶחָד יִהְיֶה לְכֻלָּנוּ
מִקְנֵינוּ וְקִנְיָנֵנוּ יִהְיוּ לָכֶם וּמִקְנֵיכֶם וְקִנְיָנֵיכֶם יִהְיוּ לָנוּ
וְאָנֹכִי שָׁפַטְתִּי אֶל־נָכוֹן לְהוֹדִיעֲכֶם אֶת־כָּל־אֵלֶּה:

VI.

Tales from the Talmud.

מוּנְבַּז הַמֶּלֶךְ פָּתַח בִּשְׁנַת בַּצּוֹרֶת אֶת אוֹצְרוֹתָיו אֲשֶׁר
אָצַר הוּא וַאֲשֶׁר אָצְרוּ אֲבוֹתָיו, וְכִלְכֵּל בָּהֶן כָּל נֶפֶשׁ
רְעֵבָה, וַיָּבוֹאוּ אֵלָיו אֶחָיו הַנְּשִׂיאִים וַיִּגְעֲרוּ בּוֹ לֵאמֹר:
אֲבוֹתֶיךָ אָצְרוּ עַל אוֹצְרוֹת אֲבוֹתֵיהֶם וְאַתָּה פִּזַּרְתָּן, וַיַּעַן
אִיתָם הַמֶּלֶךְ, אֲבוֹתַי אָסְפוּ אוֹצְרוֹת כָּלוֹת וַאֲנִי אָסַפְתִּי
אוֹצְרוֹת לָנֶצַח נְצָחִים, אֲבוֹתַי טָמְנוּ בְּמָקוֹם שָׁיָד אָדָם
מַשֶּׁנֶת, וַאֲנִי טָמַנְתִּי בְּמָקוֹם שֶׁאֵין יָד אָדָם מַשֶּׁגֶת,
אֲבוֹתַי אָצְרוּ שֶׁאֵין עוֹשֶׂה פְּרִי, וַאֲנִי אָצַרְתִּי הָעוֹשֶׂה פְּרִי,
אֲבוֹתַי טָמְנוּ כֶּסֶף וְזָהָב, וַאֲנִי רָכַשְׁתִּי נְפָשׁוֹת, אֲבוֹתַי
אָסְפוּ לַאֲחֵרִים וַאֲנִי אָסַפְתִּי לְנַפְשִׁי, אֲבוֹתַי אָצְרוּ לְעוֹלָם
הַזֶּה, וַאֲנִי אָצַרְתִּי לְעוֹלָם הַבָּא:

(See Hebrew Tales, No. xviii. p. 53).

רַבִּי נַחְמָן בִּקֵּשׁ מִן רַבִּי יִצְחָק לְבָרְכוֹ, אָמַר לִי
אֶמְשׁוֹל לְךָ מָשָׁל, אָדָם אֶחָד הָיָה הוֹלֵךְ בַּמִּדְבָּר וְהָיָה
עָיֵף וְרָעֵב וְצָמֵא, וַיִּמְצָא עֵץ פְּרִי אֲשֶׁר פִּרְיָו הָיוּ מְתוּקִים
עַד מְאֹד וְצִלּוֹ יָפֶה, וּבְרֵכַת מַיִם עָבְרָה תַחְתָּיו: וַיֹּאכַל
מִפִּרְיוֹ וַיֵּשְׁתְּ מַיִם מִן הַבְּרֵכָה וַיֵּשֶׁב בְּצִלּוֹ, כַּאֲשֶׁר הָלַךְ
לְדַרְכּוֹ אָמַר, עֵץ! עֵץ! בַּמֶּה אֲבָרֶכְךָ? אִם בִּפְרִי מָתוֹק הֲלֹא

APPENDIX

הוּא לָךְ, וְאִם בְּצֵל יָפֶה הִנּוֹ לָךְ, וְאִם בִּבְרֵכַת מַיִם הִנֵּה
הִיא לָךְ, אַף בָּזֶה אֲבָרֶכְךָ, שֶׁכָּל הָעֵצִים אֲשֶׁר יִנָּטְעוּ
מִמְּךָ, יִהְיוּ כָמוֹךְ ּ וְאַף אַתָּה בַּמֶּה אֲבָרֶכְךָ? אִם בַּתּוֹרָה,
הִנֵּה הִיא לְךָ לְתִפְאֶרֶת ּ וְאִם בָּעוֹשֶׁר, הִנֵּה יֶשׁ־לְךָ עוֹשֶׁר,
אִם בְּבָנִים, הִנֵּה יֶשׁ־לְךָ בָּנִים, אַךְ מִי יִתֵּן וְיִהְיוּ יוֹצְאֵי
יְרֵכֶיךָ כָּמוֹךְ :

(See Hebrew Tales, No. xxxiii. p. 93).

VII.

FABLES*.

מָשָׁל שְׁנֵי צְבָאִים

אֱוִיל מַחֲרִישׁ חָכָם יֵחָשֵׁב, וּבְמוֹשַׁב נְבוֹנִים יִתְיַשֵּׁב :

שְׁנֵי צְבָאִים, עָמְדוּ עַל שְׂפָיִים, מִתְלַחֲשִׁים בַּלָּט
דִּבְרֵיהֶם, אֵין שֹׁמֵעַ בֵּינֵיהֶם, וְאָזְנוֹ זֶה אֶל זֶה חִבֵּרוּ, לְהַגִּיד
לוֹ דְבָרוּ, וַיַּעֲבֹר אִישׁ עֲלֵיהֶם, וַיֵּלֶךְ לִשְׁאֹל לָהֶם, לָמָּה
דִבְּרוּ בַלָּט עֲצָתָם, כִּי אֵין מֵלִיץ בֵּינוֹתָם, גַּם כִּי יִצְעֲקוּ
בְּכָל־כֹּחָם, אֵין שׁוֹמֵעַ דִּבְרֵי שִׂיחָם, כִּי מֵאָדָם הֵם רְחוֹקִים,
וַיַּעֲנוּ הִנְנוּ נִדְבָּקִים, לְהַמְתִּיק סוֹדֵנוּ יַחַד, וּמְגַלֶּה סּוֹד
אֵין אֶחָד, אֲבָל הָעֵצָה אֲשֶׁר לָנוּ, בַּעֲבוּר כִּי נִרְפִּים אֲנַחְנוּ :

---

* These Fables are extracted from a work entitled מִשְׁלֵי שׁוּעָלִים.
It contains 107 Fables, all written in the same style. Name of the
author— *R. Berachia Hannakdan*. (See Wolf. Bib. Heb. No. 435).

חֲכַם בְּנִי וּבִין דֵּעָה, קְנֵה אֱמֶת וְתֹם דֵּעָה
חָשׁוּב אֱוִיל כִּצֵל אֱלִיל, וּמָן עֲצַת כְּסִיל שְׁעֵה
וְאִם יָצוּ הֲרֹס בְּנֵה, וְאֶל נְבוֹן דְּבַר שְׁעֵה:

מָשָׁל עוֹרֵב וְכִבְשָׂה

עֵצָה נוֹתֵן לְלֹא שׁוֹאֵל, פֶּתִי נֶחֱשָׁב וְנוֹאֵל:

עוֹרֵב יָשַׁב עַל גַּב כִּבְשָׂה, שִׁמְעוּ נָא אֶת־אֲשֶׁר עָשָׂה, מָשַׁךְ וּמָרַט הַצֶּמֶר, מֵעַל צַוָּארָהּ וַתֹּאמֶר, עוֹרֵב הַפֶּרֶד מֵעָלַי, וּשְׁמַע אֲמָרַי וּמִלַּי, וְכֵן תַּעֲשֶׂה אִם יֶשׁ־לְךָ לֵב, לֵךְ וְשֵׁב עַל גַּב הַכֶּלֶב, וּמְשֹׁךְ מֵעַל גַּבּוֹ צִמְרוֹ, וְלֹא תַשְׁאִיר לוֹ רַק עוֹרוֹ, וַיֹּאמֶר הָעוֹרֵב לֹא אֶעֱשֶׂה כָּךְ, כִּי תִרְעַצֵנִי לְפִי דַרְכֵּךְ, צִמְרֵךְ רִאשׁוֹן מְצָאתִיהָ, פֹּה אֵשֵׁב כִּי אִוִּיתִיהָ, טוֹבָה עֲצָתִי מֵעֲצָתֵךְ, בַּכֶּלֶב לֹא אַחֲלִיף וְלֹא אָמִיר אוֹתָךְ:

VIII.

Anecdotes, &c.

פִּילוֹסוֹף אֶחָד רָאָה בָחוּר מַרְבֶּה דְּבָרִים, אָמַר לוֹ בְּנִי הִזָּהֵר, הֲלֹא אֱלֹהִים עָשָׂה לָנוּ שְׁתֵּי אָזְנַיִם, וּפֶה אֶחָד, לְמַעַן נִשְׁמַע הַרְבֵּה וּנְדַבֵּר מְעָט: גַּם הוּא־לְאֶחָד אֲשֶׁר שָׁאַל כַּמָּה רָחוֹק הָאֱמֶת מִן הַשֶּׁקֶר־הֵשִׁיב, כְּמוֹ מִן הָעֵינַיִם אֶל הָאָזְנָיִם:

מֵבִיא חֵטְא הַמַּרְבֶּה דְּבָרִים
וְטוֹב לִרְאוֹת מִשְּׁמֹעַ אֲמָרִים

סוֹקְרַאטִיס הָיָה אוֹמֵר כָּל־יְדִיעָתִי הִיא שֶׁאֵינִי יוֹדֵעַ:
וַיְהִי כַּאֲשֶׁר זָקֵן וְקָרְבוּ יָמָיו לָמוּת אָטַר צַר לִי מְאֹד, כִּי
עַתָּה הָיִיתִי מַתְחִיל לִלְמֹד אוֹרַח חַיִּים ·
חָכָם, בְּעֵינָיו סָכָל
וְחָכָם בְּעֵינָיו, סָכָל:

מַטְרוֹנָה אַחַת הָיְתָה בּוֹכָה וּמִתְאַבֶּלֶת עַל בַּעֲלָהּ
הַחוֹלֶה, וּבְמַר נַפְשָׁהּ צָעֲקָה מָוֶת! מָוֶת! לוּ תִּקָּחֵנִי תַּחַת
אִישִׁי · הַמָּוֶת שָׁמַע וַיָּבֹא וַיֹּאמֶר הִנֵּנִי, וַתֶּחֱרַד הָאִשָּׁה מְאֹד
וַתֹּאמֶר אֵלָיו, לֶךְ־נָא וְאַרְאֶךָ הָאִישׁ אֲשֶׁר אַתָּה מְבַקֵּשׁ
רַבִּים מְחַפִּים לָמָוֶת וְאֵינֶנּוּ
וּבְבֹאוֹ פַּחַד יִפְחֲדוּ מִמֶּנּוּ:

שָׁאֲלוּ לְחָכָם מִי הֵם הַחֲשׁוּבִים הַחֲכָמִים אוֹ הָעֲשִׁירִים?
וַיַּעַן, הַחֲכָמִים: אָמְרוּ לוֹ אִם כֵּן לָמָּה הַחֲכָמִים בְּפִתְחֵי
הָעֲשִׁירִים יוֹתֵר מִמַּה שֶׁהָעֲשִׁירִים בְּפִתְחֵי הַחֲכָמִים?
וַיֹּאמֶר, הַחֲכָמִים יוֹדְעִים מַעֲלַת הָעֹשֶׁר, אֲבָל הָעֲשִׁירִים
אֵינָם יוֹדְעִים מַעֲלַת הַחָכְמָה:
לְמוֹר מִפִּי שֶׁיּוֹדֵעַ, וְלַמֵּד לְמִי שֶׁאֵינוֹ יוֹדֵעַ, וְאִם תַּעֲשֶׂה
זֹאת תֵּדַע מַה שֶׁלֹּא יָדַעְתָּ, וְתִזְכּוֹר אֶת אֲשֶׁר יָדַעְתָּ:

IX.

Moral Maxims*.

מוּסַר הַשָֹכֵּל בִּמְלִיצָה :

אֲמָרַי	בְּנִי רֵאשִׁית	יְרָא הָאֵל
אֲמָרַי :	וְשִׁמְעָה מַ־	לְכָה קוּמָה
תְּחִלָּה	עֲבוֹדָתָךְ	וְתֵן עַל כָּל־
תְּפִלָּה	אֱלֹהֶיךָ	בְּכָל יוֹם לְ־
שְׁחָרָךְ	לְהַשְׁכִּים כָּל־	וְעָלָיו
חֲסוֹרָךְ :	וְעָלָיו מַ־	לְהוֹדוֹת לוֹ
מְחַלֶּה	פְּנֵי הָאֵל	הֱיֵה תָמִיד
יְמַלֵּא :	אֱלוֹתֶיךָ	וְאָז כָּל־מִשְׁ־
וְתוֹרָה	שְׁמוֹר מִצְוָה	שְׁמוֹר חוּקָה
צְרוּרָה :	תְּהִי נַפְשְׁךָ	וְדַע כִּי בָם
פְּלִילִים	אֲצִילֵי עַם	וְהִתְרָע בָּךְ
כְּסִילִים :	וְאַל תֵּט אֶל	דְּבַק בָּהֶם
חֲכָמִים	נְךָ אֶל פִּי	תְּהִי נָא אָזְ־
לְשָׁמַיִם	אֲסוֹף מֵהֶם	וְעֵינָיךָ תָ־
וְגוּרָךְ	בְּכָל שִׁבְתָּךְ	וְקַנֵּא בָם
חֲבֵרָךְ :	תְּקַנֵּא בַ־	בְּכִיסְךָ אַל

---

* From מַאֲמַר הַשֹכֵּל, a didatic poem, by the celebrated *R. Hāi*, who flourished about the beginning of the eleventh century.

בְּמֶלַח פַּת	אֱכוֹל וּרְעֵה	עֲשָׂבִים
וְאַל תִּשְׁאַל	אֲגוֹרָה מְ־	נְדִיבִים :
בְּחַר מָוֶת	וְהִטָּמֵן	בְּקִבְרְךָ
וְאַל תֵּלֵךְ	לְבַקֵּשׁ מְ־	שְׁאֵרֶךָ :
וְלָמָּה תִ־	הְיֶה שׁוֹאֵל	לִשׁוֹאֵל
שְׁאַל מֵאֵל	הֲלֹא הַכֹּל	בְּיַד אֵל :

X.

The 8th Psalm Paraphrased*.

1.—יי אדנינו מה אדיר שמך וכו'

אָדוֹן עַל כָּל־נִבְרָא אָדוֹן עָלֵינוּ
כַּמָּה נוֹרָא שִׁמְךָ עַל כָּל־הָאָרֶץ
כִּי אֵלֶיךָ הַהוֹד וַיִּפְרֹץ פָּרֶץ
עַל הַשָּׁמַיִם מוּל מַרְאֵה עֵינֵינוּ :

2.—מפי עוללים ויונקים יסדת עז וכו'

מִפִּי כָּל־עוֹלֵל כָּל־יוֹנֵק יִסַּדְתָּ
עֹז מוּל כָּל־שׂנֵא וּלְמַעַן צָרֶיךָ
לְשַׁבִּית אוֹיֵב מִתְנַקֵּם מֵעָלֶיךָ
וּבְכֵן זֵדִים שׁוֹגִים רֶגַע אִבַּדְתָּ :

---

* From פְּהִנַּת אַבְרָהָם, a poetical paraphrase of the whole of the Psalms, by *R. Abraham Ben Shabthi Hacohen*. This work, written in almost every kind of metre, evinces uncommon skill and a wonderful command of language, and is therefore deservedly esteemed.

APPENDIX.

3.—כי אראה שמיך מעשה אצבעותיך וכו׳

כִּי אֵל שָׁמֶיךָ הָרָמִים תְּבַנֵּת
פֹּעַל אֶצְבַּע שַׂדַי אֶשָּׂא עֵינַיִם
כִּי מִשְׁתָּאֶה אַבִּיט גֹּבַהּ שָׁמָיִם
לִרְאוֹת יָרֵחַ כּוֹכָבִים כּוֹנַנְתָּ׃

4.—מה אנוש כי תזכרנו וכו׳

מָה אִישׁ כִּי תִזְכֹּר לוֹ בִּמְעוֹן הַקֹּדֶשׁ
וַתֵּט אוֹן אֵלָיו מֵאֶשְׁנַב שַׁחַק
מָה בֶּן־אָדָם אֱנוֹשׁ אָבָק וָשַׁחַק
לִפְקֹד אֹתוֹ כָּל־יוֹם כָּל־לֵיל כָּל־חֹדֶשׁ׃

5.—ותחסרהו טעם מאלהים וכו׳

וַתֶּחְסַר לוֹ כִּמְעַט לִהְיוֹתוֹ עֶבֶד
לָאֵל, וּכְמוֹ מַלְאָךְ וּמְשָׁרֵת צֶדֶק
כָּבוֹד עִטַּרְתָּ לּוֹ עַל אֶרֶץ חֶדֶק
כֶּתֶר הָדָר אֵלָיו נָתַתָּ זֶבֶד׃

6.—תמשילהו במעשי ידיך וכו׳

תַּמְשִׁילֵהוּ עַל כָּל־פֹּעַל יָדֶיךָ
תַּחַת רַגְלָיו כָּל־דָּבָר שַׁתָּה
הַכֹּל לִכְבוֹד שִׁמְךָ בָּרָאתָ אַתָּה
וַתִּתֶּן לוֹ כָּל־הַנִּקְרָא בְּשִׁמֶךָ׃

APPENDIX.

7.—צנח ואלפים לכם וכו׳

צֹאן וָאַלּוּף כֻּלָּם נֶגְדּוֹ יִכְרָעוּ
גַּם כָּל־חַיְתוֹ שָׂדָה יָרְדָה בַּכֹּחַ
צֶפַע תַּנִּין וּכְפִיר יִרְמֹס בַּחוּט
שַׁחַל וָפָתָן מִפָּנָיו נִכְנָעוּ :

8.—צפור שמים ודגי הים וכו׳

צִפּוֹר שָׁמַיִם לוֹ וּדְגֵי הַנָּהָר
עֹבֵר אָרְחוֹת יַמִּים אֵלָיו שׁוֹמֵעַ
יִמְשׁוֹךְ לְוָיָתָן לוֹ מַיִם נוֹבֵעַ
וּתְבוּאוֹת שֶׁמֶשׁ לוֹ עִם גֶּרֶשׁ סָהַר :

9.—יי אדנינו מה אדיר שמך וכו׳

אָדוֹן עַל כָּל־אָדוֹן אֵל חַי מַלְכֵּנוּ
כַּמָּה אַדִּיר שִׁמְךָ בִּגְדוּדֵי מַטָּה
אִם עַל הָאָרֶץ בִּרְכַּת אֵל שָׁקְטָה
כַּמָּה נוֹרָא שֵׁם אֵל עַל כָּל־אַרְצֵנוּ :

XI.

TRUTH*.

מִן הָאֲנָמִים לַעֲלוֹת יִינָעוּ
אֵידִים חֲשׁוּכִים אֶל פְּנֵי רָקִיעַ,

---

* From קוֹל מוּסָר, by *R. Simson Cohen Modun.* The work contains 50 Odes and Sonnets, all composed in the same elegant style.

APPENDIX. 275

אַךְ זָרְחָה שֶׁמֶשׁ, וְאוֹר תּוֹפִיעַ,
נָסוּ צְלָלִים, אַפְסוּ נָעוּ:

מִן הָרְשָׁעִים, כִּי בְּבֹץ הָטְבָּעוּ,
קִיטוֹר כְּזָבִים יַעֲלֶה יַרְקִיעַ,
אַךְ הָאֱמֶת תִּזְרַח וְקוֹל תָּרִיעַ,
נָסוּ שְׁקָרִים רָחֲקוּ נִכְנָעוּ:

אִמְרֵי אֱמֶת זָהָב בָּכוּר נִצְרָפוּ
יִבָּחֲנוּ הֵיטִיב וְיִתַּמָּמוּ;
יִתְכּוֹנְנוּ לָעַד וְלֹא חָלָפוּ:

סִיגֵי שְׁקָרִים נִתְּכוּ חִישׁ תַּמּוּ,
מֵעַד אֱמוּנִים יִבְרְחוּ נָגְפוּ;
אַנְשֵׁי אֱמֶת עַל כֵּן לְנֵס הוּרָמוּ:

XII.

Hope and Fear*.

יִרְאָה וְתִקְוָה תּוֹךְ לְבָבִי צָבְאוּ
יוֹם יוֹם, וְלֹא אֶשְׁקוֹט וְלֹא אַרְגִּיעַ:
זֹאת תַּחֲזִיק אוֹתִי, וְזֹאת תַּכְנִיעַ·
אַךְ זוֹ לָזוֹ צָרוֹת, וְקוֹלָן נָשָׂאוּ:

---

* See the preceding Note.

T

אִידְרָא יְמֵי רָעָה, וְלֹא יִתְמַהְמְהוּ;
אָבְטַח, וְאוֹר פִּתְחֵי עֶדֶן יוֹפִיעַ·
אֶרְעַד לְיוֹם מִיתָה לְחַי יַגִּיעַ,
אֶחְסֶה בְּאֵל חוֹנֵן, חֲסָדָיו נִפְלָאוּ:

קִוּוּ זְמַמַּי, בַּנְּעִימִים אֶשְׂמְחָה,
אָכֵן שְׂעִיפַּי יָרְאוּ נִבְהָלוּ:
מִתְהַפּוּכוֹת עֵת, וְחָכְמָה נִסְרְחָה:

עוֹד כָּל־יְמֵי אֶרֶץ, וְלֹא יֶחְדָּלוּ,
תִּקְוָה וְיִרְאָה זֹאת לָזֹאת לֹא נָצָחָה;
עַד־כִּי בְּנֵי אִישׁ לַשְׁאוֹל יוּבָלוּ:

XIII.

The Contented Shepherd.

רוֹעֶה עֲדָרָיו נַעַר
אֵין מִמֶּנַּת חֶלְקוֹ טוֹבָה בָּאָרֶץ:
כָּל־מַחְשָׁבוֹת לִבּוֹ תַּשְׁפִּילֶנָּה שָׁבַת;
בַּל־תַּחְמוֹד נַפְשׁוֹ בִּגְדוֹלוֹת לֶכֶת,
כִּי אִם רְעוֹת צֹאנוֹ אֶל עֵין הַמַּיִם,
וּלְפִיו חֲלָבָם קַחַת·
יַבִּיט כְּצֵאת אָדוֹם מַקְדִּים שֶׁמֶשׁ·

---

* From לִישָׁרִים תְּהִלָּה by *Moses Chaim Luzzato.*

מַעְיָן אֲשֶׁר נֶאֶמְנוּ
מֵימָיו, וְלֹא יְכַזְבוּ ׃
יָשׁוּר בְּלֵב שָׂמֵחַ ׃
הָלוֹךְ וְנַגֵּן כְּמִתְהַלֵּךְ אֶל רֶגֶל
צֹאנוֹ, כְּמַרְעִיתָם עֵינָיו יִבְחָנוּ
עִשְׂבֵּי הֲרָרָיו, אַף שִׂפְתוֹתָיו שֶׁבַח
אֶל יוֹצְרָם תַּבַּעֶנָה ׃
אַשְׁרָיו וּמָה טוּבוֹ, כַּמָּה יִמְתָּקוּ
לוֹ כָּל־יְמֵי חַיָּיו, כַּמָּה יַרְגִּיעַ ׃
כִּי כָּל־אֲשֶׁר תַּהְפּוֹךְ תֵּבֵל הַלֵּזוּ
עָלָיו מְסִיבּוֹתֶיהָ
יִבְזֶה וְלֹא יָחוּשׁ, לֹא יֵדַע רֹגֶז,
יִשְׂמַח בְּעָנְיוֹ, כִּי לֹא חָמַד עֹשֶׁר ׃
קִנְאָה וְכָבוֹד לֹא לִבּוֹ יַלְחָצוּ ׃
טוֹב לוֹ מְלוּנָתוֹ מֵהֵיכַל מֶלֶךְ,
מַקְלוֹ וְיַלְקוּטוֹ מִבִּגְדֵי חֹפֶשׁ ׃
עַלְמָה אֲשֶׁר לוֹ חֶבֶל
תָּפוּל, הֲלֹא לָבֶטַח
בָּהּ יַעֲלוֹז לִבּוֹ, בּוֹ לִבָּהּ יָגֵל ׃
אֵין מַחֲרִיד לָהֶם, רָע לֹא יֵדָעוּ ׃
סָבִיב לְשֻׁלְחָנָם כִּשְׁתִילֵי זַיִת
זַרְעָם מְלֵאֵי גִיל יִרְאוּ יַבִּיטוּ,
עַל נַחֲלַת חֶלְקָם כָּל־עֵת כָּל־רֶגַע,
לִמְחוֹנְנָם תּוֹדוֹת אֶלֶף יִתֵּנוּ ׃

XIV.

Rules of Life.*

מִי זֶה הָאִישׁ שֹׁחֵר שָׁלוֹם עַד קָבֶר,
לָשֶׁבֶת בֶּטַח כָּל־יָמָיו מִסַּעַר,
פֹּה בִּדְרָכַי תֵּלֵךְ אַל תֵּט אֶל עֵבֶר,
כִּי זֶה הֵיכַל כָּל־טוֹב, אַף זֶה הַשָּׁעַר:

עַל הוֹן תָּשִׂישׂ, רַק לֹא תֵחַת עַל שֶׁבֶר,
אַתָּה תִתְחַכָּם, רַק לֹא תָבוּז אִישׁ בַּעַר,
בַּנֹּעַם תִּתְרָאֶה לִקְרַאת כָּל־גֶּבֶר,
אֶת־הַיָּשִׁישׁ תֶּהְדַּר, תָּחוֹן הַנַּעַר:

אַל נָא תַּהֲגֶה אִם לֹא וְתִשְׁפֹּט כָּל־אֹמֶר,
אַל נָא תִשְׁפֹּט אִם לֹא תַחְקֹר כָּל־טַעַם,
אַל נָא תַחְקֹר אֶת־הַנִּשְׂגָּב מֵחֹמֶר:

אִם יֵשׁ עַוְלָתָה בָּךְ, אַחַר אַל תֵּכַח,
אִם זָר שִׁמְךָ נָאֵץ אַל תֵּט בַּזַעַם,
שִׁיתָה תָּמִיד יִרְאַת שַׁדַּי אֶל נֹכַח:

---

* From אֵלֶּה בְּנֵי הַנְּעוּרִים, by *Ephraim Luzzato*. This work is very scarce, and is deservedly esteemed for its elegant diction and poetic beauties.

XV.

The Metamorphosed Physician.*

יַלְדָה יָפָה אַחַת וּמְאֹד אֹהֶבֶת
בָּאָה בֵּיתָה רוֹפֵא מָזוֹר לָקַחַת,
לֵאמֹר, כִּי זֶה יָמִים נַפְשָׁהּ כּוֹאֶבֶת,
אַף בַּלֵּילוֹת רָחַק מִמֶּנָּה נַחַת:

עוֹד הַשֶּׁגַל הַזֹּאת אֶצְלוֹ נִצֶּבֶת,
שָׁלַח יָדוֹ לַחְקֹר אִם יֵשׁ קַדַּחַת:
וַתִּצַּת בְּלִבָּבוֹ פִּתְאֹם שַׁלְהֶבֶת,
אָהַב, נִלְכַּד גַּם הוּא אֶל תּוֹךְ הַפַּחַת:

נִדְהָם אַף מִשְׁתָּאֶה הָיָה הַגֶּבֶר;
עַד הַחוֹלָה שֵׁנִית הֵטִיבָה טַעַם,
בִּי הָאָדוֹן, הַאֵין מַרְפֵּא לַשֶּׁבֶר?

אָז הוּא: הָהּ רַעְיָתִי אַל נָא תַחְשׁוֹכִי
חִבְּשִׁי אַתְּ אֶת־פִּצְעִי; אָמְנָם הַפַּעַם
לֹא הָרוֹפֵא, אַךְ הַחוֹלֶה אָנֹכִי:

See the preceding note.

XVI.

Philanthropy*.

יְיָ אָהֵב גֵּר, לָתֵת לוֹ לֶחֶם
לָתֵת לוֹ שִׂמְלָה, כִּי כוֹנְנוּ בְרָחֵם
כַּאֲשֶׁר כּוֹנֵן אֶזְרָח, כּוֹנֵן מַלְכֵּהוּ,
גַּם אֲסִיר בּוֹר, יַעֲבִידוּ בוֹ בְּפָרֶךְ,
אִם יְרֵא אֱלֹהִים הוּא וּתְמִים דָּרֶךְ,
יְיָ עוֹזֵר לוֹ, יִשְׁעוֹ יַרְאֵהוּ:

כֶּחָצִיר כָּאָרֶז אֲשֶׁר יִפְרָחוּ
מִטַּל, וּמִמְּטַר שָׁמַיִם יִצְמָחוּ
עַל שָׁפֵל עַל נִשָּׂא עָבִים נָזָלוּ:
בֵּן כָּל־אָדָם, טוּבָם מֵעַל יִינָקוּ
עַמִּים כֻּלָּם בְּחֶפְצֵיהֶם יִדְבָּקוּ
וַיְיָ טוֹב לַכֹּל, אִם טוֹב פָּעָלוּ:

אִם מֵרֹאשׁ נִבְרָא הָאָדָם בַּצֶּלֶם
מַדּוּעַ נִשְׁאַל בֶּן מִי זֶה הָעֶלֶם?
מִפִּי נָחַל כָּבוֹד, מִי זֶה עִטְּרֵהוּ?

---

* From שִׁירֵי תִפְאֶרֶת, by *Hartwig Wessley*.

רוּחַ אָדָם יֵשׁ בּוֹ, חֵלֶק מִמַּעַל:
לוֹ מִמִּזְרָח שֶׁמֶשׁ—לוֹ מַיִם יַעַל,
חָכְמָתוֹ עָמְדָה לוֹ, צִדְקוֹ גִדְּלֵהוּ:

רֹאשׁ יִשְׁרֵי לֵב בֶּן־מִי הָיָה؟ בֶּן תֶּרַח—
מִנְּוֵה עֹבֵד אֵל זָר יָצָא פָּרַח
וַיְהִי לְעֵץ חַיִּים אֶל יוֹשְׁבֵי חָלֶד:
כִּי חָכְמָה תִּפְרֶה טוֹב גַּם בִּמְשׁוּכַת חֶדֶק؟
מִמֶּלֶךְ זָקֵן וּכְסִיל בּוֹזֶה צֶדֶק
מַה יָּקַר אִישׁ חָכָם מִסְכֵּן וָיָלֶד:

אִם צוּרֵי הַחַלָּמִישׁ אֵין בָּהֶם לֵיחַ ·
וּבְשׁוֹאָה וּמְשׁוֹאָה אֵין פִּרְחֵי רֵיחַ,
בֵּין כָּל־עַם שׁוֹבָב יֵשׁ מֵטִיב מַעֲשֵׂהוּ ·
אֵיפֹה אֶרֶץ רָעָה, רַבַּת אִוֶּלֶת,
אוֹ אַיֵּה מַמְלָכָה אָוֶן פּוֹעֶלֶת,
לֹא יֻלַּד בָּהּ אוֹהֵב אֵל וּמְכַבְּדֵהוּ؟

עַמִּים כֻּלָּם מֵאָב אֶחָד יָצָאוּ؛
אִם אֶל מוּסַר אֲבוֹתָם לֹא שָׁמָעוּ,
אֶת־תִּפְאֶרֶת אֲבוֹתָם לֹא אָבָדוּ:
אֶחָד מִמִּשְׁפַּחְתָּם יֵיטִיב מַעֲשֵׂהוּ
בִּדְמוּת אֲבוֹתָיו הוּא, אָהוֹב קְנֵהוּ
תּוֹעִים יָשִׁיב אֶל אֵל, צֶדֶק יְלַמְּדוּ:—וכו׳

XVII.

SEVERINII BOETII

DE CONSOLATIONE PHILOSOPHIÆ.

CARMEN QUINTUM LIBRI QUINTI.

Quam variis terras animalia permeant figuris!
Namque alia extento sunt corpore, pulveremque verrunt,
Continuumque trahunt vi pectoris incitata sulcum,
Sunt quibus alarum levitas vaga, verberetque ventos,
Et liquido longi spacia ætheris enatet volatu.

Hæc pressisse solo vestigia gressibus gaudent,
Vel virides campos transmittere, vel subire silvas.
Quæ variis videas licet omnia discrepare formis,
Prona tamen facies hebetes valet ingravare sensus.

Unica gens hominum celsum levat altius cacumen,
Atque levis recto stat corpore, despicitque terras,
Hæc nisi terrenus male desipis admonet figura.

Qui recto cœlum vultu petis, exerisque frontem,
In sublime feras animum quoque; ne gravata pessum
Inferior sidat mens corpore seltius levato.

XVII.

תרגום:

שָׁנּוּ צוּרוֹת חַיּוֹת לָזוּ מִלָּזוּ,
יֵשׁ עַל־נָחוֹן זוֹחֵל עָפָר יְלַחֵכוּ
יֵשׁ כָּנָף יִפְרְשׂוּן, מָרוֹם יְהַלֵּכוּ,
כֹּה וָכֹה יַכּוּ רוּחַ וִיפַזֵּזוּ:

יֵשׁ לִצְעֹד בָּאֲדָמָה עָלוֹ עָלָזוּ,
יָשׁוּטוּ בַיְּעָרִים, שָׂדוֹת יִדְרְכוּ:
כֻּלָּן חַיּוֹת הַחֲמָרִיּוֹת, יַהְפְּכוּ
אַרְצָה פְּנֵימוֹ, שְׂאֵת רֹאשׁ לֹא הֵעֵזוּ:

וַיַּבְדֵּל אָדָם זָקוּף לָלֶכֶת;
יִמְאַס אַדְמַת עָפָר, יַבִּיט שָׁמַיִם:
זִכְרוֹן לָנוּ בַּל־נִטְבַּע בָּרֶפֶשׁ:

אַתָּה, כִּי לִשְׁחָקִים תִּשָּׂא עֵינַיִם,
רָם הַקּוֹמָה, רוֹמֵם גַּם אֶת־הַנֶּפֶשׁ
אֵיךְ יִגְבַּהּ גֹּלֶם, וּתְהִי זֹאת מָשְׁלֶכֶת:

שמואל דוד לוצאטו

XVIII.

GOD SAVE THE KING.

God save our noble King
William! Long live the King,
  God save the King!
Send him victorious,
Happy and glorious,
Long to reign over us,
  God save the King!

O Lord our God arise,
Scatter his enemies,
  And make them fall!
Confound their politics,
Frustrate their knavish tricks,
On him our hearts are fix'd,
  O save us all!

Thy choicest gifts in store
On him be pleased to pour,
  Long may he reign!

XVIII.

אל שמר המלך

אֵל שְׁמֹר וְיִלְיָם מַלְכֵּנוּ ׃
לְעוֹלָם יְהִי מַלְכֵּנוּ ׃
אֵל שְׁמֹר הַמֶּלֶךְ ׃
שְׁלַח שָׁלוֹם בְּנָוֵהוּ ׃
בְּעֹז וְהָדָר עַטְּרֵהוּ ׃
לָעַד הַמְשִׁילֵהוּ ׃
אֵל שְׁמֹר הַמֶּלֶךְ ׃

אָנָּא אֱלֹהִים קוּמָה ׃
בְּאוֹיְבָיו תְּנָה מְהוּמָה ׃
וְהַפִּילֵמוֹ ׃
הָפֵר תַּחְבֻּלֹתָם ׃
סַכֶּל־נָא עֲצָתָם ׃
לְעַמּוֹ תֵּן מִשְׁאֲלֹתָם ׃
וְהוֹשִׁיעֵמוֹ ׃

מִבְחַר בִּרְכָתְךָ אֵל !
לְהָרִיק עָלָיו הוֹאֵל ׃
לָעַד יִמְלוֹךְ !

May he defend our laws,
And ever give us cause
To sing with heart and voice,
  God save the King!

O, grant him long to see
Friendship and unity
  Always increase!
May he his sceptre sway,
All loyal souls obey,
Join heart and voice, huzza!
  God save the King!

XIX.
LA TOURTERELLE ET LE PASSANT.

LE PASSANT.
Que fais tu dans ce bois, plaintive tourterelle?

LA TOURTERELLE.
Je gémis: j'ai perdu ma compagne fidèle.

LE PASSANT.
Ne crains tu point que l'oiseleur
Ne te fasse mourir comme elle?

LA TOURTERELLE.
Si ce n'est lui, ce fera ma douleur.

יָגֵן בְּעַד חָקֵינוּ ׃
אָז יִשְׂמַח לִבֵּנוּ ׃
וְנָשִׁיר בְּכָל מְאֹדֵנוּ ׃
אֵל שְׁמֹר הַמֶּלֶךְ ׃

עוֹד עֵינָיו תֶּחֱזֶינָה
יְדִידוּת וְאַחְוָה תִרְבֶּינָה
בְּכָל עִיר וָפֶלֶךְ ׃
יֶרֶךְ שִׁבְטוֹ בִּגְדֻלָּה ׃
נַעַבְדֶנּוּ בְּגִילָה ׃
וְנָרֹן בְּקוֹל צָהֳלָה ׃
אֵל שְׁמוֹר הַמֶּלֶךְ ׃

H.

XIX.

הַתּוֹר וְהַהֵלֶךְ ׃

החלך
מַה לְּתוֹרִי כִּי בַיַּעַר זֶה אֵבֶל הִגְדִּילָה ?
התור
נִגְדַּע הוֹדִי, רֵעִי וְדוֹדִי, לָזֹאת אֵילִילָה ׃
החלך
וְאֶת הַצַּיָּד אֲשֶׁר לָקַח מַחְמַד עֵינָיִךְ
הֲלֹא תִירָאִי, כִּי יִשְׁפּוֹךְ גַּם אֶת־דָּמַיִךְ ?
התור
אִם הוּא לֹא יְהַרְגֵנִי, הֲלֹא הַיָּגוֹן יְמִיתֵנִי ׃

H.

XX.

Morgengedanken.

Der Mond verbirgt sein Licht, der Nebel grauer Schleier
    Deckt Luft und Erde nicht mehr zu;
Der Sterne Glanz erbleicht, der Sonne reges Feuer
    Stört alle Wesen aus der Ruh.

Der Himmel färbet sich mit Purpur und Saphiren,
    Die frühe Morgenröthe lacht,
Und vor der Rosen Glanz, die ihre Stirne zieren,
    Entflieht das blasse Heer der Nacht.

Durch's rothe Morgenthor der heitern Sternenbühne
    Naht das verklärte Licht der Welt;
Die falben Wolken glühn von blitzendem Rubine,
    Und brennend Gold bedeckt das Feld.

Die Rosen öffnen sich und spiegeln an der Sonne
    Des kühlen Morgens Perlenthau;
Der Liljen Ambradampf belebt zu unsrer Wonne
    Der zarten Blätter Atlasgrau.

Der wache Landmann eilt mit Singen in die Felder,
    Und treibt vergnügt den schweren Pflug;
Der Vögel rege Schaar erfüllet Luft und Wälder
    Mit ihrer Stimm' und frühem Flug.

XX.

רַעְיוֹנֵי שַׁחַר:

הַיָּרֵחַ שׁוֹאֵף אֶל מְקוֹמוֹ לְהִסְתַּתֵּר,
וְעַרְפָּל הַמְכַסֶּה תֵבֵל הָלַךְ לוֹ;
כֹּכְבֵי שָׁמַיִם בְּמִסְפָּם אָסְפוּ נָגְהָם,
וּמוֹצָא שֶׁמֶשׁ עוֹרֵר כָּל־יְשֵׁנֵי אָרֶץ:

הַשָּׁמַיִם לָבְשׁוּ סַפִּיר וְאַרְגָּמָן,
עַפְעַפֵּי שַׁחַר שָׂשִׂים וּמְשִׂיבִים כָּל־חָי,
וְכֹכְבֵי בֹקֶר אָבְדוּ הִלָּם, נָסִים
מִלִּפְנֵי הוֹד הֲדָרַת פְּנֵיהֶם:

בְּשַׁעֲרֵי זְבוּל כּוֹכָבִים אָדְמוּ מִפְּנִינִים
הַשֶּׁמֶשׁ מֵחֻפָּתוֹ שָׂשׂ לָרוּץ אֹרַח,
עָבֵי שְׁחָקִים מַבְרִיקִים כִּבְרַק אָדֵם
וּכְזָהָב מוּפָז כִּסָּה אֶת פְּנֵי הַשָּׂדֶה:

פִּתְּחוּ הַשּׁוֹשַׁנִּים, וְנוֹצְצִים לִקְרָאתוֹ
אֶגְלֵי טַל בֹּקֶר אֲשֶׁר עֲלֵיהֶם שׁוֹכְבִים:
הַדּוּדָאִים נָתְנוּ רֵיחַ, נוֹזְלִים בְּשָׂמִים,
וְעוֹלֵז הַשָּׂדֶה וְכֹל אֲשֶׁר בּוֹ צוֹמֵחַ:

יָקִץ אִישׁ הַשָּׂדֶה לְמַהֵר לַעֲבוֹדָתוֹ
בְּקוֹל שִׁיר וְרַנֵּן מְפַתֵּחַ וּמְשַׂדֵּד אַדְמָתוֹ·
יַעַר וְכָל־עֵץ בּוֹ מְרִיעִים לְקוֹל צִפֳּרִים,
לָעוּף בְּמוּעָף, וְלָשִׁיר בְּשִׁירִים:

O Schöpfer! was ich seh', sind deiner Allmacht Werke,
    Du bist die Seele der Natur;
Der Sterne Lauf und Licht, der Sonne Glanz und Stärke,
    Sind deiner Hand Geschöpf' und Spur.

Du steckst die Fackel an, die in dem Mond' uns leuchtet,
    Du giebst den Winden Flügel zu,
Du liehst der Nacht den Thau, womit sie uns befeuchtet,
    Du theilst der Sterne Lauf und Ruh.

Du hast der Berge Stoff aus Thon und Staub gedrehet,
    Der Schachten Erz aus Sand geschmelzt;
Du hast das Firmament an seinem Ort erhöhet,
    Der Wolken Kleid darum gewälzt.

Dem Fisch, der Ströme bläs't und mit dem Schwanze stürmet,
    Hast du die Adern ausgehöhlt;
Du hast den Elephant auf Erden aufgethürmet,
    Und seinen Knochenberg beseelt.

Des weiten Himmelsraums saphirene Gewölber
    Gegründet auf den leeren Ort,
Das ungemeßne All, begrenzt nur durch sich selber,
    Hob aus dem Nichts dein einzig Wort.

אַתָּה אֱלֹהִים! לְבַדְּךָ עָשִׂיתָ כָּל־אֵלֶּה,
יָצַרְתָּ אַף עָשִׂיתָ, אַתָּה חַי עוֹלָמִים!
אוֹר כּוֹכָבִים וּמְסִלּוֹתָם, הוֹד שֶׁמֶשׁ וְעֻזּוֹ,
מַעֲשִׂים כּוֹנְנוּ יָדֶיךָ אֵל אֱלֹהִים!

אַתָּה הֲכִינוֹתָ מָאוֹר לַיָּרֵחַ,
אַתָּה הוּא הַנּוֹתֵן כְּנָפַיִם לָרוּחַ
אַתָּה מוֹרִיד שִׁכְבַת הַטַּל עַל הָאָרֶץ
תֹּאמַר לַכּוֹכָבִים, סֹבּוּ, שׁוּבוּ, וְנוּחוּ.

מֶחֱזָק וּמַאֲבָק הֶעֱמַדְתָּ הַרְרֵי עֹז,
וַתִּתִּיךְ בַּסָּתוּם חוֹל לְעָפְרוֹת זָהָב:
יָסַדְתָּ גְּבָעוֹת עוֹלָם מִימֵי קֶדֶם,
עָבֵי שְׁחָקִים כַּלְבוּשׁ כְּסִיתָם סָבִיב.

אַתָּה חָצַבְתָּ יַרְכֵי תַנִּין הַגָּדוֹל
שׁוֹפֵךְ מֵי הַיָּם בְּאַפָּיו וּבְכֹחוֹ מַרְעִישׁ:
הִפִּיל צָבַרְתָּ מֵעָפָר גָּבֹהַּ וְתָלוּל,
וַתִּתֵּן בַּעַל עַצְמוֹתָיו נֶפֶשׁ חַיָּה:

סְפוּנֵי שְׁמֵי הַשָּׁמַיִם וּצְבָאֵיהֶם,
חֲתוּלִים בִּרְצוֹנְךָ מוּסָדִים עַל בְּלִי מָה,
הָאָרֶץ הַזֹּאת אַךְ בִּגְבוּלֶיהָ מָנְבֶּלֶת,
אַתָּה אָמַרְתָּ תְּהִי, וַתְּהִי מֵאַיִן.

Doch dreimal großer Gott! es sind erschaffne Seelen
Für deine Thaten viel zu klein;
Sie sind unendlich groß, und wer sie will erzählen,
Muß, gleich wie du, unendlich seyn.

O Unbegreiflicher, ich bleib' in meinen Schranken,
Du Sonne blendst mein schwaches Licht;
Und wem der Himmel selbst sein Wesen hat zu danken,
Braucht eines Wurmes Lobspruch nicht.

Haller.

XXI.
LA PARTENZA.
(CANZONETTA DI METASTASIO.)

Ecco quel fiero istante;
   Nice, mia Nice, addio:
   Come vivrò, ben mio
   Cosi lontan da te?

   Io vivro sempre in pene,
   Io non avrò più bene;
   E tu, chi sa se mai
   Ti sovverrai di me?

Soffri che in traccia almeno
   Di mia perduta pace
   Venga il pensier seguace
   Su l'orme del tuo piè

גָּדוֹל וְנוֹרָא מַה נִפְלָאִים מַעֲשֶׂיךָ!
וּנְשָׁמוֹת עָשִׂיתָ לֹא יוּכְלוּ שַׁעֲרָם,
גָּדְלוּ עַד לִמְאֹד וְלִגְדוּלָתָם אֵין חֵקֶר,
אַךְ בְּנֵי בְּלִי קֵץ יָבוֹאוּ וִיסַפְּרוּ הוֹדָם:

נִמְצָא בְּלִי מוּשָׂג! יָדַעְתִּי אֶת־עָרְפִּי
אוֹר שִׁמְשֶׁךָ מַאֲפִיל הָאוֹר לִנְתִיבָתִי,
וְלַאֲשֶׁר הַשָּׁמַיִם רוֹפְפִים מִגַּעֲרָתוֹ
מַה יִּתֶּן־לוֹ שֶׁבַח בֶּן־אָדָם תּוֹלֵעָה?

XXI.

תרגום

הִנֵּה בָּא מוֹעֵד לְכָתְבִי:
שָׁלוֹם לָךְ וּלְשָׁלוֹם לֵכִי:
אֵיכָה נָא אֶחְיֶה מֵעַתָּה
מֵרָחוֹק מִיָּפָתִי?

הָהּ! לֹא־עוֹד אֶמְצָא מַרְגּוֹעַ,
רַק רָעוֹת אֶשְׁבַּע שָׁבוֹעַ:
וּלְבָבֵךְ מִי הַיּוֹדֵעַ
אִם־יָשׁוּב יִזְכּוֹר אוֹתִי?

אַף־אִם־בִּי עוֹד לֹא תַחְפְּצִי,
אַתְּ אַל־נָא בִּשְׁמִי תָקוּצִי:
וּבְכָל־אֶרֶץ אַתְּ נֹסַעַת
אַל־נָא תֵשִׁי עֲנוּתִי ·

Sempre nel tuo cammino,
Sempre m'avrai vicino;
E tu, chi sa se mai
Ti sovverrai di me?

Io fra remote sponde
Mesto volgendo i passi,
Andrò chiedendo ai sassi:
La ninfa mia dov' è?

Dall'una all'altra aurora
Te andrò chiamando ognora;
E tu, chi sa se mai
Ti sovverrai di me?

Io rivedrò sovente
Le amene piagge, o Nice,
Dove vivea felice,
Quando vivea con te.

A me saran tormento
Cento memorie e cento;
E tu, chi sa se mai
Ti sovverrai di me?

זִכְרוֹנִי בַּהֲלִיכוֹתֶיךָ
יִהְיֶה־נָא קָרוֹב אֵלֶיךָ:
וּלְבָבְךָ מִי הַיּוֹדֵעַ
אִם יָשׁוּב יִזְכֹּר אוֹתִי?

אָנֹכִי אָבֵל הֵלֵכָה,
עֵת בִּקְצֵה תֵבֵל אֵלֵכָה,
אֶל־כָּל־אֶבֶן וּלְכָל־סֶלַע
אָז אֶשְׁאַל, אֵי רַעֲיָתִי?

אֶקְרָאֵךְ בַּאֲשֶׁר אֶשְׁכֹּנָה
מִתֵּימָנָה הַצָּפוֹנָה;
וּלְבָבְךָ מִי הַיּוֹדֵעַ
אִם־יָשׁוּב יִזְכֹּר אוֹתִי?

הָהּ! עֵינִי, הֵן עוֹד אַתֶּנָּה
כָּל חֶלְקָה טוֹבָה תִרְאֶינָה,
זוֹ עַל־רוֹב שָׁלוֹם וָעֹנֶג
גַּרְתִּי בָהּ אֶת־יוֹנָתִי.

עַל זִכְרוֹן טוֹבוֹת תָּדְלוּ
עַצְמוֹתַי אָז יִבָּהֵלוּ:
וּלְבָבְךָ מִי הַיּוֹדֵעַ
אִם־יָשׁוּב יִזְכֹּר אוֹתִי?

Ecco, dirò, quel fonte,
>Dove avvampò di sdegno,
>Ma poi di pace in pegno
>La bella man mi diè.

Qui si vivea di speme,
>La si languiva insieme;
>E tu, chi sa se mai
>Ti sovverrai di me?

Quanti vedrai giungendo
>Al nuovo tuo soggiorno,
>Quanti venirti intorno
>A offrirti amore e fe!

Oh Dio! chi sa fra tanti
>Teneri omaggi e pianti,
>Oh Dio! chi sa se mai
>Ti sovverrai di me?

Pensa qual dolce strale,
>Cara, mi lasci in seno,
>Pensa che amò Fileno
>Senza sperar mercè:

אָז אָמַר: פֹּה עַל־הָעַיִן
הִיא הִרְחִיקָה מֶנִּי עָיִן;
הַאָמְנָם אַחַר שָׁכָכָה,
וַתָּבֹא בִּבְרִית אִתִּי:

פֹּה מָשׂוֹשׂ קָרוֹב יְחָלְנוּ,
לַהַב חֵשֶׁק שָׁם אֲכָלָנוּ:
וּלְבָבֵךְ מִי הַיּוֹדֵעַ
אִם־יָשׁוּב יִזְכֹּר אוֹתִי?

כַּמָּה אָז יָרוּצוּ, כַּמָּה,
שָׁם בַּאֲשֶׁר מִשְׁכָּנֵךְ שָׁמָּה,
לֵאמֹר לָךְ: אַל־נָא תִמְאָסִי
חִבָּתִי וֶאֱמוּנָתִי!

כִּרְאוֹתֵךְ רַבִּים יִכְרָעוּ,
וּבְמָרַת רוּחָם יִדְמָעוּ,
הָהּ! לִבֵּךְ מִי הַיּוֹדֵעַ
אִם יָשׁוּב יִזְכֹּר אוֹתִי

כִּי תַשְׂאִירִי רֹאשׁ הַנֶּשֶׁק,
בִּלְבָבִי מַחַיִן הַחֵשֶׁק;
זִכְרִי זֹאת, יָפָה; וּזְכֹרִי
כִּי הִנָּם כָּל־אַהֲבָתִי ּ

Pensa, mia vita, a questo
   Barbaro addio funesto;
   Pensa——Ah! chi sa se mai
   Ti sovverrai di me?

XXII.

SONETTO DEL MARINI.

Apre l'uomo infelice allor che nasce,
   In questa vita di miserie piena,
   Pria ch'al sol, gli occhi al pianto, e nato appena
   Va prigionier fra le tenaci fasce.

Fanciullo poi, che non più latte il pasce,
   Sotto rigida sferza i giorni mena.
   Indi, in età più ferma e più serena,
   Tra Fortuna ed Amor, more e rinasce.

Quante poscia sostien, tristo e mendico,
   Fatiche e morti, infin che curvo e lasso
   Appoggia a debil legno il fianco antico!

Chiude alfin le sue spoglie angusto sasso,
   Ratto cosi, che sospirando io dico:
   Dalla culla alla tomba è un breve passo.

צָרָתִי יָפָה, הָבִינִי;
בִּינִי נָא אֵיךְ תַּעַזְבִינִי
בִּינִי נָא—הָהּ! מִי יוֹדֵעַ
אִם־יִזְכֹּר לִבֵּךְ אוֹתִי?

כנור נעים

XXII.

יִפְתַּח אֱנוֹשׁ אָנוֹשׁ בְּיוֹם הִוָּלֶדֶת
עֵינָיו בְּקוֹל דִּמְעָה וְיִזַּל־מָיִם׃
אָז בַּשִּׁבְיִ יֵלֵךְ, וְהַמְיַלֶּדֶת
חִישׁ תַּחֲבוֹשׁ אֹתוֹ כִּבְנְחֻשְׁתַּיִם׃

יִגְדַּל, וְהַמְלַמֵּד בְּיַד שֹׁקֶדֶת
נִצָּב לְעֻמָּתוֹ כְּאִישׁ בֵּינָיִם;
אַחַר יְבַקֵּשׁ הוֹן וּבַת נֶחְמֶדֶת,
וִיהִי עֲמַל נַפְשׁוֹ מְלֹא חָפְנָיִם׃

כַּמָּה וְכַמָּה אַחֲרָיו יִדְלָקוּ,
הַוּוֹת וּמַכְאוֹבוֹת, וְרָע וְיַגִּיעַ,
עַד־אִם שָׁחוֹחַ יַחֲזִיק בַּפֶּלֶךְ!

וְיִגַּע מְהֵרָה קַל, שְׁאוֹלָה יֵלֵךְ:
עַל־כֵּן בְּאַנְחָתִי אֲנִי אַבִּיעַ:
לֵדָה וְיוֹם מִיתָה מְעַט רָחָקוּ׃

שמואל דוד לוצאטו

XXIII.

Non ebur, neque aureum &c.
   Hor. Od. 18. L. 2.

לֹא הֵיכְלֵי עֹנֶג, מִצְפֵּי שֵׁן וָכָתֶם,
לֹא אַרְמוֹנֵי שֵׁשׁ, בְּנֵי עַמּוּדֵי אָרֶז
לֹא שְׂכִיּוֹת חֶמְדָּה (מַתַּת הַשֶּׁפַע)
וּסְגֻלּוֹת מְלָכִים נְחוּנוֹתַי אָנֹכִי;
אַדֶּרֶת שִׁנְעָר גֵּוִי בְּגָאוֹן וָהוֹד
בַּל תְּכַסֶּה, וּגְלוּמֵי תְכֵלֶת;
לֵב שָׂמֵחַ חֶלְקִי, וְרוּחַ אֱמוּנָה ·
וְאֹתִי עָנִי רוֹזְנִים יִדְרְשׁוּן,
סוֹד עַמִּי לְהַמְתִּיק, עַמִּי הִתְעַלֵּס;
שָׂמֵחַ בְּחֶלְקָה קְטַנָּה אַחַת
סֶלֶף שָׂנְאָה נַפְשִׁי וַחֲלָקוֹת;
וְיוֹם חֹדֶשׁ וְשָׁנָה חִישׁ יַחְלֹפוּן
בִּנְעִימִים לִי, וְרוֹב שָׁלוֹם ·—
אַתָּה, רְחַב נֶפֶשׁ! בְּשַׁעֲרֵי מָוֶת
גְּדוֹלוֹת עוֹד תְּבַקֵּשׁ אַתָּה;
תַּחְצֹב בְּאַפְסֵי אֶרֶץ שַׁיִשׁ,
טִירָה בָּנוֹת וְאַרְמוֹן נֶצַח ·
תַּרְשִׁישׁ תְּשַׁלַּח קַחַת אַלְמוּג

הָבִיא אֶרֶז וְשֵׁן מֶרְחַקִּים ·
עָנִי תִגְזוֹל יָתוֹם הַכְּאֵת
דַּם נָקִי תִשְׁפּוֹךְ כֶּרֶם לַעֲשֹׁק
אַרְמוֹן תַּגִּיעַ בָּאַרְמוֹן פֹּה ·
כֶּרֶם שָׁם בְּכֶרֶם עַד אֵין קָצֶה ·
אֱוִיל ! הַמָּוֶת לַפֶּתַח רוֹבֵץ,
וְאַתָּה אֵין דַּי לָךְ עִיר וּמְלֹאָהּ ·
מְעוֹן צַר יִשְׁפֹּק לְךָ מְהֵרָה,
מְעוֹן רָמָה בְּחֶשְׁכַּת קָבֶר ·
נַפְשְׁךָ אֱוִיל ! בַּל תִּשְׂבַּע ؟
כְּסִיל ! בִּטְנְךָ יֶחְסַר תָּמִיד ׃
פִּיהוּ עַד אַרְגִּיעָה יִפְצֶה
הַקֶּבֶר, וְאַתָּה לֹא הָיִיתָ ! —
שֶׁקֶר הַזָּהָב הֶבֶל הַפָּז,
חִנָּם ! מִמָּוֶת לֹא יְמַלֵּט ·
גַּם מֹשֵׁל גַּם עֶבֶד יַחְדָּו
כִּי יִתֵּן קוֹלוֹ הַמָּוֶת, יִגְוָר,
וּשְׁאוֹל עַד מְהֵרָה יִבְלָעֵמוֹ ·

בּ״ר שענפעלד

REGISTER OF WORDS.

EXPLAINED IN THIS WORK.

(1) Refers to the First Part, 3rd Edition, the figures refer to the Page.
The figures without any mark before them, refer to the Etymology and Syntax, 3rd Edition.

א

50	אִשָּׁה	172	אָחוֹר	83	אֱוִיל	52	אָנֵר	I. 31	אָב
I. 16	אִישָׁה	״	אֲחֹרַנִּית	172	אוּלַי	49	אִגֶּרֶת	106	אָבַד
I. 67	אִישׁוֹן	״	אַחַר	65	אוּלָם	65	אֶגְרוֹף	״	אָבַר
172	אַךְ	״	אַחֲרֵי	70	אָוֶן	83	אִיד	81	אֲבַדּוֹן
20	אָכֹל	65	אַחֲרִית	67	אוֹפָן	26	אָדוֹן	131	אָבָה
״	אָכַל	172	אָט	171	אוֹם	201	אֲדֹנָי	״	אֹבֶה
״	אֹכֶל	I. 26	אִי	66	אוֹצָר	65	אַדִּיר	172	אֲבוֹי
78	אֲכִילָה	172	אֵי / אַיָּה	58	אוֹר, אוֹרָה	33	אָדָם	65	אֶבְיוֹן
169	אֶבֶן	״	אֵיךְ / אֵיכָה	49	אוֹת	5	אֲדֹם	I. 36	אָבֵל
63	אָפָר	137	אֹיֵב	172	אָז / אֲזַי	81	אַדֶּרֶת	45	אָבִיב
172	אַל	57	אֹיֵב	131	אֹזֶל	131	אָהֵב	172	אָבָל
4	אֵל	I. 46	אֵיבָה	63	אֶזְרָח	״	אֹהֵב	49	אֶבֶן
37	אֶל	70	אַיִל	26	אָזֵן	15	אַהֲבָה	I. 33	אַבְנֵט
79	אָלָה	I. 46	אֵיל	48	אָח	172	אָהָה	49	אָבָק
I. 37	אָלָה	170	אִין / אֵין	״	אָחוֹת	71	אֹהֶל	31	אַבְרָהָם
97	אַלֶּה	37	אֵיפָה	91	אֶחָד	172	אוֹ	141	אֱגוֹז
99	אֱלֹהִים	172	אֵיפֹה	״	אַחַת	247	אוֹדוֹת	I. 37	אֲגֻדָּה
172	אִלּוּ	״	אֵיפֹא	131	אָחוֹן	172	אוֹי	66	אֲנַם
״	אַלְלַי	33	אִישׁ	״	אָחוֹר	״	אוֹיָה	I. 37	אָגֵן

304 REGISTER OF WORDS.

אַרְמוֹן *	אֶפְרֹחַ 65	אָנוּ אֲנַחְנוּ 29	אֱמֶת 46	אֻלָם 73
אֶרֶץ 26	אֵצֶל 172	אַתָּה אַתְּ ,,	אָמוֹן 68	אַלְמָנָה 184
אִישׁ 4	אֶצְבַּע l. 67	אַתֶּם אַתֵּן ,,	אָמֹר 13	אֶלֶף 50
אֲשׁוּר 46	אֹרֵב 73	אָסִיר 57	אֹמֶר ,,	אִם 46
אֵשׁ 164	אַרְבַּע 91	אָסֹר 132	אָמְנָם 172	אִם 171
אֲשֶׁר 99	אַרְבָּעִים 92	אָסֹף 131	אָמֵשׁ 53	אָמָה 171
אֵת 172	אֲרִי/אַרְיֵה 72	אַף 75	אִמְתַּחַת 2א	אַמָּה 171
אֶתְמוֹל ,,	אֲרוֹת 50	אַף־ כִּי 172	אָן אָנָה 172	אֱמוּנָה 142
אָתוֹן 48	אַרְגָּמָן l. 33	אֶפֶס ,,	אָנָא ,,	אָמֵן 171
אַתָּה 131	אֹרֶךְ 71	אֵפֹה 131	אֱנוֹשׁ l. 73	אָמֵן 47
אוֹתִי/אוֹתִי 172	אָדָם 33	אֶפֶר 57	אֲנִי אָנֹכִי 29	אֹמֶנֶת 46

ב

בָּרוּךְ 26	בַּעֲבוּר 172	בְּבוּרָה 78	בּוֹשׁ 138	בְּאֵר 49
בֶּרֶךְ 107	בְּעַר 107	בְּכוֹר 101	בָּחוֹן 163	בָּאֵר 107
בֵּרֵךְ ,,	בָּעַר ,,	בַּל 172	בָּחוֹר 121	בְּאֵר ,,
בְּרָכָה 63	בַּקְבּוּק l. 33	בְּלִי ,,	בֶּטַח 211	בָּבֶל 133
בֵּרֵךְ 107	בִּקֵּר l. 55	בִּלְעֲדֵי ,,	בֶּטֶן l. 78	בֶּגֶד 70
בְּרִית 57	בָּקַר 53	בִּלְתִּי ,,	בִּין 16	בְּגָלָל 172
בַּרְזֶל l. 33	בִּקֵּשׁ l. 66	בֶּלַע 16	בֵּין 172	בֹּהוּ 181
בְּעַל 116	בַּר 163	בְּלִיַּעַל ,,	בִּינָה 78	בֶּהָלָה 63
בֹּשֶׁם l. 45	בַּר 75	בֵּן 27	בַּיִת 72	בְּהֵמָה 81
בִּישׁוֹר 127	בָּרָה 87	בַּת 50	בָּלַד 145	בַּהֶרֶת 63
בָּשָׂר 69	בָּרָא l. 17	בַּעַל 81א	בָּכָה 76	בוֹא 161
בְּתוּלָה 49	בָּרַח 48	בּוֹנֶה 83	בְּכִיָּה ,,	בּוֹר l. 31

ג

גִּבּוֹר 65	גְּבֶרֶת 80	גְּבִיר 61	עָבַר l. 72	גֵּאָה 77
נָבָל ,,	גְּבוּרָה 37	גְּבִירָה 81	גֶּבֶר ,,	גַּבָּה 145

* A palace.

REGISTER OF WORDS.

גָּדוֹל 47	גֵּו 3א	גִּיל 154	גַּם 173	גְּעָרָה 78
גֹּרָל 71	גֵּוִי 49	גַּל 74	גָּמָל 47	גֵּר 16
גָּדַל 116	גּוֹרָל 133	גִּלְגַּל 190	גַּן 21	גָּרַע l. 36
גָּרְלָה 7ד	גּוּר 16, 65	גָּלָה 145	גָּנַן „	גָּרֹן l. 33
גְּדִי 72	גָּוַע 137	גְּלוּגַרת 66	גַּנָּב 67	גָּזְבָּר „
גָּדַע 121	גָּזַל 70	גִּלְעָד 190	גְּנֵבָה 149	גֶּשֶׁם l. 35
גֶּדֶר 70	גִּיא l. 27	גָּלַל 154	גָּוַע l. 72	גֶּשֶׁת 128

ד

דֹּב 47	דֶּגֶל 14	דִּין 127	דָּלַג 154	דֶּרֶךְ 40
דָּבָר 13	דּוֹד l. 31	דּוֹר 49	דֶּלֶת 41	דָּרֹשׁ 161
דָּבָר „	דּוּד 65	דַּי 172	דָּם 66	דָּרַשׁ „
דְּבַשׁ 66	דָּוִד 132	דַּל 74	דַּעַת 82	דֶּשֶׁא l. 35
דָּן 67	דַּיָּן l. 37	דְּבוֹרָה l. 27	דֵּעָה l. 27	דָּרְבָּן l. 41

ה

הֵא 31	הֹוִי 172	הִנֵּה 170	הָאָרֶץ 171	הַלְלוּיָהּ 152
הֶאָח 172	הֵן 167	הָיָה 147	הָלַךְ l. 64	הַר 35
הָבָה 167	הוּא 29	הוֹן 52	הָלַךְ 161, 16	הַרְבֵּה 172
הֲדַס 66	הִיא „	הַיּוֹם 169	הָלַל 152	הָרַן l. 66
הוֹד 37	הִפֹּה „	הֵיטִיב 170	הוֹלֵל „	הֵרָיוֹן 63
הִוָּה 168	הֵנָּה „	הֲלֹם 172	הָדַק 231	הֵתֵל 102

ז

זְאֵב l. 32	זָהָב 45	זָכֹר 17	זְמָן 66	זָרָה 36
זֶבַח 83	זוּלָתִי 168	זִכָּרוֹן „	זָעַק 124	זָר 64
זֶה זוּ 97	זִיק l. 30	זָמִיר l. 69	זְעָקָה 127	זֶרַע 37
זֹאת „	זַיִת 72	זָמַם 151	זָר 63	זָקֵן 118

REGISTER OF WORDS.

ח

חֶרֶב 80	חֲמִישִׁי 94	חָלָל 133	חַי, חַיָּה 11	חָבַק 166
חָרְבָּה ,,	חֲמִישִׁית ,,	חֲלֹם 132	חַיָּה 148	חֲבוּרָה 78
חֶרֶב 187	חֵן 169	חֵלֶק 70	חַיִּים 141	חָן 1. 31
חֲרָדָה 79	חִנָּם ,,	חָלָק 88	חֵטְא 164	חָד 89
חֲרִי 72	חָנַן 164	חַם 1. 31	חַיִל 72	חֹרֶשׁ 57
חָרָן 41	חֲנִית 49	חָמוֹר 123	חֵךְ 75	חָדָשׁ 142
חֶרֶס 10	חָסַד 57	חֵמָה 51	חָכָם 69	חוֹחַ 64
חֹרֶף 37	חָסִיד 154	חֵמָה 1. 46	חָכְמָה 80	חוּט 1. 31
חֶרְפָּה 80	חֲסִידָה 47	חַמָּה 10	חָכַם 5	חוֹל ,,
חָרָשׁ 63	חָסֹר 123	חָם 48	חָלַב 11	חוּם 37
חֶרֶשׁ ,,	חֶסְרוֹן 65	חָמוֹת ,,	חֵלֶב ,,	חָגִין 172
חָשֹׁב 5	חֲצַן 119	חָמָס 166	חֶלְבְּנָה ,,	חָוָה 77
חֹשֶׁךְ 1. 45	חֲצִי 95	חֹמֶן 59	חֶלְבּוֹן ,,	חֹוָה 1. 27
חָשׁוּךְ ,,	חָצֵר 26	חֲמוֹר 48	חַלָּה 105	חִזָּיוֹן 63
חָשֹׁךְ ,,	חֲצֹצְרָה 1. 35	חֵמֶר 202	חָלָה ,,	חָזָק 107
חָשֹׂף ,,	חֹק 75	חֲבֵרִים ,,	חֲלוֹם 163	חָזַק ,,
חָתָן 49	חָקַר 154	חָמֵשׁ 91	חַלּוֹן 49	חָזְקָה 150
חֹתֵן 73	חֻקָּה 78	חֲמִשִּׁים 93	חֳלִי 72	חָזָק 88

ט

טָנֵא 1. 27	טָלֶה 1. 27	טוֹב 149	טַבַּעַת 49	טָהוֹר 68
טָעַם 150	טָמֵא 70	טוּר 1. 31	טָבַל 132	טָהֵר 107
טֶרֶם 149	טָמֵא 107	טַל ,,	טוֹב 85	טָהֵר ,,

י

יָרֵעַ 19	יְדִידוּת 57	יָדוֹת 31	יָנַר 162	יָבֵשׁ 134
יוֹם 37	יָהּ 1. 27	יָדִיד 1. 32	יָד 30, 51	יָנוֹן 68

REGISTER OF WORDS. 307

יְרִיעָה 1. 27	יָקַר 65	יָסֹד 131	יָבֵל 118	יוֹמָם 167
יָרֵךְ 70	יָרֵא 131	יָפָה 76	יָכֹלֶת 61	יוֹנָה 132, 17
יָשֵׁב 24	יִרְאָה 1. 66	יָצָא 150	יֶלֶד 135	יוֹסֵף 39
יָשֵׁן 134	יָרַד 134	יָצַב 137	יֵלֵךְ 45	יֳפִי 1. 27
יָשֵׁן 70	יַרְדֵּן 44	יצג ,,	יָלַךְ 161	יַחַד 172
יָשַׁע 154	יְרוּשָׁלַיִם 33	יצע ,,	יַלְדָּה 45	יָטֹב 162
יָשָׁר 84	יָרֹה 156	יצק ,,	יָם 74	יֵי 1. 46
יִשְׂרָאֵל 33	יֶרַח 10	יצר ,,	יָנַח 137	יַיִן 49
יָתֵד 70	יָרֵחַ ,,	יצת ,,	יָנַק 131	יָבֹחַ 166

כ

כַּפֹּרֶת 81	כְּנַעַן 44	כּוֹל 162	כֹּהֵן 41	כְּאֵב 64
כַּשְׂדִּים 126	כְּעוֹר 127	כֹּל 75	כּוּן 169	כָּבֵד 12
כָּרַת 119	כָּנָף 69	כֶּלֶב 89	כֵּן 100, 169	כָּבֵד ,,
כְּרֻב 1. 33	כְּסֵא 49	כָּלָה 21	כּוֹס 62	כָּבוֹד ,,
כֶּרֶם 154	כִּסָּה 150	כַּלָּה 78	כֹּחַ 64	כְּבֵדוּת ,,
כַּרְמֶל 44	כְּסוּת 66	כְּלִי 54	כַּחַשׁ 105	כָּבַד ,,
כָּתֵב 66	כְּסִיל 83	כְּלָיוֹת 50	כִּי 172	כֶּבֶשׂ 45
כָּתַב 107	כַּסֶּמֶת 81	כִּלְכֵּל 162	כִּים 61	כִּבְשָׂה ,,
כְּתֹנֶת 57	כֶּסֶף 45	כִּלְמָה 150	כָּכָה 37	כִּבְשָׁן 67
כָּתַף 70	כָּעַם 128	כַּפָּה 170	כּוֹכָב 67	כַּד 71
כֹּתֶרֶת 81	כַּף 1. 31	כְּמוֹ 173	כָּבַר ,,	כֹּה 37

ל

לוּחַ 65	לִבְנָה 11	לָבָן 69	לֵבָב 69	לֹא 172
לֵוִי 48	לְבָנוֹן ,,	לִבְנָה 11	לְבַד 173	לֵאָה 132
לוּן 142	לָבַשׁ 154	לִבְנָה ,,	לְבוּשׁ 65	לָאט 172
לְחִי 72	לוּ לוּלֵא 173	לִבְנָה ,,	לָבִיא 1. 27	לֵב 52

x

REGISTER OF WORDS.

לֵין 179	לַעֲנָה 88	לָמַד 107	לְכַד 149	לֶחֶם 3א
לָקַח 130	לִפְנֵי 169	לְמַעַן 173	לְבֵן 169	לַיִל 72
לָשׁוֹן 3	לְפָנִים 169	לְעֻמַּת ,,	לִמֹד 15	לַיְלָה 37

מ

מַעֲלָה 7	מִלְחָמָה 81	מָחָר 173	מָהַר 167	מָאוֹר 173
מַעֲנֶה 85	מִלִּין 68	מָחֳרָת ,,	מְהֵרָה ,,	מֵאָה 50
מְעָרָה 79	מָלַךְ 7	מָחוּן ,,	מוֹדָע l. 67	מָאוֹר 84
מַעֲשֶׂה 76	מֶלֶךְ ,,	מַחְתָּה l. 36	מוּל 173	מֵאָז 173
מַעֲצֵר 73	מַלְכָּה ,,	מַטֶּה 21	מוֹלֶדֶת 82	מֹאזְנַיִם 51
מִפְּנֵי 167	מַלְכוּת 65	מִטָּה ,,	מוֹסָד 67	מֵאַיִן 173
מַפְתֵּחַ 73	מַלְקֵשׁ 84	מַטֶּה 173	מוּסָר 66	מַאֲכָל 21
מָצָא 25	מֶלְקָחַיִם 51	מַטְמוֹן 65	מוֹעֵד 74	מַאֲכֶלֶת ,,
מַצֵּבָה 81	מַמְלָכָה 27	מַטָּע 27	מוֹעֵצָה 79	מְאֹם 154
מִצְוָה 126	מֶמְשָׁלָה 82	מַיִם 51	מוֹפֵת 74	מַבּוּל l. 37
מְצוּלָה 141	מָנָה 79	מִין 64	מוֹצָא 66	מֵבִין 68
מִצְרַיִם 101	מַנְעוּל 7	מַכָּה 77	מוֹקֵשׁ 74	מְבִישָׁה 84
מִקְדָּשׁ 189	מָנוֹעַ 52	מַפָּה 78	מוֹרָא 66	מִבַּיִת 173
מָקוֹם 68	מַסָּה 78	מָכַר 127	מוֹרָה l. 27	מַעַל l. 37
מָסוֹד 15	מָסָךְ 67	מִכְתָּב 185	מוֹרָשָׁה 79	מָגֵן 63
מַקֵּל 73	מִסְכֵּן 73	מַכְתֵּשׁ 73	מוֹשֵׁל 85	מְגִלָּה 27
מִקְנֶה 21	מִכְמָר ,,	מָלֵא 70	מָוֶת 138	מִדְבָּר 39
מִקְרָא 66	מַסָּע 67	מִלֵּא 84	מָוֶת 70	מִדָּה 18
מַר 88	מִסְפָּר l. 36	מְלָאכָה 53	מִזְבֵּחַ 73	מָרַד ,,
מֹר l. 31	מָעוֹז 75	מַלְבּוּשׁ 65	מִזְמוֹר 65	מַדּוּעַ 170
מַרְאָה 142, 75	מָעַט 66	מֻלָּה l. 37	מַחֲנֶה 47	מַדָּע 27
מַרְגֵּל 163	מְעִיל 7	מֶלַח 13	מַחֲצִית 95	מָה 100
מָרָה 41	מַעְיָן 72	מֶלַח ,,	מַחֲשָׁבָה 4	מַהְמֹרֶה 162
מַרְדּוּת l. 36	מַעֲלָה 7	מָלַח 31	מַחְתָּה 83	מָאַן 168

REGISTER OF WORDS. 309

מָתָן	3א	מִשְׁפָּט	27	מַשְׁכֹּלֶת	84	מִינָּב	67	מָרְדֳּכַי	142
מָתוֹק	84	מִשְׁנָה	77	מֵטִיל	52	מַשְׁחִית	65	מֶרְכָּבָה	63
מָתַי	171	מִשְׁמֶרֶת	81	מָשִׁיל	126	מִשְׁעָן	67	מֵישָׁא	66
מַתָּנָה	17	מִשְׁקָל	22	מִשְׁפָּחָה	53	מַעְבֹּרֶת	81	מִשְׁבָּר	19

נ

גֵּרֵךְ	I. 33	גֵּס	I. 31	נַחַת	46	נָגַע	132	נֹאד	I. 33
נִרְדָּף	5	נִסְמָךְ	55	נִחַם	124	נָד	I. 32	נָאוָה	89
נִישָּׂא	156	נַעַל	7	נָטָה	21	נְדָבָה	79	נֶאֱנָה	106
נִשָּׂא	I. 45	נַעַר	26	נָטַע	27	נָדִיב	68	נָאִין	108
נִשְׁבַּע	106	נַעֲרָה	41	נִיסָן	15	נָחַן	108	נָבוֹן	142
נָשִׂיא	I. 45	נָפַל	21	נָכָה	133	נֹחַם	85	נָבִיא	41
נָשִׁים	50	נִפְרָד	55	נִדְרִי	49	נָהָר	35	נָבָל	154
נְשָׁמָה	151	נֶקֶשׁ	128	נָבַר	123	נֹכַח	173	נְבֵלָה	79
נָשַׁף	I. 77	גַּיִן	I. 32	נָכְרִיָּה	49	נַחֲלָה	84	נֶגֶב	41
נָשַׁק	132	גֶּצַח	37	נִסּוֹף	105	נַחֲלָה	105	נִנְפָּה	..
נָתַן	130	נָצַב	132	נִלְחַם	106	נֶחָמָה	63	נֶגֶד	84
נָתִיב	52	גֵּר	61	נִמְקָה	52	נְחֹשֶׁת	45	נָגַשׁ	24

ס

סֵפֶר	154	סָס	I. 32	סִפְרָה	78	סוֹחֵר	73	סָבַב	151
סָקַל	107	סְעָרָה	11	סַל	74	סוּס	57	סָבָּה	152
סֶקֶל	..	סַף	71	סָלָם	31	סִינַי	44	סָבִיב	173
סֵתֶר	80	סָפַר	27	סֶלַע	142	סְחַרְחַר	102	סוֹד	I. 32

ע

עִבְרִית	43	עָבַר	127	עֲבוֹדָה	76	עָבַד	133	עָב	16
עַמּוֹן	..	עֵבֶר	43	עַבְטִיט	16	עֶבֶד	35	עָב	84

REGISTER OF WORDS.

עֶרֶב 1. 54	עָנָף 69	עַלְקְמָה 80	עֵוֶר 80	עִבְרִי 43
עֹרֶב 73	עָנָק 88, 66	עֹלָם 169	עֲטָרָה 79	עֵגֶל 1. 77
עָרוֹם 62	עָפָר 13	עַם 171	עֲטֶרֶת 57	עַד 60
עָרְמָה 80	עַפָּר ,,	עַם ,,	עִיר 57	עַד 173
עָרִין 65	עֹפֶרֶת 45	עָמַד 123	עַיִר 72	עוֹד ,,
עָשֹׂה 149	עַיִן 4	עַמּוּד 65	עַיִן 46, 51	עֲדִי 1. 27
עָשֵׁב 1. 57	עֵצָה 79	עָמִית 171	עוֹף 117	עוּגָב 67
עָשָׂה ,,	עִצָּבוֹן 68	עָפֳרִי 173	עֲבְכָּר 1. 33	עוֹל 7
עָשָׁן 13	עָצֵל 52	עַמְשָׁא 155	עַבְרִית 1. 32	עוֹלֵל ,,
עָשֵׁן ,,	עַצְלָה 133	עֹמֶק 203	עַל 7	עוֹף 11
עֹשֶׁר 133	עֶצֶם 65	עֲפַת 171	עָלֶן 73	עוֹר 64
עָשִׁיר 83	עָצוּם 26	עֲנָנָה 1. 27	עָלָה 7	עֲגֶל 70
עָשֵׁר 91	עָקֵב 173	עָנִי 72	עֹלָה ,,	עוֹלָה ,,
עֶשְׂרִים 92	עָקֵב 70	עֵנָב 69	עָלָה ,,	עָוֹן 127
עֵת 169	עַר 1. 70	עָנָה 29	עֲלִי ,,	עוּר 73
עַתָּה ,,	עֶרֶב 1. 69	עָנָן 36	עֶלְיוֹן ,,	עֹז 75

פ

פֹּשַׁע 126	פָּקִיד 26	פֹּעַל 71	פֶּלֶא 1. 27	פֵּאָה 79
פָּרַת 74	פָּר 1. 32	פַּעַם 173	פְּלֶגֶשׁ 76	פֶּגַע 132
פִּתְאֹם 173	פָּרַד 1. 35	פַּעֲמַיִם ,,	פֶּן 168	פֶּלַח 18
פָּתַח 108	פָּרֹכֶת 214	פַּעֲמוֹן 65	פָּנָה 149	פֶּה 1. 27
פֶּתַח ,,	פְּרִי 72	פָּקַד 110	פָּנִים 50	פֹּה 173
פֶּתִי 72	פָּרָזוֹן 68	פֹּקֵד 115	פָּעַל 22	פָּז 1. 32
פִּתְנָהֶם 16	פֶּשַׁע 127	פָּקוּד ,,	פָּעַל ,,	פַּחַד 1. 62

צ

צוּד 164	צַדִּיק 64	צַד 74	צְבִי 72	צֹאן 53
צַוָּה ,,	צְדָקָה 79	צֶדֶק 126	צִבְיָה ,,	צֶאֱצָא 66

REGISTER OF WORDS. 311

צַר 64	צָפָה 76	צָמֵא 143	צֵל 27	צַיִד 236
צָרָה 74	צָפֹה 190	צָמַח 106	צִלָּה 46	צֵידָה 78
צְרִי 72	צִפּוֹר 65	צָמַח „	צָלַל 27	צַיִן l. 32
צֳרִי „	צְפִיָּה 76	צָעִיר 88	צֶלַע 69	צִיר 127

ק

קֶרֶב 13	קְעָרָה 78	קַל 88	קוֹן l. 32	קָבַר 142
קְרָב „	קֵן 75	קָלַל 152	קוֹר 37	קֶבֶר 83
קָרְבָה „	קָצֶה 141	קֹמֶן 71	קַחַת 130	קַרְדֹּת 46
קָרְבָּן „	קָצֹר 21	קָמָה 78	קָטָן 47	קָדֹשׁ 23
קִרְיָה 83	קָצִיר „	קֵן 75	קָטֹן 87	קֶדֶם 127
קֶרֶן 149	קָצַר 70	קִנְאָה 89	קְטֹרֶת 46	קָדְשׁ 71
קָרַשׁ 204	קָצִין 52	קָנָה 21	קַיִם 139	קָדוֹשׁ 176
קָשָׁה 94	קָרָא 25	קָנָה 77	קִיר 64	קוֹל 57
קֶשֶׁת 49	קָרוֹב 13	קָנֶה „	קַיִן 52	קוּם 137

ר

רֹעָה 48	רָמָה 190	רַחִים 51	רֶגֶל 163	רָאָה 25
רַעְיָה 88	רִנָּה 83	רָחֵל 132	רֶגַע 26	רֹאֶה 76
רָצוֹן 83	רָנַן 154	רַחֲמִים 50	רָדַף 107	רֹאשׁ or רֵישׁ 62
רֶצַח 52	רַע 52	רָחוֹק 101	רָדַף „	רֹאשׁ 7
רָצַח 107	רֵעַ 83	רֵיחַ l. 69	רֻגַּח 4	רֵאשִׁית „
רִשָׁע 88	רָעָב 117	רֵיקָם 173	רוֹב 137	רִאשׁוֹן „
רַק 172	רְעָבוֹן 68	רֵישׁ 62	רִיב „	רֹב 142
רֵק l. 32	רָעָה 77	רַךְ 74	רוּחַ 52	רִבּוֹא 51
רָקָב 64	רָעָה 142	רִכּוּשׁ 133	רֹחַב 71	רְבִיעִי 94
רָקִיעַ 10	רָעָה 150	רָם 64	רְחוֹב 52	רֶגֶל 46, 11

ש

שֶׁעֲשֻׁעַ 163	שָׁמַע 48	שָׁלַח 163	שׁוֹט 83	שַׁאַר 64
שִׁפְרָה 51	שְׁמוּעָה 81	שֻׁלְחָן 63	שֶׂה 1. 32	שְׁאוֹר ,,
שִׁפְחָה 48	שָׁמַר 16	שִׁלְטוֹן 65	שַׁוְעָה 83	שְׁאֵרִית 65
שָׁפַט 27	שֶׁמֶר 14	שָׁלַל 149	שׁוּק 50	שָׁאַל 84
שֵׁבֶט 41	שֹׁמֵר 36	שָׁלֵם ,,	שׁוֹקֵק 85	שְׁאֵל 149
שִׁפְטוּת ,,	שֶׁמֶשׁ 10	שַׁלְמָה 80	שׁוֹשָׁן 67	שָׁבוּעַ 62
שָׁפָן 69	שֵׁן 75	שָׁלִישׁ 68	שׁוֹר 50	שִׁבֹּלֶת 81
שׁוֹפָר 1. 45	שָׂנֵא 15	שְׁלֹשָׁה 91	שֹׁחַד 26	שְׁבִיל 64
שַׂק 150	שֹׂנֵא 73	שְׁלִישִׁי 94	שָׁחַל 52	שֵׁבֶט 83
שָׁקָה 162	שִׂנְאָה 15	שָׁלִישִׁים 92	שַׁחַר 37	שְׁבִיעִי 94
שֶׁקֶר 54	שָׁנָה 50	שִׁלְשׁוֹם 173	שֹׁטֵר 52	שִׁבְעִים 93
שָׂר 64	שֵׁנָה 7	שֵׁם 6. 44	שֵׂיבָה 78	שָׁבַר 17
שַׂר ,,	שֵׁנִי 94	שָׁם 173	שִׁיר 42	שִׁבָּרוֹן 19
שָׂרָה 46	שְׁנַיִם 91	שִׂמְחָה 80	שִׁירָה ,,	שָׁבַע 91
שָׂרִיט 15	שְׁתַּיִם ,,	שָׁמַיִם 51	שָׁכַב 116	שַׁבָּת 76
שַׁרְבִיט 1. 33	שַׂעֲרָה 11	שִׂמְלָה 60	שָׁכַח 107	שֶׁבֶת 82
שִׁירָה 91	שָׂעִיר ,,	שֶׁמֶן 49	שֵׂכֶל 154	שָׁבוּר 19
שִׁיטִים 93	שְׂעֹרָה 45	שְׁמֹנָה 91.	שָׁכֵן 118	שֶׁבֶר ,,
שָׁשׂוֹן 68	שַׁעַר 70	שְׁמִינִי 94	שֵׁכָר 179	שָׂרָה 30
שֹׁשַׁנָּה 88	שֵׂעָר 69	שְׁמֹנִים 93	שִׁכּוֹר 65	שׁוּב 137
שָׁתָה 162	שַׁעַר 11	שָׁמַע 125	שָׁלוֹם 127	שׁוּב ,,

ת

תּוֹרָה 78	תַּבְנִית 46	תְּבוּאָה 52	תֹּאַר 71	תָּא 62
תָּנוּךְ 72	תֹּהוּ 181	תְּבוּנָה 90	תֵּבָה 1. 27	תְּאֹם 171
תּוֹחֶלֶת 82	תְּהִלָּה 31	תֶּבֶן 133	תֵּבֵל 126	תְּאוֹמִים ,,

REGISTER OF WORDS.

תִּפְאֶרֶת 46	תָּמִיד 173	תֵּל 1. 32	תַּחְתִּית 65	תּוֹלֵעָה 81		
תְּפִלָּה 31	תּוֹעֵבָה 83	תָּמוֹל 172	תִּירוֹשׁ 66	תּוֹלַעַת 57		
תַּרְדֵּמָה 133	תַּעֲלָה 7	תֹּם 75	תֹּכֶן 133	תּוֹרָה 56		
תִּשְׁעָה 91	תַּעֲנוּג 65	תָּם 171	תַּכְלִית 21	תּוֹעָב 67		
תְּשִׁיעִי 94	תֹּף 75	תָּמִים "	תְּכֵלֶת 81	תְּחִנָּה 77		
תִּשְׁעִים 93	תֹּפֶשׂ 149	תְּנוּמָה 1. 64	תַּלְמִיד 57	תַּחַת 173		

INDEX

OF

BIBLICAL PASSAGES CITED AND EXPLAINED IN THIS WORK. BY THE
REV. F. ILIFF, D.D., HEAD MASTER OF THE ROYAL
INSTITUTION SCHOOL, LIVERPOOL.

Note—The * marks the page in the First Part of the Grammar.

GENESIS.	GENESIS.	GENESIS.	GENESIS.	GENESIS.	GENESIS.	GENESIS.
1: 1. *83	2:12. *25	4: 2. 246	8: 2. 106	14: 9. 204	18:29. 204	24: 7. 252
— *87	13. *84	3. 214	5. 106	10. 202	181	12. *88
— 214	— 209	4. 219	15: 1. 232	256	14. 211
— 236	14. *84	5. 246	8. 230	2. 256	19: 2. *89	— 224
— 246	— 100	6. *88	11. 224	10. 211	— 232	33. *89
2. 181	15. *84	7. *84	12. 231	12. 214	8. 213	34. *89
— 216	16. 228	8. *87	13. 208	13. 210	9. 204	44. 209
3. *87	17. 208	9. 256	21. 247	— 222	12. 213	55. 238
— 218	— 232	10. 237	9: 2. 194	15. 222	13. 225	67. 190
4. *83	— 230	12. *84	18. 185	16: 1. 213	17. 229	226
— 249	18. 227	15. 212	23. 237	5. 253	19. 239	256
5. *85	23. *88	18. 106	24. 224	17: 5. 219	20. 121	25: 1. 231
6. 249	— 106	21. 207	10: 9. 106	18. 234	22. 227	6. 197
7. *85	24. *84	25. *84	21. *90	21. *80	20: 7. 232	9. 121
— *87	— *85	26. 209	11: 7. 201	23. 192	13. 236	28. 214
— *88	25. 206	5: 2. 106	— 233	25. *80	21: 1. 221	26: 1. 242
— 249	3: 2. 108	3. 95	9. 238	18: 1. 214	7. 235	14. 181
11. 237	3. 108	14. 214	14. 12	— 216	8. 121	18. 231
14. 236	— 246	6: 1. 228	19. 95	— 221	17. 210	27: 1. 229
15. *85	4. 106	4. 209	12: 1. *85	3. 332	24. 209	2. 215
21. *40	7. 106	15. 208	— 192	4. 232	248	— 225
26. 201	— 224	18. *10	5. 229	11. 238	22: 2. 192	4. 210
28. *83	8. 106	20. 200	12. 214	15. *89	12. 232	— 233
30. *84	13. 109	21. 106	13. *85	18. 230	20. 208	— 247
189	22. 213	— 219	19. 226	21. *89	239	6. 235
2: 4. 106	— 220	7: 4. 225	13: 2. 192	21. 220	135	20. 231
6. 225	— 233	11. 106	5. 100	24. 233	23: 6. 211	25. 233
8. 189	4: 2. 219	22. 196	9. *85	26. 233	13. 221	33. 211
10. 100	— 231	8: 2. 230	— 246	27. 120	17. *87	38. 209

314   INDEX OF BIBLICAL PASSAGES.

GENESIS.	GENESIS.	EXODUS.	JOSHUA.	1. KINGS.	PSALMS.	ISAIAH.
28:12. 223	48:20. *40	40:18. 204	2: 1. 242	19:11. 223	72:17. 232	30:20. 200
— 189	49: 1. 106	— 35. 118	3:14. 190	20: 7. 247	74:17. 193	31: 3. 181
29: 4. *58	— 8. 209	41: 4. 204	4: 4. 204		81: 5. 196	33: 9. 238
— 9. 198	— 22. 237		5: 9. 190	2. KINGS.	88:15. 168	37:28. 228
— 19. 228		LEVITICUS.	7:21. 190	1: 2. 231	94: 1. *75	51:12. 188
30:27. 247	EXODUS.	4: 2. 238	10: — 119	2: — 147	99:11. 97	52: — 121
— 34. 234	1:20. 238	7.18. 120	13:11. 119	4: 1. 180	102:27. 209	54: 1. 188
— 186	2: 6. 188	11:13. 193	— 14. 237	5: 9. 198	103:15. *73	63:11. 191
31: 6. 225	— 18. 231	— 47. 249	15:19. 210	— 26. 256	104: 3. 199	
— 8. 237	3: 1. 214	12: 4 189	24:19. 201	6:10. 207	— 5. 199	JEREMIAH.
— 13. 190	— 8. 229	13: 3. 107		— 32. 229	105:25. 239	10: 3. 237
— 24. 106	— 11. 233	— 28. 107	JUDGES.	7:12. 117	— 29. 239	— 20. 210
— — 209	— 16. 217	14: — 122	4:20. 243	10: 2. 229	114: 8. 189	17: 4. 240
— 29. 330	— 16. 232	21: — 122	8: 1. 242	13:11. 180	116: — 121	22:20. 202
— 30. 230	5: 1. 217	24: 5. 237	9:28. 233	— 17. 160	118: — 119	51: 8. 254
— 32. 201	— 10. 186	25:19. 242	11:14. 215	14:10. 119	— — 121	
— 36. *60	— 16. 221	— 50. 228	— 24. 201	15.16. 196	119:168.259	LAMENTA-
— 37. 206	— 19. 212	— — 237	— 37. 220	— 35. 252	135:17. 170	TIONS.
— 38. 145	— 42. 213	26:46. 192	12: 2. 220	16: 7. 138	— — 170	1: 1. 213
— 42. 234	7: 9. 213	27: 5. 92	13:19. 238	18:31. 189	139:7. *76	— 9. 242
— 44. 234	8: 1. 193		14:18. 234	25:27. 220		2: — 120
— — 253	— 10. 202	NUMBERS.	20:25. 92		PROVERBS.	3:29. 233
— 47. 190	9: — 135	1:47. 122	— 41. 239	1 CHRON-	1:15. 232	
— 48. 190	— 33. 226	3:46. 204		ICLES.	— 26. 229	EZEKIEL.
32: 5. 192	10: 5. 216	7:13. 204	RUTH.	9:13. 197	— — 131	3:15. 217
— — 200	— 8. 193	9. 6. 237	1: 6. 222	29: 2. 37	3:18. 237	14: 4. 121
— 8. 239	— 12. 220	— 16. 225	2: 9. 210		— 35. 199	18:23. 243
— 9. 233	— 14. 220	11:29. 234	12: 3. 120	NEHEMIAH.	5:23. 243	24: 3. 135
— 13. 204	— 24. 211	12: 4. 206		9:28. 210	6: 6. *68	27: — 131
— 15. 204	— — 120	— — 253	1. SAMUEL.		— 15. 254	31: — 119
33:13. 239	12:11. 242	— — 238	1:12. 231	ESTHER.	— 19. 249	34: 5. 212
— 19. 21	— 30. 243	13:25. 229	2: 3. 231	7: 4. 234	7: 1. *67	43: 6. 215
— — 213	— 37. 242	14:22. 214	— — 244	8: — 228	8:34. 235	
34: 5. 220	13: — 162	19:13. 200	4. 237	9: 1. 120	11:14. 243	DANIEL.
— 7. *89	14: 3. 218	20:11. 200	4:16. 200		12: 1. 234	9: — 197
— 25. 211	— 11. 228	— 13. 200	9:11. 243	JOB.	— 11. 235	
35: 3. 108	— — 244	— 4. 237	14:29. 12	1: 5. 226	— 28. 244	HOSEA.
37: 2. 213	— 25. 242	21: 8. 217	15: — 121	— 7. 229	18: 3. 229	5: 6. 232
— 3. 239	15: 9. 222	22:14. 227	16: 7. 191	— 9. 254	20:14. 203	
— 8. 205	— — 226	24: 7. *40	— 18. 198	— 14. 214	— 21. 197	AMOS.
— — 230	16: 3. 234	32: 5. 193	18: 3. 206	3: 2. 29	21: 3. 227	9: 4. 188
— 13. 243	— 29. 211		— 29. 214	12: 7. *74	27: 9. 238	
— 17. 235	17: 9. 216	DEUTER-	21. 8. 198	— — 197		ECCLE-	JONAH.
— 29. 186	18:14. 221	ONOMY.	22:10. 12	14: 1. *70	SIASTES.	2: 9. 235
38: 8. 256	20: 8. 239	1: 2. 205	25:27. 237	22: 8. 193	1: 4. 226	
— 9. 224	— 10. 212	— 11. 247		— 9. 237	6: 6. 334	MICAH.
— 16. 233	21: 2. 256	— 16. 230	2. SAMUEL.	32: — 131	12: 9. 240	6: 6. *78
— 17. 21	— 4. 236	3: 1. 117	6: — 131	34:33. 209		7: — 131
39: 5. 247	— — 238	5: 5. 255	12: 1. *63	38:21. 237	CANTICLES.	
40: 3. 196	— 5. 225	6:13. 253	17: 9. 235	42:15. 237	1: 5. 117	HABAKKUK.
— 19. 220	— 11. 253	11:30. 244	— 29. 117		— 15. 189	1:16. 237
41:10. 239	— 17. 246	12:10. 242	18:22. 232	PSALMS.	2:10. *69	
— 15. 241	— 29. 236	13:14. 231	— 23. 232	1: 1. 185	— — 29	HAGGAI.
— 53. 237	— — 121	14:12. 193	33. 202	— 5. 241	— 16. 97	2:11. 240
42: 1. 224	27:34. 198	— 21. 230	19:16. 240	6: 2. *70	5:10. 117	
— 18. 233	28:17. 197	15:13. 253	— 30. 234	8: — 197	6: 2. *70	ZECHARIAH.
— 27. 204	— 20. *40	16:20. 202	20: — 131	5: 4. 210		1: 5. 256
43:16. 210	30:33. 211	17: 8. 249	24:24. 145	6: 5. 256	ISAIAH.	7: 5. 230
44: 3. 12	— 36. 231	22: 8. 235		7:10. 233	5: 9. 242	10: 3. 222
— 25. 189	32: 1. 201	— 16. 253	1. KINGS.	8: 6. 162	8:13. 194	
45: 1. 211	— 3. 202	— 21. 244		9:19. 244	12: 3. 202	MALACHI.
— 21. 12	— 4. 201	24: 2. 193	20: — 131	15: 5. 196	14: 6. 244	
46:33. 216	— 16. 185	25: 1. 107		24:11. *66	17:10. 197	1: 6. 195
47: 4. 12	33:23. 218	— 13. 292	3: 7. 225	34: — 199	23:17. 222	— — 199
— 13. 12	34: 3. 211	28:43. 244	— — 228	36: 6. 33	26:10. 240	3: 1. 254
— 24. 95	35: 5. 208	— 67. 234	8:28. 198	51:15. 240	29:14. 117	
48: 1. 239	— 11. 193	31: 7. 214		66:17. 189		
— 2. 239	38:10. 204	32: — 119				
— 7. 229	39:33. 193	— 7. 217				
— 16. *89	40:12. 204	— 50. 233	17:15. 238			

www.ingramcontent.com/pod-product-compliance
Lightning Source LLC
Chambersburg PA
CBHW022140300426
44115CB00006B/279